Read
to Write

Exposure to the writing process, through Don Murray's work . . . has been the single most important element of my education as a writer. By teaching the lesson that writing is not magic, but a rational process that can be identified and repeated successfully, no matter what the writing task, Murray has made better writers out of me and many of my colleagues. . . . Writers are hungry for real-life examples. In our writing seminars conducted by Murray, the most successful sessions have often revolved around actual pieces of writing. *Read to Write,* I believe, will satisfy the writing student's passion for vivid illustrations of the writer at work and, thanks to Murray's incisive comments, will also reveal to them the process that can help them achieve personal writing success.

Christopher Scanlan
National Correspondent
Washington Bureau,
Knight-Ridder Newspapers

Donald M. Murray

Read
to Write

A Writing Process Reader

Second Edition

Instructor's Edition

Holt, Rinehart and Winston, Inc.
Fort Worth   Chicago   San Francisco   Philadelphia   Montreal
Toronto   London   Sydney   Tokyo

Publisher   Charlyce Jones Owen
Acquisitions Editor   Michael A. Rosenberg
Project Editor   Christine B. Caperton
Production Manager   Kathleen Ferguson
Art & Design Supervisor   John Ritland
Cover Illustration   John Hulsey

Library of Congress Cataloging-in-Publication Data

Murray, Donald Morison, 1924–
    Read to write : a writing process reader / Donald M. Murray. — 2nd ed.
    Includes index.
    1. College readers.   2. English language—Rhetoric.   I. Title.
    PE1417.M87   1990
    808'.0427—dc20   89-15470

ISBN: 0-03-030799-6

Requests for permission to make copies of any part of the work should be mailed to: Copyrights and Permissions Department, Holt, Rinehart and Winston, Inc., Orlando, FL 32887

Address editorial correspondence to: 301 Commerce Street, Suite 3700, Fort Worth, TX 76102
    Address orders to: 6277 Sea Harbor Drive, Orlando, FL 32887
        1-800-782-4479, or 1-800-433-0001 (in Florida)

Printed in the United States of America

0 1 2 3   039   9 8 7 6 5 4 3 2 1

Holt, Rinehart and Winston, Inc.
The Dryden Press
Saunders College Publishing

Woody Allen, "The Colorization of Films Insults Artists and Society," *The New York Times,* June 28, 1987. Copyright © 1987 by The New York Times Company. Reprinted by permission.
James Baldwin, from *Notes of a Native Son.* Reprinted by permission.
Amiri Baraka, from *The Autobiography of Leroi Jones/Amiri Baraka,* Copyright © 1984 by Amiri

(continued on page 436)

for
Minnie Mae
who shares both reading
and writing with me

To Student and Teacher

In my other books I have written separate introductions to student and teacher, but that is not appropriate here. In writing and reading, student and teacher are the same, or should be. I have learned as much from my students as I have taught them; often I feel I have learned more than I have taught.

We both learn from the text: our own evolving drafts and the texts of published writers. I am in my sixties but I have not yet learned to read and write; my daily delight is that I continue to learn to read and write.

And the skills of reading and writing are intertwined. School often tries to separate them, but it cannot. In writing our own drafts we read and, when the writing goes well, we read with surprise, discovering that our words mean more than we expected, or, at least, something different than we expected. Our drafts teach us what to say and how to say it. We write and learn.

Just as we see our texts for the first time as we write them, so we should come to the texts of other writers—prepared to be surprised, ready to travel to new places, to look at familiar places differently, to experience other worlds and other ideas, to become the people on the page, to question, to doubt, to think, to feel, to care, to learn.

We read as we write, with difference. Each of us brings our own knowledge, our own backgrounds, our own needs to the pages we write and read. We are individual writers and readers of individual texts.

As we each learn, in our own way, to read and write, what we learn helps us see the possibilities of reading and writing. We discover what can be done on the page by reading and can try it when we write. And by trying it we better understand, when we return to reading, how writing is made.

This text is designed to take advantage of individuality and diversity; it celebrates diversity and encourages you, student or teacher, to read and write in your own way.

A Writer's Reader

The selections in this reader are personal, from my own bookshelves or from my own file of favorite pieces. These are the pieces of writing that continue to teach me my craft. They are mostly nonfiction, often leaning toward the autobiographical in the hope that students can connect their lives with the writer's. The selections represent a diversity of writers appropriate to our culture and a variety of genre appropriate to our times.

I have paired the selections to reinforce my belief that there is not one way to write anything, but many. Seeing writers coming to a common subject or writing task in their own way is instructive, and I hope this will lead to class discussion.

A Process Reader

Read to Write is organized according to my vision of the writing process. I am surprised to find myself considered one of the founders of the writing process movement. I never thought of the writing process as more than a logical approach to teaching writing.

I enjoyed reading and writing outside school although I couldn't spell, didn't know grammar, dropped out twice, and eventually flunked out of high school. I didn't learn to write in school—where writing meant reading a piece and telling the teacher what the teacher had already told us the teacher thought the essay, poems, story meant. We were graded on regurgitation, penmanship, spelling, and formal syntax.

I learned to write by writing, submitting my work to editors and trying to figure out why it wasn't accepted. I worked for newspaper and magazine editors who took me through the entire process of writing: collecting, focusing, ordering, drafting, clarifying.

When I came to the classroom, I explored this process with my students. Teachers also became my students, and their teaching about process informed me. I also worked with professional writers and still serve as writing coach to *The Boston Globe* and *The Providence Journal*. The organization of this book is based on the experience and research of many who have studied the making of meaning in writing from the process perspective.

Each chapter presents a stage in the writing process in such a way that it can serve as an introduction to the writing process or as a review of that process.

The instructor's manual is designed to help teachers put this text in a practical and a theoretical context. I have written it myself and have included in this second edition accounts from teachers telling how they have used *Read to Write* in their classrooms in a variety of colleges and universities. Teachers who wish to pursue the pedagogical or theoretical assumptions of this work, may wish to read *A Writer Teaches Writing,* second edition, *Learning by Teaching,* or *Expecting the Unexpected.*

Reading with a Writer

My wife was trained as a singer, and when we go to a concert she hears a different performance than do I, who collects records, disks, and tapes and listens to music throughout the day. I do not read music, I play no instruments and have never performed. I played football, and when we go to a game we see different games. I see what isn't done as well as what is; I notice what happens away from the ball; I have the experience of playing that I bring to my watching. She is a perceptive fan, but we look at the same play differently.

Writers read differently from those who do not write. Many of our most perceptive readers are not writers, but they do not approach the text as writers. In other courses in language arts and English you have looked at the text as a reader, critic, or scholar. This book invites you, student and teacher, to write as you read and to look at the readings with a writer's eye.

I have written an entirely new first chapter to introduce a writer's approach to reading. The chapter introduces a writer's way of looking at a piece of writing: the promise and the promise fulfilled.

To help understand the writing process, the text includes case histories by published and student writers who share evolving drafts and a description of how the final draft was produced.

In the first three selections I make marginal comments, inviting you to share, question, challenge, contradict my personal writerly view of the text. You may, of course, ignore these comments or keep them for a second reading. Such a second reading is what I offer for the rest of the selections. After the texts there are "A Writer's Notes for a Second Reading" in which I give my writers' view of the text and invite teacher and students to return to the text and produce their own view of what the writing was doing and how well it is being done.

Argument

This edition responds to the concerns of many who used the book by providing a discussion of writing the argument and examples of argumentative writing in that strand and in other selections in the text.

Argument is the fundamental form of academic discourse and students need to see how effective arguments are made and to appreciate the range of interesting writing possible in the genre of argument. Many of the selections in the book can be viewed as argument, but I have added 15 selections, including a new case history with a response, that are specifically in this genre. I hope these selections demonstrate that argument can be a lively, graceful genre that can reach the general reader.

Case Histories of Publishing Writers

Each stage of the writing process is introduced with the case history of a professional writer—a journalist, an academic turned writing authority [new in this edition], a technical writer, a poet, a science writer—producing a piece of writing. Each also writes an account of their writing, showing how they read and write. Student and teacher are taken behind the text, into the writer's workshop.

Case Histories of Student Writers

This edition includes ten new student case histories from a Freshman English class in argument that I taught. Here you will see my students teaching themselves—and teaching me. Besides their final draft, each has completed a commentary of what they have done and how they did it.

Collaborative Reading and Writing

In recent years, we have discovered how important it is for students to work together reading and writing. Each chapter in the writing process closes with suggestions for collaborative activities making use of the selections in the book and the students' own drafts.

Learning to Write by Reading

An assumption of this text is that the student can best learn to write by writing **and reading**, that the student can best learn to read by reading **and writing**. The two activities are intertwined in this book, which can be used as a writing text. *Read to Write* is also designed to be paired with my writing text *Write to Learn*.

Discussion Questions and Activities

The discussion questions and activities at the end of each selection are designed to be used by the individual student or by the class. This edition has special collaborative writing activities. The questions and activities all show how student writing and reading may be integrated, with each skill stimulating and illuminating the other.

Other Aids to Learning

The book includes three special indexes. One allows the student to identify a writing problem and then see how other writers have solved that writing problem. Another allows the student to read what other writers have written on a theme being explored by the student. A third allows students to see examples of a genre the student is attempting. All of these indexes support a theme of this text: there is no one way to write well, but many.

Acknowledgments

I am grateful for the help of many colleagues who inspire, prod, support, suggest, and listen. Donald H. Graves of the University of New Hampshire is always a phone call away, as is Christopher Scanlan of the Washington Bureau of Knight-Ridder Newspapers. Jane Hansen and Ruth Hubbard of the University of New Hampshire and Allan Nielsen of Mount Saint Vincent University in Halifax, Nova Scotia, helped me put my views of how the writer reads in the context of reading research. Brenda Miller made important contributions to the argument strand in this edition. Thomas Newkirk is that special colleague who constantly stimulates my learning. Brock Dethier is that special resource, a careful, insightful, tough but constructive reader. Melody Graulich gave me important counsel.

This book is greatly enriched by the contributions of Joseph Freda, Denise Grady, Roy Peter Clark, Mekeel McBride, and Christopher Scanlan, who have shared their writing and reading with the students who will use this book. All of my students in English 401 made important contributions to this edition.

I also appreciate the careful, critical responses I received from my reviewers: Wendy Bishop, University of Alaska–Fairbanks; Albert DeCiccio, Merrimack College; Roy Fox, Boise State University; Carol Freeman, Cowell College; Naomi Given, Middlesex County College; Penelope Gleeson, Virginia Polytechnic Institute and State University; Carol Johnson, Virginia Wesleyan College; Candace Meier, Des Moines Area Community College; Lyle Morgan, Pittsburgh State University; Harold Nelson, Minot State University. They, and all my other colleagues and editors, should get credit for what you like in the book and not be blamed for what you do not like.

This book was the suggestion of Charlyce Jones Owen, English Editor and Publisher/Humanities at Holt, Rinehart and Winston. She has been both editor and friend. Her suggestions have consistently improved my text, as have the editorial direction of Kate Morgan on the second edition. I am fortunate in having the full support of Holt, Rinehart and Winston in attempting to write texts that others would see as unconventional. Everyone has always encouraged and never interfered. All my failures are my own.

My wife, as always, has contributed to my work in so many ways that I cannot list them. Without her, I would not be published.

Contents

3   A Focus Found   123

4   An Order Designed   236

7   Watch Out: After School May Come Reading and Writing   433

Contents by Genre and Theme

Each selection in the book is paired with another, so that the student can study two different writers dealing with a similar subject, usually in the same genre. Here I have made a personal selection of pieces that might be compared by genre or content.

Alienation

Argument

Atomic Age

Autobiography

Childhood

Death

Family

Growing Up

History

Humor

Medicine

Narrative

Poetry

Prejudice

School

Writing

1

Reading as a Writer

A little disrespect, please.

Read the pages in this book through the lens of your own experience as a writer. The writers in this collection faced the blank page you have faced, felt the same terror you have felt, explored the meaning of their lives armed with your language.

You can—and should—second-guess what they say and how they say it.

If you do, you will find reading much more fun. You will start to play in the game of making meaning in which the author plays.

Teachers and school too often leave the impression that books and writers are to be worshiped. Published texts are too often presented as unquestioned authority.

Our best writers, however, do not see their books as full of answers but as packed with questions. Writers write to participate in the great conversations of mankind. When writers read, they see a mind at the work of making meaning out of what confuses us all.

Published texts, to writers, are not cadavers on the stainless-steel autopsy table; they rise, they are alive. The pages reveal the author in the act of making meaning.

Writers bring their own experience in writing to the printed page. This allows the reading writer to see many of the choices the author made, to understand the problems the author faced, and the solutions that might have been attempted as well as the one that appears on the page.

The writer enters into a dialogue with the author—questioning, challenging the text and its maker. The experienced writer sees how the printed text was made, but the writer (and you are a writer even if you have not been published) can create an imaginary text and then compare what was said with what might have been said.

Students sometimes feel that literature is a museum, a storehouse of the dead past. But literature—the literature of science, economics, political science, military or foreign affairs, psychology, education, medicine, physical education, nutrition, even the literature of literature, all of the areas in which human beings have a need for meaning to be made—is the active record of experience and reflection upon experience.

We must pay the published author the compliment of disrespect by entering into the text with the writer: We should not leave our own experiences as writers behind when we read. The problems we each face as writers are the same problems the published writer faces. The craft of making meaning is understandable.

The only mystery comes in those rare cases where everything works so well that we lose ourselves in the text and forget that it has been made because it seems so natural, so easy, so right: the pieces of writing we call art. And we can go back and reread those to discover at least some of the craft that always lies behind art. We may not see it as readers, but we can see it as writers if we put ourselves in the shoes of the maker.

Participatory reading helps the reader become a better writer. The writer learns from the masters and from fellow apprentices the techniques of a shared craft. Later the reader turned writer can attempt the solutions of others to the writing problems encountered in an evolving draft.

The Writer's Promise

The writer is a demanding, impatient reader who knows from intimate experience that the writer makes a promise to the reader at the beginning of each piece of writing. This promise is delivered in the first line or sentence, in the first paragraph, on the first page. Readers are a cruel, busy lot. They decide to read a piece in seconds, not minutes.

You can test this yourself, or in your class, by having people go through the front page of a newspaper, a few pages of a magazine, or the selections in this book. Have people note when they decide to read or not to read. You will find that it's a matter of lines, not pages; seconds, not minutes.

The writer has to realize that it's not possible to capture every reader. The writer's promise indicates the subject of the piece of writing; it reaches out to select the audience for *this* piece of writing. In school we are all directed to read the same piece, but that assignment, like so many things in school, is artificial. It is not the way the world works. When we read we read for information, for entertainment, for understanding, on topics that interest us. The skillful writer can, with a crafty promise, entice us into subjects that do not interest us but should, some of the time but not all of the time.

Before we examine the elements of an effective promise let us look at some promises writers have made at the beginning of their texts. Some of these examples are from the beginning of books, chapters, or articles; others are excerpts;

but they are all units of writing built to attract and hold a reader. All are from selections in this book, so later you will be able to read them to see if the promise was fulfilled.

> School was classes and faces and teachers. And sometimes trouble. School was as much the playground as the classroom. For me, it was more the playground than the classroom. One grew, one had major confrontations with real life, in the playground, only rarely in the classroom. Though I had some terrible confrontations. Around discipline and what not. The only black teacher in the school at that time, Mrs. Powell, a statuesque powder-brown lady with glasses, beat me damn near to death in full view of her and my 7B class because I was acting the fool and she went off on me (which apparently was sanctioned by my mother—it probably had something to do with conflicting with the only black teacher in the whole school and that had to be revenged full-blood-flowingly at once as an example to any other malefactors). . . .
>
> Amiri Baraka

> On the 29th of July, in 1943, my father died. On the same day, a few hours later, his last child was born. Over a month before this, while all our energies were concentrated in waiting for these events, there had been, in Detroit, one of the bloodiest race riots of the century. A few hours after my father's funeral, while he lay in state at the undertaker's chapel, a race riot broke out in Harlem. On the morning of the 3rd of August, we drove my father to the graveyard through a wilderness of smashed plate glass.
>
> James Baldwin

> When I first realized that I might have cancer, I felt immediately I had entered a special place, a place I came to call "The Land of the Sick People." The most disconcerting thing, however, was not that I found the place terrifying and unfamiliar, but that I found it so ordinary, so banal. I didn't feel different, didn't feel that my life had radically changed at the moment the word cancer became attached to it. The same rules still held. What had changed, however, was other people's perceptions of me. . . .
>
> Alice Stewart Trillin

> It was in Burma, a sodden morning of the rains. A sickly light like yellow tinfoil, was slanting over the high walls into the jail yard. We were waiting outside the condemned cells, a row of sheds fronted with double bars, like small animal cages. Each cell was measured about ten feet by ten and was quite bare within except for a plank bed and a pot for drinking water. In some of them brown, silent men were squatting at the inner bars, with their blankets draped round them. These were the condemned men, due to be hanged within the next week or two.
>
> George Orwell

Elements of the Promise

It is helpful as reader and writer to look at those elements in the promise that organize and focus the subject for the writer as well as the reader. As you study these elements go back to the examples above and the ones at the end of this section as well as other promises in the book, in your own drafts, in other readings to see how writers have constructed their promises to their readers.

Voice   This is the most important and difficult element in writing. Above all else it is the quality of voice that attracts and holds a reader. Sometimes this quality is called *style,* but I prefer *voice.* Style implies something you can order off the rack, while voice is something that comes from you.

Readers hunger for an individual voice. We read alone. Reading is a form of private communication between one individual—a writer—and another individual—a reader. We respond to a voice that is concerned, personal, appropriate, individual. Reading is, in a sense, an idealized conversation. It is what we hope to hear but rarely do.

Of course, voice is an illusion. The writer's voice is similar to how the writer sounds, but not the same. We all have many voices. We speak differently in the classroom, at home, in the dormitory, in the locker room, at a party, at a funeral. And we write differently according to the purpose of the text. We may be familiar or distant, professional or casual, humorous or serious, and so I prefer to use the term **the voice of the text.**

That voice is our personal voice tuned to a written purpose. But no matter how serious the writing, we should never forget that readers respond most strongly to writing they can hear. We should write with our ears, hearing the voice as we put it on the page. This is the best guarantee that our readers will hear the text when they read.

And this heard quality is a significant part of the promise that attracts readers.

> ☞ Read the beginnings printed on pages 66 and 84 to hear the voice, the music of each author. Note the touches of street English Baraka purposefully and skillfully uses. Hear the special music of Orwell's "It was in Burma, a sodden morning of the rains." Have some of your classmates read their first lines aloud to hear their voices, and read yours to hear your own. ☜

Authority   The writer has the problem of establishing authority in the very beginning of a text. It is no accident that the words *author* and *authority* are so closely related. The reader needs evidence the writer knows the subject, that the writer can be trusted, that the writer will have something worth listening to.

Voice helps (some voices are much more authoritative and believable than others), but the reader usually wants specific information, documentation, evidence that the writer knows the subject.

> ☞ Note how Baldwin uses concrete details to establish his authority on the subject. He gives you date, place, event. Note how quickly—nine words—Alice Trillin establishes her authority: "When I first realized that I might have cancer. . . ." ☜

Tension   The energy that drives a piece of writing forward usually comes from the tension within the topic—and successful tension is established early.

Effective writing usually contains forces on a collision course or forces that belong together being driven apart. These forces are similar to those in many courtships and many marriages.

Beginning writers often conceive of topics that have no tension (school) instead of one that has some tension (how my school flunked). Experienced writers usually spend a great deal of time circling a potential subject until they discover the essential conflict or tension within it: the point at which the forces meet, the moment of decision, the time of choice. And then they communicate that immediacy to the reader right away.

❧ The selection on page 84 is a good example of establishing a forward-driving tension. Baraka is in conflict with school, but is in a special conflict as a black student with the only black teacher in the school. ❧

Significance   The effective subject doesn't float free like an untethered balloon. The piece of writing that attracts and holds us implies or states its own importance. The incident is part of a trend. The idea connects with an evolving theory. The event reveals a changing tradition.

One of the reasons we read is that authors show us the significance of events, people, ideas, or information that we normally think insignificant. We don't like to spend time reading about things that don't have some importance. Even humor needs to connect with something significant in our lives—our shyness; our difficulty in behaving the way other people want us to; the problems we have on the job, in school, or on a date. A piece of writing that attracts readers promises its own importance. We are confident the writer will answer our unspoken question "Why should I read this?"

❧ Baldwin puts his family's private history into the larger history of his race in America. He connects personal history with national history. Each of the last three selections I chose has the significance of life and death. I did not choose them for that reason, but they demonstrate that good writing is rarely involved with the trivial. It is almost always concerned with what is important to us as human beings. ❧

Technique   Questions of technique are more apparent to a fellow writer than they are to the nonwriting reader. I believe, however, that the reader senses at least some matters of technique. If the text, for example, promises a story, the reader expects a story; if the text promises an argument, the reader is ready to go head-to-head in a battle of ideas; if the writer promises entertainment, the reader sits back prepared to be entertained.

Reading writers, certainly, see in the promise in the beginning of a piece of writing the techniques the writer will use to capture and hold the reader, to state and develop the evolving text. We know, while the other readers sense, that the writer has chosen a path of craft that will be consistent and fulfilled.

> ❧ Baldwin lets the reader know immediately that his essay will be strung on a line of narrative. Trillin will write a personal essay, exploring our world from a new perspective. ❧

Surprise   I know that an effective piece of writing—for the writer—has to have an element of surprise. We write what we know and we write to know what is not known until it is written. Writing, for the writer, is a process of exploration and discovery. The writer takes us in directions we do not expect.

The element of surprise is also important for the reader. The text that attracts and holds the reader promises something extra, something more than the reader has received from what has been read before. There is a hint, at least, of surprise. Readers, in reading the promise, are caught by something they did not expect at the beginning of the page.

> ❧ Each of the examples above demonstrates surprise. We are, for example, surprised as Baraka was by the conflict between black student and black teacher. Trillin is surprised that she has not changed, but that the world sees her as changed. ❧

Not all of the elements listed, of course, need to be in each promise, and the intensity of each element may change. But some of them have to be there with enough force to make the reader start to read.

Fulfilling the Promise

In writing as in life, it isn't enough to promise: You have to deliver. Writers sometimes try to fool readers with a flashy beginning full of false promise. It doesn't work. The reader can always shut the book, toss the magazine in the trash, use the newspaper as fish wrapping.

Readers who are cheated will not trust that writer again, but when they find a writer who promises and delivers they will look to read more work by that author.

The writer's double vision allows the reading writer to read both as a reader and as a writer, following the text for information, story, enjoyment, whatever the reader needs, and also to see if—and how—the writer will fulfill the promise.

The elements of the promise change as the text moves forward. I've listed the names I've used to describe the effective promise on the left and the terms I've chosen for the elements that fulfill the writer's promise on the right in the chart below.

The rest of this chapter shows how the promise may be fulfilled, how the promise develops into satisfying text. But remember how I started: Give me a little disrespect, please. Do not take me more seriously than I take myself. This isn't TRUTH, this is theory, a hunch, an idea, an intellectual game by which I'm trying to understand an enormously complex intellectual process.

Listen to me, consider me, and then take me on. Read and write with your own way of thinking, your own experiences in life, and as a writer/reader. Enter into the game of making meaning with me.

This chart first appeared in my daybook, but not in this form. Making charts is one way I think, a way of viewing elements in a problem or solution and their relationships. This is the chapter stripped down. Printing, I hope, will help you see what I've been trying to do and may introduce you to a way of making your own meanings.

Voice	Texture
Authority	Development
Tension	Structure
Significance	Context
Technique	Solutions
Surprise	Closure

Elements of the Promise Fulfilled

To read like a writer, you have to remember the blank pages the writer faced. Writers write to be surprised, to learn, to explore and discover. E. M. Forster said, "How do I know what I think until I see what I say?" John Updike agrees: "Writing and rewriting is a constant search for what one is saying." Eudora Welty adds, "I'm working on something. I don't know exactly what." I have a collection of dozens of quotations from writers that say the same thing. What they write grows out of the evolving text.

Hemingway said that he wrote in his head. That is only partially true. The writer writes on the page. Words, lines, sentences, paragraphs—written and rewritten—lead the writer toward meaning, and in reading from our own experience in writing we can reconstruct, in part, the points at which the text surprises, turning on a word, choosing an order of meaning to pursue, selecting one form of documentation over another, changing the pace, tuning the voice, making all the decisions a writer makes—or rationalizing and polishing the choices the writer finds being made by the text.

These categories are simply my way of looking at how evolving texts fulfill the promise made to the reader in the beginning. You will notice, I hope, how they fail to remain rigid. They are not watertight compartments, entirely separate from each other. Just as argument may employ narrative and story may become an essay, the different categories I use below will run into each other and overlap. Of course. Eventually, as you become your own writer and your own reader, you will develop your own way of reading, of looking at the text you are making and that others are making. Your categories and your conclusions will not be mine. Just as we should encourage our children to become their own persons, I hope this text will encourage you through your own writing and reading to become your own reader.

The Promise: Voice

The Promise Fulfilled: Texture   The writer brings to reading a special appreciation for the way language is used because the writer is a conscious user of language. Writers notice how each piece of effective writing develops a richness that some writers like to call density. I prefer the term *texture*. It is similar to that quality of light in the early morning or at the end of the day when the sun is low and you see the changing texture of grass in a field or the patterns of brick and stone in the buildings along a city street.

Texture in writing is most often a product of the interaction between voice and information. The writer writes with specific information, information that reveals meaning. And the words, the pacing, the rhythm of those words becomes the voice of the text. Writers know the voice of writers they appreciate and they enjoy and learn from how a writer will tune that voice so it supports and reveals the writer's subject.

Effective writing satisfies our brain's hunger for information and our ears' hunger for music. The voice tells us how the world is seen by the writer.

An important part of texture is the angle of vision. Just as the sun, close to the horizon, reveals a special world, the writer's angle of vision reveals an individual view of the world. The writer invites us to stand in a particular place and to look at the world, often a familiar world, from a different point of view. As Alice Trillin's essay evolves we see her ordinary world and ours changed not so much by her perception as by others' perception of her.

Writers know only too well that poor writing can be very skillful. It is glib, slick, calculated to make us slide along the surface. Politicians and advertising writers do this in a calculated way, so that we have the illusion of meaning, or so that complicated matters are seen in a dangerously simple fashion. Excellent writing reveals complexity, contradiction, tension, individuality. We hear a writer speaking of a particular view of the world with language that is musical, complex, textured so that it makes us see and feel and think.

❧ Baraka, Baldwin, Trillin, Orwell are all master writers, and they demonstrate the quality of texture in almost every paragraph as they fulfill the promise of the lead. It is especially useful to examine the second and third paragraphs of *Notes of a Native Son* on page 151. Baldwin looks at himself looking at his father with such unflinching honesty that we are forced to read on and to look at ourselves in the process. The text has richness, depth, energy—texture. ❧

The Promise: Authority

The Promise Fulfilled: Development   One of the inexperienced writer's greatest problems is a lack of development. A beginning writer has an idea for a piece of writing, or through writing sees what needs to be written. Then the young writer states that idea or concept, believing that the idea will leap from the page to the reader's mind.

Writers know that they have to take the time to develop a text. The excellent writer, even in argument and opinion, does not so much tell the reader how to think or feel or care or experience as create a text that causes the reader to think or feel or care or experience.

The reader has a hunger for the fully developed text, for information, for feelings, for images, for quotation and dialogue, for detail, for what will give the reader the experience of the text. When writing works, the text forces the reader to see and to come to a conclusion from what has been seen. The writer does not think for the reader but causes the reader to think.

As writers read, they learn from how the text develops the subject. The writer delivers evidence and documentation for each point, in a form that is appropriate to the subject and that will communicate to the reader. Some points are made with anecdote, others with statistics, still more with scholarly reference or empathic choice of material with which the reader will be familiar.

Writers as readers see the writer on the page delivering enough information, but not too much, and pacing the text so that the reader has time to absorb, reflect, and react to what has been written.

❦ Notice how Baraka on page 87 doesn't just tell us about the games, he gives enough detail for us to experience the games with him and therefore discover their significance. We read to live in other worlds, to enter lives and minds and times other than our own. When the reader develops a piece of writing effectively, the experience of reading the text becomes a real experience, part of our life and our knowledge and our memory, influencing how we see the world and think about it from the moment of reading onward. ❧

The Promise: Tension

The Promise Fulfilled: Structure   Form is the largest element in structure. It is the outside shape of the building and represents the history of the word-buildings that have preceded it. When we choose the form, we are choosing a bulding that will fit our meaning and its purpose or audience.

Reader and writer come to the potential meaning with an unspoken but firm expectation. There is a tradition to argument, narrative, poetry, essay, memo, news story, scientific report, to each of the many forms we write and read.

Writers know that form and meaning are intimately related. Story helps us see events in the world in a particular way. There is a sequence: a beginning, a middle, and an end. Argument implies a battle of the mind, a conflict between believer and nonbeliever. Essay promises a commentary on life.

The writer knows that the selection of a form of writing will influence the way both the writer and reader view the subject, and that the form will limit, in some way, the meaning the writer sees in the subject.

The reading writer also is aware of the traditions of each form or genre. Through the years we have come to expect certain behaviors from the writers of the essay, the story, the argument. The writer may work against the traditions of the form or work to extend them, but the traditions are always there. And when the writer reads the writer sees the text working with or against the expectations of the form. It is often an interesting and revealing game. And writers who have explored these forms in their own drafts understand the game well enough to observe how it is being played.

This book is full of narrative, because personal narrative is the most common form of writing in most beginning college composition courses. The next most frequent form is argument, and so there is a strand of argument in this edition as well. In both cases I discuss narrative and argumentative writing so that we can see how the traditions of these forms are used by a variety of writers.

The traditions of each form of writing should not be a prison. That was the way I felt about tradition when I was young. I am more radical than I was forty years ago, but I am a different kind of radical. I see each genre or form as a lens, a way of looking at the world, and I hope in some small way to use those lenses with which I write to extend the reader's vision of the world. And as I seek to discover and reveal my own individual truths I hope I may influence and extend the tradition of the form in which I am writing.

Then, within each form, the writer knows there are many ways to construct the piece of writing. A story can start at the end as well as at the beginning. An essay can be personal or impersonal; the writer can be involved or detached. The builder of argument has many ways to order each point.

The writer has the ability, because of personal experience in writing, to see how each writer orders the information so that it will cause the reader to think and to care.

Writers as readers know what a skillful game it is to anticipate what information the reader will need—and the exact point at which the reader will need it. Writers who have tried this game of anticipation themselves have the experience to understand what the writer is doing as they read.

Readers who do not write are more likely to believe that there is a right or wrong way a piece should be ordered, or, in fact, to see absolutes in every element in writing. The more experienced the writer the more the writer is likely to delight in the diversity of approaches within each text the writer reads. There is not so much correct and incorrect as alternatives, a great variety of alternatives, many that work and many that do not. Through reading the writer keeps discovering new ways of writing writers may choose to adapt on their own pages.

❲ In Orwell's essay, the clock ticks. Suspense is created not by what we do not know, the amateur's misconception, but by the inevitability of what will happen. Everything moves the reader forward on the surface, to the hanging, and beneath that surface, to the implications of what that means for the author—and every single reader. ❳

The Promise: Significance

The Promise Fulfilled: Context   Each topic has a context; the writer makes that context clear so that the readers can make contact with the subject and see the subject's importance to them. A reader may not know how an environmental hazard, crime in another part of the city, a law made in Washington relates to him or her individually. The writer puts an event in context so the reader knows the impact of the event.

In many cases the context is explicit. In many magazine articles or newspaper stories it comes in the lead, the first lines of the story. In a delayed lead, the article opens with an anecdote, a scene, a quotation, a revealing fact or specific event and then, usually about the third paragraph, the writer tells the reader the context. The writer may, for example, open with the description of a specific case of child abuse and then, once the reader is involved, point out how prevalent child abuse is in the reader's community.

In more artful writing, the context is implied. The writing may be subtle but the connection is not. Writing enters the reader's world and makes the reader pay attention by showing the direct significance of the subject.

❲ Go back to the lead of Baldwin's piece, reprinted on pages 150–151. He establishes the context in the ninth line; as you read the entire piece you will see how Baldwin weaves the context both explicitly and implicitly throughout the entire piece. ❳

The Promise: Technique

The Promise Fulfilled: Solutions   When writers read they see the problems the writer faced and the solutions available. They read the writer's choices, seeing which solution was selected or occasionally even invented or redesigned. They learn from writing and reading which solutions work.

The writer's knowledge of writing problems *and solutions* gives a richness and depth to each writer's reading. They bring their knowledge to the text, and when they read effective pieces of writing they often add to their own knowledge in a way that can help their own writing.

Writers, through reading, keep extending their inventory of solutions. Many times writers will read just to see how other writers have solved a problem that has appeared on the writer's own page. They look in the toolbox of another writer to see what they may use in their situation.

To get behind the scenes and really understand how a text has been made, it can be helpful to identify the writer's problems, defining them in the margin, then going through the text to see the solutions the writer has attempted. Then you can second-guess the writer, listing other solutions to the writer's problems and perhaps even trying one or two out in your own words, getting into the text with the writer and messing around. In this way you will appreciate what the writer has done, and not done, as well as what you can do in your own writing.

☞ The most obvious technique used by Baraka, Baldwin, Trillin, and Orwell is to use specific, revealing detail to give the piece authority and to recreate experience in your mind. Note on page 161 how Baldwin takes you to the funeral from his dressing—and drinking—before he went, presented with a terrible fullness. The reader has the promise of the lead fulfilled. ☜

The Promise: Surprise

The Promise Fulfilled: Closure   In the beginning I talked about the importance of surprise, that element in the promise that raises the reader's expectation. By the end of the piece of writing, however, that expectation must be satisfied. An effective piece of writing has closure, or resolution.

This doesn't mean that the tension has to be completely resolved, that there is always a happy ending, that every theory is proved, every argument won.

Effective writing does not mean oversimplification. Writing can and should reflect the complications of the world. Effective writing may define a problem rather than solve it, propose a theory rather than prove it, reveal a complication that cannot yet be simplified.

The reader, however, needs a sense of forward movement, a feeling that everything in the piece of writing has advanced the reader's experience with the subject, and that this experience has been completed for the moment. The resolution, or ending, of the piece of writing may occur in the reader's mind, but that feeling must have been purposefully caused by a writer who has skillfully brought the reader to the point of continuing the text beyond the last page.

The reader, in other words, must be satisfied at the end of the piece of writing. The questions that have to be answered must be answered. The piece of writing has to be complete. And the reader who is a writer will begin, through writing and reading, to see how this can be accomplished.

☞ Trillin's ending on page 224 is a fine example of closure. We are taken into a world where we did not want to go, the world of those who have fatal disease, but we are given a working conclusion to the sentence we may receive. It is not the dishonest promise of a miracle cure but the resolution of reality. "We will never kill the dragon. But each morning we confront him. Then we give our children breakfast, perhaps put a bit more mulch on the peas, and hope we can convince the dragon to stay away for a while longer.'' We experience the temporary closure the author finds in each day of continued life. ⚑

The Writer's Double Vision

The more you write and read the more the writer's double vision will become natural. It will increase your enjoyment for reading and your skill at writing.

As we write we are readers. The words and sentences and paragraphs that appear under our hand are read. We see our own attempts to capture meaning. And we remember as we make these attempts how other writers have faced these problems and solved them, how they have tuned their voice, how they have reached their readers, established their authority, developed and ordered their meaning.

And as we read we remember ourselves writing, and we see the writer behind the text, an individual who does not yet know completely what is being written and how it is being written. We share in the excitement of meaning being made.

The purpose of this book is to give you this double benefit, to allow you to read as a writer and write as a reader.

And remember: a little disrespect. Read as a writer playing in the game of making meaning.

2

Information Collected

Writing is an act of exploration. Writers do not so much write what they know as write to learn what they may know. There is a mystery to be investigated.

Beginning writers—and not-so-beginning writers—share the terror of emptiness, that there is nothing to write about and that when there is something to write about, there is nothing to say. I felt it this morning and performed all sorts of virtuous evasions—answering mail, making phone calls, neatening up—to avoid the emptiness. But the emptiness is the starting point of writing and I have to remind myself of that. After all, I don't want to write what I've written before—and write it in the same way. I have to remember that in despair, in terror, in hopelessness I have come to the beginning of my writing. Now I can find a new country to explore or a new way to explore a familiar land.

In this chapter we will read writers who have found and developed a subject—but never forget that they started with the same emptiness you feel, that there was writing before the final draft, and before the first draft fragments and notes and plans that were used and many more that were not used. You will see some of this process in Christopher Scanlan's piece, but only a sample. Most articles, if they were published with all their notes and drafts, would be as long as a book.

Finding the Subject to Explore

There are some subjects, of course, that are assigned to you, and then the problem is how to collect the information that will allow you to develop the subject. There are also subjects that attach themselves to you; they seek you out and arrive as insistent and uncalled-for as an itch. (Examples in this chapter include work by Woody Allen, Anna Quindlen, Lisa Keiski, and Maureen Hurley.) Pay attention to those subjects. They have an intensity and immediacy that other subjects do not have. You have a need to explore such a subject and good writing is often the product of such a demanding subject: "Write me, write me!"

Still, there are times when you need to seek out a subject. You have to look at the world beyond yourself and within yourself to find material that may be developed and become worthy of being shared with a reader.

The Outward Search

We begin to examine the world from the point at which we are standing, connecting what we observe with our own experience first of all. We often start with questions that make a connection between ourselves and our world:

- What would I like to know more about?
- Who would I like to know better?
- What process interests me?
- How is my world changing?
- What needs to be changed?
- What is happening that should—and why?
- What is *not* happening that should—and why?
- What process should I know more about?
- What do I need to know?
- What do I want to know?
- What don't I want to know?
- What event is affecting my world?
- What caused the event?
- What will result because of the event?
- What surprises me?

The questions can go on and on as we study our world, asking who, what, where, and especially why and how. The more we see the more we will see, and we will begin to look carefully at what is taking place—has taken place and will take place—in our world. Soon we begin to look at the interactions in the world around us:

- What forces are attracted to each other?
- What forces are resisted by each other?
- What forces are in conflict?
- What forces will be in conflict?
- What problems need solutions?
- What solutions will lead to new problems?
- What are those new problems?
- How may they be solved?

The writer is constantly scanning the world the way radar rotates across the horizon, and the writer keeps seeing new blips, new points of potential subject. Most of them begin with a necessary self-interest. The writer is open to the world, concerned with what the writer is seeing, hearing, smelling, tasting, touching. Every sense is in contact with the world outside the writer. Note the way in which many of the selections in this chapter—Scanlan, Caro, Orwell, Didion, and Baraka—show the writer observing and recording the world, building a significant piece of writing from the specific information the writer has collected.

The Inward Search

Writers looks inward as well as outward, for writers are not only observers of society, but members of society. They know their feelings and thoughts are an integral part of the subject-seeking process. The writer's own lives and own histories often provide important material. Writers know that what they feel and think will be felt and thought by other individuals.

In some cases—autobiography, the personal narrative, the familiar essay, the opinion—the writer will speak directly of the writer's inner world. In other cases the inner feelings or reactions will be the starting point for a writer's explorations of the world outside.

Some of the questions that will help the writer discover subjects within himself or herself are:

- What makes me worry?
- What makes me angry?
- Why am I reacting so strongly to this incident?
- Why am I *not* reacting strongly?
- What is making me nostalgic?
- What is making me laugh?
- What is making me sad?
- Why am I making these connections?
- Why do I think the result will be good?
- Why do I think the result will be bad?

Combining the Two

It should be obvious that it is hard—in fact impossible—to make a clear separation between the personal and the impersonal. The writer may respond to an outside stimulus, as Christopher Scanlan did, and end up revealing the personal impact of what he discovered. Or the writer may feel something in a very personal way and write about it in an objective manner, as Robert Caro has in "The Sad Irons."

In many cases, the writer combines both the outside and the inside world in a single piece of writing, moving back and forth between external observation and inward reflection as Joseph Mitchell and most of the writers in this section do in the excerpts reprinted here.

Finding the Information through Exploration

Once writers have a subject or territory to explore, they move across the countryside like a monster vacuum cleaner, gobbling up everything that may help them understand the subject. Writers know that they need far more information than they will be able to use. You can see evidence of this in Christopher Scanlan's notes, and you should realize that, as detailed as Robert Caro's piece may seem to be, the published details are selected from a necessary inventory of many more details.

Written Sources

Librarians are often the writer's best friends, They collect, organize, and can recover huge amounts of written information. Writers draw on books, newspaper clippings, magazine articles, monographs, reports, statistical collections, government reports, the publications of professional organizations, scientific papers, speeches—a vast smorgasbord of material that may reveal significant specifics that can be connected and woven into a meaning.

Librarians, public information offices, public relations officers, professional associations, government agencies, and legislative committees are but a few of the sources writers use to get information. And these are all sources that are available to the inquisitive student, who can contact them by mail, telephone, or in person.

Live Sources

In school we forget that the best source of information is often a live authority. The policeman, the judge, the social worker, the victim, the defense attorney, the prosecuting attorney, the accused, the doctor, the neighbor, the parent are all sources from which the writer can get important information. Robert Caro and his wife traveled through the Texas hill country, interviewing live sources. Christopher Scanlan and Thomas French use information from live sources in their selections.

These people all used the interview to collect information. The effective interviewer prepares for the interview by finding out as much as possible about the interviewee ahead of time and tries, whenever possible, to make appointments at the subject's convenience. Interviewers take careful notes or tape-record the interviews.

The key to an information-producing interview is good questions. I like to prepare for the interview by writing down the four to six questions that the reader has to have answered if I am to produce a good story. I work on these questions and, of course, change them as the story evolves. The best questions cannot be answered by yes or no. I try not to ask, "Did you win the game?" but "Why did you win the game?" "How did you win the game?" "What was the key play and why did it work?" I want quesitons that will force the interviewee to think and respond with concrete details.

The interviewer tries to make the interview a relaxed experience. He or she tries to create an environment that is as casual as a conversation. But it is an intense experience. Behind the relaxed manner of the person asking questions is an intense listener who is trying to put each answer into context, trying to see what question needs to be asked next, trying to notice how the answers are being answered, and paying close attention to what isn't being said as well as what is said. And all the time the writer remains prepared to be surprised, to discover meaning, as Christopher Scanlan did when he interviewed the French farmer and found the real significance of the story when he did not expect to find it.

Observation

Firsthand observation is another skill that is essential to the writer. All of the writers in this section have seen the story with their own eyes. The careful observation of the world will produce much of the raw material we use in writing. I find it helpful to observe even if I do not use the material directly. If I am writing about teaching I need to sit in a class as a student and I need to teach my own classes. I may not use any of that material, but the firsthand experience helps me put the material I have in context.

While observing, the writer is always looking for revealing details—the specific anonymity of the way the graves were numbered in Scanlan's story, for example. The writer wants the detail that gives off extra meaning. The writer wants to hear the quotation, such as when the old farmer told Scanlan, "That the young who died delivered us." Such a quotation brings another voice and a special authority to the story. The writer needs to see the place in which the story is taking place. Scanlan describes a U.S. military cemetery in France as "4,313 white crosses and Stars of David lined up on a manicured field like a marching band at half time." The mention of the marching band, of course, gives the reader a double vision of the high school Saturday game in the world of expectation and possibility that these young men had left, and the vision of the cemetery in which they were buried only months later. And seeing does not only mean seeing the physical world, but seeing the meaning in what is visualized. Scanlan and the other writers in this chapter make us see.

Memory

A writer's memory is a special contraption. In fact, the writer's memory is so special that it would be worth it to be a writer just to enjoy the product of this memory. Few writers have TV game-show recall. I am typical, I think, in having a rather poor memory in that I cannot recall many names or facts or details out of context. But the act of writing stimulates my memory, and I find that information appears on the page that I didn't know I knew. I remember little about being in combat years ago, but as I write about combat, I am once more in combat and my pages flood with an excess of detail that has been imprisoned in my skull for decades.

Most of us, I believe, have this writer's memory. When I collect a group of strangers in a room, class, or writing workshop who do not believe they are writers, and get them writing, either just free-writing or writing freely and fast about something they care about, information that they had forgotten or were not aware of remembering, tumbles out of their brains onto the page. When Amiri Baraka writes autobiography his history is recreated in enormous detail on the page. That history has not been remembered before writing, but it is remembered by writing, in the way that details come out of your mouth when you are describing an experience to a good listener, details you "discover" by the act of sharing the experience.

The student writer should be impressed by the abundance of remembered detail, especially in the autobiographical pieces by such writers as James Baldwin, William Gibson, Alice Trillin, Richard Ford, Charles Simic, Theodore Roethke, Maya Angelou, John Updike, George Orwell, E. B. White, Jean Shepherd, Enrique Hank Lopez, and Maxine Hong Kingston in this book. To share their experience and learn from them how to make use of it, you should write at least a scene from your own biography—taking a few minutes when you first witnessed a death, or were especially scared by a place, or felt hatred, love, pity, or resentment for a person—and describe that event, place, or person in detail, giving yourself 10 pages, or 20, and writing as fast as possible to see what tumbles out of your own brain onto the page. You will discover that you also have a writer's memory, and that the act of writing stimulates your brain to reveal what you didn't know you knew.

In all these ways, and many others, of examining your outer and inner worlds and the connections between them, you will see how many subjects you have to write about and to see how many ways there are to discover the material that will develop those subjects. You will understand, through your own writing, the problems of the writers we have reprinted here and discover, through your reading, how your fellow writers have solved their problems.

A Note on Collaborative Writing

The myth of the lonely writer is no myth. Writing is normally an individual act—a single writer speaking to an individual reader. The writer usually composes in private, working alone, even if a journalist working in a city room packed with other lonely writers.

But it doesn't have to be this way. Writers can work in pairs or small groups, producing a text that has the benefits of teamwork. Studies of college graduates show that most of them have to write in teams when they work on the job in corporations, for government agencies, in laboratories, in law firms. Students need experience in producing a joint text.

In recent years many writing instructors have also studied the advantages of students working together, learning together as they share writing problems and solutions, often producing texts that are better than the single writer could produce without the help of others.

Some of the patterns of collaboration writers practice include:

Collecting

- The team discusses the writing project, dividing up the research tasks, then pooling their findings in written or oral form.
- The team works together: working in the library stacks, interviewing sources as a pair or group, continually integrating their questions and their findings.

Focusing and Ordering

- Each member works separately at each stage of the planning process, then the team meets to incorporate what each has produced into a single plan.
- The team talks through the entire planning process, producing a series of co-written plans.

Drafting

- One writer produces a draft and another writer [or writers] take that draft as a basis for another draft. A variation is to assign each team member a section of the text to draft alone, then meeting to glue it together.
- The writers talk their way through a draft. One writer may be the secretary [not always a female, please] but the evolving text is the integrated product of the team, different from what any team member would produce alone.

Clarifying

- The draft is handed from one team member to another, with each person revising and editing the text.
- The team talks its way through the text, revising, then editing together, line by line.

Within this range of working in parallel or with total integration, all sorts of patterns are possible, depending on the task and the working/thinking habits of the participants.

In every case there are obvious difficulties and not-quite-so-obvious advantages. When I have collaborated I have not only learned from the other person (and I have learned a very great deal from them) but I have also discovered how to detach myself from the text and to serve its own evolving meaning.

Collaboration has freed me from the limitations of ego and the false concept that I possess the text. The text is not owned by the writer or the reader. It has its own evolving meaning, and the writer must learn how to listen to the text and help it say what it has to say in its own way. The text is the child of the writer, not a possession of the writer. It is of the writer but has its own life to lead. Collaboration has helped me detach myself from my text and work to make that text fulfill itself.

To Collaborate

- Work in parallel as described above, dividing tasks, then coming together to deal with material produced individually.
- Work closely together in the pattern described above so that all your work is the product of the pair or team.
- After you have completed the project, discuss the advantages and disadvantages of working this way with your team members or the class. And next time you perform collaborative writing, work in a different pattern to discover what you learn.

A Note on Writing Argument

You don't have to be angry to argue. And you don't have to get mad when someone argues with you.

Imagine an argument, and most of us see two monster mouths, both projecting noise, from heads that have no ears. We have observed argument at home, in school, on the playground, in church, on the street, at work. We have argued and been argued at. For most of us argument is something to be avoided.

But argument is the form of writing society uses to participate in the world of ideas. Through argument we present, develop, test, and communicate our ideas, discover the ideas of others, and respond.

The World of Ideas

Ideas are invisible until they are written down, and even then most people do not see them as having the strength and reality of bridges, roads, walls. But your world and mine is not controlled by things, but ideas. There was the idea of a bridge, of a road, of a wall before any were built. And ideas caused their need.

Ideas are the thoughts, concepts, beliefs, imaginings, speculations, dreams, theories, truths that govern our personal and social lives.

These ideas usually begin with an individual using interior language to talk to himself or herself; then the idea-maker (usually tentatively, hesitantly) mentions the idea to another individual. That person listens and responds. The idea-maker goes back to the laboratory inside the head, considers the response, accepts it, rejects it, or makes use of it to develop the idea more completely.

Again and again the idea is brought out. Others respond to it, and the idea becomes changed and stronger in the process. Usually the idea gets written down, for by writing down an idea we give it precision. The idea-maker can study the written idea, stand back from it, move in close, make changes. The written idea also allows those around the idea-maker to study and respond with greater care. And writing, ultimately, allows the idea-maker or the community of people who now believe in the idea to reach out to others.

The written idea wins acceptance from larger and larger groups of people or it is adapted and changed, influencing the world that receives it. Or it is rejected. But many times the thinking that produces rejection causes those who do the rejecting to change their ideas.

We all live in many worlds of ideas. We are governed by ideas of family and friendship and love and hate. We are ruled more by the ideas of the society with which we identify than we are by the police and the courts that enforce some of those ideas. A church, a club, a political party, or a union is above all a community of ideas. And in school we are introduced to the worlds of ideas that govern the subjects we study. The idea of history is what we learn from the facts of history; the idea of science is what we learn from the process of experimentation.

Playing the Game of Ideas

One of the great ideas of our society is that we should not be passive citizens in the worlds of ideas in which we dwell. This is an idea to which everyone we know would swear allegiance—in the abstract. We should not just receive ideas and believe them; we should question, doubt, adapt, qualify those ideas by developing, testing, and sharing our own ideas. No world of ideas should be static, but it should always change, moving forward on the thinking of those who precipitate and participate in the ever-changing code of beliefs by which each world of ideas is governed.

Much of the most influential writing is never published. You will almost certainly find yourself writing argument after graduation. The ideas that change the direction of a business or a corporation are usually presented in reports and memoranda. Judges change the law through their opinions. Scientists use laboratory reports and scientific papers; literary critics use essays and reviews; poets argue with poems, lawyers with briefs, legislators with proposals for new or amended laws.

Is Argument Male?

Yes.

But don't women argue?

My wife, my daughters, my women friends and colleagues certainly do. But the world of formal, academic argument has been dominated by the attitudes and forms of male display.

Men have dominated our worlds, and it should be no surprise that the ways in which men have thought it proper to argue have been the forms imposed on both men and women.

No matter how ridiculous male display is—the hoof pawing the ground, the shaking of the horns, the roar, the line in the dust, the conflict—it is the way that has been imposed on those who want to change the ideas in our world.

Women and men who may not want to argue in that way have been forced to go to the extremes of positions in the belief that the truth can evolve from a conflict between two opposing forces. I was an introverted, shy little coward, who had to learn to be a man. For a while I overcompensated, played right tackle, jumped out of planes, and shot at people, competed on the newspaper for stories, valuing victory over the way in which the victory was achieved.

As I began to grow up and learn the complexities of the world, I saw that the forms of argument through which people were trying to influence ideas were too simple.

We live in complex worlds. Ideas do not exist in isolation. It is the nature of ideas to influence our vision of the present and of the future, to affect the relationship of overlapping and interacting ideas.

It is always uncomfortable for a male to argue in favor of feminism. It can be at best patronizing. And yet I am a male, and I am writing on argument, and the feminist movement has greatly influenced my writing, my teaching of writing—and my life.

As I have studied argument, even books written by women, I realized the masculine nature of traditional argument. Its purpose seemed victory at almost any cost; its language macho; its images male (note how *I* talk about playing the game of ideas); its procedures combative; its language militaristic—"take a position and defend it."

When I taught the freshman class in argument, from which the student examples in this text are drawn, 21 of the 26 students were female. They were bright, committed, opinionated, and yet they all resisted writing argument. They saw argument as an alien form of expression, and they taught me because of their beliefs. The five males all seemed to feel comfortable with the idea and the form of argument. I had to pay attention to this.

The implications for women in the fact that academic and professional argument has been a male domain is another twist on the old double standard. If women want to achieve in school and afterward as scholars, corporate executives, legistlators, scientists, lawyers, engineers, as influencing members of the professions, then they have to learn to use male-designed methods of argument.

This, unfortunately, will be no surprise to women. My women students generally write better than the men and I believe this is due, in part, to the fact that women have to speak two languages: the language of women and the language of men. They have greater linguistic skills because they have to move back and forth from one language to another.

Of course many men do not realize there are two languages. Men can succeed, for the time being, by just speaking their own language, not realizing there is another. And it is their loss. Men will be richer—better writers, better thinkers—if they realize there are two languages and at least two ways to argue, to listen and respond, to make a case, to persuade and convince—and if they learn these other ways in addition to their own.

Men may continue to draw a line in the dust and dare their opponents to step across it, but such simplistic, confrontational argument has less and less effectiveness in a diverse and complex modern world. Women are working out their own collaborative rhetoric of argument based on listening first, then responding, sharing and learning, absorbing and integrating the views of others into a position that will not defeat but persuade.

And if men are not wise enough to see the value of this alternative to confrontational, militaristic argument for their own enrichment, they will have to learn it for their own survival. Women will achieve power by speaking the male language and following the traditions of male argument, but once they have power, women will—and should—start adapting and enriching the language of their professions and modifying and enhancing the methods of argument.

Today women are lawyers and judges, bosses and executives, professors and administrators, editors as well as writers (I have had only one male book editor for more than a dozen books), men's colleagues and increasingly their superiors in almost every career. Change may be slow in coming but it *is* coming and men must realize that they will work with women and for women and they will have to persuade women as well as men if they want to participate in the game of ideas.

What then does the fact that argument is male imply? That women have to learn the modes of male discourse, and then work to change them; that men have to work with women to develop new ways of speaking, writing, and arguing that are appropriate in a pluralist society. And both sexes should work together to develop methods of thinking and communicating that encourage a great diversity of ideas.

What Should I Argue About?

The best arguments usually come from the subjects we know about and care about. All effective writing must speak with authority. We need to know our subject to document our writing with appropriate and accurate information.

And we need to remember the caring. Sometimes, in fact, the caring comes first. We see a stream polluted, and it makes us mad. We have to go back and investigate the causes, learning about the reason for the pollution, the effects of stopping the pollution that may cost jobs as well as profits. We may have to learn a great deal about how laws are made, how they are enforced, and what their influence is. We may, in other words, have to learn economics and sociology, chemistry and biology, law and medicine.

Your subjects should rise out of your own personal concerns. You should challenge those ideas that seem unproductive or harmful in the worlds you inhabit. In other words, you should scratch what itches.

And when you are assigned to make an argument in school, in the corporation, in the government agency, you should look for an itch. You should try to find a way to deal with the subject on your own terms, or through your own investigations find a point of view from which you can examine the subject.

What Makes an Effective Argument?

An effective argument has six principal elements. The importance of each element will vary from argument to argument: logic may dominate one argument, facts another, and voice a third. But all the elements usually work together to make the case in an effective argument.

A Point   The reader must know the point of the argument, the single dominant message the writer wants to deliver. An argument may have several points or messages, but they should each support and advance the main point. The writer must communicate authority and purpose, convincing the reader that the writer knows what to do and is doing it.

Empathy   The writer must be able to enter the world of the reader and see the argument from the point of view of the reader. The writer must be able to make the reader connect with the topic and shape all the other elements of the argument (for example, evidence and voice) so the reader will be interested and convinced.

A Structure   An effective argument carries the reader from point to point in a logical sequence. Indeed, one thing leads to another. Each point is presented; the reader is given time to absorb it; then a new point is built on it. The structure moves forward with the momentum and energy of an evolving meaning.

Evidence   The readable, believable writer builds prose with information. This information should be specific and accurate. The specifics give the text vitality, clarity, authority. Each specific sparks meaning in the reader's mind and memory.

Voice   The tone, style, and manner of the argument are not cosmetic parts of the argument, they are essential to the effectiveness of the message. The writer's voice must be appropriate to the writer's subject and the writer's opinion of that subject. The voice should also be close enough to the reader's voice for the reader to "hear" the message and feel that the writer has articulated the reader's own beliefs.

An Invitation   The argument should invite the reader to act. That invitation may be explicit or implicit, but it should be there. The reader wants to know what to do by the end of a persuasive argument. That act may be external—a vote, a decision—or it may be internal, inviting the reader to think, reflect, feel, believe differently than before.

The principal purpose of written argument is to persuade others, over the barriers of time, culture, and distance, to accept your ideas into their thinking. Sometimes they will accept your ideas as truth; other times—without knowing it—they will believe they have thought your ideas themselves; sometimes they will reject what you have to say outright. Most of the time they will accept part of what you have to say, drafting it onto their own beliefs or adding new questions to their thinking. Then you will respond to their ideas: accepting, rejecting, adapting what they say to your own thinking.

Truth—those ideas in which a group of people agree to believe for the moment—does not often arrive complete and believed but is hammered out through the interaction of written argument: the articles and books that change the nature of our lives. If you learn the craft of written argument, you will influence the world of ideas and the "truths" by which we live.

Case Study: A Journalist Writes and Reads

Christopher Scanlan

Every writer builds a small writing community on which the writer depends for support, stimulation, criticism, and encouragement during the writing process. Christopher Scanlan is one of the most important members of my personal writing community. Every week we are in touch with each other by mail and phone, sharing drafts that work and don't work, listening, counseling, discussing the craft of writing that forever fascinates us.

I first met Scanlan when I was brought to the Providence, Rhode Island, *Journal/Bulletin* as a writing coach. At the first workshop I noticed his skepticism and his tough-minded interest in how writing was made. I read what he wrote and was impressed, and as I got to know him I learned with him and from him. Later, he moved to the *St. Petersburg* (Florida) *Times* and our phone calls continued—and the phone bills went up. He is editor of a book on newswriting, *How I Wrote the Story,* published by the Providence Journal Book Club.

Scanlan is above all a pro. He takes his turn at rewrite and covering hard news, although he is both an investigative reporter digging out material authorities do not want to divulge and a feature writer known for his sensitive stories. He is a graduate of the Columbia University School of Journalism, has worked on newspapers in Delaware and Connecticut, as well as Rhode Island, and has been a contributing editor of *Connecticut Magazine.* His nonfiction has been published in more than a dozen other publications and he was won awards for investigative reporting, spot news, business, and feature writing. Scanlan has been honored for the best series and the best feature story by the New England Associated Press News Executives Association.

In this case study he shares some of his notes and drafts with us as well as a draft revised after publication for reprinting. It is fascinating to see how many writers can't let go but keep improving their work even after it has been published. He has also written an account of how he collected, selected, and wove the information into a story that has been reprinted in five publications.

You may want to follow the history of this article as we have printed it, seeing the work evolve, or jump ahead and read the article or the account of its writing and then work through the material from which the article evolved.

❧ Most writers keep journals, daybooks, or logs in which they talk to themselves
about what they may write and store up material for that writing. One page
from Scanlan's "Traveler's Log" follows. ❧

~~pilgrimage   a journey, especially a long one, undertaken
in quest of something for a particular purpose; as to pay
homage.~~

From a Traveler's Log.

June 23. 8:50 a.m.

We are on the train at Gare St. Lazaee bound for Lison-
Marigny to find Pat Callahan's half-brother's grave. It
is first class- like an American commuter- except that most
of the seats are reserved. We found two "non reserve" next
to two "mutile." I notice the French don't take the "mutile"
which are by the windows so we moved out of them . If no
mutile shows perhaps we can reclaim them.
It's a nice day- light sky with mild breezes and a promise
of a warm sunny day. We gave a bag with camera. This is the
train to Cherbourg from which we would leave for Ireland but
we really don't have the time. As of midnight last night
we have just 7 full daYS OF Eurail travelling left and we want
to spend at least one more day in Paris which means at the
soonest we wont leave Paris until Thursday and with that
just doesn't give us enough time so we'll proably head west
again to Germany and Austria...Leaving Paris now on this
Turbotrain to Cherbourg, fiie filled mostly with businessmen
one of whom seems to have a gimp;y gimpy leg from the way it's
sticking out and the way he almost lost his balance when he
changed seats. This train is comfortable and quick. I hope
we can find the grave. I'd hate for this to be a wild goosh
goosechase...
11:03 a.m. Arrive in Lison in 23 minutes. I'm nervous, anxious
about switching trains - whether we have to buy a ticket or
what- and hungry. We passed villages and cities, orchards and
green fields and fields of baled hay. A beautiful Cathedral
in Lisieux. It is a beautiful day.
1:13 p.m. Took bus from Lison to St. Lo and then a taxi to
Marigny (100 francs) but the American cemetery is no longer
there - only a German one. A long time ago, the taxi driver
said, they moved the graves we go no to St. Laurent to find
it.
Interview with Pedro Rivere (sp) superintendent of Normandy
cemetery:
He's from Albugurque, NM, a radio operatsor and tail gunner
in a B-26 who flew 40 missions over North African and Italy
who has been working for cemetery commission for 26 years,
with service at cemeteries in Luxembourgh and North Carthage,
Tunishxix Tunisia.
He pulled out the book of the dead from a shelf in his office
and looked down the columns of tiny print.
"Here it is. Juba, John Jr. from Pa. He's in Brittany Cemetery
at St James." He gave us the information. Section D, Row 10
Grave 8. Killed Aug. 4, 1944. Rank Private First Class.
Serial Number 33673674. Outfit: 12 Inf. 4 Division. Winner
of Purple Heart.

☞ The lead is a journalistic term for the first sentence, paragraph, or paragraphs that lead the reader into the story. Few journalists will proceed with a draft until they have a working lead that establishes the voice or tone of the article, its focus, and direction. What follows is Scanlan's first attempt at a lead. The professional writer knows how important it is to get something down, to write badly—not wanting to write badly—to write well. ☜

IT was to be our firSt trip to Europe.~ _together_ After almost six years of dreaming and hoping and wishing we had enough money, we had enough. What if it was the downpayment for a house or enough for the IBM typewriter we wanted to buy? ~~Europe~~ Some day we would have that house, ~~andxthatxxxiting~~ someday that typewriter, but when would we ever have that first trip to Eruopex together if we didn't take it now. That's what we told each other as Kathy and I planned our itinerary _and going_. Germany, ~~wherexherx~~ to the Rhine Balley where her mother was born and grew up, where she lived until an American airmen married her and brought her to the United States. Ireland, ~~Wherexmyxgreatxgranparentsx~~ in search of my roots. France, because it was in the middle ~~ofxthosextwoxcountries~~, and whatever side trips we could manage ~~in~~ on our 15 day Eurail Pass. It was all fiarly vague which was how we wanted it. It was a vacation after all, not a pilgrimage. Or so we thought.

~~LikexeveryonexwextoldxaboutxourxtripyxPatxCallahanxxx~~ ~~axcoxworkerxxinxthexnewsroomyxwasxenthusiasticxx~~

A couple of weeks before we left, Pat Callahan came up to me at my desk in the newsroom. ~~Likextherxfriendsxx~~ ~~andxcoxworkersyx~~ I had told him about the trip and like other friends and co-workers, he'd been enthusiastic. _You said_ "You're going to France, right?" he asked now.

~~XYesyxxxYesyxIxIxsaidxxXParisxandxthenxwestxtoxx~~ ~~CherbourgxxWhenxIxnoddedyxhexsontinuedxxx~~

I nodded and he said, "You know, I have a half-brother _he was only 18._ whose buried in France. He died in the Normandy invasion.X The ~~XNsxkiddingx~~ thing is, nobody in family has ever been able to visit his grave and I was wondering since you're going to be in France, that maybe you could visit the grave. If it's on your way, of course."

~~WhyxnotyxIxthoughtxxIfxitxsxnearby~~

Why not, I thought. ~~Ifxwexcould Itxmightxmakexanx~~ ~~interestingxsidextrip~~ I imagined Kathy and I getting off a train with a bouquet of flowers and walking down a dusty country road~~xxiinedxwith~~ shaded by tall leafy trees _I saw us_ to the cemetery, standing before the soldier's grave, sabin

The writer has been reading notes, reading drafts imagined in the writer's head and reads what has been written to see what may be written, then reads it again and again, not so much to see what doesn't work and has to be crossed out or tossed away but to see what may work on future drafts. The writer reads with surprise while writing and after writing, not thinking before writing as much as thinking by writing. Here are the first and fourth pages of a discovery draft which reveal a writer thinking by writing.

```
SLUG: JUBA      VER:            DATE: 25-SEP 81  TIME: 13:42
PAP:  DAY:      ED              PG:        ORIG  SCAN ;12/09,09-1MSG
FMT: NEWS6HJ:   HD:                        OU:   SCAN   FR: SCAN ;12/SD
```

war's ouch a drag.
you get the day
for it.

It was to be our first trip to Europe. After almost six years of dreaming
and hoping -- and working -- we had enough money to go. ~~What If it was the
downpayment for a house,~~ or enough for the ~~IBM~~ typewriter ~~we wanted to buy. Some
day we would have a house~~ someday that typewriter. ~~But when would we have even
that first trip to Europe if we didn't take it now?~~ That's What Kathy and I
told each other. last spring ~~x~~ we planned our itinerary. Germany, where her
mother was born. Ireland, in search of my roots. France, because it was in the
middle, plus whatever other side trips e could manage on a 15-day Eurail Pass.
Our plans were vague, but that's how we wanted it. It was a vacation, after
all, not a pilgrimage. ~~Or so we thought.~~

<BO> [UPstars]   *stet*

<RO> A couple of weeks before we left, I mentioned the trip to a ~~co-worker~~
Pat Callahan, *a coworker in the newsroom at the paper,*

"You're not going to France, are you?" ~~he said~~ *he said*

"The reason I ask, ~~he said~~ "is I've got a half brother buried there.
He was in the Normandy invasion and never made it home. Nobody in my family has
ever been able to visit his grave. *get over there so we'll* ~~and I was wondering if maybe~~ you would
visit the cemetery, if it ~~were~~ *i'd not* out of your way."

"Sure," I said. "I'd be glad to try. I'm not really sure where we're
going in France, but if we're close enough, it shouldn't be too much trouble to
stop."

"Great," Pat said. "We've got the location where he's buried. I'll get
it from my mother." A few days later, he handed me a slip of paper ~~with this
message:~~

                              (MORE)

if we're close, I'd be glad to try
```
```

It was lunchtime when we got off in Lison ~~taxtransfer~~ to change for
the ~~xtexxxmxxxdxjxllyxxxx~~ spread butter and jelly
~~x~~ bus to St. Lo. We ~~finishedxxurxbreakfast~~ crossants ~~xxdx inx~~

~~iaftharkxx~~ left over from breakfast ~~xxdxxhxxxxx~~ as we bumped along

on the back seat of the bus as it rolled up and down narrow ~~rxadsxx~~

country roads and squeezed through ~~txwnxxxx~~ Main Streets hedged by

~~bulletxpxrked~~ stone houses. It was a hot summer day.~~xxdxfliexxbuxxxdx~~

~~xrxundxxurxhexdxx~~ Flies buzzed around our heads. ~~I Stxkxxxx~~
                                                    lay
~~laxxinxxxvalleyxxxx~~ The city of St Lo ~~lxy~~ in a valley~~yxxxx~~

~~industrialxsasisxxhrxxdxdxinxdxxtx~~
                miles of
After riding past ~~hedgxgx~~ fields latticed with hedegrows ~~wx~~

we came upon St Lo spread out on the floor of a ~~dxxtryx~~

valley and ended the bus ride at the train station. Marigny
                    but wasnt on a train or bus line,
was about 20 kilomters away, the ticket agent told us. There
                    either but the agent got on the phone
were no cabs in sight so he called us one and within a minute

a cream Mercedes pulled up ~~xndxwxxxpxdxxwxyxxx~~ at the door.

    The driver was in his fifties, ~~xxgrxyxx~~ gray-haired,
            He hit 120 Kms.   passed lorries + cars
and taciturn, ~~butxhexdrxvexthextxxixtikexxxixngxx~~ but he raced

the ~~Itxwxxxxxxhxrtxxidxx~~ taxi as if it were Le MaNS instead of
            uкр   Show
this rural highway. ~~A~~ What sounded like the Salty Brine of

St Lo chattered on the radio.

    ~~XWxtrxxgxingxtxx~~

    ~~"NxuxxchxrchxnxxlxxximtixrxxAmericxnxyXxIxtxidxhimxxxx~~

    ~~"xWxtrxxgxingxtxxthexAmericxnxcxmxtxryyXxIxtxidxhimxxxxxxxxxxx~~

    ~~X~~ After we had ridden in silence for a few minutes, I leaned

fotward and in my rusty French told him our destination. For the

first time he turned around.

    ~~XWhxtx~~ "There's no American cemetery in Marigny," ~~b~~e said.

    Just then we turned off the highway and he pointed at

a sign in a grassy ~~g~~raffic island. "Cimtiere allemands," it

said. There's a German cemetery there," he said. "But no

Americans."

❧ Scanlan read the last draft and wrote a number of handwritten attempts before starting the new second draft. We have reprinted the first page of the "final" second draft.❧

SLUG: JUBA   PAGE: 2

    "U.S. Military Cemetery.

Marigny, France.

Plot K, Row 9, Grave 10.

9 miles west of St. Lo, France.

PFC John Juba Jr. 12 Inf. Reg.

Died Aug. 12, 1944 (18 years old)"

    ⟨BO⟩ [UFstars]

⟨RO⟩   On the Michelin map the French Tourist Office ⟨NO⟩ check name ⟨RO⟩ sent

us, Marigny was a pinhead circle that looked to be about a 50-mile detour off the train

route from Paris to the port of Cherbourg where we planned to sail to Ireland.   We could

get off the train, we figured, catch a bus or a taxi to the cemetery, maybe have lunch in

the country and still make an evening boat to Rosslare.   When we flew out of Logan Airport

on June 6, our Lufthansa 777 ⟨NO⟩ check ⟨RO⟩ leaving thunderstorms behind, the map was

in one of our bags, an X inked beside Marigny.

❧ We have reprinted the first, seventh, and eighth pages of the third draft. ❧

~~Cream Mercedes hurtled through the Normandy countryside,~~

The taxi ~~sped~~ along the country highway and for the

10th time since we left Paris thatm morning, I looked at the

piece of paper in my hand.

"U.S. Military Cemetery.

Marigny, France.
9 miles west of StLo
Row DGrave 10.
9 mil

PFc John Juba Jr.   12 Inf. 4 Reg.

Killed Agu12, 1944.   18 yeaRS old."

xxxfxjxxx xgxixxk xxxxgxery xxxt x xkxxjxjtxjx xgxixxkpxx xxxfxxpxxxxjtxxgk xxtxxdpxxjpxx x

~~We~~ *my wife* Kathy and I ~~were taking a day from our~~ *as a favor to a*

vacation in Europe to do ~~x a x~~ favor for a friend back home *friend back*
last summer *home, my wife and*
half-brother *I were on my*
by visiting the grave of a ~~relative~~ killed two months after *way to visit the grave*
of a man we never
D-Day and buried in the Normandy countryside. *knew—a young*
American soldier
"Wait a minute," our cabbie said, "there's no American *killed in Normandy*
France 2 months
~~cemetery in Marigny."~~ ~~I read him the directions.~~ ~~He was~~ *later, on HisD-Day.*
I didn't know there
~~unim pressedxxxxxxxxxxxxxxxgfxxxkxxxxxxxxxxxxxxpxxgxxxxxxx~~ *were any American*
s buried in
~~xxkxxxx and when we turned off the highway at Marigny, he~~ *Marigny,"*
our
~~pointed to a sign in the grassy traffic island.~~ /"German *cabbie said our*
cabbie who
soldier's cemetery" a sign safid in French and German.   When *picked us up*
at the train
we reached the town, he stopped on the sleepy Main Street and *station in StLo.*

~~xxdkxdxxxxuxxxxpxdxxxxxxxxxxxxxxxxxxxxxxykixgxxxuxxxpxxxthxxpxxxx~~

called to a woman ~~watxxingxxxxpxxxxxx~~ on the sidewalk *and asked if there*
was an America cemetry in town.
"There's no Americans cemetery," ~~she said too.~~ "There

used to be one, but it's not there anymore. There's only Germans

there now." ^s

He slowed up to turn and pointed to a white sign in a
grassy traffic island, and pointing in the direction of
Marigny

The graves at Brittany Cemetery lie beyond the
Wall of the Missing – 4,313 marble crosses and ~~Stars~~
Stars of David ~~lined up~~ lined
up like a ~~marble~~ marching band at half-time. ~~Section~~
Section D was on the right.

"Kathy, over here," ~~I called~~ I called, ~~someone~~
~~breaking~~ breaking the stillness of the afternoon. A man
appeared in the window of a house ~~beside~~ beside the cemetery and
within moments ⌄emerged wearing a tan raincoat⌄ and introduced
himself as Donald Davis, the superintendent.

"D-10-8," he said, "That's right down here ~~~~ He led
(ws) down nine rows of graves, turned off down the tenth and
~~~~ began counting off crosses.
At the eighth ⌄we stopped and found John Juba Jr's name
cut into the marble.

              blossoms up
I laid the flowers⌄ in front of the ✱ cross to take
a ~~~~ picture ~~~~ for the boy's mother.

"Wait," Mr. Davis ~~~~ said. He bent down
and rearranged the bouquet so the ~~~~ flowers ~~~~ would face
the camera. "Otherwise, all you'll get is a ~~~~ picture of the
stems." Every trade has its secrets, ~~I thought, and prayed~~

The old ~~~~ Frenchman was outside
trimming his rose bushes when we returned. ~~~~ He
invited us into his kitchen, ~~~~ where the
air was tangy with the smell of woodsmoke and ~~~~ poured
wine into three china cups.

His name was Pierre Letrachant, ~~~~ he was
72 years old and he had lived most of his life in ~~this~~ the farm
country outside the village of St. James.

~~██████~~, his wife's family had owned the 27 acres of land where John Juba was buried until the Americans bought it after the war. In those days, it was a dairy farm. Now his wife was dead and, except for his chickens and his garden, he was retired from farming.

"The cemetery is very ~~████~~beautiful, isn't it," ~~██~~ he said. It was quiet most of the time, except on the last day of May ~~████████████████████████████~~ ~~███████████████~~ "That's one of your holidays, isn't it."

But young people like you, he said, they ~~█~~ never come to visit. "The young have forgotten all this."

What have they forgotten, we asked him.

"That the young who died delivered us," he said.."The ~~█████████~~ young, they should come here."

We rode back to Paris on the train later that afternoon. ~~████████████████████████~~ I thought of the flowers from the old man's garden, lying at the foot of John Juba's grave, and I knew I ~~█████~~ would never forget.

Writers, as we have said, are members of a writing community. Scanlan showed his piece to Barbara Carton, a fellow writer on the *Providence Journal/Bulletin* who is now on the staff of the *Washington Post*. Here is her comment about the beginning of this late draft.

```
SLUG: JUBA2      VER:          DATE: 28-SEP 81  TIME: 16:47
PAP:  DAY:       ED            PG:          ORIG   SCAN  ;25/09.16:4MSG
FMT: NEWS6HJ:           HD:                 OU:    SCAN   FR: SCAN ;2 /SD



        <NC> I think this is a really neat story. Because it's so neat and because

was such a wonderful, unusual thing to take time out of your two week a year

vacation.   i want to know lmore about why you did it and how you felt, without

being sappy.   Just the way you told it to me when you got back   Otherwise,

great.   <RO>

        The Mercedes taxi sped along the country highway.   For the tenth time since

we left Paris that morning, I looked at the piece of paper in my hand.

        "U.S. Military Cemetery.

        Marigny, France.

        9 miles west of St. Lo.

        Row D. Grave 10.

        Pfc. John Juba Jr. 12 Inf. 4 Reg.

        Killed Aug. 1944. 18 years old."

        That was all I knew about the man whose grave my wife and I were on our

way to visit.   Kathy and I were on a delayed honeymoon in Europe last June, a
```

❧ Now Scanlan has read his draft with Carton's comments in mind and then he writes the draft from which we have reprinted the first and last pages. ❧

```
SLUG: GRA E     VER:          DATE: 29-SEP 81  TIME: 12:15
PAP:  DAY:        ED          PG:        ORIG   SCAN  ;29/09.10:3MSG
FMT:  NEWS6HJ:   0052.2/0HD          OU:  SCAN    FR: SCAN ;29/SD
```

⟨BO⟩ By Christopher Scanlan ⟨RO⟩

  The Mercedes taxi sped along the _c_ountry highway.   For the tenth time since we left Paris that morning, I looked at the piece of paper in my hand.

  "U.S. Military Cemetery.

  Marigny, France.

  9 miles west of St. Lo.

  Row D. Grave 10.

  Pfc. John Juba Jr. 12 I f. 4 Reg.

  Killed Aug. 1944. 18 years old."

  That was all I knew about the man whose grave my wife and I were on our way to visit.   Kathy and I were on a delayed honeymoon in Europe last June. a month-long trip that had already taken us to Germany, Holland and Paris.   Now, with a week left before we headed home, we were making good on a promise to a friend back in Rhode Island.

  Pat Callahan, a co-worker in the ⟨IT⟩ Journal ⟨RO⟩ newsroom didn't know much about John Juba either; his half brother had been killed before he was born.   Pat didn't know how he died, only that he was buried in France in a grave no one in the family had ever seen.   He asked if my wife and I would mind visiting the cemetery on our vacation, maybe take a picture of the gravestone for his mother.   "If it's on your way, of course," Pat said when he handed me the directions and that was how we left it.

  It wasn't on our way, as it turned out, but all through our vacation, the X e'd marked beside Marigny on our map _o_f France

         (MORE)

woodsmoke and poured port wine into three china cups.

His name was Pierre Letrachant.   He was 72 years old and for most of his life he had lived in this farm country outside St. James.   His wife's family, in fact, had once owned the 27 acres of land where John Juba was buried.   It had been a dairy farm in those days, until the Americans bought it after the war.

The cemetery was quiet most of the time, he said, except on the last day of May when crowds came.   That's one of your holidays, isn't it.''

''But young people like you,'' he said, shaking his head, ''they never come to visit.   The young have forgotten all this.''   He didn't sound angry, just a little sad.

What have they forgotten, we asked.

''That the young who died delivered us,'' he said.   ''The young, they should come here.''

We rode back to Paris on the train later that afternoon. I thought of the flowers from the old man's garden lying at the foot of John Juba's grave and I knew that I would never forget.

(END)

❦ The article appeared in the *Sunday Journal Magazine,* but when it was reprinted, Scanlan touched it up some more and here is that final draft. ❧

The Young Who Died Delivered Us

1   The Mercedes taxi sped along the country highway. For the tenth time since we left Paris that morning, I looked at the piece of paper in my hand.

2   "U.S. Military Cemetery
Marigny, France.
9 miles west of St. Lô.
Row D Grave 10.
Pfc. John Juba Jr. Inf. 4 Div.
Killed Aug. 4, 1944, 20 years old."

3   That was all I knew about the man whose grave my wife and I were on our way to visit. Kathy and I were on a delayed honeymoon in Europe, a month-long trip that had already taken us to Germany, Holland and Paris. Now, with a week left before we headed home, we were making good on a promise to a friend back home.

    ❦Notice how quickly Scanlan gets you into the story. You are in the taxi and you know where you are and where you are going and why in just 21 lines. Also note how Scanlan uses narrative—the ancient skill of storytelling—to carry the reader through the article. Finally, you should study how Scanlan has gotten out of the way. You are there. You are discovering the story with Scanlan. George Orwell, master to all journalists, tells us that "Good writing is like a window pane." Scanlan has the craft to construct a pane of glass so clear the reader does not even know it is there. ❧

4   Pat Callahan didn't know much about John Juba either; his half-brother had been killed before he was born. Pat didn't know how he died, only that he was buried in France in a grave no one in the family had ever seen. He asked if my wife and I would mind visiting the cemetery on our vacation, maybe take a picture of the gravestone for his mother. "If it's on your way, of course," Pat said when he handed me the directions, and that was how we left it.

5   It wasn't on our way, as it turned out, but all through our vacation the "X" we'd marked beside Marigny on our map of France nagged at us. I'd never met Pat's mother. Was she wondering if we'd found the cemetery? Did she wait to hear what the place where her son was buried looked like? In the end, we didn't want to disappoint a woman who'd lost her first son in a war and never had the chance to pray at his grave. The day after we arrived in Paris we set out by train for Marigny, about 200 miles to the west.

6   Four hours later, the taxi we hired at the St. Lô station raced through the rolling Normandy countryside, quickly eating up the nine miles left of our jour-ney. For the first time that day I began to relax. We'd find the grave, take some

pictures and make it back to Paris for a boat ride on the Seine without any problem.

7   "I didn't know there were any Americans buried in Marigny anymore," the taxi driver said over his shoulder.

8   I was still trying to explain, in my rusty French, about the directions in my hand and how there had to be an American cemetery there because that's where this soldier was buried, when the cabbie turned off the highway towards Marigny and pointed to a sign planted in a grassy traffic island.

9   "German military cemetery," it said in French and German. Kathy and I were staring at each other now, beginning to panic. They just don't pick up cemeteries and move them, I said. It's got to be there.

10   We came to a sleepy Main Street of stone shops, and the cabbie stopped to consult a woman on the sidewalk.

11   "American cemetery?" she said. "Yes, there used to be one outside of town, but it's not there anymore. There are only Germans there now."

12   I wasn't ready to give up yet. "Maybe the Americans are buried *with* the Germans," I suggested to the driver. He shook his head, but drove on. A few miles out of town, on a narrow road that wound its way through apple orchards and pastures, he turned onto a dirt driveway and pulled up in front of a tall, stone fence.

13   Behind it, we found a tree-shaded meadow lined with neat rows of yellow rosebushes, like Normandy's hedgerows, stretching to the horizon, This was a curious cemetery.

14   There weren't many gravestones visible, just groups of brown crosses set in a row and staggered among the rosebushes. The graves—11,169 of them, we learned from a brochure in the chapel—were marked by stone rectangles set into the earth. We only needed to read a few of the names inscribed on them—Heinz, Friedrich, Gunther—to realize that our search for John Juba's grave hadn't ended. It had just begun.

❡ Note how neatly he works in the transition. ❡

15   "I think it was about 15 years ago they moved all the American graves," the cabbie told us on the way back to St. Lô. "As far as I know, there's only one American cemetery in Normandy now. It's a big one up north at Colleville sur Mer, on the shore. You could take a train to Bayeux and get a taxi out there. It's only about 30 kilometers."

16   We were hot, tired and hungry, but neither of us wanted to stop yet. We got on another train, and in less than an hour, a taxi deposited us in front of the visitors' building at the Normandy American Cemetery and Memorial.

17   In the office we found Pedro Rivera, a New Mexico native who was the cemetery's superintendent, and asked for his help. Yes, he told us, there had been an American cemetery at Marigny once, but it was a temporary one. After the war, the graves were moved to permanent cemeteries like this one perched on a cliff overlooking Omaha Beach and the English Channel.

18   He reached up to a wall shelf lined with half a dozen thick, black books, pulled one down and began flipping pages lined with columns of tiny print. If John Juba were buried overseas, Rivera said, his name would be in here. The books contained the names of American war dead buried overseas or commemorated as unknown or missing—35,000 names from World War I and more than 182,000 from World War II.

> ❦ Now he works in exposition, information that puts this particular veteran in context of other American war dead. ❧

19   American war dead lie in cemeteries around the world, Rivera told us, but a Normandy casualty could be found in only two places. Here, on the site of the largest amphibious assault in the history of the world, or in another cemetery about 60 miles south, in the province of Brittany.

20   "Here he is," the superintendent said, his finger stopping at the bottom of a page." John Juba Jr. He was a Pfc." He paused and then looked up at us.

21   "Oh, I'm sorry," he said, "He's in Brittany."

22   "At least we'll be able to tell his mother where he is buried," I told Kathy outside the visitor's building. She nodded, but we were both disappointed. We had a few hours to catch our train back to Paris, so we strolled in the cemetery, mixing with the crowds of schoolchildren, families of tourists and a contingent of French soldiers. The cemetery draws more than a million people a year, Rivera told us.

23   We passed by a 22-foot bronze statue of a young man, "The Spirit of American Youth Rising from the Waves." The dead at Normandy lie under a carpet of grass kept green by lawn sprinklers waving back and forth over the white-marble headstones, 9,386 of them, set in single-file rows that reach to infinity. Beyond them, we came to the cliffs of Normandy and gazed down at the beach hundreds of yards below.

24   From books and movies, I knew something about the history made on this spot, but it was hard to imagine it then.

25   It was raining on D-Day. Today the sun was warm, the sky as blue as the water and dotted with puffy white clouds. Not an armada of ships, just a single sailboat; no dead, just a lone family sunbathing on the beach.

> ❦ Scanlan uses this peaceful scene to highlight the horror of war. He doesn't write with flowery language—especially adjectives and adverbs, but with specific detail. ❧

26   "You know, if we stop now," Kathy said, "all we can bring back is what they gave us in the first place—an address."

27   I was surprised she wanted to go on. By now, we knew that visiting John Juba's grave was going to mean spending another vacation day doing it. We'd have to return to Paris first and then set out again—this time for Brittany. "I wouldn't blame you if you wanted to quit," I said. "We tried."

28   "I know," she said, "but we can't stop now." She smiled. "It's become a pilgrimage, like going to Lourdes."

29   The train back to Paris was crowded, and we had to take seats apart. Kathy sat opposite two American college kids who, it turned out, had been at Normandy that day too. Omaha Beach attracted them for a reason different from ours though.

30   "We went," said the taller of the pair, otherwise identical in shorts and nylon backpacks, "to lie on the beach, you know, catch some rays."

31   John Juba was 18 years old—about the same age as these two college kids—when he was drafted out of trade school in 1942. Everyone called him Johnny. He loved to play football and baseball. He was engaged to a girl named Dorothy.

32   We didn't know any of this when we were searching for his grave last summer. It wasn't until we returned home that I learned more about him from his mother, Mrs. Ann Callahan, 76, who lives in the Hartford Park Housing Project in Providence.

33   Johnny grew up in New Kensington, Pa., where the family lived at the time. He wasn't happy to be drafted, his mother said. But she recalled a letter he once wrote from overseas. "I'd rather be here," he wrote, "than see a man that has a family."

34   "He stepped on a mine and it blew his legs off," his mother said, "He was still alive in the hospital, but when he found he lost his legs, the shock killed him."

35   It was raining two days later when we stepped out of a taxi at the gate to the Brittany American Cemetery and Memorial. There was no one is sight and the visitors' building was locked. We were headed for the graves when I realized that I had forgotten to bring flowers.

36   It had taken 17 years for someone to visit John Juba's grave and I wanted it to be a special occasion. Kathy was right. This was a pilgrimage, a journey to the grave of a soldier who could have been anyone's son, brother, father, husband. In some unspoken way, I felt that we had become his family, at least for this one day, and I knew that his family would have brought flowers.

37   "Wait here," I told Kathy and set off the rural highway in search of wildflowers. I was about to settle for a flowering carrot weed when I heard a radio through the open window of a stone farmhouse and saw beside it a garden bursting with white roses and snapdragons.

38   The old man who answered the back door wore scuffed black clogs, gardening clothes and a cap. His apple cheeks were whiskery with white stubble. I had interrupted his lunch; behind him, in the spartan stone kitchen, a bowl of bread, cheese and cherries sat on a table covered with an oilcloth.

❧ How quickly that man—who will be vital to the story—is made to come alive. ❧

39   In my clumsy French, I told him about our search for the American soldier's grave and asked for permission to pick a few flowers from his garden. He turned away without a word.

40   I was about to leave myself—ready to believe that the French do hate all Americans—when he reappeared with a pair of pruning shears. He waved away my suggestion of payment. Bring your wife back with you after you've seen the grave, he said. We'll visit and drink some wine.

41   The graves at Brittany lie beyond the Wall of the Missing—4,313 white crosses and Stars of David lined up on a manicured field like a marching band at half time. Five varieties of grass keep it green all year round. The cemetery was empty and so quiet we could hear the rain falling on the flower beds bordering the graves.

42   Granite stones in the grass marked each section. I saw one labelled "D" on the right side and ran over, excited and nervous at the same time. What if he wasn't here either?

43   "Over here," I yelled to Kathy, a hundred yards behind me. I cringed as my shout broke the stillness, and a man appeared in the window of a house next door. Within moments he emerged, a middle-aged man in a tan raincoat who introduced himself as Donald Davis, the superintendent of the cemetery.

44   "D-10-8," he said, "That's right down here." He led us down nine rows of graves, turned down the tenth and began to count off crosses. At the eighth, we stopped and found John Juba's name cut into the white marble.

45   I laid the flowers in front of the cross and knelt to take a picture for his mother.

46   "Wait." Davis bent down and turned the bouquet around so the flowers faced the camera. "Otherwise, all you'll get is a picture of the stems." Every trade has its secrets.

    ❡ That nice touch in the last sentence is a good example of voice. It relieves the tension and gives the writer and the reader a chance to express anger at what has happened to all these young men. ❡

47   "Rest in peace, John," I said under my breath.

48   The old Frenchman was outside trimming his rosebushes when we returned. He invited us into the kitchen, where the air was tangy with wood smoke, and poured port wine into three china cups.

49   His name was Piere Letranchant. He was 72 years old and for most of his life he had lived in this farm country outside St. James. His wife's family, in fact, had once owned the 27 acres of land where John Juba was buried. It had been a dairy farm until the Americans bought it after the war.

50   The cemetery was quiet most of the time, he said, except on the last day of May when crowds come. "That's one of your holidays, isn't it?"

51   "But young people like you," he said, shaking his head, "they never come

to visit. The young have forgotten all this." he said. He didn't sound angry, just a little sad.

52   "What have they forgotten?" we asked.

53   "That the young who died delivered us," he said. "The young, they should come here."

❦ Scanlan has found the title and the meaning of the piece. And he avoids sentimentality by getting out of the way—Orwell's counsel again—and allowing the quotation to do the job. ❧

Here is Scanlan's account of how he read and wrote to produce that article.

Learning to Read Writing

1   "The Young Who Died Delivered Us" went through six drafts before it was published. That in itself makes it an unusual piece of writing for a working journalist like myself.

2   Journalism has been called "history in a hurry," and it is a discipline that teaches a writer to write fast and concentrate more on accuracy and clarity than style. Depending on the deadline, a reporter may only have time to try out a few leads and then forge ahead, making small changes as the writing is completed with an eye on the ticking clock.

3   While this nonfiction magazine story—a personal account of a search for a soldier's grave in Europe—gave me a luxury of time usually absent in most newsrooms, it taught me that time is not the secret in good writing: The real key to writing success is learning how to read a manuscript with a discriminating eye—and ear.

4   Studying how I wrote the story suggests the following rules to remember for the writer struggling to develop the necessary skills of "reading writing."

5
- Much of what you write will be discarded. Only a phrase on some draft pages will remain in the published version.
- In the beginning, lower your critical standards and accept whatever pap flows from your pen or typewriter.
- The writing you think is fantastic will later prove to be dreck. The stuff you know is dreck will point you in the direction of better writing.
- The only way to improve a piece of writing is to rewrite and rewrite and rewrite and. . . .

6   I wish I could say that I knew all this when I began writing this story, but that would be a lie. The importance of "reading writing" only became evident after I examined all of my drafts and the writing journal I keep.

7   The first draft of "The Young Who Died Delivered Us" was 2300 words long. The published version was slightly longer, about 2600 words. But a comparison of the two versions reveals that less than half of what I wrote in the first draft made it to the final version. A study of the writing process shows how

crucial the reading of the text was to the changes between the beginning and end of the making of this story.

8   As a professional writer, my process generally begins with an assignment, either from an editor or one I generate.

9   The story at hand began with a promise to a co-worker to look up the grave of a relative killed in World War II and buried in France. Before we left, I had a vague idea that it might make a good freelance story for my paper's Sunday Magazine.

10   Armed with an idea, I always begin by collecting voluminous amounts of information, much more than I will ever use. Much of it never appears in the final version, but I have a compulsion to learn as much about a subject as possible. I believe saturating myself gives me a confidence to write about subjects I know very little about. Journalists are expected to become instant experts, which is why a check with the newspaper's library is always one of my first, and most important, stops on any story.

11   During the trip chronicled in "The Young Who Died Delivered Us," I took careful notes in a travel diary, jotting down impressions and quotes from interviews. I collected brochures and other printed material at the military cemeteries we visited. After we returned home, I supplemented the field reporting with trips to the library where I consulted histories of D-Day and World War II and travel books about the regions of France we visited.

12   Two months passed before I sat down for my first writing session one evening at the end of August. By then, I had told the story to friends so many times I was bored with it.

13   I can remember staring at the blank page for a while until I seized on an idea; transcribe your notes. That's always a good time-waster. I did that for about 45 minutes until I got bored again. I turned to my journal:

14   *One of the themes I'd like to explore is pacifism. War and Peace. What's it all about? Destroyed lives and lost chances. The cost of war. Was it worth it.*

15   Noble aims, but they didn't get me any closer to my story. Now I started talking to myself. "Can I tell you a story," I wrote.

16   "Thanks," I replied. But after a couple more exchanges like that, that bored me too.

17   Write a title. That's always a good beginning.

18   "In Search of John Juba."

19   "Searching for Juba."

20   Searching but getting nowhere. I stopped. Next morning, I tried titles again.

21   "Visiting a Soldier's Grave." Nope.

22   The only thing to do would be start at the beginning.

23   I wrote:

24   *One day in late May, I mentioned to Pat Callahan, a co-worker at the newspaper where I work, that my wife and I were going to Europe in June.*

25   After about two pages of longhand I reached the point where "Pat handed me a slip of paper with the address: U.S. Military Cemetery, Marigny, France, Plot K. Row 9, Grave 170. Pfc John Juba Jr. Died Aug. 12, 1944 (20 years old)"

26   "The quest," I wrote now, "had begun."

27   I was amazed to find this passage staring out from my journal. The slip of paper with the address of John Juba's grave would eventually become my lead but at the time I didn't even recognize it.

28   During the writing I was experiencing the usual hair-pulling crises of confidence, mood swings and depression that accompany most of the writing I do, convinced almost until the end that I was incapable of writing anything worthwhile.

29   I know now that I was in the middle of the "rehearsal period," which follows the reporting. Like an actor practicing different deliveries, I was trying out leads and endings, hoping to discover my story and develop it by writing. I tell myself frequently to leave the judging until later (I used to keep that line taped to my typewriter. Now I use a word processor and the line that stares at me from my VDT is one attributed to a Spanish poet: "Traveler, there is no path. Paths are made by walking.") I need to keep reminding myself that at this stage of any story, I must follow poet William Stafford's advice and lower my standards. I have to remember that to write well I must discover what a story is by writing it and rewriting it and not spend so much time hating the early drafts because they contain the promise of the final one.

30   At this point in the process, reading other writers is important. I read for knowledge and inspiration, trying to prime the writing engine.

31   For instance, here is the first lead I wrote:

32   *It was to be our first trip to Europe. After almost six years of dreaming and hoping—and working—we had enough money to go. What if it was the downpayment for a house or enough for the IBM typewriter we wanted to buy. Someday we would have a house, someday that typewriter. But when would we ever have that first trip to Europe if we didn't take it now? That's what Kathy and I told each other last spring as we planned our itinerary. Germany, where her mother was born. Ireland, in search of my roots. France, because it was in the middle, plus whatever other sidetrips we could manage on a 15-day Eurail Pass. Our plans were vague, but that's how we wanted it. It was a vacation after all, not a pilgrimage.*

33   My journal tells me that this lead was "inspired by Don Murray's essay on his daughter's rubber tree." Inspired by the voice, the emotion and his phrase "drunk on the possibility," a line came to me: "It was to be our first trip to Europe." I raced to the typewriter and in about 15 minutes wrote a lead which I like though I worry a bit about its apparent violation of some writing canons. But at least it gives me a beginning that persuades me to go on and that's all that counts.

34   Eventually I expanded that lead to eight legal-size pages that became my first full-length draft. This was my "discovery draft." Reading this shapeless

mass of prose, I discovered several things. I saw the skeleton of a story, which I used as the basis of an outline for my next draft. This draft also showed me what I wanted to say, often by the fact that I had not said it, and what I didn't want to say because I had said it and found it lacking.

35   For instance, by the time the next draft was finished, the opening paragraph about our first trip to Europe was discarded. Only one element remains in the final version, the notion of a pilgrimage. All the other background—the house we wanted, the typewriter, our ethnic origins, I realized on rereading, was superfluous since this story was not about our vacation, but about the search that took it over for a few days in France.

36   A pilgrimage, that was the focus, the point, of the story I was struggling to write. Focus may be the most important *point* of all when you're reading your writing because in it lies the answers to those crucial questions a writer has about a draft: Does this line work? Is my organization sound? How do I begin my story? How do I end it?

37   As a journalist, my first responsibility is to the news, the information I am trying to convey. But in this complicated age of ours, information without context is meaningless. If the Public Utility Commission approves a rate increase for the electric company, that is the news, but the context, the focus, the point of my story, must take the news one step further in an effort to make it meaningful. Rather than write a lead that says "The PUC approved a $13 million rate hike yesterday," I would write it this way: "The electric bill for an average residential customer will go up $45 a month in January as a result of a rate increase approved yesterday by the PUC."

38   Two questions help me keep track of the focus of my stories as I write and read and rewrite. I write them at the top of my video display screen, even before the dateline. They are: What's the news? What's the point? Answering the first is usually easy. The second is often more difficult, probably because it is more crucial. The rewards are greater too, though, because forcing yourself to state the single dominant meaning may not only give you the focus. You may also hear the voice of your story.

39   A third question is essential when I know, the way a piano tuner recognizes discord, that a line just doesn't sound right. "What am I trying to say?" I ask myself. Often I type my answer and lo and behold, the problem is solved.

40   Every step along the way is critical, but for me, revision seems the most crucial. I am rarely satisfied with my writing, as this passage from my writing journal demonstrates.

41   *Session 9. 9 a.m. "Outlined a new draft (the 2nd) which I'll type today. Time is running out but the piece is getting more concise . . .:*

42   *11 a.m. Second draft completed. Now six pages, double-spaced about 1200 words, a far cry from the 2300 words of the first draft. It's closer now, but God it takes time.*

43   *3 p.m. Second draft edited. Ready to type. Still not happy with the lead, worried I'm leaving too much out. Why can't I just hand in what I've got?"*

44   *4 p.m. "My central fear right now is that the editors at the magazine will not like the piece, will have criticism of it and decide I'm no good and never will want my stuff again."*

45   By now I had typed the piece several times and was getting sick of it.
46   But I still wasn't satisfied.

47   *7:23 p.m. "Copy-edited. It stinks."*

48   *8:12 p.m. Retold the story in a tape recorder. It's better now."*

49   For a long time, I thought my self-flagellation during the writing process was a weakness, the sign of a hopeless neurotic. Now I see it as a strength because it forces me to keep working on a story until the meaning is clear. The effort has its rewards.

50   At one point, I had to push myself to type another draft and for my pains I discovered a line that is one of my favorites. After the cemetery superintendent told me to turn the flowers around for the picture of the grave, the line "Every trade has its secrets" popped into my head. So besides a clean draft, I got a good line from the drudgery of typing.

51   Rewriting is like rubbing a dusty window with a cloth. The more you rub the clearer the vision on the other side becomes.

52   Comparing an early draft with the published version of "The Young Who Died Delivered Us" inspired a list of rules I try to remember every time I write:

53   • Read your story with an eye out for what is missing. You may need to do more reporting.

54   When we went to Europe, we knew next to nothing about the man whose grave we hunted. This is how I handled that paucity of information in the early draft.

55   *But that was about all we knew—or to this day know—about John Juba. We don't know how he died or what he wanted to be if he had made it back home. We don't know and in the end, we don't think it really matters. What we learned standing in those cemeteries was the price a nation pays when it goes to war.*

56   That was a copout for not having the goods. A week before the final deadline I called John Juba's mother and after our conversation I knew I had the perfect juxtaposition for those two college kids we met at Normandy who went "to catch some rays."

John Juba was 18 years old—about the same age as the two college kids on the train—when he was drafted out of trade school in 1942. Everyone called him Johnny. He loved to play football and baseball. He was engaged to a girl named Dorothy.

It was one thing to say "What we learned standing in those cemeteries was the price a nation pays when it goes to war." It was quite another to use the details—trade school, a sports fan, a girl back home, and the awful details of death in wartime ("He stepped on a mine and it blew his legs off," his mother said. "He was still alive in the hospital, but when he found he lost his legs, the shock killed him.")

59   In three paragraphs, Juba became Everyman.

60   • Find co-readers of your work who can help you improve it.

61   While I wrote "The Young Who Died Delivered Us" credit for several important changes must be shared with people I think of as "co-readers." A co-reader is someone who has the unique capability of being able to read a piece of writing critically, and communicate their criticism in a way that does not make the writer want to push the typewriter out the window.

62   Here for example is how Barbara Carton, my newspaper colleague, encouraged me to write what is for me the most poignant passage in the story.

63   In the draft version I explained how I went off in search of flowers outside the Brittany cemetery and came across the old Frenchman who gave me my title.

64   Barbara could have said simply, "This passage doesn't work. It's too superficial and I just can't believe it. Needs work."

65   Instead she wrote, "This was such a nice thing to do." . . . "I think you should explain more about how you felt too. Why you wanted to bring flowers for somebody you had never met. Without getting too maudlin, which is tough and I've never learned how to do this right."

66   And instead of ripping up the page, I found myself trying very hard to understand why I had felt it was so important to bring flowers.

67   *It had taken 37 years for someone to visit John Juba's grave and I wanted it to be a special occasion. Kathy was right. This was a pilgrimage, a journey to the grave of a soldier who could have been anyone's son, brother, father, husband. In some unspoken way, I felt that we had become his family, at least for this one day, and I knew that his family would have brought flowers.*

68   • Read with your ears as well as your eyes.

69   The most important changes between drafts occurred after I read the story aloud, either to my wife and once, even to a taperecorder. For instance, in the draft version, I wrote:

70   *I was just about to leave, ready to finally accept the tourist truism that the French hate Americans—when he reappeared with a pair of pruning shears and added an invitation to return with my wife for a visit and some wine.*

71   Now there was a run-on sentence with definitely fatal syntactical symptoms. Don Murray suggests three different types of reading of drafts. First, a fast reading for context, at a distance, like a reader. Have I left any questions unanswered? Have I supported my points? Is the focus clear? (Could I say it in a single sentence?) The second reading is slower and aimed at questions of form. Have I caught the reader with a vivid lead that keeps its promise? Does my

ending carry the reader back through the story? Does the story have a logical basis, answering questions and raising new ones to answer?

72   The third reading is line by line. The writer is a mechanic now, reading to fine-tune. It is at this stage that I am looking for passive verbs to replace with active ones, for run-on sentences to break up.

73   Here is how I rewrote that offending paragraph.

74   *I was about to leave myself—ready to believe that the French do hate all Americans—when he reappeared with a pair of pruning shears. He waved away my suggestion of payment. Bring your wife back with you after you've seen the grave. We'll have a vist and some wine.*

75   By now, "The Young Who Died Delivered Us" has been published five times, in *The Providence Journal, Catholic Digest, The Milwaukee Journal, The Pittsburgh Press* and *The Sacramento Bee*. What has given me the most satisfaction, however, are the letters I have received from readers who were touched by the story. "You seem to have caught the feelings experienced by us who were there," wrote one man who served with an Army Graves Registration unit and who helped lay out the cemetery where John Juba is buried. A letter like that makes all the effort worthwhile.

76   But writers never stop "reading writing."

77   An editor at a writing seminar I attended a couple of years ago read the story and liked it too. But one passage needed work, he thought.

78   *I'd never met Pat's mother, but I kept wondering if we'd found the cemetery, waiting to hear what the place where her son was buried looked like.*

79   He was right. It was clumsy, which is why in the version I am sending out to editors this spring hoping they will publish it to mark the 40th anniversary of D-Day, that passage now reads:

80   *I'd never met Pat's mother. Was she wondering if we'd found the cemetery? Did she wait to hear what the place where her son was buried looked like?*

81   Is that an improvement? Well, at least it reads better.

Discussion

- What surprised you about this case study and Scanlan's writing methods? What is similar to the way you write? What is different?
- What do you think was Scanlan's most difficult problem in writing the piece? Did he solve it? How?
- What are the advantages of a taut, disciplined news style? The disadvantages? Compare his style to Caro's. What are the advantages and disadvantages of each style?
- Scanlan wrote a personal narrative of his search. What are the advantages of that approach? The disadvantages? What other ways could it have been written?
- How can you apply what Scanlan was teaching himself—according to his

account—during the writing of this piece to the last piece you have written or the piece you are writing?

• Compare Scanlan's use of specific detail with Caro's in the following piece. (You may also wish to compare Scanlan to other writers in the book who build on journalistic training. These include Orwell, Didion, Laurence, and Hersey.)

Activities

• Write a different lead for the article by using something else in the piece or by changing the "I" into the third person, "he" or "she." You may even imagine some research that might have been in your notes had you been Scanlan.

• Apply one of Scanlan's "rules" to a draft of your own, and write a paragraph saying how it has affected your draft.

• Search for a person or a place that is important to the history of where you are living and write an account of that search. Do not imitate Scanlan, but find your own way; then compare your version to his.

• Interview a veteran of World War II, Korea, or Vietnam to discover what people of your age need to know about the price of war.

• Take a draft of your own and imagine you are a journalist like Scanlan. See what happens if you use the discipline of the journalist as you rewrite your draft.

• Take a draft of your own and use specific details, as Scanlan does and as Caro does in the piece that follows. Write a paragraph describing what that does for your article.

• Ask a classmate to be a "co-reader" for a draft of your own. If someone asks you to be a co-reader, try to achieve the tone of Barbara Carton in your response.

Robert A. Caro

Writers are constantly sharing the news of other writers who have done an especially good job at our craft. John Monahan of the Worcester, Massachusetts, *Telegram/Gazette* shared his excitement at reading the chapter "The Sad Irons" in Robert A. Caro's biography *The Path to Power—The Years of Lyndon Johnson.* I went out the next day, bought the book, and read the chapter. Monahan had raved about the reporting that lay behind the chapter. He was right. It is a magnificent job of reporting and writing. Caro and his wife, Ina Joan Caro, who works with him, dig out details that reveal significance. This volume, the first of three, is one of the best political biographies I have read. When it was published it received the National Book Critics Circle award as the best nonfiction work of 1982.

Caro, who received the Pulitzer Prize for his biography of Robert Moses, *The Power Broker,* uses an enormous amount of detail, yet always remains the master of it, and writes with such grace that the reader is never lost in the density with which he explores the political world.

The Sad Irons

1   The source of water could be either a stream or a well. If the source was a stream, water had to be carried from it to the house, and since, in a country subject to constant flooding, houses were built well away from the streams, it had to be carried a long way. If the source was a well, it had to be lifted to the surface—a bucket at a time. It had to be lifted quite a long way; while the average depth of a well was about fifty feet in the valleys of the Hill Country, in the hills it was a hundred feet or more.

2   And so much water was needed! A federal study for nearly half a million farm families even then being conducted would show that, on the average, a person living on a farm used 40 gallons of water every day. Since the average farm family was five persons, the family used 200 gallons, or four-fifths of a ton, of water each day—73,000 gallons, or almost 300 tons, in a year. The study showed that, on the average, the well was located 253 feet from the house— and that to pump by hand and carry to the house 73,000 gallons of water a year would require someone to put in during that year 63 eight-hour days, and walk 1,750 miles.

❧ First he uses statistics, then he connects them with people below. ❧

3   A farmer would do as much of this pumping and hauling as possible himself, and try to have his sons do as much of the rest as possible (it was Lyndon Johnson's adamant refusal to help his mother with the pumping and hauling that touched off the most bitter of the flareups with his father during his youth). As soon as a Hill Country youth got big enough to carry the water buckets (which held about four gallons, or thirty-two pounds, of water apiece), he was assigned the job of filling his mother's wash pots before he left for school or the field. Curtis Cox still recalls today that from the age of nine or ten, he would, every morning throughout the rest of his boyhood, make about seven trips between his house and the well, which were about 300 feet apart, on each of these trips carrying two large buckets, or more than 60 pounds, of water. "I felt tired," he says. "It was a lot of water." But the water the children carried would be used up long before noon, and the children would be away—at school or in the fields—and most of the hauling of water was, therefore, done by women. "I would," recalls Curtis' mother, Mary Cox, "have to get it, too—more than once a day, more than twice; oh, I don't know how many times. I needed water to wash my floors, water to wash my clothes, water to cook. . . . It was hard work. I was always packing (carrying) water." Carrying it—after she had wrestled off the heavy wooden lid which kept the rats and squirrels out of the well; after she had cranked the bucket up to the surface (and cranking—lifting thirty pounds fifty feet or more—was very hard for most women even with a pulley; most would pull the rope hand over hand, as if they were climbing it, to get their body weight into the effort; they couldn't do it with their arms alone). Some Hill Country women make wry jokes about getting water. Says Mrs. Brian

Smith of Blanco: "Yes, we had running water. I always said we had running water because I grabbed those two buckets up and ran the two hundred yards to the house with them." But the joking fades away as the memories sharpen. An interviewer from the city is struck by the fact that Hill Country women of the older generation are noticeably stooped, much more so than city women of the same age. Without his asking for an explanation, it is given to him. More than once, and more than twice, a stooped and bent Hill Country farm wife says, "You see how round-shouldered I am? Well, that's from hauling the water." And, she will often add, "I was round-shouldered like this well before my time, when I was still a young woman. My back got bent from hauling the water, and it got bent when I was still young."

❧ The bent shoulders of these hill wives and their quotations make a historical situation contemporary. ❧

4   The Hill Country farm wife had to haul water, and she had to haul wood.
5   Because there was no electricity, Hill Country stoves were wood stoves. The spread of the cedar brakes had given the area a plentiful supply of wood, but cedar seared bone-dry by the Hill Country sun burned so fast that the stoves seemed to devour it. A farmer would try to keep a supply of wood in the house, or, if he had sons old enough, would assign the task to them. (Lyndon Johnson's refusal to chop wood for his mother was another source of the tension between him and Sam.) They would cut down the trees and chop them into four-foot lengths that could be stacked in cords. When wood was needed in the house, they would cut it into shorter lengths and split the pieces so they could fit into the stoves. But as with the water, these chores often fell to the women.
6   The necessity of hauling the wood was not, however, the principal reason so many farm wives hated their wood stoves. In part, they hated these stoves because they were so hard to "start up." The damper that opened into the fire-box created only a small draft even on a breezy day, and on a windless day, there was no draft—because there was no electricity, of course, there was no fan to move the air in the kitchen—and a fire would flicker out time after time. "With an electric stove, you just turn on a switch and you have heat," says Lucille O'Donnell, but with a wood stove, a woman might have to stuff kindling and wood into the firebox over and over again. And even after the fire was lit, the stove "didn't heat up in a minute you know," Lucille O'Donnell says—it might in fact take an hour. In part, farm wives hated wood stoves because they were so dirty, because the smoke from the wood blackened walls and ceilings, and ashes were always escaping through the grating, and the ash box had to be emptied twice a day—a dirty job and dirtier if, while the ashes were being carried outside, a gust of wind scattered them around inside the house. They hated the stoves because they could not be left unattended. Without devices to regulate the heat and keep the temperature steady, when the stove was being used for baking or some other cooking in which an even temperature was important, a woman would have to keep a constant watch on the fire, thrusting logs—or

corncobs, which ignited quickly—into the firebox every time the heat slackened.

7   Most of all, they hated them because they were so hot.

❧ Caro varies the lengths of his paragraphs, using the the short ones for emphasis and the longer to carry a packed load of information to the reader. ❧

8   When the big iron stove was lit, logs blazing in its firebox, flames licking at the gratings that held the pots, the whole huge mass of metal was so hot that it was almost glowing, the air in the kitchen shimmered with the heat pouring out of it. In the Winter the heat was welcome, and in Spring and Fall it was bearable, but in the Hill Country, Summer would often last five months. Some time in June the temperature might climb to near ninety degrees, and would stay there, day after day, week after week, through the end of September. Day after day, week after week, the sky would be mostly empty, without a cloud as a shield from the blazing sun that beat down on the Hill Country, and on the sheet-iron or corrugated tin roofs of the box-like kitchens in the little dog-run homes that dotted its hills and valleys. No matter how hot the day, the stove had to be lit much of the time, because it had to be lit not only for meals but for baking; Hill Country wives, unable to afford store-bought bread, baked their own, an all-day task. (As Mrs. O'Donnell points out, "We didn't have refrigerators, you know, and without refrigerators, you just about have to start every meal from scratch.") In the Hill Country, moreover, Summer was harvest time, when a farm wife would have to cook not just for her family but for a harvesting crew—twenty or thirty men, who, working from sun to sun, expected three meals a day.

9   Harvest time, and canning time.

❧ Again and again, Caro uses the natural process of what he is discussing, to carry his prose forward—getting water, washing, canning, ironing. He also uses process and process analysis to reveal political strategies and tactics and you can use it in writing about business, sports, engineering, science. ❧

10   In the Hill Country, canning was required for a family's very survival. Too poor to buy food, most Hill Country families lived through the Winter largely on the vegetables and fruit picked in the Summer and preserved in jars.

11   Since—because there was no electricity—there were no refrigerators in the Hill Country, vegetables or fruit had to be canned the very day they came ripe. And, from June through September, something was coming ripe almost every day, it seemed; on a single peach tree, the fruit on different branches would come ripe on different days. In a single orchard, the peaches might be reaching ripeness over a span as long as two weeks; "You'd be in the kitchen with the peaches for two weeks," Hill Country wives recall. And after the peaches, the strawberries would begin coming ripe, and then the gooseberries, and then the blueberries. The tomatoes would become ripe before the okra, the

okra before the zucchini, the zucchini before the corn. So the canning would go on with only brief intervals—all Summer.

12   Canning required constant attendance on the stove. Since boiling water was essential, the fire in the stove had to be kept roaring hot, so logs had to be continually put into the firebox. At least twice during a day's canning, more-over—probably three or four times—a woman would have to empty the ash container, which meant wrestling the heavy, unwieldy device out from under the firebox. And when the housewife wasn't bending down to the flames, she was standing over them. In canning fruit, for example, first sugar was dropped into the huge iron canning pot, and watched carefully and stirred constantly, so that it would not become lumpy, until it was completely dissolved. Then the fruit—perhaps peaches, which would have been peeled earlier—was put in the pot, and boiled until it turned into a soft and mushy jam that would be packed into jars (which would have been boiling—to sterilize them—in another pot) and sealed with wax. Boiling the peaches would take more than an hour, and during that time they had to be stirred constantly so that they would not stick to the pot. And when one load of peaches was finished, another load would be put in, and another. Canning was an all-day job. So when a woman was can-ning, she would have to spend all day in a little room with a tin or sheet-iron roof on which a blazing sun was beating down without mercy, standing in front of the iron stove and the wood fire within it. And every time the heat in that stove died down even a bit, she would have to make it hotter again.

13   "You'd have to can in the Summer when it was hot," says Kitty Clyde Ross Leonard, who had been Johnson's first girlfriend. "You'd have to cook for hours. Oh, that was a terrible thing. You wore as little as you could. I wore loose clothing so that it wouldn't stick to me. But the perspiration would just pour down my face. I remember the perspiration pouring down my mother's face, and when I grew up and had my own family, it poured down mine. That stove was so hot. But you had to stir, especially when you were making jelly. So you had to stand over that stove." Says Bernice Snodgrass of Wimberley: "You got so hot that you couldn't stay in the house. You ran out and sat under the trees. I couldn't stand it to stay in the house. Terrible. Really terrible. But you couldn't stay out of the house long. You had to stir. You had to watch the fire. So you had to go back into the house."

☞ Note how Caro uses quotation for authority and to bring in the voices of the Hill Country women as a variation on his own voice.☜

14   And there was no respite. If a bunch of peaches came ripe a certain day, that was the day they had to be canned—no matter how the housewife might feel that day. Because in that fierce Hill Country heat, fruit and vegetables spoiled very quickly. And once the canning process was begun, it could not stop. "If you peeled six dozen peaches, and then, later that day, you felt sick, you couldn't stop," says Gay Harris. "Because you can't can something if it's rotten. The job has to be done the same day, no matter what." Sick or not, in

the Hill Country, when it was time to can, a woman canned, standing hour after hour, trapped between a blazing sun and a blazing wood fire.'' We had no choice, you see,'' Mrs. Harris says.

15   Every week, every week all year long—every week without fail—there was washday.

16   The wash was done outside. A huge vat of boiling water would be suspended over a larger, roaring fire and near it three large "Number Three" zinc washtubs and a dishpan would be placed on a bench.

17   The clothes would be scrubbed in the first of the zinc tubs, scrubbed on a washboard by a woman bending over the tub. The soap, since she couldn't afford store-bought soap, was soap she had made from lye, soap that was not very effective, and the water was hard. Getting farm dirt out of clothes required hard scrubbing.

18   Then the farm wife would wring out each piece of clothing to remove from it as much as possible of the dirty water, and put it in the big vat of boiling water. Since the scrubbing would not have removed all of the dirt, she would try to get the rest out by "punching" the clothes in the vat—standing over the boiling water and using a wooden paddle or, more often, a broomstick, to stir the clothes and swish them through the water and press them against the bottom or sides, moving the broom handle up and down and around as hard as she could for ten or fifteen minutes in a human imitation of the agitator of an automatic—electric—washing machine.

19   The next step was to transfer the clothes from the boiling water to the second of the three zinc washtubs: the "rinse tub." The clothes were lifted out of the big vat on the end of the broomstick, and held up on the end of the stick for a few minutes while the dirty water dripped out.

20   When the clothes were in the rinse tub, the woman bent over the tub and rinsed them, by swishing each individual item through the water. Then she wrung out the clothes, to get as much of the dirty water out as possible, and placed the clothes in the third tub, which contained bluing, and swished them around in it—this time to get the bluing all through the garment and make it white—and then repeated the same movements in the dishpan, which was filled with starch.

21   At this point, one load of wash would be done. A week's wash took at least four loads: one of sheets, one of shirts and other white clothing, one of colored clothes and one of dish towels. But for the typical, large, Hill Country farm family, two loads of each of these categories would be required, so the procedure would have to be repeated eight times.

22   For each load, moreover, the water in each of the three washtubs would have to be changed. A washtub held about eight gallons. Since the water had to be warm, the woman would fill each tub half with boiling water from the big pot and half with cold water. She did the filling with a bucket which held three or four gallons—twenty-five or thirty pounds. For the first load or two of wash, the water would have been provided by her husband walking—over and over—

that long walk to the spring or well, hauling up the water, hand over laborious hand, and carrying those heavy buckets back.*

23   Another part of washday was also a physical effort: the "punching" of the clothes in the big vat. "You had to do it as hard as you could—swish those clothes around and around and around. They never seemed to get clean. And those clothes were heavy in the water, and it was hot outside, and you'd be standing over that boiling water and that big fire—you felt like you were being roasted alive." Lifting the clothes out of the vat was an effort, too. A dripping mass of soggy clothes was heavy, and it felt heavier when it had to be lifted out of that vat and held up for minutes at a time so that the dirty water could drip out, and then swung over to the rinsing tub. Soon, if her children weren't around to hear her, a woman would be grunting with the effort. Even the wringing was, after a few hours, an effort, "I mean, wringing clothes might not seem hard," Mrs. Harris says, "but you have to wring every piece so many times— you wring it after you take it out of the scrub tub, and you wring it after you take it out of the rinse tub, and after you take it out of the bluing. Your arms got tired." And her hands—from scrubbing with lye soap and wringing—were raw and swollen. Of course, there was also the bending—hours of bending— over the rub boards. "By the time you got done washing, your back was broke," Ava Cox says. "I'll tell you—of the things of my life that I will never forget, I will never forget how much my back hurt on washdays." Hauling the water, scrubbing, punching, rinsing: a Hill Country farm wife did this for hours on end—while a city wife did it by pressing the button on her electric washing machine.

24   Washday was Monday, Tuesday was for ironing.

25   Says Mary Cox, in words echoed by all elderly Hill Country farm wives; "Washing was hard work, but ironing was the worst. Nothing could ever be as hard as ironing."

26   The Department of Agriculture finds that "Young women today are not aware of the origin of the word 'iron,' as they press clothes with lightweight appliances of aluminum or hollow stainless steel." In the Hill Country, in the 1930s an iron was IRON—a six- or seven-pound wedge of iron. The irons used in the Hill Country had to be heated on the wood stove, and they would retain their heat for only a few minutes—a man's shirt generally required two irons; a farm wife would own three or four of them so that several could be heating while one was working. An iron with a wooden handle cost two dollars more than one without the handle, so Hill Country wives did their weekly loads of ironing—huge loads because, as Mary Cox puts it, "in those days you were expected to starch and iron almost everything"—with irons without handles. They would either transfer a separate wooden handle from one iron to another, or they would protect their hands with a thick potholder.

*Because so much water was required in washing, the introduction of a gas-operated washing machine by the Maytag Company in 1935 did not help the farm wife much, even if she could afford to buy it, which most Hill Country wives could not: she still had to fill and refill the machine with water.

27   Since burning wood generates soot, the irons became dirty as they sat heating on the stove, Or, if any moisture was left on an iron from the sprinkled clothes on which it had just been used, even the thinnest smoke from the stove created a muddy film on the bottom. The irons had to be cleaned frequently, therefore, by scrubbing them with a rag that had been dipped in salt, and if the soot was too thick, they had to be sanded and scraped. And no matter how carefully you checked the bottom of the irons, and sanded and scraped them, there would often remain some little spot of soot—as you would discover when you rubbed it over a clean white shirt or dress. Then you had to wash that item of clothing over again.

28   Nevertheless, the irons would burn a woman's hand. The wooden handle or the potholder would slip, and she would have searing metal against her flesh; by noon, she might have blister atop blister—on hands that had to handle the rag that had been dipped in salt. Ironing always took a full day—often it went on into Tuesday evening—and a full day of lifting and carrying six- or seven-pound loads was hard on even these hardy Hill Country women. "It would hurt so bad between the shoulders," Elsie Beck remembers. But again the worst aspect of ironing was the heat. On ironing day, a fire would have to be blazing in the wood stove all day, filling the kitchen, hour after hour, with heat and smoke. Ironing had to be done not only in the Winter but in the Summer— when the temperature outside the kitchen might be ninety or ninety-five or one hundred, and inside the kitchen would be considerably higher, and because there was no electricity, there was no fan to so much as stir the air. In a speech in Congress some years later, Representative John E. Rankin described the "drudgery" a typical farm wife endured, "burning up in a hot kitchen and bowing down over the washtub or boiling the clothes over a flaming fire in the summer heat." He himself remembered, he said, "seeing his mother lean over that hot iron hour after hour until it seemed she was tired enough to drop." Rankin was from Mississippi, but his description would have been familiar to the mothers of the Edwards Plateau. The women of the Hill Country never called the instruments they used every Tuesday "irons," they called them "sad irons."

29   Washing, ironing—those were chores that were performed every week. Then, of course, there were special occasions—harvest time and threshing time, when a woman had to cook not just for her family but for a crew of twenty or thirty men; the shearing, when, because there was no electricity and her husband had to work the shears, she had to crank the shearing machine, pedaling as if she were pumping a bicycle up a steep hill, pedaling, with only brief pauses, hour after hour; "He was always yelling 'Faster, faster,'" Mrs. Walter Yett of Blanco recalls. "I could hardly get up the next morning, I was so tired after that." Washing, ironing, cooking, canning, shearing, helping with the plowing and the picking and the sowing, and every day, carrying the water and the wood, and because there was no electricity, having to do everything by hand by the same methods that had been employed by her mother and grandmother

and great-great-great-grandmother before her—"They wear these farm women out pretty fast," wrote one observer. In the Hill Country, as many outside observers noted, the one almost universal characteristic of the women was that they were worn out before their time, that they were old beyond their years, old at forty, old at thirty-five, bent and stooped and tired.

❧ Caro repeats the description of stooped women, reminding you of the reasons for it. Effective writers are always weaving such threads through their drafts. ❧

30   A Hill Country farm wife had to do her chores even if she was ill—no matter how ill. Because Hill Country women were too poor to afford proper medical care, they often suffered perineal tears in childbirth. During the 1930's, the federal government sent physicians to examine a sampling of Hill Country women. The doctors found that, out of 275 women, 158 had perineal tears. Many of them, the team of gynecologists reported, were third-degree tears, "tears so bad that it was difficult to see how they stand on their feet." But they WERE standing on their feet, and doing all the chores that Hill Country wives had always done—hauling the water, hauling the wood, canning, washing, ironing, helping with the shearing, the plowing and the picking.

31   Because there was no electricity.

Discussion

- List the techniques Caro has used to make statistics come alive. Discuss how these techniques might be used in something you are writing.
- Take a paragraph which has been packed with detail by another writer in the book—for example, Baldwin or Didion—and discuss the similarities and differences in their technique.
- Discuss what techniques Caro uses to keep the reader interested. How does he use them? How could you use them on a draft you are writing?
- Make a list of the different types of details you would need to write a persuasive government report, business proposal, scientific paper, or another form of writing. If you do not know the kind of writing you will have to do after school, interview someone in the field or a professor in the area in which you may work after school.
- Outline a page of Caro to see how he has made his case. Discuss how a similar pattern of development could be used on a page of a classmate's draft.

Activities

- Take a page of Caro that is filled with detail and write it with generalizations, then compare the two versions to see the difference that makes to the reader. Which would make you care?

- Take a paragraph from a draft you are working on and develop it with detail as Caro would.
- Interview people in your family, neighbors, and other survivors you can find to discover the kind of details Caro uses so you can recreate a moment in the Depression, the Civil Rights Movement, the Holocaust, World War II, the Korean or the Vietnam War, the Internment of Japanese Americans during World War II, or some other historic moment.
- Use library sources to recreate a time far enough in the past so that there are no living survivors. Limit your subject. For example, an hour in the journey when people pulled wagons on a Mormon trek to Utah, an hour at a witch trial in colonial Massachusetts, an hour fighting the great Chicago fire.
- Imagine that you are a Caro 50 years from now trying to recreate the present time. Choose an activity or process or place in your life and describe it in as much detail as Caro uses.

To Collaborate

- Take a local event from the recent past, investigate it from at least three points of view—a crime from the point of view of the criminal, the police, the victim; the family of the criminal, of the victim; a social worker; defense and prosecuting attorneys; judge and jury. Decide the best way to reveal the most important lesson from the event.
- Write a quick report of the same historical moment viewed from the present and at the time it happened. Devise a way to combine both points of view in a text.

George Orwell

Although George Orwell is known for his novels such as *1984,* he will be best remembered for the power and style of his political reporting and his essays. Anyone who is a serious nonfiction writer in our time has learned from Orwell.

In one of his best-known essays, "Politics and the English Language," he gives a famous list of rules for writing:

   (i) Never use a metaphor, simile, or other figure of speech which you are used to seeing in print.
  (ii) Never use a long word where a short one will do.
 (iii) If it is possible to cut the word out, always cut it out.
 (iv) Never use the passive where you can use the active.
  (v) Never use a foreign phrase, a scientific word, or a jargon word if you can think of an everyday English equivalent.
 (vi) Break any of these rules sooner than say anything outright barbarous.

Why I Write

1   From a very early age, perhaps the age of five or six, I knew that when I grew up I should be a writer. Between the ages of about seventeen and twenty-four I tried to abandon this idea, but I did so with the consciousness that I was outraging my true nature and that sooner or later I should have to settle down and write books.

2   I was the middle child of three, but there was a gap of five years on either side, and I barely saw my father before I was eight. For this and other reasons I was somewhat lonely, and I soon developed disagreeable mannerisms which made me unpopular throughout my schooldays. I had the lonely child's habit of making up stories and holding conversations with imaginary persons, and I think from the very start my literary ambitions were mixed up with the feeling of being isolated and undervalued. I knew that I had a facility with words and a power of facing unpleasant facts, and I felt that this created a sort of private world in which I could get my own back for my failure in everyday life. Nevertheless the volume of serious—i.e., seriously intended—writing which I produced all through my childhood and boyhood would not amount to half a dozen pages. I wrote my first poem at the age of four or five, my mother taking it down to dictation. I cannot remember anything about it except that it was about a tiger and the tiger had "chair-like teeth"—a good enough phrase, but I fancy the poem was a plagiarism of Blake's "Tiger, Tiger." At eleven, when the war of 1914–18 broke out, I wrote a patriotic poem which was printed in the local newspaper, as was another, two years later, on the death of Kitchener. From time to time, when I was a bit older, I wrote bad and usually unfinished "nature poems" in the Georgian style. I also, about twice, attempted a short story which was a ghastly failure. That was the total of the would-be serious work that I actually set down on paper during all those years.

3   However, throughout this time I did in a sense engage in literary activities. To begin with there was the made-to-order stuff which I produced quickly, easily and without much pleasure to myself. Apart from school work I wrote *vers d'occasion,* semi-comic poems which I could turn out at what now seems to me astonishing speed—at fourteen I wrote a whole rhyming play, in imitation of Aristophanes, in about a week—and helped to edit school magazines, both printed and in manuscript. These magazines were the most pitiful burlesque stuff that you could imagine, and I took far less trouble with them than I now would with the cheapest journalism. But side by side with all this, for fifteen years or more, I was carrying out a literary exercise of a quite different kind: this was the making up of a continuous "story" about myself, a sort of diary existing only in the mind. I believe this is a common habit of children and adolescents. As a very small child I used to imagine that I was, say, Robin Hood, and picture myself as the hero of thrilling adventures, but quite soon my "story" ceased to be narcissistic in a crude way and became more and more a mere description of what I was doing and the things I saw. For minutes at a time this

kind of thing would be running through my head: "He pushed the door open and entered the room. A yellow beam of sunlight, filtering through the muslin curtains, slanted on to the table, where a matchbox, half open, lay beside the inkpot. With his right hand in his pocket he moved across to the window. Down in the street a tortoiseshell cat was chasing a dead leaf," etc., etc. This habit continued till I was about twenty-five, right through my non-literary years. Although I had to search, and did search, for the right words, I seemed to be making this descriptive effort almost against my will, under a kind of compulsion from outside. The "story" must, I suppose, have reflected the styles of the various writers I admired at different ages, but so far as I remember it always had the same meticulous descriptive quality.

4   When I was about sixteen I suddenly discovered the joy of mere words, *i.e.,* the sounds and associations of words. The lines from *Paradise Lost*—

5   *So hee with difficulty and labour hard*
      Moved on: with difficulty and labour hee,

6 which do not now seem to me so very wonderful, sent shivers down my backbone; and the spelling "hee" for "he" was an added pleasure. As for the need to describe things, I knew all about it already. So it is clear what kind of books I wanted to write, in so far as I could be said to want to write books at that time. I wanted to write enormous naturalistic novels with unhappy endings, full of detailed descriptions and arresting similes, and also full of purple passages in which words were used partly for the sake of their sound. And in fact my first completed novel, *Burmese Days,* which I wrote when I was thirty but projected much earlier, is rather that kind of book.

7   I give all this background information because I do not think one can assess a writer's motives without knowing something of his early development. His subject matter will be determined by the age he lives in—at least this is true in tumultuous, revolutionary ages like our own—but before he ever begins to write he will have acquired an emotional attitude from which he will never completely escape. It is his job, no doubt, to discipline his temperament and avoid getting stuck at some immature stage, or in some perverse mood: but if he escapes from his early influences altogether, he will have killed his impulse to write. Putting aside the need to earn a living, I think there are four great motives for writing, at any rate for writing prose. They exist in different degrees in every writer, and in any one writer the proportions will vary from time to time, according to the atmosphere in which he is living. They are:

8   (1) Sheer egoism. Desire to seem clever, to be talked about, to be remembered after death, to get your own back on grownups who snubbed you in childhood, etc., etc. It is humbug to pretend that this is not a motive, and a strong one. Writers share this characteristic with scientists, artists, politicians, lawyers, soldiers, successful businessmen—in short, with the whole top crust of humanity. The great mass of human beings are not acutely selfish. After the age of about thirty they abandon individual ambition—in many cases, indeed, they almost abandon the sense of being individuals at all—and live chiefly for others,

or are simply smothered under drudgery. But there is also the minority of gifted, wilful people who are determined to live their own lives to the end, and writers belong in this class. Serious writers, I should say, are on the whole more vain and self-centered than journalists, though less interested in money.

9   (2) Esthetic enthusiasm. Perception of beauty in the external world, or, on the other hand, in words and their right arrangement. Pleasure in the impact of one sound on another, in the firmness of good prose or the rhythm of a good story. Desire to share an experience which one feels is valuable and ought not to be missed. The esthetic motive is very feeble in a lot of writers, but even a pamphleteer or a writer of textbooks will have pet words and phrases which appeal to him for non-utilitarian reasons; or he may feel strongly about typography, width of margins, etc. Above the level of a railway guide, no book is quite free from esthetic considerations.

10   (3) Historic impulse. Desire to see things as they are, to find out true facts and store them up for the use of posterity.

11   (4) Political purpose—using the word "political" in the widest possible sense. Desire to push the world in a certain direction, to alter other people's idea of the kind of society that they should strive after. Once again, no book is genuinely free from political bias. The opinion that art should have nothing to do with politics is itself a political attitude.

12   It can be seen how these various impulses must war against one another, and how they must fluctuate from person to person and from time to time. By nature—taking your "nature" to be the state you have attained when you are first adult—I am a person in whom the first three motives would outweigh the fourth. In a peaceful age I might have written ornate or merely descriptive books, and might have remained almost unaware of my political loyalties. As it is I have been forced into becoming a sort of pamphleteer. First I spent five years in an unsuitable profession (the Indian Imperial Police, in Burma), and then I underwent poverty and the sense of failure. This increased my natural hatred of authority and made me for the first time fully aware of the existence of the working classes, and the job in Burma had given me some understanding of the nature of imperialism: but these experiences were not enough to give me an accurate political orientation. Then came Hitler, the Spanish civil war, etc. By the end of 1935 I had still failed to reach a firm decision. I remember a little poem that I wrote at that date, expressing my dilemma:

13   *A happy vicar I might have been*
Two hundred years ago,
To preach upon eternal doom
And watch my walnuts grow;

14   *But born, alas, in an evil time,*
I missed that pleasant haven,
For the hair has grown on my upper lip
And the clergy are all clean-shaven.

15   *And later still the times were good,*
      We were so easy to please,
      We rocked our troubled thoughts to sleep
      On the bosoms of the trees.

16   *All ignorant we dared to own*
      The joys we now dissemble;
      The green finch on the apple bough
      Could make my enemies tremble.
      But girls' bellies and apricots,
      Roach in a shaded stream,
      Horses, ducks in flight at dawn,
      All these are a dream.

17   *It is forbidden to dream again;*
      We maim our joys or hide them;
      Horses are made of chromium steel
      And little fat men shall ride them.

18   *I am the worm who never turned,*
      The eunuch without a harem;
      Between the priest and the commissar
      I walk like Eugene Aram;

19   *And the commissar is telling my fortune*
      While the radio plays,
      But the priest has promised an Austin Seven,
      For Duggie always pays.

20   *I dreamed I dwelt in marble halls,*
      And woke to find it true;
      I wasn't born for an age like this;
      Was Smith? Was Jones? Were you?

21   The Spanish war and other events in 1936–7 turned the scale and there-after I knew where I stood. Every line of serious work that I have written since 1936 has been written, directly or indirectly, *against* totalitarianism and *for* democratic socialism, as I understand it. It seems to me nonsense, in a period like our own, to think that one can avoid writing of such subjects. Everyone writes of them in one guise or another. It is simply a question of which side one takes and what approach one follows. And the more one is conscious of one's political bias, the more chance one has of acting politically without sacrificing one's esthetic and intellectual integrity.

22   What I have most wanted to do throughout the past ten years is to make political writing into an art. My starting point is always a feeling of partisanship, a sense of injustice. When I sit down to write a book, I do not say to myself, "I am going to produce a work of art." I write it because there is some lie that I want to expose, some fact to which I want to draw attention, and my initial

concern is to get a hearing. But I could not do the work of writing a book, or even a long magazine article, if it were not also an esthetic experience. Anyone who cares to examine my work will see that even when it is downright propaganda it contains much that a full-time politician would consider irrelevant. I am not able, and I do not want, completely to abandon the world-view that I acquired in childhood. So long as I remain alive and well I shall continue to feel strongly about prose style, to love the surface of the earth, and to take a pleasure in solid objects and scraps of useless information. It is no use trying to suppress that side of myself. The job is to reconcile my ingrained likes and dislikes with the essentially public, non-individual activities that this age forces on all of us.

23   It is not easy. It raises problems of construction and of language, and it raises in a new way the problem of truthfulness. Let me give just one example of the cruder kind of difficulty that arises. My book about the Spanish civil war, *Homage to Catalonia,* is, of course, a frankly political book, but in the main it is written with a certain detachment and regard for form. I did try very hard in it to tell the whole truth without violating my literary instincts. But among other things it contains a long chapter, full of newspaper quotations and the like, defending the Trotskyists who were accused of plotting with Franco. Clearly such a chapter, which after a year or two would lose its interest for any ordinary reader, must ruin the book. A critic whom I respect read me a lecture about it. "Why did you put in all that stuff?" he said. "You've turned what might have been a good book into journalism." What he said was true, but I could not have done otherwise. I happened to know, what very few people in England had been allowed to know, that innocent men were being falsely accused. If I had not been angry about that I should never have written the book.

24   In one form or another this problem comes up again. The problem of language is subtler and would take too long to discuss. I will only say that of late years I have tried to write less picturesquely and more exactly. In any case I find that by the time you have perfected any style of writing, you have always outgrown it. *Animal Farm* was the first book in which I tried, with full consciousness of what I was doing, to fuse political purpose and artistic purpose into one whole. I have not written a novel for seven years, but I hope to write another fairly soon. It is bound to be a failure, every book is a failure, but I do know with some clarity what kind of book I want to write.

25   Looking back through the last page or two, I see that I have made it appear as though my motives in writing were wholly public-spirited. I don't want to leave that as the final impression. All writers are vain, selfish and lazy, and at the very bottom of their motives there lies a mystery. Writing a book is a horrible, exhausting struggle, like a long bout of some painful illness. One would never undertake such a thing if one were not driven on by some demon whom one can neither resist nor understand. For all one knows that demon is simply the same instinct that makes a baby squall for attention. And yet it is also true that one can write nothing readable unless one constantly struggles to efface one's own personality. Good prose is like a window pane. I cannot say with

certainty which of my motives are the strongest, but I know which of them deserve to be followed. And looking back through my work, I see that it is invariably where I lacked a *political* purpose that I wrote lifeless books and was betrayed into purple passages, sentences without meaning, decorative adjectives and humbug generally.

A Hanging

1   It was in Burma, a sodden morning of the rains. A sickly light, like yellow tinfoil, was slanting over the high walls into the jail yard. We were waiting outside the condemned cells, a row of sheds fronted with double bars, like small animal cages. Each cell measured about ten feet by ten and was quite bare within except for a plank bed and a pot for drinking water. In some of them brown, silent men were squatting at the inner bars, with their blankets draped round them. These were the condemned men, due to be hanged within the next week or two.

2   One prisoner had been brought out of his cell. He was a Hindu, a puny wisp of a man, with a shaven head and vague liquid eyes. He had a thick, sprouting moustache, absurdly too big for his body, rather like the moustache of a comic man on the films. Six tall Indian warders were guarding him and getting him ready for the gallows. Two of them stood by with rifles and fixed bayonets, while the others handcuffed him, passed a chain through his handcuffs and fixed it to their belts, and lashed his arms tight to his sides. They crowded very close about him, with their hands always on him in a careful, caressing grip, as though all the while feeling him to make sure he was there. It was like men handling a fish which is still alive and may jump back into the water. But he stood quite unresisting, yielding his arms limply to the ropes, as though he hardly noticed what was happening.

3   Eight o'clock struck and a bugle call, desolately thin in the wet air, floated from the distant barracks. The superintendent of the jail, who was standing apart from the rest of us, moodily prodding the gravel with his stick, raised his head at the sound. He was an army doctor, with a grey toothbrush moustache and a gruff voice. "For God's sake hurry up, Francis," he said irritably. "The man ought to have been dead by this time. Aren't you ready yet?"

4   Francis, the head jailer, a fat Dravidian in a white drill suit and gold spectacles, waved his black hand. "Yes sir, yes sir," he bubbled. "All iss satisfactorily prepared. The hangman iss waiting. We shall proceed."

5   "Well, quick march, then. The prisoners can't get their breakfast till this job's over."

6   We set out for the gallows. Two warders marched on either side of the prisoner, with their rifles at the slope; two others marched close against him, gripping him by arm and shoulder, as though at once pushing and supporting him. The rest of us, magistrates and the like, followed behind. Suddenly, when

we had gone ten yards, the procession stopped short without any order or warning. A dreadful thing had happened—a dog, come goodness knows whence, had appeared in the yard. It came bounding among us with a loud volley of barks and leapt round us wagging its whole body, wild with glee at finding so many human beings together. It was a large woolly dog, half Airedale, half pariah. For a moment it pranced round us, and then, before anyone could stop it, it had made a dash for the prisoner, and jumping up tried to lick his face. Everybody stood aghast, too taken aback even to grab the dog.

7   "Who let that bloody brute in here?" said the superintendent angrily. "Catch it, someone!"

8   A warder detached from the escort, charged clumsily after the dog, but it danced and gambolled just out of his reach, taking everything as part of the game. A young Eurasian jailer picked up a handful of gravel and tried to stone the dog away, but it dodged the stones and came after us again. Its yaps echoed from the jail walls. The prisoner, in the grasp of the two warders, looked on incuriously, as though this was another formality of the hanging. It was several minutes before someone managed to catch the dog. Then we put my handkerchief through its collar and moved off once more, with the dog still straining and whimpering.

9   It was about forty yards to the gallows. I watched the bare brown back of the prisoner marching in front of me. He walked clumsily with his bound arms, but quite steadily, with that bobbing gait of the Indian who never straightens his knees. At each step his muscles slid neatly into place, the lock of hair on his scalp danced up and down, his feet printed themselves on the wet gravel. And once, in spite of the men who gripped him by each shoulder, he stepped lightly aside to avoid a puddle on the path.

10   It is curious; but till that moment I had never realized what it means to destroy a healthy, conscious man. When I saw the prisoner step aside to avoid the puddle I saw the mystery, the unspeakable wrongness of cutting a life short when it is in full tide. This man was not dying, he was alive just as we are alive. All the organs of his body were working—bowels digesting food, skin renewing itself, nails growing, tissues forming—all toiling away in solemn foolery. His nails would still be growing when he stood on the drop, when he was falling through the air with a tenth-of-a-second to live. His eyes saw the yellow gravel and the grey walls, and his brain still remembered, foresaw, reasoned—even about puddles. He and we were a party of men walking together, seeing, hearing, feeling, understanding the same world; and in two minutes, with a sudden snap, one of us would be gone—one mind less, one world less.

11   The gallows stood in a small yard, separate from the main grounds of the prison, and overgrown with tall prickly weeds. It was a brick erection like three sides of a shed, with planking on top, and above that two beams and a crossbar with the rope dangling. The hangman, a greyhaired convict in the white uniform of the prison, was waiting beside his machine. He greeted us with a servile crouch as we entered. At a word from Francis the two warders, gripping the

prisoner more closely than ever, half led, half pushed him to the gallows and helped him clumsily up the ladder. Then the hangman climbed up and fixed the rope round the prisoner's neck.

12   We stood waiting, five yards away. The warders had formed in a rough circle round the gallows. And then, when the noose was fixed, the prisoner began crying out to his god. It was a high, reiterated cry of "Ram! Ram! Ram! Ram!" not urgent and fearful like a prayer or cry for help, but steady, rhythmical, almost like the tolling of a bell. The dog answered the sound with a whine. The hangman, still standing on the gallows, produced a small cotton bag like a flour bag and drew it down over the prisoner's face. But the sound, muffled by the cloth, still persisted, over and over again: "Ram! Ram! Ram! Ram! Ram!"

13   The hangman climbed down and stood ready, holding the lever. Minutes seemed to pass. The steady, muffled crying from the prisoner went on and on, "Ram! Ram! Ram!" never faltering for an instant. The superintendent, his head on his chest, was slowly poking the ground with his stick; perhaps he was counting the cries, allowing the prisoner a fixed number—fifty, perhaps, or a hundred. Everyone had changed colour. The Indians had gone grey like bad coffee, and one or two of the bayonets were wavering. We looked at the lashed hooded man on the drop, and listened to his cries—each cry another second of life; the same thought was in all our minds; oh, kill him quickly, get it over, stop that abominable noise!

14   Suddenly the superintendent made up his mind. Throwing up his head he made a swift motion with his stick. "Chalo!" he shouted almost fiercely.

15   There was a clanking noise, and then dead silence. The prisoner had vanished, and the rope was twisting on itself. I let go of the dog, and it galloped immediately to the back of the gallows; but when it got there it stopped short, barked, and then retreated into a corner of the yard, where it stood among the weeds looking timorously out at us. We went round the gallows to inspect the prisoner's body. He was dangling with his toes pointed straight downwards, very slowly revolving, as dead as a stone.

16   The superintendent reached out with his stick and poked the bare brown body; it oscillated slightly. "*He's* all right," said the superintendent. He backed out from under the gallows, and blew out a deep breath. The moody look had gone out of his face quite suddenly. He glanced at his wrist-watch. "Eight minutes past eight. Well, that's all for this morning, thank God."

The warders unfixed bayonets and marched away. The dog, sobered and conscious of having misbehaved itself, slipped after them. We walked out of the gallows yard, past the condemned cells with their waiting prisoners, into the big central yard of the prison. The convicts, under the command of warders armed with lathis, were already receiving their breakfast. They squatted in long rows, each man holding a tin pannikin, while two warders with buckets marched round ladling out rice; it seemed quite a homely, jolly scene, after the hanging. An enormous relief had come upon us now that the job was done. One felt an impulse to sing, to break into a run, to snigger. All at once everyone began chattering gaily.

18   The Eurasian boy walking beside me nodded towards the way we had come, with a knowing smile: "Do you know, sir, our friend (he meant the dead man) when he heard his appeal had been dismissed, he pissed on the floor of his cell. From fright. Kindly take one of my cigarettes, sir. Do you not admire my new silver case, sir? From the boxwallah, two rupees eight annas. Classy European style."

19   Several people laughed—at what, nobody seemed certain.

20   Francis was walking by the superintendent, talking garrulously: "Well, sir, all has passed off with the utmost satisfactoriness. It was all finished—flick! Like that. It iss not always so—oah, no! I have known cases where the doctor wass obliged to go beneath the gallows and pull the prissoner's legs to ensure decease. Most disagreeable!"

21   "Wriggling about, eh? That's bad," said the superintendent.

22   "Arch, sir, it iss worse when they become refractory! One man, I recall, clung to the bars of hiss cage when we went to take him out. You will scarcely credit, sir, that it took six warders to dislodge him, three pulling at each leg. We reasoned with him, 'My dear fellow,' we said 'think of all the pain and trouble you are causing to us!' But no, he would not listen! Ach, he wass very troublesome!"

23   I found that I was laughing quite loudly. Everyone was laughing. Even the superintendent grinned in a tolerant way. "You'd better all come out and have a drink," he said quite genially. "I've got a bottle of whiskey in the car. We could do with it."

24   We went through the big double gates of the prison into the road. "Pulling at his legs!" exclaimed a Burmese magistrate suddenly, and burst into a loud chuckling. We all began laughing again. At that moment Francis' anecdote seemed extraordinarily funny. We all had a drink together, native and European alike, quite amicably. The dead man was a hundred yards away.

A Writer's Notes for a Second Reading

The first paragraph of this essay is so filled with promise. Each time I read that paragraph I am drawn into the piece and read it even when I don't want to. Orwell fulfills the promise of the beginning, and it is worth reading it again and again to see how the piece grows out of that lead, how it develops and deepens, how we are all drawn into the pain of our human condition.

I am always struck by Orwell's compassion, how he does not stand aside from the killers but realizes how he is—we are—involved.

On a second or third reading I am struck again by how much Orwell can do with a detail:

> . . . *And once, in spite of the men who gripped him by each shoulder, he stepped lightly aside to avoid a puddle on the path.*
>
> *It is curious; but till that moment I had never realized what it means to destroy a healthy, conscious man. When I saw the prisoner step aside to avoid the puddle I saw the mystery, the unspeakable wrongness of cutting a life short when it is in full tide. This man was not dying, he was alive just as we are alive. All the organs of his body were working—bowels digesting food, skin renewing itself, nails growing, tissues forming—all toiling away in solemn foolery. His nails would still be growing when he stood on the drop, when he was falling through the air with a tenth-of-a-second to live. His eyes saw the yellow gravel and the grey walls, and his brain still remembered, foresaw, reasoned—even about puddles. He and we were a party of men walking together, seeing, hearing, feeling, understanding the same world; and in two minutes, with a sudden snap, one of us would be gone—one mind less, one world less.*

As a writer, pay attention to that puddle. If you want to know what a specific can do, reread the lines reprinted above. We see through the specific, through the revealing detail, the small significant act. The artist makes us see the importance of what seems trivial and is not.

Discussion

- Discuss what Orwell has said about why he is a writer. Relate it to your own experience with writing, relate it to the other writers in the text, relate it to what Updike says about creativity in the quotation cited in the introduction to his selection in Chapter 5.
- Consider the standards of good writing Orwell has established in his six rules and in "Why I Write." Does he live up to them in "A Hanging"?
- Consider if other writers in the text have lived up to his standards.
- Discuss how Orwell implicates himself. He doesn't stand apart from the human race but criticizes himself as he criticizes others. How does he manage to be both participant and critical observer at the same time? Does it work?
- Relate what Orwell has said to current political speeches and statements as well as political reporting.
- Consider how other writers in the text might have covered the hanging.
- Discuss how the hanging might have been covered on television. What would be the advantages of film? The limitations?

Activities

- Apply Orwell's rules and his suggestion that "good prose is like a windowpane" to several pages of another writer in this text, editing those pages to fulfill Orwell's counsel. Do the same thing to one of your own drafts.

- Write a short essay on "Why I Write," "Why I Don't Write," "Why I Should Write," "What Happens When I Write."
- Write the lead and then outline a piece that might be similar to "A Hanging." For example, a funeral where people walk away laughing and joking. Consider the proportions in the piece.
- Edit "A Hanging" to make it an essay by an uninvolved observer or an insensitive participant.
- Revise a piece of your own using Orwell's technique of participant-observer.
- Create your own list of six rules for clear, vigorous writing.

To Collaborate

- Work together to draft a paragraph or two for a speech against capital punishment, using a quote from the Orwell essay to support your point.
- Write a report showing how Orwell practices—or does not practice—what he preaches in his essay on writing.

Joan Didion

Joan Didion, like Orwell, writes both fiction and nonfiction, and both forms are marked with the precision of vision and her language. Her caring and concern are honed by the discipline of her prose. "My writing is a process of rewriting," she has said, "of going back and changing and filling in. In the rewriting process you discover what's going on, and you go back and bring it up to that point." Since she is so skilled at her trade the rewriting never shows to the ordinary reader, but the writer knows that such clear, well-organized prose could only be the result of expert polishing.

Why I Write

1   Of course I stole the title for this talk from George Orwell. One reason I stole it was that I like the sound of the words: *Why I Write.* There you have three short unambiguous words that share a sound, and the sound they share is this:

2   *I*
           I
           I

3   In many ways writing is the act of saying I, of imposing oneself upon other people, of saying *listen to me, see it my way, change your mind.* It's an aggressive, even a hostile act. You can disguise its aggressiveness all you want with veils of

subordinate clauses and qualifiers and tentative subjunctives, with ellipses and evasions—with the whole manner of intimating rather than claiming, of alluding rather than stating—but there's no getting around the fact that setting words on paper is the tactic of a secret bully, an invasion, an imposition of the writer's sensibility on the reader's most private space.

4   I stole the title not only because the words sounded right but because they seemed to sum up, in a no-nonsense way, all I have to tell you. Like many writers I have only this one "subject," this one "area"; the act of writing. I can bring you no reports from any other front. I may have other interests: I am "interested," for example, in marine biology, but I don't flatter myself that you would come out to hear me talk about it. I am not a scholar. I am not in the least an intellectual, which is not to say that when I hear the word "intellectual" I reach for my gun, but only to say that I do not think in abstracts. During the years when I was an undergraduate at Berkeley I tried, with a kind of hopeless late-adolescent energy, to buy some temporary visa into the world of ideas, to forge for myself a mind that could deal with the abstract.

5   In short I tried to think. I failed. My attention veered inexorably back to the specific, to the tangible, to what was generally considered, by everyone I knew then and for that matter have known since, the peripheral. I would try to contemplate the Hegelian dialectic and would find myself concentrating instead on a flowering pear tree outside my window and the particular way the petals fell on my floor. I would try to read linguistic theory and would find myself wondering instead if the lights were on in the bevatron up the hill. When I say that I was wondering if the lights were on in the bevatron you might immediately suspect, if you deal in ideas at all, that I was registering the bevatron as a political symbol, thinking in shorthand about the military-industrial complex and its role in the university community, but you would be wrong. I was only wondering if the lights were on in the bevatron and how they looked. A physical fact.

6   I had trouble graduating from Berkeley, not because of this inability to deal with ideas—I was majoring in English, and I could locate the house-and-garden imagery in *The Portrait of a Lady* as well as the next person, "imagery" being by definition the kind of specific that got my attention—but simply because I had neglected to take a course in Milton. For reasons which now sound baroque I needed a degree by the end of that summer, and the English department finally agreed, if I would come down from Sacramento every Friday and talk about the cosmology of *Paradise Lost,* to certify me proficient in Milton. I did this. Some Fridays I took the Greyhound bus, other Fridays I caught the Southern Pacific's City of San Francisco on the last leg of its transcontinental trip. I can no longer tell you whether Milton put the sun or the earth at the center of his universe in *Paradise Lost,* the central question of at least one century and a topic about which I wrote 10,000 words that summer, but I can still recall the exact rancidity of the butter in the City of San Francisco's dining car, and the way the tinted windows on the Greyhound bus cast the oil refineries around

Carquinez Straits into a grayed and obscurely sinister light. In short my attention was always on the periphery, on what I would see and taste and touch, on
the butter, and the Greyhound bus. During those years I was traveling on what
I knew to be a very shaky passport, forged papers: I knew that I was no legiti-
mate resident in any world of ideas. I knew I couldn't think. All I knew then
was what I couldn't do. All I knew then was what I wasn't, and it took me some
years to discover what I was.

7   Which was a writer.

8   By which I mean not a "good" writer or a "bad" writer but simply a writer,
a person, whose most absorbed and passionate hours are spent arranging words
on pieces of paper. Had my credentials been in order I would never have
become a writer. Had I been blessed with even limited access to my own mind
there would have been no reason to write. I write entirely to find out what I'm
thinking, what I'm looking at, what I see and what it means. What I want and
what I fear. Why did the oil refineries around Carquinez Straits seem sinister to
me in the summer of 1956? Why have the night lights in the bevatron burned
in my mind for twenty years? *What is going on in these pictures in my mind?*

9   When I talk about pictures in my mind I am talking, quite specifically,
about images that shimmer around the edges. There used to be an illustration
in every elementary psychology book showing a cat drawn by a patient in varying stages of schizophrenia. This cat had a shimmer around it. You could see
the molecular structure breaking down at the very edges of the cat: the cat
became the background and the background the cat, everything interacting,
exchanging ions. People on hallucinogens describe the same perception of
objects. I'm not a schizophrenic, nor do I take hallucinogens, but certain images
do shimmer for me. Look hard enough, and you can't miss the shimmer. It's
there. You can't think too much about these pictures that shimmer. You just lie
low and let them develop. You stay quiet. You don't talk to many people and
you keep your nervous system from shorting out and you try to locate the cat
in the shimmer, the grammar in the picture.

10   Just as I meant "shimmer" literally I mean "grammar" literally. Grammar
is a piano I play by ear, since I seem to have been out of school the year the
rules were mentioned. All I know about grammar is its infinite power. To shift
the structure of a sentence alters the meaning of that sentence, as definitely and
inflexibly as the position of a camera alters the meaning of the object photographed. Many people know about camera angles now, but not so many know
about sentences. The arrangement of the words matters, and the arrangement
you want can be found in the picture in your mind. The picture dictates the
arrangement. The picture dictates whether this will be a sentence with or without clauses, a sentence that ends hard or a dying-fall sentence, long or short,
active or passive. The picture tells you how to arrange the words and the
arrangement of the words tells you, or tells me, what's going on in the picture.
Nota bene:

11   It tells you.

12   You don't tell it.

13   Let me show you what I mean by pictures in the mind. I began *Play It as It Lays* just as I have begun each of my novels, with no notion of "character" or "plot" or even "incident." I had only two pictures in my mind, more about which later, and a technical intention, which was to write a novel so elliptical and fast that it would be over before you noticed it, a novel so fast that it would scarcely exist on the page at all. About the pictures the first was of white space. Empty space. This was clearly the picture that dictated the narrative intention of the book—a book in which anything that happened would happen off the page, a "white" book to which the reader would have to bring his or her own bad dreams—and yet this picture told me no "story," suggested no situation. The second picture did. This second picture was of something actually witnessed. A young woman with long hair and a short white halter dress walks through the casino at the Riviera in Las Vegas at one in the morning. She crosses the casino alone and picks up a house telephone. I watch her because I have heard her paged, and recognize her name: she is a minor actress I see around Los Angeles from time to time, in places like Jax and once in a gynecologist's office in the Beverly Hills Clinic, but have never met. I know nothing about her. Who is paging her? Why is she here to be paged? How exactly did she come to this? It was precisely this moment in Las Vegas that made *Play It as It Lays* begin to tell itself to me, but the moment appears in the novel only obliquely, in a chapter which begins:

14   *Maria made a list of things she would never do. She would never: walk through the Sands or Caesar's alone after midnight. She would never ball at a party, do S-M unless she wanted to, borrow furs from Abe Lipsey, deal. She would never carry a Yorkshire in Beverly Hills.*

15   That is the beginning of the chapter and that is also the end of the chapter, which may suggest what I meant by "white space."

16   I recall having a number of pictures in my mind when I began the novel I just finished, *A Book of Common Prayer*. As a matter of fact one of these pictures was of that bevatron I mentioned, although I would be hard put to tell you a story in which nuclear energy figured. Another was a newspaper photograph of a hijacked 707 burning on the desert in the Middle East. Another was the night view from a room in which I once spent a week with paratyphoid, a hotel room on the Colombian coast. My husband and I seemed to be on the Colombian coast representing the United States of America at a film festival (I recall invoking the name "Jack Valenti" a lot, as if its reiteration could make me well), and it was a bad place to have fever, not only because my indisposition offended our hosts but because every night in this hotel the generator failed. The lights went out. The elevator stopped. My husband would go to the event of the evening and make excuses for me and I would stay alone in this hotel room, in the dark. I remember standing at the window trying to call Bogota (the telephone seemed to work on the same principle as the generator) and watching the night wind come up and wondering what I was doing eleven degrees off the equator

with a fever of 103. The view from that window definitely figures in *A Book of Common Prayer,* as does the burning 707, and yet none of these pictures told me the story I needed.

17   The picture that did, the picture that shimmered and made these other images coalesce, was the Panama airport at 6 A.M. I was in this airport only once, on a plane to Bogota that stopped for an hour to refuel, but the way it looked that morning remained superimposed on everything I saw until the day I finished *A Book of Common Prayer.* I lived in that airport for several years. I can still feel the hot air when I step off the plane, can see the heat already rising off the tarmac at 6 A.M. I can feel my skirt damp and wrinkled on my legs. I can feel the asphalt stick to my sandals. I remember the big tail of a Pan American plane floating motionless down at the end of the tarmac. I remember the sound of a slot machine in the waiting room. I could tell you that I remember a particular woman in the airport, an American woman, a *norteamericana,* a thin *norteamericana* about 40 who wore a big square emerald in lieu of a wedding ring, but there was no such woman there.

18   I put this woman in the airport later. I made this woman up, just as I later made up a country to put the airport in, and a family to run the country. This woman in the airport is neither catching a plane nor meeting one. She is ordering tea in the airport coffee shop. In fact she is not simply "ordering" tea but insisting that the water be boiled, in front of her, for twenty minutes. Why is this woman in this airport? Why is she going nowhere, where has she been? Where did she get that big emerald? What derangement, or disassociation, makes her believe that her will to see the water boiled can possibly prevail?

19   *She has been going to one airport or another for four months, one could see it, looking at the visas on her passport. All those airports where Charlotte Douglas's passport had been stamped would have looked alike. Sometimes the sign on the tower would say "Bienvenidos" and sometimes the sign on the tower would say "Bienvenue," some places were wet and hot and others dry and hot, but at each of these airports the pastel concrete walls would rust and stain and the swamp off the runway would be littered with the fuselages of cannibalized Fairchild F-227's and the water would need boiling.*

20   *"I knew why Charlotte went to the airport even if Victor did not."*

21   *"I knew about airports."*

22   These lines appear about halfway through *A Book of Common Prayer,* but I wrote them during the second week I worked on the book, long before I had any idea where Charlotte Douglas had been or why she went to airports. Until I wrote these lines I had no character called "Victor" in mind: the necessity for mentioning a name, and the name "Victor," occurred to me as I wrote the sentence. *I knew why Charlotte went to the airport* sounded incomplete. *I knew why Charlotte went to the airport even if Victor did not* carried a little more narrative drive. Most important of all, until I wrote these lines I did not know who "I" was, who was telling the story. I had intended until that moment that the

"I" be no more than the voice of the author, a 19th-century omniscient narrator. But there it was:

23   *"I knew why Charlotte went to the airport even if Victor did not."*

24   *"I knew about airports."*

25   This "I" was the voice of no author in my house. This "I" was someone who not only knew why Charlotte went to the airport but also knew someone called "Victor." Who was Victor? Who was this narrator? Why was this narrator telling me this story? Let me tell you one thing about why writers write: had I known the answer to any of these questions I would never have needed to write a novel.

Salvador

1   The three-year-old El Salvador International Airport is glassy and white and splendidly isolated, conceived during the waning of the Molina "National Transformation" as convenient less to the capital (San Salvador is forty miles away, until recently a drive of several hours) than to a central hallucination of the Molina and Romero regimes, the projected beach resorts, the Hyatt, the Pacific Paradise, tennis, golf, water-skiing, condos, *Costa del Sol;* the visionary invention of a tourist industry in yet another republic where the leading natural cause of death is gastrointestinal infection. In the general absence of tourists these hotels have since been abandoned, ghost resorts on the empty Pacific beaches, and to land at this airport built to service them is to plunge directly into a state in which no ground is solid, no depth of field reliable, no perception so definite that it might not dissolve into its reverse.

2   The only logic is that of acquiescence. Immigration is negotiated in a thicket of automatic weapons, but by whose authority the weapons are brandished (Army or National Guard or National Police or Customs Police or Treasury Police or one of a continuing proliferation of other shadowy and overlapping forces) is a blurred point. Eye contact is avoided. Documents are scrutinized upside down. Once clear of the airport, on the new highway that slices through green hills rendered phosphorescent by the cloud cover of the tropical rainy season, one sees mainly underfed cattle and mongrel dogs and armored vehicles, vans and trucks and Cherokee Chiefs fitted with reinforced steel and bulletproof Plexiglas an inch thick. Such vehicles are a fixed feature of local life, and are popularly associated with disappearance and death. There was the Cherokee Chief seen following the Dutch television crew killed in Chalatenango province in March of 1982. There was the red Toyota three-quarter-ton pickup sighted near the van driven by the four American Catholic workers on the night they were killed in 1980. There were, in the late spring and summer of 1982, the three Toyota panel trucks, one yellow, one blue, and one

green, none bearing plates, reported present at each of the mass detentions (a "detention" is another fixed feature of local life, and often precedes a "disappearance") in the Amatepec district of San Salvador. These are the details—the models and colors of armored vehicles, the makes and calibers, the particular methods of dismemberment and decapitation used in particular instances—on which the visitor to Salvador learns immediately to concentrate, to the exclusion of past or future concerns, as in a prolonged amnesiac fugue.

3   Terror is the given of the place. Black-and-white police cars cruise in pairs, each with the barrel of a rifle extruding from an open window. Roadblocks materialize at random, soldiers fanning out from trucks and taking positions, fingers always on triggers, safeties clicking on and off. Aim is taken as if to pass the time. Every morning *El Diario de Hoy* and *La Prensa Grafica* carry cautionary stories. *Una madre y sus dos hijos fueron asesinados con arma cortante (corvo) por ocho sujetos desconocidos el lunes en la noche":* A mother and her two sons hacked to death in their beds by eight *desconocidos,* unknown men. The same morning's paper, the unidentified body of a young man, strangled, found on the shoulder of a road. Same morning, different story: the unidentified bodies of three young men, found on another road, their faces partially destroyed by bayonets, one face carved to represent a cross.

4   It is largely from these reports in the newspapers that the United States embassy compiles its body counts, which are transmitted to Washington in a weekly dispatch referred to by embassy people as "the grimgram." These counts are presented in a kind of tortured code that fails to obscure what is taken for granted in El Salvador, that government forces do most of the killing. In a January 15, 1982 memo to Washington, for example, the embassy issued a "guarded" breakdown on its count of 6,909 "reported" political murders between September 16, 1980 and September 15, 1981. Of these 6,909, according to the memo, 922 were "believed committed by security forces," 952 were "believed committed by leftist terrorists," 136 "believed committed by rightist terrorists," and 4,889 "committed by unknown assailants," the famous *desconocidos* favored by those San Salvador newspapers still publishing. (The figures actually add up not to 6,909 but to 6,899, leaving ten in a kind of official limbo.) The memo continued:

5   *The uncertainty involved here can be seen in the fact that responsibility cannot be fixed in the majority of cases. We note, however, that it is generally believed in El Salvador that a large number of the unexplained killings are carried out by the security forces, officially or unofficially. The Embassy is aware of dramatic claims that have been made by one interest group or another in which the security forces figure as the primary agents of murder here. El Salvador's tangled web of attack and vengeance, traditional criminal violence and political mayhem make this an impossible charge to sustain. In saying this, however, we make no attempt to lighten the responsibility for the deaths of many hundreds, and perhaps thousands, which can be attributed to the security forces. . . .*

6   The body count kept by what is generally referred to in San Salvador as "the Human Rights Commission" is higher than the embassy's, and documented periodically by a photographer who goes out looking for bodies. These bodies he photographs are often broken into unnatural positions, and the faces to which the bodies are attached (when they are attached) are equally unnatural, sometimes unrecognizable as human faces, obliterated by acid or beaten to a mash of misplaced ears and teeth or slashed ear to ear and invaded by insects. *"Encontrado en Antiguo Cuscatlan el dia 25 de Marzo 1982: camison de dormir celeste,"* the typed caption reads on one photograph: found in Antiguo Cuscatlan March 25 1982 wearing a sky-blue nightshirt. The captions are laconic. Found in Soyapango May 21 1982. Found in Mejicanos June 11 1982. Found at El Playon May 30 1982, white shirt, purple pants, black shoes.

7   The photograph accompanying that last caption shows a body with no eyes, because the vultures got to it before the photographer did. There is a special kind of practical information that the visitor to El Salvador acquires immediately, the way visitors to other places acquire information about the currency rates, the hours for the museums. In El Salvador one learns that vultures go first for the soft tissue, for the eyes, the exposed genitalia, the open mouth. One learns that an open mouth can be used to make a specific point, can be stuffed with something emblematic; stuffed, say, with a penis, or, if the point has to do with land title, stuffed with some of the dirt in question. One learns that hair deteriorates less rapidly than flesh, and that a skull surrounded by a perfect corona of hair is a not uncommon sight in the body dumps.

8   All forensic photographs induce in the viewer a certain protective numbness, but dissociation is more difficult here. In the first place these are not, technically, "forensic" photographs, since the evidence they document will never be presented in a court of law. In the second place the disfigurement is too routine. The locations are too near, the dates too recent. There is the presence of the relatives of the disappeared: the women who sit every day in this cramped office on the grounds of the archdiocese, waiting to look at the spiral-bound photo albums in which the photographs are kept. These albums have plastic covers bearing soft-focus color photographs of young Americans in dating situations (strolling through autumn foliage on one album, recumbent in a field of daisies on another), and the women, looking for the bodies of their husbands and brothers and sisters and children, pass them from hand to hand without comment or expression.

9   *One of the more shadowy elements of the violent scene here [is] the death squad. Existence of these groups has long been disputed, but not by many Salvadorans. . . . Who constitutes the death squads is yet another difficult question. We do not believe that these squads exist as permanent formations but rather as ad hoc vigilante groups that coalesce according to perceived need. Membership is also uncertain, but in addition to civilians we believe that both on- and off-duty members of the security forces are participants. This was unofficially confirmed by right-wing spokesman Maj. Roberto D/Aubuisson who*

stated in an interview in early 1981 that security forces members utilize the guise of the death squad when a potentially embarrassing or odious task needs to be performed.

10   —From the confidential but later declassified January 15, 1982 memo previously cited, drafted for the State Department by the political section at the embassy in San Salvador.

11   The dead and pieces of the dead turn up in El Salvador everywhere, every day, as taken for granted as in a nightmare, or a horror movie. Vultures of course suggest the presence of a body. A knot of children on the street suggests the presence of a body. Bodies turn up in the brush of vacant lots, in the garbage thrown down ravines in the richest districts, in public rest rooms, in bus stations. Some are dropped in Lake Hopango, a few miles east of the city, and wash up near the lakeside cottages and clubs frequented by what remains in San Salvador of the sporting bourgeoisie. Some still turn up at El Playon, the lunar lava field of rotting human flesh visible at one time or another on every television screen in America but characterized in June of 1982 in the *El Salvador News Gazette,* an English-language weekly edited by an American named Mario Rosenthal, as an "uncorroborated story . . . dredged up from the files of leftist propaganda." Others turn up at Puerta del Diablo, above Parque Balboa, a national *Turicentro* described as recently as the April-July 1982 issue of *Aboard TACA,* the magazine provided passengers on the national airline of El Salvador, as "offering excellent subjects for color photography."

12   I drove up to Puerta del Diablo one morning in June 1982, past the Casa Presidencial and the camouflaged watch towers and heavy concentrations of troops and arms south of town, on up a narrow road narrowed further by landslides and deep crevices in the roadbed, a drive so insistently premonitory that after a while I began to hope that I would pass Puerta del Diablo without knowing it, just miss it, write it off, turn around and go back. There was however no way of missing it. Puerta del Diablo is a "view site" in an older and distinctly literary tradition, nature as lesson, an immense cleft rock through which half of El Salvador seems framed, a site so romantic and "mystical," so theatrically sacrificial in aspect, that it might be a cosmic parody of nineteenth-century landscape painting. The place presents itself as pathetic fallacy: the sky "broods," the stones "weep," a constant seepage of water weighting the ferns and moss. The foliage is thick and slick with moisture. The only sound is a steady buzz, I believe of cicadas.

13   Body dumps are seen in El Salvador as a kind of visitors' must-do, difficult but worth the detour. "Of course you have seen El Playon," an aide to President Alvaro Magana said to me one day, and proceeded to discuss the site geologically, as evidence of the country's geothermal resources. He made no mention of the bodies. I was unsure if he was sounding me out or simply found the geothermal aspect of overriding interest. One difference between El Playon and Puerta del Diablo is that most bodies at El Playon appear to have been killed

somewhere else, and then dumped; at Puerta del Diablo the executions are believed to occur in place, at the top, and the bodies thrown over. Sometimes reporters will speak of wanting to spend the night at Puerta del Diablo, in order to document the actual execution, but at the time I was in Salvador no one had.

14   The aftermath, the daylight aspect, is well documented. "Nothing fresh today, I hear," an embassy officer said when I mentioned that I had visited Puerta del Diablo. "Were there any on top?" someone else asked. "There were supposed to have been three on top yesterday." The point about whether or not there had been any on top was that usually it was necessary to go down to see bodies. The way down is hard. Slabs of stone, slippery with moss, are set into the vertiginous cliff, and it is down this cliff that one begins the descent to the bodies, or what is left of the bodies, pecked and maggoty masses of flesh, bone, hair. On some days there have been helicopters circling, tracking those making the descent. Other days there have been militia at the top, in the clearing where the road seems to run out, but on the morning I was there the only people on top were a man and a woman and three small children, who played in the wet grass while the woman started and stopped a Toyota pickup. She appeared to be learning how to drive. She drove forward and then back toward the edge, apparently following the man's signals, over and over again.

15   We did not speak, and it was only later, down the mountain and back in the land of the provisionally living, that it occurred to me that there was a definite question about why a man and a woman might choose a well-known body dump for a driving lesson. This was one of a number of occasions, during the two weeks my husband and I spent in El Salvador, on which I came to understand, in a way I had not understood before, the exact mechanism of terror.

16   Whenever I had nothing better to do in San Salvador I would walk up in the leafy stillness of the San Benito and Escalon districts, where the hush at midday is broken only by the occasional crackle of a walkie-talkie, the click of metal moving on a weapon. I recall a day in San Benito when I opened my bag to check an address, and heard the clicking of metal on metal all up and down the street. On the whole no one walks up here, and pools of blossoms lie undisturbed on the sidewalks. Most of the houses in San Benito are more recent than those in Escalon, less idiosyncratic and probably smarter, but the most striking architectural features in both districts are not the houses but their walls, walls built upon walls, walls stripped of the usual copa de oro and bougainvillea, walls that reflect successive generations of violence: the original stone, the additional five or six or ten feet of brick, and finally the barbed wire, sometimes concertina, sometimes electrified, walls with watch towers, gun ports, closed-circuit television cameras, walls now reaching twenty and thirty feet.

17   San Benito and Escalon appear on the embassy security maps as districts of relatively few "incidents," but they remain districts in which a certain oppressive uneasiness prevails. In the first place there are always "incidents"— detentions and deaths and disappearances—in the *barrancas,* the ravines lined with shanties that fall down behind the houses with the walls and the guards

and the walkie-talkies; one day in Escalon I was introduced to a woman who kept the lean-to that served as a grocery in a *barranca* just above the Hotel Sheraton. She was sticking prices on bars of Camay and Johnson's baby soap, stopping occasionally to sell a plastic bag or two filled with crushed ice and Coca Cola, and all the while she talked in a low voice about her fear, about her eighteen-year-old son, about the boys who had been taken out and shot on successive nights recently in a neighboring *barranca*.

18   In the second place there is, in Escalon, the presence of the Sheraton itself, a hotel that has figured rather too prominently in certain local stories involving the disappearance and death of Americans. The Sheraton always seems brighter and more mildly festive than either the Camino Real or the Presidente, with children in the pool and flowers and pretty women in pastel dresses, but there are usually several bulletproofed Cherokee Chiefs in the parking area, and the men drinking in the lobby often carry the little zippered purses that in San Salvador suggest not passports or credit cards but Browning 9 mm. pistols.

19   It was at the Sheraton that one of the few American *desaparecidos,* a young free-lance writer named John Sullivan, was last seen, in December of 1980. It was also at the Sheraton, after eleven on the evening of January 3, 1981, that the two American advisers on agrarian reform, Michael Hammer and Mark Pearlman, were killed, along with the Salvadoran director of the Institute of Agrarian Transformation, José Rodolfo Viera. The three were drinking coffee in a dining room off the lobby, and whoever killed them used an Ingram MAC-10, without sound suppressor, and then walked out through the lobby, unapprehended. The Sheraton has even turned up in the investigation into the December 1980 deaths of the four American churchwomen, Sisters Ita Ford and Maura Clarke, the two Maryknoll nuns; Sister Dorothy Kazel, the Ursuline nun; and Jean Donovan, the lay volunteer. In *Justice in El Salvador: A Case Study,* prepared and released in July of 1982 in New York by the Lawyers' Committee for International Human Rights, there appears this note:

20   *On December 19, 1980, the [Duarte government's] Special Investigative*
      Commission reported that 'a red Toyota 3/4-ton pickup was seen leaving (the
      crime scene) at about 11:00 P.M. on December 2' and that 'a red splotch on the
      burned van' of the churchwomen was being checked to determine whether the
      paint splotch 'could be the result of a collision between that van and the red
      Toyota pickup.' By February 1981, the Maryknoll Sisters' Office of Social
      Concerns, which has been actively monitoring the investigation, received word
      from a source which it considered reliable that the FBI had matched the red
      splotch on the burned van with a red Toyota pickup belonging to the Sheraton
      hotel in San Salvador. . . . Subsequent to the FBI's alleged matching of the paint
      splotch and a Sheraton truck, the State Department has claimed, in a
      communication with the families of the churchwomen, that 'the FBI could not
      determine the source of the paint scraping.'

21   There is also mention in this study of a young Salvadoran businessman named Hans Christ (his father was a German who arrived in El Salvador at the

end of World War II), a part owner of the Sheraton. Hans Christ lives now in Miami, and that his name should have even come up in the Maryknoll investigation made many people uncomfortable, because it was Hans Christ, along with his brother-in-law, Ricardo Sol Meza, who in April of 1981, was first charged with the murders of Michael Hammer and Mark Pearlman and José Rodolfo Viera at the Sheraton. These charges were later dropped, and were followed by a series of other charges, arrests, releases, expressions of "dismay" and "incredulity" from the American embassy, and even, in the fall of 1982, confessions to the killings from two former National Guard corporals, who testified that Hans Christ had led them through the lobby and pointed out the victims. Hans Christ and Ricardo Sol Meza have said that the dropped case against them was a government frame-up, and that they were only having drinks at the Sheraton the night of the killings, with a National Guard intelligence officer. It was logical for Hans Christ and Ricardo Sol Meza to have drinks at the Sheraton because they both had interests in the hotel, and Ricardo Sol Meza had just opened a roller disco, since closed, off the lobby into which the killers walked that night. The killers were described by witnesses as well dressed, their faces covered. The room from which they walked was at the time I was in San Salvador no longer a restaurant, but the marks left by the bullets were still visible, on the wall facing the door.

22   Whenever I had occasion to visit the Sheraton I was apprehensive, and this apprehension came to color the entire Escalon district for me, even its lower reaches, where there were people and movies and restaurants. I recall being struck by it on the canopied porch of a restaurant near the Mexican embassy, on an evening when rain or sabotage or habit had blacked out the city and I became abruptly aware, in the light cast by a passing car, of two human shadows, silhouettes illuminated by the headlights and then invisible again. One shadow sat behind the smoked glass windows of a Cherokee Chief parked at the curb in front of the restaurant, the other crouched between the pumps at the Esso station next door, carrying a rifle. It seemed to me unencouraging that my husband and I were the only people seated on the porch. In the absence of the headlights the candle on our table provided the only light, and I fought the impulse to blow it out. We continued talking, carefully. Nothing came of this, but I did not forget the sensation of having been in a single instant demoralized, undone, humiliated by fear, which is what I meant when I said that I came to understand in El Salvador the mechanism of terror.

A Writer's Notes for a Second Reading

If I had to pick one document that would articulate my feelings about writing, it would be Didion's essay. It captures the experience of writing for me. I read it with that special satisfaction we all feel when someone says what we feel, speaking for us and with us.

Read it from your own experience of writing to see if she speaks for you.

In "Salvador" Didion shows the writer how to weave a great variety of forms of documentation through a piece of writing while maintaining the flow of the text with clarity and grace. It is worthwhile to consider all the forms of evidence and how she builds her case with them.

Discussion

- Compare Didion's "Why I Write" to Orwell's. What statements in each essay give you insights to your own writing and your own writing experience?
- Discuss how what Didion says about writing relates to her own writing.
- Consider how Orwell's counsel about writing relates to the excerpts from Didion's "Salvador."
- Reverse the situation and consider how Didion's "Why I Write" illuminates or relates to Orwell's "A Hanging."
- Discuss how Didion's essay on writing relates to the work of other writers in the text.
- Compare her political reporting in "Salvador" to "A Hanging" and to the writing of others, such as Baldwin, who are concerned with political issues.
- Discuss how the movie and television camera has influenced writers, such as Didion, and how it has influenced the way in which readers read today.

Activities

- Write a brief description of how you write, trying to get inside the experience of writing, as Didion does.
- Cover a political event in your school or community, or visit an area in your neighborhood or across town and report on it, the way Didion has, mixing revealing details of observation with objective documentation.
- Write a review of Didion for a publication of the right and of the left.
- Since Didion is also a novelist, imagine the journal notes she might write herself if she considered using the material in the excerpt in a novel.
- Write a page of Didion's "Salvador" as she might write it for an essay rather than a piece of reportage.

To Collaborate

- Using "Salvador," work together to create a checklist of the forms of evidence or documentation a writer can use to support a position or advance an argument.
- Go to the library and take out some other articles or books on Central America. Compare Didion's treatment with them and report to the class on what you have learned about political writing.

Amiri Baraka

The professional writer, such as Robert Caro—who spent years researching for the first volume of his biography of Lyndon Johnson—has the financial support to gather enormous quantities of information. The pro can write from abundance but many of us do not know enough about a specific subject to write from abundance, and we do not have the resources or the time to gather that information. Yet, when we write later during our educational career and afterward in other careers, we have to know how to collect an abundance of information and select meaningful pertinent pieces of information from it. The answer for most of us is autobiography. We have an enormous inventory of experience recorded in our minds. Each of us has thousands of times as much information in our memory as we remember.

Amiri Baraka wrote first as LeRoi Jones, and his has been one of the strongest black voices in our literature in this century. He has written 24 plays, two works of fiction, seven of nonfiction, and eleven books of poetry. In his autobiography he shares his life and his reactions to that life with his readers. In the selection below he tells of his experiences in going to school.

School

1   School was classes and faces and teachers. And sometimes trouble. School was as much the playground as the classroom. For me, it was more the playground than the classroom. One grew, one had major confrontations with real life, in the playground, only rarely in the classroom. Though I had some terrible confrontations. Around discipline and what not. The only black teacher in the school at that time, Mrs. Powell, a statuesque powder-brown lady with glasses, beat me damn near to death in full view of her and my 7B class because I was acting the fool and she went off on me (which apparently was sanctioned by my mother—it probably had something to do with conflicting with the *only* black teacher in the whole school and that had to be revenged full-blood-flowingly at once as an example to any other malefactors). But Mrs. Powell was one of the only teachers to take us on frequent trips to New York. And she had us publish a monthly newspaper that I was one of the cartoonists for. But apparently I did something far out and she took me out.

2   But when I was in kindergarten I got sick (went off with the whooping cough, then the measles). And I learned to read away from school—my first text, Targeteer comics—and when I came back I was reading—and haven't stopped since.

3   I skipped 3B a few years later—I can't tell you why. But the 3A teacher was drugged for some reason or more likely I drugged her with my perpetual-

motion mouth and she made me *skip* around the room. (For some reason it makes me think of my son, Amiri!)

4 I have distorted in various books and stories and plays and what not iron confrontations in the school with the various aspects recalled at different times. The seventh-grade beating by Mrs. Powell. The weird comic strip I created, semi-plagiarized, called "The Crime Wave," which consisted of a hand with a gun sticking out of strange places holding people up. For instance, as a dude dived off the diving board the ubiquitous hand would be thrust up out of the water holding a gun and in the conversation balloon the words "Your money!" A series of those all over the goddam place and only "Your money!"

5 I think I saw the concept somewhere else but I was attracted to it and borrowed it and changed it to fit my head. But why "Your money!"?

6 When the curious old Miss Day, the white-haired liberal of my early youth, shuffled off into retirement as principal, there came Mr. Van Ness, hair parted down the middle, sallow-faced and sometimes seeming about to smile but sterner-seeming than Miss Day. We loved Miss Day, we seemed to fear Mr. Van Ness, probably because he seemed so dressed up and stiff. (The irony of this is that I just had drinks with old man Van Ness two months ago, up at his apartment with my wife and a lady friend of his—a black woman!—and we went over some of these things. Because, as it turns out, Van Ness was an open, investigating sort, actually a rather progressive person!)

7 Van Ness even took some interest in the fact that my mother had been to Fisk and Tuskegee. And on the basis of those startling credentials he could ask me what was proper, "Negro" or "colored." I said, "Negro," and Van Ness told the students, "Remember, there's a right and a wrong way of saying that." You bet!

8 In the eighth grade we had a race riot. And in them days race riot meant that black and white "citizens" fought each other. And that's exactly what happened in Newark. It was supposed to have jumped off when two white boys stopped a guy in my class named Haley (big for his age, one of the Southern blacks put back in school when he reached "Norf") and asked him if he was one of the niggers who'd won the races. He answered yes and they shot him. They were sixteen, Haley about the same age even though he was only in 8B and most of us in our earlier teens—I was about twelve.

9 The races they'd talked about were part of the citywide elementary school track meet. The black majority schools had won most of those races and this was the apparent payoff. So rumbles raged for a couple weeks on and off. Especially in my neighborhood, which confronted the Italian section. The Black Stompers confronted The Romans—a black girl was stripped naked and made to walk home through Branch Brook Park (rumor had it). A white girl got the same treatment (the same playground rumor said). But two loud stone- and bottle-throwing groups of Americans did meet on the bridge overpassing the railroad tracks near Orange Street. The tracks separating the sho-nuff Italian streets from the last thrust of then black Newark. The big boys said preachers tried to break it up and got run off with stones. It was the battle of the bridge.

10   Beneath that fabric of rumor and movement. The bright lights of adventure flashing in my young eyes and the actual tension I could see, the same tensions had rose up cross this land now the war was over and blacks expected the wartime gains to be maintained and this was resisted. Probably what came up on the streets of Newark was merely a reflection of the Dixiecrats who declared that year for the separation of the races. But whatever, that year New Jersey became the first state to declare a statute against all discrimination.

11   As a child the world was mysterious, wondrous, terrible, dangerous, sweet in so many ways. I loved to run. Short bursts, medium cruises, even long stretched-out rhythm-smooth trips. I'd get it in my head to run somewhere—a few blocks, a mile or so, a few miles through the city streets. Maybe I'd be going somewhere, I wouldn't take the bus, I'd just suddenly get it in my head and take off. And I dug that, the way running made you feel. And it was a prestigious activity around my way, if you was fast you had some note. The street consensus.

12   I only knew what was in my parents' minds through their practice. And children can't ever sufficiently "sum that up," that's why or because they're children. You deal with them on a perceptual level—later you know what they'll do in given situations (but many of their constant activities you know absolutely nothing about). Later, maybe, deadhead intellectuals will try to look back and sum their parents up, sometimes pay them back for them having been that, one's parents. Now that we are old we know so much. But we never know what it was like to have ourselves to put up with.

13   My family, as I've tried to tell, was a lower-middle-class family finally. For all the bourgeois underpinnings on my mother's side, the Depression settled the hash of this one black bourgeois family. And those tensions were always with us. My mother always had one view, it seemed even to me. A forward forward upward upward view, based on being conscious and taking advantage of any opening. I cannot even begin to describe the love factor in my mother and father's relationship, what brought them together aside from their bodies and some kind of conversation.

14   My father from the widowed wing of the lower middle class, a handsome high school graduate from the South, a barber, a truck driver, who tells the old traditional black lie that he thought Newark was New York . . . and it wasn't until much later that . . . His family was upwardly mobile, of course, that's the ideological characteristic of the class. But what if the ruined sector of the black bourgeoisie and the bottom shadow of the petty bourgeoisie come together, the feudings in that, the fumings, the I-used-to-be's and We-would've-been's and the many many If-it-wasn't-for's . . . oh boy oh boy all such as that. The damaged aristocracy of ruined dreams. The open barn door of monopoly capitalism. What a laugh. I mean, if some big-eyed dude was to step in and give a lecture, no, if suddenly there in the darkness of my bedroom I (or whoever could pull this off sleeping in my bed) could have stepped forward into the back-and-forth of sharp voices trying to deal with their lives, in our accepted confusion of what life is, and say, "Look, the bourgeoisie of the oppressed nation always faces a

tenuous existence, the petty bourgeoisie of any nation is always shaky. And yeh, they can get thrown down, like in a fixed rasslin match, thrown down among that black bubbling mass. Yeh, they can get thrown down . . . and all the lit-up fantasies of Sunday School picnics in the light-skinned church of yellow dreams could get thrown down, by the short trip home, to the vacant lots and thousands of dirty Davises, and what you-all is doin is class struggle . . . of a sort, yeh, it's only that, translated as it has to be through the specifics of your life, the particular paths, crossroads and barricades, but that's all it is . . . you know?''

15   I guess their, my parents', eyes would've lit up for a second and then a terrible hard loss would've settled there, because they would've figured the goddam kid is crazy, he's babbling outta his wits. What? And they'd look at each other in the half-dark, and exchange looks about what to do. I'm glad I wasn't that smashed up. What I did do, with a taste of Krueger's beer in my mouth my mother had let me sip out of her glass earlier that night when they had friends over, I just opened my eyes so they glowed softly bigly in the dark and said nothing. I heard my sister's slow deep breathing in the bed under mine.

16   The games and sports of the playground and streets was one registration carried with us as long as we live. Our conduct, strategies and tactics, our ranking and comradeship. Our wins and losses. (Like I was a terrible terrible loser and still am.) I would fight, do anything to stop losing, I would play super-hard, attacking, with endless energy, to stop a loss. I would shout and drive my team on. Stick my hands in the opponents' faces, guard them chest to chest, or slash through the line from the backfield and catch them as they got the pass back from center. Or take the passes and cut around end and streak for the goal. Or double-step, skip, stop, leap, jump back, ram, twist, hop, back up, duck, get away, hustle, and rush into the end zone. I could leap and catch passes one-handed, backwards, on my back, on the run, over someone's shoulder, and take it in. And mostly I never got hurt. I had a fearlessness in games and sports. A feeling that I could win, that I could outrun or outhustle or outscramble or rassle or whatever to pull it out. I would slide head first into home, even first. On tar and cement. I would turn bunts into home runs, by just putting my head down and raging around the bases.

17   In ring-a-leerio, I was always with the little guys and I actually liked that. There was always more of us allowed on the team, cause we were little. But our secret was that we were fast and shifty. I had one move where just as the big boy would be about to snatch me after the run, I'd stop short very suddenly and duck down, and this would send this big dude literally flying over my shoulders. Me, Johnny Boy Holmes, Skippy, and a few others patented that move. So they had to be wary and not run so hard after you and instead try to hem you in and get a couple or three of them to run us down. So we were the dangerous ringy players. And sometimes we'd even break loose and slide into the box and free the others already caught. Streaking into the box, which was marked on the ground, and against the fence of one side of the playground, ''Ring-a-leerio,'' we'd scream, whoever got that honor of charging through the ring of big boys

to free the others. Sometimes we'd form a kind of flying wedge and come barreling in. But some other times them big dudes would smash us, block us, knock us down. Or if we didn't have our thing together, some of the really fast and shifty dudes wasn't playing for instance, they'd chop us off one by one and you had a hell of a time if it was the big boys' time to run out to stop those dudes. But we could and did. If there was enough of us we'd roam in twos and threes and tackle them suckers and sit on them. But you also had to get them back to the box, and they'd be struggling and pulling and that could be worse than just catching them.

18   But ringy was the top game for my money. It involved all the senses and all the skills and might and main of little-boydom. We played everything, baseball, basketball, football, all day every day, according to what season it was (though we'd play basketball all the time, regardless of what the big leagues was doing). But ringy was something else again. I'd like to see a big-league ringy game and league. It's just war pursuit and liberation without weapons. Imagine a ringy game in Yankee Stadium, with karate, boxing, wrestling, great speed, evasion tactics, plus the overall military strategy and tactics that would have to be used. That would really be something.

19   Ringy got you so you could get away from any assault and at the same time fear no one in terms of running directly against big odds trying to free your brothers in the box. And sometimes if you were the only one left, and could keep the bigs darting and running and twisting, and outspeeding them, with the whole playground watching, that was really something, really gratifying.

20   Another teaching experience I had was the game "Morning." It had its variations, "Afternoon," and perhaps there was also an "Evening," though I don't think so. "Morning" happened in the mornings. The first time we came in contact with each other the first one to see the other could hit him, saying, "Morning." And though the other variations probably could be played, "Morning" was most happening I guess because at that time it was the first confrontation of the day and folks just getting up could be unawares and thus bashed.

21   And these suckers who most liked to play "Morning" were not kidding. When they hit they was trying to tear your shoulder off. The shoulder was the place most often hit. The real killers like this dude Big Shot would sneak up on you and hit you in the small of the back and that would take most people down and rolling on the ground in pain. Sometimes actual tears.

22   Close friends wouldn't actually play it or they wouldn't actually hit each other and if they did it wouldn't be a crushing blow. They'd just make believe they were playing it to keep you on your toes. But killers like Shot and some other dudes, little ugly Diddy and dudes like that, would actually try to take you off the planet.

23   If there was a slight tension, an outdoing or competitive thing, between dudes they would use "Morning" as an excuse to get off. But then the only thing that meant is that the other guy would come creeping around looking for an opening to bash the other one. I got hit a couple times, most times not hard—these were my main men who did it, cause I'd be watching, jim. I was not going

to get "Morninged" too often. And I caught a couple of them terrible snake-ass niggers a couple times and tried to tear 'em up, though they were taller and huskier, so my mashing punch was more embarrassment and aggravation than physical wipeout. I got Shot one time and jumped off my feet punching this sucker in his back and he got mad (which was supposed to be against the "rules") and he started chasing me around the playground. But then he really got embarrassed, because his ass was too heavy to catch me. I motored away from him, ducking and twisting, just like in ringy. And finally he got tired and people was laid out on the fence of the playground laughing at his sorry ass.

24   But then he runs over to my main man Love and catches him. You see, you were supposed to say, "Morning," then the other dude couldn't hit you. So Shot zooms over and catches Love right between the shoulder blades and damn near killed him. Love and Shot were always on the verge of going around anyway. Love had a close-cut haircut and a funny, bony-looking head, according to us. And we called him bonehead or saddlehead or some such. But it was the usual joke time. With Shot it was some kind of bitter rebuke, cause Love could play ball—any kind of ball—Shot couldn't do nothing but terrorize people with his ugly-ass self.

25   Love was hurt but when he come up a fight almost started, and then goddam Shot wanted to talk about the "rules." "Like how come Love wanna fight . . . he just don't know how to play the goddam game. If you a sissie you can't play."

26   "How come you can play then, Shot?" And people cracked up, knowing he could not catch me. But from then on I had to watch Shot very close.

27   The "rules." And he had just broke 'em himself. People like that I knew about early. And also I learned how to terrorize the terrorizers.

28   The Dozens. You know the African Recrimination Songs!! Yeh yeh see, I gotta anthropological tip for you as well. But Dozens always floated around every whichaway, around my way, when you was small. Or with close friends, half lit, when you got big. But that was either fun, for fun-connected folks, or the sign that soon somebody's blood would be spilt.

29   The lesson? The importance of language and invention. The place of innovation. The heaviness of "high speech" and rhythm. And their *use*. Not in abstract literary intaglios but on the sidewalk (or tar) in the playground, with everything at stake, even your ass. How to rhyme. How to reach in your head to its outermost reaches. How to invent and create. Your mother's a man— Your father's a woman. Your mother drink her own bath water—Your mother drink other people's. Your mother wear combat boots—Your mother don't wear no shoes at all with her country ass, she just come up here last week playing a goddam harmonica. Or the rhymed variations. I fucked your mama under a tree, she told everybody she wanted to marry me—I fucked your mama in the corner saloon, people want to know was I fucking a baboon. Or: Your mother got a dick—Your mother got a dick bigger than your father's! Point and Counterpoint. Shot and Countershot. Up and One Up.

30   (In the late 60's I was going through some usual state harassment—to wit,

I had supposedly cussed out a policeman in a bank. The truth being that this dude had been harassing us every few evenings, riding by the house, making remarks to the women, creep gestures at us, etc. So he comes in this bank with a shotgun out on "bank patrol" and starts talking loudly about George Wallace, who was running for President. Hooking him up with some local creep, Imperiale, and saying he was voting for Wallace. I said, "You should, it's your brother!" Or something like that. There was an ensuing baiting, a scuffle, more cops summoned, and three of us who'd been in this bank talking bad to the cop, then cops, got taken away. But it was later thrown out because the prosecution said I'd baited the cop by talking about his father. My attorney and I pointed out that while that might be the mores of Irish Americans [the prosecutor] African Americans focused on de mama, so it was an obvious frame. The judge blinked, hmmm, case dismissed. Some street anthropology. And if you could've been there, Judge, in them playgrounds, and heard it, you'd see my point. But, miraculously, he did.)

31   I learned that you could keep people off you if you were mouth-dangerous as well as physically capable. But being Ebony Streak also helped just in case you had to express some physical adroitness. Cause your mouth might get your ass into a situation it could not handle! In which case it was the best thing to rapidly change your landscape.

32   Fighting, avoiding fights, observing fights, knowing when and when not to fight, were all part of our open-air playground-street side education. And fights were so constant, a kind of staged event of varying seriousness. Sometimes very serious. Sometimes just a diversion, for everyone. Like two dudes or girls woofing. Woof woof woof woof woof. They'd be standing somewhere, maybe the hands on the hips, the chicks especially, hands on hips. Maybe one hand gesturing. Or each with one hand on the hip and one hand gesturing. Or they'd get closer and closer. In the purely jive fights the audience would get drugged and push the would-be combatants into each other and that could either start a real fight or it would reveal the totally jive nature of the contest.

A Writer's Notes for a Second Reading

Voice is that vital element in writing that is almost impossible to describe but easy to recognize. Baraka has voice, a casual-appearing but carefully cultivated voice that is tuned to capture and communicate his experience. He is an intellectual. He can—and has—written formal, traditional English. He can also speak, easily and naturally, the language of the street. He is bilingual, can write in White English and Black English. The voice of this text is a masterly combination of all of his languages, tuned to his subject. I hear him speaking on the page and I feel the emotions that rise off his page.

        I also learn from his pacing, the way he builds up an event, carrying the reader forward in a strong flow of revealing detail. And as a reader, he takes me back to my own school and the streets on which I learned to survive. As I read his text, I write the text of my own childhood and see it a bit differently because of what he has said of his own growing up.

Discussion

- Consider how Baraka uses the point of view of the child, the point of view of the adult looking back at childhood, and the two. Discuss examples of where it works well and where it doesn't work.
- Discuss how Baraka uses specific information to make you think and feel.
- Discuss how Baraka uses his street voice and his educated voice. Why does he do this? Does it work?
- List the ways Baraka makes people come alive on the page, both himself and those he describes. Consider which are the most effective.

Activities

- Read a section aloud to hear Baraka's voice in your voice. Ask classmates to read sections aloud so you can hear Baraka's voice in theirs. Notice how their own backgrounds and language affect the reading.
- Take one of the experiences that Baraka writes about and write about a similar experience of your own in your own way, and compare it with his.
- Choose something that is special in your background—a Puerto Rican christening, a Greek wedding, an Italian street festival, an hour at a country club pool, a locker-room at half-time, a sorority meeting—and take the reader who is unfamiliar with your culture inside that experience.
- Write a brief sketch of a relative showing, as Baraka does, how that person's story tells us something significant about the people that person represents.
- Take a paragraph or two from Baraka and rewrite it with the same facts in your own tone of voice, then compare the two versions to see how voice is expressed in print and how it affects the reader.

To Collaborate

- Have each member of the team find a common school experience, then work together to create a school legend written in a voice that supports and reinforces the meaning of the experience.
- Write a joint memo to a first-year teacher who is going to have 26 Barakas in class, helping the teacher to understand the world of the students and how the teacher might reach them.

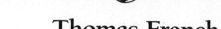

Thomas French

Thomas French knew he wanted to be a writer when he was ten years old and in the fifth grade. At Pike High School in Indianapolis, he was editor of his high school paper; he went to the University of Indiana, where he studied and practiced journalism.

Now he is one of the top writers on the *St. Petersburg Times* in Florida, where he also works with high school journalists through the Poynter Institute. When the incident described in the following article occurred, he sat down and wrote the following commentary in four or five hours. His biggest problem, he says, was "keeping a balance between personal recollections and present observations."

It didn't surprise French when he heard from many high school students. What did surprise him is that he heard "from adults in their fifties, sixties, and one in his seventies. They still carried resentment from the way they were treated in high school."

Long Live High School Rebels

1   Ten years ago I was in high school. It was the most absurd and savage place I have ever been.

2   To listen to the morning announcements, you'd have thought the most pressing crisis in the world was our student body's lack of school spirit. Seniors were grabbing freshmen, dragging them into the bathrooms and dunking their heads in the toilets—a ritual called "flushing." Basketball players were treated like royalty; smart kids were treated like peasants. And the administrators worshipped the word "immature." Inevitably, they pronounced it "imma-tour." Inevitably, they used it to describe us.

3   The principal and his assistants told us to act like adults, but they treated us like children. Stupid children. They told us what we could wear, when we could move, how close we could stand to our girlfriends, how fast we could walk to lunch and what topics were forbidden to write about in our school newspaper.

4   When I went out for the tennis team, I remember, the coach told me to cut my hair. It was down to my shoulders and looked terrible, but I loved it. I asked the coach what was the point. Just do it, he said.

5   If we were taught anything, it was that high school is not about learning but about keeping quiet. The easiest way to graduate was to do what you were told, all of what you were told, and nothing but what you were told. Most of us did just that. I smiled at the principal, stayed out of trouble, avoided writing articles critical of the administration, asked only a few smart-alecky questions

and cut my hair as ordered. I was so embarrassed afterwards that I wore a blue ski cap all day every day for weeks.

6   I admit to some lingering bitterness over the whole affair. I'd still like to know, for one thing, what the length of my hair had to do with my forehand. Maybe that's why, to this day, I almost always root for high school students when they clash intelligently with administrators. High school needs a good dose of dissension. If you've been there in recent years, and I have because I work with student newspapers around Pinellas County, you'd know it needs dissension more than ever.

7   A reminder of this came with the news that one day last month an assistant principal at St. Petersburg High was rummaging through a student's car in a school parking lot. When the assistant principal found three empty wine-cooler bottles and what was suspected to be some spiked eggnog inside the car, the student was suspended for five days.

8   Though the student has argued that the search was an unconstitutional violation of his rights, the incident should not have come as any huge surprise. High school officials around this county have been searching through kids' cars and lockers for some time. One day a couple of years ago, a teacher tells me, officials at Lakewood High allowed police to search for drugs with dogs. At the time, students were gathered at an assembly on God and patriotism.

9   Searches tell students plainly enough what administrators think of them. But in this county, such incidents are only part of a larger tradition of control. Some memorable moments over the years:

10   • In 1983, a group of boys at Lakewood High decided it was unfair that they weren't allowed to wear shorts to school but that girls were allowed to wear miniskirts. The rationale for the rule was that shorts—but not miniskirts—were too "distracting." To make fun of the rule, the boys began wearing miniskirts to school.

11   Administrators laughed at first, but once the rebellion began attracting publicity, the principal suspended the ringleader. When dozens of students staged further protest in front of the school and refused to go to class, the principal suspended 37 of them, too. Later, although close to 1,400 signatures were gathered on a petition against the rule, the Pinellas County School Board bore down and decided to ban shorts from all middle and high schools. Miniskirts, however, were still allowed.

12   "We need to set a moral standard for our children," explained board member Gerald Castellanos.

13   • Last year, William Grey, the principal of St. Petersburg High, suspended a ninth-grader who dyed her hair purple. "I just don't think school is the place for multi-colored heads," Grey said. He did acknowledge that he allowed students to dye their hair green for special events—the

school's colors are green and white—but he insisted that was different because it was "promoting school spirit."

14 • Earlier this year at Pinellas Park High, two of the school's top students—they're number one and two in their class academically—were criticized by the principal when they wrote articles in the student newspaper pointing out that many of the school's students are sexually active and do not use birth control. I was working with the staff that year, and I know the two students wrote the articles in an effort to prevent teen-age pregnancies. But the principal called their work irresponsible—he disagreed with their methodology—and told the newspaper staff it should write more "positive" articles.

15 • This fall, says a teacher at Pinellas Park, the administration cracked down on cafeteria infractions by warning that anyone caught leaving a lunch tray on a table would be suspended.

16 • Last year, 16-year-old Manny Sferios and a group of other students from public and private high schools put together an underground magazine called *Not For Profit* and distributed several issues to students around the county. The magazine ridiculed apartheid, protested the proliferation of nuclear weapons and tried to prod students into thinking about something more than their next pair of designer jeans.

17   *Not For Profit* also contained a variety of swear words and ridiculed the small-mindedness of many school officials, and when administrators saw it, they began confiscating copies from kids and warning that those caught with the publication risked suspension.

18   Though the officials said their main objection to *Not For Profit* was its language, the magazine's activist stance also came under fire. Gerald Castellanos, the school board member, said he did not believe students were sophisticated enough to put together such a magazine.

19   "I sincerely sense the hand of some very anti-American, anti-free enterprise types in here," he said. "And I don't believe they're students."

20   Castellanos' attitude was not surprising. Too often the people who run our high schools and sit on our school boards are not prepared to accept or deal with students who think for themselves and stand up for themselves. It would mean a loss of some control, increased resistance to petty rules and a slew of hard questions for those officials who'd rather present a "positive image" than openly confront the real problems in our schools.

21   There are plenty of real problems that need confronting. Alcohol. Drugs. Broken families. Teen-age pregnancies. Not to mention what's happening in some of our classrooms.

22   While working on an article published earlier this year, I sat in a couple of classes at St. Petersburg High—the school run by William Grey, the principal who took a stand on purple hair—and what I saw were rows and rows of kids who were bored beyond description. They were trading jokes while the teachers tried to speak. They were literally falling asleep at their desks. One boy who

had no interest in the subject matter—it was American history, by the way— was allowed to get up and leave. Another sat in his seat, strumming his finger across his lips, making baby noises.

23   Dealing with apathy as deep as this is challenge enough for anyone. It requires more teachers, more money, inspiration, real change—all of which are hard to come by. Throw that in with the other problems in our high schools, and the task becomes monumental.

24   I'm not saying that administrators aren't trying to cope with that task. I know they are. But frequently they waste time and distance themselves from students by exerting their authority in other ways. Make sure the kids don't wear shorts. See to it they put away their lunch trays. Bring in the dogs every once in a while and let them sniff around the lockers. In the face of everything else, keep the school quiet. It's a way the adults tell themselves they're in charge. It's a way they tell themselves they're making a difference.

25   In the meantime, the ideas that our high schools should promote—free-dom of thought and expression, for one—get shoved aside. And the students whom we should be encouraging—the ones who have the brains and spirit to start their own magazine, to protest silly rules, to ask what the color of one's hair has to do with an education—are lectured, suspended and told to get back in line.

26

Kids know it stinks. Once in a while, they find the guts to step forward and say so, even if it means getting in trouble. I think they should do it more often. Because if there's anything I regret about my own days in high school, it's that more of us didn't fight against the absurdity with every ounce of ado-
27 lescent ingenuity and irreverence we had.

We should have commandeered the p.a. system one morning and read aloud from Thoreau's *Civil Disobedience.* We should have boycotted the food in the cafeteria for a solid week. We should have sent a note home to the princi-pal's parents informing them he was suspended until he grew up. We should have boned up on our rights in a law library and published what we found in the school paper. And every time an adult said "imma-tour," we should have pulled kazoos out of our pockets and blown on them to our heart's content.

A Writer's Notes for a Second Reading

Our high school newspaper made money for the school and, since the administration didn't know how to accept or use money from students, they closed us down.

That's this writer's first reaction to this piece—and a compliment to the writer when I connect this topic with my own experience. It shows I have made use of what I have read.

Tom French maintains the balance between personal experience and fresh obser-vation. Rereading the text, I am impressed at how he weaves the personal and the reported.

His voice is interesting to me. It is the journalistic voice of a person trained to report the stories of others with detachment and economy. His prose is clean, specific, vigorous. Now he tunes that professional voice to a subject filled with emotion.

I'm also interested in the way the commentary develops. In the beginning it is packed with documentation, but in the last eight paragraphs he writes almost pure opinion, a position he hopes he has earned by the authority he has established in the previous 19 paragraphs.

Discussion

• In a commentary French does not have to give each side an equal voice. He is allowed to have a personal opinion he would not be allowed in a news story, but is he fair to both sides? Should he be?

• What techniques does French use to establish his authority? To make his position clear? To support his position?

• How are Baraka and French different in the way they look back at school? How are they the same? What are the strengths and weaknesses of each approach?

• Who is French's audience? Imagine different audiences for his article. What would he have to change to appeal to those audiences?

Activities

• Look back at a high school gripe and write your own brief commentary. Write a response to it from the point of view of a teacher or administrator.

• Propose a policy based on personal experience.

• Write a page of French's commentary as Baraka might have written it; write a page of Baraka's text as French might have written it.

• Go through French's piece and describe how each paragraph advances and supports the writer's opinion. Do the same thing with a draft of your own or a classmate's.

To Collaborate

• Write a committee proposal for a change in a school policy based on personal and objective evidence.

• Create a publishable written dialogue between people on both sides of an issue.

Woody Allen

Woody Allen is a writer of both short stories and films, an actor, a movie director, and a jazz clarinet player. His career began after he was rejected by both New York University and City College. He has written, directed, and appeared in 16 films, beginning in 1964 with *What's New, Pussycat?* He is also a regular contributor to *The New Yorker*.

His formula for productivity is simple: "If you work only three to five hours a day, you become quite productive. It's the steadiness that counts. Getting to the typewriter every day is what makes for productivity."

The Colorization of Films Insults Artists and Society

1   In the world of potent self-annihilation, famine and AIDS, terrorists and dishonest public servants and quack evangelists and contras and Sandinistas and cancer, does it really matter if some kid snaps on his TV and happens to see "The Maltese Falcon" in color? Especially if he can simply dial the color out and choose to view it in its original black and white?

2   I think it does make a difference and the ramifications of what's called colorization are not wonderful to contemplate. Simply put, the owners of thousands of classic American black and white films believe that there would be a larger public for the movies, and consequently more money, if they were reissued in color. Since they have computers that can change such masterpieces as "Citizen Kane" and "City Lights" and "It's A Wonderful Life" into color, it has become a serious problem for anyone who cares about these movies and has feelings about our image of ourselves as a culture.

3   I won't comment about the quality of the color. It's not good, but probably it will get better. Right now it's like elevator music. It has no soul. All faces are rendered with the same deadening pleasance. The choices of what colors people should be wearing or what colors rooms should be (all crucial artistic decisions in making a film) are left to caprices and speculations by computer technicians who are not qualified to make those choices.

4   Probably false, but not worth debating here, is the claim that young people won't watch black and white. I would think they would, judging from the amount of stylish music videos and MTV ads that are done in black and white, undoubtedly after market research. The fact that audiences of all ages have been watching Charlie Chaplin, Humphrey Bogart, Jimmy Stewart, Fred Astaire—in fact, all the stars and films of the so-called Golden Age of Hollywood—in black and white for decades with no diminution of joy also makes me wonder about these high claims for color. Another point the coloroids make is that one can

always view the original if one prefers. The truth is, however, that in practical terms, what will happen is that the color versions will be aired while token copies of the original black and white will lie around preserved in a vault, unpromoted and unseen.

5   Another aspect of the problem that one should mention (although it is not the crucial ground on which I will make my stand) is that American films are a landmark heritage that do our nation proud all over the world, and should be seen as they were intended to be.

6   One would wince at defacing great buildings or paintings, and, in the case of movies, what began as a popular entertainment has, like jazz music, developed into a serious art form. Now, someone might ask: "Is an old Abbott and Costello movie art? Should it be viewed in the same way as 'Citizen Kane'?" The answer is that it should be protected, because all movies are entitled to their personal integrity and, after all, who knows what future generations will regard as art works of our epoch?

7   Yet another question: "Why were directors not up in arms about cutting films for television or breaking them up for commercials, insulting them with any number of technical alterations to accommodate the television format?" The answer is that directors always hated these assaults on their work but were powerless to stop them. As in life, one lives with the first few wounds, because to do battle is an overwhelmingly time-consuming and pessimistic prospect.

8   Still, when the assaults come too often, there is a revolution. The outrage of seeing one's work transformed into color is so dramatically appalling, so "obvious"—as against stopping sporadically for commercials—that this time all the directors, writers and actors chose to fight.

9   But let me get to the real heart of the matter and to why I think the issue is not merely one that affronts the parties directly involved but has a larger meaning. What's at stake is a moral issue and how our culture chooses to define itself. No one should be able to alter an artist's work in any way whatsoever, for any reason, without the artist's consent. It's really as simple as that.

10   John Huston has made it clear that he doesn't want "The Maltese Falcon" seen in color. This is his right as an artist and certainly must be his choice alone. Nor would I want to see my film "Manhattan" in color. Not if it would bring in 10 times the revenue. Not if all the audiences in the world begged or demanded to see it that way.

11   I believe the people who are coloring movies have contempt for the audience by claiming, in effect, that viewers are too stupid and too insensitive to appreciate black and white photography—that they must be given, like infants or monkeys, bright colors to keep them amused.

12   They have contempt for the artist, caring little for the moral right these directors have over their own creations.

13   And, finally, they have contempt for society because they help define it as one that chooses to milk every last dollar out of its artists' work, even if it means mutilating the work and humiliating the culture's creative talent..

14   This is how we are viewed around the world and how we will be viewed by future generations. Most civilized governments abroad, realizing that their society is at least as much shaped and identified by its artists as by its businessmen, have laws to protect such things from happening. In our society, merchants are willing to degrade anything or anyone so long as it brings in a financial profit.

15   Allowing the colorization of films is a good example of our country's regard for its artists, and why I think the issue of moral rights requires legislative help and protection.

16   The recent Federal copyright decision says that if a human being uses a certain minimum amount of creativity in coloring a black and white film, the new color version is a separate work that can be copyrighted. In short, if a man colors "Citizen Kane," it becomes a new movie that can be copyrighted. This must be changed. How? By making sure that Representative Richard A. Gephardt's film integrity bill is passed. It would legalize the moral rights of film artists and, in the process, make colorization without consent illegal.

17   It is, after all, a very short step to removing the score from "Gone With the Wind" and replacing it with a rock score under the mistaken notion that it will render it more enjoyable to young people.

A Writer's Notes for a Second Reading

I'm first of all struck at Woody Allen's empathic understanding of the audience he wants most to reach: those who think the issue of colorization is trivial. He makes his opponents' strongest argument against his position and by so doing effectively takes it away from them, a traditional and clever argumentative strategy.

He goes on, again and again, to dismiss his opponents' arguments—that the color will get better, that young people won't watch black and white—and *then* launches his attack, working from the least controversial positions to the most extreme but saving for the end a specific situation on which he can be pretty sure the reader and he would agree.

It's not fancy writing, but a direct, disciplined, and traditional example of argument.

Discussion

- What are the strengths of Allen's argument? The weaknesses?
- How would you argue *for* colorization? What would be your strong and weak points?
- What other arguments might Allen have employed?
- What other sequences of arguments might he have used? What would be the strengths and weaknesses of each?

Activities

• In class or in a small group, rent a black-and-white and a colored version of the same movie. Through discussion, develop a written class position for both sides of the issue.

• Draft as many beginnings for Allen's article as you can imagine and discuss the advantages and disadvantages of each.

• Rewrite a scene from a Woody Allen movie (many of the scripts are available in paperback) and see how "updating" the characters, action, or language changes the movie.

• Turn the color off on a classic color film to see the effect black and white has, how it changes the film and your experience in watching the movie.

• Using Allen's technique, write a brief argument on an issue important to you and submit it for publication.

To Collaborate

• View a colorized film with your teammates. List all the elements in the film that are affected by the change of color. Work together to build an argument showing how colorization influences other aspects of a film.

• Prepare a marketing questionnaire as a team and use it to interview VCR renters or videotape stores to see how people feel on the issue and just how popular colorized films are over black and white. Write a collaborative report on your findings.

Anna Quindlen

Anna Quindlen has had an outstanding career as a journalist. She was a reporter for the *New York Post* and was recruited by the *New York Times*. Later, when she was in her 20s, she was given a prestigious assignment—to write the "About New York" column. During her three years on that assignment, Anna Quindlen earned a national reputation as a writer.

At 31 she was promoted to deputy metropolitan editor. After a stint in that position, she left to write free-lance articles and a novel. Then she was hired back by the *New York Times* to write the "Life in the 30s" column from which this selection was taken. Once again she has left the *Times* to write books.

This Child I Carry, Like My Other Two, Is Wanted. Healthy or Not.

1   It's interesting to note the way medical miracles can go from brave new world to simple acceptance almost overnight. Once it was a major news event when a heart from one person was placed in the chest of another. Once it stopped the presses when a baby was born of an egg fertilized outside a woman's body. Today, there have been many heart transplants and many babies conceived in vitro, and people speak knowledgeably of donating organs, or of infertility.

2   It was not so many years ago that few of us could pronounce, much less talk about, amniocentesis. It is a procedure in which amniotic fluid is withdrawn with a needle from the uterus of a pregnant woman; the fluid is then tested to see if the child within has certain abnormalities.

3   The procedure is now routinely recommended to women over the age of 35, and almost everyone has heard of it. I know this because I am almost 36 years old, I am expecting a baby and soon after "Congratulations" and "Was it an accident?"—this is, after all, my third child in a 1.8 children per family country—I am sure to be asked whether I am having amnio, as it is now familiarly called. The assumption is that I am.

4   The reality is that I am not. I have had a good long time to think about it, knowing since the birth of my second that I wanted more and that I would slip into the danger zone over 35 before I became pregnant again. My husband and I have had some good long talks about it, too, about how much stress and disappointment our family could stand, about when life begins and under what circumstances it should be ended.

5   This has nothing to do with our being Roman Catholics, although people always seem to suspect that our religion and our decision are inextricably linked. For while some people use amniocentesis to prepare for bad news, for most it is an issue of abortion. You have the test so that you can find out if the child will be impaired. And if it will, you can . . . well, what I'm supposed to write here is terminate the pregnancy. But that's not what I feel. If I were talking about doing something as clinical as "terminating" something as disembodied as "a pregnancy," I wouldn't have a problem.

6   It's interesting how we have managed to move the bottom line of the question to the back of our minds. The other day, I was talking to a woman who said that she never let her mind get that far; that she underwent the procedure for peace of mind and forced her thoughts to make a sharp S-curve around the possibility that the results would not be soothing.

7   I think that's natural. There are two questions here, and both are terrify-

ing. One is about abortion itself, and about when and why we can bear it. Some of my friends have suggested that I have a newer diagnostic test, something called chorionic villi sampling, that gives earlier results than amnio, and so allows for earlier abortion. But timing is not truly my concern. Perhaps if this child were unwanted, I could think of it as a fetus. But my children—three of them now—have all been wanted; they were babies from the moment I knew they were coming. I do not know what it would take for me to stop their lives.

8   What would it take? That is the other question. If a test could tell that the child I carry is schizophrenic or autistic, conditions that are my two personal demons, what would I do then? Or if I were Jewish and a carrier of Tay-Sachs, the vile disease that reduces children to insensate husks before they die at the age of 3 or 4? I suspect I might make a different decision here.

9   But for Down's syndrome, in which the baby would be moderately to severely retarded and have medical problems ranging from persistent ear infections to heart disease? Or spina bifida, which can cause lifelong paralysis and often necessitates corrective surgery? Trying to explain to my doctor, who is wise and sensitive, I raised my arms from the too-large armholes of the paper gown as though I were begging him to finish my sentence. "It's not . . . It's not . . . " I repeated. "Sufficient impediment?" he said. Right, as usual.

10   How much can you handle? People tell me that's the real question: whether a family has sufficient resources, both emotional and financial, to fit the extraordinary needs of a handicapped child into its web. But here's the real answer: I haven't a clue what I could handle. I do know that I would have blighted my life if I had turned away from all the things I thought I was not big enough to do.

11   I once tried to have my tubes tied because I was convinced I could never handle children. On a bad night, when my children were young, I have been convinced that I couldn't handle another. And despite our decision, I pray that the third will be as wonderful and healthy as the first two have been—in, I should add, that order.

12   It all comes down to our other children. If I decided to abort this baby because it was going to be retarded, or unable to walk, or in need of extraordinary amounts of medical care, I could not find the words to explain it to them. The only compelling argument anyone has made to us for amnio, which is not entirely without risk, was made by my doctor, who asked us to consider the possibility that we could not devote sufficient time to the needs of the children we have now if we were looking after those of someone so much needier. We considered that argument, and let it go. Having more than one child always means a willingness either to give less to the others or to stretch yourself more.

13   The first two children have taught us that, and they have taught us that life is nothing but hard questions, and that we answer them as best we can. In some sense, the future's already writ. This child is already something: boy, girl,

healthy, ill—perhaps, if you are a devotee of nature over nurture, even good or bad. I do not know yet. I know only one thing now. This child is ours, for better or for worse, in sickness and in health.

―――――――――――――――――――――――

❦Anna Quindlen's column caused an unusual reaction among *New York Times* readers and the newspaper published the following examples:❧

A Conscience Plagued

To The Home Section:

1   There is an aspect of the possibility of the birth of a handicapped child that Ms. Quindlen seems to have overlooked. And that is the quality of life of the child itself.

2   She seems very concerned with how she would handle this child's disability, how she would cope, how her family would react. And she reassures herself that all sorts of love and compassion would be there. This child would be to her as dear as the others.

3   I urge Ms. Quindlen to give a thought to the life she is asking this child to lead. After all, she will only react to the disability. The child is the one who will have to live this life.

4   If I knowingly brought a handicapped child into this less-than-compassionate world, with no guarantee of the permanent presence of loving parents, my conscience would plague me with that, not the more merciful abortion. And if the child knew, would it not be justified in saying,"*You* did *this* to me?"

5   Ms. Quindlen should stop dwelling on herself and her feelings and think of the child, and have the amnio.

MARIE R. KLEIN
Port Washington, L.I.

Moral Dilemma

To The Home Section:

1   We had our first child when my wife was 29, too young for routine prenatal genetic screening. Our child, now 5, has Down's syndrome, and I often shudder at the thought of perhaps ignorantly terminating that pregnancy if we had known beforehand of her handicap. She is a great kid who has been a wonderful gift to our family in many unexpected ways. Most people with Down's syndrome are only mildly retarded, incidentally.

2   Three trends are converging that make Ms. Quindlen's column very timely. The genetic markings of more and more disorders and even personality traits are being identified. Prenatal genetic screening is becoming cheaper, safer, and is being done earlier in the pregnancy. Medical malpractice claims

increasingly encourage doctors to recommend screening. It will become standard procedure within a few years, which is certain to pose profound moral dilemmas for society in general and childbearing families in particular.

3   I wish more people had Ms. Quindlen's attitude on this issue.

RICHARD H. BARRY
Dallas

Competence of Parents

To the Home Section:

1   I had amniocentesis when I was pregnant. The results came back just fine. Four months later I gave birth to my son, who had a birth defect known as radial aplasia. He has a very short arm and a hand with only three fingers. There are also potentially serious problems with his spine.

2   I had the amnio done because I was 35 and my husband and I knew that we probably could not cope with a child with spina bifida or Down's syndrome. Since amnio can only alert you to certain problems like neural tube defects, we still took a chance and something did indeed turn out to be wrong.

3   As a result I learned that we could cope with far more than we thought, and while we are more aware of how vulnerable to disaster parenting is, we also have a sense of competency as parents that is special.

4   I believe in a woman's right to abortion, not as a casual means of birth control but as a decision related to how well she feels she can raise a child given certain difficult circumstances. In fact, I wish that pro-life advocates would concern themselves more with the rights of children already born.

5   I applaud, however, Ms. Quindlen's discussion of her decision. She has been fortunate so far and has not had to experience the problems of having a physically imperfect child. She and her husband are obviously thoughtful and deliberate in their determination and they know what they feel they can deal with, if necessary.

6   We have raised our son to see himself as a whole person—with a difference. But then, there are no truly physically perfect people. If someone said I could trade my son for another child with two arms the same length, but told me that he would not be the same child I know and love, I wouldn't do it.

SUSAN GOODE
Teaneck, N.J.

Selfish Decisions

To The Home Section:

1   I am disturbed and incredulous at the conclusions drawn by Anna Quindlen. She declares that a possible future of "lifelong paralysis" is not "sufficient impediment" to her developing fetus to warrant an abortion because the child is "wanted," yet schizophrenia, autism and Tay-Sachs disease would most likely be reason enough to abort.

2   How selfish for her to decide for this child which of the vast array of severe physical and mental incapacities is "sufficient impediment." And how selfish to eschew chorionic villus sampling or amniocentesis to determine the presence of Down's syndrome, and the blood test to screen for the insidious disease spina bifida.

3   What about the rights of this fetus to not be destined to a life in a wheelchair or without limbs, something detected easily and early via sonogram.

4   Taking my cue from Ms. Quindlen's self-congratulations for deciding against prenatal testing at the age of 36, I would like to congratulate myself. At the age of 38, after weighing the decision to bring another human being into this chaotic cosmos, I am in my 25th week of my first pregnancy.

5   I know my daughter will not have Down's syndrome or spina bifida. And during the future sonogram, I will know whether she will be burdened with a cleft palate, so I can have a surgeon waiting in the delivery room.

6   Ms. Quindlen's logic escapes me. Does she really believe that not having tests after the age of 35, when women automatically go into the high-risk pregnancy category, shows that she wants her baby more than I want mine?

SUSAN BATTLES
Washington

A Writer's Notes for a Second Reading

I am struck by the personal honesty of this piece, almost not an argument because the author does not seem to want to influence others but simply to share the private decision of her husband and herself.

Her motive? Who can say what a writer's motives are—or anyone else's motives? I have seen so much hurt delivered by good motives that I am no longer interested in motives. Anna Quindlen is a writer. She has chosen to report on the life she is leading, articulating the problems and decisions faced by those who fit the title of her column, "Life in the 30s."

On rereading I am struck by her tone. It is quiet, almost hesitant, yet direct. The kind of tone appropriate to a morning talk with a friend over a mug of coffee at the kitchen table or a late-night talk on a summer porch with old friends.

It is a voice that does not seek confrontation and so may reach those who would not normally read about the subject, either because of their position on the subject or their disinterest. I feel that she would listen, that she invites other views. Whether that is the reason or it is simply her subject and her decision, she certainly caused others to respond—as the letters attest.

I was once told that a letter written in response to a newspaper article meant that 100 intended to write and 1000 were concerned enough to think of writing. I don't know if that's accurate, but I do know that editors pay attention. When I wrote for *Time* I believe we had more than four million subscribers and newsstand purchasers, many more readers. Yet one or two letters on a story would cause the editor and the writer to pause and reconsider what had been written and how. Critical letters could cause change and, just as important, positive letters support what was being done. Write to writers and their publications when you feel strongly. Your voice will be heard.

Discussion

- Do you think there is a difference between male and female modes of argument, as suggested in *A Note on Writing Argument?* If so, does Anna Quindlen demonstrate qualities that might be called feminist?
- How could her argument be made stronger?
- What are the similarities and differences between the structure of Allen's argument and Quindlen's? What other elements are strikingly the same or different?
- Would Allen or Quindlen persuade you most effectively? Why?

Activities

- Collect some other written arguments or articles on Quindlen's topic. Compare their effectiveness with hers.
- Take another controversial issue in which you have strong beliefs and write it with Quindlen's tone, then with a confrontational tone.
- Revise her article so it would connect with a different audience: doctors, young mothers, parents of children with severe birth handicaps, clergy.
- List the questions you'd like to ask Quindlen and answer them to see if they could be incorporated in the article.

To Collaborate

- Have your team interview a number of people interested in this topic. You might interview sources from different categories or concentrate on one—for example, pregnant women 35 and over. Sources might include doctors, clergy, social workers, birth-control-clinic staff members. Write a piece revealing what you have discovered.
- Team up with someone who takes a position on a significant issue that is opposite yours. Then each write an argument for *the other person's position;* read and compare what you have written to discover what you have learned about writing argument.

Notes on a Course in Argument

I am reprinting ten student papers written in a Freshman English course in argument I taught at the University of New Hampshire. In each case, I have included the student writer's final commentary on the entire process and, in some cases, drafts and notes written during the process that may illuminate how the final draft was created. The following paragraphs from the syllabus—and my notes on those paragraphs—will explain the course in which the papers were produced.

- *"This is an experimental course in the basic academic discipline of writing argument. To counter the usual fragmentation of university courses, students will spend the entire semester developing an extensive, well-developed argument. Students will pick their own topics and their own audience. There will be a written assignment due at the beginning of each Tuesday class. I will keep the original and you will keep a copy of it, and bring that copy both to class and to conference."*

☞ I have taught Freshman English with daily papers five days a week, four days a week, three days a week, at each class period, and usually with a weekly paper. I have, however, been concerned with the fragmentation of student work. I have encouraged students to work on one topic and once taught a basic composition course in which the students wrote eighteen papers during the semester, all on the same topic. In the course described in this syllabus I did with Freshmen what I have done in advanced writing courses, and had the students write every week, but work toward one final paper. ☜

> • *"In addition to the written assignment you will bring enough copies of a one-page, single-spaced typed commentary for everyone in the class. The instructor and the student will share their experiences writing and reading during the week. These commentaries will provide the basis for most class discussion."*

☞ I have found that asking students to write about their writing process each week forces them to be more reflective about how they are writing. They also teach themselves, each other, and me. When I have these commentaries passed in just to me they are tossed off, but when their classmates are going to read them they are much more considered and helpful. I also write a commentary each week about my writing, whatever it is, and this allows me to say what I think needs to be said as a colleague, without the excess formality and power that comes with most lectures. The students are prepared for discussion with each other, in small groups and large groups,m and they are also prepared for conference.

> • *"Class attendance is required. If you stop attending class you will be dropped from the course. If there is an emergency and you cannot make class, notify the English Department or me at home in advance of class."*

☞ If I'm going to make class then my students, by God, are going to make ☜ class.

> • *"Weekly conferences are required. You are expected to come to the conference on time and come to my office door. It is up to you to keep me on schedule. In the conference you will comment on your work, and I will respond to your comments. Miss conferences, and you will be dropped."*

☞ At the University of New Hampshire every student in every Freshman English class has a weekly conference with the instructor. The conferences are short, but they are central to the way I teach. The student speaks first, then I read the paper and the student's commentary, and respond to what the student has said about the writing and to the writing in that order. ☜

> • *"Grades will be given only at the end of the course, and will depend on class participation, with emphasis on your final paper."*

❦ I do not believe in grading what the student has learned in previous courses but on the work the student produces by the end of my course.❧

- *"This plan has been carefully thought out, but no syllabus should stand in the way of your education. You should feel free to question everything in the course. We will learn from each other and with each other."*

❦ In this Freshman course everyone held to the syllabus, but I have had courses in which everyone by the middle of the course has written their new personal syllabus. Each, of course, has to be approved by me, but I find that they demand more of themselves than I would have required. I haven't had to reject one yet.❧

The subjects in which the students chose to write were grim, and this caused me the following September at the beginning of school and the beginning of my retirement to write an *Over Sixty* column, arguing, I suppose, for understanding of the world in which young people live.

I have chosen the selections for this book because I have been able to pair them so that the reader can see two student writers dealing with similar topics. I would have been happy, however, to publish all but one or two from the class of more than twenty. There were many excellent papers that I have not been able to publish, and I apologize to their authors.

Donald M. Murray

The column I write for *The Boston Globe* appears every other Tuesday and is aimed at people like myself who are over sixty. Some columns are nostalgic, others humorous, some serious. I like to imagine myself a foreign correspondent not assigned to the Middle East, China, or Russia but to the land of aging and retirement. It is a personal column but I hope, as all writers hope, to articulate the unspoken concerns of my readers.

The columns are usually about 12 or 13 paragraphs long—this one is 16—and they are written quickly. I do not write until I have a line. I prefer that term to *idea*. Of course it is an idea but it is more, a fragment of language which contains some tension and that conflict or tension will compel me to write the piece to find out what I have to say.

Once I have the line I write the lead, the first paragraph or so. That will take me 15 minutes or less. I may let that sit overnight or I will write as fast as I can. In about 45 minutes I finish the draft, then spend another 45 minutes that day or next, jiggling things around, cutting, developing. I show it to my wife and she points out my errors in spelling, grammar, and punctuation as well as my errors in thinking. If she approves, I send it off my modem to the *Globe*.

Victims of the Age of Prosperity

1   The students are back in school but not I. I came to teaching late and I'm leaving early, well, slightly early. First the no-necks return, the football players in cut-off T-shirts and cut-off shorts, walking with rehearsed menace, their arms hung away from their sculptured torsos. How few mirrors they must pass without posing.

2   Then the freshman camp counselors, the campus politicians, the fraternity and sorority insiders, tans by Wianno, uniforms by North Conway. Then the freshmen and the freshwomen, their parents, proud, worried, relieved, looking at their watches and kissing goodbye at the same time.

3   At last the upperclass scholars, the hope of the future, heads unbalanced by huge earrings on only one side; wearing clothes left to rot in Cuban mountains by Castro generations ago; sporting skin heads and rooster heads and swooped skulls and pink hair. They swirl around, speak no language taught in school and are rarely caught carrying a book. It is easy to despair.

4   But I have seen beneath their disguises for years, and I am a bit sad they will not write for me this fall semester, and I will not sit reading and listening as they come, one by one, unable to keep their masks from slipping bit by bit.

5   As they write and reveal themselves to themselves on the page, their secrets will be revealed. Behind the sophistication is innocence—and fear and hope and longing and pain and a thirst for the answers to the questions we have always asked and an idealism that may not be ours but is real to them, embarrassing for them to admit and nothing less than inspiring to observe.

6   They do not appear to be like us, and that can spark fear and anger and worry and even disgust—some would like nothing more than to inspire disgust in someone of our age. We must remember that these college students are the survivors of wars most of us do not know, and these young veterans deserve our understanding, compassion and respect.

7   Many are the victims not of Depression but of a prosperity that brings its own aching hunger. To have a car, a computer, a portable compact disc player and speakers that can crack ledge, to wear the correct sneakers and have been at the right beach does not bring peace—or happiness or security or comfort.

8   They are often surprised to discover that, and such a pain may be all right. A little—even a great—discomfort may be just fine in university students. It may spark questions that will bring the answers we need. Certainly, our generation cannot be smug about our values, whatever they are.

9   Our children—or our children's children—have emigrated from a world far different from ours. At an educational meeting to plan for the future of the study of reading, writing and language, the participants were told that 93 percent of the students in elementary school right now come from homes that are radically different from the imaginary environments for which our curriculums are designed. Ninety-three percent!

10   Five students out of 25 or more in the classrooms I visit live with their biological parents, and the teacher knows that some of those marriages will break up next year or the year after. A "normal" home is now abnormal.

11   I personally know of several parents who have left town to live with companions—and left teenagers alone and unsupervised in the house—for years. Many of my students come from a world that seems far different from—and often far harsher than—my Depression, prewar years.

12   My last freshman section was composed of well-educated—and often well-heeled (a historic cliche that comes from a time when you had old shoes resoled if you were lucky) young people who have survived in a suburban world that seems to deny reality and therefore makes dealing with it all the more difficult. They did not live on the street. They lived in homes that were supposed to look stable and, indeed, have the appearance of happiness, success and belonging.

13   I only know a little of the lives of these freshmen, but in one section alone I had a glimpse behind their premature sophistication. One student had to miss several classes for the latest in a series of difficult operations. Another gave an anniversary present to her parents as she left for school. They rejected it, telling their daughter their marriage was over—a common freshman trauma. A student leaves for college and the parents take off—some don't even tell their children where they have gone for weeks or months. Other students spent their first semester on the phone playing counselor to parents who were thinking of breaking up.

14   Two students had friends who tried suicide—one made it. Five—that I knew of—had a parent, a sibling, or a close friend institutionalized for drug treatment. A student, whose mother died when he was 15, lived in the homes of friends or slept on the floor where he worked for most of the last two years of high school, although his father was a successful businessman.

15   None of the stories surprised me. I'd heard them all before. Your children, perhaps your grandchildren, are survivors. Most of them are not immigrants, exploited in mills, but will make it as those who came before us made it.

16   This fall I'll smile at some of their get-ups, get angry at their rudeness, worry at examples of stupidity, but I hope I will remember the struggles they have had to get this far. I'll remember—I hope—that they are remarkably like I was at their age—scared, eager, rude, impatient, full of concerns and empty of knowledge, clumsy, idealistic and young, wonderfully young.

A Writer's Notes for a Second Reading

I find it hard to reread my own writing. I always seem to feel I could do it better, but I've tried to read with less destructive criticism and I'll try to point out what I think works in this essay.

I am struck by the humor. Until I started the column I thought of myself as a grump, a dour Scot, a person who was probably boringly serious. But the columns are fun to write and I remember the fun I had describing the students returning to the college town where I live.

I hope I haven't tricked the reader—but I suppose I have because I turn serious, looking into the lives of my students. I am saying that, yes, young people are often funny-looking and funny-acting, as funny as we were and are, but don't be fooled by appearances. They have a tough life. Actually, the attitude of many elderly toward the young—fear and disgust—makes me very angry, but I don't think anger will carry the day. I want to speak in a voice that will encourage and allow those who don't agree with me to read on. And at the end, I try to make my serious point with a touch of humor. I hope I succeeded.

Discussion

- How does Murray's argument compare with Allen's and Quindlen's? What is similar? What is different?
- What are the strengths of Murray's piece? Its weaknesses?
- Do you agree with Murray's view of his students, remembering that his class was not a "normal" college Freshman English class. These students were younger and more homogeneous than most Freshman English classes. Still, do you believe his vision of his students? If not, what could he have done to convince you?
- Are there any significant differences between Murray's voice in the column and in the text? Are they accidental or purposeful?

Activities

- Rewrite Murray's column for an audience of freshmen, for a parents' newsletter, as a reply to a politician describing students in radically different terms or proposing a curriculum for students from an imaginary Disney world.
- Respond to Murray's description of freshmen with a letter of agreement or disagreement. Write your own column in response.
- Rewrite Murray's column in your own voice.
- Take a technique Allen, Quindlen, or Murray uses and apply it to a draft of your own.

To Collaborate

- Do a class survey of your fellow students to see how they agree with or differ from the students Murray describes.
- Write a committee report, suggesting changes in the college (or high school) curriculum based on the backgrounds of the students attending classes now.

A Note on Student Writing

These papers deal with the problems with which students of this generation have to deal. As I point out in my column, they do not live in a Walt Disney world. They confront drinking, drugs, suicide, and death head on. And when you read pieces that are written close to the bone, the reader can—and should—become involved. Readers will hurt as well as the writers. I have had to remove extraordinary means and give the gift of death to my father, my mother, and my 20-year-old daughter, Lee. But I think writers must write of what is important to them and to us, the elemental human problems we experience as individuals and as a society. I hope that any discomfort or pain readers experience will be constructive and that they will understand, as I did, that the writers meant well.

I applaud these ten student writers of mine for the courage of their writing and their double courage in being willing to expose their struggle and their final drafts to scrutiny by other students and their instructors. They will make a valuable contribution by so doing, but it is difficult for them. I have not found my students over-confident, just the opposite. They know they have a great deal to learn, but they also know that the only way to learn it is by writing. Those who go on to become writers will gain a professionalism that will make their writing far different from these student papers but, in gaining command of their craft, they may lose something of the natural, raw talent they display here. That is the nature of craft and art.

Maureen Hurley
STUDENT ESSAY

Temptations of Death

1   "To exist on a level that is yet unknown." You may be thinking that this is very deep, or you may not really understand the meaning of it at all. The first time I read it, I cried. My friend, William, who took his own life in his senior year of high school, submitted this as his quote in the yearbook. That is how he wanted people to remember him. Little did I know that this was a foreshadow of what was to come three months later—that William would deliberately drive his car into the wall of a supermarket. Little did I know that when I received the yearbook six months after his death I would cry as I looked at his picture, his sad, clear-blue eyes staring out at me from the page of a book. How blank, how empty, but this is all that I had left. This and my own special memories.

2   William was only one of approximately 50,000 persons who die each years as suicides. It is now the third leading killer of Americans between the ages of fifteen and twenty-four, and the seventh leading cause of death overall. More than two million Americans have made suicide attempts. Four out of every five people who have succeeded have made previous attempts. For every person who succeeds, there are eight to ten times as many people who make attempts that fail.

3   These statistics are all very intriguing, but they do not give me comfort when I think of William. He was only one person in a considerable amount of people, but he was my friend. That is why his death was unique; and that is why I am opposed to suicide as the solution for one's problems.

4   There is not one race, age group, gender, or social class that is more susceptible to committing suicide than another. Nonetheless, there have been connections between certain groups and the reasons behind the deaths. For example, teenagers often commit suicide as a revenge tactic—to "get back at" someone. William did not have a very happy family life; he did not have a strong parent-son relationship. Although he had a car of his own, the night that he committed suicide William was driving his father's car. This, among other things, leads me to believe that he wanted to make his family suffer.

5   There are a number of warning signs which can signify that a person has suicidal tendencies:

- Changes in eating or sleeping habits, such as anorexia, bulimia, and insomnia.
- Withdrawal, especially from family, friends, and social activities.
- Boredom with school, friends, activities.
- Changes in personality, including sudden mood swings.
- Rebellious, violent behavior, sometimes accompanied by drug or alcohol abuse.
- Neglect of one's self in regard to appearance or schoolwork.
- Giving away of prized possessions; for example, a favorite piece of jewelry, a stamp collection, a piece of clothing, etc.
- Updating of finances or wills, especially final payments of mortgages, loans, etc.
- Expressions of suicidal thoughts, threats, or previous attempts. (Even a simple statement such as "What use is it to live anyway?" could be a definite clue.)
- Recent loss: death or suicide of a family member or a friend.
- Over- or underprotected children. This most likely played a role in William's death.
- "Perfect" person who "has everything." (This type of person will usually crack sooner, feeling enormous pressures to live up to others' expectations.)

6   If you notice any of these signs, act immediately. Here are some methods that can be helpful in preventing a suicide—or, in more simple terms, to save someone's life:

- If someone wants to talk, accept what is said and take it seriously.
- Do not pass off suspicions.
- Do not give advice; do not lecture.
- Do not say that everything will be all right.
- Do not make the person feel guilty. (For example, do not say anything to the effect of "Think of how your family will feel.")
- Deal with the matter immediately. Every minute could be a matter of life or death.
- Help deal with emotions, explore feelings.
- Talk openly and freely, asking about the person's intentions.
- Ask directly if suicide seems to be the only solution. This will not give the person an idea that has not already been pondered.
- Say that you truly care. This could mean more than you think to an unstable person.
- Get the person to agree to constructively try to make changes for the better.
- Arrange to make contact in the near future. This will make a definite plan the person will not want to break.
- Do not leave the person alone if the problem is immediate. Call the police.
- Encourage professional help even if the problem does not appear to be severe.

7   Professional help is available to those cases which are severe—along with those which may not be. There are crisis or suicide centers, mental health centers, doctors, priests, ministers, school counselors, principals, teachers, and state and local mental health associations. If the problem cannot be dealt with by a family member or a friend alone, the person should be directed to a professional to insure proper care and assistance. Still, support from family and friends remains an important factor.

8   It seems so simple when I write about the ways to recognize a problem and the methods of preventing a suicide. It is not that easy. Some people may show their depression, but those individuals may not be calling out for help. Some people truly want to die—they are not trying to get attention. One woman wrote a note before committing suicide saying: "This is a terrible thing for me to do, but perhaps in the end it will be all for the best. I hope so—Mary."

9   I do not know, to this day, if William truly wanted to die or if he had been sending out signals for help. I cannot accept the fact that William sent out clues and foreshadows, that he truly wanted help, but that we did not realize it; but on the other hand, I cannot accept the fact that there may not have been any

warnings, that he truly wanted to die, just like that. It is so much more complicated than that. A life-or-death decision cannot be so simple.

10   I spoke to Francis, one of William's best friends, about the circumstances
surrounding his death. I asked Francis if he believed that William had actually
committed suicide. He replied, "There's not a doubt in my mind. He never
talked about it and I never saw any warnings, but his family life was so screwed
up that he couldn't deal with it any longer."

11   One evening last month, Francis and I went to the cemetery where William is buried. I looked at the dates on the stone. June 14, 1967–January 28,
1985. I suddenly realized that I am older now than William was when he drove
his car into the wall of the supermarket. He had always seemed so much older
to me, in my mind; although, in reality, he will never be older than me again.
Life does not go on after suicide—not that we know of, at least. Some people
have an unrealistic view of the finality of death. When I look at the fact that my
age has surpassed William's, I see the shocking reality.

History of the Essay

Maureen Hurley was the fortunate student who found her subject immediately
by brainstorming—in class and out—to find what subjects demanded her
attention. In the second week of the course she wrote:

> I was very excited while writing the detailed description of my topic for the paper
> for this semester. I had many ideas about which I wanted to write, but each time
> I brainstormed, I kept referring back to one particular subject. I have been very
> interested in the topic which I chose. I have been involved in groups dealing with
> it, and I have had some personal experiences also. These experiences affected me
> greatly. When an incident has such impact on me, I want to research it more in
> order to understand it as best I can. I feel that this paper is giving me the
> opportunity to deal with the feelings I have been experiencing. I am eager to
> explore various areas involved with the topic also.

Her paper that week was a model of planning:

> After much contemplation, I have chosen a topic for my paper for this semester. I
> am planning to write about suicide. I realize that I will have to limit this subject.
> I have not decided exactly how I will go about this, but I know that I am going to
> use case histories.
>
> I plan to use a case history of a friend of mine who took his own life.
>
> I plan to use a case history of another friend who was suspected of having
> suicidal tendencies.
>
> I plan to attend a suicide support group.
>
> I plan to find statistics on the age groups most commonly involved in suicide.

I plan to see if there is a realtionship between the time of the year and the amounts of suicides at that particular time by researching at the library.

I plan to write to suicide prevention groups.

I plan to call the Samaritans for information on the aid of a suicidal person.

I plan to survey people anonymously.

I plan to talk to a psychologist that I know who deals with suicide frequently.

I plan to collect brochures and pamphlets concerning suicide.

I plan to study the emotional strains reported to be involved in suicides (or attempts) by researching at the library.

I plan to attend lectures about suicide.

I chose suicide as the topic for my paper because I was involved in a support group in my high school for a short time. I want to become knowledgeable in the field in order to be able to prevent a suicide, if there is ever that need. I feel very strongly about this subject because of my personal interactions in the past.

Hurley's weekly notes document her writerly work habits. Samples:

I wrote this paper late one night. I had not done any homework that day, and I wanted to write about the information I had gained while it was still fresh in my mind. I sat in the lounge and began writing. My boyfriend listened to each part in order to assure me that I was getting my point across. I have found that I need someone to aid me when I am writing a paper. I do not like when people try to change my thoughts, however.

One of my morning classes was cancelled, so I had an extra hour during the day. I had gotten up early and eaten breakfast, and I was ready to "tackle the world"—or at least my English paper. I had gathered quite a bit of information already, so I sat in my room—alone—with the cool breeze blowing through the window. I was finished in almost half an hour.

I was not sure what I was supposed to do for the paper this week, so I thought about the information that I have gathered, and I wrote freestyle. At first, I was going to tell about how I was going to write my first draft, but then I began writing a short piece of argument.

I wrote this paper with the thought in mind that a person with suicidal tendencies would be persuaded not to commit suicide after reading my piece of argument. I do not feel that I have completely accomplished this task, but I have an idea as to how I will do it. I can already see where I would have to go on to explain my point in some areas.

In the "first attempt," I brainstormed and wrote quickly, just to get my thoughts onto the paper. I was sitting alone in my room. I could not believe how quickly I wrote the paper! I have decided that it is much easier for me to write when I am pressed for time and I have the room to myself. I like to sit at my desk: My chair is comfortable, although it forces me to sit up straight and be alert. I have to use my desk lamp when I write. The paper itself is clearer to me, and somehow, my thoughts seem to be clearer, too. A sharp pencil is also a necessity. Before typing the draft, I organize the material by drawing arrows, stars, brackets, and numbers.

I was much more pleased with The Second Draft then I was with The First Draft. The workshop in class helped me realize what areas needed work. Although I did not change some of the things that people did not like in my paper, I was happy to see the positive and the negative remarks. I believe that a writer must keep what he believes is right most of the time, but must always consider what the readers did not like about a certain part. If the writer changes something for everyone, he will end up with a paper that is not his own.

In the commentary for The First Draft, I said that I was having trouble deciding what to keep and what to leave out, but that I thought I just needed to take the time to organize my material in order to make it work. I found that this was true. I feel that this paper is much more organized. Each section was thought-out, planned, and considerably edited.

I worked on the revision just about every day since we had the workshop in class. Each time I had a free moment, I took out my draft and made notes on small sections at a time. Then, one night, I went through the entire paper at least six times and deleted, added, changed, moved, changed back, reworded, etc. I really felt good about the changes. I think that the paper reads much easier now.

One section that I had to work on a great deal was the paragraphs on recognizing the warning signs of and preventing a suicidal person. I was not sure if I should use lists in this part. When it was in paragraph form, I found myself skimming over these parts, due to lack of interest. I did not want that to happen. These parts are very important and should "stick out" to the reader. That is why I decided to use lists.

Final Commentary

Writing this paper, Temptations of Death, was very helpful to me. I not only learned a great deal about writing, but I also learned how to deal with my feelings.

Suicide is a very delicate subject to write about, especially because this paper was so personal. The death of my friend affected me so much. I realized this even more since I began writing about it. When an incident has such impact on me, I want to research it more in order to understand it as best I can. I was forced to confront the fears that I had been suppressing.

In order to obtain more information about suicide, I called and visited many centers on the University of New Hampshire campus. In doing this, I have become very aware of how people deal differently with the topic of suicide. I also gathered facts and case histories which were useful to the writing of my paper.

Writing argument is not as difficult as I thought it would be. At first, I thought it would be impossible. Then, I realized that when I feel strongly about a subject, as I did in this case, I am able to write about it more easily. In effect, I convey my message to the reader more effectively.

I have found some factors which are helpful to me in writing a paper. I often need another person to aid me by listening to different parts of the paper and by giving me advice. I do not like it when people try to change my thoughts, however, so I am careful about whom I choose. It is important to keep in mind what the reader will want to learn, but I must first write for myself. It is easier for me to write when I am alone, sitting at my desk with a bright light and a sharp pencil. Interruptions are not good for me. Once I have started to write, I am usually "on a roll" until I finish. When I revise, I do it a little at a time, though.

Revision is something that I enjoy now. I like to organize my material by drawing arrows, stars, brackets, and numbers. This final draft was not my biggest revising step—that was the second draft. The final draft was just the "polishing" step.

After I finished the final draft of Temptations of Death, I was relieved and disapppointed. I am very proud of all the work I have done in order to write this paper, but I felt as though a part of my life had "ended." So much time and effort has been put into this one paper and now it is finished!

Lisa Keiski
STUDENT ESSAY

Suicide's Forgotten Victims

1   I didn't panic when Sue, my best friend, tried to commit suicide. A college freshman, she had been trying to manage five courses and an off-campus job. The pressure became too much for her and late on Wednesday night she over-dosed on sleeping pills. Approximately an hour later, she got scared and came up to my room. She wouldn't tell me directly what she had done, but it wasn't too hard to figure out. Fifteen minutes later, policemen and EMT's were crowding into my room to take care of her. She needed them—and so did I. I needed someone to tell me that my friend was not going to die, that everything was going to be all right, and that the world was not permanently screwed up.

2   But they took her away in the ambulance and left me standing by myself. Intense grief, still masked by shock, flooded over me. I wanted to cry, but the tears couldn't, or wouldn't, come. I felt that I still had to be in control of the situation, to mask my feelings and to be strong.

3   The burden of concealing my feelings grew worse. I wasn't sleeping well, lost my appetite, and had no energy or interest in doing anything. The pressure

increased until it was unbearable and I broke down. I was lucky to have someone supportive to listen to me. Not everyone is so fortunate.

4   For all too many people, there is no one to talk to when a loved one tries
or succeeds in committing suicide. Other family members and friends are in a
similar position and therefore unable to offer much support. Mental health
professionals rarely make any effort to contact these forgotten victims, and the
social stigma of having a friend or relative commit suicide, fear of exposing the
buried feelings, or simple monetary considerations can all keep the other victims from seeking the needed help. Nearly every community has some sort of
support system for suicidal people, but very few offer specialized help for those
individuals who have lost a friend or relative through suicide. We, as a society,
need to stop stigmatizing the friends and relatives of a suicide victim and start
helping them.

5   Social stigma may not seem like a big problem for a suicide victim's family,
but it has in the past been extremely vicious. For example, the bodies of suicide
victims were often buried in unmarked graves, denied burial in churchyards,
buried at night with a stake driven through their hearts, or thrown into the
bushes for animals to devour. None of these rituals happen now, at least not in
Western countries, but many life insurance companies will not pay benefits for
those who die by their own hands—perhaps a remnant of the tradition of confiscating a suicide victim's property.

6   Pressure can also come from the condemnation of others who seem to
blame those closest to the victim for letting the suicide happen and not doing
something to prevent it. Somehow they should have known what was going to
happen. That is quite a natural impulse—to want to find some rational explanation for the seemingly irrational act. An easy way to do it is to pin the blame
on someone else. I had some of those feelings myself. I knew that Sue was
suicidally depressed. She had been for four days. When she came out into the
dorm's kitchen to fill a coffee cup with water and suddenly gave me a hug, I
had a strong feeling that something was very wrong. I went to a mutual friend
who was going to stay with her that night and indicated my worry. He had been
around Sue too and said that she'd be all right for the few hours that he worked
at his computer. I wasn't convinced and went over to her room, intending to
knock and ask her how she was doing. But I was too tired and stressed. So I
left without knocking. It was during that time when we were all busy taking
care of ourselves that she took the pills.

7   I knew that it was not my "fault" any more than it was my friend's. I knew
that it was solely Sue's responsibility. Still, I kept tormenting myself with the
"what ifs." What if I had knocked on her door? What if we had not left her
alone those few hours? I'll never know for sure the answers to these questions,
but I do know that at best we could only have delayed a crisis. Her problems
were too big for us to handle and there was no need for guilt. Even so, guilt can
be a tremendous burden for people to carry and it can at times lead to serious
complications of its own.

8   Mrs. D.'s story is an example of one such case. After 23 years of marriage

to an abusive, alcoholic husband, she left him and moved to another state. He phoned and wrote frequently, begging her to return to him. Ten months later, after making one last call threatening suicide, he smashed his car into a stone wall and died.

9   Her first feelings were of guilt and great depression. She felt that she should have done something about her husband's suicide threat, told someone. Partly because of her inability to express her feelings to her daughters, one of them developed several phobias. The situation worsened for eight months until Mrs. D. sought help from a therapist.

10   Individual therapy with a psychologist or psychiatrist is probably the most common form of treatment available for people suffering from any sort of depression or needing help through a crisis. And it can be remarkably effective in helping those closest to a suicide victim deal with their own unique problems. Mrs. D.'s therapy encouraged her to explore the marriage and its sadomaso-chistic qualities freely. The therapist reassured her that she had taken all she could and was justified in leaving her husband. After learning to express her feelings, she took more interest in herself, began to dress more attractively, and decreased her need for penance and self-punishment. Her daughter's phobias improved as her mother's depression eased.*

11   My own therapy has been immensely helpful, perhaps lifesaving. The morning after Sue's attempted suicide, I went to see a psychologist at the cam-pus mental health care center and discussed my feelings as best I could. One of the first questions she asked was "What is this doing to you?" She forced me to start thinking of myself and how I was handling the situation instead of just how Sue was doing and how I could help take care of her.

12   Later therapy continued along these lines. I began to understand the myr-iad of different feelings I was experiencing and where they were coming from. I was mentally exhausted from having such traumatic issues to deal with. I was physically exhausted from having run myself ragged trying to take care of Sue. I was shocked at what had happened and grieved that my best friend had so much pain inside that she felt compelled to try and end her own life. And I was scared—scared of being alone forever without any friends, and yet scared of being around my friends because they too might abandon me.

13   To get rid of these feelings and find peace with myself, I had to live through them. I would not have been able to do it myself. I would have buried them all and tried to forget that they had ever existed. Many people try to do that and find their lives disrupted by a drastic change in sleeping habits, loss of appetite, and/or loss of energy and interest in everyday activities. That doesn't have to happen. For those people who have lost someone through suicide, indi-vidual therapy (which costs only as much as you can afford to pay) is possible. There is also a free support group run by the Samaritans which can help people who have undergone this particular trauma. Perhaps if these mental health

---

*Mrs. D.'s story is taken from *Survivors of Suicide,* edited by Albert Cain, pp. 183–85.

professionals went directly to the victims, instead of waiting for the victims to come to them, we could reduce the amount of tragedy and suffering a single suicide brings.

History of the Essay

Lisa Keiski was working on a paper about the peace movements on campus and in the sixth week she passed in a traditional outline—"A Brief History of Peace Movements on College Campuses"—but her commentary included the following paragraph:

> To be honest, I really haven't done anything this week. I've been far too busy trying to take care of my friend after her attempted suicide and trying to get my own life back in order. I have a lot of feelings which were crying to be heard and recognized. I think that it might be helpful for me to write about what happened and how I feel. She's in the hospital now for an indefinite period of time, and I'm left behind with my feelings about what she did and the loneliness of being left without such a good friend.

Next week her commentary said:

> Ever since my friend's attempted suicide, I felt a great need to find some way to let my own feelings out. Once the original shock had worn off, I was in a constant state of tension and tiredness, because there was no way for me to express how I felt. There is so much support for someone who attempts suicide, and of course there should be. But the people left behind, the friends of the victim, also need help and that is much harder to come by.
>
> Once I realized my need to express how I was feeling, I tried to talk about it with other friends, with only limited success. Everyone had their own reaction to what had happened, and many people just preferred to forget that it had ever occurred.
>
> I couldn't do that. I was far too close to my friend to be able to. Besides, I was constantly being reminded because she would call and ask me to bring her certain forgotten items, etc.
>
> In the end, I decided writing was the only way for me to be able to get at my feelings. While writing, I wouldn't have to worry about people talking back, and I hoped that the act would not only help me realize my feelings, but also free myself of the worst ones. And it worked. I tried to write a fictional story and did a few pages. I felt more strongly though that the pure truth with no disguise would help me the best. So that's what I did.

The students wrote two complete drafts before the final paper and had written comments on each from most of the students in class in addition to conferences on each draft. Fellow students are asked to tell the writer what works and what needs work. While we are reading the papers and commenting on them in class, I'm reading and commenting as well. Keiski received constructive, supportive, and candid criticism from her classmates.

On her first draft some of the responses were:

> "*Your case histories work great! They are powerful and thought-provoking. I don't know why you worried about melodrama.*"

> "*Yes, the ending is abrupt—but so is suicide.*"

> "*The only thing that needs work is your word choice in a few places—I've shown you where I think it needs it.*"

> "*Your paper is thought-provoking and informative—but what point are you trying to make? It seems to be a broad picture of suicides in general.*"

> "*What audience are you talking to? . . . What is your argument? I have no clue!*"

On the second draft some responses were:

> "*This was the most informative of any paper I've read. I can relate.*"

> "*Good paper and topic! Like variety of things discussed. Between the end of pg. 2 and the top of pg. 3 you need a transition paragraph, it would make it clearer. Page 3, second paragraph, who is Mrs. S? Last paragraph 4th page needs clarifying. Since your friend lived, perhaps you could include if communicating with her has helped at all or how it has affected your friendship.*"

Final Commentary

One of the most important things I learned is what I can write about. I can write most powerfully about those issues which are of direct, personal importance to me. I can write clearly about a topic which doesn't directly concern me, but it lacks the power of conviction that drives the other paper forward. When I really believe in the idea, the paper demands to be written and the job is fairly easy. All writing students are familiar with trying to write on assigned topics—it's not easy. I like to compare the experience with getting my teeth pulled; the paper doesn't come out any easier than the teeth.

I also learned to write simply. Well, at least I learned to try and write simply. I'm not quite sure if I do a good enough job of it or not.

I hadn't intended to make this such a personal paper. When I began the first draft, I used lots of case histories—most of which were removed from mine. I wanted to make it general enough so that everyone could identify with it. At the time I didn't realize that readers identify best with real people and that I could best represent a "real" person by narrowing the outlook and actually making it more specific. That's why in this paper, the final draft, I devoted nearly all of my consideration to my own story and that of my friend.

All of these elements go into making a good argument and a good piece of writing. Caring is the most important, but practice is also necessary. I never used to do any more than one or two drafts at the most. Having done three for this paper, I believe that the end product is more articulate and concise than it would have been had I stuck to my old ways. When writing argument, I just try to be willing to make use of new ideas.

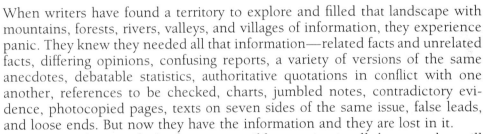

3

A Focus Found

When writers have found a territory to explore and filled that landscape with mountains, forests, rivers, valleys, and villages of information, they experience panic. They knew they needed all that information—related facts and unrelated facts, differing opinions, confusing reports, a variety of versions of the same anecdotes, debatable statistics, authoritative quotations in conflict with one another, references to be checked, charts, jumbled notes, contradictory evidence, photocopied pages, texts on seven sides of the same issue, false leads, and loose ends. But now they have the information and they are lost in it.

Writers have to find a focus, a possible meaning in all the mess that will allow them to explore the subject in a relatively orderly fashion so they can continue through the writing process to find out if they have anything worth saying—and worth a reader's hearing.

I must back off at this stage of the exploration so I can think about what the material means. I sit, notebook or clipboard in hand, where I cannot see the mess of research and try to write a note that tells me the single most important thing I have to say. If nothing comes, I go for a walk or a drive, daydreaming, half thinking, half not thinking about the subject until a potential focus surfaces.

If neither of those techniques works, I interview myself, asking questions similar to the ones I asked to find the subject:

- What information have I discovered that surprised me the most?
- What will surprise my reader?
- What one thing does my reader need to know?
- What one thing have I learned that I didn't expect to learn?
- What can I say in one sentence that tells me the meaning of what I have explored?

- What one thing—person, place, event, detail, fact, quotation—have I found that contains the essential meaning of the subject?
- What is the pattern of meaning I have discovered?
- What can't be left out of what I have to write?
- What one thing do I need to know more about?

There are a number of different ways to focus on a subject. The writer, of course, only uses the techniques that are necessary to achieve a focus. The focus may be obvious to the writer, or the writer may need to use one, two, three, or more of these techniques. The writer does not consciously go through these every time, but the experienced writer rarely proceeds until a focus is felt or known. Some of the ways writers achieve focus are:

1. *Voice* is one of the most common ways that writers find their focus. As they make notes about what they may write—in their heads or on the page— or rehearse how they may write it, their language may reveal a special intensity or tone that points out a focus for the subject. Too often voice is thought of as a matter of style that follows the writing, icing that is put on the cake, when it may come early in the planning process and indicate the direction in which the writer may head. In all of the selections in this chapter the writer may have heard a voice, scholarly, angry, detached, nostalgic, evangelical, that could have provided a focus.

2. *Frame* is another way to achieve focus. It tells the writer what is left out. A good subject, as we have seen, usually has a rich abundance of material. It may include not only one potential subject, but many. When the writer decides to deal only, for example, with the death of a grandmother and to exclude the death of a pet, a life-threatening illness, the brother who almost died as the result of an accident, then the writer has achieved a potential focus and can write about death in terms of one death.

3. *Distance* is a vital and often overlooked element in focusing on a subject. Barbara Tuchman in this chapter stands at a historic distance from the Black Death. Alice Trillin writes of her personal experience with cancer. In each case the distance of the author, and therefore the reader, from the subject helps the writer achieve a focus. Notice also that the distance at which Trillin wrote is a matter of subtle adjustment. If she stands too close to her subject the reader will be embarrassed and feel uncomfortable because of the intimacy with which she is revealing her experience and her feelings. If she stands at too far a distance the reader will not care, not feel with the writer. It is often helpful to consider distance in looking for focus.

4. *Question* is extremely helpful in finding a potential focus. What is *the* question the reader will ask? What is *the* reader's question that must be answered if the writing is to work? It may help for the writer to role-play a specific reader; often I stand back from my desk and physically mimic the mannerisms and voice of a reader to see my subject from the point of view of a reader. Then I can ask of myself a tough question that makes me realize the

focus. Alice Trillin, speaking and then writing for an audience of doctors, may have asked, for her readers, "What's it like to have cancer?" or "What should I know in treating a patient with a life-threatening illness?" James Baldwin may have made himself white and said, "What's it like to grow up black in America?"

5. *Statement* is the traditional way of finding focus. It's often called a thesis statement or a statement of potential meaning. A thesis is a proposition that will be defended by the writing. The danger is that many teachers or students believe that thesis means conclusion, and that in a thesis statement the writer has to state the final meaning of the piece that has yet to be written. The thesis statement is a guess or an estimate; it is a proposition that may or *may not* be proved by the drafts that follow. There must be room for discovery. Baldwin knew a lot about being black in America before he wrote his famous *Notes of a Native Son,* but he knew more through the act of writing.

6. *Problem* is a helpful way of finding the focus. If we can identify the problem that is to be solved, or at least explored, in the piece of writing, then we may be well along the road toward a working draft. Each of the selections in this chapter has problems that are dealt with in the text.

7. *Conflict* is an effective way of finding what to focus on in an argument, in an essay, in a news story, in a play, in a social worker case study, in a management memo. The point of conflict is the place at which the forces and the subject meet; it is the point at which we can see those forces most clearly; it is the point from which the causes or the implications of the conflict can be best studied.

8. *Tension* is related to conflict, but it is a way of looking at those forces that are related to each other but not yet in conflict. They may be drawn together or forced apart, but if we can see, for example, in Alice Trillin's piece the forces of death and life held in a fragile suspension, then we can see a way of dealing with that subject.

9. *Happening* is a term playwright William Gibson uses in his wise book, *Shakespeare's Game,* when he writes, "A play begins when a world in some state of equipoise, always uneasy, is broken into by a happening." This event provides a focus which initiates the action of the play. I find that fine counsel when looking for a way to focus on a short story, a novel, an essay, a ghostwritten corporate speech, a news story, a memo to a dean about a problem, and many other forms of writing. The happening can provide a way in which to deal with many different forms of information relating to a single subject.

10. *Organizing item* is the technique I use most often to find a productive focus for what I'm writing. I look for an event, a quotation, a statistic, an anecdote, an individual, a place, a process, a revealing detail which can be the seed from which the entire piece of writing will grow. For example, I was once in a high school classroom in which both the teacher and I were working individually with students. Neither of us was behind the teacher's desk. A messenger from the front office came in, looked at the 27 human beings in the room

quickly, did not spot the "teachers," and said out loud, "There's nobody here," and left without delivering the message. That incident could, obviously, spark an essay on how students are perceived in some schools.

11. *Opinion* is an important way of achieving focus in many forms of writing. Note the example I just gave above. The incident could have led me to an opinion, or I could have had the opinion that students are invisible to the administration of some schools, and used that to provide me with a focus for my essay. All of these techniques, of course, overlap. Many times, however, the writer's opinion of the subject will provide the focus. In each of the following selections the writer has an opinion. In some it is more clearly expressed than others, but it is there, and it may have provided the author with a way of approaching the subject.

12. *Sequence* is another way that can show the writer a focus that may lead the writer, and therefore the reader, through the forest of information. There is a sequence of events leading to the deaths of Baldwin's and Gibson's fathers. That sequence of inevitability provides a focus for the mountains of information they had in their memories. Sometimes I call this a trail, or a thread that I can see leading me through information that was contradictory or jumbled up in my mind, until I found the trail or a thread.

13. *Point of view* is the place that the subject is seen by the writer and the reader. It is a good way of focusing on a subject. We may have, for example, an enormous amount of material about a sport, a season, and a particular team. We may not know how to deal with that material, and we may find out how to deal with it when we look at the subject from the point of view of the athletic director, an alumnus, the coach, a player, the trainer, an orthopedic surgeon, a fan, a pro scout, a star, a bench-warming substitute, the referee, a sports equipment manufacturer, the coach of an opposing team, last year's star, next year's high school recruit. Every subject may be seen from many different points of view, and it can be helpful to identify one as a way of achieving focus.

14. *Image* often gives a writer the focus for a piece of writing. The Vietnam images of a young girl running in terror down the street with her clothes burned off and of a South Vietnam officer holding a pistol to the head of another human being were images that brought that war home to Americans. I was constantly surprised by the power of those images, for such powerful images had been burned into my memory from my experience in combat in World War II, but without television, the people at home saw only a romantic, heroic Hollywood war. A powerful image is often the organizing element around which a piece of writing can be collected. It is a magnet that draws information into a pattern of meaning clear to both writer and reader.

Having spotted a focus for the drafts which will follow, the writer has not concluded the process of exploration. Seeing the mountain does not eliminate the adventure of climbing to its peak.

Case Study: A Writer Writes and Reads

Roy Peter Clark

Roy Peter Clark's dissertation was on Chaucer, and after he received his doctorate from the University of New York at Stony Brook he took a job teaching literature and Freshman English at Auburn University at Montgomery, Alabama. He seemed destined for a conventional academic career, but he had a radical idea: since he was teaching writing, he should try writing.

Dr. Clark sold some essays to *The New York Times* and that led to his being chosen to write a report on writing in newspapers for the American Society of Newspaper Editors, to write for the *St. Petersburg Times,* to serve as its writing coach, and then to leave the university and join the Poynter Institute for Media Studies in St. Petersburg, Florida, where he developed its writing program.

That program not only offers seminars in writing to writers and editors, it also offers summer programs for college students and, separately, for journalism teachers. Dr. Clark works with local high school newspapers and a summer camp for local students and language arts teachers. That summer program led to the publication of his book *Free to Write: A Journalist Teaches Young Writers* by Heinemann.

Roy Peter Clark agreed to keep a record of the following argumentative essay from idea to publication. It demonstrated how a piece grows and changes even more than Dr. Clark believed it could when he began. His argument has an additional significance because the essay was developed, in part, as a talk and he learned from the experience of "rehearsing" in public and reading his audience's response.

The essay began when Clark wrote a three-page memo to himself on a Radio Shack lap computer in an airplane. The most interesting factor is that it was written *and forgotten*—he discovered it after finishing the piece. That has often happened to me and it is demonstration that the subconscious, perhaps even the unconscious, is writing away at the pieces of writing most important to us. We find the subject that itches.

The issue of victims had been on his mind for years; he and his family had been victims themselves and he hadn't been able to put the issue to rest. The issue of *Press Photographer's Magazine* tapped into his personal concern as a victim and his personal concern as an authority of journalistic ethics and writing.

Here is the first page of that memo, forgotten but (as we shall see) not lost. He was obviously working on the piece long before he knew he would write it.

```
ETHICS ON THE FLY

A recent edition of Press Photographer's magazine devoted
itself to controversial news photos, the kind that copy
editors most hate on deadline. Many of the photos pictured
are by now well-travelled examples of journalistic excess. A
nude young woman, the victim of a kidnapping, flees a
building, a look of terror on her face, clutching only a
small towel to cover herself. A grieving father weeps over
the visible body of his drowned son, draped in a body bag. A
brother stands over the body his head thrown back and his
hand clutching his face in agony. A woman looks up with
terrible fear in her eyes as she gapes at the burning
building in which her son is trapped.

Such photos inspire impassioned debates among journalists as
to the responsible course of action. Those who defend
publication of such photos would argue that they are part of
life, that they tell a dramatic story in a dramatic way,
that they warn people about real dangers in their lives, or
that they direct the sympathy of the public toward innocent
victims of tragedy.

People who oppose publication might argue that newspapers
should not sensationalize private grief, that readers hate
such photos, that an insensitive press loses credibility, or
that, while dramatic, the photos lack any serious news
content....
```

Then, on May 29, 1986, Clark received a letter from Texas Christian University giving his assignment at a symposium on media treatment of victims:

> *Roy does the first session, an overview of the problem. Roy will show examples of the various forms the problem takes. It's his job to give everyone an idea of the various issues involved and to show them examples from actual stories and pictures of how the media might victimize victims.*

The following page shows Clark brainstorming the subject, looking for a focus.

Victims:

① what is a victim? Innocent victim of tragedy.
   Person who has suffered pain and humiliation
   through no fault of his/her own. Someone
   very close to such a person.

② How ~~are professionals~~ does the press expect   * deserve
   professionals to deal with such individuals.   special
                                                       consideration?

③ what is the news here; what is the journalistic
   purpose for publishing the story.   – price of narrative
                                          – warning to society
                                          – visceral reaction
                                          – real life

④ Two questions :– ✓ acquiring information
                  –✓ publishing

⑤ Is people's reaction based on how the story
   turned out?

⑥ Problem of individual approach vs.
              group or pack approach.

⑦ cameras more invasive
          TV images more fleeting

⑧ red light
       consequences of publication

⑨ reasons not to publish ⟨ technique for gathering is invasive
                            person is specially vulnerable
                            grief in many cases does not need to be public
                            serves the public ✗ not necessarily
                            causes additional grief to family members + victims

⑩ choices → application of professional judgment

TV – news   tension →
    first voices   bystander + help
      2 photos

① red light go off?

② what bothers you about picture?

③ would you publish as is?

④ ~~if yes~~, what journalistic purpose would
   publication serve.

⑤ how would you feel if about publication
   if person in the photo were you or
   a close relative.

⑥ can you anticipate any
   direct or indirect consequences
   of publication?

⑦ would your behavior change if you

slot editor

Clark made further notes and then created a handwritten draft he used as notes for the presentation. Here are pages one and two of six.

Slides 5-6

Unbelievable Statement # 1:

Reporters and editors are dedicated, caring individuals, many of whom have been victims in their personal lives. They hate necessary parts of their jobs. One fear: going to the home of the family of a victim. I'm now collecting examples: its up to 4 of reporters who lied to their editors → people not true, or wouldn't talk.

Principal choices

Principal #2 Journalists are often confronted on deadline by conflicting duties: logo docility This conflict right to know / right to privacy → transform equation: Duty to Inform vs. Duty to Protect the Vulnerable or Comfort the afflicted.

David Hungate

Principal #3 / They can do a better job of both if they can pursue their jobs too as individuals: take advantage of their humanity, suffer with the victim, participate in the catharsis. Problem occurs when the journalist becomes part of a group — a pack. It is the public vision of the voracious insensitive pack that dehumanizes us, hurts victims, and makes us unpopular.

❦ Clark's presentation was taped and Clark had the text typed so he could use it as a draft for a piece of writing. What follows are the first two pages of that typed text so that you can compare what he said to his speaking notes. ❧

J.R. : "*Once* ~~When~~ you give up your integrity, the rest is a piece of cake."

Personal account of being a victim.

Definition of a victim:

     a person who through no fault of his own suffers direct physical harm, pain, emotional trauma as a result of a crime, an accident, or a natural disaster -- or the relative or loved one of such a person.

Is there a special class of people, asked ethicist Lou Hodges whome we can call "innocent victims of tragedy.?" *trauma*

Do these people deserve our special attention and protection whether they ask for it or not?

slides 1, 2, 3

Principle #1: [No one who has never been an innocent victim of tragedy can know what it feels like to be one.] Victims have different feelings no doubt, whether they have been victimized by a criminal, an accident, or a natural disaster. I read stories about the victims of crimes which says "so and so was not injured." That may be the best way to say it, but even though it may be accurate to say that no one in my family was "injured" the results of that crime were a sense of violation, a loss of innocence, a changed perception of human nature, feelings of guilts, anxiety, paranoia, and a range of psychosomatic illnesses. At the moment of trauma the victim may need any combination of companionship, consolation, medical care, psychological counselling, a renewed sense that justice is still possible, and a restored sense of balance. And you need protection from additional trauma which in some cases may mean protection from the press. If I had opened the Charlotte Observer the day after our robbery and seen a photograph of our tortured expressions -- I'm not sure how I would have felt.

4

(ring of robberys)

Principle #2: [News people, I am convinced, recognize this and would be the first to expose medical professionals or law enforces who were callous to the needs of victims.] Reporters and editors I know tend to be dedicated, caring individuals, many of whom have been victims in their personal lives. They hate certain parts of their jobs. One of the worst assignments is to go to the house of a dead child to interview the parents and, perhaps, to obtain a photograph. I don't know anyone who savors the opportunity to do this. In fact, I'm now collecting examples, the list is up to 4, of reporters who have lied to their editors, telling them that the families were not home, or would not talk. (Gretta Tilley? made up quote?)

5-6

Principle #3. [Journalists are often confronted on deadline with conflicting duties.] They may not be able to choose between a simple good and a simple evél. Logo for conference describes the conflict between the public's right to know and the victim's right to privacy. I would like to transform the equation to emphasize the conflicting duties of the journalist, which I would describe as the Duty to inform the public about things it needs to know and the Duty to help protect the vulnerable and in an old defintion of news to comfort the afflicted.

" To afflict the comfortable,
to comfort the afflicted "

❧ Clark took the typed notes and began the process of turning a talk into an essay. Here is the first page of that effort.❧

I remember watching the television program Dallas a couple of years ago. In one episode J.R. Ewing was confronted by a man whose life he had just ruined through some shady deal. The man said something like: "J.R., how can any one person be so despicable?" J.R. just smiled and said, "Heck, once you give up integrity, the rest is a piece of cake."

I think we will find that when it comes to the pursuit of ethics in journalism, even if you have integrity, the rest is still going to be difficult, especially in the conflicts that inevitably arise between the working press and the victims of crime and other tragedies.

I understand something of these conflicts from both sides of the street, from the perspective of a working journalist and teacher of journalists, and from the special perspective of a victim.

In 1976 I was travelling with my family (my wife and two young daughters) from our home in Montgomery, Alabama, to visit grandparents in New York. We stopped for a night in a motel along the Interstate in Charlotte, North Carolina. The next morning we were robbed in our room by a man with a gun. He threatened to blow my daughter's brains out, herded us into the bathroom, and robbed us of our belongings. Although he never laid a hand on us, he changed our lives forever. And although there was nothing written about the robbery in the Charlotte newspapers, I have often wondered how I would have greeted a reporter or photographer at that devastating moment.

For the purposes of this conference, let me offer a working definition of a victim: A person who through no fault of his own suffers direct physical harm, pain, or emotional trauma as a result of a crime, an accident, or a natural disaster -- or the relative or loved one of such a person.

From the perspective of the journalist, is there a special class of people which ethicist Lou Hodges has described as the innocent victims of tragedy and trauma? And do these people deserve our special attention and protection whether they ask for it or not?

Principle #1: <u>No one who has never been an innocent victim of tragedy can know what it feels like to be one.</u> Victims differ in their feelings, no doubt, depending on whether they are old or young, have been raped or robbed, or have suffered through a bank robbery or skijacking. What they share, I believe, is a sense of violation, a loss of innocence, a changed perception of human nature, feelings of guilt, anxiety, paranoia, and a range of psychosomatic illnesses. At the moment of trauma, the victim may need any combination of companionship, consolation, medical care, pscyhological counseling, the feeling that justice is possible, and a restored sense of balance. In some cases victims need the press to hear their stories as part of a cathartic process of healing. But in other cases, victims need protection from additional trauma, which in some cases may mean protection from the press.

Principle #2: <u>News people, I am convinced, recognize the vulnerability of victims and would be the first to expose medical professionals or law enforcers who were callous to the needs of victims.</u> Reporters and editors I know tend to be caring individuals, many of whom have been victims in their personal lives. They hate certain parts of their jobs. One of the worst assignments, traditionally, is to go to the house of a dead child to interview

❧Clark wrote the argument and showed it to his colleague Don Fry, who made notes and discussed the draft with him. Here is the first page of that draft.❧

---

audience?

a:victims

Mr. Dooley

The job of the journalist, according to an old saying, is to afflict the comfortable and comfort the afflicted. But to read some contemporary newspapers and to watch local television news is to believe that journalists thrive on comforting the comfortable and afflicting the afflicted.

The journalism that people hate most in America is the journalism that panders to the public's fascination with violence and its aftermath. This is the journalism of bodybags and stretchers, of funerals and sobbing mothers, of missing teenage girls and bloodstains in car trunks. Francis X. Clines calls it "telling the morbid truth." George Will calls it "the pornography of grief."

motel?

A woman in Florida is kidnapped from her office by her estranged husband. He forces her to his apartment, strips her of her clothing, and holds off police at gunpoint for several hours. Finally, a shot explodes. The cops rush in to discover that the man has blown his brains out. The woman, covering herself with only a dishtowel, is hustled to safety by police. The next day, a photo of the woman, her nudity barely concealed by the towel, her face contorted by fear, appears on the front page of the local newspaper.

Responding to tradition and gut instinct, some editors rush such photos hell-bent into print. The photos rivet a reader's attention. They capture the essential drama of violent public events. And unlike the fleeting images of television news, the photo on page one, fear and humiliation frozen in time, lingers to haunt readers throughout the day. *printed*

Picture the close-up of a mother, her mouth agape, watching in anguish as firemen try to rescue her children from a burning building. Picture family members twisted in grief over the corpse of a drowned child, now half exposed in a body bag. Perhaps the photos have special news value in their own communities. But these are the kinds of photos that are picked up by wire services and run all over the country. Why does a Boston newspaper run the photo of the grieving mother in Kentucky? Why does the Florida newspaper run the photo of the drowned child in California? Because there are fires in Boston? Because children swim in Florida? *good*

Listening to some editors defend these photos, one imagines that they really believe that shocking images on page one can magically transform the society, and that from henceforth children will never again play with matches and that parents will protect little ones who skinny-dip in local ponds. These editors remind me a little of my high school driver education teacher who showed films of automobile accidents, replete with charred and decapitated bodies, to inspire safety in young drivers. They did little to deter the future drag racers in the class. *They deterred future drag racers only until the end of the class.*

Too often, editors concoct excuses to rationalize the use of sensational photos the day after publication, when an unexpected torrent of protest floods the newspaper. Then, about 12 hours late, news judgment is discussed, along with questions of taste and consequences. The reasons for publication are often couched in formulas which hide, rather than reveal, true motivation. The editor says, "This photo is a slice of life. People should not be protected from the truth." Or "this was a violent, public event. We would be remiss in our duty if we did not share it with readers."

what is the true motivation?

(you need agent(s) in this passive construction. Who discusses?

❧ He cut the lead, made other changes and polished the following draft, which was published in the *St. Petersburg Times* November 22, 1987.❧

The Underside of Journalism

The journalism that people hate most in America is the journalism that panders to the public's fascination with violence and its aftermath. This is the journalism of body bags and stretchers, of funerals and sobbing mothers, of missing teen-age girls and bloodstains in car trunks. George Will calls it "the pornography of grief."

> ❦Clark focuses immediately on the issue, in specific details and images. His first paragraph describes the photographs we have seen in newspapers and on the TV screen from our memories. Then he gives us an example, making sure we "see" the issue and establishing both the topic and his authority.❧

A woman in Florida is kidnapped from her office by her estranged husband. He forces her to his apartment, strips her of her clothing and holds off police at gunpoint. Finally, a shot explodes. The cops rush in to discover that the man has killed himself. The woman, covering herself with only a dish towel, is hustled to safety by police. The next day, a photo of the woman, her nudity barely concealed by the towel, her face contorted by fear, appears on the front page of the local newspaper.

Driven by tradition and gut instinct, some hell-bent editors rush such photos into print. The photos rivet a reader's attention. They capture the essential drama of violent public events. And unlike the fleeting images of television news, the photo printed on page one, fear and humiliation frozen in time, lingers to haunt readers throughout the day.

To be sure, editors face tough choices on deadline. Readers expect a good photo to illustrate a dramatic story. But editors usually reject the most grisly, those showing a dead body. They also reject static photos of the scene, perhaps a field where the body was found, because such photos don't tell a story or focus on people. What is left, then, but close-ups of the grieving family?

Picture the close-up of a mother, her mouth agape, watching in anguish as firefighters try to rescue her children from a burning building. Picture family members twisted in grief over the corpse of a drowned child, now half exposed in a body bag.

Perhaps the photos have special news value in their own communities. But such photos are picked up by wire services and run all over the country. Why does a Boston newspaper run the photo of the grieving mother in Kentucky? Why does the Florida newspaper run the photo of the drowned child in California? Because there are fires in Boston? Because children swim in Florida?

> ❦Notice how Clark anticipates what editors will say in their defense and attempts to answer each defense before it is given. He is also engaging a dialogue with the reader, implying what the reader will say and responding.❧

Listening to some editors defend these photos, one imagines that they really believe that shocking images on page one can magically transform the society, and that henceforth children will never again play with matches or skinny dip in dangerous swimming holes.

8   These editors remind me of my high school driver education teacher who showed films of automobile accidents, replete with charred and decapitated bodies, to inspire safety in young drivers. They deterred the future drag racers only until the moment they revved up their customized Chevys.

9   Too often, editors concoct excuses to rationalize the use of grief photos the day after publication, when an unexpected torrent of protest floods the newspaper. Then, about 18 hours late, editors discuss news judgment, taste and privacy. They couch reasons for publication in formulas that hide, rather than reveal, motivation.

10   The editor says, "This photo is a slice of life. People should not be protected from the truth." Or "This was a violent, public event. We would be remiss in our duty if we did not share it with readers."

11   Readers suspect such responses, assuming that they veil the real motive for publication: greed. They open the newspaper and encounter the photo of a crazed man dangling his child by the feet out a window. They are fascinated, but also repulsed, and hide the page from their own children.

12   In their anger, they envision the meeting in which it was decided to run the photo. They see a smoky room filled with drooling journalists sitting elbow to elbow with accountants and ad managers. They hear the ringing of cash registers.

13   Of course, these readers are wrong.

14   The real reasons for publication of these photos are not economic, but aesthetic. They involve questions of personal ambition and peer approval. The photographer desires to get his or her best work, a memorable photo, on the front page.

15   The pressures of the newsroom place the demands of the photo and the story above the needs of the victim. In that sense, the victims are sacrificed to the necessities of art. The photographer and editor see them not as vulnerable human beings for whom publicity brings certain consequences, but as *objets d'art*.

16   Newsroom conversation about such photos rarely centers on the plight of those pictured or on the consequences of publication to them and their families.

17   The talk is more likely to concern which photo out of several works best, where the photo will run in the paper and in what size, or whether cropping the photo will improve its composition. Evaluation is expressed immediately and viscerally: "Great photo" or "We're talking Pulitzer here."

❡ Notice how Clark broadens the issue at this point. ❡

18   The danger comes in the erosion of common sympathy. In that sense, a newsroom is like a M*A*S*H unit, in which dark humor becomes the remedy for the cyclical exposure to violence, tragedy and grief. In one newsroom, the

most horrible photos, the dismembered bodies that never make the paper, are saved and used as decorations for the office Christmas tree.

19   All journalists, like all police officers or emergency room physicians, risk hardening of the heart. One symptom is the inability to understand readers' objections to the publication of disturbing news. Another is an indifference to the plight of victims and their loved ones, who through no fault of their own, find themselves thrust into the spotlight.

20   I have heard the family members of victims of homicide testify of their ordeals. First they suffer the heinous acts of murderers. Then they face the humiliation of moving through a system designed to protect the rights of the criminal.

21   A father cannot get the police to keep him informed on the progress of an investigation into the murder of his son. A daughter is left to clean the blood off the walls and floors of the room in which her mother was shot to death. A wife almost has a heart attack when she sees on television the picture of her husband being carted to the morgue in a body bag. A mother complains when a newspaper refers to her murdered teen-age daughter as a waitress. "She was a waitress," says the mother, "but she was also an honors student."

22   Victims share a profound sense of violation, a loss of innocence, a changed perception of human nature, feelings of guilt, anxiety, paranoia and a range of psychosomatic illnesses. At the moment of trauma, the victim may need any combination of companionship, consolation, medical care, psychological counseling, the feeling that justice is possible and a restored sense of balance.

23   In some cases victims need the press to hear their stories as part of a cathartic process of healing. The families of missing children or hostages, for example, often seek out all the publicity they can get. But, in other cases, victims need protection from additional trauma, which may mean protection against the press.

❝Too many arguers are good at pointing out a problem but stop short of proposing a solution. Clark suggests what might be done—by victims as well as editors.❞

24   If journalists are going to fulfill their traditional role of comforting the afflicted, the first thing they may need is some sensitivity training. Reporters, editors, photographers, student journalists and teachers should meet with former victims, their advocates and psychologists who work with them.

25   Such meetings should convince reporters that the most sensitive and responsible journalists also get the best stuff. The victim may turn to the reporter for consolation; he may need some advice or merely someone to listen; he may want to talk at length, not about the death of a murdered daughter, but about her life. The process may produce for the victim a purging of emotions and for the journalist the story of the year.

26   Along with the sensitivity training should come some assertiveness train-

ing. Victims want justice and journalists, in their aggressive watchdog role, might help bring it about. Stories about victims may involve aspects of police misbehavior, raise questions of public safety, or explore the inefficiency of the criminal justice system.

27   Some journalists behave as if the least responsible among them get the best stuff. Maybe the best photos go to the photographer who is willing to keep the camera clicking during the most painful moments of private grief. Or maybe the best quotations go to the reporter who nags family members into a rage. Maybe the race is not to the kind, but to the rude. If so, we deserve to cry out in despair and grief, like the victims we photograph.

Commentary

When I write straight narrative, the story of how my Italian aunt came to America, for example, I usually know the structure of what I want to say before I sit at the keyboard. The main parts of the story take shape in my mind. I rehearse them until they take such a visible form that I can envision how the story will look in the newspaper. I can even fantasize about a particular reader coming upon my story over a bowl of Cheerios and reading parts of it out loud to her family. When I am writing very well, I seem to be able to project such stories from my mind right onto the page.

Argument is much more difficult for me. When I used to review films for the St. Petersburg Times, I would return from a screening and my colleagues would ask with eager curiosity what I thought of The Deerhunter *or* The Attack of the Killer Tomatoes. *My answer would always be: "I'll tell you in an hour."*

That hour constituted my writing time. I was saying to my friends: "I need to write the review before I know what I think about the movie." For me, writing is thinking, and I may not have realized that before I put the period at the end of this sentence.

I would never be able to say that I project an argument onto the page. I would use two other words: discover and build.

When I was a college student, I usually felt pretty stupid when I sat down to write a persuasive essay. I would have only the vaguest notion of what I wanted to say, so I spent long hours procrastinating, or feeling guilty about not getting the work done, or worrying about the grade. You would think twenty years of writing would change all that, but not so. I still wonder what I'm going to say, I still procrastinate, and I worry about meeting my deadlines. The difference is that I now accept those stages of ignorance/waiting/anxiety as the normal conditions of beginning to write. I always tell myself that if I can lower my bottom into the chair and get my hands moving, things will get better, and they always do.

In the case of "Shooting Victims" I had both to discover my argument and to build it. The story of my interest in this argument goes back several years, to the day I saw the photo of the terrified woman covered only with a dishtowel. I've used this photo as a case study in ethics seminars for professional journalists. The photo always inspires lively discussion among journalists. In the role of discussion leader, I would routinely direct the argument between those who object to what the photo does to the victim and those who regret that but vote in favor of the public's opportunity to see it.

I quickly became a collector of such photos, taking advantage as an educator of the emotional response they inspired. In a strange sense, I was doing what I accused the photographers and editors of in my essay: I was publishing photos of victimized people for my own purposes—to look like a better teacher.

I realized only later that, although I found the photos engaging, I had not formed a clear opinion on their use. When someone would ask me, "Do you think that photo should be used?" I would routinely turn it back on the questioner: "You're the editor. What do you think?

After conducting such discussions dozens of times, I was invited to give a major speech at Texas Christian University on the topic of "Victims and the Media." This would be a gathering of journalists, journalism educators, students, and the families of victims who had to deal with the media in their grief. Since I was the keynote speaker, I felt a responsibility to touch on both sides of the issue: What good things journalists were trying to do when they published stories about victims and the consequences of such publication for victims and their families.

I came to this presentation from an unusual perspective: that of journalist and victim. Through my teaching and writing, I know how journalists think and work, so it was easy to demonstrate how most journalists hate the parts of their job that deal with violence and grief, how many journalists are remarkably sensitive and helpful to families that have suffered, and how they feel a powerful duty to inform the public about important events, even if they are unsettling or disturbing.

But I had also been a victim in my life. In 1976 my family had been robbed at gunpoint in a motel room by a man who threatened to blow my daughter's brains out if we resisted him. I talked at TCU about how that event had changed our lives, and about how, if you had not had such an experience, you could not really understand what it meant to be a victim.

There was testimony at this conference from family members of murder victims. They spoke powerfully about their victimization by the system, and what surprised me was they had much less rancor for the media than they had for the criminal justice system, which they perceive as cruelly slow.

As in my own classroom, my job was not the persuader, but the facilitator of argument. I needed to represent the positions of the journalist and the victim in some sort of balance, so that they could spend two days talking to each other with some civility. I think I succeeded, but once again, it gave me the chance to avoid the decision of whether I would publish certain gruesome photos.

Two things happened to me in Texas that made me want to write again. First was the poignant testimony of the victims themselves. You could not listen to these stories without sympathizing with people who had lost parents and children to the cruelest murderers. Some of them left in tears from the lecture hall during my slide presentation, because the photos of dead bodies and sobbing parents reminded them of their grief. In the face of their suffering my lukewarm, carefully balanced, let-us-reason-together arguments seemed insufficient to the reality I was describing. I felt the urge to go after the mavericks in journalism, to raise the temperature of my argument, and to embrace it more passionately.

The other thing that happened was that something came out of my mouth in response to a question at the conference that was worth arguing about. At one point, I uttered a simple, unproven assertion: "The most sensitive journalists get the best stuff." I'm still not sure that is true, by the way, but I wanted now to assert it and to argue that the opposite—"The most irresponsible journalists get the best stuff"—was unthinkable. And so at least four years after I saw the photo of the naked woman with the dishtowel, I had discovered what I wanted to say.

But, a crucial point worth repeating, the discovery came not before I sat down to write my draft, but while I was writing it. And it took me a full draft of writing—which I accomplished in a day—to discover it fully. I used no outline, and the only material on my desk was the draft of the TCU lecture, which I kept wanting to turn to, but did only once. In that sense, my essay was completely new, buttressed by my previous writing and thinking, but not a sequel to them.

The drafting came very slowly. I was never able to see ahead more than a paragraph at a time, and sometimes more than a sentence or word at a time. In that sense I was building my argument unit by unit from the top down. Writing a paragraph, and letting that paragraph teach me where the next paragraph should begin to go. This requires for me more concentration than when I am writing narrative. Physiologically it feels more like reading difficult music than playing by ear. It's as if I am engaged in a higher dimension of thinking.

That is why it is especially important for me to follow poet William Stafford's advice to "lower your standards" rather than fall victim to writer's block. This kind of writing and thinking is so hard for me that I've got to let my hands do a lot of the thinking, instead of my head. I am not projecting a polished argument onto the page. I am building it, and then rebuilding it, to learn what I think, and to consider how to lead readers in the same direction.

My original lead, which I kept through several drafts, was: "The job of the journalist, according to an old saying, is to afflict the comfortable and comfort the afflicted. But to read some contemporary newspapers and to watch local television news is to believe that journalists thrive on comforting the comfortable and afflicting the afflicted." It took me a long time to cut this first paragraph and to begin the story with the second: "The journalism that people hate most. . . ." The saying about afflicting the comfortable is one of my favorites and I always looked for an opportunity to use it in a story. But eventually it was clear to me that the lead wouldn't work:

1. The story would be about comforting the afflicted, but would be nothing about afflicting the comfortable, except a brief mention of the press's watchdog role.
2. I would focus the argument on press matters, especially news photos, so the reference to television seemed broadly misleading.
3. The first paragraph didn't tell me anything that wasn't in the second paragraph, and that second paragraph turned out to be more direct, more specific, and a more gripping opener.

So my original lead turned out to be "scaffolding." I needed to erect it in order to begin to build my argument. But at the end, I had to tear it down to let the purer elements of argument be revealed.

I'm sure I violate some important rule of argument by beginning my essay with an unproven generalization: "The journalism that people hate most. . . ." Do I know for sure that the exploitation of victims is the journalism Americans hate most? No. But I base my statement on: (1) A personal aversion to such exploitation; (2) years of listening to outraged denunciations of such acts by family, friends, and other nonjournalists; (3) public opinion polls criticizing the press for violating people's privacy. If I had been writing an essay for a scholarly journal, perhaps I would have been tempted to load up my first paragraph with evidence and qualifiers: "A series of recent public opinion surveys reveals what seems to be a disturbing trend in the public's attitude toward the press. . . ." There is a place for such a piece, but it is not the one I wanted to write. I wanted to be direct, lean, and engaging. If you, the reader, disagree that this is the journalism people hate most, so be it, That is part of the transaction.

I learned something years ago that has helped me in many ways as a writer. It's a model of thinking and communicating described by semanticist S. I. Hayakawa called the "ladder of abstraction." When you're writing an argument, imagine you're climbing up and down a ladder. At the very top of the ladder you reach the abstract and the general (freedom, goodness); descend the ladder and you reach the concrete and specific (a teenager's car, Mother Teresa). As a reader and journalist, I much prefer to write on the level of dirt than the level of ideas. So in argument, I make sure that ideas are supported by concrete evidence; or that generalizations flow from hard, specific information. John Updike once began a one-paragraph essay this way: "We live in an era of gratuitous inventions and negative improvements. Consider the beer can."

So I make sure my second sentence supports my first by going from violence to body bags and bloodstains. And throughout the piece I try to reward my reader with specific cases and concrete descriptions that are more lively and compelling than my generalizations.

I've got a collection of dozens of news photos and stories about victims, so I took some of the best for use in this essay. Remember that I use these slides in lectures all the time. My challenge in this essay was to use my descriptive powers to recreate the scenes for readers. I realized I couldn't make a word worth a thousand pictures, but I tried to turn this problem into a subtle advantage. First, by describing the pictures in words, I could call attention to key highlights, such as the skimpy dishtowel or the mouth agape. I could do this without having to show the pictures once again, running the risk of one more act of publicity which might, in some remote way, hurt the victims. (I'm nervous about turning tortured people into perpetual case studies.)

In addition, I would hope that my brief descriptions would allow readers to fill in the blanks, that is, to remember from their own experience dozens of similar photos which might have fascinated or repulsed them.

Before my first draft, I thought that the hammer of my argument would be the weight of my own personal experience. In an early draft, I devoted a full paragraph to our terrible experience in the robbery: "He threatened to blow my daughter's brains out, herded us into the bathroom, and robbed us of our belongings. Although he never laid a hand on us, he changed our lives forever."

I had written about this event recently in a number of contexts. On its tenth anniversary, I wrote a personal essay about my relationship with my father and how the robbery had shaped my own sense of fatherly responsibility. Of course, I referred to it at TCU and was able, in so doing, to identify with victims.

But in developing "Shooting Victims," something nagged at me. It was clear from my first draft that the paragraph about the robbery was not central to my argument. I tucked it in about two-thirds of the way down. Placing it in such an unemphatic position in the story made me wonder about whether I should use it at all. I had purged myself in my other writing of having to deal with it, and frankly worried that too many references to it in too many stories would make me seem obsessive, and undercut my argument. Another problem: although I was a victim, I was not a victim who had to deal with the press. I worried that the incongruities would show and distort the focus of the piece.

Here's another way to say it: My personal experience as a victim is in the story, all through it, in fact. It's just not visible. It's the mass of the iceberg below the surface. Take the paragraph that begins with "Victims share a profound sense of violation. . . ." I could not have written that with such conviction if I had looked it up in a book or consulted an expert. That is the only paragraph, by the way, that comes out of my TCU lecture. But, this time, the first person is removed, and the argument improved.

I used to think that a writer had to use the first person completely, or not at all. Like a poker game, you were either in or you were out. But now I have no problem with dropping the "I" into the story to make it more personal or to provide a bit of evidence, and then shift out just as quickly. I retained the first person, for example, in the anecdote about driver's education. I could have recounted that in the third person, but I wanted to draw the reader closer by using "I." The larger philosophical question is whether publicity changes behavior. Do gruesome photos make people more careful? Since my honest answer would be "I don't know," my strategy was to allude to an analogous, more common experience: horror films in driver's education.

You may notice, that I not only use the third and first person in my argument, but I also drop briefly into the second: you understood. "Picture the close-up of a mother, moth agape. . . ." "Picture family members twisted in grief. . . ." Addressing the reader directly at points of high emotion in the story attempts to create a sense of charged intimacy, that they cannot escape the force of your argument. This is, in both senses of the word, a manipulation. The writer is laying hands on the reader, invading the safety of the reader's common distance.

Once again, I imagine I am violating unwritten canons of responsible argument, but the most fun for me in building and refining an argument are the points of manipulation, the slightly unfair loading of language, the spinning of words and allusions to create an undertow of persuasion.

For example, I have in three places (three always seems to be the magic number in writing) used religious imagery or language to reinforce my argument. The word "hell-bent" to describe impetuous editors came out of nowhere, but I liked its playful connotations of damnation. In fact, both elements seemed to fit: hell and bent.

My favorite anecdote concerns the profanation of the office Christmas tree. What you hang on your Christmas tree says something about your values. For Hugh Hefner's tree, I imagine ornaments in the shape of naked women. That journalists would display their grotesqueries in such an unlikely context is either an act of unparalleled theological sophistication (victims suffer like Christ), or, more likely, a shameful blasphemy, reflective of the worst values of journalists.

My final religious allusion comes near the end, in the sentence "Maybe the race is not to the kind, but to the rude." Some will recognize in it an allusion to the book of Ecclesiastes, "The race is not to the swift, nor the battle to the strong." When I wrote my parody of that, I only had the rhythm of it in my head and had to look it up in a book of quotations. I didn't plan the allusion at this point in the story, I merely stumbled upon it. But having stumbled, it seemed to me not a bad thing to plant a reference to the Bible right near the end. I don't want such an allusion to stop the reader. If the reader says, "I wonder why he alluded to the Bible?" I've failed. I want the reference to work almost subliminally.

What I really wanted, too, was a strong ending. In journalism we call them "kickers." In journalism, more than in academic writing, we try to grab the reader early, and in an opinion column, to leave the reader with a final blast. To end with "If so, we deserve to cry out in despair and grief, like the victims we photograph" serves a number of purposes. It saves my clearest, most passionate argument until last. It rewards the reader who has followed me to the end. It reminds the reader of the plight of victims. I guess I'm always disappointed when a final sentence falls flat, and always thrilled when a writer leads me to a special ending.

Discussion

- What are the strongest points in Clark's argument? The weakest?
- What surprises you in reading the case history and his commentary?
- What would you have used from the earlier drafts that Clark didn't?
- Clark dropped his personal experience because he wasn't a victim of the press. Did he lose anything by moving away from his personal experience? Gain anything?
- What are the strengths and weaknesses of Clark's piece compared to those by Allen, Quindlen, Hurley, and Keiski?
- What are some of the problems common to all writers of argument?

Activities

- Take a personal experience of your own and list the ways you could argue about it—the issues that the experience reveals.
- Research a personal experience or an issue that bothers you as Clark did to see what other cases reveal about the topic.

- Write a response to Clark, playing the role of photographer, editor, or victim.
- Clip a story from a local newspaper. Interview one of the people involved and the writer or editor to see what issues are involved.

To Collaborate

- Make plans with another classmate or two to keep case histories of a piece of writing so you can compare your experiences in making meaning, the problems and solutions you share in the process of researching and writing the topic.
- Work as a team to develop a policy on treatment of victims for your college newspaper or a local paper.

Daryl Frazell

Daryl Frazell is now editing coach at the *St. Petersburg Times* in Florida, where his job is to pass on the skills and wisdom he has learned in a distinguished career as an editor.

He received his bachelor's and master's degrees from the Medill School of Journalism at Northwestern University and was a reporter for the famous *City News Bureau* in Chicago. He was an editor for the *Minneapolis Star,* the *Detroit Free Press,* and the *New York Times* before going to St. Petersburg. He has also been a Visiting Professional at the School of Journalism at the University of Kansas.

Photo Decisions Are Careful, Deliberate

1   I plead guilty. Having been a "hell-bent editor" in my time, I confess that I have rushed photos into print that I would not want in my family album.

2   That's because a newspaper is not a family album—and shouldn't be. The pictures we print are meant to help tell the story of what's going on in the world. If we printed only rose gardens and seascapes, we wouldn't deserve the respect and trust of our readers. They would know we weren't telling the truth.

> ☞ Note how Frazell takes one of Clark's most aggressive charges and turns it to his advantage—to make his own point. Also, the direct, take-charge language is appropriate to the person who has to make difficult decisions under pressure. The voice supports the writer's argument. ☜

3   Of course we can't tell the truth in the pure sense. We can only disclose what we know. Often we have to go to press with incomplete facts, and when

we learn more the next day the story sometimes changes. So we correct ourselves if necessary and keep on telling what we know.

4   We never have to correct a picture. Unless they are tampered with, pictures don't lie. They are vital to the credibility of our daily report.

5   Pictures bring a sense of human drama to what might otherwise be a dry,
emotionless collection of words. Suppose a major earthquake strikes California
this afternoon. Los Angeles goes up in flames. Press photographers are going to
take a lot of shocking photos.

6   Should the *Times* editors throw these photos away because the event is a
long way from St. Petersburg? Would you want to pick up your paper tomorrow
morning and find headlines about the quake but only pictures of wind surfers
on the Gulf?

7   I think not. I think *Times* readers would expect to find a selection of photos
that depicted the devastation while avoiding the worst stomach-turning scenes
of horror and gore.

8   Would our coverage of this disaster constitute pandering to the public's
fascination with violence and its aftermath?

9   For a few readers, perhaps, but not for the vast majority of people hungry
for every scrap of information they could get. When it comes to disasters, California is not really so far away after all, especially for those who have loved
ones there.

10   I don't contend that every news photo from California, or any other distant place, deserves to be published in the *Times*. Pictures that focus strictly on
the grieving faces of bereaved people are usually in bad taste, in my view. Yet
sometimes we publish photos that go far beyond the limits of good taste, and
I'm strongly in favor of it. These are pictures that shouldn't be withheld because
they are of compelling interest. I can think of several examples:

- A naked little girl running down a road toward the camera after her
  clothes were burned off in a napalm attack in Vietnam.

- A South Vietnamese official executing a Viet Cong prisoner on the street
  by shooting him in the head with a handgun.

- Buddhist monks setting themselves afire on Saigon streets to protest
  South Vietnamese government policies in the 1960s.

11   I am proud of the press for taking those pictures and having the courage
to print them. They probably affected the course of history.

> ☞ Frazell has specific examples of his own to balance Clark's. Then he turns to
> make his case with specific accounts of careful decisions. Note the progression
> of cases carefully placed in the sequence the author believes will make his case. ☜

12   Assistant managing editor George Sweers, the *Times'* director of illustrations, has helped make some hard decisions about controversial photos over
the years. He says he believes *Times* editors have made the right moves most of

the time, but there are a couple of cases that bother him—not because photos were published but because they were withheld.

13   One of these showed charred bodies of U.S. airmen lying on the desert sand with some wrecked U.S. equipment after the 1980 attempt to rescue hostages failed in Iran. The *Times* eventually printed the picture, but only after sitting on it for a day.

14   "This picture told the story, and we should have published it right away," Sweers says.

15   The other showed Vice President Nelson A. Rockefeller making an obscene gesture at a heckler at a political rally in 1976.

16   "Our decision at the time was that there was no need to publish the photo because the words in the story adequately described what Rockefeller had done," says Sweers. "We thought there was no need to offend our readers with that sort of gesture.

17   "But later, we realized it was not the gesture that was important, but who was making it. He was, after all, vice president of the United States. And it wasn't something he did inadvertently, or just once—he did it repeatedly. There was no question he meant to do what he did. Most of us now think we made a mistake in withholding the photo."

18   Other newspapers printed the picture. Some played it big on the front page. Not all editors think alike. Some will do things with pictures the others would consider irresponsible. But it is a myth that newspaper photo decisions are made by a panel of slobbering Neanderthals whose only ethical standard is printed in dollar signs.

19   There is a heightened sensitivity in newsrooms today. We have come a long way since a photographer sneaked a camera into the death chamber and snapped a picture of an execution in the 1920s. We have also come a long way since the press made a circus of the Lindbergh kidnapping case and eventually drove one of America's most beloved heroes to move his family out of the country.

20   In making photo decisions, today's editors take a lot of factors into consideration, including the sensibilities of their readers and the feelings of the victims. The editors talk to one another and seek the opinions of others in the newsroom. Seldom is a decision made on a controversial photo without collective deliberation.

21   Aesthetics are part of it, along with the photographer's labor and the possibility of prizes. But in essence it usually comes down to this: Are the arguments against publishing the picture strong enough to outweigh the natural journalistic tendency to disclose as much as possible? Editors are here to reveal what they know, not cover it up.

22   Does this mean the prevailing philosophy is one of "hold your nose and slap it in the paper"? By no means.

23   The self-restraint of editors was demonstrated earlier this year when the state treasurer of Pennsylvania called a news conference and shot himself to

death in front of video and still cameras. Editors were presented with a shocking sequence of pictures of the act. All but a few around the nation opted not to print the most harrowing ones, which showed the man's face just as he fired the gun into his mouth.

24   The *St. Petersburg Times,* for example, published only one picture, showing the man holding the gun in front of his chest. The story simply wasn't deemed important enough to *Times* readers to justify more extensive coverage.

25   On the other hand, sometimes even photos of the grief-stricken have their place in the newspaper. When race driver Jim Fitzgerald was killed in the St. Petersburg Grand Prix earlier this month, *Times* photographer Joe Walles took a moving photo of Fitzgerald's racing partner, actor Paul Newman, staring into the camera in stunned disbelief.

26   No amount of words could have rivaled that picture in expressing the shock and pain everybody felt at the scene. Some readers may disagree, but I think it was a fine example of responsible journalism.

27   Editors know their readers stand ready to criticize what they do. They also know the easiest way to avoid criticism is not to print anything controversial. But what value would there be in a newspaper edited by that sort of standard?

Discussion

- Who wins, Clark or Frazell? Why and how?
- Is argument always a case of winning or losing? How have these arguments led to a position in the middle? Is that wimpism or responsibility?
- What examples of photos, TV pictures, or news stories bothered you? Why? What might have been done differently?
- How does Frazell's voice reinforce and advance his meaning? What is the role of voice in argument?
- What are the elements of news style? What are its advantages and limitations?

Activities

- Interview local writers and editors to discover their positions on the issues raised by Clark and Frazell.
- Write a defense of something you have done in a voice as effective and appropriate as Frazell's.
- Take a local story and interview all the participants. Write a story about the effect of the story on their lives.
- Your editor has told you that the stories by Clark and Frazell will appear on page 1 in a box, pro and con, but that there will only be room for six paragraphs each. Cut both stories to six paragraphs.

To Collaborate

- Imagine that Clark and Frazell are on a committee to establish a new photo policy. Draft a policy statement combining their views.
- Work as a group to develop a class presentation on an ethical issue in another field—business, medicine, politics, pollution, religion, vivisection, race relations, psychology, the arts, child care, sports—whatever interests you and your classmates.

James Baldwin

The late James Baldwin was a major American writer who took his particular human experience and used it to speak both of the black experience in America and the universal experience of people of all races, sexes, and conditions. He was an important writer from early youth, and his voice changed and developed, but it was always his own. He spoke with his own particular hurt and rage in a language that is disciplined and effective. I have never been able to read his pages untouched, first as a human being and second as a writer. He reaches my gut, and then engages me as a writer, admiring the technical skill with which he has spoken.

One of his strongest pieces is the one I have selected to include in this book, a classic essay written at a special moment in our history. But it is just as alive today as it was when it was written. Baldwin once said, "When you're writing, you're trying to find out something which you don't know. The whole language of writing for me is finding out what you don't want to know, what you don't want to find out." At another time he said, "You go into a book and you're in the dark, really. You go in with a certain fear and trembling. You know one thing. You know that you will not be the same person when this voyage is over." In this piece you can sense the author, hurt, angry, mourning, searching for meaning in what is happening within him and around him.

Notes of a Native Son

❡ Note the irony right away in the title. Baldwin was alienated from his father and from his country. At the time he published this he had been living in Europe for eight years. The title establishes the focus and the tone of the essay. ❡

1   On the 29th of July, in 1943, my father died. On the same day, a few hours later, his last child was born. Over a month before this, while all our energies were concentrated in waiting for these events, there had been, in Detroit, one of the bloodiest race riots of the century. A few hours after my father's funeral, while he lay in state in the undertaker's chapel, a race riot

broke out in Harlem. On the morning of the 3rd of August, we drove my father to the graveyard through a wilderness of smashed plate glass.

> ❧ This is a superb example of a lead that puts the reader right into the story. The writer dares you not to read on. As a writer I am impressed by the fact that Baldwin has understated the terrible personal and public events that are described. The events themselves are so strong that he can write of them in an almost flat tone. I'm also impressed as a writer with the power of the specific at the end of the paragraph. ❧

2   The day of my father's funeral had also been my nineteenth birthday. As we drove him to the graveyard, the spoils of injustice, anarchy, discontent, and hatred were all around us. It seemed to me that God himself had devised, to mark my father's end, the most sustained and brutally dissonant of codas. And it seemed to me, too, that the violence which rose all about us as my father left the world had been devised as a corrective for the pride of his eldest son. I had declined to believe in that apocalypse which had been central to my father's vision; very well, life seemed to be saying, here is something that will certainly pass for an apocalypse until the real thing comes along. I had inclined to be contemptuous of my father for the conditions of his life, for the conditions of our lives. When his life had ended I began to wonder about that life and also, in a new way, to be apprehensive about my own.

3   I had not known my father very well. We had got on badly, partly because we shared, in our different fashions, the vice of stubborn pride. When he was dead I realized that I had hardly ever spoken to him. When he had been dead a long time I began to wish I had. It seems to be typical of life in America, where opportunities, real and fancied, are thicker than anywhere else on the globe, that the second generation has no time to talk to the first. No one, including my father, seems to have known exactly how old he was, but his mother had been born during slavery. He was of the first generation of free men. He, along with thousands of other Negroes, came North after 1919 and I was part of that generation which had never seen the landscape of what Negroes sometimes called the Old Country.

4   He had been born in New Orleans and had been a quite young man there during the time that Louis Armstrong, a boy, was running errands for the dives and honky-tonks of what was always presented to me as one of the most wicked of cities—to this day, whenever I think of New Orleans, I also helplessly think of Sodom and Gomorrah. My father never mentioned Louis Armstrong, except to forbid us to play his records; but there was a picture of him on our wall for a long time. One of my father's strong-willed female relatives had placed it there and forbade my father to take it down. He never did, but he eventually maneuvered her out of the house and when, some years later, she was in trouble and near death, he refused to do anything to help her.

5   He was, I think, very handsome. I gather this from photographs and from

my own memories of him, dressed in his Sunday best and on his way to preach
a sermon somewhere, when I was little. Handsome, proud, and ingrown, ''like
a toe-nail,'' somebody said. But he looked to me, as I grew older, like pictures
I had seen of African tribal chieftains: he really should have been naked, with
war-paint on and barbaric mementos, standing among spears. He could be
chilling in the pulpit and indescribably cruel in his personal life and he was
certainly the most bitter man I have ever met; yet it must be said that there was
something else in him, buried in him, which lent him his tremendous power
and, even, a rather crushing charm. It had something to do with his blackness,
I think—he was very black—with his blackness and his beauty, and with the
fact that he knew that he was black but did not know that he was beautiful. He
claimed to be proud of his blackness but it had also been the cause of much
humiliation and it had fixed bleak boundaries to his life. He was not a young
man when we were growing up and he had already suffered many kinds of ruin;
in his outrageously demanding and protective way he loved his children, who
were black like him and menaced, like him; and all these things sometimes
showed in his face when he tried, never to my knowledge with any success, to
establish contact with any of us. When he took one of his children on his knee
to play, the child always became fretful and began to cry; when he tried to help
one of us with our homework the absolutely unabating tension which emanated
from him caused our minds and our tongues to become paralyzed, so that he,
scarcely knowing why, flew into a rage and the child, not knowing why, was
punished. If it ever entered his head to bring a surprise home for his children,
it was, almost unfailingly, the wrong surprise and even the big watermelons he
often brought home on his back in the summertime led to the most appalling
scenes. I do not remember, in all those years, that one of his children was ever
glad to see him come home. From what I was able to gather of his early life, it
seemed that this inability to establish contact with other people had always
marked him and had been one of the things which had driven him out of New
Orleans. There was something in him, therefore, groping and tentative, which
was never expressed and which was buried with him. One saw it most clearly
when he was facing new people and hoping to impress them. But he never did,
not for long. We went from church to smaller and more improbable church, he
found himself in less and less demand as a minister, and by the time he died
none of his friends had come to see him for a long time. He had lived and died
in an intolerable bitterness of spirit and it frightened me, as we drove him to
the graveyard through those unquiet, ruined streets, to see how powerful and
overflowing this bitterness could be and to realize that this bitterness now was
mine.

> ❧ As a writer I reread and reread this spectacular paragraph that covers so many
> complicated matters, interweaving them. Many of us have had very complicated
> relations with our parents, and we can identify with the difficulty the author is
> feeling in confronting his father after his death. ❧

6   When he died I had been away from home for a little over a year. In that year I had had time to become aware of the meaning of all my father's bitter warnings, had discovered the secret of his proudly pursed lips and rigid carriage: I had discovered the weight of white people in the world. I saw that this had been for my ancestors and now would be for me an awful thing to live with and that the bitterness which had helped to kill my father could also kill me.

7   He had been ill a long time—in the mind, as we now realized, reliving instances of his fantastic intransigence in the new light of his affliction and endeavoring to feel a sorrow for him which never, quite, came true. We had not known that he was being eaten up by paranoia, and the discovery that his cruelty, to our bodies and our minds, had been one of the symptoms of his illness was not, then, enough to enable us to forgive him. The younger children felt, quite simply, relief that he would not be coming home anymore. My mother's observation that it was he, after all, who had kept them alive all these years meant nothing because the problems of keeping children alive are not real for children. The other children felt, with my father gone, that they could invite their friends to the house without fear that their friends would be insulted or, as had sometimes happened with me, being told that their friends were in league with the devil and intended to rob our family of everything we owned. (I didn't fail to wonder, and it made me hate him, what on earth we owned that anybody else would want.)

8   His illness was beyond all hope of healing before anyone realized that he was ill. He had always been so strange and had lived, like a prophet, in such unimaginably close communion with the Lord that his long silences which were punctuated by moans and hallelujahs and snatches of old songs while he sat at the living-room window never seemed odd to us. It was not until he refused to eat because, he said, his family was trying to poison him that my mother was forced to accept as a fact what had, until then, been only an unwilling suspicion. When he was committed, it was discovered that he had tuberculosis and, as it turned out, the disease of his mind allowed the disease of his body to destroy him. For the doctors could not force him to eat, either, and, though he was fed intravenously, it was clear from the beginning that there was no hope for him.

9   In my mind's eye I could see him, sitting at the window, locked up in his terrors; hating and fearing every living soul including his children who had betrayed him, too, by reaching towards the world which had despised him. There were nine of us. I began to wonder what it could have felt like for such a man to have had nine children whom he could barely feed. He used to make little jokes about our poverty, which never, of course, seemed very funny to us; they could not have seemed very funny to him, either, or else our all too feeble response to them would never have caused such rages. He spent great energy and achieved, to our chagrin, no small amount of success in keeping us away from the people who surrounded us, people who had all-night rent parties to which we listened when we should have been sleeping, people who cursed and drank and flashed razor blades on Lenox Avenue. He could not understand

why, if they had so much energy to spare, they could not use it to make their lives better. He treated almost everybody on our block with a most uncharitable asperity and neither they, nor, of course, their children were slow to reciprocate.

10   The only white people who came to our house were welfare workers and bill collectors. It was almost always my mother who dealt with them, for my father's temper, which was at the mercy of his pride, was never to be trusted. It was clear that he felt their very presence in his home to be a violation; this was conveyed by his carriage, almost ludicrously stiff, and by his voice, harsh and vindictively polite. When I was around nine or ten I wrote a play which was directed by a young, white schoolteacher, a woman, who then took an interest in me, and gave me books to read and, in order to corroborate my theatrical bent, decided to take me to see what she somewhat tactlessly referred to as "real" plays. Theater-going was forbidden in our house, but, with the really cruel intuitiveness of a child, I suspected that the color of this woman's skin would carry the day for me. When, at school, she suggested taking me to the theater, I did not, as I might have done if she had been a Negro, find a way of discouraging her, but agreed that she should pick me up at my house one evening. I then, very cleverly, left all the rest to my mother, who suggested to my father, as I knew she would, that it would not be very nice to let such a kind woman make the trip for nothing. Also, since it was a schoolteacher, I imagine that my mother countered the idea of sin with the idea of "education," which word, even with my father, carried a kind of bitter weight.

11   Before the teacher came my father took me aside to ask *why* she was coming, what *interest* she could possibly have in our house, in a boy like me. I said I didn't know but I, too, suggested that it had something to do with education. And I understood that my father was waiting for me to say something—I didn't quite know what; perhaps that I wanted his protection against this teacher and her "education." I said none of these things and the teacher came and we went out. It was clear, during the brief interview in our living room, that my father was agreeing very much against his will and that he would have refused permission if he had dared. The fact that he did not dare caused me to despise him; I had no way of knowing that he was facing in that living room a wholly unprecedented and frightening situation.

12   Later when my father had been laid off from his job, this woman became very important to us. She was really a very sweet and generous woman and went to a great deal of trouble to be of help to us, particularly during one awful winter. My mother called her by the highest name she knew; she said she was a "christian." My father could scarcely disagree but during the four or five years of our relatively close association he never trusted her and was always trying to surprise in her open, Midwestern face the genuine, cunningly hidden, and hideous motivation. In later years, particularly when it began to be clear that this "education" of mine was going to lead me to perdition, he became more explicit and warned me that my white friends in high school were not really my friends and that I would see, when I was older, how white people would do

anything to keep a Negro down. Some of them could be nice, he admitted, but none of them were to be trusted and most of them were not even nice. The best thing was to have as little to do with them as possible. I did not feel this way and I was certain, in my innocence, that I never would.

13   But the year which preceded my father's death had made a great change in my life. I had been living in New Jersey, working in defense plants, working and living among southerners, white and black. I knew about the south, of course, and about how southerners treated Negroes and how they expected them to behave, but it had never entered my mind that anyone would look at me and expect *me* to behave that way. I learned in New Jersey that to be a Negro meant, precisely, that one was never looked at but was simply at the mercy of the reflexes the color of one's skin caused in other people. I acted in New Jersey as I had always acted, that is as though I thought a great deal of myself—I had to *act* that way—with results that were simply unbelievable. I had scarcely arrived before I had earned the enmity, which was extraordinarily ingenious, of all my superiors and nearly all my co-workers. In the beginning, to make matters worse, I simply did not know what was happening. I did not know what I had done, and I shortly began to wonder what *anyone* could possibly do, to bring about such unanimous, active, and unbearably vocal hostility. I knew about jim-crow but I had never experienced it. I went to the same self-service restaurant three times and stood with all the Princeton boys before the counter, waiting for a hamburger and coffee; it was always an extraordinarily long time before anything was set before me; but it was not until the fourth visit that I learned that, in fact, nothing had ever been set before me; I had simply picked something up. Negroes were not served there, I was told, and they had been waiting for me to realize that I was always the only Negro present. Once I was told this, I determined to go there all the time. But now they were ready for me and, though some dreadful scenes were subsequently enacted in that restaurant, I never ate there again.

14   It was the same story all over New Jersey, in bars, bowling alleys, diners, places to live. I was always being forced to leave, silently, or with mutual imprecations. I very shortly became notorious and children giggled behind me when I passed and their elders whispered or shouted—they really believed that I was mad. And it did begin to work on my mind, of course; I began to be afraid to go anywhere and to compensate for this I went places to which I really should not have gone and where, God knows, I had no desire to be. My reputation in town naturally enhanced my reputation at work and my working day became one long series of acrobatics designed to keep me out of trouble. I cannot say that these acrobatics succeeded. It began to seem that the machinery of the organization I worked for was turning over, day and night, with but one aim: to eject me. I was fired once, and contrived, with the aid of a friend from New York, to get back on the payroll; was fired again, and bounced back again. It took a while to fire me for the third time, but the third time took. There were no loopholes anywhere. There was not even any way of getting back inside the gates.

❦ Notice all through this piece how Baldwin uses point of view—the adult looking back and reflecting upon experience—to control the flood of all the material of his life and to put it in context. We can walk beside him as he tries to record, and then to understand, his life. ❧

15   That year in New Jersey lives in my mind as though it were the year during which, having an unsuspected predilection for it, I first contracted some dread, chronic disease, the unfailing symptom of which is a kind of blind fever, a pounding in the skull and fire in the bowels. Once this disease is contracted, one can never be really carefree again, for the fever, without an instant's warning, can recur at any moment. It can wreck more important things than race relations. There is not a Negro alive who does not have this rage in his blood— one has the choice, merely, of living with it consciously or surrendering to it. As for me, this fever has recurred in me, and does, and will until the day I die.

❦ The following anecdote is a powerful form of documentation. Here Baldwin writes a one-paragraph anecdote about his experience in the diner, then follows it with an extended anecdote of his experience in a restaurant. The anecdote is a little narrative similar to the biblical parable that tells a story and makes a point. ❧

16   My last night in New Jersey, a white friend from New York took me to the nearest big town, Trenton, to go to the movies and have a few drinks. As it turned out, he also saved me from, at the very least, a violent whipping. Almost every detail of that night stands out very clearly in my memory. I even remember the name of the movie we saw because its title impressed me as being so patly ironical. It was a movie about the German occupation of France, starring Maureen O'Hara and Charles Laughton and called *This Land Is Mine*. I remember the name of the diner we walked into when the movie ended; it was the "American Diner." When we walked in the counterman asked what we wanted and I remember answering with the casual sharpness which had become my habit: "We want a hamburger and a cup of coffee, what do you think we want?" I do not know why, after a year of such rebuffs, I so completely failed to anticipate his answer, which was, of course, "We don't serve Negroes here." This reply failed to discompose me, at least for the moment. I made some sardonic comment about the name of the diner and we walked out into the streets.

17   This was the time of what was called the "brown-out," when the lights in all American cities were very dim. When we re-entered the streets something happened to me which had the force of an optical illusion, or a nightmare. The streets were very crowded and I was facing north. People were moving in every direction but it seemed to me, in that instant, that all of the people I could see, and many more than that, were moving toward me, against me, and that everyone was white. I remember how their faces gleamed. And I felt, like a physical sensation, a *click* at the nape of my neck as though some interior string connecting my head to my body had been cut. I began to walk. I heard my friend

call after me, but I ignored him. Heaven only knows what was going on in his mind, but he had the good sense not to touch me—I don't know what would have happened if he had—and to keep me in sight. I don't know what was going on in my mind, either; I certainly had no conscious plan. I wanted to do something to crush these white faces, which were crushing me. I walked for perhaps a block or two until I came to an enormous, glittering, and fashionable restaurant in which I knew not even the intercession of the Virgin would cause me to be served. I pushed through the doors and took the first vacant seat I saw, at a table for two, and waited.

18   I do not know how long I waited and I rather wonder, until today, what I could possibly have looked like. Whatever I looked like, I frightened the waitress who shortly appeared, and the moment she appeared all of my fury flowed towards her. I hated her for her white face, and for her great, astounded, frightened, eyes. I felt that if she found a black man so frightening I would make her fright worthwhile.

19   She did not ask me what I wanted, but repeated, as though she had learned it somewhere, "We don't serve Negroes here." She did not say it with the blunt, derisive hostility to which I had grown so accustomed, but, rather, with a note of apology in her voice, and fear. This made me colder and more murderous than ever. I felt I had to do something with my hands. I wanted her to come close enough for me to get her neck between my hands.

20   So I pretended not to have understood her, hoping to draw her closer. And she did step a very short step closer, with her pencil poised incongruously over her pad, and repeated the formula: " . . . don't serve Negroes here."

21   Somehow, with the repetition of that phrase, which was already ringing in my head like a thousand bells of a nightmare, I realized that she would never come any closer and that I would have to strike from a distance. There was nothing on the table but an ordinary watermug half full of water, and I picked this up and hurled it with all my strength at her. She ducked and it missed her and shattered against the mirror behind the bar. And, with that sound, my frozen blood abruptly thawed, I returned from wherever I had been, I saw, for the first time, the restaurant, the people with their mouths open, already, as it seemed to me, rising as one man, and I realized what I had done, and where I was, and I was frightened. I rose and began running for the door. A round, potbellied man grabbed me by the nape of the neck just as I reached the doors and began to beat me about the face. I kicked him and got loose and ran into the streets. My friend whispered, *"Run!"* and I ran.

22   My friend stayed outside the restaurant long enough to misdirect my pursuers and the police, who arrived, he told me, at once. I do not know what I said to him when he came to my room that night. I could not have said much. I felt, in the oddest, most awful way, that I had somehow betrayed him. I lived it over and over and over again, the way one relives an automobile accident after it has happened and one finds oneself alone and safe. I could not get over two facts, both equally difficult for the imagination to grasp, and one was that I could have been murdered. But the other was that I had been ready to commit

murder. I saw nothing very clearly but I did see this: that my life, my *real* life, was in danger, and not from anything other people might do but from the hatred I carried in my own heart.

23   I had returned home around the second week in June—in great haste because it seemed that my father's death and my mother's confinement were both but a matter of hours. In the case of my mother, it soon became clear that she had simply made a miscalculation. This had always been her tendency and I don't believe that a single one of us arrived in the world, or has since arrived anywhere else, on time. But none of us dawdled so intolerably about the business of being born as did my baby sister. We sometimes amused ourselves, during those endless, stifling weeks, by picturing the baby sitting within in the safe, warm dark, bitterly regretting the necessity of becoming a part of our chaos and stubbornly putting it off as long as possible. I understood her perfectly and congratulated her on showing such good sense so soon. Death, however, sat as purposefully at my father's bedside as life stirred within my mother's womb and it was harder to understand why he so lingered in that long shadow. It seemed that he had bent, and for a long time, too, all of his energies towards dying. Now death was ready for him but my father held back.

24   All of Harlem, indeed, seemed to be infected by waiting. I had never before known it to be so violently still. Racial tensions throughout this country were exacerbated during the early years of the war, partly because the labor market brought together hundreds of thousands of ill-prepared people and partly because Negro soldiers, regardless of where they were born, received their military training in the south. What happened in defense plants and army camps had repercussions, naturally, in every Negro ghetto. The situation in Harlem had grown bad enough for clergymen, policemen, educators, politicians, and social workers to assert in one breath that there was no "crime wave" and to offer, in the very next breath, suggestions as to how to combat it. These suggestions always seemed to involve playgrounds, despite the fact that racial skirmishes were occurring in the playgrounds, too. Playground or not, crime wave or not, the Harlem police force had been augmented in March, and the unrest grew—perhaps, in fact, partly as a result of the ghetto's instinctive hatred of policemen. Perhaps the most revealing news item, out of the steady parade of reports of muggings, stabbings, shootings, assaults, gang wars, and accusations of police brutality, is the item concerning six Negro girls who set upon a white girl in the subway because, as they all too accurately put it, she was stepping on their toes. Indeed she was, all over the nation.

25   I had never before been so aware of policemen, on foot, on horseback, on corners, everywhere, always two by two. Nor had I ever been so aware of small knots of people. They were on stoops and on corners and in doorways, and what was striking about them, I think, was that they did not seem to be talking. Never, when I passed these groups, did the usual sound of a curse or a laugh ring out and neither did there seem to be any hum of gossip. There was certainly, on the other hand, occurring between them communication extraordi-

narily intense. Another thing that was striking was the unexpected diversity of the people who made up these groups. Usually, for example, one would see a group of sharpies standing on the street corner, jiving the passing chicks; or a group of older men, usually, for some reason, in the vicinity of a barber shop, discussing baseball scores, or the numbers, or making rather chilling observations about women they had known. Women, in a general way, tended to be seen less often together—unless they were church women, or very young girls, or prostitutes met together for an unprofessional instant. But that summer I saw the strangest combinations: large, respectable, churchly matrons standing on the stoops or the corners with their hair tied up, together with a girl in sleazy satin whose face bore the marks of gin and the razor, or heavy-set, abrupt, no-nonsense older men, in company with the most disreputable and fanatical "race" men, or these same "race" men with the sharpies, or these sharpies with the churchly women. Seventh Day Adventists and Methodists and Spiritualists seemed to be hobnobbing with Holy Rollers and they were all, alike, entangled with the most flagrant disbelievers; something heavy in their stance seemed to indicate that they had all, incredibly, seen a common vision, and on each face there seemed to be the same strange, bitter shadow.

> ❮ Do you hear echoes of the boy preacher in his style? I do. I hear the preachers of my childhood as they recited lists of events or verses to work up to a moral point. I also hear parables, the anecdotes or little stories by which the Bible preaches. And I hear fragments of the music of the preacher, the pacing, rhythm, sound of churchly speech. ❯

26   The churchly women and the matter-of-fact, no-nonsense men had children in the Army. The sleazy girls they talked to had lovers there, the sharpies and the "race" men had friends and brothers there. It would have demanded an unquestioning patriotism, happily as uncommon in this country as it is undesirable, for these people not to have been disturbed by the bitter letters they received, by the newspaper stories they read, not to have been enraged by the posters, then to be found all over New York, which described the Japanese as "yellow-bellied Japs." It was only the "race" men, to be sure, who spoke ceaselessly of being revenged—how this vengeance was to be exacted was not clear—for the indignities and dangers suffered by Negro boys in uniform; but everybody felt a directionless, hopeless bitterness, as well as that panic which can scarcely be suppressed when one knows that a human being one loves is beyond one's reach, and in danger. This helplessness and this gnawing uneasiness does something, at length, to even the toughest mind. Perhaps the best way to sum all this up is to say that the people I knew felt, mainly, a peculiar kind of relief when they knew that their boys were being shipped out of the south, to do battle overseas. It was, perhaps, like feeling that the most dangerous part of a dangerous journey had been passed and that now, even if death

should come, it would come with honor and without the complicity of their countrymen. Such a death would be, in short, a fact with which one could hope to live.

27   It was on the 28th of July, which I believe was a Wednesday, that I visited my father for the first time during his illness and for the last time in his life. The moment I saw him I knew why I had put off this visit so long. I had told my mother that I did not want to see him because I hated him. But this was not true. It was only that I *had* hated him and I wanted to hold on to this hatred. I did not want to look on him as a ruin: it was not a ruin I had hated. I imagine that one of the reasons people cling to their hates so stubbornly is because they sense, once hate is gone, that they will be forced to deal with pain.

28   We traveled out to him, his older sister and myself, to what seemed to be the very end of a very Long Island. It was hot and dusty and we wrangled, my aunt and I, all the way out, over the fact that I had recently begun to smoke and, as she said, to give myself airs. But I knew that she wrangled with me because she could not bear to face the fact of her brother's dying. Neither could I endure the reality of her despair, her unstated bafflement as to what had happened to her brother's life, and her own. So we wrangled and I smoked and from time to time she fell into a heavy reverie. Covertly, I watched her face, which was the face of an old woman; it had fallen in, the eyes were sunken and lightless; soon she would be dying, too.

29   In my childhood—it had not been so long ago—I had thought her beautiful. She had been quick-witted and quick-moving and very generous with all the children and each of her visits had been an event. At one time one of my brothers and myself had thought of running away to live with her. Now she could no longer produce out of her handbag some unexpected and yet familiar delight. She made me feel pity and revulsion and fear. It was awful to realize that she no longer caused me to feel affection. The closer we came to the hospital the more querulous she became and at the same time, naturally, grew more dependent on me. Between pity and guilt and fear I began to feel that there was another me trapped in my skull like a jack-in-the-box who might escape my control at any moment and fill the air with screaming.

30   She began to cry the moment we entered the room and she saw him lying there, all shriveled and still, like a little black monkey. The great, gleaming apparatus which fed him and would have compelled him to be still even if he had been able to move brought to mind, not beneficence, but torture; the tubes entering his arm made me think of pictures I had seen when a child, of Gulliver, tied down by the pygmies on that island. My aunt wept and wept, there was a whistling sound in my father's throat; nothing was said; he could not speak. I wanted to take his hand, to say something. But I do not know what I could have said, even if he could have heard me. He was not really in that room with us, he had at last really embarked on his journey; and though my aunt told me that he said he was going to meet Jesus, I did not hear anything except that whistling in his throat. The doctor came back and we left, into that unbearable train again, and home. In the morning came the telegram saying that he was dead.

Then the house was suddenly full of relatives, friends, hysteria, and confusion and I quickly left my mother and the children to the care of those impressive women, who, in Negro communities at least, automatically appear at times of bereavement armed with lotions, proverbs, and patience, and an ability to cook. I went downtown. By the time I returned, later the same day, my mother had been carried to the hospital and the baby had been born.

> ❨ All the way through this powerful piece of writing, Baldwin speaks of a race by speaking of individuals. He presents the particulars of private, family conflict and tragedy against the backdrop of national crisis and tragedy. This is what the writer does: the abstract is made particular and the specific is put in context so its significance may be understood. ❩

31   For my father's funeral I had nothing black to wear and this posed a nagging problem all day long. It was one of those problems, simple, or impossible of solution, to which the mind insanely clings in order to avoid the mind's real trouble. I spent most of that day at the downtown apartment of a girl I knew, celebrating my birthday with whiskey and wondering what to wear that night. When planning a birthday celebration one naturally does not expect that it will be up against competition from a funeral and this girl had anticipated taking me out that night, for a big dinner and a night club afterwards. Sometime during the course of that long day we decided that we would go out anyway, when my father's funeral service was over. I imagine *I* decided it, since, as the funeral hour approached, it became clearer and clearer to me that I would not know what to do with myself when it was over. The girl, stifling her very lively concern as to the possible effects of the whiskey on one of my father's chief mourners, concentrated on being conciliatory and practically helpful. She found a black shirt for me somewhere and ironed it and, dressed in the darkest pants and jacket I owned, and slightly drunk, I made my way to my father's funeral.

32   The chapel was full, but not packed, and very quiet. There were, mainly, my father's relatives, and his children, and here and there I saw faces I had not seen since childhood, the faces of my father's one-time friends. They were very dark and solemn now, seeming somehow to suggest that they had known all along that something like this would happen. Chief among the mourners was my aunt, who had quarreled with my father all his life; by which I do not mean to suggest that her mourning was insincere or that she had not loved him. I suppose that she was one of the few people in the world who had, and their incessant quarreling proved precisely the strength of the tie that bound them. The only other person in the world, as far as I knew, whose relationship to my father rivaled my aunt's in depth was my mother, who was not there.

33   It seemed to me, of course, that it was a very long funeral. But it was, if anything, a rather shorter funeral than most, nor, since there were no overwhelming, uncontrollable expressions of grief, could it be called—if I dare to use the word—successful. The minister who preached my father's funeral sermon was one of the few my father had still been seeing as he neared his end.

He presented to us in his sermon a man whom none of us had ever seen—a man thoughtful, patient, and forbearing, a Christian inspiration to all who knew him, and a model for his children. And no doubt the children, in their disturbed and guilty state, were almost ready to believe this; he had been remote enough to be anything and, anyway, the shock of the incontrovertible, that it was really our father lying up there in that casket, prepared the mind for anything. His sister moaned and this grief-stricken moaning was taken as corroboration. The other faces held a dark, non-committal thoughtfulness. This was not the man they had known, but they had scarcely expected to be confronted with *him;* this was, in a sense deeper than questions of fact, the man they had not known, and the man they had not known may have been the real one. The real man, whoever he had been, had suffered and now he was dead; this was all that was sure and all that mattered now. Every man in the chapel hoped that when his hour came he, too, would be eulogized, which is to say forgiven, and that all of his lapses, greeds, errors, and strayings from the truth would be invested with coherence and looked upon with charity. This was perhaps the last thing human beings could give each other and it was what they demanded, after all, of the Lord. Only the Lord saw the midnight tears, only He was present when one of His children, moaning and wringing hands, paced up and down the room. When one slapped one's child in anger the recoil in the heart reverberated through heaven and became part of the pain of the universe. And when the children were hungry and sullen and distrustful and one watched them, daily, growing wilder, and further away, and running headlong into danger, it was the Lord who knew what the charged heart endured as the strap was laid to the backside; the Lord alone who knew what one *would* have said if one had had, like the Lord, the gift of the living word. It was the Lord who knew of the impossibility every parent in that room faced; how to prepare the child for the day when the child would be despised and how to *create* in the child—by what means?—a stronger antidote to this poison than one had found for oneself. The avenues, side streets, bars, billiard halls, hospitals, police stations, and even the playgrounds of Harlem—not to mention the houses of correction, the jails, and the morgue—testified to the potency of the poison while remaining silent as to the efficacy of whatever antidote, irresistibly raising the questions of whether or not such an antidote existed; raising, which was worse, the question of whether or not an antidote was desirable; perhaps poison should be fought with poison. With these several schisms in the mind and with more terrors in the heart than could be named, it was better not to judge the man who had gone down under an impossible burden. It was better to remember: *Thou knowest this man's fall; but thou knowest not his wrassling.*

34   While the preacher talked and I watched the children—years of changing their diapers, scrubbing them, slapping them, taking them to school, and scolding them had had the perhaps inevitable result of making me love them, though I am not sure I knew this then—my mind was busily breaking out with a rash of disconnected impressions. Snatches of popular songs, indecent jokes, bits of books I had read, movie sequences, faces, voices, political issues—I thought I

was going mad; all these impressions suspended, as it were, in the solution of the faint nausea produced in me by the heart and liquor. For a moment I had the impression that my alcoholic breath, inefficiently disguised with chewing gum, filled the entire chapel. Then someone began singing one of my father's favorite songs and, abruptly, I was with him, sitting on his knee, in the hot, enormous, crowded church which was the first church we attended. It was the Abyssinia Baptist Church on 138th Street. We had not gone there long. With this image, a host of others came. I had forgotten, in the rage of my growing up, how proud my father had been of me when I was little. Apparently, I had had a voice and my father had liked to show me off before the members of the church. I had forgotten what he had looked like when he was pleased but now I remembered that he had always been grinning with pleasure when my solos ended. I even remembered certain expressions on his face when he teased my mother—had he loved her? I would never know. And when had it all begun to change? For now it seemed that he had not always been cruel. I remembered being taken for a haircut and scraping my knee on the footrest of the barber's chair and I remembered my father's face as he soothed my crying and applied the stinging iodine. Then I remembered our fights, fights which had been of the worst possible kind because my technique had been silence. . . .

35   I remembered the one time in all our life together when we had really spoken to each other.

36   It was on a Sunday and it must have been shortly before I left home. We were walking, just the two of us, in our usual silence, to or from church. I was in high school and had been doing a lot of writing and I was, at about this time, the editor of the high school magazine. But I had also been a Young Minister and had been preaching from the pulpit. Lately, I had been taking fewer engagements and preached as rarely as possible. It was said in the church, quite truthfully, that I was "cooling off."

37   My father asked me abruptly, "You'd rather write than preach, wouldn't you?"

38   I was astonished at his question—because it was a real question. I answered, "Yes."

39   That was all we said. It was awful to remember that that was all we had *ever* said.

40   The casket now was opened and the mourners were being led up the aisle to look for the last time on the deceased. The assumption was that the family was too overcome with grief to be allowed to make this journey alone and I watched while my aunt was led to the casket and, muffled in black, and shaking, led back to her seat. I disapproved of forcing the children to look on their dead father, considering that the shock of his death, or, more truthfully, the shock of death as a reality, was already a little more than a child could bear, but my judgment in this matter had been overruled and there they were, bewildered and frightened and very small, being led, one by one, to the casket. But there is also something very gallant about children at such moments. It has something to do with their silence and gravity and with the fact that one cannot help them.

Their legs, somehow, seem *exposed,* so that it is at once incredible and terribly clear that their legs are all they have to hold them up.

41   I had not wanted to go to the casket myself and I certainly had not wished to be led there, but there was no way of avoiding either of these forms. One of the deacons led me up and I looked on my father's face. I cannot say that it looked like him at all. His blackness had been equivocated by powder and there was no suggestion in that casket of what his power had or could have been. He was simply an old man dead, and it was hard to believe that he had ever given anyone either joy or pain. Yet his life filled that room. Further up the avenue his wife was holding his newborn child. Life and death so close together, and love and hatred, and right and wrong, said something to me which I did not want to hear concerning man, concerning the life of man.

42   After the funeral, while I was downtown desperately celebrating my birthday, a Negro soldier, in the lobby of the Hotel Braddock, got into a fight with a white policeman over a Negro girl. Negro girls, white policemen, in or out of uniform, and Negro males—in or out of uniform—were part of the furniture of the lobby of the Hotel Braddock and this was certainly not the first time such an incident had occurred. It was destined, however, to receive an unprecedented publicity, for the fight between the policeman and the soldier ended with the shooting of the soldier. Rumor, flowing immediately to the streets outside, stated that the soldier had been shot in the back, an instantaneous and revealing invention, and that the soldier had died protecting a Negro woman. The facts were somewhat different—for example, the soldier had not been shot in the back, and was not dead, and the girl seems to have been as dubious a symbol of womanhood as her white counterpart in Georgia usually is, but no one was interested in the facts. They preferred the invention because this invention expressed and corroborated their hates and fears so perfectly. It is just as well to remember that people are always doing this. Perhaps many of those legends, including Christianity, to which the world clings, began their conquest of the world with just some such concerted surrender to distortion. The effect, in Harlem, of this particular legend was like the effect of a lit match in a tin of gasoline. The mob gathered before the doors of the Hotel Braddock simply began to swell and to spread in every direction, and Harlem exploded.

43   The mob did not cross the ghetto lines. It would have been easy, for example, to have gone over Morningside Park on the west side or to have crossed the Grand Central railroad tracks at 125th Street on the east side, to wreak havoc in white neighborhoods. The mob seems to have been mainly interested in something more potent and real than the white face, that is, in white power, and the principal damage done during the riot of the summer of 1943 was to white business establishments in Harlem. It might have been a far bloodier story, of course, if, at the hour the riot began, these establishments had still been open. From the Hotel Braddock the mob fanned out, east and west along 125th, 135th, and so on—bars, stores, pawnshops, restaurants, even little luncheonettes had been smashed open and entered and looted—looted, it might

be added, with more haste than efficiency. The shelves really looked as though a bomb had struck them. Cans of beans and soup and dog food, along with toilet paper, corn flakes, sardines and milk tumbled every which way, and abandoned cash registers and cases of beer leaned crazily out of the splintered windows and were strewn along the avenues. Sheets, blankets, and clothing of every description formed a kind of path, as though people had dropped them while running. I truly had not realized that Harlem *had* so many stores until I saw them all smashed open; the first time the word *wealth* ever entered my mind in relation to Harlem was when I saw it scattered in the streets. But one's first, incongruous impression of plenty was countered immediately by an impression of waste. None of this was doing anybody any good. It would have been better to have left the plate glass as it had been and the goods lying in the stores.

> ❦ Study how Baldwin brings order to the confusion he is describing so that the reader can understand the confusion. If Baldwin just records confusion, we will have a confused text and not be able to understand it. If the text is too ordered, we will not experience the riot. It seems to me that he maintains an impressive balance between both extremes—an example of the tension between freedom and discipline that is central to the creative process. Also note the expert use of detailed context. ❧

44   It would have been better, but it would also have been intolerable, for Harlem had needed something to smash. To smash something is the ghetto's chronic need. Most of the time it is the members of the ghetto who smash each other, and themselves. But as long as the ghetto walls are standing there will always come a moment when these outlets do not work. That summer, for example, it was not enough to get into a fight on Lenox Avenue, or curse out one's cronies in the barber shops. If ever, indeed, the violence which fills Harlem's churches, pool halls, and bars erupts outward in a more direct fashion, Harlem and its citizens are likely to vanish in an apocalyptic flood. That this is not likely to happen is due to a great many reasons, most hidden and powerful among them the Negro's real relation to the white American. This relation prohibits, simply, anything as uncomplicated and satisfactory as pure hatred. In order really to hate white people, one has to blot so much out of the mind— and the heart—that this hatred itself becomes an exhausting and self-destructive pose. But this does not mean, on the other hand, that love comes easily: the white world is too powerful, too complacent, too ready with gratuitous humiliation, and, above all, too ignorant and too innocent for that. One is absolutely forced to make perpetual qualifications and one's own reactions are always canceling each other out. It is this, really, which has driven so many people mad, both white and black. One is always in the position of having to decide between amputation and gangrene. Amputation is swift but time may prove that the amputation was not necessary—or one may delay the amputa-

tion too long. Gangrene is slow, but it is impossible to be sure that one is read-ing one's symptoms right. The idea of going through life as a cripple is more than one can bear, and equally unbearable is the risk of swelling up slowly, in agony, with poison. And the trouble, finally, is that the risks are real even if the choices do not exist.

45   "But as for me and my house," my father had said, "we will serve the Lord." I wondered, as we drove him to his resting place, what this line had meant for him. I had heard him preach it many times. I had preached it once myself, proudly giving it an interpretation different from my father's. Now the whole thing came back to me, as though my father and I were on our way to Sunday school and I were memorizing the golden text: *And if it seem evil unto you to serve the Lord, choose you this day whom you will serve; whether the gods which your fathers served that were on the other side of the flood, or the gods of the Amorites, in whose land ye dwell: but as for me and my house, we will serve the Lord.* I suspected in these familiar lines a meaning which had never been there for me before. All of my father's texts and songs, which I had decided were meaningless, were arranged before me at his death like empty bottles, waiting to hold the meaning which life would give them for me. This was his legacy: nothing is ever escaped. That bleakly memorable morning I hated the unbe-lievable streets and the Negroes and whites who had, equally, made them that way. But I knew that it was folly, as my father would have said, this bitterness was folly. It was necessary to hold on to the things that mattered. The dead man mattered, the new life mattered; blackness and whiteness did not matter; to believe that they did was to acquiesce in one's own destruction. Hatred, which could destroy so much, never failed to destroy the man who hated and this was an immutable law.

❦ In the next paragraph Baldwin writes a formal conclusion in which he states directly what he believes is the meaning he has discovered in the experiences he has shared with us. Notice the care with which he balances two complicated ideas and the vigor of the language he chooses for the conclusion of the essay. ❧

46   It began to seem that one would have to hold in the mind forever two ideas which seemed to be in opposition. The first idea was acceptance, the acceptance, totally without rancor, of life as it is, and men as they are: in the light of this idea, it goes without saying that injustice is a commonplace. But this did not mean that one could be complacent, for the second idea was of equal power: that one must never, in one's own life, accept these injustices as commonplace but must fight them with all one's strength. This fight begins, however, in the heart and it now had been laid to my charge to keep my own heart free of hatred and despair. This intimation made my heart heavy and, now that my father was irrecoverable, I wished that he had been beside me so that I could have searched his face for the answers which only the future would give me now.

Discussion

- Choose a page in which Baldwin's voice is especially strong. Discuss the elements in voice and compare his voice to Baraka's.
- Baldwin once said, "I remember standing on a streetcorner with the black painter Beauford Delaney down in the Village, waiting for the light to change, and he pointed down and said, 'Look.' I looked and all I saw was water. And he said, 'Look again,' which I did, and I saw oil on the water and the city reflected in the puddle. It was a great revelation to me. I can't explain it. He taught me how to see, and how to trust what I saw. Painters have often taught writers how to see. And once you've had that experience, you see differently . . . I'm still learning how to write. I don't know what technique is. All I know is that you have to make the reader *see* it." Discuss how Baldwin makes the reader see.
- Discuss other methods Baldwin could have used to describe his alienation.
- What could Baldwin have used to focus on his subject instead of his father's death? How would that focus have changed the piece?
- Baldwin has said, "Writing for me must be a very controlled exercise, formed by passions and hopes. . . . The act of writing itself is cold." Discuss what Baldwin meant. Is there evidence of control and coldness in the text? If so, is it effective?
- Baldwin also said, "You learn how little you know. It becomes more difficult because the hardest thing in the world is simplicity. And the most fearful thing, too. It becomes more difficult because you have to strip yourself of all your disguises, some of which you didn't know you had. You want to write a sentence as clean as a bone. That is the goal." Pick a sentence or a paragraph that demonstrates what Baldwin means. Is this simplicity effective?

Activities

- Write a short draft about an emotional experience in your life, such as the death of a parent. Write another paragraph stating what you learned by writing about that experience.
- Take a description you have written, imagine what Baldwin would add to it, and then add it.
- Go through a page of Baldwin and take out the specific details to see what happens to the prose.
- Go back to the anecdote with the waitress and write it from the point of view of the waitress or the friend outside, or someone in the restaurant to see how an incident can be viewed from different angles and how each angle of vision may provide a different meaning.

To Collaborate

- Read Baldwin with one or two classmates with backgrounds different from yours. Prepare a written or oral group report on your different responses to the text.
- Write a team report reviewing Baldwin's piece.

William Gibson

William Gibson is a poet, novelist, nonfiction writer, and playwright. His plays include *Two for the Seesaw, The Miracle Worker,* and *Golda.* And although he is best known for his work for the theater, he confessed to me that he shared a special feeling for his book *A Mass for the Dead,* which was published in 1968 but has been out of print for years. I had told him that my edition is worn and battered from reading and rereading, and that I would teach it, as I once did, if it were in print again. Unfortunately it isn't, but this excerpt will give you an idea of the quality of the book.

Gibson and Baldwin are of the same generation and come from the same city. Both are writers and both here focus on the death of their father. These pairings through the book, and this one certainly, should make it clear that there is no right, no single correct way to deal with a subject in writing, and there is no wrong, no single, ineffective way to deal with a subject in writing. What we can appreciate are two sons writing of their different backgrounds and their similar problems in coming to terms with their fathers and their fathers' deaths. Both are powerful pieces of writing, and we should not try to rate one over the other, but to learn from both of them.

Sunset I Saw By

1   Downtown, in a neighborhood grimy with warehouses and bridges, the old hospital was our gathering place for fifteen days. My father was in a room with two beds, and whoever lay in the other I hardly saw; at his bedside near the window my mother and I met—my sister was away on her vacation—for idle chats, making light of his stay, until the period of tests was done. I was there when our doctor in a careful choice of words explained to my father, propped up in a bedgown, that the nature of his ulcer made surgery a wise procedure, and my father said with a twitch of fear in his downward smile, "All kinds of ulcers, I have to have the worst kind." I knew the fear was unnecessary, but my mother called my sister home from the country, and the three of us were in the hospital corridor the morning my father was wheeled out. The surgeon had informed us the chances were fifty-fifty it was an ulcer he could cut out, in which case the operation would take several hours, else my father would soon be back; we sat in a small corner room, all restive, but I with a book was counting on a long wait, and my sister talked with my mother, still on the edge of a chair. It was not an hour when my mother, now in and out of the corridor, appeared with her face stricken and said, "Daddy's back." I walked in a confusion to his doorway and saw a nurse busy at his bed, with a substance of legs beneath the white spread, but half guessed the surgery was simpler than predicted, and after I returned to our corner room the three of us stood in uncer-

tainty, five minutes, ten minutes, until the surgeon came to find my mother. Courteous and prompt, he said he could do nothing for her husband, it was a stomach cancer and inoperable. Yet only when she stammered, "Doctor, how long does he have?" and the surgeon said, "Six months," did I comprehend the truth: the earth that opened at my feet in that minute was never to close. In the unreal hour that followed my tremulous mother instructed us my father was not to know, and that afternoon it was she who through his fog of anesthesia delivered the good news to him, the ulcer was cured and he would soon be getting better at home.

2   For out of my sickly mother now came a rigor, not unpredictable, which was to cope with whatever befell. Old neighbors, relatives, fellows from the bank, came to congratulate my father in the week he was recovering from the knife, and one took a snapshot of my mother in a rattan chair on the hospital roof; with her children standing beside her—a healthy blonde miss in a summerprint frock, dangling a white purse, and a lank youth in unpressed wool slacks and jacket, shirt wide open—she sits in a neat polka-dot dress, a lean lady of fifty with legs crossed, looking forty in her pearl earrings, and a white chrysanthemum at her bodice; all the feet are sporty in white shoes on the roof tiles, underneath which my father convalesces in his bed, unseen and doomed. It is the faces that baffle me, the youth's in a surly grin, the girl's prettily beaming, my mother's eager with a lipsticked smile to please the camera, all caught in the family lie from which I had fled to my suffering minorities. Only, my mother's hands are knotted against her stomach, and I was to watch how her bright denial of the underworld was armor to carry her through it; back of the brittle smile, which for half a year she wore for my father, was the durable will of an older mother who had buried a husband and fourteen sons.

3   I was at the hospital with the Ford the morning my father was discharged, and the four of us rode home together; I drove in the slow lane of traffic, not to jar his abdominal wound. Still in some pain, but out again in the air of life, my father at a back window gazed contentedly at whatever we passed, and with her gay chatter my mother beside him shared his view of the towering city in which he had been born, of the midtown streets they had strolled in the horsecar days of their courtship, of the bridge over the islanded river and the green ballpark where Sundays in the benchstands they would not again sit with orange pop and franks, of the boulevard they had often crossed from the prosperity in their winebrick colony to the poverty in her sister Minnie's flat, and at last the parkway, pleasant with grass and woodland and the vision they first had together from it of rooftops in a suburban multitude below, and among these, in a street still young with saplings, the little house in which he was to die. I parked at the curb, my mother hurried up the driveway to unlock the front door from within, my sister stood by with his suitcase, and I helped my father out of the back seat; with him bent on my forearm we advanced up the steps, past my mother, and through the sun porch into the comfort of the living room, where my father, welcomed home by us as he looked around at his easy chair, the sofa and twin lamptables, his piano and stool, startled us with a half-

sob and, still upon my arm, cried tears. Seated with him on the sofa, my mother was all cheery banter, promising his strength back. I then supported him up the staircase, along the hallway to the front room, and onto the twin bed that waited with coverlet turned down, where I left him to be undressed by my mother and put to bed.

4   So began the six months of an old sorrow, but new to us. I took a step so natural that only now it seems a choice, I broke up my flat and came back to live in my room. My sister turned to the faith that moved mountains, was unfailingly at mass on Sunday, in the city prayed in a church before work each morning, and, making novena after novena at night with other petitioners on their knees, read from her prayerbook that "all you ask the Father in My name He will give you"; a literal believer, she asked that hers not die. I was to make the same prayer, but only in my dreams. My mother's lips, whatever the hope of holy miracle in her head, were tight; she told the truth to almost nobody, not even to my father's mother and sisters in Jersey, lest someone in a slip let it out in his hearing, and month after month the air in the house was heavier with our secret.

5   For all, the first month was the easiest. My father was incapacitated most by the wound, which knitted, and aided at the outset by whosever arm was handy, but soon unhelped, he was back and forth the dozen steps to the toilet, dressed himself, shaved, and was of good cheer; a higher official from the bank, visiting, bade him not to hurry his return to work. Downstairs, my mother and the official sat on the sun porch in a low-voiced conversation, in which he told her of the bank's decision to continue my father on salary until his death. Though weekdays my sister and I left for work, neighbors and other visitors came in and my mother was not always alone, except in her thoughts; half the time the housework was shared by her "oldest and dearest friend" Nelie, who at night slept on the sofa in a dusting cap, and Minnie arriving by subway and bus for the day would fill the house with her "for Gawd's sake" joshing of her brother-in-law. Only these two women, the one monosyllabic, the other our generous bungler, knew what my mother knew. My father grew strong enough to make his way downstairs, a gala day; now the household was almost normal, he tuned the radio to baseball, tried the piano, and in the flowering backyard sat on the springy chair my mother brought him, head back and eyes closed, renewing himself in the sun. The boys from the bank who visited in threes and fours found him there, all smiles to see them, and hale enough for a cigarette— forbidden on the ulcer diet, cigarettes were again permitted by the merciful doctor—which my father explained as a success of the surgery. For such guests my mother was blithe, and for the first time kept liquor in the house to serve, instead of pineapple juice; new to bartending, she made highballs with ginger ale in her tallest tumblers, half whiskey, and the visits were gay indeed. On the weekend I chauffeured my parents on gentle rides of a few miles out of one community into another, replicas, but a change of scene for my father . . .

6   Without appetite, he was growing thin, and the strength was reluctant to come into his legs, but it came. It would have been less difficult to see him

worse; what was grievous was to watch his gratitude in the abortive recoveries. Once again on my mother's arm, setting himself distances, he left the bedpan behind, and for a week sat at open windows in his pants, shirt, slippers, and then worked his way down the banister to the living room, to the sun porch, to the backyard, and the color of pleasure returned to his face, each day a restoral, each destination a further reach: the next shock of hemorrhage erased it all. My mother settled him in the bed, her hands quick with the ice-bag, and quick in the kitchen to boil and assemble the parts of the hypodermic, but upstairs she was timid to pierce his arm with it, and I took over the task. In bed my father lay with eyes closed, the rubber ice-bag on his belly, a blanket keeping him warm in the heat of the summer day, and slept; and I walked the five blocks to my store, where I put aside the play and undertook to write him my parting word, or loveletter, which was a poem.

7   I was three weeks over it; he was bedridden still, or again, the morning I took the typed page in, said I had written something for him, and left it in his hands. Back now on the job, I could not linger but in any case was embarrassed to, the forty lines were too frank an avowal of how much of him I hoped was in me, named his goodness as the homework of my knowledge of man, and, muted by what I could not mention except as the fate all must share, said neither of us was to enter the silence with my debt unspoken. Home at five-thirty, I went upstairs to his room to say hello, as always, and saw my page on the night table between the twin beds; his eyes following mine, my father said, "Bill, it's beautiful," and I said I was glad, there was a pause, and he said, "What does it mean?" So, in some despair at the isolateness even of my art, I sat upon the other bed, and with the poem in hand explained it word by word in prose.

8   Summer went under, the year was ebbing and so too the outer edge of my father's world; the last time he took to his chair in the backyard he grew uneasy, and shuffled indoors, not to emerge again. I was not in the house the evening he forewent the downstairs half, and with it the brotherly companion of his life, the Horace Waters piano. Up or down the ten steps to the bedroom, he would now sit upon them midway, for breath; on a visit to my sister the giant youth who was once her beau saw my father at the stairfoot pause, hand on newel, awaiting the will to climb, and simply carried him in his arms up the stairs.

9   At the bedside there stood henceforth an enamelled white bucket, containing a few inches of water, for the next spewing of blood. It was not yet frequent, but my father was enfeebled by loss of hunger and abdominal pain, glum that the incision was so slow to heal, and critical of the city doctor who he said was "not doing me any good"; at the doctor's advice we called in a local "consultant," and on the sun porch my mother confided the facts to his suave face. For a month my father's hopes were up as the new doctor wrote out a variety of prescriptions, my mother observed to my sister only that the pharmacist was his brother, and the bottles of expensive medicine accumulated on the night table, to no effect. Exhausted by a third and fourth vomiting my father said, "He doesn't understand my case," and my mother called in another doctor to add encouragement; this man said bluntly he "hated like hell" to have

such a patient, sat at my father's bedside with his bagful of useless instruments, scribbled a prescription for sugar pills, and that autumn lent his burly comfort more to us than to my father, who, emptier of faith, said indifferently, "He's a fake."

10   Nothing in the weariness of his day upstairs could distract him from the gnawing ache in his stomach. Off for work, my sister and I were in the bedroom each morning to say goodbye—I was old enough to kiss him again, the sweet odor of his brow at my lips recalling the Sunday mornings when as children we climbed into bed with him to giggle over his nonsensical stories, all forgotten, but not how we loved the odor of his pillow dent—and until evening my mother, in the midst of housecleaning, tried to lighten his pain with a diversity of moves. She would plump up two bed-pillows for the mahogany rocker so my father, sitting at the window, could have a view of the red-tinned roof of our sun porch with the bit of tranquil street beyond, and in my sister's room she plumped up pillows for another chair at the rear window to which he came to see his backyard garden, kept trim by her for his eyes; back and forth between the two chairs, in one soon restless for the other, my father travelled on her arm, and in them an hour of the long morning, an hour of the longer afternoon, would pass. The pillows were needed because the flesh was leaving him, his buttocks were bony, and more often he was at rest upon one of the twin beds. On good days, with my mother's support he would get into the old pants and shirt that now hung loose on him, and feel more optimistic for being dressed; other days he kept to his bed, in pajamas, where my mother would bathe him with alcohol, and twice daily unmake and remake the bed to freshen it for his back. Left alone, my father would read for an hour—a newspaper, a cheap novel his chick or I brought him from the drugstore library—or dial around my little radio for some daytime music, find only the soap operas, and click it off. Visitors came, to pass another hour. My mother would use it for downstairs work, but whatever chores she could bring up to the bedroom she saved for their departure, peeling vegetables then in the rocker, brightly gossiping and misquoting the doctor in prediction of an upturn tomorrow to perk up his spirits. It was all in vain, the heel of his hand pressing was futile to ease the bellyache always under his ribs, and worsening; his one desire was for the morphine.

11   My father disrespected himself for asking it of us, and my mother and I were uncertain when to grant it. In the kitchen the doctor had counselled us to be sparing, how insufferable the cancer might grow was not known, and if we habituated his body to morphine in the beginning we could give him no help at the end; concerned thus, my mother and I would conspire to talk him out of it. My father at first was with us, still expecting nature to mend what the surgeon had somehow botched, and to be a "hophead" when on his feet again was a worry to him. All day he bit down the words, until I was home to boil the needle; but the interludes of numbness to the pain grew briefer. It was less often we heard him say he "wouldn't want to get to depend on it," and what in August was a contest of my father with himself had by September turned into

one between him and us. I was acceding to his wish for the morphine before I
left in the morning, and my mother withstood his pleas throughout the afternoon as best she could, then yielded too, overcoming her finickiness about the
needle. To see my father relax after it—going limp, murmuring "how good that
felt," letting his eyebrows unknit at last—eased us too, but we bargained with
him to put it off, for two hours, one hour, half an hour, and would agree to a
time by the clock upon his night table; he would lie with eyes sidelong to it,
and be unable not to plead with us again, too early. I injected his arm a few
times with sterile water or a solution of half a pellet, but he was not deceived,
accused me of it, and distrusted my denials; our needs had parted company,
and the candor in his blue eyes was clouded with a new doubt of us. . . .

12   I had gone on a second leave from my job, and was hanging around the
house. I ran errands to the avenue for my mother, like taking a suit of my
father's to be cleaned and pressed, and three days later fetched it again to put
in the downstairs closet, knowing it would next be worn by him in a coffin. I
shovelled coal into the furnace, and fed the dog, and settled to work at my play,
and wrote a letter to my teacher apologizing that I could not; I read until my
head was dulled, and waited for my father to die.

13   Daily I was in the mahogany rocker in his sickroom to keep him company,
but the talk was a trickle. I would ask could I get him anything, he woud say
no; I was not in his focus, another of the liars, and I sat in a misery of silence
with fifty years of him to ask into, too late, my begetter was dying with the riddle
of our life untold; I would ask was he comfortable enough, he would say yes;
bedridden, his head awry to the window like a plant to the thin sunlight, he lay
with eyes large as a child's and blank, lost in whatever a dying man thinks, why
me, and I was of the enemy who would outlive him, tonguetied with it, too
craven to say a word that would confess the last of our differences and let us
share it for an hour; I would ask did he want the radio on, he would say no.
Dumb in that bedroom with the alarm clock ticking, the cottonlace curtains
moveless, the boudoir suite of twin beds with ruffles and chifforobe and mir-
rored vanity-table so feminine around us, every surface with its doily, I felt an
ennui that would not let me breathe, and what was in my heart I hardly knew,
so never said, that he was my true love and I could not forgive it in my mother
that she was forever between us. I would fix the needle whenever he spoke for
it now, lulling his organs to sleep, but not the scatter of outlaw cells in them
that had shrunk his flesh to this, so close to inhuman earth again; whatever
flowering had been possible to it was at an end. One such afternoon he asked
what time it was and I told him, he seemed asleep, two minutes later he asked
again what time it was and I told him, and after some thought he said in a
murmur, "Almost the same time." Interminably in the ebb of sunlight the clock
ticked on, afternoon into afternoon, and I would think, Die, let me go.

14   Poor as it was, my father clung to consciousness. Downstairs at lunch my
mother and I were interrupted by a dreadful thud in the ceiling; with her at my
heels, I was up the stairs three at a time and into the sickroom, where on the
floor between the twin beds I saw my father inert on his back, and knowing the

scream I heard was my own, an oddity I had read of, I ran to lift, pull, push him onto the bed, but he was dead weight and I was too rattled; my mother helped, the two of us falling upon the blankets with more than a corpse, he was breathing. My mother nursed him back to an awareness of us which was confused, and after that he was rarely without a bedside watcher. In December he lay so skeletal that his bones poked at his skin, chafing it to bedsores, and these nagged him in every which position; my mother laved him with alcohol, and cut up rolls of absorbent cotton to tape as pads onto his shoulders, elbows, hips, and with pillows under the blankets kept their burden from his shins. Morning, afternoon, night, she "took wonderful care of him," her own face a wedge of worn flesh, pale and inexhaustible. I was not loath when, the leave up, I could escape to my job; and after six weeks in Mt. Vernon my grandmother was taken home by Ada for Christmas in Trenton, not to see her son again, but it was a suffering to sit with him now. Yet my mother sat with him, and supported his head in her hands when every few days he retched over the white bucket until "all his insides came out" in great bloody chunks, and death would not them part.

15   It was my sister's habit, after frost killed off the backyard garden, to bring her father home a handful of flowers she bought in the subway, but toward the end his mind was too errant for such tokens; one evening he stared at me and asked who I was. I tried not to be hurt when for two days he would not have me in the room, yet I took it as the rebuke for my life. In and out of a half-delirium my father more than once called for all the lights on, the frilly lamps and the pink ceiling fixture, and required everyone in the household to sit where he could see us; abruptly then he would banish lights and family, to lie in the dark, and we heard him muttering to himself that he was "too young to die," the spectre was out now, and my father with his fist banged on the wall, intoning, "I don't want to die, I don't want to die," banged methodically on the wall till that hammering unnerved us. My mother, putting on the lamp to dissuade him, would be pained with the sight of his knuckles bleeding.

16   In the last week he went blind. Christmas was with us again, and in the sickroom—grown brilliant with the arrival of poinsettias, other plants, bouquets, and a hundred greeting cards propped everywhere, even atop the radiators—my mother set up a diminutive fir and hung it with a few of the ornaments that had been ours for two decades; my father was unable to make any of it out. Of that joyless day I retain little, but my sister remembers how our mother described each plant in the room to him. Presents too were there, a vestige of the old spill of plenty, and become a bitterness; we put into my father's fingers such things as the soft new pajamas he would never wear, and earlier he had instructed his chick to shop with his money from the vanity drawer, so my mother unwrapped the three or four packages he could not see, stockings, a waffle iron, a slip, his last gifts to her. Or not quite, for in that week when her face was gone my father held to her fingers, said, "Oh God, how I love you," and left her that too.

17   Two days passed, and my sister and I at the bedside each morning, kissing

his brow and taking with us the word or two he murmured, saw no change; that he was sleeping the third morning was not unusual. Yet a few hours later my mother, seated in the rocker in the quiet sickroom, heard a break in the rhythm of his breathing. She called to her spinster schoolmate, and for some minutes the two women kept watch at the bed with its burden of skin and bone, which breathed, and faltered, took in a mouthful of air, exhaled, left off; my mother said, "Is he gone?" and the emaciated head on the pillow breathed again, and the spinster said almost but told her not to "cry or talk to him, you'll only bring him back," and so my mother stood over him, dumb, waiting for the next breath. It never came, and when she knew the discoloring body was at the end of its effort to live my mother said, "Now I can cry."

18   Around his unseeing corpse, the household which was his lifework slowly set about its business of survival. My mother went into the neighbor's phone, and throughout the afternoon the front and back doors let in a traffic of doctor, undertaker and assistants, women of the family, neighbors, a houseful simmering with the suppressed excitement of death; at work my sister was interrupted by word her father was "very ill," knew, and travelled home, where she found my mother red-eyed over a cup of tea in the kitchen and the funeral arrangements in the expert hands of Will's widow, who had buried a second husband in recent years; upstairs in the bedroom with pails, scalpels, tubes, the embalmers were at their labors over my father's cadaver on a table, disembowelling it, draining off its corruptible fluids, and repacking its refuse of viscera, disinfected. My sister escorted my mother away to buy the first of the black clothes that she would wear for a year.

19   Inaccessible by phone, I knew none of this, served out my workday among storage bins, and, homecoming at dusk to the monotony of leafless hedge and stoops, saw the door to our house was hung with a lamentation of flowers. Inside, the downstairs was lively enough with others moving the furniture back for the wake, and after I talked with my mother I took my way up the carpeted steps to the hall; here all was still, and I stood in the doorway of the bedroom. The embalmers gone, nothing in the room was different since morning except that now on the twin bed my father, clad in his gray suit, pallid hands clasped, lay forever dead, and his good face which was like no other in the world was a stranger to me. I went no nearer, and I had no tears, something in me had become stony in those six months, and it would be weeks before I cried, but once begun, was never quite done, for of course he never let me go. After a time I rejoined the living, and when later the coffin was delivered the men carried my father downstairs in a wicker basket, to create a flowery retreat of the living room with his corpse as its centerpiece, and my mother shut the keyboard lid of the piano; upstairs she stripped the deathbed, and remade it with clean sheets. It was occupied that night by the spinster in her dusting cap, and in the adjacent bed my mother for the first time slept without the sound of her husband's breathing in the room, or perhaps did not sleep.

20   In the morning the undertaker was at our door with his discreet box of cosmetics, to touch up the unstable face of my father, and so opened the wake.

For three days and nights the little house was crowded with people, all the other faces of my life, the half-forgotten neighbors of childhood, my aunts, uncles, cousins, clerks by the score from the bank, each of whom stood his silent minute at the coffin and then lingered, in muted conversation, from dining room to sun porch; the sheaves of flowers they sent so swamped the house that everywhere they were stepped upon, and were even hung on the walls. In the sickly fragrance my father's mother for three days immovably filled the easy chair opposite the body, hardly speaking, hardly caring, sat. In the kitchen, with its swingdoor closed, the talk was more cheerful. The coffee pot was always perking on the range, the tablecloth was set with platterfuls of cold cuts, salads, cakes brought in by the neighbors, my mother was in and out anxious that everyone eat, and the visitors on chairs, or squeezed into the breakfast nook, or standing with cups in hand against the refrigerator and sink, gossiped of other matters; I sat with them chatting, nodding, smiling, until a sudden widening of my inner eye saw what lay beyond the swingdoor, my father already forgotten, and I condemned us all. Only once was my mother somewhat beside herself, upstairs, when she and Ben's minx collapsed in a hysteria of laughing, excusable as "something Irv must want us to do." I had asked one friend to come, and so at the coffin my mother first received the girl who would bear two of her grandsons, and led her from the dead man to introduce her to the family and the food; the girl in wonder took in how gentiles mourned. By ten o'clock at night the house was emptied, save for a relative or two who slept over, ourselves, and the body. On the eve of the funeral the bedroom allotments put me downstairs on the sofa not far from the coffin; I awoke in the small hours to lie with eyes open and breath held, listening, half afraid of the waxen effigy that so unreasonably had befriended me, and I had somehow let die.

21   It was an icy day when the hearse waited at the curb and barren tree, with a black limousine behind, and from our house in both directions the cars of relatives and friends waited one after the other along the street. In the living room some folding chairs had been delivered by the undertaker, but too few, and the fifty or so who had come for the minister's valediction were backed into doorways, stood against walls, sat two on each step of the staircase that led up from the dining room; on the top step, unseen of all, sat my mother. I have no recollection of anything said by the minister, a stranger to us, but when the brief ceremony died into silence I heard from above me a scream, bulletlike, abruptly sent and broken off, and knew it was my mother. I was embarrassed by it, yet now realize she chose that step because from nowhere else could she see over heads down into the coffin and take leave of my father's face as the lid was shut upon it. So he disappeared finally from our sight, and was carried in the coffin out the front door, and was placed in the elegant hearse, and the sidewalk was busy with the dispersal of people to cars, and at the limousine a gathering of women in black—his mother, sisters, wife, daughter—was helped in, I joined them, and the headlights of the many cars came on, pale and dreamlike in the day; in slow procession we followed the hearse that bore my father's body out of the dream the four of us had lived in together.

22   The cemetery gates were a dozen miles away, and here, at a tombstone among others in a field patchy with snow, the grave was open. At the edge of this pit in the frozen earth my mother, with my sister and me at either elbow, and roundabout a silent party of watchers, saw the coffin lowered by straps until it came to rest, with something in it that was and was not her husband, and not in virgin clay; deeper were the remains of my uncle Will and his two children, in ground offered by his widow, and the women who stood in survival near that pit wept for more than my father, who was the oldest in it, having lived for fifty years, nine months, and twenty-five days; in her black half-veil my mother endured the last minute of rite and prayer, the flower tossed in, the first shov-elful of dirt, and then turned away to the icy lane and the limousine. It drove us out of the gates, no headlights of procession now, a single carful of mourners going back to an empty house.

23   Yet it was late night before we were alone in it. Other carfuls returned to the street, and people again, food, a distraction of voices, filled the downstairs till dusk came, some of my mother's kin and her in-laws stayed for supper, and she sent my sister with her suitor off to the movies, common sense was the mood, but the hour was inevitable when all the dishes were washed, dried, put away, the comforters were gone, and my sister and I sat with our mother in a house which had disowned us. It was the last day of the year, and in the living room, so void of its coffin, the three of us with our tired talk saw the old year out, the worst we had known and good riddance, but with it came to another end; the decorum around our eyes, in chintz drapes, sofa and coffee table, con-sole radio, easy chair, the upright piano and its stool, had been set to rights and was as before, only its heartbeat was done, the house too was dead, and not one of us but through its walls saw the reality of winter on the plot of earth under which my father in his gray suit was laid to rot. We had come to the end of our tale as a family, now each of us must find his own and other place in the world.

24   So in the first hour of the new year we separated for bed, upstairs, and hereafter lay not quite apart either, when in the dark of different rooms, and under a dozen other roofs, in each of our dreaming heads my father lived again, and died too, over and over.

A Writer's Notes for a Second Reading

As a writer, I am particularly impressed by the texture of this piece of writing. Gibson, line by line, creates the world in which he lived and the relationship between the peo-ple in that world in all their complexity.

    This is never a piece of glib, superficial writing. It is significant and painful as he explores his own reactions to the death of his father. He is specific, honest, revealing in his writing. And the more specific he is about his own world, his writing takes on that quality of art and becomes more universal.

When I read this piece I often stop, not so much to admire his writing but to reflect and to think upon my reflections. I remember my family, our life together and what it has meant to me, good and bad. He takes me deeply into his world and in doing that I see my own world a little better than before.

Discussion

• Describe Gibson's voice, the style with which he writes. How is it different from or similar to Baldwin, Trillin, Tuchman?

• Discuss the techniques Gibson uses to describe the people in his piece and their world. How do his descriptions change at those times of the greatest horror?

• Discuss the way in which Gibson and Baldwin each put their father's dying in the context of a specific time and place.

• Discuss the techniques Gibson and Baldwin use to put themselves in the piece of writing and to get out of the piece of writing. What are the advantages and disadvantages of the writer being there or not being there?

• Can you imagine some of the changes that Gibson would have to make to turn this chapter into a scene in a play?

• Gibson writes in fully developed paragraphs. What is similar between his paragraphs writing about personal experience and Allen's and Quindlen's paragraphs writing argument?

Activities

• Take a paragraph of a piece of your own and try to write it as Gibson might, to see how his voice differs from yours. You should not adopt his voice, but merely do this to see another way you might write.

• Take a 1000-word chunk of Gibson and cut it to 250 words to see what is lost and what is gained.

• Write about your relationship with a parent or someone with whom you have lived. Reread it to make sure that the reader will see the general issues in your specific account. If you have to make changes, make them, but try not to tell the reader directly how to think or feel.

• Take a scene within this chapter and write it as a scene in a play or movie or television production. Make up the dialogue, of course. By doing this you may discover some important differences between drama and prose.

To Collaborate

• Go through the text with a fellow reader to find the best examples of texture in writing. Work together to make an oral report to the class on writing with texture, citing your examples.

• Work together to revise a page of the text as it might have been written by the father, his wife, a priest, a social worker, the doctor.

Charles Simic

Imagine that you pick up the telephone one morning and someone asks you if you'll accept a grant for the next five years. They will pay you a thousand dollars for each year of your life and add another. Each year they will increase it by another thousand dollars. And what do I have to do, you ask? Whatever you have been doing, whatever you want to do.

Charlie Simic accepted. It was from the MacArthur Foundation and he had won an award for which you cannot apply, the so-called genius grant.

It was not his first award. He has won the Di Castagnola Award, the Harriet Monroe Poetry Award, the Edgar Allan Poe Award, the P.E.N. Translation Prize, and awards from the American Academy of Arts and Letters and the National Institute of Arts and Letters. He continued to teach at the University of New Hampshire after he received the MacArthur grant (I have known him as a concerned teacher and responsible, involved colleague) and he has continued to write more poetry, extending the horizons of his craft. He has also begun an autobiography, the beginning of which I am reprinting here.

Simic was born in Yugoslavia in 1938, and his story is that old American story of people who survive war and political changes and come to a new world. In this selection he tells the story of a boy during war that has been told in the movies *Hope and Glory* and *Empire of the Sun*. It is a story that particularly fascinates me because in combat I often fought while children played in the same streets or fields. I wondered how they would survive and how they would be affected if they did. Simic tells us of his own war and his own survival, the story being told in Asia, Africa, Central America, the Middle East, the story that probably will be told and retold during our lifetime.

In the Beginning . . .

I

1   The radio. It sits on the table by my bed. It has a dial which lights up. The stations have names. I can't read yet, but I make others read them to me. There's Oslo, Lisbon, Moscow, Berlin, Budapest, and many more. One moves the red arrow to a spot and hears a strange language or unfamiliar music. At ten o'clock the stations sign off. The war is on. The year is 1943.

2   The nights of my childhood were spent in the company of that radio. I attribute the insomnia from which I still suffer to its temptations. I couldn't keep my hands off it. Even after the stations went silent, I kept turning the dial and listening to various noises. Once I heard beeps in Morse code. Spies, I thought. Often I'd catch a distant station so faint I'd have to turn the sound all

the way up and press my ear against the rough burlap that covered the speaker. Somewhere dance music was playing or the language was so attractive I'd listen to it for a long time, as if on the verge of understanding.

3   All this was strictly forbidden. I was supposed to be asleep. Come to think of it, I must have been afraid to be alone in that big room. The war was on. Terrible things happened at night. There was a curfew. Someone was late. Someone else was pacing up and down in the next room. Black paper curtains hung on the windows. It was dangerous even to peek between them at the street—the dark and empty street.

4   I see myself standing on tiptoes, one hand on the curtain, wanting to look but afraid of the light the radio tubes cast dimly through its trellised back onto the bedroom wall. My father is late and outside the roofs are covered with snow.

5   The Germans bombed Belgrade in April of 1941 when I was three years old. The building across the street was hit and destroyed. I don't remember anything about that bomb. The next day we left the city on foot. I remember a beautiful meadow, great clouds overhead, and then suddenly a plane flying very low.

6   Did we leap into a ditch by the railroad tracks, or was that some other time? How many of us were there? I remember my mother but not my father. There were strangers, too. I see their hunched backs, see them running with their bundles, but no faces . . . My film keeps breaking. An image here and there, but not much continuity. And poor lighting. I have to strain my eyes, and then the match goes out, so to speak.

7   Was the world really so gray then? In my early memories, it's almost always late fall. The soldiers are gray and so are the people.

8   The Germans are standing on the street corner. We are walking by. "Don't look at them," my mother whispers. I look anyway, and one of them smiles. For some reason that makes me afraid.

9   One night the Gestapo came to arrest my father. This time I was asleep and woke suddenly to the bright lights. They were rummaging everywhere and making a lot of noise. My father was already dressed. He was saying something, probably making a joke. That was his style. No matter how bleak the situation he'd find something funny to say. Years later, surrounded by doctors and nurses and in the throes of a heart attack, he asked for pizza and beer. The doctors were afraid that he had suffered brain damage.

10   I guess I went back to sleep after he was taken away. In any case, nothing much happened that time. He was released. It wasn't his fault his kid brother stole a German army truck to take his girlfriend for a spin. He didn't even get shot, that brother of his. The Germans were astonished—almost amused—by his stupidity. They shipped him off to work in Germany. They tried to, that is, but he wiggled through their fingers.

11   In the meantime, we kids were playing war. All the kids were playing war. We took prisoners. We fell down dead. We machinegunned a lot. How we loved the sound of a machine gun!

12   This kind of playing drove the grown-ups crazy. All the real shooting—and these kids kept firing their imaginary guns. It didn't take much to make our parents fly off the handle. They'd look so serious, so preoccupied, and then all of a sudden—pop! You'd see a woman stop on the street and slap her child, seemingly for no reason at all, and with everybody watching.

13   You couldn't blame them, really. I had a friend who could imitate an air-raid siren perfectly. Every time his parents locked him in, he'd stand on his sixth-floor balcony and wail. People on the street below would plead with him to stop. He wouldn't. In fact, he'd get even louder, even better. We thought it was very funny and a little scary, too.

14   The building we lived in was in the center of the city on a small side street near the main post office and the parliament. A dangerous place to be. That's what we thought in the spring of 1944 when the English and the Americans started bombing the city.

15   It was Easter Sunday. The dining-room table was set with our best china when the planes came. We could hear them. The windows were open since it was such a nice spring day.

16   "Americans are throwing Easter eggs," my father said. Then, it started thundering. We ran down to the cellar. The building shook. People huddled on the floor. One could hear glass breaking up above. Some kid ran to the stairs to take a look. His mother screamed.

17   Then it was all over. We came out. The street was dark. All the dust of the city had risen in the air. The buildings in sight were still standing. A man covered with fallen plaster walked by telling everybody that a certain neighborhood had been levelled. That was astonishing. It was one of the poorest neighborhoods in the city. There were no Germans there.

18   The next day the Allies came again and it was the same. They never hit anything of military importance. A bomb landed on our sidewalk. It didn't explode. My mother was for clearing out immediately; my father was for staying. She prevailed.

19   The roads out of the city were full of refugees. The planes kept returning. We approved of Americans and the English bombing Germans. I never heard anyone complain. They were our allies. We loved them. Still, with their poor marksmanship, it was dangerous to remain in the city.

20   My grandfather had a summer house twenty miles from Belgrade. When we arrived there, my father's side of the family had already assembled. They argued all the time. In addition to the German occupation, there was a civil war in Yugoslavia. There were at least half-a-dozen factions made up of Royalists, Communists, Fascists, collaborators, fighting. The family was divided bitterly between the Royalists and the Communists. My grandfather remained neutral. They were all the same, in his opinion.

21   As for my mother, she said nothing. She disliked my father's people. She came from an old middle-class family while they were bluecollar workers. She was educated in Paris while they spent their time getting drunk in low dives.

It's astonishing that she and my father ever got married. My father had gone to the university, was a successful engineer now, but he hated my mother's world.

22   It wasn't long before he left us. Early one morning my mother and I accompanied him to the small and crowded train station. By the way he looked at me and by the way he hugged me I knew this was no ordinary journey. I was told nothing. Ten years would pass before I would see my father again. People would ask, "Where's your father?" I couldn't tell them. All my mother knew that day was that he was going to try to get to Italy, but there was no news of him for a long time.

23   We stayed with my grandparents. Summer came. The bombing of Belgrade continued. We could see the planes high up over the city. Our house was on a hill overlooking the river Sava and we had a fine view in that direction. Columns of smoke went up as bombs fell. We'd be eating watermelon in our garden watching the city burn. My grandmother would cross herself repeatedly. The dogs would get restless.

24   The fighting was intensifying. The Russian Army was in southern Romania pushing toward Belgrade along the Danube. Locally, the various factions were settling old scores. There was a lot of indiscriminate killing. After I found some bodies early one morning in a roadside ditch, they did not let me go out any more. Our neighbors were executed in their own home. The people across the street just disappeared. Nothing happened to us. My mother was very pregnant and wobbled around. She had no politics, neither did my grandfather. That doesn't explain it, of course. We were just lucky.

25   It was a relief when the Russians came. At least now there were only two sides fighting. The Germans had retreated across the river from us. One could see them go about their business. Then they brought some artillery pieces. The Russians had their own big guns. You didn't have to be a genius to figure that if they both start shooting we'd be right in the middle.

26   Pregnant as she was, my mother decided to flee with me to a village further up beyond the hills, where we had a friend. My grandparents retreated to the cellar.

27   It was early October 1944. The road to the village was empty and so was the farmhouse of our friend where we found just a very old woman who gave us goat's milk. The whole of that day we sat and waited in silence. Toward dusk we heard steps. A dishevelled and bloodied peasant told us, without even stopping, that the Germans were coming this way and killing everybody in sight.

28   There was nothing else to do but hurry back to my grandfather. The old woman stayed behind. We were back on that empty road lined with poplars. It was so quiet we could hear our steps. All of a sudden there were shots. A bullet whizzed by. My mother pulled me to the ground and threw herself over me. Then it was quiet again. Just our hearts beating. No more shots.

29   After a long, long time, we looked up. The sky was cloudless. The first few evening stars were in place. We got up and stood for a while in the long shadow of a tree. When we entered my grandfather's house, he was at the table drinking a toast with a Russian officer and grinning at us.

30   My wartime adventures really began the day the Russians liberated Belgrade. We had gotten back to our apartment quickly since my mother wanted to be near her doctor. The very next day she managed somehow to get herself a cot in the basement of a private clinic to await the termination of her pregnancy. As it turned out, she stayed there a month. I was entrusted to the care of an aunt of my mother, the only relative we had left in the city.

31   Nana was the black sheep in that family. It was said that she cheated on her old husband, had spent money recklessly, and used bad language. That's what I loved about her. She would swear often and shamelessly.

32   I've no idea where Nana's husband was, or why she was still in the city. I suspect she had her own private reasons. This was the second day of the liberation and there was still some street fighting. To my surprise she let me go out on the street alone. There were other children out there, to be sure, but, still, this was strange. Often I'd return home and find no one. Later I'd see her walking down the street, extremely elegant with her gloves and high heels, on the sidewalk strewn with the rubble of recent fighting. She'd be glad to see me, and would have something special for me to eat. I've no memory of what we did in the evenings. Our building was almost empty. The lights were often out. There was nothing to do but sleep a lot. One morning, on waking early, I saw my aunt washing her breasts in a pail of cold water. She caught me watching her and turned around. Then she did a little dance, naked like that.

33   I was happy. My friends and I had plenty to do during the day and plenty of time to do it. There was no school and our parents were either absent or busy. We roamed the neighborhood, climbed over the ruins, and watched the Russians and our Partisans at work. There were still Germans holed up in a couple of places. We'd hear shots and take off running. There was a lot of military equipment lying around. The guns were gone, but there was other stuff. I got myself a German helmet. I wore empty ammo belts. I had a bayonet.

34   One day I was sitting with a friend in front of our building when a column of German prisoners came by escorted by some women soldiers. "Let's go and shoot Germans, kids!" said one cheerily. Well, this was a bit too much. We said no. Actually, I doubt we gave them a straight answer. One learned early to be circumspect and cautious. We followed them as far as the corner and then turned back. I remember one tall blonde German straight as a broomstick. The others looked humpbacked in comparison.

35   Later we went anyway. There was a large old cemetery nearby with a huge church, and beyond it the fairgrounds where, supposedly, they were shooting Germans. We met some children on the way who said that they were from the circus. It was true. There used to be a circus tent on the fairgrounds, but now only a few trailers were left on its edge. These were odd looking children, barely dressed, and they spoke a foreign language among themselves.

36   "Show him what you can do," said my friend who had met them before. They obliged. A little boy stood on his hands. Then, he removed one hand, and was left standing on the other. A dark-eyed girl leaned back until her head emerged from between her legs.

37   "They have no bones," my friend said. The dead have no bones, I thought. They fall over like sacks of flour.

38   The war went on. The Germans had dug-in west of the city on the other side of the rivers Sava and Danube. The Russians had left the fighting to the Yugoslavs while they advanced north toward Hungary. All able men were conscripted and the fighting was fierce. Belgrade was a city of the wounded. One saw people on crutches on every street. They walked slowly, at times carrying a mess kit with their daily ration. There were soup kitchens where such people got their meals.

39   Once, chased by a friend, I rounded the street corner at top speed and collided with one of these invalids, spilling his soup on the sidewalk. I won't forget the look he gave me. "Oh child!" he said softly. I was too stunned to speak. I didn't even have the sense to help him pick up his crutch. I watched him do it himself.

40   By the time my brother was born, and he and my mother came home, I was in business, selling gunpowder. It worked this way. Many of us kids had stashes of ammunition we had collected after the street fighting. The gunpowder from these rounds was sold to older kids who in turn were selling it to the fishermen on the Danube. This last part I cannot guarantee. "Selling" is also the wrong word. We exchanged gunpowder for old comic books, cans of food, and God-knows-what-else? I remember a particularly tasty can of American corned beef which I devoured all by myself sitting in the winter sunlight behind the great Byzantine church of St. Mark.

41   I've no idea how long this went on. I had a large laundry basket full of ammunition hidden in the cellar. Removing the gunpowder was a one-man job. I placed the bullet part into the kitchen spigot and yanked the round sideways. Absolute secrecy, of course, was required. My mother had no idea how I spent my time until one of the kids on our block lost his hands. He was trying to remove the long black sticks of gunpowder from some sort of grenade. That's what he told me later, while I tried to avoid looking at his two newly healed and still red stumps.

42   I started school in spring of 1945, but don't remember much of it. My parents taught me how to read early on, and I breezed through the first few grades. The classes that spring were sporadic. My interests, in any case, were elsewhere. The streets were full of semi-abandoned children. Gangs were being formed. Legendary toughs held whole neighborhoods in terror.

43   There was so much to worry about. We had no news of my father. Unknown to us, he had been locked up as a spy by the Germans in Italy and was about to be liberated by the Americans. He had no desire to return. He didn't like the Communists and he didn't get along with my mother. Before the war he had worked for an American company, had many American business connections, and had always wanted to see that country.

44   There were other reasons, too, for concern. The Communists were firmly in power. People were being arrested left and right. In school there was indoctrination.

45   I remember a young man coming to talk to us about Communism. The subject of religion came up. He said there was no God, and asked if anyone of us believed in God. Everybody kept their mouths shut except one kid who said he did. The fellow asked the kid what can God do? Everything, the kid said. Well, the fellow said, if you were to ask him to help you pick this table up, would he do it? I wouldn't ask him, said the kid, eyeing the heavy table. Why not, insisted the man. It'd be a dumb thing to ask for, replied the kid barely audibly.

46   That ended that. But there were other, more sinister things. One day the same man asked if our parents at home complained about the new regime. No one said anything. When I described to my mother what happened, she told me, in no uncertain terms, that she would kill me if I ever opened my mouth. In any case, she didn't take any chances. Anytime I walked into a room, the grown-ups would shut up and eye me suspiciously. I had plenty to be guilty about and it must have shown in my face, for there would be a long cross-examination: "What did you say?" "Nothing! I swear it!" And so it went.

47   My life on the street was also getting more complicated. I hung around with older boys. If I was seven, they must have been ten, twelve years old. Gang territories were being charted. If you left your neighborhood unaccompanied, you could get hurt. Even going to school was complicated since I had to pass through several enemy areas. We travelled in groups everywhere, fists at the ready, glaring, looking mean. I had so many fights then and later on. Mostly I got beat up, since I was the youngest.

48   Then there was stealing. We stole for profit and for the fun of it. We took things from people's yards mostly. If it was valuable, we sold it to the older boys, if not, we'd throw it away. I was usually the one to make the snatch since I was the smallest and the nimblest. I remember being chased by an ax-wielding man whose bicycle pump I'd stolen. I remember walking into a grocery store, grabbing something from the counter, and running away. This was for practice. There was not much to be had in those stores. Most of the food was rationed. If you took someone's monthly ration of sugar, you were committing an unforgivable crime.

49   My mother never heard about my exploits. She had a lot on her mind. I don't know when exactly it was that we heard that my father was alive and well in Trieste. She was determined we should join him. The frontier between Yugoslavia and Italy was still open, as the area around Trieste was disputed by the two countries. There was still a chance we could leave, but it was dangerous. One could get arrested. One could get shot in those days for nothing.

50   We left Belgrade for the coast in the fall of 1945. That train journey took forever. The tracks were still in terrible shape. All along the way one could see the derailed railroad cars and bombed-out stations.

51   When we reached Opatia-Fiume, that once fashionable Austro-Hungarian sea-resort, we heard the border was closed. Still, if one knew the right people one could cross illegally. We stayed in a near-empty grand hotel for a week. I remember the high ornate ceilings, the crystal chandeliers, and mirrors everywhere. We took our meals in a large, immaculately set and deserted dining room which looked out at the gray sea. I've wondered since, who the few other guests were? They had a secretive air about them, didn't speak to each other, and rarely acknowledged our nods. I could walk for hours down the long hallways without meeting anyone, or hearing a sound. Once I heard sobs, muffled sobs, and even got my eyes on the keyhole, but could see nothing. Just the gray sea through the open balcony door, and the silence of the hotel around me. The woman had stopped crying.

52   We went back to Belgrade but my mother was stubborn. She found someone who knew someone else who, for a price, could take us across the border into Austria. Again, I was told nothing. I thought we were going on vacation in the mountains of Slovenia since once more we found ourselves in an elegant, half-empty chalet, sleeping late and taking long mountain walks. One evening we walked farther than was our custom. We sat on a couple of rocks in the woods, and my mother told me that that very night we'd be going to my father.

53   It was almost pitch dark when a man came to take us to a farmhouse where two other men waited. The rest of the night we spent climbing the mountains with my mother carrying my infant brother in her arms. They had given him something so he would sleep.

54   We couldn't see much for most of the way. The moon only came out when we crossed the border. We were on the side of a hill and Yugoslavia was down below. We sat on the grass talking and the men smoked. That was a mistake, as it turned out. We heard someone shout in German. One of our guides opened fire and the two of them took off in the direction of Yugoslavia leaving us in the hands of an Austrian-American patrol. That wasn't so bad. The Americans treated us well. They took us to their post where we spent the rest of the night. In the morning they fed us and asked no questions.

55   The problems started when the Americans handed us over to the English Army whose zone of occupation it was. A colonel asked my mother for our passports. My mother laughed. After all that mountainclimbing, our clothes were in tatters, our faces and hands were covered with scratches. My mother even tried a bit of humor. She told him, in the best English she could summon, that if we had a passport we would have taken a sleeping car. The fellow was not amused. What he did then—and it took us a while to grasp his intentions— was to put us in a jeep and deliver us to the Yugoslav border officials. We were back in Yugoslavia and under arrest.

56   We didn't know, of course, that this kind of thing happened often. The English were deporting the Russian war prisoners and anybody else they got their hands on. They didn't care what happened to these people. Stalin, as everybody now knows, sent them to labor camps where many perished. Our

case wasn't so tragic. We were transported from prison to prison for the next two weeks until we reached Belgrade. There, my brother and I were released into the hands of my grandmother, and my mother was kept in prison for another four months. Her defense was that she simply wanted to be with her husband and was not given the legal means to do so. This was true enough, although probably not the reason they let her go so quickly. The jails at that time were full of people with more interesting political transgressions. We were small fry. They slapped my mother around a few times, but that was all.

As for me, I thoroughly enjoyed being in jail. They put me in with the men. The cell doors opened at some wee hour and a little kid stood there. The prisoners were stunned. The cells were packed. They'd have to make room for me, make sure I had plenty of covers. They also wanted to hear my story. I obliged, of course. The bedbugs made it hard to sleep. I embroidered, how I embroidered! At home, too, all our relatives and friends were waiting to hear what happened. I don't remember the details of what I said, but there was a lot of shooting in my reenactment. I cocked my finger and fired for the benefit of all those grim and wary faces.

A Writer's Notes for a Second Reading

I delight in the diversity I find in my craft. Not right and wrong, but fascinating possibility. Reading Gibson I revel in the texture he creates with his complex sentences and fully packed sentences. Then I turn to Simic, poet turned prose writer, and delight in the texture he creates with his spare, imagistic writing.

His work is born of the discipline of his poetry, the eye that selects the revealing moment, the ear that catches the line that reveals the revealing moment. This autobiography seems like a wonderful movie, a series of quick scenes that draw me in and make me experience Simic's world.

He is also a master of what I like to call the angle of vision. He manages to recreate the world as seen by a child, yet, at the same time, put that child's view in context. The author does not interfere but he is there viewing the child, viewing the world.

Discussion

- What techniques does Simic use to recreate his world in the reader's mind?
- What are the advantages and disadvantages of Simic's and Gibson's voices?
- Discuss how movie techniques may have influenced Simic and other writers.
- Discuss the possibility that movies and television have prepared the reader for fast-moving, quick-transition, imagistic writing.

Activities

- Look up some of Simic's poetry in the library or in poetry-course anthologies. Share the poetry with the class and discuss the influence of his poetry technique on his prose.
- Use resources from the history department and library to report on what was happening in Yugoslavia in World War II.
- Show Simic's piece to a survivor of a war to discover that person's reaction to this text.
- Take a paragraph of Simic's writing and see if you can arrange the lines, not the sentences, into a poem.
- Write of your own first memories in Simic's spare, disciplined style.
- Write two paragraphs of Simic's piece as Gibson might have written it; write two paragraphs of Gibson in Simic's style.

To Collaborate

- Interview some survivors who have come to this country recently or in the past. Tape their stories and make a presentation telling their stories of survival and escape.
- Work with a young person who has recently arrived in this country to help record his or her own story so it can be read by others.

Richard Ford

"People say all sorts of things to you about making it as a writer, but there's no it to make. There's no gradient, no step ladder. I've just given everything I've ever written my very best—my absolute, greatest best shot. And that's all. Sometimes people like you and sometimes they don't. Now they like me. Next year, who knows what they'll do?"

But we know what Richard Ford will do. He'll keep on writing. "A lot of people could be novelists," he says, "if they were willing to devote their lives to their own responses to things."

And that is what we see one of the best fiction writers of our time do in the following selection from an article remembering his mother and celebrating her memory. Writers see Ford as a master of our craft. I am particularly impressed by the fact that each of his novels and his book of short stories are all different. I often speak of the voice of the text rather than the voice of the writer; Ford demonstrates that. His voice is very much in his books, but it is always tuned to tell the story, to call attention to the world of the story—not to the skill of the writer.

Ford says, "Just to write a good sentence—that's the postulate I go by. I guess I've always felt that if you keep a kind of fidelity toward the individual sentence, that you could work toward the rest." Enjoy his good sentences.

My Mother, in Memory

1   My mother's name was Edna Akin, and she was born in 1910, in the far northwest corner of the state of Arkansas—Benton County—in a place whose actual location I am not sure of and never have been. Near Decatur or Centerton, or a town no longer a town. Just a rural place. That is near the Oklahoma line there, and in 1910 it was a rough country, with a frontier feel. It had only been ten years since robbers and outlaws were in the landscape. Bat Masterson was still alive and not long gone from Galina.

2   I remark about this not because of its possible romance, or because I think it qualifies my mother's life in any way I can relate now, but because it seems like such a long time ago and such a far-off and unknowable place. And yet my mother, whom I loved and knew quite well, links me to that foreignness, that other thing that was her life and that I really don't know so much about and never did. This is one quality of our lives with our parents that is often overlooked and so, devalued. Parents link us—closeted as we are in our lives—to a thing we're not but they are; a separateness, perhaps a mystery—so that even together we are alone.

3   The act and practice of considering my mother's life is, of course, an act of love. And my incomplete memory of it, my inadequate relation to the facts, should not be thought incomplete love. I loved my mother the way a happy child does, thoughtlessly and without doubts. And when I became an adult and we were adults who knew one another, we regarded each other highly; could say "I love you" when it seemed necessary to clarify our dealings, but without pausing over it. That seems perfect to me now and did then, too.

4   My mother's life I am forced to piece together. We were not a family for whom history had much to offer. This fact must have to do with not being rich, or with being rural, or incompletely educated, or just inadequately aware of many things. For my mother there was simply little to history, no heroics or self-dramatizing—just small business, forgettable residues, some of them mean. The Depression had something to do with it, too. My mother and father were people who lived for each other and for the day. In the thirties, after they were married, they lived, in essence, on the road. They drank some. They had a good time. They felt they had little to look back on, and didn't look.

5   My father's family came from Ireland and were Protestants. This was in the 1870s, and an ocean divided things. But about my mother's early life I don't know much. I don't know where her father came from, or if he too was Irish, or Polish. He was a carter, and my mother spoke affectionately about him, if elliptically and without a sense of responsibility to tell anything at all. "Oh,"

she would say, "my daddy was a good man." And that was it. He died of cancer in the 1930s, I think, but not before my mother had been left by her mother and had lived with him a time. This was before 1920. My sense is that they lived in the country, back near where she was born—rural again—and that to her it had been a good time. As good as any. I don't know what she was enthusiastic for then, what her thoughts were. I cannot hear her voice from that time long ago, though I would like to be able to.

6   Of her mother there is much to say—a story of a kind. She was from the country, with brothers and sisters. There was Indian blood on that side of the family, though it was never clear what tribe of Indian. I know nothing about her parents, though I have a picture of my great-grandmother and my grandmother with her new, second husband, sitting in an old cartage wagon, and my mother in the back. My great-grandmother is old then, witchy looking; my grandmother, stern and pretty in a long beaver coat; my mother, young, with piercing dark eyes aimed to the camera.

7   At some point my grandmother had left her husband and taken up with the younger man in the picture—a boxer and roustabout. A pretty boy. Slim and quick and tricky. "Kid Richard" was his ring name. (I, oddly enough, am *his* namesake.) This was in Fort Smith now. Possibly 1922. My grandmother was older than Kid Richard, whose real name was Bennie Shelley. And to quickly marry him and keep him, she lied about her age, took a smooth eight years off, and began to dislike having her pretty daughter—my mother— around to date her.

8   And so for a period—everything in her life seemed to happen for a period and never for long—my mother was sent to live at the Convent School of St. Ann's, also in Fort Smith. It must've seemed like a good idea to her father up in the country, because he paid her tuition, and she was taught by nuns. I don't exactly know what her mother—whose name was Essie or Lessie or just Les— did during that time, maybe three years. She was married to Bennie Shelley, who was from Fayetteville and had family there. He worked as a waiter, and then in the dining-car service on the Rock Island. This meant living in El Reno and as far out the line as Tucumcari, New Mexico. He quit boxing, and my grandmother ruled him as strictly as she could because she felt she could go a long way with him. He was her last and best choice for something. A ticket out. To where, I'm not sure.

9   My mother often told me that she'd liked the sisters at St. Ann's. They were strict. Imperious. Self-certain. Dedicated. Humorous. It was there, I think, as a boarding student, that my mother earned what education she ever did— the ninth grade, where she was an average good student and was liked, though she smoked cigarettes and was punished for it. I think if she had never told me about the nuns, if that stamp on her life hadn't been made, I might never have ordered even this much of things. St. Ann's cast a shadow into later life. In her heart of hearts my mother was a secret Catholic. A forgiver. A respecter of rituals and protocols. Reverent about the trappings of faith; respecter of inner disciplines. All I think about Catholics I think because of her, who was never

one at all, but who lived among them at an early age and seemingly liked what she learned and those who taught her. Later in life, when she had married my father and gone to meet his mother, she would always feel she was thought of as a Catholic by them, and that they never truly took her in as they might have another girl.

10   But when her father, for reasons I know nothing about, stopped her tuition, her mother—now demanding they be known as sisters—took her out of St. Ann's. And that was it for school, forever. She was not a welcome addition to her mother's life, and I have never known why they took her back. It is just one of those inexplicable acts that mean everything.

11   They moved around. To K.C. To El Reno again. To Davenport and Des Moines—wherever the railroad took Ben Shelley, who was going forward in the dining-car service and turning himself into a go-getter. In time, he would leave the railroad and go to work as a caterer at the Arlington Hotel in Hot Springs. And there he put my mother to work in the cigar shop, where a wider world opened an inch. People from far away were here for the baths, Jews from Chicago and New York. Foreigners. Rich people. She met baseball players, became friends with Dizzy Dean and Leo Durocher. And during that time, sometime when she was seventeen, she must've met my father.

12   I, of course, know nothing about their courtship except that it took place—mostly in Little Rock, probably in 1927. My father was twenty-three. He worked as a produce stocker for a grocery concern there. I have a picture of him with two other young clerks in a grocery store. He is wearing a clean, white apron and a tie, and is standing beside a bin of cabbages. I don't even know where this is. Little Rock. Hot Springs—one of these. It is just a glimpse. What brought him down from the country to Little Rock I'll never know, nor what he might've had on his mind then. He died in 1960, when I was only sixteen. And I had not by then thought to ask.

13   But I have thought of them as a young couple. My mother, black-haired, dark-eyed, curvaceous. My father, blue-eyed like me, big, gullible, honest, gentle. I can think a thought of them together. I can sense what they each must've sensed pretty fast—here was a good person, suddenly. My mother knew things. She had worked in hotels, been to boarding school and out. Lived in cities. Traveled some. But my father was a country boy who quit school in the seventh grade. The baby of three children, all raised by their mother—the sheltered son of a suicide. I can believe my mother wanted a better life than working for her ambitious stepfather and contrary mother, at jobs that went no place; that she may have believed she'd not been treated well, and thought of her life as "rough"; that she was tired of being her mother's sister; that it was a strange life; that she was in danger of losing all expectation; that she was bored. And I can believe my father simply saw my mother and wanted her. Loved her. And that was how that went.

14   They were married in Morrilton, Arkansas, by a justice of the peace, in 1928, and arrived at my father's home in Atkins the next morning, newlyweds. I have no correct idea what anyone thought or said about any of that. They acted

independently, and my mother never felt the need to comment. Though my guess is they heard disapproval.

15   I think it is safe to say my parents wanted children. How many they wanted or how soon after they were married I do not know. But it was their modest boast that my father had a job throughout the Depression. And I think there was money enough. They lived in Little Rock, and for a while my father worked as a grocer, and then, in 1932, he was fired, and went to work selling starch for a company out of Kansas City, The Faultless Company: Huey Long had worked for them, too. It was a traveling job, and most of the time they just traveled together. New Orleans. Memphis. Texarkana. They lived in hotels, spent their off-hours and off-days back in Little Rock. But mostly they traveled. My father called on groceries, wholesalers, prisons, hospitals, conducted schools for housewives on how to starch clothes without boiling the starch. My mother, typically, never characterized that time except to say he and she had "fun" together—that was her word for it—and had begun to think they couldn't have a child. No children. This time lasted fifteen years. A loose, pick-up-and-go life. Drinking. Cars. Restaurants. Not paying much attention. There were friends they had in New Orleans, Memphis, in Little Rock, and on the road. They made friends of my grandmother and Bennie, who was not much older than my father—four years, at most. I think they were just caught up in their life, a life in the South, in the thirties, just a kind of swirling thing that didn't really have a place to go. There must've been plenty of lives like that then. It seems a period now to me. A specific time, the Depression. But to them, of course, it was just their life.

16   Something about that time—to my mother—must've seemed unnarratable. Unworthy of or unnecessary for telling. My father, who was not a teller of stories anyway, never got a chance to recall it. And I, who wasn't trained to want the past filled in—as some boys are—just never asked. It seemed a privacy I shouldn't invade. And I know that my mother's only fleeting references to that time, as if the thirties were just a long weekend—drinking too much, wildness, rootlessness—gave me the impression something possibly untidy had gone on, some recklessness of spirit and attitude, something that a son would be better off not to think about and be worried with. In essence, it had been *their* time, for their purposes and not mine. And it was over.

17   But looked at from the time of my birth, 1944, all that life lived childless, unexpectant, must've come to seem an odd time to her; a life encapsulatable, possibly even remembered unclearly, pointless, maybe in comparison to the pointedness of life *with* a child. Still, an intimacy established between the two of them that they brought forward into more consequential life—a life they had all but abandoned any thought of because no children had come.

18   All first children, and certainly all only children, date the beginning of their lives as extraspecial events. For my parents my arrival came as a surprise and coincident with the end of World War II—the event that finished the thirties in this country. And it came when my mother had been married to my

father fifteen years; when, in essence, their young life was over. He was thirty-nine. She was thirty-three. They, by all accounts, were happy to have me. It may have been an event that made their life together seem conventional for once, that settled them; made them think about matters their friends had thought about years ago. Staying put. The future.

19 They had never owned a house or a car, although my father's job gave him a company car. They had never had to choose a "home," a place to be in permanently. But now, they did. They moved from Little Rock down to Mississippi, to Jackson, which was the geographic center of my father's territory and a place he could return most weekends with ease, since my mother wouldn't be going with him now. There was going to be a baby.

20 They knew no one in Jackson except the jobbers my father had called on and a salesman or two he knew off the road. I'm not sure, but I think it was not an easy transition. They rented and then bought a brick duplex next to a school. They joined a church. Found a grocery. A bus stop—though you could walk to the main street in Jackson from 736 North Congress. Also to the library and the capitol building. They had neighbors—older citizens, established families hanging on to nicer, older, larger houses in a neighborhood that was itself in transition. This was life now, for them. My father went off to work Monday morning and came back Friday night. He had never exactly done that before, but he liked it, I think. One of my earliest memories is of him moving around the sunny house on Monday mornings, whistling a tune.

21 And so what my beginning life was was this. A life spent with my mother—a shadow in a picture of myself. Days. Afternoons. Nights. Walks. Meals. Dressing. Sidewalks. The movies. Home. Radio. And on the weekend, my father. A nice, large, sweet man who visited us. Happy to come home. Happy to leave.

22 I don't think my mother longed for a fulfilling career or a more active public life. I don't think my father had other women on the road. I don't think the intrusion of me into their lives was anything they didn't think of as normal and all right. I know from practice that it is my habit to seek the normal in life, to look for reasons to believe this or that is fine. In part, that is because my parents raised me that way and lived lives that portrayed a world, a private existence, that *could* be that way. I do not think even now, in the midst of my own life's concerns, that it is a bad way to see things.

23 So then, the part of my life that has to do with my mother.

24 The first eleven years—the Korean War years, Truman and Eisenhower, television, bicycles, one big snowstorm in 1949—we lived on North Congress Street, down a hill from the state capitol and across from the house where Eudora Welty had been a young girl thirty-five years before. Next door to Jefferson Davis School. I remember a neighbor stopping me on the sidewalk and asking me who I was; this was a thing that could happen to you. Maybe I was nine or seven then. But when I said my name—Richard Ford—she said, "Oh, yes. Your mother is the cute little black-headed woman up the street." And that

affected me and still does. I think this was my first conception of my mother as someone else, as someone whom other people saw and considered: a cute woman, which she was not. Black-haired, which she was. She was, I know, five feet five inches tall. But I never have known if that is tall or short. I think I must have always believed it was normal. I remember this, though, as a signal moment in my life. Small but important. It alerted me to my mother's— what?—public side. To the side that other people saw and dealt with and that was there. I do not think I ever thought of her in any other way after that. As Edna Ford, a person who was my mother and also who was someone else. I do not think I ever addressed her after that except with such a knowledge—the way I would anyone I knew.

25   It is a good lesson to learn. And we risk never knowing our parents if we ignore it. Cute, black-headed, five-five. Some part of her was that, and it didn't harm me to know it. It may have helped, since one of the premier challenges for us all is to know our parents, assuming they survive long enough, are worth knowing, and it is physically possible. This is a part of normal life. And the more we see them fully, as the world sees them, the better all our chances are.

26   About my mother I do not remember more than pieces up until the time I was sixteen: 1960, a galvanizing year for us both—the year my father woke up gasping on a Saturday morning and died before he could get out of bed; me up on the bed with him, busy trying to find something to help. Shake him. Yell in his sleeping face. Breathe in his soft mouth. Turn him over onto his belly, for some reason. Feeling terror and chill. All this while she stood in the doorway to his bedroom in our new house in the suburbs of Jackson, pushing her knuckles into her temples, becoming hysterical. Eventually she just lost her control for a while.

27   But before that. Those pieces. They must make a difference or I wouldn't remember them so clearly. A flat tire we all three had, halfway across the Mississippi bridge at Greenville. High, up there, over the river. We stayed in the car while my father fixed it, and my mother held me so tightly to her I could barely breathe. I was six. She always said, "I smothered you when you were little. You were all we had. I'm sorry." And then she'd tell me this story. But I wasn't sorry. It seemed fine then, since we were up there. "Smothering" meant "Here is danger." "Love protects you." They are still lessons I respect. I am not comfortable on bridges now, but my guess is I never would've been.

28   I remember my mother having a hysterectomy and my grandfather, Ben Shelley, joking about it—to her—about what good "barbers" the nuns at St. Dominic's had been. That made her cry.

29   I remember once in the front yard on Congress Street something happened, something I said or did—I don't know what—but my mother began running out across the schoolyard next door. Just running away. I remember that scared me and I yelled at her, "No," and halfway across she stopped and came back. I've never known how serious she was about that, but I have understood from it that there might be reasons to run off. Alone, with a small child, knowing no one. That's enough.

30   There were two fights they had that I was present for. One on St. Louis Street, in the French Quarter in New Orleans. It was in front of Antoine's Restaurant, and I now think they were both drunk, though I didn't know it, or even know what drunk was. One wanted to go in the restaurant and eat. The other didn't and wanted to go back to the hotel around the corner. This was in 1955. I think we had tickets to the Sugar Bowl—Navy vs. Ole Miss. They yelled at each other, and I think my father yanked her arm, and they walked back separately. Later we all got in bed together in the Monteleone and no one stayed mad. In our family no one ever nagged or held grudges or stayed mad, though we could all get mad.

31   The other fight was worse. I believe it was the same year. They were drinking. My father invited friends over and my mother didn't like it. All the lights were on in the house. She swore. I remember the guests standing in the doorway outside the screen, still on the porch looking in. I remember their white faces and my mother shouting at them to get the hell out, which they did. And then my father held my mother's shoulders up against the wall by the bathroom and yelled at her while she struggled to get free. I remember how harsh the lights were. No one got hit. No one ever did except me when I was whipped. They just yelled and struggled. Fought that way. And then after a while, I remember, we were all in bed again, with me in the middle, and my father cried. "Boo hoo hoo. Boo hoo hoo." Those were the sounds he made, as if he'd read somewhere how to cry.

32   A long time has passed since then, and I have remembered more than I do now. I have tried to put things into novels. I have written things down and forgotten them. I have told stories. And there was more, a life's more. My mother and I rode with my father summers and sat in his hot cars in the states of Louisiana and Arkansas and Texas and waited while he worked, made his calls. We went to the coast—to Biloxi and Pensacola. To Memphis. To Little Rock almost every holiday. We *went*. That was the motif of things. We lived in Jackson, but he traveled. And every time we could we went with him. Just to be going. The staying part was never stabilized. Only being with them, and mostly being with her. My mother.

33   And then my father died, which changed everything—many things, it's odd to say, for the better where I was concerned. But not for my mother. Where she was concerned, nothing after that would ever be quite good again. A major part of life ended for her February 20, 1960. He had been everything to her, and all that was naturally implicit became suddenly explicit in her life, and she was neither good at that nor interested in it. And in a way I see now and saw almost as clearly then, she gave up.

34 Not that she gave up where I was concerned. I was sixteen and had lately been in some law scrapes, and she became, I'd say, very aware of the formal features of her life. She was a widow. She was fifty. She had a son who seemed all right, but who could veer off into trouble if she didn't pay attention. And so, in her way, she paid attention.

35   Not long after the funeral, when I was back in school and the neighbors had stopped calling and bringing over dishes of food—when both grief and real mourning had set in, in other words—she sat me down and told me we were now going to have to be more independent. She would not be able to look after me as she had done. We agreed that I had a future, but I would have to look after me. And as we could, we would do well to look after each other. We were partners now, is what I remember thinking. My father had really never been around that much, and so his actual absence was, for me (though not for her), not felt so strongly. And a partnership seemed like a good arrangement. I was to stay out of jail because she didn't want to get me out. *Wouldn't get me out.* I was to find friends I could rely on instead. I could have a car of my own. I could go away in the summers to find a job in Little Rock with my grandparents. This, it was understood but never exactly stated (we were trying not to state too much then; we didn't want *everything* to have to be explicit, since so much was now and so little ever had been), *this* would give her time to adjust. To think about things. To become whatever she would have to become to get along from there on out.

36   I don't exactly remember the time scheme to things. This was 1960, '61, '62. I was a tenth-grader and on. But I did not get put in jail. I did live summers with my grandparents, who by now ran a large hotel in Little Rock. I got a black '57 Ford, which got stolen. I got beaten up and then got new friends. I did what I was told, in other words. I started to grow up in a hurry.

37   I think of that time—the time between my father's death and the time I left for Michigan to go to college—as a time when I didn't see my mother much. Though that is not precisely how it was. She was there. I was there. But I cannot discount my own adjustments to my father's death and absence, to my independence. I think I may have been more dazed than grieved, and it is true my new friends took me up. My mother went to work. She got a job doing something at a company that made school pictures. It required training and she did it. And it was only then, late in 1960, when she was fifty, that she first felt the effects of having quit school in 1924. But she got along, came home tired. I do not think she had trouble. And then she left that. She became a rental agent for a new apartment house, tried afterward to get the job as manager but didn't get it—who knows why? She took another job as night cashier in a hotel, the Robert E. Lee. This job she kept maybe a year. And after that she was the admitting clerk in the emergency room at the University of Mississippi Hospital, a job she liked very much.

38   And there was at least one boyfriend in all that time. A married man, from Tupelo, named Matt, who lived in the apartment building she worked at. He was a big, bluff man, in the furniture business, who drove a Lincoln and carried a gun strapped to the steering column. I liked him. And I liked it that my mother liked him. It didn't matter that he was married—not to me, and I guess not to my mother. I really have no idea about what was between them, what they did alone. And I don't care about that, either. He took her on drives. Flew her to Memphis in his airplane. Acted respectfully to both of us. She may have told

me she was just passing time, getting her mind off her worries, letting someone be nice to her. But I didn't care. And we both knew that nothing she told me about him either did or didn't have to match the truth. I would sometimes think I wished she would marry Matt. And at other times I would be content to have them be lovers, if that's what they were. He had boys near my age, and later I would even meet them and like them. But this was after he and my mother were finished.

39   What finished them was brought on by me but was not really my doing, I think now. Matt had faded for a time. His business brought him in to Jackson, then out for months. She had quit talking about him, and life had receded to almost a normal level. I was having a hard time in school—getting a D in algebra (I'd already failed once) and having no ideas for how I could improve. My mother was cashiering nights at the Robert E. Lee and coming home by eleven.

40   But one night for some reason she simply didn't come home. I had a test the next day. Algebra. And I must've been in an agitated state of mind. I called the hotel to hear she had left on time. And for some reason this scared me. I got in my car and drove down to the neighborhood by the hotel, a fringe neighborhood near a black section of town. I rode the streets and found her car, a gray and pink '58 Oldsmobile that had been my father's pride and joy. It was parked under some sycamore trees, across from the apartments where she had worked as a rental agent and where Matt lived. And for some reason I think I panicked. It was not a time to panic but I did anyway. I'm not sure what I thought, but thinking of it now I seem to believe I wanted to ask Matt—if he was there—if he knew where my mother was. This may be right, though it's possible, too, I knew she was there and just wanted to make her leave.

41   I went in the building—it must've been midnight—and up the elevator and down the hall to his door. I banged on it. Hit it hard with my fists. And then I waited.

42   Matt himself opened the door, but my mother was there in the room behind him. She had a drink in her hand. The lights were on, and she was standing in the room behind him. It was a nice apartment, and both of them were shocked by me. I don't blame them. I didn't blame them then and was ashamed to be there. But I was, I think, terrified. Not that she was there. Or that I was alone. But just that I didn't know what in the hell. Where was she? What else was I going to have to lose?

43   I remember being out of breath. I was seventeen years old. And I really can't remember what anybody said or did except me, briefly. "Where have you been?" I said to her. "I didn't know where you were. That's all."

44   And that *was* all. All of that. Matt said very little. My mother got her coat and we went home in two cars. She acted vaguely annoyed at me, and I *was* mad at her. We talked that night. Eventually she said she was sorry, and I told her I didn't care if she saw Matt only that she tell me when she would be home late. And to my knowledge she never saw Matt Matthews, or any other man, again as a lover as long as she lived.

45   Later, years later, when she was dying, I tried to explain it all to her

again—my part, what I thought, *had* thought—as if we could still open it and repair that night. All she needed to do was call me or, even years later, say she would've called me. But that was not, of course, what she did or how she saw it. She just looked a little disgusted and shook her head. "Oh, that," she said. "My God. That was just silliness. You had no business coming up there. You were out of your mind. Though I just saw I couldn't be doing things like that. I had a son to raise." And here again she looked disgusted, and at everything, I think. All the cards the fates had dealt her—a no-good childhood, my father's death, me, her own inability to vault over all of this to a better life. It was another proof of something bad, the likes of which she felt, I believe, she'd had plenty.

46   There are only these—snapshot instances of a time lived indistinctly, a time that whirled by for us but were the last times we would ever really live together as mother and son. We did not fight. We accommodated each other almost as adults would. We grew wry and humorous with each other. Cast glances, gave each other looks. Were never ironic or indirect or crafty with anger. We knew how we were supposed to act and took pleasure in acting that way.

47   She sold the new house my father had bought, and we moved into a high-rise. Magnolia Towers. I did better in school. She was switching jobs. I really didn't register these changes, though based on what I know now about such things they could not have been easy.

48   I did not and actually do not know about the money, how it was, then. My father had a little insurance. Maybe some was saved in a bank. My grand-parents stepped forward with offers. They had made money. But there was no pension from his job; it was not that kind of company. I know the government paid money for me, a dependent child. But I only mean to say I don't know how much she needed to work; how much money needed to come through; if we had debts, creditors. It may have been we didn't, and that she went to work just to thrust herself in the direction life seemed to be taking her—indepen-dence. Solitariness. All that that means.

49   There were memorable moments. When my girlfriend and I had been experimenting in one kind of sexual pleasure and another, quite suddenly my girlfriend—a Texas girl—sensed somehow that she was definitely pregnant and that her life and mine were ruined. Mine, I know certainly, felt ruined. And there was evidence aplenty around of kids marrying at fourteen, having babies, being divorced. This was the South, after all.

50   But I once again found myself in terror, and on a Sunday afternoon I just unburdened myself to my mother; told her *all* we'd done, all we hadn't. Spoke specifically and methodically in terms of parts and positions, extents and degrees. All I wanted from her was to know if Louise *could* be pregnant, based upon what she knew about those things (how much could that really have been?). These were all matters a boy should take up with his father, of course. Though, really whoever would? I know I wouldn't have. Such a conversation

would've confused and embarrassed my poor father and me. We did not know each other that well at our closest moments. And in any case, he was gone.

51   But my mother I knew very well. At least I acted that way and she did, too. She was fifty-two. I was eighteen. She was practiced with me, knew the kind of boy I was. We were partners in my messes and hers. I sat on the couch and carefully told her what scared me, told her what I couldn't get worked out right in my thinking, went through it all; used the words *it, hers, in*. And she, stifling her dread, very carefully assured me that everything was going to be fine. Nobody got pregnant doing what we were doing, and I should forget about it. It was all a young girl's scare fantasies. Not to worry. And so I didn't.

52   Of course, she was wrong. Couldn't possibly have been wronger. My girl-friend didn't get pregnant, but only because a kind fate intervened. Thousands of people get pregnant doing what we were doing. Thousands more get preg-nant doing much less. I guess my mother just didn't know that much, or else understood much more: that what was done was done now, and all the worry and explaining and getting-straight wouldn't matter. I should be more careful in the future if I was to have one. And that was about it. If Louise was pregnant, what anybody thought wouldn't matter. Best just not to worry.

53   And there is, of course, a lesson in that—one I like and have tried ever since and unsuccessfully to have direct me. Though I have never looked at the world through eyes like hers were then. Not yet. I have never exactly felt how little all you can do can really matter. Full understanding will come to me, and undoubtedly to us all. But my mother showed that to me first, and best, and I think I may have begun to understand it even then.

54 In the sixties after that I went away to college, in Michigan. It was a choice of mine and no one else's, and my mother neither encouraged nor discouraged me. Going to college in Mississippi didn't enter my mind. I wanted, I thought, to be a hotel manager like my grandfather, who had done well at it. I do not, in fact, remember my mother and me ever talking about college. She hadn't been and didn't know much about it. But the assumption was that I was simply going, and it would be my lookout. She was interested, but in a way that was not vital or supervisory. I don't think she thought that I would go away for good, even when it happened that Michigan State took me and I said I was going. I don't know what she thought exactly. She had other things on her mind then. Maybe she thought Michigan wasn't so far from Mississippi, which is true and not true, or that I wouldn't stay and would come home soon. Maybe she thought I would never go. Or maybe she thought nothing, or nothing that was clear; just noticed that I was doing this and that, sending and getting letters, setting dates, and decided she would cross that bridge when the time came.

55   And it did come.

56   In September 1962, she and I got on the Illinois Central in Jackson and rode it to Chicago (our first such trip together). We transferred crosstown to the old La Salle Street Station and the Grand Trunk Western, and rode up to

Lansing. She wanted to go with me. I think she wanted just to see all that. Michigan. Illinois. Cornfields. White barns. The Middle West. Wanted to see from a train window what went on there, how that was. What it all looked like, possibly to detect how I was going to fit myself among those people, live in their buildings, eat their food, learn their lingo. Why this was where I had chosen to go. Her son. This was how she saw her duty unfolding.

57   And, too, the ordinary may have been just what she wanted: accompanying her son to college, a send-off; to see herself and me, for a moment in time, fitted into the pattern of what other people were up to, what people in general did. If it could happen to her, to us, that way, then maybe some normal life had reconvened, since she could not have thought of her life as normal then.

58   So, at the end of that week, late September 1962, when I had enrolled, invaded my room, met my roomies, and she and I had spent days touring and roaming, eating motel dinners together until nothing was left to say, I stood up on a bus-stop bench beside the train tracks, at the old GTW station in Lansing, and held up my arms in the cool, snapping air for her to see me as she pulled away back toward Chicago. And I saw her, her white face recessed behind the tinted window, one palm flat to the glass for me to see. And she was crying. Good-bye, she was saying. And I waved one arm in that cool air and said, "Good-bye. I love you," and watched the train go out of sight through the warp of that bricky old factory town. And at that moment I suppose you could say I started my own life in earnest, and whatever there was left of my childhood ended.

59   After that the life that would take us to the end began. A fragmented, truncated life of visits long and short. Letters. Phone calls. Telegrams. Meetings in cities away from home. Conversations in cars, in airports, train stations. Efforts to see each other. Leaving dominating everything—my growing older, and hers, observed from varying distances.

60   She held out alone in Mississippi for a year, moved back into the house on Congress Street. She rented out the other side, worked at the hospital, where for a time, I think, the whole new life she'd been handed worked out, came together. I am speculating, as you can believe, because I was gone. But at least she said she liked her job, liked the young interns at the hospital, liked the drama of the ER, liked working even. It may have started to seem satisfactory enough that I was away. It may have seemed to her that there was a life to lead. That under the circumstances she had done reasonably well with things; could ease up, let events happen without fearing the worst. One bad thing did finally turn into something less bad.

61   This, at least, is what I wanted to think. How a son feels about his widowed mother when he is far away becomes an involved business. But it is not over-simplifying to say that he wants good to come to her. In all these years, the years of fragmented life with my mother, I was aware (as I have said) that things would never be completely all right with her again. Partly it was a matter of choosing; partly it was a matter just of her own character—of just how she could see her life without my father, with him gone and so much life left to be

lived in a not ideal way. Always she was resigned somewhere down deep. I could never plumb her without coming to that stop point—a point where expectation simply ceased. This is not to say she was unhappy after enough time had passed. Or that she never laughed. Or that she didn't see life as life, didn't regain and rejoin herself. All those she did. Only, not utterly, not in a way a mother, any mother, could disguise to her only son who loved her. I always saw that. Always felt it. Always felt her—what?—discomfort at life? Her resisting it? Always wished she could relent more than she apparently could; since in most ways my own life seemed to spirit ahead, and I did not like it that hers didn't. From almost the first I felt that my father's death surrendered to me at least as much as it took away. It gave me my life to live by my own designs, gave me my own decisions. A boy could do worse than to lose his father—a good father, at that—just when the world begins to display itself all around him.

62   But that is not the way it was with her, even as I can't exactly say how it *was*. I can say that in all the years after my father died, twenty-one years, her life never seemed quite fully engaged. She took trips—to Mexico, to New York, to California, to Banff, to islands. She had friends who loved her and whom she spoke well of. She had an increasingly easy life as her own parents died. She had us—my wife and me—who certainly loved her and included her in all we could. But when I would say to her—and I did say this—"Mother, are you enjoying your life? Are things all right?" she would just look at me impatiently and roll her eyes. "Richard," she'd say, "I'm never going to be ecstatic. It's not in my nature. You concentrate on your life. Leave mine alone. I'll take care of me."

63   And that, I think, is mostly what she did after his death and my departure, when she was on her own: she maintained herself, made a goal of that. She became brisk, businesslike, more self-insistent. Her deep voice became even deeper, assumed a kind of gravity. She drank in the evenings to get a little drunk, and took up an attitude (particularly toward men, whom she began to see as liabilities). She made her situation be the custom and cornerstone of her character. Would not be taken advantage of by people, though I suspect no one wanted to. A widow had to look out, had to pay attention to all details. No one could help you. A life lived efficiently wouldn't save you, no; but it would prepare you for what you couldn't really be saved from.

64   Along the way she also maintained me and my wife, at a distance and as we needed it. She maintained her mother, who finally grew ill, then crippled, but never appreciative. She maintained her stepfather—moved, in fact, back to Little Rock. She sold her house, hers and my father's first house, and lived with my grandparents in the hotel, and later—after Ben died—in apartments here and there in the town. She became a daughter again at fifty-five, one who looked after her elderly mother. They had money enough. A good car. A set of friends who were widowed, too—people in their stratum. They accompanied each other. Went to eat in small groups, played canasta afternoons, spoke on the phone, watched TV, planned arguments; grew bored, impatient, furious. Had

cocktails. Laughed about men. Stared. Lived a nice and comfortable life of waiting.

65   Our life during this time—my mother's and mine—consisted of my knowledge of what her life was like. And visits. We lived far away from each other. She in Little Rock. I, and then I and Kristina, in New York, California, Mexico, Chicago, Michigan again, New Jersey, Vermont. To us she arrived on trains and planes and in cars, ready to loan us money and to take us to dinner. To buy us this and that we needed. To have a room painted. To worry about me. To be there for a little while wherever we were and then to go home again.

66   It must be a feature of anyone's life to believe that particular circumstances such as these are not exactly typical of what the mass of other lives are like. Not better. Not worse. Only peculiar in some way. Our life, my mother's and mine, seemed peculiar. Or possibly it is just imperfect that it seemed. Being away. Her being alone. Our visits and departings. All this consumed twenty years of both our lives—her last twenty, my second, when whatever my life was to be was beginning. It never felt exactly right to me that during all these years I could not see my mother more, that we did not have a day-to-day life. That the repairs we made to things after my father's death could not be shared entirely. I suppose that nowhere in time was there a moment when life for us rejoined itself as it had been before he died. This imperfection underlay everything. And when she left again and again and again, she would cry. And that is what she cried about. That we would never rejoin, that that was gone. This was all there was. Not quite enough. Not a full enough repaying of all that time together lost. She told me once that in an elevator a woman had asked her, "Mrs. Ford, do you have any children?" And she had said, "No." And then thought to herself, "Well, yes, I do. There's Richard."

67   Our conversations over these years had much to do with television, with movies we had seen and hadn't, with books she was reading, with baseball. The subject of Johnny Bench came up often, for some reason. My wife and I took her to the World Series, where she rooted for the team we didn't like and complained about the seats we'd moved mountains to get—for her, we thought. We took her on the Universal Tour. We took her back to Antoine's. We drove her to California and to Montreal. To Maine. To Vermont. To northern Michigan. To wherever we went that we could take her. We, she and I, observed each other. She observed my wife and my marriage and liked them both. She observed my efforts to be a writer and did not fully understand them. "But when are you going to get a job and get started?" she asked me once. She observed the fact that we had no children and offered no opinion. She observed her life and ours and possibly did not completely see how one gave rise to the other.

68   I observed that she grew older; saw that life was not entirely to her liking and that she made the most of its surfaces—taking a job once in a while, then finally retiring. I observed that she loved me; would sometimes take me aside early on a morning when we could be alone together as two adults and say: "Richard, are *you* happy?" And when I told her I was, she would warn, "You must be happy. That's so important."

69   And that is the way life went on. Not quite pointlessly. But not pointedly, either. Maybe this is typical of all our lives with our parents—a feeling that some goal should be reached, then a recognition of what that goal inevitably is, and then returning attention to what's here and present today. To what's only here.

70   Something, some essence of life, is not coming clear through these words. There are not words enough. There are not events enough. There is not memory enough to give a life back and have it be right, exact. In one way, over these years apart, my mother and I lived toward one another the way people do who like each other and want to see each other more. Like friends. I have not even said about her that she didn't interfere. That she agreed my life with Kristina had retired a part of her motherhood. That she didn't cultivate random judgments. That she saw her visits as welcome, which they were. Indeed, she saw that what we'd made of things—she and I—was the natural result of prior events that were themselves natural. She was now, as before, not a psychologist. Not a quizzer. She played the cards she was dealt. By some strange understanding, we knew that this was life. This is what we would have. We were fatalists, mother and son. And we made the most of it.

71   In 1973, my mother discovered she had breast cancer. It must've been the way with such things, and with people of her background. A time of being aware that something was there. A time of worry and growing certainty. A mention to a friend, who did nothing. Finally a casual mention to me, who saw to it immediately that she visit a doctor, who advised tests and did not seem hopeful.

72   What I remember of that brief period, which took place in Little Rock, is that following the first doctor visit, when all the tests and contingencies were stated and planned, she and I and my wife took the weekend together. She would "go in" on Monday. But Saturday we drove up to the country, visited my father's family, his cousins whom she liked, his grave. She stated she was "going in for tests," and they—who were all older than she was—put a good face on it. We drove around in her Buick and just spent the time together. It was, we knew somehow, the last of the old time, the last of the period when we were just ourselves, just the selves we had made up and perfected, given all that had gone before. Something in those tests was about to change everything, and we wanted to act out our conviction that, yes, this has been a life, this adroit coming and going, this health, this humor, this affection expressed in fits and starts. This has been a thing. Nothing would change that. We could look back, and it would seem like we were alive enough.

73   Death starts a long time before it ever ends. And in it, in its very self, there is life that has to be lived out efficiently. There were seven years to go, but we didn't know it. And so we carried on. We went back to being away. To visiting. To insisting on life's being life, in the conviction that it could easily be less. And to me it seems like the time that had gone on before. Not exactly. But mostly. Talking on the phone. Visits, trips, friends, occasions. A more pointed need to know about "how things were," and a will to have them be all right for now.

74   My mother, I think, made the very best of her bad problems. She had a breast removed. She had some radiation. She had to face going back to her solitary life. And all this she did with a minimum of apparent fear and a great deal of dignity and resignation. It seemed as if her later years had been a training for bad news. For facing down disasters. And I think she appreciated this and was sharply aware of how she was dealing with things.

75   This was the first time I ever thought seriously that my mother might come to live with me, which was a well-discussed subject all our life, there having been precedent for it and plenty of opportunity to take up a point of view. My mother's attitude was very clear. She was against it. It ruined lives, spoiled things, she thought, and said no in advance. She had lived with her mother, and that had eventuated in years of dry unhappiness. Bickering. Impossibilities. Her mother had resented her, she said, hated being looked after. Turned meaner. Vicious. It was a no-win, and she herself expected nothing like that, wanted me to swear off the idea. Which I did. We laughed about how high and dry I would leave her. How she would be in the poorhouse, and I'd be someplace living it up.

76   But she was practical. She made arrangements. Someplace called Presbyterian Village, in Little Rock, would be her home when she was ready, she said. She'd paid money. They'd promised to do their duty. And that was that. "I don't want to have to be at anybody's mercy," she said, and meant it. And my wife and I thought that was a good arrangement all the way around.

77   So then it was back to regular life, or life as regular as could be. We had moved to New Jersey by then. We had a house. And there were plenty of visits, with my mother doing most of the visiting—walking out in our shady yard, afternoons, talking to our neighbors as if she knew them, digging in the flower beds. She seemed healthy. In high spirits. Illness and the possibility of illness had made her seize her life harder. She wanted to do more, it seemed. Take cruises. Visit Hawaii. Go. She had new friends, younger than she was. Loud, personable Southerners. We heard about them by name. Blanche. Herschel. Mignon. People we never met, who drank and laughed and liked her and were liked by her. I had pictures in my mind.

78   The year was counted from medical exam to medical exam, always these in the late winter, not long after my birthday. But every year there was good news after worrying. And every year there was a time to celebrate and feel relief. A reprieve.

79   I do not mean to say that any of our lives then were lived outside the expectation and prism of death. No one, I think, can lose his parent and not live out his life waiting for the other one to drop dead or begin to die. The joy of surviving is tainted by squeamish certainty that you can't survive. And I read my mother's death in almost all of her life during those days. I looked for illness. Listened to her complaints too carefully. Planned her death obscurely, along with my own abhorrence of it—treated myself to it early so that when the time came I would not, myself, go down completely.

80   At first there were backaches. It is hard to remember exactly when. The spring, 1981—six years since her first operation. She came to New Jersey to visit, and something had gone wrong. She was seventy, but pain had come into her life. She looked worn down, invaded by hurting. She'd seen doctors in Little Rock, but none of this had to do with her cancer, she said they said. It was back trouble. Parts were just wearing out. She went home, but in the summer she hurt more. I would call her and the phone would ring a long time, and then her answering voice would be weak, even barely audible. "I hurt, Richard," she'd tell me, wherever I was. "The doctor is giving me pills. But they don't always work." I'll come down there, I'd say. "No. I'll be fine," she'd say. "Do what you have to do." And the summer managed past that way, and the fall began.

81   I started a job in Massachusetts, and then one morning the phone rang. It was just at light. I don't know why anyone would call anyone at that hour unless a death was involved; but this wasn't the case. My mother had come to the hospital the night before, in an ambulance. She was in pain. And when she got there her heart had paused, briefly, though it had started again. She was better, a nurse said over the phone from Little Rock. I said I'd come that day, from Massachusetts; find people to teach my classes, drive to the airport in Albany. And that's how I did it.

82   In Little Rock it was still summer. A friend of my mother's, a man named Ed, met me and drove me in. We went by old buildings, over railroad tracks and across the Arkansas River. He was in a mood to comfort me: this would not turn out well, he said. My mother had been sicker than I knew; had spent days in her apartment without coming out. She had been in bed all summer. It was something I needed to prepare myself for. Her death.

83   But really it was more than her death. Singular life itself—hers in particular, ours—was moving into a new class of events now. These things could be understood, is what he meant to say to me. And to hold out against them was hopeless and also maybe perverse. This all was becoming a kind of thing that happens. It was inevitable, after all. And it was best to see it that way.

84   Which, I suppose, is what I then began to do. That ride in the car, across town, to the hospital, was the demarking line for me. A man I hardly knew suggested to me how I should look at things; how I should consider my own mother, my own life. Suggested, in essence, I begin to see *myself* in all this. Stand back. Be him or like him. It was better. And that is what I did.

85   My mother, it turned out, was feeling better. But something very unusual had happened to her. Her heart had stopped. There had been congestion in her lungs, the doctor told me and her. He had already performed some more tests, and the results weren't good. He was a small, curly-headed, bright-eyed young man. He was soft-spoken, and he liked my mother, remembered how she'd looked when she first came to see him. "Healthy," he said, and he was confused now by the course of a disease he supposedly knew about. I do not remember his name now. But he came into her room, sat down in the chair with some papers, and told us bad news. Just the usual bad news. The back pain was can-

cer, after all. She was going to die, but he didn't know when she would. Sometime in the next year, he imagined. There didn't seem to be any thought of recovering. And I know he was sorry to know it and to say it, and in a way his job may even have been harder than ours was then.

86   I do not really remember what we said to him. I'm sure we asked very good questions, since we were both good when the chips were down. I do not remember my mother crying. I know I did not cry. We knew, both of us, what class of events *this* was, this message. This was the message that ended one long kind of uncertainty. And I cannot believe we both, in our own ways, did not feel some relief, as if a curiosity had been satisfied and other matters begun. The real question—how serious is this?—can be answered and over with in a hurry. It is actually an odd thing. I wonder if doctors know how odd it is.

87   But still, in a way, it did not change things. The persuasive powers of normal life are strong, after all. To accept less than life when it is not absolutely necessary is stupid.

88   I think we had talks. She was getting out of the hospital again, and at least in my memory I stayed around and got out with her before I had to go back to my job. We made plans for a visit. More going. She would come to Massachusetts when she was strong enough. We could still imagine a future, and that was exactly all we asked for.

89   I went back to teaching, and talked to her most days, though the thought that she was getting worse, that bad things were going on there and I couldn't stop them, made me miss some days. It became an awful time, then, when life felt ruined, futureless, edging toward disappointments.

90   She stayed out of the hospital during that time, took blood transfusions, which seemed to make her feel better, though they were ominous. I think she went out with her friends. Had company. Lived as if life could go on. And then in early October she came north. I drove down to New York, picked her up and drove us back to my rented house in Vermont. It was misty, and most of the leaves were down. And in the house it was cold and bleak, and I took her out to dinner in Bennington just to get warm. She said she had had another transfusion for the trip and would stay with me until its benefits wore off and she was weak again.

91   And that was how we did that. Just another kind of regular life between us. I went to school, did my work, came home nights. She stayed in the big house with my dog. Read. Cooked lunches for herself. Watched the World Series. Watched Sadat be assassinated. Looked out the window. At night we talked. I did my school work, went out not very much. With my wife, who was working in New York and commuting up on weekends, we went on country drives, invited visitors, paid visits, lived together as we had in places far and wide all those years. I don't know what else we were supposed to do, how else that time was meant to pass.

92   On a sunny day in early November, when she had been with me three weeks and we were, in fact, out of things to do and talk about, she sat down

beside me on the couch and said, "Richard, I'm not sure how much longer I can look out after myself. I'm sorry. But it's just the truth."

93   "Does that worry you?" I said.

94   "Well," my mother said, "yes. I'm not scheduled to go into Presbyterian Village until way next year. And I'm not quite sure what I'm going to be able to do until then."

95   "What would you like to do?" I said.

96   "I don't exactly know," she said. And she looked worried then, looked away out the window, down the hill, where the trees were bare and it was foggy.

97   "Maybe you'll start to feel better," I said.

98   "Well, yes. I could. I suppose that's not impossible," she said.

99   "I think it's possible," I said. "I do."

100   "Well. O.K.," my mother said.

101   "If you don't," I said, "if by Christmas you don't feel you can do everything for yourself, you can move in with us. We're moving back to Princeton. You can live there."

102   And I saw in my mother's eyes, then, a light. A *kind* of light, anyway. Recognition. Relief. Concession. Willingness.

103   "Are you sure about that?" she said and looked at me. My mother's eyes were very brown, I remember.

104   "Yes, I'm sure," I said. "You're my mother. I love you."

105   "Well," she said and nodded. No tears. "I'll begin to think toward that, then. I'll make some plans about my furniture."

106   "Well, wait," I said. And this is a sentence I wish, above all sentences in my life, I had never said. Words I wish I'd never heard. "Don't make your plans yet," I said. "You might feel better by then. It might not be necessary to come to Princeton."

107   "Oh," my mother said. And whatever had suddenly put a light in her eyes suddenly went away then. And her worries resumed. Whatever lay between then and later rose again. "I see," she said. "All right."

108   I could've not said that. I could've said, "Yes, make the plans. In whatever way all this works out, it'll be just fine. I'll see to that." But that is what I didn't say. I deferred instead to something else, to some other future, and at least in retrospect I know what that future was. And, I think, so did she. Perhaps you could say that in that moment I witnessed her facing death, saw it take her out beyond her limits, and feared it myself, feared all that I knew; and that I clung to life, to the possibility of life and change. Perhaps I feared something more tangible. But the truth is, anything we ever could've done for each other after that passed by then and was gone. And even together we were alone.

109   What remains can be told quickly. In a day or two I drove her to Albany. She was cold, she said, in my house, and couldn't get warm, and would be better at home. That was our story, though there was not heat enough anywhere to get her warm. She looked pale. And when I left her at the airport gate she cried

again, stood and watched me go back down the long corridor, waved a hand. I waved. It was the last time I would see her that way. On her feet. In the world. We didn't know that, of course. But we knew something was coming.

110   And in six weeks she was dead. There is nothing exceptional about that to tell. She never got to Princeton. Whatever was wrong with her just took her over. "My body has betrayed me" is one thing I remember her saying. Another was, "My chances now are slim and none." And that was true. I never saw her dead, didn't care to, simply took the hospital's word about it when they called. Though I saw her face death that month, over and over, and I believe because of it that seeing death faced with dignity and courage does not confer either of those, but only pity and helplessness and fear.

111   All the rest is just private—moments and messages the world would not be better off to know. She knew I loved her because I told her so enough. I knew she loved me. That is all that matters to me now, all that should ever matter.

112   And so to end.

113   Does one ever have a "relationship" with one's mother? No. I think not. The typical only exists in the minds of unwise people. We—my mother and I—were never bound together by guilt or embarrassment, or even by duty. Love sheltered everything. We expected it to be reliable, and it was. We were always careful to say it—"I love you"—as if a time might come, unexpectedly, when she would want to hear that, or I would, or that each of us would want to hear ourselves say it to the other, only for some reason it wouldn't be possible, and our loss would be great—confusion. Not knowing. Life lessened.

114   My mother and I look alike. Full, high forehead. The same chin, nose. There are pictures to show that. In myself I see her, even hear her laugh. In her life there was no particular brilliance, no celebrity. No heroics. No one crowning achievement to swell the heart. There were bad ones enough: a childhood that did not bear strict remembering; a husband she loved forever and lost; a life to follow that did not require comment. But somehow she made possible for me my truest affections, as an act of great literature would bestow upon its devoted reader. And I have known that moment with her we would all like to know, the moment of saying, "Yes. This is what it is." An act of knowing that certifies love. I have known that. I have known any number of such moments with her, known them even at the instant they occurred. And now. And, I assume, I will know them forever.

A Writer's Notes for a Second Reading

I'm fascinated by the way Ford moves around the subject, exploring that mystery that draws us all into wonder. Who was that person who gave us birth, what was she like before we were born, when she was our age; how did she meet the man who made her a mother, what attracted them to each other, how like me were they? The questions continue through our lives.

I'm also impressed how much Ford can do in a paragraph—no surprise to an admirer of his fiction. Study the fourth paragraph, in which his father dies. How quickly he goes into the scene, puts the reader right there, and yet keeps the focus at the beginning and the end of this paragraph on his mother, the focus of the piece.

I admire the orchestration of the piece—his mother with Matt, Ford with the girl who might be pregnant and his talking to his mother about it.

Discussion

• Discuss the differences in the autobiographical pieces written by Baraka, French, Baldwin, Gibson, and Simic.
• Consider the distances at which the autobiographical writers stand from their subject. What are the advantages and disadvantages of the different distances?
• What are the techniques Ford and Simic use to focus their readers' attention on their subject?
• Consider how the scene with Matt or when Ford talked about his possibly pregnant girlfriend could be made into a story or a movie scene.

Activities

• Interview a parent or someone of similar influence in your life, then tell their story in a brief biography.
• Draft your own memories of someone who brought you up. Compare your tone with Ford's.
• Read an example of Ford's fiction and report on how his fictional techniques compare with how this selection is written.
• Write one of the scenes in Ford's piece in your own style; draft a scene from your life in Ford's style.

To Collaborate

• Interview another student about a parent or someone who has had a great influence in the student's life and write a sketch of that person. Reverse roles, then compare what the interviewer heard you say with what you thought you said.
• Work as a committee to draft guidelines for the writing of biography from your study of Ford, Simic, and the other autobiographical writers in this book.

Barbara W. Tuchman

Barbara Tuchman, who twice won the Pultizer Prize, published seven books of history and a collection of essays. In her writing and talking about writing she gave us all good counsel:

- "Research is endlessly seductive; writing is hard work. One has to sit down on that chair and think and transform thought into readable, conservative, interesting sentences that both make sense and make the reader turn the page. It is laborious, slow, often painful, sometimes agony. It means rearrangement, revision, adding, cutting, rewriting. But it brings a sense of excitement, almost of rapture; a moment on Olympus. In short, it is an act of creation."
- "Structure is chiefly a problem of selection, an agonizing business because there is always more material than one can use or fit into a story. The problem is how and what to select out of all that happened without, by the very process of selection, giving an over- or underemphasis which violates truth. One cannot put in everything: The result would be a shapeless mass."
- ". . . blocks (for me) generally come from difficulty of organization— that the material is resistant, or that I don't adequately understand it; it needs rethinking or additional research and a new approach."
- "I try for motion in every paragraph. I hate sentences that begin, 'There was a storm.' Instead, write, 'A storm burst.'"
- "After seven years' apprenticeship in journalism I discovered that an essential element for good writing is a good ear. One must *listen* to the sound of one's own prose."
- ". . . short words are always preferable to long ones; the fewer syllables the better, and monosyllables, beautiful and pure like 'bread' and 'sun' and 'grass' are the best of all."

- And my favorite:

- ". . . nothing is more satisfying than to write a good sentence. It is no fun to write lumpishly, dully, in prose the reader must plod through like wet sand. But it is a pleasure to achieve, if one can, a clear running prose that is simple yet full of surprises. This does not just happen. It requires skill, hard work, a good ear, and continued practice. . . ."

The following selection is taken from *A Distant Mirror: The Calamitous 14th Century*.

"This Is the End of the World": The Black Death

1   In October 1347, two months after the fall of Calais, Genoese trading ships put into the harbor of Messina in Sicily with dead and dying men at the oars. The ships had come from the Black Sea port of Caffa (now Feodosiya) in the Crimea, where the Genoese maintained a trading post. The diseased sailors showed strange black swellings about the size of an egg or an apple in the armpits and groin. The swellings oozed blood and pus and were followed by spreading boils and black blotches on the skin from internal bleeding. The sick suffered severe pain and died quickly within five days of the first symptoms. As the disease spread, other symptoms of continuous fever and spitting of blood appeared instead of the swellings or buboes. These victims coughed and sweated heavily and died even more quickly, within three days or less, sometimes in 24 hours. In both types everything that issued from the body—breath, sweat, blood from the buboes and lungs, bloody urine, and blood-blackened excrement—smelled foul. Depression and despair accompanied the physical symptoms, and before the end "death is seen seated on the face."

2   The disease was bubonic plague, present in two forms: one that infected the blood stream, causing the buboes and internal bleeding, and was spread by contacts; and a second, more virulent pneumonic type that infected the lungs and was spread by respiratory infection. The presence of both at once cause the high mortality and speed of contagion. So lethal was the disease that cases were known of persons going to bed well and dying before they woke, of doctors catching the illness at a bedside and dying before the patient. So rapidly did it spread from one to another that to a French physician, Simon de Covino, it seemed as if one sick person "could infect the whole world." The malignity of the pestilence appeared more terrible because its victims knew no prevention and no remedy.

3   The physical suffering of the disease and its aspect of evil mystery were expressed in a strange Welsh lament which saw "death coming into our midst like black smoke, a plague which cuts off the young, a rootless phantom which has no mercy for fair countenance. Woe is me of the shilling in the armpit! It is seething, terrible . . . a head that gives pain and causes a loud cry . . . a painful angry knob . . . Great is its seething like a burning cinder . . . a grievous thing of ashy color." Its eruption is ugly like the "seeds of black peas, broken fragments of brittle sea-coal! . . . the early ornaments of black death, cinders of the peelings of the cockle weed, a mixed multitude, a black plague like halfpence, like berries . . ."

4   Rumors of a terrible plague supposedly arising in China and spreading through Tartary (Central Asia) to India and Persia, Mesopotamia, Syria, Egypt, and all of Asia Minor had reached Europe in 1346. They told of a death toll so devastating that all of India was said to be depopulated, whole territories covered by dead bodies, other areas with no one left alive. As added up by Pope Clement VI at Avignon, the total of reported dead reached 25,840,000. In the

absence of a concept of contagion, no serious alarm was felt in Europe until the trading ships brought their black burden of pestilence into Messina while other infected ships from the Levant carried it to Genoa and Venice.

5   By January 1348 it penetrated France via Marseille, and North Africa via Tunis. Shipborne along coasts and navigable rivers, it spread westward from Marseille through the ports of Languedoc to Spain and northward up the Rhone to Avignon, where it arrived in March. It reached Narbonne, Montpellier, Carcassonne, and Toulouse between February and May, and at the same time in Italy spread to Rome and Florence and their hinterlands. Between June and August it reached Bordeaux, Lyon, and Paris, spread to Burgundy and Normandy, and crossed the Channel from Normandy into southern England. From Italy during the same summer it crossed the Alps into Switzerland and reached eastward to Hungary.

6   In a given area the plague accomplished its kill within four to six months and then faded, except in the larger cities, where, rooting into the close-quartered population, it abated during the winter, only to reappear in spring and rage for another six months.

7   In 1349 it resumed in Paris, spread to Picardy, Flanders, and the Low Countries, and from England to Scotland and Ireland as well as to Norway, where a ghost ship with a cargo of wool and a dead crew drifted offshore until it ran aground near Bergen. From there the plague passed into Sweden, Denmark, Prussia, Iceland, and as far as Greenland. Leaving a strange pocket of immunity in Bohemia, and Russia unattacked until 1351, it had passed from most of Europe by mid-1350. Although the mortality rate was erratic, ranging from one fifth in some places to nine tenths or almost total elimination in others, the overall estimate of modern demographers has settled—for the area extending from India to Iceland—around the same figure expressed in Froissart's casual words: "a third of the world died." His estimate, the common one at the time, was not an inspired guess but a borrowing of St. John's figure for mortality from plague in Revelation, the favorite guide to human affairs of the Middle Ages.

8   A third of Europe would have meant about 20 million deaths. No one knows in truth how many died. Contemporary reports were an awed impression, not an accurate count. In crowded Avignon, it was said, 400 died daily; 7,000 houses emptied by death were shut up; a single graveyard received 11,000 corpses in six weeks; half the city's inhabitants reportedly died, including 9 cardinals or one third of the total, and 70 lesser prelates. Watching the endlessly passing death carts, chroniclers let normal exaggeration take wings and put the Avignon death toll at 62,000 and even at 120,000, although the city's total population was probably less than 50,000.

9   When graveyards filled up, bodies at Avignon were thrown into the Rhone until mass burial pits were dug for dumping the corpses. In London in such pits corpses piled up in layers until they overflowed. Everywhere reports speak of the sick dying too fast for the living to bury. Corpses were dragged out of homes and left in front of doorways. Morning light revealed new piles of bodies. In

Florence the dead were gathered up by the Compagnia della Misericordia—founded in 1244 to care for the sick—whose members wore red robes and hoods masking the face except for the eyes. When their efforts failed, the dead lay putrid in the streets for days at a time. When no coffins were to be had, the bodies were laid on boards, two or three at once, to be carried to graveyards or common pits. Families dumped their own relatives into the pits, or buried them so hastily and thinly "that dogs dragged them forth and devoured their bodies."

10   Amid accumulating death and fear of contagion, people died without last rites and were buried without prayers, a prospect that terrified the last hours of the stricken. A bishop in England gave permission to laymen to make confession to each other as was done by the Apostles, "or if no man is present then even to a woman," and if no priest could be found to administer extreme unction, "then faith must suffice." Clement VI found it necessary to grant remissions of sin to all who died of the plague because so many were unattended by priests. "And no bells tolled," wrote a chronicler of Siena, "and nobody wept no matter what his loss because almost everyone expected death . . . And people said and believed, 'This is the end of the world.'"

11   In Paris, where the plague lasted through 1349, the reported death rate was 800 a day, in Pisa 500, in Vienna 500 to 600. The total dead in Paris numbered 50,000 or half the population. Florence, weakened by the famine of 1347, lost three to four fifths of its citizens, Venice two thirds, Hamburg and Bremen, though smaller in size, about the same proportion. Cities, as centers of transportation, were more likely to be affected than villages, although once a village was infected, its death rate was equally high. At Givry, a prosperous village in Burgundy of 1,200 or 1,500 people, the parish register records 615 deaths in the space of fourteen weeks, compared to an average of thirty deaths a year in the previous decade. In three villages of Cambridgeshire, manorial records show a death rate of 47 percent, 57 percent, and in one case 70 percent. When the last survivors, too few to carry on, moved away, a deserted village sank back into the wilderness and disappeared from the map altogether, leaving only a grass-covered ghostly outline to show where mortals once had lived.

12   In enclosed places such as monasteries and prisons, the infection of one person usually meant that of all, as happened in the Franciscan convents of Carcassonne and Marseille, where every inmate without exception died. Of the 140 Dominicans at Montpellier only seven survived. Petrarch's brother Gherardo, member of a Carthusian monastery, buried the prior and 34 fellow monks one by one, sometimes three a day, until he was left alone with his dog and fled to look for a place that would take him in. Watching every comrade die, men in such places could not but wonder whether the strange peril that filled the air had not been sent to exterminate the human race. In Kilkenny, Ireland, Brother John Clyn of the Friars Minor, another monk left alone among dead men, kept a record of what had happened lest "things which should be remembered perish with time and vanish from the memory of those who come after us." Sensing "the whole world, as it were, placed within the grasp of the Evil One," and

waiting for death to visit him too, he wrote, "I leave parchment to continue this work, if perchance any man survive and any of the race of Adam escape this pestilence and carry on the work which I have begun." Brother John, as noted by another hand, died of the pestilence, but he foiled oblivion.

13   The largest cities of Europe, with populations of about 100,000, were Paris and Florence, Venice and Genoa. At the next level, with more than 50,000, were Ghent and Bruges in Flanders, Milan, Bologna, Rome, Naples, and Palermo, and Cologne. London hovered below 50,000, the only city in England except York with more than 10,000. At the level of 20,000 to 50,000 were Bordeaux, Toulouse, Montpellier, Marseille, and Lyon in France, Barcelona, Seville, and Toledo in Spain, Siena, Pisa, and other secondary cities in Italy, and the Hanseatic trading cities of the Empire. The plague raged through them all, killing anywhere from one third to two thirds of their inhabitants. Italy, with a total population of 10 to 11 million, probably suffered the heaviest toll. Following the Florentine bankruptcies, the crop failures and workers' riots of 1346–47, the revolt of Cola di Rienzi that plunged Rome into anarchy, the plague came as the peak of successive calamities. As if the world were indeed in the grasp of the Evil One, its first appearance on the European mainland in January 1348 coincided with a fearsome earthquake that carved a path of wreckage from Naples up to Venice. Houses collapsed, church towers toppled, villages were crushed, and the destruction reached as far as Germany and Greece. Emotional response, dulled by horrors, underwent a kind of atrophy epitomized by the chronicler who wrote, "And in these days was burying without sorrows and wedding without friendschippe."

14   In Siena, where more than half the inhabitants died of the plague, work was abandoned on the great cathedral, planned to be the largest in the world, and never resumed, owing to loss of workers and master masons and "the melancholy and grief" of the survivors. The cathedral's truncated transept still stands in permanent witness to the sweep of death's scythe. Angelo di Tura, a chronicler of Siena, recorded the fear of contagion that froze every other instinct. "Father abandoned child, wife husband, one brother another," he wrote, "for this plague seemed to strike through the breath and sight. And so they died. And no one could be found to bury the dead for money or friendship . . . And I, Angelo di Tura, called the Fat, buried my five children with my own hands, and so did many other likewise."

15   There were many to echo his account of inhumanity and few to balance it, for the plague was not the kind of calamity that inspired mutual help. Its loathsomeness and deadliness did not herd people together in mutual distress, but only prompted their desire to escape each other. "Magistrates and notaries refused to come and make the wills of the dying," reported a Franciscan friar of Piazza in Sicily; what was worse, "even the priests did not come to hear their confessions." A clerk of the Archbishop of Canterbury reported the same of English priests who "turned away from the care of their benefices from fear of death." Cases of parents deserting children and children their parents were

reported across Europe from Scotland to Russia. The calamity chilled the hearts of men, wrote Boccaccio in his famous account of the plague in Florence that serves as introduction to the *Decameron*. "One man shunned another . . . kinsfolk held aloof, brother was forsaken by brother, oftentimes husband by wife; nay, what is more, and scarcely to be believed, fathers and mothers were found to abandon their own children to their fate, untended, unvisited as if they had been strangers." Exaggeration and literary pessimism were common in the 14th century, but the Pope's physician, Guy de Chauliac, was a sober, careful observer who reported the same phenomenon: "A father did not visit his son, nor the son his father. Charity was dead."

16   Yet not entirely. In Paris, according to the chronicler Jean de Venette, the nuns of the Hôtel Dieu or municipal hospital, "having no fear of death, tended the sick with all sweetness and humility." New nuns repeatedly took the places of those who died, until the majority "many times renewed by death now rest in peace with Christ as we may piously believe."

17   When the plague entered northern France in July 1348, it settled first in Normandy and, checked by winter, gave Picardy a deceptive interim until the next summer. Either in mourning or warning, black flags were flown from church towers of the worst-stricken villages of Normandy. "And in that time," wrote a monk of the abbey of Fourcarment, "the mortality was so great among the people of Normandy that those of Picardy mocked them." The same unneighborly reaction was reported of the Scots, separated by a winter's immunity from the English. Delighted to hear of the disease that was scourging the "southrons," they gathered forces for an invasion, "laughing at their enemies." Before they could move, the savage mortality fell upon them too, scattering some in death and the rest in panic to spread the infection as they fled.

18   In Picardy in the summer of 1349 the pestilence penetrated the castle of Coucy to kill Enguerrand's mother, Catherine, and her new husband. Whether her nine-year-old son escaped by chance or was perhaps living elsewhere with one of his guardians is unrecorded. In nearby Amiens, tannery workers, responding quickly to losses in the labor force, combined to bargain for higher wages. In another place villagers were seen dancing to drums and trumpets, and on being asked the reason, answered that, seeing their neighbors die day by day while their village remained immune, they believed they could keep the plague from entering "by the jollity that is in us. That is why we dance." Further north in Tournal on the border of Flanders, Gilles li Muisis, Abbot of St. Martin's, kept one of the epidemic's most vivid accounts. The passing bells rang all day and all night, he recorded, because sextons were anxious to obtain their fees while they could. Filled with the sound of mourning, the city became oppressed by fear, so that the authorities forbade the tolling of bells and the wearing of black and restricted funeral services to two mourners. The silencing of funeral bells and of criers' announcements of deaths was ordained by most cities. Siena imposed a fine on the wearing of mourning clothes by all except widows.

19   Flight was the chief recourse of those who could afford it or arrange it. The rich fled to their country places like Boccaccio's young patricians of Florence, who settled in a pastoral palace "removed on every side from the roads" with "wells of cool water and vaults of rare wines." The urban poor died in their burrows, "and only the stench of their bodies informed neighbors of their death." That the poor were more heavily afflicted than the rich was clearly remarked at the time, in the north as in the south. A Scottish chronicler, John of Fordun, stated flatly that the pest "attacked especially the meaner sort and common people—seldom the magnates." Simon de Covino of Montpellier made the same observation. He ascribed it to the misery and want and hard lives that made the poor more susceptible, which was half the truth. Close contact and lack of sanitation was the unrecognized other half. It was noticed too that the young died in greater proportion than the old; Simon de Covino compared the disappearance of youth to the withering of flowers in the fields.

20   In the countryside peasants dropped dead on the roads, in the fields, in their houses. Survivors in growing helplessness fell into apathy, leaving ripe wheat uncut and livestock untended. Oxen and asses, sheep and goats, pigs and chickens ran wild and they too, according to local reports, succumbed to the pest. English sheep, bearers of the precious wool, died throughout the country. The chronicler Henry Knighton, canon of Leicester Abbey, reported 5,000 dead in one field alone, "their bodies so corrupted by the plague that neither beast nor bird would touch them," and spreading an appalling stench. In the Austrian Alps wolves came down to prey upon sheep, and then, "as if alarmed by some invisible warning turned and fled back into the wilderness." In remote Dalmatia bolder wolves descended upon a plague-stricken city and attacked human survivors. For want of herdsmen, cattle strayed from place to place and died in hedgerows and ditches. Dogs and cats fell like the rest.

21   The dearth of labor held a fearful prospect because the 14th century lived close to the annual harvest both for food and for next year's seed. "So few servants and laborers were left," wrote Knighton, "that no one knew where to turn for help." The sense of a vanishing future created a kind of dementia of despair. A Bavarian chronicler of Neuberg on the Danube recorded that "Men and women . . . wandered around as if mad" and let their cattle stray "because no one had any inclination to concern themselves about the future." Fields went uncultivated, spring seed unsown. Second growth with nature's awful energy crept back over cleared land, dikes crumbled, salt water reinvaded and soured the lowlands. With so few hands remaining to restore the work of centuries, people felt, in Walsingham's words, that "the world could never again regain its former prosperity."

22   Though the death rate was higher among the anonymous poor, the known and the great died too. King Alfonso XI of Castile was the only reigning monarch killed by the pest, but his neighbor King Pedro of Aragon lost his wife, Queen Leonora, his daughter Marie, and a niece in the space of six months. John Cantacuzene, Emperor of Byzantium, lost his son. In France the lame

Queen Jeanne and her daughter-in-law Bonne de Luxemburg, wife of the Dauphin, both died in 1349 in the same phase that took the life of Enguerrand's mother. Jeanne, Queen of Navarre, daughter of Louis X, was another victim. Edward III's second daughter, Joanna, who was on her way to marry Pedro, the heir of Castile, died in Bordeaux. Women appear to have been more vulnerable than men, perhaps because, being more housebound, they were more exposed to fleas. Boccaccio's mistress Fiammetta, illegitimate daughter of the King of Naples, died, as did Laura, the beloved—whether real or fictional—of Petrarch. Reaching out to us in the future, Petrarch cried, "Oh happy posterity who will not experience such abysmal woe and will look upon our testimony as a fable."

23   In Florence Giovanni Villani, the great historian of his time, died at 68 in the midst of an unfinished sentence; ". . . e dure questo pistolenza fino a . . . (in the midst of this pestilence there came to an end . . .)," Siena's master painters, the brothers Ambrogio and Pietro Lorenzetti, whose names never appear after 1348, presumably perished in the plague, as did Andrea Pisano, architect and sculptor of Florence. William of Ockham and the English mystic Richard Rolle of Hampole both disappear from mention after 1349. Francisco Datini, merchant of Prato, lost both his parents and two siblings. Curious sweeps of mortality afflicted certain bodies of merchants in London. All eight wardens of the Company of Cutters, all six wardens of the Hatters, and four wardens of the Goldsmiths died before July 1350. Sir John Pulteney, master draper and four times Mayor of London, was a victim, likewise Sir John Montgomery, Governor of Calais.

24   Among the clergy and doctors the mortailty was naturally high because of the nature of their professions. Out of 24 physicians in Venice, 20 were said to have lost their lives in the plague, although, according to another account, some were believed to have fled or to have shut themselves up in their houses. At Montpellier, site of the leading medieval medical school, the physician Simon de Covino reported that, despite the great number of doctors, "hardly one of them escaped." In Avignon, Guy de Chauliac confessed that he performed his medical visits only because he dared not stay away for fear of infamy, but "I was in continual fear." He claimed to have contracted the disease but to have cured himself by his own treatment; if so, he was one of the few who recovered.

25   Clerical mortality varied with rank. Although the one third toll of cardinals reflects the same proportion as the whole, this was probably due to their concentration in Avignon. In England, in strange and almost sinister procession, the Archbishop of Canterbury, John Stratford, died in August 1348, his appointed successor died in May 1349, and the next appointee three months later, all three within a year. Despite such weird vagaries, prelates in general managed to sustain a higher survival rate than the lesser clergy. Among bishops the deaths have been estimated at about one in twenty. The loss of priests, even if many avoided their fearful duty of attending the dying, was about the same as among the population as a whole.

26   Government officials, whose loss contributed to the general chaos, found,

on the whole, no special shelter. In Siena four of the nine members of the governing oligarchy died, in France one third of the royal notaries, in Bristol 15 out of the 52 members of the Town Council or almost one third. Tax-collecting obviously suffered, with the result that Phillip VI was unable to collect more than a fraction of the subsidy granted him by the Estates in the winter of 1347–48.

27   Lawlessness and debauchery accompanied the plague as they had during the great plague of Athens of 430 B.C., when according to Thucydides, men grew bold in the indulgence of pleasure: "For seeing how the rich died in a moment and those who had nothing immediately inherited their property, they reflected that life and riches were alike transitory and they resolved to enjoy themselves while they could." Human behavior is timeless. When St. John had his vision of plague in Revelation, he knew from some experience or race memory that those who survived "repented not of the work of their hands. . . . Neither repented they of their murders, nor of their sorceries, nor of their fornication, nor of their thefts."

A Writer's Notes for a Second Reading

The writer can choose the lens with which to view the subject. Historian Barbara Tuchman demonstrates what can be done with a wide-angle lens as she stands back and surveys the scope of the Bubonic Plague.

As a writer, I am impressed at how she can, standing at such a distance from her subject, still manage to work so well with specific details, keeping the text moving forward and mixing her forms of evidence and documentation with such skill.

We stand before a mural along an entire wall and yet she manages to make us feel and fear as well as to learn and understand.

Discussion

• Select one of the pieces of Tuchman's advice about writing reprinted in the introduction and consider if she followed her own advice. Cite examples where she did or did not.

• Discuss the techniques Tuchman used to keep the text moving forward so that the reader will turn the page. How can you do the same thing with your writing?

• Do you believe Tuchman's version of the plague? Why? How has she convinced you?

• How did Tuchman make another time come alive to readers living centuries later?

• Did Tuchman underwrite, almost coldly presenting the facts. If so, why did she do this? Does it work? Where might it work in a piece of your own?

• Discuss how Tuchman achieved focus in the entire selection. In a paragraph.

Activities

• Look up a newspaper account of a catastrophe—an explosion, earthquake, famine, fire—and compare it to Tuchman's. What could the author of that piece and Tuchman teach each other?

• Write an account of an event in your world—an accident, a game, a party, an election—as if you were a historian writing 500 years from now.

• Take a piece of your own or one from a classmate and put it in historical perspective.

• Write about something that interests you that requires statistics and other documentation as if you were Barbara Tuchman. If you have such a piece in your folder, edit it as if you were she.

• You have 250 words to report on the Black Death. Choose the words from Tuchman or use her material to write your own 250-word report.

To Collaborate

• Work together on a report comparing the Black Death and the AIDS epidemic. See if there are lessons from the past that can be applied to the present.

• Go through the Tuchman text with your partner and identify each form of documentation she uses. Write guidelines for the class, giving a good example of each form of evidence she gives the reader.

Alice Stewart Trillin

Ever since Alice Trillin gave me this article, I have reread it regularly for wisdom and for technique, but never at the same time. Read it first to hear what she has to say about living, then read it again to learn from how she said it. I have used it in many classes and we have all spent some time, time well spent, to talk about the important issues of life and death and the meaning of life that are usually not allowed in the classroom. But the power of the content should not obscure the skill with which the author writes.

The article has an interesting history. It was a talk addressed to medical students at both Cornell and Albert Einstein medical schools. It meant so much to the medical profession that it was published in the March 19, 1981, issue of the distinguished journal, *The New England Journal of Medicine*.

Of Dragons and Garden Peas

1   When I first realized that I might have cancer, I felt immediately that I had entered a special place, a place I came to call "The Land of the Sick People."

The most disconcerting thing, however, was not that I found that place terrifying and unfamiliar, but that I found it so ordinary, so banal. I didn't feel different, didn't feel that my life had radically changed at the moment the word *cancer* became attached to it. The same rules still held. What had changed, however, was other people's perceptions of me. Unconsciously, even with a certain amount of kindness, everyone—with the single rather extraordinary exception of my husband—regarded me as someone who had been altered irrevocably. I don't want to exaggerate my feeling of alienation or to give the impression that it was in any way dramatic. I have no horror stories of the kind I read a few years ago in the *New York Times;* people didn't move their desks away from me at the office or refuse to let their children play with my children at school because they thought that cancer was catching. My friends are all too sophisticated and too sensitive for that kind of behavior. Their distance from me was marked most of all by their inability to understand the ordinariness, the banality of what was happening to me. They marveled at how well I was "coping with cancer." I had become special, no longer like them. Their genuine concern for what had happened to me, and their complete separateness from it, expressed exactly what I had felt all my life about anyone I had ever known who had experienced tragedy.

2   When asked to speak to a group of doctors and medical students about what it was like to be a cancer patient, I worried for a long time about what I should say. It was a perfect opportunity—every patient's fantasy—to complain about doctors' insensitivity, nurses who couldn't draw blood properly, and perhaps even the awful food in hospitals. Or, instead, I could present myself as the good patient, full of uplifting thoughts about how much I had learned from having cancer. But, unlike many people, I had had very good experiences with doctors and hospitals. And the role of the brave patient troubled me, because I was afraid that all the brave things I said might no longer hold if I got sick again. I had to think about this a great deal during the first two years after my operation as I watched my best friend live out my own worst nightmares. She discovered that she had cancer several months after I did. Several months after that, she discovered that it had metastasized; she underwent eight operations during the next year and a half before she died. All my brave talk was tested by her illness as it has not yet been tested by mine.

3   And so I decided not to talk about the things that separate those of us who have cancer from those who do not. I decided that the only relevant thing for me to talk about was the one thing that we all have most in common. We are all afraid of dying.

4   Our fear of death makes it essential to maintain a distance between ourselves and anyone who is threatened by death. Denying our connection to the precariousness of others' lives is a way of pretending that we are immortal. We need this deception—it is one of the ways we stay sane—but we also need to be prepared for the times when it doesn't work. For doctors, who confront death when they go to work in the morning as routinely as other people deal

with balance sheets and computer printouts, and for me, to whom a chest x-ray or a blood test will never again be a simple, routine procedure, it is particularly important to face the fact of death squarely, to talk about it with one another.

5 Cancer connects us to one another because having cancer is an embodiment of the existential paradox that we all experience: we feel that we are immortal, yet we know that we will die. To Tolstoy's Ivan Ilyich, the syllogism he had learned as a child, "'Caius is a man, men are mortal, therefore Caius is mortal,' had always seemed . . . correct as applied to Caius but certainly not as applied to himself." Like Ivan Ilyich, we all construct an elaborate set of defense mechanisms to separate ourselves from Caius. To anyone who has had cancer, these defense mechanisms become talismans that we invest with a kind of magic. These talismans are essential to our sanity, and yet they need to be examined.

6 First of all, we believe in the magic of doctors and medicine. The purpose of a talisman is to give us control over the things we are afraid of. Doctors and patients are accomplices in staging a kind of drama in which we pretend that doctors have the power to keep us well. The very best doctors—and I have had the very best—share their power with their patients and try to give us the information that we need to control our own treatment. Whenever I am threatened by panic, my doctor sits me down and tells me something concrete. He draws a picture of my lung, or my lymph nodes; he explains as well as he can how cancer cells work and what might be happening in my body. Together, we approach my disease intelligently and rationally, as a problem to be solved, an exercise in logic to be worked out. Of course, through knowledge, through medicine, through intelligence, we do have some control. But at best this control is limited, and there is always the danger that the disease I have won't behave rationally and respond to the intelligent argument we have constructed. Cancer cells more than anything else in nature, are likely to behave irrationally. If we think that doctors and medicine can always protect us, we are in danger of losing faith in doctors and medicine when their magic doesn't work. The physician who fails to keep us well is like an unsuccessful witch doctor; we have to drive him out of the tribe and look for a more powerful kind of magic.

7 The reverse of this, of course, is that the patient becomes a kind of talisman for the doctor. Doctors defy death by keeping people alive. To a patient, it becomes immediately clear that the best way to please a doctor is to be healthy. If you can't manage that, the next best thing is to be well-behaved. (Sometimes the difference between being healthy and being well-behaved becomes blurred in a hospital, so that it almost seems as if being sick were being badly behaved.) If we get well, we help our doctors succeed; if we are sick, we have failed. Patients often say that their doctors seem angry with them when they don't respond to treatment. I think that this phenomenon is more than patients' paranoia or the result of overdeveloped medical egos. It is the fear of death again. It is necessary for doctors to become a bit angry with patients who

are dying, if only as a way of separating themselves from someone in whom they have invested a good bit of time and probably a good bit of caring. We all do this to people who are sick. I can remember being terribly angry with my mother who was prematurely senile, for a long time. Somehow I needed to think that it was her fault that she was sick, because her illness frightened me so much,. I was also angry with my friend who died of cancer. I felt that she had let me down, that perhaps she hadn't fought hard enough. It was important for me to find reasons for her death, to find things that she might have done to cause it, as a way of separating myself from her and as a way of thinking that I would somehow have behaved differently, that I would somehow have been able to stay alive.

8   So, once we have recognized the limitations of the magic of doctors and medicine, where are we? We have to turn to our own magic, to our ability to "control" our bodies. For people who don't have cancer, this often takes the form of jogging and exotic diets and transcendental meditation. For people who have cancer, it takes the form of conscious development of the will to live. For a long time after I found out that I had cancer, I loved hearing stories about people who had simply decided that they would not be sick. I remember one story about a man who had a lung tumor and a wife with breast cancer and several children to support; he said, "I simply can't afford to be sick." Somehow the tumor went away. I think I suspected that there was a missing part to this story when I heard it, but there was also something that sounded right to me. I knew what he meant. I also found the fact that I had cancer unacceptable; the thought that my children might grow up without me was as ridiculous as the thought that I might forget to make appointments for their dental checkups and polio shots. I simply had to be there. Of course, doctors give a lot of credence to the power of the will over illness, but I have always suspected that the stories in medical books about this power might also have missing parts. My friend who died wanted to live more than anyone I have ever known. The talisman of will didn't work for her.

9   The need to exert some kind of control over the irrational forces that we imagine are loose in our bodies also results in what I have come to recognize as the "brave act" put on by people who have cancer. We all do it. The blood-count line at Memorial Hospital can be one of the cheeriest places in New York on certain mornings. It was on this line, during my first visit to Memorial, that a young leukemia patient in remission told me, "They treat lung cancer like the common cold around here," (Believe me, that was the cheeriest thing anyone had said to me in months.) While waiting for blood counts, I have heard stories from people with lymphoma who were given up for dead in other hospitals and who are feeling terrific. The atmosphere in that line suggests a gathering of knights who have just slain a bunch of dragons. But there are always people in the line who don't say anything at all, and I always wonder if they have at other times felt the exhilaration felt by those of us who are well. We all know, at least, that the dragons are never quite dead and might at any time be around, ready for another fight. But our brave act is important. It is one of the ways we stay

alive, and it is the way that we convince those who live in "The Land of the Well People" that we aren't all that different from them.

10   As much as I rely on the talisman of the will, I know that believing in it too much can lead to another kind of deception. There has been a great deal written (mostly by psychiatrists) about why people get cancer and which personality types are most likely to get it. Susan Sontag has pointed out that this explanation of cancer parallels the explanations for tuberculosis that were popular before the discovery of the tubercle bacillus. But it is reassuring to think that people get cancer because of their personalities, because that implies that we have some control over whether we get it. (On the other hand, if people won't give up smoking to avoid cancer, I don't see how they can be expected to change their personalities on the basis of far less compelling evidence.) The trouble with this explanation of cancer is the trouble with any talisman: it is only useful when its charms are working. If I get sick, does that mean that my will to live isn't strong enough? Is being sick a moral and psychological failure? If I feel successful, as if I had slain a dragon, because I am well, should I feel guilty, as if I have failed, if I get sick?

11   One of the ways that all of us avoid thinking about death is by concentrating on the details of our daily lives. The work that we do every day and the people we love—the fabric of our lives—convince us that we are alive and that we will stay alive. William Saroyan said in a recent book, "Why am I writing this book? To save my life, to keep from dying, of course. That is why we get up in the morning." Getting up in the morning seems particularly miraculous after having seriously considered the possibility that these mornings might be limited. A year after I had my lung removed, my doctors asked me what I cared about most. I was about to go to Nova Scotia, where we have a summer home, and where I had not been able to go the previous summer because I was having radiation treatments, and I told him that what was most important to me was garden peas. Not the peas themselves, of course, though they were particularly good that year. What was extraordinary to me after that year was that I could again think that peas were important, that I could concentrate on the details of when to plant them and how much mulch they would need instead of thinking about platelets and white cells. I cherished the privilege of thinking about trivia. Thinking about death can make the details of our lives seem unimportant, and so, paradoxically, they become a burden—too much trouble to think about. This is the real meaning of depression: feeling weighed down by the concrete, unable to make the effort to move objects around, overcome by ennui. It is the fear of death that causes that ennui, because the fear of death ties us too much to the physical. We think too much about our bodies, and our bodies become too concrete—machines not functioning properly.

12   The other difficulty with the talisman of the moment is that it is often the very preciousness of these moments that makes the thought of death so painful. As my friend got closer to death she became rather removed from those she loved the most. She seemed to have gone to some place where we couldn't reach her—to have died what doctors sometimes call a "premature death." I

much preferred to think of her enjoying precious moments. I remembered the almost ritualistic way she had her hair cut and tied in satin ribbons before brain surgery, the funny, somehow joyful afternoon that we spent trying wigs on her newly shaved head. Those moments made it seem as if it wasn't so bad to have cancer. But of course it was bad. It was unspeakably bad, and toward the end she couldn't bear to speak about it or to be too close to the people she didn't want to leave. The strength of my love for my children, my husband, my life, even my garden peas has probably been more important than anything else in keeping me alive. The intensity of this love is also what makes me so terrified of dying.

13   For many, of course, a response to the existential paradox is religion— Kierkegaard's irrational leap toward faith. It is no coincidence that such a high number of conversions take place in cancer hospitals; there is even a group of Catholic nurses in New York who are referred to by other members of their hospital staff as "the death squad." I don't mean to belittle such conversions or any help that religion can give to anyone. I am at this point in my life simply unqualified to talk about the power of this particular talisman.

14   In considering some of the talismans we all use to deny death, I don't mean to suggest that these talismans should be abandoned. However, their limits must be acknowledged. Ernest Becker, in *The Denial of Death,* says that "skepticism is a more radical experience, a more manly confrontation of potential meaninglessness than mysticism." The most important thing I know now that I didn't know four years ago is that this "potential meaninglessness" can in fact be confronted. As much as I rely on my talismans—my doctors, my will, my husband, my children, and my garden peas—I know that from time to time I will have to confront what Conrad described as "the horror." I know that we can—all of us—confront that horror and not be destroyed by it, even, to some extent, be enhanced by it. To quote Becker again: "I think that taking life seriously means something such as this: that whatever man does on this planet has to be done in the lived truth of the terror of creation, of the grotesque, of the rumble of panic underneath everything. Otherwise it is false."

15   It astonishes me that having faced the terror, we continue to live, even to live with a great deal of joy. It is commonplace for people who have cancer— particularly those who feel as well as I do—to talk about how much richer their lives are because they have confronted death. Yes, my life is very rich. I have even begun to understand that wonderful line in *King Lear,* "Ripeness is all." I suppose that becoming ripe means finding out that none of the really important questions have answers. I wish that life had devised a less terrifying, less risky way of making me ripe. But I wasn't given any choice about this.

16   William Saroyan said recently, "I'm growing old! I'm falling apart! And it's VERY INTERESTING!" I'd be willing to bet that Mr. Saroyan, like me, would much rather be young and all in one piece. But somehow his longing for youth and wholeness doesn't destroy him or stop him from getting up in the morning and writing, as he says, to save his life. We will never kill the dragon. But each

morning we confront him. Then we give our children breakfast, perhaps put a bit more mulch on the peas, and hope that we can convince the dragon to stay away for a while longer.

A Writer's Notes for a Second Reading

Tuchman chose the wide-angle lens; Trillin uses a close-up, moving in on the experiences of a single person with the feared disease of our time, cancer.

I am struck by how she is able to be personal without being melodramatic. She is candid, specific, and never wallows in self-pity. Some writers embarrass the reader with excessive intimacy, but Trillin never does. She is direct and effective.

Her writing is a demonstration of character. Note the compassion with which she writes. She is not attacking those whose reaction she deplores. She understands but tries to make them understand her position.

Note the way she ends the essay. The larger the topic—and none is larger than death—she turns to the ordinary, the revealing detail, the specific metaphor.

Discussion

- Discuss the ways in which Trillin gives the reader room and keeps the reader from being unnecessarily uncomfortable in confronting this subject.
- Note how the author mentions, but gets beyond, the bad aspects of her treatment in the hospital early in the piece. Notice other examples of where she does this.
- Discuss how she weaves the death of her friend and her feelings for that friend and about that death through the piece as a counterpoint to her own experience and feelings. What does that enable her to do as a writer?
- The paper was first given to instruct doctors in how to deal with patients with serious illness. What does she tell the doctors to do? How well does she get her message across? What other ways could she have done it? How effective would they have been?
- What is the focus of this piece? What role does the title, which comes from the last paragraph, play in the focus? Most times we think of focus as coming from the beginning. Can the focus come from the end? And can reader and writer work toward the focus?
- Discuss how Tuchman and Trillin use voice to carry much of the meaning of what they have to say. Is each voice appropriate to each subject? If the voice in each piece is "natural" to each author, how might Tuchman and Trillin write each other's pieces?
- Discuss the distance at which Trillin and Tuchman stand from their subject. How does the distance help the writer and the reader?
- Imagine how the piece might have been written if it were given to an audience of people who fear they might have cancer, or people who have had cancer, rather than an audience of doctors.

Activities

- Imagine the last paragraph as the lead, and outline the piece that would be written as the result.
- Imagine the first paragraph as the ending, and outline the piece that would be written as the result.
- Write a piece of your own that deals with an issue of life or death in your experience.
- Rewrite a paragraph from Trillin, using your own voice to speak of her subject.
- Draft a lead for a piece that would report on what Trillin said for a newspaper; that would use what Trillin said for a lead on a magazine article about people who have had cancer; that would use Trillin's experience for the lead of a brochure raising money for cancer research; or that would use her experience for the lead of a short story about someone similar to Trillin.

To Collaborate

- Work as a committee to interview medical counselors and lay out a brochure using their material and Trillin's piece which might be used to help families of victims of life-threatening disease.
- Work together from Trillin's text to compose a letter to a friend or family member who has a serious illness, deciding what to say and what not to say after you have just heard the news.

Anonymous
STUDENT ESSAY

The Addiction

1   Jeremy is a nineteen-year-old drug addict. For six years alcohol and marijuana have played a major part in his life. He is from a two-parent upper-middle-class family with two older siblings who are not involved with drugs. Having been in two drug rehabilitation centers, Jeremy knows and admitted his problems. He realizes he can't drink or use drugs without losing control. However, since being out of the second rehabilitation center, he has gotten drunk four or five times. He is scared, worried, and angry at himself and others. Feeling he has no control in his life, he has begun fantasizing about death.

2   If this person or one with similar problems was a large part of your life, how would you handle his problems in relation to yours? Would you blame yourself?

3   Jeremy is a real person and he is a large part of my life. Before I had known him, I had heard rumors about how much of a partier he was. I was told that

he was always being chased by gang members who had been cheated by Jeremy's drug dealing. It flashed through my mind that Jeremy needed to be loved and helped.

4   For more than the first half of our relationship we would get drunk and stoned together. He told me all about his escapades, such as when he was chased by our hometown police down back roads at 90 miles an hour. He and his friend had just bought a large amount of pot and they wanted to smoke as much as possible before they were arrested. It turned out that the police had only wanted him because the inspection sticker on his beat-up forest green car had expired.

5   I was fascinated. Here was someone who was so different from me. As the summer slowly went on, I was pretty sure that he had a drug problem, but I didn't feel I knew him well enough to tell him.

6   When I decided to stop using drugs, he became even more addicted. I began to get scared and we started talking about his problems he was having at home and with his friends. He felt that his friends were using him. He didn't know what for, though. I realized that his troubles were a result of his addictions. I began to be his "therapist" by helping him with his problems. I thought that if his problems could be solved, then he would stop drinking and smoking pot and going back to his friends who also smoke and drink heavily.

7   It didn't work that way. After a night of heavy drinking, Jeremy was picked up by the police. He had been walking home from my house. Later his mother asked why I hadn't driven him home. Being 18, he had a choice of getting arrested or going to a treatment center. He chose the center. I gave him all the support I could. My life had become dedicated to helping Jeremy overcome his problems. I would write inspiring letters to tell him how much he meant to me and how much better life would be when he got out. I made him brownies and brought him grape Fruit-Roll-Ups, which are his favorite. I was also able to visit him once, which made me even more determined to "rescue" him from drugs. The people that he lived with were a lot worse off than he was. One woman who had never come down from an acid trip would sit in front of a blank television screen and rub her hands together all day long. On the drive home, I cried because I felt so bad.

8   He'd call me every night after 9 o'clock. I would stay home to accept his collect calls. When his friends deserted him because they thought he was weak, I stood by and defended him. I was so happy when Jeremy was finally discharged. I felt that he was cured and that maybe I had helped a little.

9   A few weeks later we both went away to school. He would call and tell me he was fine and that he could handle drinking again. I was devastated that he had started again. I felt like a failure.

10   Two weeks later he was in another drug rehabilitation center. His voice reflected his depression and disgust with himself. He told me that he had learned. He didn't want to drink anymore. I was so relieved. I hadn't failed. I kept thinking that the reason he had gone back to drinking at school was because I wasn't there to listen and help all the time like I had been before.

However, during this time I had become emotionally dependent on Jeremy. When he called from the center in a bad mood, I felt guilty. I thought that I hadn't written him enough letters. Once when he called and told me that he didn't want to see or hear from me anymore, I contemplated suicide. I had truly failed him. I kept asking myself how can I help him now? He did eventually change his mind.

11   After getting out, he was so happy to be straight and I was just as happy and proud as he was. He'd call and tell me about the Alcoholics Anonymous meeting he'd gone to. He even gave me all his A.A. literature to read.

12   But soon I didn't hear any more about the meetings. He told me that he didn't need to go anymore and that he could have a drink once in a while. I didn't know what to do. I thought of dropping out of college to go home and help him. By this point, I realized how much his problems had become mine. I began reading pamphlets from Al-Anon, the organization that helps those who know an alcoholic. I read how an alcoholic has to want to stop drinking for himself and not for others. That helped me a bit, but by now it was too late.

13   One night, while home for the weekend from school, he showed up at a party I was at. I wasn't sure what to do. I didn't want him to drink, but I also knew he wasn't going to pay attention to my nagging. Jeremy got drunk. I got upset and began crying. Jeremy just told me to shut up and that he was going home. The next day I told him how guilty I felt about his drinking. He told me not to worry, that he could handle it.

14   Obviously he can't and I think he knows this. I still feel guilty; as if there was something I could do or say that would shock him into the reality of how much he is hurting himself. I don't know how long this is going to go on.

15   Not too long ago, I had an experience that showed me how fearful I was for him. One night Jeremy and I were driving when I looked over at him. I'm not sure if it was a shadow or what, but he looked like a skeleton with the black hollow eyes and white melted waxlike bones. He saw the horror in my face and asked me what was wrong. I began crying and told him. He became silent and drove me home. A few days later he called me. He explained that the reason he hadn't wanted to talk was because he was scared. He had seen himself as a skeleton, too. He told me that lately he had been having dreams that he was changing into a skeleton and a few times when looking in a mirror, he saw the same skeleton that I had described.

16   This shows how caught up in Jeremy's life I have become. I hope with time our lives will get straightened out.

History of the Essay

The student's first commentary on an extremely brief and undeveloped paper was:

"This paper is very poorly written, I know. There are somewhat painful circumstances, however, that I hope will be understood. I don't think I can write them down as yet because it is too upsetting to me. I will try to explain them to you. If this is not acceptable, then I will write them."

In conference, I listened to what she wanted to write about and told her that she was welcome to explore the topic but that if it became too painful, she could drop it without penalty. She would be the judge.

I have found that it is good therapy to write about painful subjects, but I am not a therapist, and the writer has to be the person who decides if it is constructive to write on a topic. There have been times when I could not bear to write about the death of my daughter, and times when I had to write about it.

Writing is a way of getting distance and dealing with a subject, and also a way of reaching out and helping other people. It was her decision, week by week, to go on with this. It was not a subject from which she was detached. I knew, however, that we don't learn to write by dealing with subjects with which we are not involved. We sometimes forget that scholars, supermarket managers, engineers, and everyone else in the real world who writes are writing about issues that are of vital importance to them. The writer has to learn how to deal with information that is close to the writer.

During the weeks ahead the writer was on a roller coaster in her personal life, but continued to do solid, anchoring research on drug rehabilitation. Her commentary on her first completed draft included the following statements:

"Drug rehabilitation is a topic I'm still interested in. I thought that I would be sick of it after spending so much time researching, thinking, and writing about it. . . . The process of writing this paper was an emotional one. As you know, I am very personally involved with the subject. Before writing it, I tried to block out all my personal feelings and write from the facts, but used the perspective of one involved with the subject. I don't know if that was the right thing to do or not, but I was afraid that I would make my paper a dramatic sob story."

Her draft began:

Drug rehabilitation is an important process in a drug addict's fight for freedom from his addiction. At most rehabilitation centers the concepts and ideas of Alcoholics Anonymous/Narcotics Anonymous and the use of group therapy show the addicts how to adapt and change their thinking of themselves so they can overcome their addiction.

The student readers were amazingly consistent in their response:

"Your descriptions, short and to-the-point, of the various programs worked well because they did not last forever. They explained to the reader the programs without overstating or overemphasizing. Perhaps you should have included a case study or anecdote. Such a story would have made the paper more interesting to read and perhaps it would have more strongly supported your argument."

"It reads quite well. It flows smoothly from paragraph to paragraph. . . . What what was your argument? You should strengthen your opinion with more personal feelings."

"It totally captures the behavior of addicts and provides me with some good information. Don't be afraid to be more personal and put more of yourself into it. . . ."

The next draft began like the one we have published. In her commentary she said, "This is a personal paper, probably the most personal I have ever written or ever will write. Well, it's not probably the most personal paper—it is. I had to write it like this because I don't want anyone ever to get into a situation like mine. It is the hardest and most painful thing that has ever happened to me. The funny thing is that it wasn't that hard to write. I guess I know my subject."

Again there was consistency in the student response.

"This is awesome! The only suggestion that I have is maybe you need a little more in it about how you stand—more of a position . . ."

"Your paper is definitely one of the best I've read. You bring the reader into the problem very easily. The only thing that may need some improvement is bringing the points that are made at the end and incorporating them into the body of the paper."

"Try to incorporate your argument into the beginning of the paper . . ."

Final Evaluation

The Addiction is my personal history of what my life has been like for the past year and a half. I hope that I have argued effectively enough to show people not to take on the responsibility of a loved one's problem. Life for both will soon be hell.

The first draft was entitled Processes of Drug Rehabilitation *and it was as boring as the title implies. It wasn't much of an argument since I don't truly believe in it. To revise it, I took on a different strategy. I wanted to show how difficult it can be to see someone you love go through the difficult and never-ending process of rehabilitation. I have become too involved (maybe) with Jeremy's life of problems, but this paper has certainly helped me to see in writing how much and hard I have worked to help Jeremy. On the third revision, I didn't change much except trying to get across more of my feelings of guilt. The ending is the most extreme example of my strong feelings of worry and impending tragedy. I can't explain mine and Jeremy's vision of himself as a skeleton except that maybe he is scared of what he's going to do with his life and that I sensed the same feeling of confusion and doom.*

I don't like the term argument. I'd rather think that I persuaded someone than argued with them. But I have learned how to argue or persuade by using my experiences and opinions rather than a typical "I think that this should be true" statement. I've learned how important it is to use personal knowledge effectively to convince an audience of your expertise in a subject. Through the argument writing, I've learned how to organize my thoughts better by making lists of what exactly I want to say. I've learned to take time to make sure that sentences flow together and that they pertain to my subject. The weird thing is that I had heard how to do this many times before, but I never really took as much time to work at writing until now. I've gained confidence and want to write like never before.

Pamela DeKoning
STUDENT ESSAY

Come on Trust Me, Would I Lie to You?

1   Come on, just one little hit—it's not gonna' hurtcha—I promise—trust me, it'll make ya' feel good. Don't be such a fag, everyone's doin' it—just one hit—come on, what can one hit do? You don't believe all that crap on TV—do ya'? They don't know what they're talking about, they've never done drugs. Come on trust me, would I lie to you? I promise, listen—it's not gonna' hurtcha. Look at me, I've done a lot more than one hit and it hasn't done nothin' to me, come on don't be such a wimp.

2   Okay, maybe that one hit won't hurt you. Maybe, just maybe you'll walk away unharmed, after all, just one hit's no big deal, right? Maybe your one hit won't lead you to two hits to three hits to too too many hits. Maybe it won't invite and entice you to try things that will make you feel better. There are pills, from uppers to downers to get you off the uppers to coke, crack, shrooms, X, acid, heroin, to combinations of coke and acid and booze and . . . but maybe it would. It could. It does. Every day.

3   I forgot. It can't happen to you or your family. Drug addiction and over-doses are like teenage pregnancies, murders, and scandals, they happen to other people, not to you. That's what I thought, that's what my sister thought, that's what my boyfriend thought, that's what everyone thinks. Guess agains. It happens.

4   It can happen to anyone, you just don't know, it doesn't matter what your parents are like or where you grow up or how much money you have, don't ever think you're immune, it really does happen. Sure, certain factors can increase your chances; there are more drug addicts who come from violent, broken homes and city environments, but there are plenty of wealthy drug addicts. There are plenty of drug addicts who come from loving families and

happy homes. Addiction doesn't follow a pattern, it strikes randomly, and painfully.

5   Drug dealers aren't picky. Anyone with the determination, desire, and cash can get them; doctors, lawyers, kids, moms, dads, millionaires, athletes, housewives, movie stars, welfare recipients; you can even get them, if you want them.

6   "After you've tried it [pot] once, even if you want to stop, it's so hard to say no the second or third time. You, or at least I always say to myself, 'Okay, this is the last time,' but as long as you hang around with the same kids you got it from in the first place, there just always seems to be another chance to do it one more time," said Peter, a sophomore at UNH, adding, "If you've done pot, it's so easy to get involved in other things, it's just that you've said yes once to it [drugs], and then it just seems like, well the pot was great, let's move up just one more step, to speed, then coke, it's all just like a natural process."

7   Peter, like many other drug users interviewed, agreed that there is a process, a cycle by which the harder drugs come. This natural process includes some potent drugs. Coke. Crack. Acid. Heroin.

8   I saw this process destroy my sister. The drugs stripped her of her dignity, her personality, her smile, her laughter, her logic. The sparkle in her eye turned to glass, a stranger possessed her body, she's gone now, she'll never get out, she's stuck in the game for good.

9   At twelve, she started smoking pot, she began to change, she was no longer outgoing, she gave up sports, clubs, music, changed her friends, and became quiet and withdrawn.

10   Eventually, a teacher said something to my mother. Like most parents, she didn't want to believe her daughter would do such a thing. Unlike most parents, she did. She was calm about it and was able to get Kelly to stop.

11   Kelly's attitude and appearance improved, and things were normal for a while, but not for long. She could never stop for long, she isn't strong enough, she's stuck, she hasn't the will or the determination to beat it. She just doesn't want it bad enough. It's easier to consider herself a failure than to face reality and straighten out.

12   If you could see the effects of drug abuse through my eyes, you would never be tempted by them. Although I have never taken drugs, I have been through the pain, hurt, and horror many times. I saw my sister, my boyfriend, and uncle possessed by their habits while the innocent people that love them suffer with their helplessness.

13   Watching someone you love fall into the trap of drugs is more terrifying than any horror movie; it's painfully real, there are no special effects.

14   Imagine the betrayal and confusion when you think someone is at work, or school, and they're really getting stoned or tripping or stealing money to pay for the next time.

15   You can't know how horrible it is to wait up all night waiting for someone you know is on drugs to come home. Sitting up on a stormy winter night until 3:00 A.M. is not a pleasurable experience. You wonder if they're dead or alive,

you pray to God, hoping they're okay, and not wrapped around a tree some-where freezing. Imagine watching your mother crying for days because your sister ran away without leaving a note or a word, just sneaking away in the middle of the night.

16   The frustration of trying to help someone kick a drug habit is incredible. You sit up with them all night, holding their hand, talking and crying with them for hours, only to realize they've got coke hidden and are getting high, not sick every few hours in the bathroom.

17   The most frustrating and difficult part of drug addiction is trying to help someone who doesn't really want help yet. If they don't want it, it's like trying to pull someone out of the water with a rope that's growing. It's impossible, it can't be done. The harder you try, the faster it grows.

18   If you are going to help someone kick drugs, you have to realize that there's only a limited amount you can do. You can't, no matter how much you love someone, help them by yourself. There are no miracle cures. Giving up drugs when you're hooked is like walking through hell, and unless someone is really committed to kicking it, there's nothing you can do. No matter what they say, if they aren't totally committed to it, it's just not going to happen. If the need and desire for the drugs is still there, there's little chance of staying straight. It's like trying to break up with someone when you still love them, you're still dependent on them, and that need haunts you day and night.

19   When you're trying to help someone you really love, you take it personally when they fail; this is what's frustrating, because they're not doing it to hurt you, they're sick, drug addiction is a disease, just like alcoholism. You can't say, "If you loved me you'd stop." It just doesn't work, and it's not fair to anyone. The guilt trips and ultimatums don't work either, they only make it worse. You have to remember, drug users are the best damned liars in the world, they've had plenty of practice and they've even got themselves fooled.

20   So what do you do? Well, you don't stop loving them; they're sick, you have to support them. Tell them you think they need help, spend a lot of time with them, prove to them that there are other things to do and that their lives can be happy without drugs. As corny as it may sound, get them high on life, introduce new hobbies, tell them you love them, try anything to keep them busy; if they're busy and having fun, they don't have as much time to think about the drugs.

21   Drug use has become the norm rather than the exception in today's Amer-ican society. The kid who did drugs thirty years ago was the geek, the weirdo, the social misfit—not anymore. The tables have turned, the tides have shifted, the game is up and it's time to change the rules again. Now.

22   We need to hang tough, because we can beat it. The I's and the me's can't but we can. We can educate kids before they think it's cool. Pull out a few horror stories, scare them, it will spare them the pain later on. We can apply peer pressure against drug use, and we can bust the drug dealers and suppliers. They're the ones who are supplying the ammunition, the ammunition that's killing, and destroying, and they're making money doing it. We don't have to

put up with it, but we have been. Now we can turn the tables, drugs are out there, they're here. They're now. They kill.

History of the Essay

Pam DeKoning faced the same dilemmas as the author of the preceding essay in deciding whether to deal with a personal subject in a personal manner. In her second commentary of the course she wrote:

> *"This was very difficult for me to write but . . . I realized it was something I had to do, I had to get it out. It is something I hardly ever talk about, it is too painful. I had to stop many times because I got so depressed and emotional . . . I was very relieved after I finished this article. It took me four days to write this . . . I know that it is not my best writing, and I know it needs a lot of revision, but for now it was all I could do to finish it. . . ."*

The draft was brief, undeveloped, hard-edged. It showed the discipline of a student journalist, but it certainly wasn't a piece of writing to be published yet. It was what I call a discovery draft.

During the course her comments on her work were perceptive and professional:

> *"I wrote and rewrote leads and leads and leads and ended up using four of them, or revisions of them as the first four paragraphs—for now. I've also worked on the conclusion quite a bit, knowing that when I write I need to know what I'm leading up to, where I'm going so that the piece will be easier to stay on track.*

> *"I'm undecided on how to approach it, I know the more I put into it [about her sister] the better it's going to be, but I don't want to make it melodramatic. I tried writing it like a news story, just presenting the facts, but it was too impersonal, clinical.*

> *"Another problem is in the voice, I think I want to make it sound like I'm talking to the reader, not documenting. In this approach, I'm not sure if I'm coming off sounding like a jerk who thinks she's got all the answers, or maybe I'm being too laid back, or maybe it's melodramatic. I'm just not sure yet, I guess what I'm grasping for is a little confidence. . . ."*

Final Commentary

The paper came fast at times and slowly at other times. I think writing this paper has helped me tremendously in dealing with my own personal problems with drug abuse and how it affected me.

I have learned a lot about writing argument through this project. I don't know where to start explaining it, though. I was surprised at first that I chose the topic, but as I worked with it, it didn't surprise me at all, because I realized that it was something I really did want to do. It was very emotional at times, but I really think that it was also therapeutic, as writing has always been to me.

At first, I planned to base my essay on my research and on other people's experiences, but then I realized that my own personal experiences were the strongest points and feelings I could use. That is the biggest thing I learned about argument, that your own experiences and opinions are the best things to write about, because they are things that you feel strongly about, and therefore can write more strongly about.

The paper started with a short one-page opinion paper about drug laws. I was surprised at how strong the paper came out. I could not believe that I had written it. Now, I really think that the best thing to write about is something that just comes to you, you just sort of think about something and work it through your head a bit, and then just sit down and write whatever comes, no matter how ridiculous or silly it may seem; you have to experiment, you can always start again.

I then decided to write my semester paper on drugs. Originally I wanted to focus on what made people turn to drugs in the first place, but this was too hard for me to deal with; I was on a hunt to try to find instant solutions as to why the people I knew had turned to and become drug addicts. So, I deserted this path and just kind of went with what came. The research I did I didn't really end up using that much, although the general information and knowledge is reflected in my authority of the subject. My original project outline changed a lot, and I did not end up using a lot of those sources, although I did use some of them.

My first draft was hard to write, because it was a very emotional time for me, things in my personal life dealing with the subject were really mixed up and I really wasn't in the mood to deal with any of it. The first draft reflects my confused and shaken state when writing it, as it was choppy and rambled quite recklessly at times.

The second draft was much better, I thought. It was better organized, and I worked on it carefully, omitting a lot of reckless rambling. I was happy with the additions I made, I felt they added a lot to the text, and were more applicable than my outline of health courses and such.

The draft still needed work, and like everything, it still isn't perfect, and I could probably write 12 more drafts before I was happy with it, but I think it's come along well, and I'm pleased with my efforts.

4

An Order Designed

The writer who has found the focus for a piece of writing is like a sailor who is lost in a stormy sea and then glimpses, through the clouds, the North Star. Once that point of reference is found, the sailor can navigate the ocean. And once the writer has the focus it is possible to create a design that will carry the writer through the text.

Of course that plan will have to be changed as the experience of the writing blows the writer off course, causes the draft to slow down or speed up, even makes it necessary to change the destination and head for port along the way. But a plan—altered according to changing conditions—is essential if the voyage is to be successful.

Sometimes the plan is obvious once the focus is seen. The experienced writer—drawing on familiarity with the subject, the reader, the task—knows instinctively what has to be done. Most of the time, however, the writer has to have a sketch of the voyage that may be taken in the writer's head or scribbled down on a notebook page. Sometimes these sketches are precise, detailed, and as formal as the "Harvard Outline," in which each element is a complete sentence. But I have never known a writer who needs such a detailed plan. Most designs or outlines are loose enough to allow discovery or change in midcourse. They do not eliminate exploration, but encourage it. Some of the methods writers use to design a piece of writing will be discussed in the following pages.

Titles are a favorite planning device of mine. I may draft as many as 150 titles, but that doesn't take me much time, for I can play with lists of titles when turning from a commercial during a television show, waiting for a meeting to start, sitting in a traffic jam, waiting for my wife to come out of the supermarket, doodling while waiting for a long-distance phone call to be completed. I don't want to write titles with great intensity during long periods of time; I want to

236

play with a variety of possible titles, and then spend time refining a title that may work.

Each draft title contains the seed for the meaning that may grow in the draft. The poet John Ashberry, who writes titles before he writes his poems, says, "I feel it's a kind of opening into a potential poem, a door that suddenly pops open and leads into an unknown space." Each title establishes the potential horizons and structure of the draft. Most of all, each title hints at the voice in which the draft may be written. In the selections for this chapter note how Richard Selzer's title, "Letters to a Young Surgeon III," not only targets the reader but helps establish the voice of an experienced surgeon speaking to an inexperienced one.

Leads are more helpful to me than any other single planning device. The lead, first cousin of the promise described in Chapter 1, is a journalistic term that refers to the first sentence, paragraph, or paragraphs of a piece of writing. The lead catches the reader's attention, and readers—even sometimes when they are assigned reading by a teacher—will not continue to read unless the lead reaches out to them. John L'Heureux says, "The first lines of the story teach us how to read it. Tone gives us the clue. It prepares us for the story we are going to read." He could also have said that the lead tells how to write the story. Read the beginnings of pieces in this book to see how the first lines or paragraphs help you decide how to read—and the writer to write—the piece. Notice how important for the writer and the reader Selzer's lead is: "All right. You fainted in the operating room, had to go sit on the floor in a corner and put your head down." Note Jordon's lead: "Caesar was right. Thin people need watching. I've been watching them for most of my adult life, and I don't like what I see." And look at McMillan's lead: "'I want to be white, like Brant,' my 3-year-old said to me the other day." I dare you not to read on. Read the first sentence of the Toni Morrison story: "Nuns go by as quiet as lust, and drunken men and sober eyes sing in the lobby of the Greek hotel." Stand in awe before the tiny surprises and significant contradictions that help establish the beat and music of her prose.

But the lead is just as important for the writer. The lead makes it possible for the writer to see and hear how the piece may be written. John McPhee says, "Leads, like titles, are flashlights that shine down into the story." Joan Didion says, "What's so hard about that first sentence is that you're stuck with it. Everything else is going to flow out of that sentence. And by the time you've laid down the first *two* sentences your options are all gone." Some of the techniques experienced lead writers use include the anecdote or brief story, a statement of news or surprise, a quotation, a statistic, a scene, a significant fact, the introduction of a person important to the story. Study the leads in the selections in this chapter, in the other selections in the book, and my own leads to see how those crucial first sentences have helped the writer find a way of writing the piece. In my case the lead may come early, but I often do not know that that early lead is the right one until I have drafted dozens of others in my head and on my notebook page. I write these mostly in fragments of time, the way I write titles, but I do not start a draft until I have a written and polished lead that I think will work.

Endings are almost as important as leads. In talking with the best writers on the newspapers where I have served as writing coach, I find that they have a good idea of where they will end before they begin. William Gibson, playwright, poet, novelist, and nonfiction writer, who has a selection in this book, says, "I always know the end. The end of everything I write is somehow always implicit from the beginning. What I don't know is the middle. I don't know how I'm going to get there." And John McPhee says, "I generally know what the last line of the story will be before I know the first. The purpose of building a structure is to try to know where you are going."

Writers may not end up where they plan to go—the Saturday afternoon trip to the beach may turn into a party at a lake along the way—but the sense of destination, at the very least, gets the trip started. There would be no party at the lake unless we were headed for the beach. Sometimes I merely have an idea of where I will end that is too vague to be written down, but clear enough for me to aim at it. Other times I will have a note reminding me of an anecdote or a statistic or a quotation, or some such ending point which allows me not so much to conclude as to give readers a piece of information that allows them to draw the conclusion I want in their own minds. Study the endings in the pieces in this book to see how the writer draws what is written to a conclusion, and note how those techniques, which are often good techniques for writing leads, can help the writer develop the text.

Sequence is a trail of information that may lead the writer and the reader from the lead to the end. In my case this is usually three to five points that have to be made, developed, and documented if I am going to arrive at a believable conclusion, and if the reader is going to travel forward with me. Identify the main points made in the selections in this chapter to see how the knowledge of those points may have helped the writer during the draft. I say may, because we cannot always recreate the process of development. Study what Joseph Freda has to say in the case history to see how he worked. But then imagine how the writers of the other pieces may have worked. Don't believe that the imaginary history of the draft is the real one. The writers may have discovered those points during the writing; they may have inserted them during a revision, or they may, indeed, have known them before they began the draft. The point is that it can be a help to know the main points in a text before beginning the draft.

Outlines come in many forms. They can be formal and informal. Sometimes I use Roman numerals and Arabic numbers, capital letters and small letters to design something I may write. Other times I simply write the crossheads and subtitles first, as I have in these chapters, and then add other ones, such as "Outlines" as I go along. Sometimes I put the items to be included in the text on separate 3 × 5 cards and rearrange them into a meaningful pattern, the technique used most frequently by movie scriptwriters. Often I sort the piles of materials I have on a nonfiction piece of writing into file folders and rearrange the folders themselves into an effective order. Share your outlining techniques with your classmates, and listen to the methods they used that helped them *before* the first draft or *after* a draft is completed and they are planning a revision.

The Reader's Questions is such a powerful form of outlining that I am including it as a separate item. Each piece of effective writing may be described as a conversation between reader and writer, in which the writer anticipates the reader's questions and answers them just before they are asked. To test this go through the selections of this chapter or in this book and write down in the margin the questions that the writer has answered. You will find that effective writers have known when you will need a definition; a clarifying description of a process; an answer to such questions as what does this mean, is this a common problem, who says, why should I believe you, what can I do about it?

If you role-play your reader, you will find that you can anticipate the four, five, or six questions the reader must have answered. Then you can put those questions in the order the reader will ask them. Occasionally in writing a text or a brochure you may even want to use the questions as crossheads, but most of the time they are invisible—but very much there.

Design is an effective way of seeing the order with which a piece of writing may be developed. The visual pattern or structure of a piece of writing may be seen in the writer's head, or actually written down on the page. My daybooks, or journals, are filled with the shapes I may use to develop a piece of writing. John Updike, who is reprinted in this text, has said, "I really begin with some kind of solid, coherent image, some notion of the shape of the book and even of its texture. The *Poorhouse Fair* was meant to have a sort of Y shape. *Rabbit Run* was a kind of zig-zag. The *Centaur* was sort of a sandwich." One of my novels became clear to me when I saw it as a sort of fever chart, with the actions and emotions of the main characters rising to peaks and falling into valleys, with crucial actions taking place when the lines on the fever chart intersected.

One of my nonfiction books appeared to me as a stone thrown into a pond, with each chapter being a concentric circle.

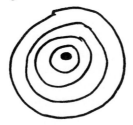

I often use a cone lying on its side to show me a pattern of development from a point or development to a point.

Sometimes I use a sequence of building blocks or stairs.

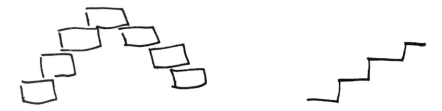

The important thing is not that anybody else understands my designs, but that I do, that they help me see how I may develop a piece of writing.

Genre is the form or type of writing that will help the writer discover meaning and share it with the reader. Some of the genre you may read and write include argument, poetry, expository essay, news story, science report, short story, research or term paper, autobiography. Each genre has its own traditions. These traditions should not be seen as absolute rules, but as lessons or counsel from explorers who have gone before. We do not have to follow their advice, but we are wise if we know when we are departing from it and aware of the hazards that entails. Effective writers have the illusion, I think, that they are writing the first short story or the first research paper, because they need to feel that they are not just filling in the blanks in a formula but using the genre to help them say something new. I like to think of genre as a lens, a way of seeing how I may find out what I have to say. In this chapter we have many genres— Freda's pages from a software manual; Suzanne Britt Jordan's, Terry McMillan's, and Richard Selzer's essays; part of novels by Alice McDermott and Toni Morrison. Look at these different genres not as forms that restricted them but as forms which helped the writers explore their subjects.

All the pieces in this book have found an order, for structure is as important to effective writing as skeletons are to human beings. Take away your bones and you'd be a messy heap of stuff. To learn how to write it is helpful to strip away the text from the structures upon which they are built. Outline some of these pieces of writing, realizing that the outline you create may not be an outline the writer needed. But you should have in your mind a number of structures that will help you design the one you need to create your text for your reader.

Case Study: A Technical Writer Writes and Reads

Joseph Freda

Joseph Freda, who was a Senior Software Writer for Digital Equipment Corporation, one of the largest computer manufacturers in the world, is now Publications Manager for Tegra Corporation in Billerica, Massachusetts.

Before going to work for Digital he worked as a carpenter, railroad trackman, canoe guide, and writing teacher at the University of New Hampshire, where he received a master's degree in writing. He is a novelist, but he has also become an award-winning technical writer. Technical writing has become an expanding career for writers in an age of high technology. These writers provide the link between our marvelous new machines and the people who use them. He has written books for Digital on typesetting and publishing software, and has also written instructional manuals and textbooks for software, such as text editors and programming languages. Freda designed and edited Digital's best-selling book, *Introduction to BASIC,* which won a regional Award of Excellence from the Society of Technical Communication. He also won an international Award of Distinction from the same organization for a set of books he designed and edited, *BASIC for Beginners* and *More BASIC for Beginners.*

Canoe Paddling and the Craft of Communicating Concepts

Writing on a Straight Course

1   I used to teach canoeing on the Delaware River. For some time, I started my training session by explaining the paddle: choosing the appropriate length, holding the paddle, stroking. Then I dispatched everybody to the canoes, where, I assumed, they would paddle down the river on a perfectly straight course. Instead, they struggled to haul their canoes over the rocks at the river's edge. They pondered which end of the canoe was which, tipped over on getting in, sat on thwarts instead of seats. Wet, frustrated, and sure of their imminent demise, they gripped the paddles much as they would rakes or snow shovels or vacuum wands and then hacked and flailed at the river. One young husband-and-wife team sat at either end of the canoe, backs toward each other, paddling furiously in opposite directions.

2   What was wrong? I had explained the parts of the paddle, had carefully demonstrated forward strokes and backwatering, had overseen their practice

on dry land. The husband and wife churning away in opposite directions gave me my clue: even though I had told them how to *move* the canoe, I hadn't told them a thing about the craft itself. I hadn't distinguished the bow from the stern, hadn't shown them how to float the canoe through the shallows or how to get into it. Of course they had forgotten my paddling instruction—they had enough trouble just confronting a canoe for the first time. They didn't know a thing about it, and *that* was my fault. In teaching how to paddle a canoe, I hadn't started at the beginning.

3   The concept of paddling a canoe, I realized, could be broken into a hierarchy of its parts: the canoe, the paddle, paddling the canoe. By starting out teaching about the paddle, I had simply started out too low in the hierarchy. So I changed my method, started with the canoe—describing its parts, showing how to get in and out—and *then* went on to teach paddling. It worked. Although nobody ever paddled off on that perfectly straight course I pictured in my mind, subsequent students usually avoided the confusion and ineptitude that their forbears had felt while getting underway.

4   Teaching a person to paddle a canoe is not that different from teaching a person to do just about anything: make pea soup, write an essay, or use computer software, which is what I do now as a technical writer. Concepts exist in hierarchies, and to explain a concept, you need to break it into a hierarchy of its parts. Then you present each part in logical sequence, working from the top of the hierarchy toward the bottom. Think of this as *linear* writing, or writing on a straight course.

5   To do this, you should:

1. Define the concept in simple terms.
2. Divide the concept into its parts.
3. Show how the parts work together.

6   If you were to follow these steps in writing a book on how to paddle a canoe, they might look like this:

1. Define the concept of paddling a canoe. Show pictures of a person paddling a canoe. This is a simple definition; it fixes the concept in readers' minds.
2. Divide the concept into its parts—canoe and paddle.
   Canoe: show a diagram of the canoe, labeling bow, stern, thwarts, gunwales, seats, and so on. Explain how each of these parts functions toward the overall performance of the canoe.
   Paddle: show a diagram of a paddle, labeling grip, shaft, and blade. Show how to hold the paddle. Explain how each part functions toward the overall performance of the paddle.
3. Explain how the paddle and canoe work together. Show diagrams of strokes and their effects on the movement of the canoe.

7   By fleshing out this outline with explanations and diagrams, you would give your readers a fair idea of how to paddle a canoe. If, however, you were to

begin your explanation with a description of a paddle—as I used to do—your readers would have no *context* in which to place the explanation. This is the key to describing technical information to a nontechnical audience: by working your way down the hierarchy, you give readers a context into which they can place each new piece of information.

8   The hierarchies of many concepts are not so easy to spot as that of paddling a canoe. You cannot simply look at a concept and *shazam!* determine its parts in their correct order. To discover these parts you have to do plenty of brainstorming, freewriting, rewriting, and just plain stumbling around. (I perceived the hierarchy in canoe paddling only in the midst of splashing water, banging aluminum, and shouting people—an extremely nonlinear method of discovery.) But after you have discovered the hierarchy—and you should use any means available to do this—your *presentation* will be much clearer if you follow a logical sequence.

9   The piece of writing that follows is an introductory chapter from a manual I wrote for Digital Equipment Corporation. It describes how to use a software product called DECpage, which is a system that typesets text and prints it on a laser printer. The three drafts show how I tried to explain the concepts of DEC-page in a hierarchical fashion, and how I used certain devices to do this. A discussion of these devices follows the final draft.

FIRST DRAFT

What is DECpage?

DECpage is a text-processing system that produces typeset, paginated text on the [crossed out] laser printer.

[Before DECpage,] If you wanted to typeset text, you had to go through a [laborious, lengthy process.] You had to type your text on a typewriter or word processor and take it to a typesetter, who retyped it all into his or her computerized text composition system. In this step the typesetter also had to type in a lot of lengthy markup commands to tell the composition system how to format the text. This step ended when the composed text came out of the phototypesetter in the form of typeset galley. The typesetter then sent the galley to the printer, who ran off the necessary number of copies on a printing press.

This process was labor-intensive, time-consuming, and hence, very expensive. With DECpage, you don't have to go through all this. You simply type your text on a Digital word processor, and DECpage handles the rest. It's easier, quicker, and cheaper.

[From your point of view,] DECpage has two main [components: text] you type in and text DECpage prints out. There are two concepts you need to learn to use DECpage: keying conventions and styles.

What are Keying Conventions?

Every document can be subdivided into its component parts. For instance, a report is made up of chapters, a chapter is made up of paragraphs, headings, tables, lists, and so on. We can recognize these and other components in any piece of text, whether it be a technical manual, a novel, or a magazine article.

By following certain keying conventions, you enable DECpage to recognize certain text components and format your documents accordingly. When DECpage recognizes the convention for a list, for instance, it formats the text that follows as a list. DECpage continues to format text as a list until it encounters a different convention. By using the conventions for paragraphs, lists, and other text components, you enable DECpage to format your text according to a certain style. You need not be concerned with the style of the document while you are creating it, however. With DECpage, you can concentrate on the content of your document and let the software worry about the style.

The following chapter explains keying conventions more fully.

Handwritten margin notes:

- too much like B.C./A.D.
- vague
- The steps are all here, but it's not as clear as it could be. Make a list?
- Weak — doesn't really convey the power the user has.
- Sounds condescending, or like I'm hiding something. not really parallel — try to get across impact + output without sounding technical.
- gives a non-computer touch, but it's not really necessary. But should I give up the friendly tone to gain efficiency?
- Something feels wrong here. The shift in these lines it seems clunky. Is there a way to reorganize it in a "synopsis"?
- gets off the track — gets into the next section too early.
- Because I got off the track with the soft stuff, this sentence seems jammed in.

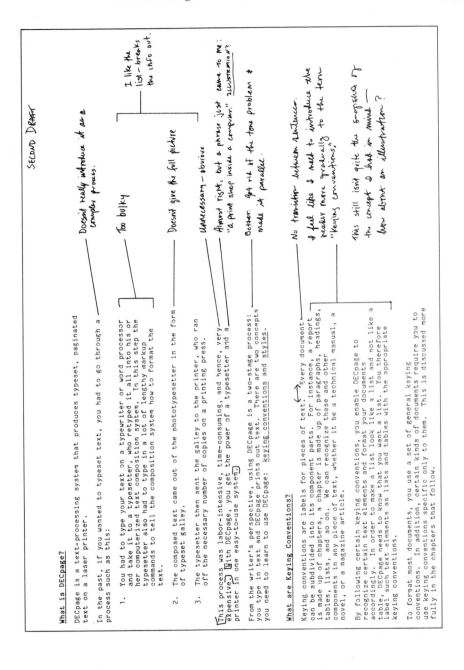

SECOND DRAFT

What is DECpage?

DECpage is a text-processing system that produces typeset, paginated text on a laser printer.

In the past, if you wanted to typeset text, you had to go through a process such as this:

Doesn't really introduce it as a complex process.

1. You had to type your text on a typewriter or word processor and take it to a typesetter, who retyped it all into his or her computerized text composition system. In this step the typesetter also had to type in a lot of lengthy markup commands to tell the composition system how to format the text.

Too bulky

I like the list – breaks the info out.

2. The composed text came out of the phototypesetter in the form of typeset galley.

Doesn't give the full picture

3. The typesetter then sent the galley to the printer, who ran off the necessary number of copies on a printing press.

Unnecessary — obvious

This process was labor-intensive, time-consuming, and hence, very expensive. With DECpage, you get the power of a typesetter and a printer in one easy-to-use system.

Almost right, but a phrase just came to me: "a print shop inside a computer." illustration?

From the writer's perspective, using DECpage is a two-stage process: you type in text and DECpage prints out text. There are two concepts you need to learn to use DECpage: keying conventions and styles.

Better. Get rid of the two problem & made it parallel.

What are Keying Conventions?

Keying conventions are labels for pieces of text. Every document can be subdivided into its component parts. For instance, a report is made up of chapters, a chapter is made up of paragraphs, headings, tables, lists, and so on. We can recognize these and other components in any piece of text, whether it be a technical manual, a novel, or a magazine article.

No transition between sentences

I feel like I need to introduce the reader more gradually to the term "keying conventions."

By following certain keying conventions, you enable DECpage to recognize certain text elements and format your documents accordingly. In order to make a list look like a list and not like a table, DECpage needs to know that you want a list. You therefore label such text elements as lists and tables with the appropriate keying conventions.

This still isn't quite the emphasis I had in mind — how about an illustration?

To format most documents, you use a set of general keying conventions. In addition, certain kinds of documents require you to use keying conventions specific only to them. This is discussed more fully in the chapters that follow.

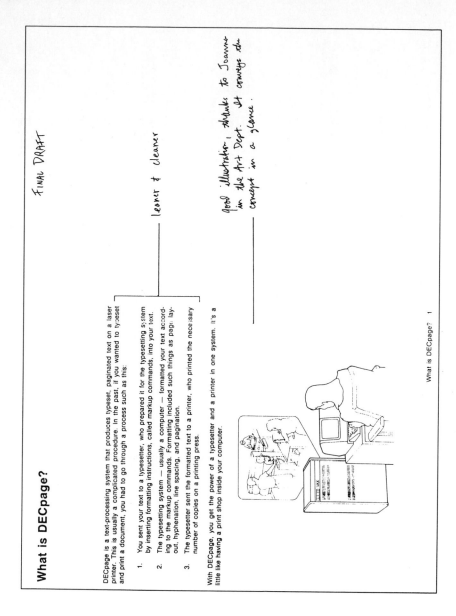

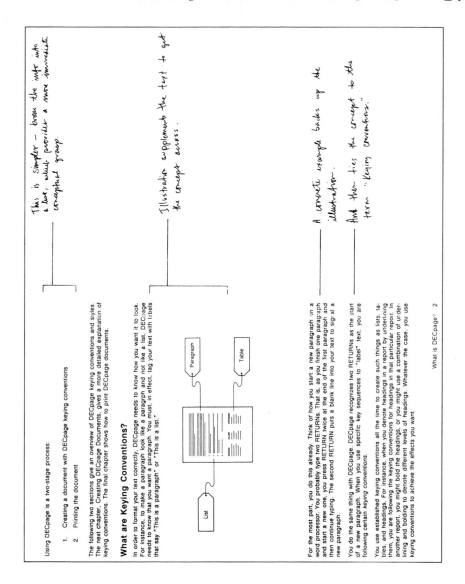

Using DECpage is a two-stage process:

1. Creating a document with DECpage keying conventions and styles
2. Printing the document

The following two sections give an overview of DECpage keying conventions and styles. The next chapter, Creating DECpage Documents, gives a more detailed explanation of keying conventions. The final chapter shows how to print DECpage documents.

What are Keying Conventions?

In order to format your text correctly, DECpage needs to know how you want it to look. For instance, to make a paragraph look like a paragraph and not like a list, DECpage needs to know that you want a paragraph. You must, in effect, tag your text with labels that say "This is a paragraph" or "This is a list."

List

Paragraph

Table

For the most part, you do this already. Think of how you start a new paragraph on a word processor. You probably type two RETURNs. That is, as you finish one paragraph and start a new one, you press RETURN twice at the end of the first paragraph and then continue typing. The second RETURN puts a blank line into your text to signal a new paragraph.

You do the same thing with DECpage. DECpage recognizes two RETURNs as the start of a new paragraph. When you use specific key sequences to "label" text, you are following certain *keying conventions*.

You use established keying conventions all the time to create such things as lists, tables, and headings. For instance, when you denote headings in a report by underlining them, you are following the keying conventions for headings in that particular report. In another report, you might bold the headings, or you might use a combination of underlining and bolding to denote different levels of headings. Whatever the case, you use keying conventions to achieve the effects you want.

What is DECpage?   2

Handwritten annotations:

This is simpler — break the info into a text, which provides a more immediate grasp.

Illustration supplements the text to get the concept across.

A concrete example backs up the illustration.

And then ties the concept to the term "keying conventions."

What is DECpage?

DECpage is a text-processing system that produces typeset, paginated text on a laser printer. This is usually a complicated procedure. In the past, if you wanted to typeset and print a document, you had to go through a process such as this:

1.   You sent your text to a typesetter, who prepared it for the typesetting system by inserting formatting instructions, called markup commands, into your text.

2.   The typesetting system — usually a computer — formatted your text according to the markup commands. Formatting included such things as page layout, hyphenation, line spacing, and pagination.

3.   The typesetter sent the formatted text to a printer, who printed the necessary number of copies on a printing press.

With DECpage, you get the power of a typesetter and a printer in one system. It's a little like having a print shop inside your computer.

Using DECpage is a two-stage process:

1. Creating a document with DECpage keying conventions
2. Printing the document

The following two sections give an overview of DECpage keying conventions and styles. The next chapter, Creating DECpage Documents, gives a more detailed explanation of keying conventions. The final chapter shows how to print DECpage documents.

What are Keying Conventions?

In order to format your text correctly, DECpage needs to know how you want it to look. For instance, to make a paragraph look like a paragrph and not like a list, DECpage needs to know that you want a paragraph. You must, in effect, tag your text with labels that say "This is a paragraph" or "This is a list."

For the most part, you do this already. Think of how you start a new paragraph on a word processor. You probably type two RETURNs. That is, as you finish one paragraph and start a new one, you press RETURN twice at the end of the first paragraph and then continue typing. The second RETURN puts a blank line into your text to signal a new paragraph.

You do the same thing with DECpage. DECpage recognizes two RETURNs as the start of a new paragraph. When you use specific key sequences to "label" text, you are following certain *keying conventions*.

You use established keying conventions all the time to create such things as lists, tables, and headings. For instance, when you denote headings in a report by underlining them, you are following the keying conventions for headings in that particular report. In another report, you might bold the headings, or you might use a combination of underlining and bolding to denote different levels of headings. Whatever the case, you use keying conventions to achieve the effects you want.

What is DECpage? 2

A Technical Writer's Toolkit

10   The preceding excerpt attempts to communicate a fairly technical computer concept to a nontechnical audience. To do this, the technical writer usually has to present information in the hierarchical fashion described earlier. There are several devices to help with this job, including:

- Headings
- Analogies
- Illustrations
- Examples
- Lists
- Tables

11   The following sections discuss each of these.

12   *Headings*—One of the most obvious ways to direct readers through the hierarchy of a concept is with headings. In the sample chapter, there is one main heading and two subheadings:
    What is DECpage?
    What are Keying Conventions?
    What are Styles?

13   The structure of the chapter, and hence its hierarchical organization, is obvious: DECpage is the overriding concept, and keying conventions and styles are the components that constitute it. By quickly scanning the headings, readers see that the overall concept is explained first, and that two supporting concepts are also explained.

14   In this sample, I phrased the headings as questions because I figured these would be foremost in readers' minds. If readers see their own questions laid out in headings, they assume answers will appear in the text. They begin to trust the piece of writing. This is always a primary concern in writing about computer software: people have a lot of anxiety, mistrust, and insecurity about computers; it is usually up to the written material—called *documentation*—to allay these feelings.

15   *Analogies*—It often helps to describe a technical concept in easily recognizable terms. Analogies work well for this. Consider the print shop analogy from the sample. By explaining the traditional process of typesetting and printing a document, and then telling readers that a similar process goes on inside their computers, I defined the concept of DECpage. The reader then had a context into which all other information would fit.

16   *Illustrations*—Illustrations provide a "snapshot" of a concept. We are visual as well as verbal beings, so many times a simple picture can help us envision a concept that might take several paragraphs to explain. The first illustration in the sample reinforces the print shop analogy by providing a visual image of the concept. The second illustration does the same thing for the concept of keying conventions.

17   *Examples*—As in any kind of writing, specific examples are essential to give readers a concrete grasp of a concept. If, after defining a concept by analogy and/or illustration, you follow with a specific example of the concept, you marry the *idea* of the concept to the real thing. For example, look at the paragraph immediately after the illustration of keying conventions. With the illustration in front of them, readers get a concrete example of a keying convention: typing two RETURNs to begin a paragraph.

18   *Lists*—Another device that communicates concepts is the list. In most kinds of writing, when we need to list a few items, we simply list them in a sentence and separate them with commas or semicolons. In technical writing we use a vertical list, which separates the items more clearly. For example, consider the following list:

19   *DECpage allows you to typeset and print three types of letters, including block letters, the most common style in business correspondence; modified block letters, also a business style but less frequently used; and informal letters, used in personal correspondence.*

20   Compare that paragraph with the following vertical list:

21   DECpage allows you to typeset and print three types of letters:
- Block letters—most common style in business correspondence
- Modified block letters—also a business style, but less frequently used
- Informal letters—a style for personal correspondence

22   The information in the vertical list is clearly more accessible than that in the paragraph. Notice again that the information is broken into a hierarchy, and that the parts of the hierarchy are presented in logical sequence.

23   *Tables*—Tables also help break information into parts that are easily grasped. In this manual on DECpage, I wanted to provide a way for readers to fix problems they might have in printing their documents. What should they do, for instance, when they pick up their letter or memo from the laser printer, and the paragraphs run into each other or are too narrow? If I could provide a guide to problem solving, readers would be less confused and frustrated when they had problems. I started doing this in conventional paragraph form:

24   *If your paragraphs run into each other, it is because you didn't insert the paragraph convention at the beginning of a new paragraph. To fix this problem, simply insert two RETURNs between paragraphs.*

25   *If your paragraph margins are too narrow, it is because the paragraph is preceded by a list or table with narrower paragraphs, and the convention to end the list or table is missing. To fix this problem, reset the ruler at the end of the list or table.*

26   The problems and their solutions were there, but they weren't as obvious as they could have been. The paragraphs seemed dense, and I worried about losing readers in thickets of words—not a very good way to solve their problems. Then I remembered my Volkswagen repair manual—it contained a trou-

bleshooting guide that had broken the information into logical blocks. I looked it up, and applied the technique to my manual. The result is a chapter called Troubleshooting, a long table that looks like this:

Symptom	Possible Cause	Suggested Solution
Paragraphs run into each other.	Paragraph convention wasn't inserted between paragraphs.	Insert two RETURNs between paragraphs.
Paragraph margins are too narrow.	Paragraph is preceded by a list or table with narrower paragraphs, and the convention to end the list or table is missing.	Reset the ruler at the end of the list or table.

Thinking on a Straight Course

27   We've heard a lot about the coming of the "Information Age." Well, it's here. But information can only have value if it is transmitted from a source to a terminus, and we as writers are often cast in the role of transmitter. We fill this role whether we are teachers, reporters, business managers, real estate agents, biological researchers, or graphic artists. And we don't do it only on the job. We must communicate information to spouses, parents, postal clerks, insurance agents, and auto mechanics. We will be more successful on our jobs and in our private lives if we not only *communicate* logically and clearly, but also *think* that way.

28   I have never seen an analysis of the kinds of thinking that go on in the human mind, so I can only hypothesize on the test subject I know best. For every ordered, structured idea I have, there are hundreds—thousands—that are scattered, fuzzy, or somehow muddled enough to keep me from using them in a productive way. I realize that sometimes, in order to be productive, thoughts should be free-ranging and unencumbered by structure—while writing fiction or poetry, for example. Or during the beginning stages of any kind of writing. And without daydream, fantasy, and imagination, we would cease to be what we consider human. But for handling many kinds of day-to-day information, I work best if I can apply the kind of logical, hierarchical analysis I've discussed here.

29   It doesn't come easy. Overcoming chaos demands work. One of the best ways I've found to think logically is to write logically. It is practice for logical thought, so when I discuss my job performance with my boss or argue about a parking ticket with the town clerk or explain paddling a canoe to a novice, I can better communicate my ideas.

Discussion

• Compare the kind of directed, practical writing that Freda does with the argumentative writing of Allen and Quindlen. What do each have to teach the other?

• List the forms of writing you have to do in school and apply the lessons Freda has to teach to those tasks.

• Investigate the kind of writing you will have to do on the job after you graduate. Apply Freda's techniques to those writing tasks.

• Consider what typographical techniques you can use to make your meaning clear. Remember that writers are influenced by how they see writing on the page.

• Using Freda as a beginning point, make a class checklist to help you make a complicated subject clear. Discuss the checklist in terms of the kind of writing you and your classmates have to do in school and out.

• Discuss how the writing tasks of the technical writer are similar and different from writers in other genres.

• Discuss what we can all learn from technical writers.

• Bring a manual or a computer or a software program to class. Compare it to Freda's pages. Decide what works and what needs work.

Activities

• Take part of a technical subject you know well (how to sit in a chair if you're a nontechnical person like myself) and give clear instructions to a person who has never done it before.

• Take a page you have written previously and see if you can apply Freda's techniques to it.

• Take a technical manual for a computer, car repair, setting of a digital watch, hi-fi assembly, whatever, and apply Freda's techniques to increase its clarity.

• Rewrite Freda's instructions in normal prose style to see which form is most effective.

• How could Freda's piece be turned into an argument?

To Collaborate

• Interview computer experts at your school to see what qualities they appreciate in the writing of software manuals. Make a class presentation on what you discover, relating it to all forms of writing.

• Break into small groups representing as many diverse majors or career goals as possible. Poll the group to find out the role of writing in that discipline or career. Report to the class what you find out.

Richard Selzer

Richard Selzer is a writer who, until recently, was a practicing surgeon and a professor at Yale Medical School. He writes of surgery from the point of view of an insider. His powerful essays and short stories are collected in *Letters to a Young Doctor,* from which the following selection is taken, and *Rituals of Surgery, Mortal Lessons: Notes on the Art of Surgery,* and *Confessions of a Knife.* If you have trouble finding time to write, consider his schedule. "I go to bed early—9 o'clock—and wake up without an alarm clock at 1 in the morning and write from 1 to 3," Selzer says. "Then I go to sleep until 6. I keep to this regimen unless there is a family commitment." It is clear that Selzer writes as a means to explore his experience, to try to discover meaning in what he sees and does in the operating room. He says, "One sits down and writes a sentence and then one writes another. I, for one, don't know where I'm going." Because of his explorations the reader has the opportunity to go into the mind of the surgeon and follow that mind as it tries to order experience into meaning.

Letter to a Young Surgeon III

1   All Right. You fainted in the operating room, had to go sit on the floor in a corner and put your head down. You are making altogether too much of it. You have merely announced your humanity. Only the gods do not faint at the sight of the MYSTERIUM TREMENDUM; they have too jaded a glance. At the same place in the novitiate I myself more than once slid ungracefully to the floor in the middle of things. It is less a sign of weakness than an expression of guilt. A flinching in the face of the forbidden.

2   The surgeon is an explorer in the tropical forest of the body. Now and then he reaches up to bring closer one of the wondrous fruits he sees there. Before he departs this place, he knows that he must pluck one of them. He knows, too, that it is forbidden to do so. But it is a trophy, no, a SPOIL that has been demanded of him by his patron, the patient, who has commissioned and outfitted him for this exploration. At last the surgeon holds the plucked organ in his hand, but he is never wholly at ease. For what man does not grow shy, fearful, before the occult uncovered?

3   Don't worry. The first red knife is the shakiest. This is as true for the assassin as it is for the surgeon. The assassin's task is easier, for he is more likely to be a fanatic. And nothing steadies the hand like zeal. The surgeon's work is madness icily reined in to a good purpose. Still I know that it is perverse to relieve pain by inflicting it. This requires that the patient give over to you his

free will and his trust. It is too much to ask. Yet we do every day, and with the arrogance born of habit and custom, and grown casual, even charming.

> ❦ Pay attention to his voice and how he uses that voice to take you inside the experience of surgery. And then notice the ways in which he puts that experience in context. He never forgets how unnatural it is to commit surgery. This is one of the ways that the piece develops density and is much more than a superficial account of surgery. ❧

4   "Come, lie down on this table," you say, and smile. Your voice is soft and reasonable.

5   "Where will you cut me open?" the patient asks. And he grips his belly as though he and it were orphan twins awaiting separate adoption. The patient's voice is NOT calm; it trembles and quavers.

6   "From here . . . to here," you reply, and you draw a fingernail across his shuddering flesh. His navel leaps like a flushed bird. Oh, God! He has heard the knell of disembowelment. You really DO mean to do it! And you do, though not with the delectation that will be attributed to you by those who do not do this work.

7   The cadaver toward which I have again and again urged you is like an abundant nest from which the birds have long since flown. It is a dry, uninhabited place—already dusty. It is a "thing" that the medical student will pull apart and examine, seeking evidence, clues from which he can reconstruct the life that once flourished there. The living patient is a nest in which a setting bird huddles. She quivers, but does not move when you press aside leaves in order to see better. Your slightest touch frightens her. You hold your breath and let the leaves spring back to conceal her. You want so much for her to trust you.

8   In order to do good works throughout his lifetime, a man must strive ever higher to carry out his benefices; he must pray, defer pleasure and steel himself against temptation. And against fainting. The committing of surgery grows easier and easier, it seems, until the practice is second nature. Come, come! You fainted! Why don't you admit that you are imperfect, and that you strain to appeal to yourself and to others? Surgery is, in one sense, a judicious contrivance, like poetry. But . . . it is an elect life, here among the ranting machinery and brazen lamps of the operating room, where on certain days now the liquidity of the patient reminds me of the drought that is attacking my own flesh. Listen, I will tell you what you already know: There is nothing like an honest piece of surgery. Say what you will, there is nothing more satisfying to the spirit than . . . the lancing of a boil!

9   Behold the fierce, hot protuberance compressing the howling nerves about it. You sound it with your fingers. A light tap brings back a malevolent answering wave, and a groan from the patient. Now the questing knife rides your hand. Go! And across the swelling gallops a thin red line. Again! Deeper, plowing. All at once there lifts a wave of green mud. Suddenly the patient's breathing comes

more easily, his tense body relaxes, he smiles. For him it is like being touched by the hand of God. It is a simple act, requiring not a flicker of intellect nor a whisker of logic. To outwit disease it takes a peasant's cunning, not abstract brilliance. It is like the felling of a tree for firewood. Yet not poetry, nor music nor mathematics can bring such gladness, for riding out upon that wave of pus has come the black barque of pain. Just so will you come to love the boils and tumors of your patients.

10   I shall offer you two antidotes to fainting in the operating room.

11   1. Return as often as possible to the Anatomy Laboratory. As the sculptor must gain unlimited control over his marble, the surgeon must "own" the flesh. As drawing is to the painter, so is anatomy to the surgeon. You must continue to dissect for the rest of your life. To raise a flap of skin, to trace out a nerve to its place of confluence, to carry a tendon to its bony insertion, these are things of grace and beauty. They are simple, nontheoretical, workaday acts which, if done again and again, will give rise to that profound sense of structure that is the birthplace of intuition.

12   It is only at the dissecting table that you can find the models of your art. Only there that you will internalize the structure and form of the body so that any variations or anomalies or unforeseen circumstances are not later met with dismay and surprise. Unlike the face, the internal organs bear a remarkable sameness to one another. True, there are differences in the size of normal kidneys, livers and spleens, and there are occasional odd lobulations and unusual arrangements of ducts and vessels, but by and large, one liver is very like another. A kidney is a kidney. Unlike a face, it bears no distinctive mark or expression that would stamp it as the kidney of Napoleon Bonaparte, say, or Herman Melville. It is this very sameness that makes of surgery a craft that can be perfected by repetition and industry. Therefore, return to the Anatomy Laboratory. Revere and follow your prosector. The worship and awe you show the cadavers will come back to you a thousandfold. Even now, such an old knife as I goes to that place to dissect, to probe, to delve. What is an operating room but a prosectorium that has been touched into life?

13   2. Do not be impatient to wield the scalpel. To become a surgeon is a gradual, imperceptible, subtle transformation. Do not hurry from the side of the one who instructs you, but stay with your "master" until he bids you to go. It is his office to warm you with his words, on rounds and in the operating room, to color the darkness and shade the brilliance of light until you have grown strong enough to survive. Then, yes, leave him, for no sapling can grow to fullness in the shade of a big tree.

14   Do these things that I have told you and you will not faint in the operating room. I do not any longer faint, nor have I for thirty years. But now and then, upon leaving the hospital after a long and dangerous operation has been brought to a successful close, I stroke the walls of the building as though it were a faithful animal that has behaved itself well.

Discussion

• Discuss how Selzer, by going so deeply into his subject, establishes a universality. Consider how the piece could be written as a letter to a young soldier, teacher, salesman, lawyer, carpenter, mother, father, farmer, pilot, writer.

• Think of other ways the piece could be organized around an incident or a single operation, for example.

• Consider the language he uses and whether or not the words with which we are not familiar are clear in the context he establishes.

• Consider techniques other than personal, human experience a writer can use to make a technical subject clear to the general reader.

• Note the ways in which the author establishes his authority to speak on this subject.

Activities

• Take a job or a skill you know and write a letter of advice to someone just starting out in the same area.

• Choose a technical subject with which you are familiar and make it clear to someone who does not know the subject.

• List the ways an author can establish authority within a text, using a specific subject on which you are an authority.

• Outline three other ways Selzer could have organized his essay. Outline three other ways you could organize one of your own essays.

• Rewrite a few paragraphs of the essay from the point of view of the young doctor, the patient, or a nurse observing the doctor.

To Collaborate

• Using Selzer as a starting point, work together on a letter of advice to an incoming freshman.

• Share a draft of yours with a classmate while the classmate shares one with you. Each respond in a letter, perhaps answering, as the students in the case histories in this text did, the questions: What works? What needs work?

Suzanne Britt Jordan

Ever see a fat person? Of course.

Ever see a thin person? Of course.

Ever become a fat person looking at a thin person? Well, no.

That's the writer's magic. They can enter a stranger's skin. In this essay, Suzanne Britt Jordan, who wrote a book called *Skinny People Are Dull and Crunchy Like Carrots,* becomes a fat person who looks at a thin person—not with the envy the reader expects, but with extreme prejudice.

Her prejudiced view surprises, yet entertains because it runs opposite to our present social prejudices that fat is bad (ugly, unhealthy, stupid, lazy, embarrassing) and that thin is good (beautiful, healthy, intelligent, hard working, proud).

But notice that as we laugh, we are educated. We see, or should see, that prejudice is stupid, that we should never generalize from a person's appearance.

This light, humorous form of argument is not lighthearted. The touch is light but the pain is real, and because of the light touch the reader may both read and learn.

It takes enormous skill to write so that the humor is always there and that the serious message in the humor is delivered just as effectively to the reader. Suzanne Britt Jordan demonstrates that rare ability to combine humor and seriousness with extraordinary grace.

That Lean and Hungry Look

1   Caesar was right. Thin people need watching. I've been watching them for most of my adult life, and I don't like what I see. When these narrow fellows spring at me, I quiver to my toes. Thin people come in all personalities, most of them menacing. You've got your "together" thin person, your mechanical thin person, your condescending thin person, your tsk-tsk thin person, your efficiency-expert thin person. All of them are dangerous.

2   In the first place, thin people aren't fun. They don't know how to goof off, at least in the best, fat sense of the word. They've always got to be adoing. Give them a coffee break, and they'll jog around the block. Supply them with a quiet evening at home, and they'll fix the screen door and lick S&H green stamps. They say things like "there aren't enough hours in the day." Fat people never say that. Fat people think the day is too damn long already.

3   Thin people make me tired. They've got speedy little metabolisms that cause them to bustle briskly. They're forever rubbing their bony hands together and eyeing new problems to "tackle." I like to surround myself with sluggish, inert, easygoing fat people, the kind who believe that if you clean it up today, it'll just get dirty again tomorrow.

4   Some people say the business about the jolly fat person is a myth, that all of us chubbies are neurotic, sick, sad people. I disagree. Fat people may not be chortling all day long, but they're a hell of a lot *nicer* than the wizened and shriveled. Thin people turn surly, mean, and hard at a young age because they never learn the value of a hot-fudge sundae for easing tension. Thin people don't like gooey soft things because they themselves are neither gooey nor soft.

They are crunchy and dull, like carrots. They go straight to the heart of the matter while fat people let things stay all blurry and hazy and vague, the way things actually are. Thin people want to face the truth. Fat people know there is no truth. One of my thin friends is always staring at complex, unsolvable problems and saying, "The key thing is. . . ." Fat people never say that. They know there isn't any such thing as the key thing about anything.

5   Thin people believe in logic. Fat people see all sides. The sides fat people see are rounded blobs, usually gray, always nebulous and truly not worth worrying about. But the thin person persists. "If you consume more calories than you burn," says one of my thin friends, "you will gain weight. It's that simple." Fat people always grin when they hear statements like that. They know better.

6   Fat people realize that life is illogical and unfair. They know very well that God is not in his heaven and all is not right with the world. If God was up there, fat people could have two doughnuts and a big orange drink anytime they wanted it.

7   Thin people have a long list of logical things they are always spouting off to me. They hold up one finger at a time as they reel off these things, so I won't lose track. They speak slowly as if to a young child. The list is long and full of holes. It contains tidbits like "get a grip on yourself," "cigarettes kill," "cholesterol clogs," "fit as a fiddle," "ducks in a row," "organize," and "sound fiscal management." Phrases like that.

8   They think these 2,000-point plans lead to happiness. Fat people know happiness is elusive at best and even if they could get the kind thin people talk about, they wouldn't want it. Wisely, fat people see that such programs are too dull, too hard, too off the mark. They are never better than a whole cheesecake.

9   Fat people know all about the mystery of life. They are the ones acquainted with the night, with luck, with fate, with playing it by ear. One thin person I know once suggested that we arrange all the parts of a jigsaw puzzle into groups according to size, shape, and color. He figured this would cut the time needed to complete the puzzle by at least 50 percent. I said I wouldn't do it. One, I like to muddle through. Two, what good would it do to finish early? Three, the jigsaw puzzle isn't the important thing. The important thing is the fun of four people (one thin person included) sitting around a card table, working a jigsaw puzzle. My thin friend had no use for my list. Instead of joining us, he went outside and mulched the boxwoods. The three remaining fat people finished the puzzle and made chocolate, double-fudged brownies to celebrate.

10   The main problem with thin people is they oppress. Their good intentions, bony torsos, tight ships, neat corners, cerebral machinations, and pat solutions loom like dark clouds over the loose, comfortable, spread-out, soft world of the fat. Long after fat people have removed their coats and shoes and put their feet up on the coffee table, thin people are still sitting on the edge of the sofa, looking neat as a pin, discussing rutabagas. Fat people are heavily into fits of laughter, slapping their thighs and whooping it up, while thin people are still politely waiting for the punch line.

11   Thin people are downers. They like math and morality and reasoned eval-

uation of the limitations of human beings. They have their skinny little acts together. They expound, prognose, probe, and prick.

12   Fat people are convivial. They will like you even if you're irregular and have acne. They will come up with a good reason why you never wrote the great American novel. They will cry in your beer with you. They will put your name in the pot. They will let you off the hook. Fat people will gab, giggle, guffaw, gallumph, gyrate, and gossip. They are generous, giving, and gallant. They are gluttonous and goodly and great. What you want when you're down is soft and jiggly, not muscled and stable. Fat people know this. Fat people have plenty of room. Fat people will take you in.

A Writer's Notes for a Second Reading

All right, I'm prejudiced. I was, well, chubby for the first five years of my life; then I became elongated and skinny. That lasted until football and the paratroops. For about five years there I was not exactly muscular but then, one morning, the muscles left. I was 23 and portly. Since then I have varied between my doctor's obscene term *obese* and plump. Suzanne Britt Jordan is a great writer.

Humor is the most difficult form of writing. It is always a high-wire act. Usually the humorist plays against a popular idea as Jordan has—that thin is good.

The humorist often exaggerates, but like the leader who cannot get too far ahead of the followers, the humorist must stay close enough to reality to be funny.

One writer said that a good style is full of tiny surprises. Note how Jordan does this right away: "thin people *need watching*" and "*narrow* fellows." The piece is full of words and phrases that are unexpected—and accurate within the world of her essay.

Discussion

- Consider how Jordan differs from Art Buchwald, Garrison Keiler, Erma Bombeck, and other humorists. What are the strengths and weaknesses of each style?
- How serious is Jordan? How important is her subject?
- How will the piece be read by someone who is overweight or underweight?
- How might the piece be written as a serious essay?

Activities

- Rewrite the beginning of Jordan's piece as an angry attack on thin people or a detached essay on the problem of obesity to better understand the problems she faced and their solution.

- Take a piece of humorous writing—Jordan's essay or another—and list the different humor techniques employed.
- Listen to a tape or a record of a humorist and compare written and oral techniques.
- Write an essay of your own in a humorous voice on a subject that you feel strongly about.

To Collaborate

- Write a brief humorous piece with a partner or a team and compare the different ways each person uses humor.
- Work with other writers to produce a humorous essay on a topic familiar to you, all under pseudonym.

Terry McMillan

The best reading by a writer I have ever attended was in Laramie, Wyoming, where a visiting professor of writing, read from her new work and then, for more than an hour, answered an enormous range of questions with patience, humor, directness, and extraordinary candor.

This was a writer laying it on the line: here was the truth as she knew it. And, more important, here was a human being, a black single mother, laying it on the line: here was the truth as she lived it.

Now a professor at the University of Arizona, McMillan is a writer of powerful novels and short stories. She has been a fellow at both Yaddo and the MacDowell Colony. She has received grants from the PEN American Center, The Authors League, the Carnegie Fund, The New York Foundation for the Arts, and the National Endowment for the Arts.

This essay was one of several she wrote for the "Hers" column in *The New York Times*.

What Is Perfect Anyway? Simply Being Beautiful?

1   "I want to be white, like Brant," my 3-year-old said to me the other day. We were on our way home from the Denver Zoo. "Look, Mommy, I'm turning white," he said, pointing to the inside of his palms.

2   We passed through the red mountains. I blinked. Then I said: "The color of your skin is beautiful, Solomon. Brant just told me yesterday that he wants to be black, but both colors are beautiful. That's why God made people all over the world different."

3   "Oh," was all he said. He didn't buy it.

4   This made me think of all the things I've always wanted to be but never was. I always wanted to be 5 foot 8, but I'm 2 inches shy. My teeth could be bigger, too. They're perfectly straight, and I never needed braces. I wish I were smarter, but there are women who aren't as smart as I am. My biggest fear after having my first child at 32 was that my body would fall apart. It didn't, and I rarely exercise. Still, I wish my breasts were about 3 inches higher, and firmer.

5   "I pray I look half as good as Raquel Welch or Cicely Tyson when I'm their age," a girlfriend says. We are at the health spa, undressing. Some teenage girls walk in, wearing miniskirts. Their legs are long, their hips slender, their buttocks firm. They take off their clothes, and my girlfriend and I stare at them. Their breasts are still firm, like everything else. They look good. Perfect.

6   "I used to wear minis," I say to her.

7   "But we can't anymore," she says.

8   "Who wants to?"

9   "Me. I'm beginning to feel my age."

10   "I know what you mean," I say as we wrap our towels tightly around us, holding everything in.

11   I have a dream. I win the Pulitzer for fiction. Then, for some reason, I find myself making an acceptance speech at the Academy Awards with my Oscar gripped in my hand. I am in a white buglebeaded gown. My makeup is perfect, although I don't have very much on because I've taken such good care of myself I don't need it. When I walk offstage, my hips swing, but nothing shakes except the beads. My husband, who has no face, only hands, is so proud of me. We sit next to Madonna, who looks at me and says, "You're gorgeous."

12   The next day, I am on the swimsuit cover of Sports Illustrated. No one can believe I'm 40! I give women hope. Raquel and Jane both call to ask what *my* secret is. That's when I wake up and walk into the bathroom to brush my teeth, and before my eyes is a brown-skinned witch. "Some dream," I say to myself. I shower and stand on the toilet seat to look at myself in the mirror. "My breasts don't sag that much," I say out loud. My cheekbones are high without blush. I turn sideways to see if my buttocks sag. They do, but not all that much. I look for stretch marks. I see a few. I jump down off the seat and turn out the light. I'm not as bad off as I thought.

13   The fact is none of us are.

14   As women, it seems that we are always comparing ourselves with other women, for God only knows how many reasons. Always wishing we had something we don't. Never satisfied with what we've already got.

15   I used to sit on New York subways, looking at women who weren't as

attractive as I was and staring at the big diamonds on their fingers. "How come they can get a husband and I can't?" I would ask. Never wondered whether they were happy or miserable, just that they had something I didn't. And never mind that I chose not to be married and wasn't miserable.

16   For a long time I wished I were perfect. But after looking at national women's magazines month after month, cover after cover, ad after ad, it occurred to me that I didn't know what perfect really meant. Is it simply being beautiful? Having a great body? Being smart? A good mother? A good lover? Successful? Sensitive and compassionate? Or all of the above? How many of us haven't tried to overcompensate in at least two of these areas? I know I have, but after years of envying other women, it has occurred to me that I will never look like Madonna or Raquel or Lena or Cicely. But so what? I look good being me. No one else can do that.

17   Of course, these days, if you always wanted blue eyes, you can buy them. Fix the nose, chin or cheeks; pay for a new look. Cher has changed who she was to who she wanted to be. I don't knock it—the most important thing is to feel good about yourself. If buying it will do the trick, then do it.

18   All my sisters have Angie Dickinson legs. They could do commercials. I got stuck with my father's football knees and chicken feet. I thought of surgery to correct them, but I'm too scared. Besides, I know that there will always be something about myself that I'd like to change.

19   The second week of classes, I wore a pair of tight jeans. As I looked over my notes, I noticed one of the students staring at me nervously.

20   "Did the professor give us homework already?" she asked.

21   I couldn't wipe the grin off my face. "I'm the professor," I said.

22   "You've got to be kidding," she said. "You don't look old enough. You could be a student."

23   "Thanks," I said.

24   She had made my day.

25   My son is taking a bath. I'm buttoning up my pajama top. "Mommy," he said, "I'm a girl."

26   I laughed. "Solomon, you are not a girl."

27   "Yes I am—look at my boobs."

28   I laughed again but tried to hide it. "That's your chest."

29   He looked disappointed, then amazed. "Mommy, will you have a baby girl for me?"

30   "Maybe one day," I said.

31   "Right now," he said. "Please."

32   "First, Mommy's belly will have to get very, very big."

33   "It's already big," he said.

34   "So what," I said, as I prepared to stand on the toilet and look in the mirror. But then I changed my mind. I already knew what was there.

A Writer's Notes for a Second Reading

McMillan deals with the same general topic as Jordan, but she raises the ante in the first line. As a writer I am impressed by the power and directness of her beginning. What a promise! Will she be able to deliver?

She delivers honesty and directness in the next three paragraphs—and a kind of humor, not yak-yak but a quiet, sad, not quite bitter humor. Then she develops that humor until she has us hooked and then turns up the seriousness again in the brief transition paragraph: "The fact is none of us are."

And then she returns to her son at the end in a scene that is both humorous and sad. You want to read voice? Read this. You want to read a writer who has exquisite control of voice, flawless pacing, well-crafted tone? Read it again.

Discussion

- What is this essay about? Race, fashion, what?
- What are examples of voice and how does McMillan control and use voice?
- What works most effectively and least effectively in Jordan's and McMillan's essays?
- What are the fictional techniques McMillan, the novelist, uses in her essay?
- Are these essays argument? Why? Why not? If so, what is each writer's argument?

Activities

- Write the first page of Jordan's essay in McMillan's voice, McMillan's in Jordan's.
- Make notes on what you'd have to do to make McMillan's essay a story.
- Take an incident from your life as McMillan took the incident with her son and write fast to see where it will take you.

To Collaborate

- Turn McMillan's essay into a scene in a movie or play. Act it out for the class. Discuss narrative and its relationship to nonfiction.
- Work with your partner or team to see how many different ways Jordan and McMillan could have approached their common topic.

A Note on Narrative

I can't tell, sitting here behind the page, if you are black or white, tall or short, portly or scrawny, young or old, eat liver and onions or ginger ice cream, but I do know that when you were young you demanded "Tell me a story." The hunger for story seems born within us; the need for story must go far back beyond the cave paintings of the hunt.

Narrative, the grown-up word for story, retells experience so that it has the flavor of experience but contains a meaning that is clearer than life. Story is the fundamental writing form, the most powerful genre, and yet it is often left out of the college writing course as if it were a childish form of writing, something inferior to argument, the expository essay, the research paper.

Narrative uses time to organize events in sequence. In the beginning, the structure of story is simple and children tell the breakfast to bed story in which all events—the putting on of socks, the way Uncle Herbert was gobbled up by the whale, the eating of the peanut butter sandwich—all are given equal time and importance. This pattern continues with inexperienced writers and causes many college instructors to scorn personal narratives by students. Their complaint should not be with the form but its use. The personal narrative that has no meaning, that reveals no significance, does not need to be outlawed so much as to be developed.

To reveal meaning, the narrative distorts time, giving more space to one event and compressing the time given to less important events. Eventually the student may learn how to jump ahead in time and "flashback" in time. I find students and readers are able to move more quickly through time because of the experience of viewing TV commercials which can flash through a series of events in seconds.

Once students become masters of time, they can begin to experiment with point of view and then with the significant shift from first person to third. These questions of technique all force the student to achieve distance from the subject, to become more objective, to evaluate, to think. Narrative is certainly not the only form of writing, but it's basic and sophisticated, a form worthy of study in any writing class.

This book includes many nonfiction examples of narrative—biography and autobiography, history and chronicles of events, travel narrative and poetic narrative—and it has in the selections which follow some examples of fictional narrative, story-telling that is made up but which tells the truth. It may be a good idea to reread Joan Didion's "Why I Write," for she is both a nonfiction and a fiction writer, and that essay talks about the writing of fiction as well as nonfiction. We've also published an excerpt from Toni Morrison's first novel and an excerpt from an Alice McDermott novel.

You should read and study these narratives—and the poems in the next chapter—for delight first of all. These writers, masters of our craft, are fun to read. They create a make-believe world that is more real many times than the world in which we live. It is so real that we can enter and live in their manufactured experience. By doing this we see and understand and experience a special kind of living. We also, by hearing their voices, hear the music of our language and see how it can be pushed to the edge of meaning by Toni Morrison or used in a more traditional manner by Alice McDermott.

We should also read narrative as practiced by masters of narrative, because all writers of nonfiction have their roots in poetry and fiction. In one sense all forms of prose writing are a variation on narrative. In many forms of writing—the lawyer's brief, the analysis of supermarket sales, the political argument, the news story, the critical essay, even the research paper—there is a narrative embedded in the text, and the reader follows that embedded narrative to find out what happens.

We also use narrative when writing in other forms, such as exposition. We use little anecdotes or incidents to document or illuminate the text. We use a narrative of process in a scientific paper, or a narrative of a case history to make an argument. Each of the writers whose drafts we have printed here has written a narrative of his or her own writing, even though they may not seem to be narratives at first glance.

We cannot understand the nonfiction writing craft and perform it with skill unless we appreciate narrative, learn from it, and use the lessons of narrative, when appropriate, in all forms of our writing.

Alice McDermott

When Alice McDermott came to the University of New Hampshire's graduate writing program, we all recognized her exceptional talent. We soon realized that talent was matched by the discipline that would guarantee she would become a published writer.

It did. This excerpt is from her second novel, which was greeted with a page-one review in *The New York Times Book Review* and all sorts of other critical acclaim.

McDermott also developed into a fine teacher of writing and these days teaches at the University of California at San Diego as well as continues to write.

That Night

1   On the morning after the fight, I left Leela and my mother and little Jake in our kitchen and stepped outside, where Diane Rossi, Georgie Evers and the Meyer twins were already searching the sidewalk and street in front of Sheryl's house. I knew precisely what they were looking for, and without comment I joined them. In each of our basements and attics, in grimy shoeboxes and old footlockers, in paper bags as limp as cloth, our fathers, we knew, had iron crosses and silver swastikas, tarnished medals marked with bright red suns, heavy foreign coins and black-and-white postcards fading to yellow and brown, and what we searched for that morning was in some way our own version of

those souvenirs: mementos of a battle, a night of high drama we were not likely to see again.

2   As we searched, we discussed what had happened to Sheryl.

3   Diane said, "They got married secretly, her and her boyfriend. And when her mother found out, she sent her away."

4   "To Ohio," Georgie said. He crouched to touch a piece of mica that gleamed up from the road. He already held a small shard of black glass. I held another.

5   "They didn't get married," one of the Meyer twins said, his voice full of scorn. "She's going to have a baby."

6   "Yeah," the other said. Both of them had long, thin, freckled faces and only the slightest brown fuzz of a crew cut. Their voices, too, were identical. "She's pregnant," he said.

7   The word alone startled us.

8   We were silent for a moment and then, together, Diane, Georgie and I said, "We know that," although I'm not sure any of us knew it with such certainty until then. The night before, parents all up and down the block had offered their children short, contingency courses in the birds and the bees, just as my mother had done for me and apparently with as much detail and tact. They were of that generation who spelled the words they couldn't speak and followed strict rules regarding what could be discussed in mixed company, so this morning, we, their children, were more confused than ever about just what was involved.

9   We studied the tire tracks on the grass by the curb and then crossed the sidewalk and stepped only one inch at a time onto Sheryl's torn lawn. We were all thinking about sex.

10   "But they got married, too," Diane finally added.

11   "No they didn't," the Meyer twins told her.

12   She paused and squinted at them, "Yesss," she said. "My mother told me."

13   They stuck out their chins. "Nooo," they answered. "Your mother's wrong."

14   She put her hands on her hips. "How could she have a baby if they weren't married?"

15   The Meyer twins stopped in their tracks and then slowly staggered backward, their hands on their stomachs, their mouths wide open. Then they threw their arms around one another and whooped with laughter.

16   Georgie and I moved closer to Diane. We knew she had made a terrible mistake, but we knew our own parents, in explaining Sheryl's dilemma, had said an awful lot about marriage as well. ("When people get married," my own mother had begun, "they do what Sheryl did . . ." as if it were Sheryl herself who had established the trend.)

17   "Don't you know anything?" Mickey Meyer asked, still holding his stomach but bending now, as if her stupidity had given him appendicitis.

18   "How old are you?" Ricky cried. "Two or something? You don't have to be married to have a baby, dope."

19   "Yes you do," she said weakly. She turned to me, "Right?"

20   Wanting to stay on her side but fairly certain she was wrong, I merely shrugged. This spun Mickey and Ricky around with delight.

21   "Two idiots!" they cried. I saw Mrs. Rossi glance out her window, and I told them both to hush. "I know you don't have to be married," I told them.

22   "You just have to go to sleep with someone," Georgie suddenly added. "That's all."

23   But the Meyer twins were too delighted with our ignorance to let it go at that. "Oh yeah, sure" Mickey said. He folded his hands under his cheek, closed his eyes and pretended to snore—"gnaa-shew, gnaa-shew"—then he opened his eyes and said in a high-pitched voice, "Uh-oh, I'm going to have a baby."

24   Ricky threw himself on the edge of Sheryl's lawn and rocked with laughter, touching his shoulder to one of the ripped places on the grass. His own marriage in another ten years' time would be to a girl whom everyone, including his parents, had believed to be Italian until a prenuptial barbecue in the Meyers' backyard had filled our street with cries of *"Mira, mira,"* and the Meyers' lawn chairs with three out of five grandparents who were definitely not white.

25   "You better take No-Doz," he told us now. In another ten years' time he would leave his parents and their house for good—choosing to be dead to them, as his mother put it to mine, rather than give up the love of his mongrel girl.

26   Georgie looked crestfallen and I, too, was confused. We had both thought sleeping with someone was a valid enough explanation but the Meyers' laughter filled us with doubt.

27   Diane had chosen to ignore them both and had returned to her search. She walked slowly along the edge of the curb, touching the toe of her sneaker to every pebble or bit of debris. Between her fingers she rolled what had been thus far the morning's best find: the dark black earpiece to one of the hoods' sunglasses.

28   Mickey Meyer was saying, "It doesn't take more than five minutes. The guy gets on top of the girl"—he slammed his fist into his palm three times, imitating some adult—"and she's going to have a baby."

29   I thought of my parents and their breathless nights and early mornings. Of Leela's ruined marriage. "Maybe," I added.

30   "What do you mean *maybe?*" Mickey asked.

31   "Not always," I said. "It doesn't always work out."

32   From the curb where he sat, Ricky added, "Only if the guy sweats."

33   We all turned to him, even Mickey. This was a new part of the puzzle.

34   "What?" Georgie said, returning some of the Meyers' own scorn.

35   Ricky shrugged nonchalantly. "The guy's got to sweat, and the lady's got to drink it."

36   Diane, who was still pretending not to listen, was the first to say, "Does not," but we all quickly followed.

37   "Does," Ricky insisted.

38   "Who told you that?" I asked.

39   "My father," Ricky said.

40   "He did not!" Mickey cried.

41   "Yes he did," Ricky told him calmly.

42   "When?" Mickey demanded.

43   "Once," Ricky said, vague and arrogant with our attention. "When you weren't around."

44   Mickey squinted at him. "When wasn't I around?" He said it as if the very idea of his ever not being around was ludicrous.

45   "Last night," Ricky said regally, "When Dad got home from the police. You were sleeping. That's when he told me."

46   "Baloney!" Mickey cried.

47   Diane said, "That makes me sick just to think of it."

48   Ricky shrugged. "Glad I'm not a girl."

49   Georgie suddenly sat down beside him, chunky and puzzled, his round little mouth wide open and his brown shorts pulling against his white thighs. I recalled sometimes seeing light beads of sweat on his upper lip. "Is that what Sheryl did?" he asked.

50   "I guess," Ricky said.

51   "She did not," I told them impatiently. I knew the Meyers were notorious liars, but I also knew they usually collaborated on their tales. Their disagreement had given Ricky's story new authority. "It doesn't happen like that," I said.

52   "How, then, Miss Smarty?" Ricky asked.

53   I was about to say they kissed each other and breathed a baby into life but knew even before I spoke the words that it was a weak and fanciful explanation. I recalled my parents' voices, my mother's desperate headstand, Leela's tears and what Sheryl herself had told me. I knew something more difficult was involved.

54   Diane sighed loudly as if she hadn't wanted to reveal this but could no longer resist. "It has to do with where you go to the bathroom," she said quickly. "But you have to be married."

55   Now Georgie, his face lightening, changed his allegiance once more. Yes, he said. Diane was right. When his mother had her babies they tried to get out her behind, but the doctor cut open her stomach and took them out that way instead.

56   Mickey Meyer, still subdued by the possibility that their father had told Ricky something he hadn't told him, perked up a bit at this. "They cut open her stomach?" he cried. "Didn't all the food fall out?"

57   "Stupid," Diane whispered, and Ricky once more commanded center stage. "That's how they get out," he said. "But I'm talking about how they get in." He leaned forward and made each word emphatic. "The guy sweats and the lady drinks it, I swear."

58   "They do not," Diane said again, and Mickey suddenly leaned closer to her. He wore that look he got whenever he had something disgusting to show you: a blackened fingernail, a festering cut, a green opaque marble that he could hold in his nostril. "Maybe it's not sweat she drinks." he said, leering as effectively as a nine-year-old can leer. "Maybe it has to do with where you go to the bathroom."

59   We all cried out at this, suddenly moving around as if our revulsion were physical. Georgie stood and walked halfway up Sheryl's lawn. Diane and I stepped up on the curb and then down again and then, to show our true indignation, crossed to the curb on the other side of the street. Georgie then skirted Ricky, who was crawling along the grass pretending to choke, and joined us. Mickey danced after him (Diane and I shouting, "Get out of here," all the while he approached) and then Ricky followed.

60   Now Sheryl's house was before us and we held our small mementos in our hands or rested them on our bare knees. Sitting on the curb, we began again, slowly and more seriously now, trying words the way a locksmith might go through a large set of keys. I said *womb* and *seed* and *conception,* and Diane contributed *kissing, petting* and *blood.* Ricky insisted on repeating *sweat,* and Mickey would not give up *bathroom,* although it had been Diane's contribution from the start. (I recalled my parents' hollow voices, the swish of tub water.) Georgie tried *bed* and *sleeping* a few times but then conceded them when I said *car* and *darkness.*

61   We stretched our legs, bare and summer-brown, out into the street before us. We touched each other at our elbows and shoulders as we tried words as we might try key after key. Across the street, the ragged lawn and the drawn shades had already become for us just one more desolate sign of that household's manlessness, and it was Mickey Meyer who first said, "I wonder if she'll have a boy."

62   We paused to think about this for a moment, realizing for the first time, I think, that whatever difficult and extravagant feat had to be performed, whatever painful acrobatics, whatever horror, we, the children, were after all the end, the desired result—the culmination of our poor parents' most difficult task, their very motive.

63   Georgie said a boy would be the right age to play with his youngest brother. Diane and I said we'd soon be old enough to baby-sit. Although we'd heard it a hundred times, the Meyer twins began to recount for us the elaborate story of their surprise birth, how in the first minute of life, according to their father, they had both spat in each eye of the doctor, who had failed to predict twins.

64   Slowly, we began to see what poor things our parents' lives would have been had we not, after their urging and acrobatics and pain, agreed to arrive, stumbling as we did upon the one consolation it seemed no one had yet offered Sheryl: a child as marvelous as any one of us would be born.

A Writer's Notes for a Second Reading

I am struck, as a writer, first of all, by the discipline of McDermott's style, how spare and yet rich it is, how daring she is to say it one time and say it well—just the right word, just the right phrase—no saying the same thing over and over again in the hope the reader will get it.

I am also aware of the way she gets into the heads of her characters. Their dialogue and their actions are right because she knows their world. This is no adult speaking as a child, but the child, himself or herself.

Pace is important in all writing, but especially in narrative. I learn from the way she allows information to come out in its own way, in its own time.

Compassion is the mark of a good, responsible writer—and although there is much that is hilarious in this chapter, McDermott does not laugh at her characters. She respects them but reveals them or, rather, allows them to reveal themselves.

Here is a universal story told again in such a way that it is as new as if it had never been told before.

Discussion

- How does McDermott pace out the story?
- We usually tell fiction and drama writers to "show, not tell." Imagine an essay on the same subject or a personal-experience paper that tells us about the subject. Describe how McDermott has shown instead of told so that the subject is revealed to us, not told to us.
- Elizabeth Bowen said, "Dialogue is action." Discuss this dialogue to see if it is true.
- Discuss how McDermott makes sure the reader knows what is going on without her characters knowing.
- Discuss what you have learned from McDermott's writing of fiction that could be applied to nonfiction.

Activities

- Imagine you are a movie scriptwriter. Take a page or three of McDermott's text and edit it so that it could become a screenplay. You *may* have to add some dialogue.
- Chart the interaction between the characters to see how this interaction moves the story forward.
- Write a page or two of McDermott's text in the language of the world in which you grew up.
- Read another piece of narrative—fiction or nonfiction—from the book and compare the two, not to see which is better but to discover the different ways narrative can work.
- Speculate on the changes you would have to make if the "I" were younger or older, or a boy.

To Collaborate

- Write a report for a topic in your major, in your job, or for a campus activity, using narrative to reveal the situation so that the reader will respond in the manner you want.
- Act out a scene from the short story to see how dramatic action works.

Toni Morrison

I can still remember my excitement when I read the first pages of Toni Morrison's first novel. You are going to read some of these pages. They took off like a jet plane, and I felt that I was standing at the edge of the runway feeling the power and the force of her prose. For a while this first novel was out of print, and I went to the library and xeroxed the whole novel and kept it in a notebook until it came back into print. Now Toni Morrison is recognized as one of our major novelists. She has published *Sula, Song of Solomon,* and *Tar Baby,* but I have a particularly warm spot for this first novel.

"After my first novel, *The Bluest Eye,*" Morrison has said, "writing became a way to be coherent in the world. It became necessary and possible for me to sort the past, and the selection process, being disciplined and guided, was genuine thinking as opposed to simple response or problem-solving. Writing was the only work I did that was for myself and by myself. In the process, one exercises sovereignty in a special way. All sensibilities are engaged, sometimes simultaneously, sometimes sequentially. While I am writing, all of my experience is vital and useful and possibly important. It may not appear in the work, but it is valuable. Writing gives me what I think dancers have on stage in their relation to gravity and space and time. It is energetic and balanced, fluid and in repose. And there is always the possibility of growth; I could never hit the highest note so I'd never have to stop. Writing has for me everything that good work ought to have, all the criteria. I love even the drudgery, the revision, the proofreading."

From *The Bluest Eye*

1   Nuns go by as quiet as lust, and drunken men and sober eyes sing in the lobby of the Greek hotel. Rosemary Villanucci, our next-door friend who lives above her father's cafe, sits in a 1939 Buick eating bread and butter. She rolls down the window to tell my sister Frieda and me that we can't come in. We stare at her, wanting her bread, but more than that wanting to poke the arrogance out of her eyes and smash the pride of ownership that curls her chewing mouth. When she comes out of the car we will beat her up, make red marks on her white skin, and she will cry and ask us do we want her to pull her pants down. We will say no. We don't know what we should feel or do if she does,

but whenever she asks us, we know she is offering us something precious and that our own pride must be asserted by refusing to accept.

2   School has started, and Frieda and I get new brown stockings and cod-liver oil. Grown-ups talk in tired, edgy voices about Zick's Coal Company and take us along in the evening to the railroad tracks where we fill burlap sacks with the tiny pieces of coal lying about. Later we walk home, glancing back to see the great carloads of slag being dumped, red hot and smoking, into the ravine that skirts the steel mill. The dying fire lights the sky with a dull orange glow. Frieda and I lag behind, staring at the patch of color surrounded by black. It is impossible not to feel a shiver when our feet leave the gravel path and sink into the dead grass in the field.

3   Our house is old, cold, and green. At night a kerosene lamp lights one large room. The others are braced in darkness, peopled by roaches and mice. Adults do not talk to us—they give us directions. They issue orders without providing information. When we trip and fall down they glance at us; if we cut or bruise ourselves, they ask us are we crazy. When we catch colds, they shake their heads in disgust at our lack of consideration. How, they ask us, do you expect anybody to get anything done if you all are sick? We cannot answer them. Our illness is treated with contempt, foul Black Draught, and castor oil that blunts our minds.

4   When, on a day after a trip to collect coal, I cough once, loudly, through bronchial tubes already packed tight with phlegm, my mother frowns. "Great Jesus. Get on in that bed. How many times do I have to tell you to wear something on your head? You must be the biggest fool in this town. Frieda? Get some rags and stuff that window."

5   Frieda restuffs the window. I trudge off to bed, full of guilt and self-pity. I lie down in my underwear, the metal in my black garters hurts my legs, but I do not take them off, for it is too cold to lie stockingless. It takes a long time for my body to heat its place in the bed. Once I have generated a silhouette of warmth, I dare not move, for there is a cold place one-half inch in any direction. No one speaks to me or asks how I feel. In an hour or two my mother comes. Her hands are large and rough, and when she rubs the Vicks salve on my chest, I am rigid with pain. She takes two fingers' full of it at a time, and massages my chest until I am faint. Just when I think I will tip over into a scream, she scoops out a little of the salve on her forefinger and puts it in my mouth, telling me to swallow. A hot flannel is wrapped about my neck and chest. I am covered up with heavy quilts and ordered to sweat, which I do—promptly.

6   Later I throw up, and my mother says, "What did you puke on the bed clothes for? Don't you have sense enough to hold your head out the bed? Now, look what you did. You think I got time for nothing but washing up your puke?"

7   The puke swaddles down the pillow onto the sheet—green-gray with flecks of orange. It moves like the insides of an uncooked egg. Stubbornly clinging to its own mass, refusing to break up and be removed. How, I wonder, can it be so neat and nasty at the same time?

8   My mother's voice drones on. She is not talking to me. She is talking to

the puke, but she is calling it my name: Claudia. She wipes it up as best she can and puts a scratchy towel over the large wet place. I lie down again. The rags have fallen from the window crack, and the air is cold. I dare not call her back and am reluctant to leave my warmth. My mother's anger humiliates me; her words chafe my cheeks, and I am crying. I do not know that she is not angry at me, but at my sickness. I believe she despises my weakness for letting the sickness "take holt." By and by I will not get sick; I will refuse to. But for now I am crying. I know I am making more snot, but I can't stop.

9   My sister comes in. Her eyes are full of sorrow. She sings to me: "When the deep purple falls over sleepy garden walls, someone thinks of me . . ." I doze, thinking of plums, walls, and "someone."

10   But was it really like that? As painful as I remember? Only mildly. Or rather, it was a productive and fructifying pain. Love, thick and dark as Alaga syrup, eased up into that cracked window. I could smell it—taste it—sweet, musty, with an edge of wintergreen in its base—everywhere in that house. It stuck, along with my tongue, to the frosted windowpanes. It coated my chest, along with the salve, and when the flannel came undone in my sleep, the clear, sharp curves of air outlined its presence on my throat. And in the night, when my coughing was dry and tough, feet padded into the room, hands repinned the flannel, readjusted the quilt, and rested a moment on my forehead. So when I think of autumn, I think of somebody with hands who does not want me to die.

11   It was autumn too when Mr. Henry came. Our roomer. Our roomer. The words ballooned from the lips and hovered about our heads—silent, separate, and pleasantly mysterious. My mother was all ease and satisfaction in discussing his coming.

12   "You know him," she said to her friends. "Henry Washington. He's been living over there with Miss Della Jones on Thirteenth Street. But she's too addled now to keep up. So he's looking for another place."

13   "Oh, yes." Her friends do not hide their curiosity. "I been wondering how long he was going to stay up there with her. They say she's real bad off. Don't know who he is half the time, and nobody else."

14   "Well, that old crazy nigger she married up with didn't help her head none."

15   "Did you hear what he told folks when he left her?"

16   "Uh-uh. What?"

17   "Well, he run off with that trifling Peggy—from Elyria. You know."

18   "One of Old Slack Bessie's girls?"

19   "That's the one. Well, somebody asked him why he left a nice good church woman like Della for that heifer. You know Della always did keep a good house. And he said the honest-to-God real reason was he couldn't take no more of that violet water Della Jones used. Said he wanted a woman to smell like a woman. Said Della was just too clean for him."

20   "Old dog. Ain't that nasty!"

21   "You telling me. What kind of reasoning is that?"

22   "No kind. Some men just dogs."

23   "Is that what give her them strokes?"

24   "Must have helped. But you know, none of them girls wasn't too bright. Remember that grinning Hattie? She wasn't never right. And their Auntie Julia is still trotting up and down Sixteenth Street talking to herself."

25   "Didn't she get put away?"

26   "Naw. County wouldn't take her. Said she wasn't harming anybody."

27   "Well, she's harming me. You want something to scare the living shit out of you, you get up at five-thirty in the morning like I do and see that old hag floating by in that bonnet. Have mercy!"

28   They laugh.

29   Freida and I are washing Mason jars. We do not hear their words, but with grown-ups we listen to and watch out for their voices.

30   "Well, I hope don't nobody let me roam around like that when I get senile. It's a shame."

31   "What they going to do about Della? Don't she have no people?"

32   "A sister's coming up from North Carolina to look after her. I expect she wants to get aholt of Della's house."

33   "Oh, come on. That's a evil thought, if ever I heard one."

34   "What you want to bet? Henry Washington said that sister ain't seen Della in fifteen years."

35   "I kind of thought Henry would marry her one of these days."

36   "That old woman?"

37   "No, but he ain't no buzzard, either."

38   "He ever been married to anybody?"

39   "No."

40   "How come? Somebody cut it off?"

41   "He's just picky."

42   "He ain't picky. You see anything around here you'd marry?"

43   "Well . . . no."

44   "He's just sensible. A steady worker with quiet ways. I hope it works out all right."

45   "It will. How much you charging?"

46   "Five dollars every two weeks."

47   "That'll be a big help to you."

48   "I'll say."

49   Their conversation is like a gently wicked dance: sound meets sound, curtsies, shimmies, and retires. Another sound enters but is upstaged by still another: the two circle each other and stop. Sometimes their words move in lofty spirals; other times they take strident leaps, and all of it is punctuated with warm-pulsed laughter—like the throb of a heart made of jelly. The edge, the curl, the thrust of their emotions is always clear to Frieda and me. We do not, cannot, know the meanings of all their words, for we are nine and ten years

old. So we watch their faces, their hands, their feet, and listen for truth in timbre.

50   So when Mr. Henry arrived on a Saturday night, we smelled him. He smelled wonderful. Like trees and lemon vanishing cream, and Nu Nile Hair Oil and flecks of Sen-Sen.

51   He smiled a lot, showing small even teeth with a friendly gap in the middle. Frieda and I were not introduced to him—merely pointed out. Like, here is the bathroom; the clothes closet is here; and these are my kids, Frieda and Claudia; watch out for this window; it don't open all the way.

52   We looked sideways at him, saying nothing and expecting him to say nothing. Just to nod, as he had done at the clothes closet, acknowledging our existence. To our surprise, he spoke to us.

53   "Hello there. You must be Greta Garbo, and you must be Ginger Rogers."

54   We giggled. Even my father was startled into a smile.

55   "Want a penny?" He held out a shiny coin to us. Frieda lowered her head, too pleased to answer. I reached for it. He snapped his thumb and forefinger, and the penny disappeared. Our shock was laced with delight. We searched all over him, poking our fingers into his socks, looking up the inside back of his coat. If happiness is anticipation with certainty, we were happy. And while we waited for the coin to reappear, we knew we were amusing Mama and Daddy. Daddy was smiling, and Mama's eyes went soft as they followed our hands wandering over Mr. Henry's body.

56   We loved him. Even after what came later, there was no bitterness in our memory of him.

57   She slept in bed with us. Frieda on the outside because she is brave—it never occurs to her that if in her sleep her hand hangs over the edge of the bed "something" will crawl out from under it and bite her fingers off. I sleep near the wall because that thought *has* occurred to me. Pecola, therefore, had to sleep in the middle.

58   Mama had told us two days earlier that a "case" was coming—a girl who had no place to go. The county had placed her in our house for a few days until they could decide what to do, or, more precisely, until the family was reunited. We were to be nice to her and not fight. Mama didn't know "what got into people," but that old Dog Breedlove had burned up his house, gone upside his wife's head, and everybody, as a result, was outdoors.

59   Outdoors, we knew, was the real terror of life. The threat of being outdoors surfaced frequently in those days. Every possibility of excess was curtailed with it. If somebody ate too much, he could end up outdoors. If somebody used too much coal, he could end up outdoors. People could gamble themselves outdoors, drink themselves outdoors. Sometimes mothers put their sons outdoors, and when that happened, regardless of what the son had done, all sympathy was with him. He was outdoors, and his own flesh had done it. To be put outdoors by a landlord was one thing—unfortunate, but an aspect of life over which you had no control, since you could not control your income. But to be

slack enough to put oneself outdoors, or heartless enough to put one's own kin outdoors—that was criminal.

60   There is a difference between being put *out* and being put out *doors*. If you are put out, you go somewhere else; if you are outdoors, there is no place to go. The distinction was subtle but final. Outdoors was the end of something, an irrevocable, physical fact, defining and complementing our metaphysical condition. Being a minority in both caste and class, we moved about anyway on the hem of life, struggling to consolidate our weaknesses and hang on, or to creep singly up into the major folds of the garment. Our peripheral existence, however, was something we had learned to deal with—probably because it was abstract. But the concreteness of being outdoors was another matter—like the difference between the concept of death and being, in fact, dead. Dead doesn't change, and outdoors is here to stay.

61   Knowing that there was such a thing as outdoors bred in us a hunger for property, for ownership. The firm possession of a yard, a porch, a grape arbor. Propertied black people spent all their energies, all their love, on their nests. Like frenzied, desperate birds, they over-decorated everything; fussed and fidgeted over their hard-won homes; canned, jellied, and preserved all summer to fill the cupboards and shelves; they painted, picked, and poked at every corner of their houses. And these houses loomed like hothouse sunflowers among the rows of weeds that were the rented houses. Renting blacks cast furtive glances at these owned yards and "some nice little old place." In the meantime, they saved, and scratched, and piled away what they could in the rented hovels, looking forward to the day of property.

62   Cholly Breedlove, then, a renting black, having put his family outdoors, had catapulted himself beyond the reaches of human consideration. He had joined the animals; was, indeed, an old dog, a snake, a ratty nigger. Mrs. Breedlove was staying with the woman she worked for; the boy, Sammy, was with some other family; and Pecola was to stay with us. Cholly was in jail.

63   She came with nothing. No little paper bag with the other dress, or a nightgown, or two pair of whitish cotton bloomers. She just appeared with a white woman and sat down.

64   We had fun in those few days Pecola was with us. Frieda and I stopped fighting each other and concentrated on our guest, trying hard to keep her from feeling outdoors.

65   When we discovered that she clearly did not want to dominate us, we liked her. She laughed when I clowned for her, and smiled and accepted gracefully the food gifts my sister gave her.

66   "Would you like some graham crackers?"

67   "I don't care."

68   Frieda brought her four graham crackers on a saucer and some milk in a blue-and-white Shirley Temple cup. She was a long time with the milk, and gazed fondly at the silhouette of Shirley Temple's dimpled face. Frieda and she had a loving conversation about how cu-ute Shirley Temple was. I couldn't join them in their adoration because I hated Shirley. Not because she was cute, but

because she danced with Bojangles, who was *my* friend, *my* uncle, *my* daddy, and who ought to have been soft-shoeing it and chuckling with me. Instead he was enjoying, sharing, giving a lovely dance thing with one of those little white girls whose socks never slid down under their heels. So I said, "I like Jane Withers."

69   They gave me a puzzled look, decided I was incomprehensible, and continued their reminiscing about old squint-eyed Shirley.

70   Younger than both Frieda and Pecola, I had not yet arrived at the turning point in the development of my psyche which would allow me to love her. What I felt at that time was unsullied hatred. But before that I had felt a stranger, more frightening thing than hatred for all the Shirley Temples of the world.

71   It had begun with Christmas and the gift of dolls. The big, the special, the loving gift was always a big, blue-eyed Baby Doll. From the clucking sounds of adults I knew that the doll represented what they thought was my fondest wish. I was bemused with the thing itself, and the way it looked. What was I supposed to do with it? Pretend I was its mother? I had no interest in babies or the concept of motherhood. I was interested only in humans my own age and size, and could not generate any enthusiasm at the prospect of being a mother. Motherhood was old age, and other remote possibilities. I learned quickly, however, what I was expected to do with the doll: rock it, fabricate storied situations around it, even sleep with it. Picture books were full of little girls sleeping with their dolls. Raggedy Ann dolls usually, but they were out of the question. I was physically revolted by and secretly frightened of those round moronic eyes, the pancake face, and orangeworms hair.

72   The other dolls, which were supposed to bring me great pleasure, succeeded in doing quite the opposite. When I took it to bed, its hard unyielding limbs resisted my flesh—the tapered fingertips on those dimpled hands scratched. If, in sleep, I turned, the bone-cold head collided with my own. It was a most uncomfortable, patently aggressive sleeping companion. To hold it was no more rewarding. The starched gauze or lace on the cotton dress irritated any embrace. I had only one desire: to dismember it. To see of what it was made, to discover the dearness, to find the beauty, the desirability that had escaped me, but apparently only me. Adults, older girls, shops, magazines, newspapers, window signs—all the world had agreed that a blue-eyed, yellow-haired, pink-skinned doll was what every girl child treasured. "Here," they said, "this is beautiful, and if you are on this day 'worthy' you may have it." I fingered the face, wondering at the single-stroke eyebrows; picked at the pearly teeth stuck like two piano keys between red bowline lips. Traced the turned-up nose, poked the glassy blue eyeballs, twisted the yellow hair. I could not love it. But I could examine it to see what it was that all the world said was lovable. Break off the tiny fingers, bend the flat feet, loosen the hair, twist the head around, and the thing made one sound—a sound they said was the sweet and plaintive cry, "Mama," but which sounded to me like the bleat of a dying lamb, or, more precisely, our icebox door opening on rusty hinges in July. Remove the cold and stupid eyeball, it would bleat still, "Ahhhhh," take off the head,

shake out the sawdust, crack the back against the brass bed rail, it would bleat still. The gauze back would split, and I could see the disk with six holes, the secret of the sound. A mere metal roundness.

73   Grown people frowned and fussed: "You-don't-know-how-to-take-care-of-nothing.   I-never-had-a-baby-doll-in-my-whole-life-and-used-to-cry-my-eyes-out-for-them.   Now-you-got-one-a-beautiful-one-and-you-tear-it-up-what's-the-matter-with-you?"

74   How strong was their outrage. Tears threatened to erase the aloofness of their authority. The emotion of years of unfulfilled longing preened in their voices. I did not know why I destroyed those dolls. But I did know that nobody ever asked me what I wanted for Christmas. Had any adult with the power to fulfill my desires taken me seriously and asked me what I wanted, they would have known that I did not want to have anything to own, or to possess any object. I wanted rather to feel something on Christmas day. The real question would have been, "Dear Claudia, what experience would you like on Christmas?" I could have spoken up, "I want to sit on the low stool in Big Mama's kitchen with my lap full of lilacs and listen to Big Papa play his violin for me alone." The lowness of the stool made for my body, the security and warmth of Big Mama's kitchen, the smell of the lilacs, the sound of the music, and, since it would be good to have all of my senses engaged, the taste of a peach, perhaps, afterward.

75   Instead I tasted and smelled the acridness of tin plates and cups designed for tea parties that bored me. Instead I looked with loathing on new dresses that required a hateful bath in a galvanized zinc tub before wearing. Slipping around on the zinc, no time to play or soak, for the water chilled too fast, no time to enjoy one's nakedness, only time to make curtains of soapy water careen down between the legs. Then the scratchy towels and the dreadful and humiliating absence of dirt. The irritable, unimaginative cleanliness. Gone the ink marks from legs and face, all my creations and accumulations of the day gone, and replaced by goose pimples.

76   I destroyed white baby dolls.

77   But the dismembering of dolls was not the true horror. The truly horrifying thing was the transference of the same impulses to little white girls. The indifference with which I could have axed them was shaken only by my desire to do so. To discover what eluded me: the secret of the magic they weaved on others. What made people look at them and say, "Awwwww," but not for me? The eye slide of black women as they approached them on the street, and the possessive gentleness of their touch as they handled them.

78   If I pinched them, their eyes—unlike the crazed glint of the baby doll's eyes—would fold in pain, and their cry would not be the sound of an icebox door, but a fascinating cry of pain. When I learned how repulsive this disinterested violence was, that it was repulsive because it was disinterested, my shame floundered about for refuge. The best hiding place was love. Thus the conversion from pristine sadism to fabricated hatred, to fraudulent love. It was a small step to Shirley Temple. I learned much later to worship her, just as I learned to

delight in cleanliness, knowing, even as I learned, that the change was adjustment without improvement.

79   "Three quarts of milk. That's wha was *in* that icebox yesterday. Three whole quarts. Now they ain't none. Not a drop. I don't mind folks coming in and getting what they want, but three quarts of milk! What the devil does *any*body need with three quarts of milk?"

80   The "folks" my mother was referring to was Pecola. The three of us, Pecola, Frieda, and I, listened to her downstairs in the kitchen fussing about the amount of milk Pecola had drunk. We knew she was fond of the Shirley Temple cup and took every opportunity to drink milk out of it just to handle and see sweet Shirley's face. My mother knew that Frieda and I hated milk and assumed Pecola drank it out of greediness. It was certainly not for us to "dispute" her. We didn't initiate talk with grown-ups; we answered their questions.

81   Ashamed of the insults that were being heaped on our friend, we just sat there: I picked toe jam, Frieda cleaned her fingernails with her teeth, and Pecola finger-traced some scars on her knee—her head cocked to one side. My mother's fussing soliloquies always irritated and depressed us. They were interminable, insulting, and although indirect (Mama never named anybody—just talked about folks and *some* people), extremely painful in their thrust. She would go on like that for hours, connecting one offense to another until all of the things that chagrined her were spewed out. Then, having told everybody and everything off, she would burst into song and sing the rest of the day. But it was such a long time before the singing part came. In the meantime, our stomachs jellying and our necks burning, we listened, avoided each other's eyes, and picked toe jam or whatever.

82   ". . . I don't know what I'm suppose to be running here, a charity ward, I guess. Time for me to get out of the *giving* line and get in the *getting* line. I guess I ain't sup *posed* to have nothing. I'm sup *posed* to end up in the poorhouse. Look like nothing I do is going to keep me out of there. Folks just spend all their time trying to figure out ways to send *me* to the poorhouse. I got about as much business with another mouth to feed as a cat has with side pockets. As if I don't have trouble enough trying to feed my own and keep out the poorhouse, now I got something else in here that's just going to *drink* me on in there. Well, naw, she ain't. Not long as I got strength in my body and a tongue in my head. There's a limit to everything. I ain't got nothing to just throw *away*. Don't *no* body need *three* quarts of milk. Henry *Ford* don't need three quarts of milk. That's just downright *sin* ful. I'm willing to do what I can for folks. Can't nobody say I ain't. But this has got to stop, and I'm just the one to stop it. Bible say watch as *well* as pray. Folks just dump they children off on you and go on 'bout they business. Ain't nobody even *peeped* in here to see whether that child has a loaf of bread. Look like they would just *peep* in to see whether I had a loaf of bread to give her. But naw. That thought don't cross they mind. That old trifling Cholly been out of jail *two* whole days and ain't been here *yet* to see if his own

child was 'live or dead. She could be *dead* for all he know. And that *mama* neither. What kind of something is that?''

83 When Mama got around to Henry Ford and all those people who didn't care whether she had a loaf of bread, it was time to go. We wanted to miss the part about Roosevelt and the CCC camps.

84 Frieda got up and started down the stairs. Pecola and I followed, making a wide arc to avoid the kitchen doorway. We sat on the steps of the porch, where my mother's words could reach us only in spurts.

85 It was a lonesome Saturday. The house smelled of Fels Naptha and the sharp odor of mustard greens cooking. Saturdays were lonesome, fussy, soapy days. Second in misery only to those tight, starchy, cough-drop Sundays, so full of ''don'ts'' and ''set'cha self downs.''

86 If my mother was in a singing mood, it wasn't so bad. She would sing about hard times, bad times, and somebody-done-gone-and-left-me times. But her voice was so sweet and her singing-eyes so melty I found myself longing for those hard times, yearning to be grown without ''a thin di-i-ime to my name.'' I looked forward to the delicious time when ''my man'' would leave me, when I would ''hate to see that evening sun go down . . .'' 'cause then I would know ''my man has left this town.'' Misery colored by the greens and blues in my mother's voice took all of the grief out of the words and left me with a conviction that pain was not only endurable, it was sweet.

87 But without song, those Saturdays sat on my head like a coal scuttle, and if Mama was fussing, as she was now, it was like somebody throwing stones at it.

88 ''. . . and here I am poor as a bowl of yak-me. What do they think I am? Some kind of Sandy Claus? Well, they can just take they stocking down 'cause it *ain't* Christmas . . .''

89 We fidgeted.

90 ''Let's do something,'' Frieda said.

91 ''What do you want to do?'' I asked.

92 ''I don't know. Nothing.'' Frieda stared at the tops of the trees. Pecola looked at her feet.

93 ''You want to go up to Mr. Henry's room and look at his girlie magazines?''

94 Frieda made an ugly face. She didn't like to look at dirty pictures. ''Well,'' I continued, ''we could look at his Bible. *That's* pretty.'' Frieda sucked her teeth and made a *phttt* sound with her lips. ''O.K., then. We could go thread needles for the half-blind lady. She'll give us a penny.''

95 Frieda snorted. ''Her eyes look like snot. I don't feel like looking at them. What *you* want to do, Pecola?''

96 ''I don't care,'' she said. ''Anything you want.''

97 I had another idea. ''We could go up the alley and see what's in the trash cans.''

98 ''Too cold,'' said Frieda. She was bored and irritable.

99 ''I know. We could make some fudge.''

100   "You kidding? With Mama in there fussing? When she starts fussing at the walls, you know she's gonna be at it all day. She wouldn't even let us."

101   "Well, let's go over to the Greek hotel and listen to them cuss."

102   "Oh, who wants to do *that*? Besides, they say the same old words all the time."

103   My supply of ideas exhausted, I began to concentrate on the white spots on my fingernails. The total signified the number of boyfriends I would have. Seven.

104   Mama's soliloquy slid into the silence ". . . Bible say feed the hungry. That's fine. That's all right. But I ain't feeding no elephants . . . Anybody need three quarts of milk to *live* need to get out of here. They in the wrong place. What is this? Some kind of *dairy* farm?"

105   Suddenly Pecola bolted straight up, her eyes wide with terror. A whinnying sound came from her mouth.

106   "What's the matter with *you*?" Frieda stood up too.

107   Then we both looked where Pecola was staring. Blood was running down her legs. Some drops were on the steps. I leaped up. "Hey. You cut yourself? Look. It's all over your dress."

108   A brownish-red stain discolored the back of her dress. She kept whinnying, standing with her legs far apart.

109   Frieda said, "Oh. Lordy! I know. I know what that is!"

110   "What?" Pecola's fingers went to her mouth.

111   "That's ministratin'."

112   "What's that?"

113   "You know."

114   "Am I going to die?" she asked.

115   "Noooo. You won't die. It just means you can have a baby!"

116   "What?"

117   "How do *you* know?" I was sick and tired of Frieda knowing everything.

118   "Mildred told me, and Mama too."

119   "I don't believe it."

120   "You don't have to, dummy. Look. Wait here. Sit down, Pecola. Right here." Frieda was all authority and zest. "And you," she said to me, "you go get some water."

121   "Water?"

122   "Yes, stupid. Water. And be quiet, or Mama will hear you."

123   Pecola sat down again, a little less fear in her eyes. I went into the kitchen.

124   "What you want, girl?" Mama was rinsing curtains in the sink.

125   "Some water, ma'am."

126   "Right where I'm working, naturally. Well, get a glass. Not no clean one neither. Use that jar."

127   I got a Mason jar and filled it with water from the faucet. It seemed a long time filling.

128   "Don't nobody never want nothing till they see me at the sink. Then everybody got to drink water. . . ."

129 When the jar was full, I moved to leave the room.

130 "Where you going?"

131 "Outside."

132 "Drink that water right here!"

133 "I ain't gonna break nothing."

134 "You don't know what you gonna do."

135 "Yes, ma'am. I do. Lemme take it out. I won't spill none."

136 "You bed' not."

137 I got to the porch and stood there with the Mason jar of water. Pecola was crying.

138 "What you crying for? Does it hurt?"

139 She shook her head.

140 "Then stop slinging snot."

141 Frieda opened the back door. She had something tucked in her blouse. She looked at me in amazement and pointed to the jar. "What's that supposed to do?"

142 "You told me. You *said* get some water."

143 "Not a little old jar full. Lots of water. To scrub the steps with, dumbbell!"

144 "How was I supposed to know?"

145 "Yeah. How was you. Come on." She pulled Pecola up by the arm. "Let's go back here." They headed for the side of the house where the bushes were thick.

146 "Hey. What about me? I want to go."

147 "Shut uuuup," Frieda stage-whispered. "Mama will hear you. You wash the steps."

148 They disappeared around the corner of the house.

149 I was going to miss something. Again. Here was something important, and I had to stay behind and not see any of it. I poured the water on the steps, sloshed it with my shoe, and ran to join them.

150 Frieda was on her knees; a white rectangle of cotton was near her on the ground. She was pulling Pecola's pants off. "Come on. Step out of them." She managed to get the soiled pants down and flung them at me. "Here."

151 "What am I supposed to do with these?"

152 "Bury them, moron."

153 Frieda told Pecola to hold the cotton thing between her legs.

154 "How she gonna walk like that?" I asked.

155 Frieda didn't answer. Instead she took two safety pins from the hem of her skirt and began to pin the ends of the napkin to Pecola's dress.

156 I picked up the pants with two fingers and looked about for something to dig a hole with. A rustling noise in the bushes startled me, and turning towards it, I saw of pair of fascinated eyes in a dough-white face. Rosemary was watching us. I grabbed for her face and succeeded in scratching her nose. She screamed and jumped back.

157 "Mrs. MacTeer! Mrs. MacTeer!" Rosemary hollered. "Frieda and Claudia are out here playing nasty! Mrs. MacTeer!"

158   Mama opened the window and looked down at us.

159   "What?"

160   "They're playing nasty, Mrs. MacTeer. Look. And Claudia hit me 'cause I seen them!"

161   Mama slammed the window shut and came running out the back door.

162   "What you all doing? Oh. Uh-huh. Uh-huh. Playing nasty, huh?" She reached into the bushes and pulled off a switch. "I'd rather raise pigs than some nasty girls. Least I can slaughter *them!*"

163   We began to shriek. "No, Mama. No, ma'am. We wasn't! She's a liar! No, ma'am, Mama! No, ma'am, Mama!"

164   Mama grabbed Frieda by the shoulder, turned her around, and gave her three or four stinging cuts on her legs. "Gonna be nasty, huh? Naw you ain't!"

165   Frieda was destroyed. Whippings wounded and insulted her.

166   Mama looked at Pecola. "You too!" she said. "Child of mine or not!" She grabbed Pecola and spun her around. The safety pin snapped open on one end of the napkin, and Mama saw it fall from under her dress. The switch hovered in the air while Mama blinked. "What the devil is going on here?"

167   Frieda was sobbing. I, next in line, began to explain. "She was bleeding. We was just trying to stop the blood!"

168   Mama looked at Frieda for verification. Frieda nodded. "She's ministratin'. We was just helping."

169   Mama released Pecola and stood looking at her. Then she pulled both of them toward her, their heads against her stomach. Her eyes were sorry. "All right, all right. Now, stop crying. I didn't know. Come on, now. Get on in the house. Go on home, Rosemary. The show is over."

170   We trooped in, Frieda sobbing quietly, Pecola carrying a white tail, me carrying the little-girl-gone-to-woman pants.

171   Mama led us to the bathroom. She prodded Pecola inside, and taking the underwear from me, told us to stay out.

172   We could hear water running into the bathtub.

173   "You think she's going to drown her?"

174   "Oh, Claudia. You so dumb. She's just going to wash her clothes and all."

175   "Should we beat up Rosemary?"

176   "No. Leave her alone."

177   The water gushed, and over its gushing we could hear the music of my mother's laughter.

178   That night, in bed, the three of us lay still. We were full of awe and respect for Pecola. Lying next to a real person who was really ministratin' was somehow sacred. She was different from us now—grown-up-like. She, herself, felt the distance, but refused to lord it over us.

179   After a long while she spoke very softly, "Is it true that I can have a baby now?"

180   "Sure," said Frieda drowsily. "Sure you can."

181   "But . . . how?" Her voice was hollow with wonder.

182   "Oh," said Frieda, "somebody has to love you."
183   "Oh."
184   There was a long pause in which Pecola and I thought this over. It would involve, I supposed, "my man," who, before leaving me, would love me. But there weren't any babies in the songs my mother sang. Maybe that's why the women were sad: the men left before they could make a baby.
185   Then Pecola asked a question that had never entered my mind. "How do you do that? I mean, how do you get somebody to love you?" But Frieda was asleep. And I didn't know.

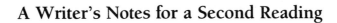

A Writer's Notes for a Second Reading

A writer hears voices—voices that rise from the page. The voices of the characters, the speakers in the story, of course, but over it all the voice of the writer who is orchestrating it all.

I reread this story for the authentic voices of the speakers within the story. I believe those voices. Too often the characters in a story, the authorities cited in non-fiction all sound the same—and inappropriately similar to the author. Morrison's characters are individual and they speak the way people speak.

But I hear another voice, the powerful voice of the author telling me the story in a manner that line by line does not only tell me the story but reinforces it, the way that movie background music tells the story as well as action, dialogue, and description.

Read this story for that voice, then read writing you like in the world of your major, your hobby, your religion, your career and you will hear that text, hear the music of a voice supporting what is being said.

Discussion

- Discuss how what Toni Morrison does relates to Alice McDermott.
- As nonfiction writers we continue to learn our craft from our poets and our fiction writers. What can you learn from this selection and apply to your nonfiction?
- Compare this novel about growing up to the autobiographical writing of Baraka, Baldwin, Gibson. In what ways are they similar and in what ways do they differ?
- What surprised you about Morrison's writing? How is it different from what you expected? How does it involve you? How does it make you feel? How does it make you think?
- How does Morrison use detail? Where does it work for you? Where doesn't it?
- How does Morrison use point of view?
- What gives her writing such force and energy?

Activities

- Rewrite a page of your prose as Morrison might.
- "I write out of ignorance," Morrison has said. "I write about the things I don't have any resolutions for, and when I'm finished, I think I know a little bit more about it. I don't write out of what I know. It's what I don't know that stimulates me. I merely know enough to get started." Grace Paley has said something that seems to clarify what Morrison means. Paley said, "We write about what we don't know about what we know." Write a draft about something in your life which you don't fully understand and need to understand.
- Morrison should liberate you. Don't write the way she writes, but write with the courage she displays to reveal herself, to hear herself, to use her language to explore her world. Create a free-writing draft to hear the voice you do not yet know that you have.
- Take a page from McDermott and write it as Morrison might. Then let McDermott go to work on a page of Morrison.

To Collaborate

- Work with someone who shares a major, a career, a hobby with you; take a document from that field and tune the voice so that it does a better job of supporting and communicating the meaning of the text.
- Each of your team should write a page from Morrison in your own voice, then combine the texts into a collaborative text that has its own consistent and appropriate voice.

Valerie Gillam
STUDENT ESSAY

An Infant's Right to Die

1   On October 11, 1983, an infant named Baby Jane Doe was born in a Long Island hospital with spina bifida, an abnormally small head, and fluid on the brain. In addition, she had a malformed brain stem, was missing parts of her cerebral cortex, and exhibited weak face, a condition which prevents the child from being able to fully close her eyes or make a full suck with her tongue. A few years before this a child in Baby Jane Doe's condition would have died naturally within two years.

2   New medical advances enabled doctors to prolong Baby Jane Doe's life for as much as twenty years with an operation to close the opening in her spine and drain the fluids from her head. This operation could increase the quantity of her life but not the quality. Baby Jane Doe would always remain severely retarded, unable to speak or learn, epileptic, paralyzed, incontinent, and unable to ever leave her bed.

3   Baby Jane Doe's parents consulted numerous religious and medical advisors and understood that the operation could do no more than prolong her condition. After careful consideration, the child's parents decided not to authorize the operation because they felt that it would not benefit their daughter.

4   Due to the growth of medical technology, there was a great deal of turmoil in the early 1980s concerning the care of deformed infants. A lawyer named Lawrence Washburn felt that Baby Jane Doe's parents had made the wrong decision and brought them to court to force the hospital into giving the child the operation. Washburn was a member of the Right to Life activists who believed that all children should be provided with maximum care despite the extent of their illness. The judicial branch traditionally in favor of parental choice in these matters rejected Washburn's suit terming it "offensive" and "distressing." The judges involved in this case did not feel that the court had the right to override the decision made by the child's parents and doctors without conclusive evidence proving that the decision was made contrary to the child's best interests.

5   At the same time, the legislative and executive branches were passing guidelines that would cut parental choice in these matters completely. The guidelines stated that no child should be denied medical treatment due to present or anticipated handicaps. If a hospital violated this in any way federal funding for that hospital would be cut. To ensure that these guidelines were followed, a 24-hour hotline was set up for anyone who wished to report a violation.

6   The judicial branch once again sided with the parents and rejected these guidelines, stating that they were so general that they were unlawful. For some infants, maximum treatment could cause undue pain. For example, in one case, a child named Terri was born prematurely with severe lung disease and brain damage. During birth a blood vessel in the child's brain had ruptured, causing internal bleeding. Due to Terri's lung disease, doctors were unable to get her to breathe in the first moments of her life and the lack of oxygen greatly increased her brain damage.

7   Terri was immediately placed on a respiratory machine which controlled her breathing by means of a tube down her throat. The child was in obvious discomfort and pain and her life expectancy with maximum care was only six months. The doctors involved in the case and Terri's parents decided to discontinue care and allow the child to die an earlier death.

8   According to [President Ronald] Reagan's guidelines, this action was not permissible. They simplistically stated that all children should be provided with

maximum care, without taking into account the wide range of individuality in each case. This led the judicial branch to uphold their view that those closest to and personally involved with the infant are best able to decide what is best for her.

9   The parents are closest to the child emotionally and would have to bear the burden of caring for an invalid child or the guilt involved in allowing a child to die, so legally they should have the power to decide what is best for their baby. Parents usually feel a natural love for their child despite its health and therefore are not likely to make a hasty decision.

10   The child's doctor should be available to provide the parents with advice and information. The doctor should also have the power to monitor the parents' decision to ensure that it was made solely to benefit the child. Occasionally, the parents became too distressed to make a decision or other concerns such as the cost of caring for an invalid child or other children cloud the integrity of their choices.

11   In one case, a baby was born with Down's syndrome and an intestinal blockage which could be routinely removed. If the blockage was not removed, the child could not be fed and would die of starvation. The child's mother was a 34-year-old nurse and his father was a 35-year-old lawyer. They had two other children. Though well-informed that a child with Down's syndrome could lead a long and happy life, the parents refused to authorize the operation on the grounds that it would be unfair to the other children in the family to raise them with a retarded sibling. In this case, the parents believed that the well-being of their two older children was more important than the life of their new-born.

12   Usually, the natural love a parent has for a child along with the high regard for life among medical professionals is enough to ensure that the decisions are made in the child's best interests. Their personal involvement with the infant and familiarity with its needs make them by far more qualified to decide what is best for the infant than the government or courts.

13   The struggle for control in these cases will continue to surface in courts around the country because so many children who would have died can now be kept alive with new medical treatments. Though this gives many children a welcome second chance at life, there are other children like Baby Jane Doe and Terri with such irreversible conditions as severe brain damage or paralysis. For them, advanced medical technology can only provide prolonged suffering. In these cases, the rapid growth in the field of medicine has taken their life out of the hands of nature and placed it into the hands of its parents and doctors who now have the agonizing responsibility to decide what is best for that child.

14   It is important to note that the decision concerning the life of a child should be made solely for the welfare of the child; not society's welfare or the welfare of the child's parents or siblings. How does one decide whether it would benefit a child to prolong its life? We can ask ourselves if the child will ever

grow to place value on his own life. To answer this, we must look at what we find valuable in our own lives; perhaps the ability to experience happiness or pleasure, to form friendships and know how to love, or to be able to learn and be curious.

15   Obviously, there is much more to life than simply being able to breathe. In the case of Baby Jane Doe and Terri, the infants would never grow to experience those elements in life that give it value. With care and attention, these infants could be kept alive for a time, but would they ever grow to value their existence?

16   The government would like to have all infants born defective or diseased given maximum treatment. On the face of it, this proposal sounds rather noble—but unfortunately prolonged life is not noble for every child. Baby Jane Doe would be forced to live bedridden and severely retarded for as long as twenty years and Terri would be resuscitated over and over until her lungs finally collapsed forever. Medical technology can't give these children a second chance at life because they weren't born with a first chance at life. The government seems unable to recognize the extent of individuality in each case. Could an official in Washington possibly understand the torment of a diseased infant better than the parents who love it and the doctors who care for it?

History of the Essay

Valerie Gillam started out with a good topic but one that was too broad. She would have to find her own way, however, to narrow it. Her first paper stated the topic:

> "I chose the topic, euthanasia, basically because I plan to enter the medical profession and have had a lot of trouble understanding why the majority of people in this profession seem to be against the legalization of euthanasia for badly suffering, chronically ill patients."

The next week she worked in the library, and in the third week she wrote:

> "This week, I decided to narrow my topic down to instances where the decision was to put a child through an operation or not. In the majority of case studies concerning euthanasia and infants this seems to be the main question."

She also had a plan in the fourth week:

> "In the introduction of my argument paper, I plan to describe a case or two that show instances where a child is born in such a condition that it would be merciless to force it to live with an operation. I want to open my paper in this

way to grab my audience's attention and to stir their feelings. I have not decided exactly which case study to use but I plan to choose a case where the state or the doctors forced an operation on a child despite what seemed most humane to give my audience a sense that an injustice was being done to the infant, therefore swaying them to my viewpoint.

"In my next couple of paragraphs, I want to discuss my opinion that the parents should be the major decision makers for their child because of their emotional investment in the situation. I believe that above all decisions should be made solely for the well being of the child. So, in my next couple of paragraphs, I plan to attempt to define what a worthwhile life is and use some diseases and deformities as examples which prevent a child from living a worthwhile life. Throughout my paper, the theme will be that forcing a child to live with an operation is at times not in the best interests of the infant."

Next week Gillam wrote a lead, an outline, and an ending, and the week after that produced her first draft for class publication. Her commentary is a good example of a writer demonstrating her learning about writing.

"As a freshman college student with experiences limited to a rather sheltered middle-class childhood, I feel that I have no right to be writing this paper. I can very well form an opinion from the things I've read and what people with more experience in the matter have told me but my opinion feels rather shallow. In fact I am unsure if I will have this present opinon years from now or would even follow this opinion now if faced with a life-or-death decision concerning a deformed infant. It is easy to have an opinion, but carrying that opinion out is another matter altogether.

"I feel that my rough draft is poorly done despite the work I put into it. After reading my argument points over I was left with a sense that they weren't convincing. In future drafts, I think that these points will have to be built up and drawn out more carefully to give my argument any effect at all.

"I wanted to use a case study to grab the attention of the reader. Since the information of all available cases concerning deformed infants is so fact-orientated, I couldn't make my case study too stirring without lying. The case I introduced my paper with seems sort of cold since I could only tell the story with facts and not emotions. This doesn't give the effect I wanted at all. The factual way I am forced to present my case makes it seem rather unreal to me and it doesn't seem to be able to draw the reader into the story as I had hoped a case study would. I think that if I made it more storylike and added the emotion that fits the story, though, I would be on the verge of lying.

"Since my entire paper is opinion-orientated it is hard to lead the reader to my viewpoint subtly. Unfortunately, I've found myself stating my opinions instead of illustrating them and allowing the reader to draw his own conclusion. In my further revisions, I plan to cut down on the direct statements of my position and try to show my readers what my point is instead of telling them.

"Finally, I feel that my opinion concerning what position a judge, doctor, or parent should play in the decision-making process sorely needs clarification. People who have read this draft of my paper are never sure exactly what my viewpoint is on this issue. Also I think that the paragraphs in that part of my paper need some rearranging to clarify my point and make my paper run more smoothly towards the ending."

The students were supportive of her draft, and the tone of her commentaries, which the students read as well as the draft, allowed her readers to be critical in a constructive way.

Final Commentary

I chose my topic, passive euthanasia and infants, because it was a subject that I had an opinion on yet I actually knew little about. My ignorance on the topic was most obvious when I began to feel my opinions changing as my research became more involved.

I began my research by reading everything available on my topic. I had planned to take notes but there was simply too much information to deal with. I abandoned my hopes of taking notes and ended up writing my paper from memory. After I had built up a working knowledge of my topic, I began interviewing people who had experience in matters concerning deformed infants. The interviews did not add anything to my argument but they did provide me with information on alternate opinions.

After three weeks of reading and interviewing, it was time to begin writing. In class, we were walked through the steps of writing an argument. We were taught how to make use of lists to aid in the difficult task of choosing titles, endings, and leads. We were also shown the importance of anticipating the audience's responses to the argument. Once we were able to think like our audience, we could answer their questions in the paper to give them the sense that all bases had been covered.

Starting a paper was always the most difficult part for me so I used a tactic discussed in class and wrote leads in short periods of free time. When I had enough time to write the entire paper, I got started by choosing which lead I liked best.

I was disappointed with my first draft. It seemed much too boring and unfocused. I had used only one case study and was advised to add a few more to the paper to add evidence to the argument. Extra case studies just didn't seem to fit into my paper as I had written it so I put away the first draft and wrote a new paper.

I felt that the second paper was much better than the first. It was more focused and more interesting to read. For my final draft, I edited the paper and shortened the paragraphs to make the essay easier on the reader.

Lori Parsons
STUDENT ESSAY

A Pathway to Peace

1   She silently slips away without any commotion or attempted rescue. Only the EKG shows a change. Her life has ended without complication. Although they did not save her heart, they did save her dignity.

2   Sounds fairly easy, you might say. The truth is that it can be easy—that is, with the proper ingredients. The woman in our example, Marion Jordan, was 78 years old and suffering from cancer and chronic cardiac malfunctionings. Her physician, seeing her poor prognosis of survival, took the initiative in discussing with her ways of handling the situation, as there are usually several routes to take. The result was a "no-code" DNR order, which stands for do not resuscitate. Because of this order, CPR was not performed when she had a cardiac arrest, thus she died.

3   A DNR order is often found to be in the patient's best interest if he/she has some terminal illness by which death is imminent. However there are, as one may expect, complications. One of the prevalent problems is that although DNR is supported by hospital administration as well as in the courts, the initiative to introduce and designate a DNR order is not performed often enough. This may lead to weak policies concerning the subject as well as the way by which the physicians go about handling the situation.

4   The most important step in reaching a decision consists of communication. When Marion Jordan suffered from a cardiac arrest, which left her not only in the intensive care unit but also weaker and in more pain than before, her physician took notice. He took the initiative to discuss with her the need to make some decisions in light of her prognosis. Together they were able to reach an understanding.

5   Without communication, wishes may be either misunderstood or unknown. In a study done in 1984 on patients in the Medical Intensive Care Unit of a Cleveland hospital, ⅓ of those surviving from resuscitative measures later revealed that they would have preferred not to be resuscitated. In most cases, the patients weren't familiar with any such order as DNR. The responsibility rests on the attending physician to bring up the subject with the patient.

6   Obviously, every patient who is admitted is not automatically a candidate. For the most part, the patients who are admitted to an intensive care unit are often likely candidates according to their prognoses. In a combined study of 13 different hospital ICU patients conducted in 1986, of those patients diagnosed for a DNR order, more than half were over 65 years of age and 40 percent were severely failing before their admission to ICU. Patients receiving an immediate

DNR order were found to be suffering from intercranial hemorrhage or cardiac arrest followed by respiratory arrest and a localized or systemic infection.

7   Although the patient's wishes take precedence in the final decision, the family will sometimes aid in the decision, especially if the patient is comatose or mentally incompetent. In such a case, the physician works with the immediate family in reviewing the patient's diagnosis as well as medical history, chances of long-term survival, and any known personal views which would help lead to a satisfactory decision. Hospitals often have special committees to work with the physician and the family to help in the decision-making process. These Ethics Committees usually consist of social workers and some medical staff.

8   One aspect of a DNR order that should be stressed to the patient and any prevalent family members is the fact that this order is not synonymous with no care. All treatment is continued as usual; and in some cases, the patient actually receives more attention. Once the decision to accept a DNR order has been made, the patient's comfort, both physicially and mentally, is the primary concern, not the imminent death.

9   The final step in the process is the one in which much discrepancy has been found. It consists of writing the order. Simple enough is what many physicians make it, by simply putting down "DNR" or "no code" on the patient's chart. This carelessness may result in future confusion, especially if the other attending medical staff is not fully aware of the order or of its implementations.

10   After the discussions with Marion Jordan, her physician not only made certain that her family was in accordance with and understanding of the decision, he also presented the case to the head medical staff. He then made the order known to the attending medical staff. Beside all of that, he also completed the order in writing.

11   The final order should be written carefully and completely on the charts as well as in the progress notes. The formal order as written in the progress notes should not only include the patient's prognosis and situation, but all other considerations such as the patient's wishes and concerns, the family's role and any discussions which were relevant in the decision-making process.

12   Marion Jordan was lucky. She was in just the right situation with an understanding physician in a hospital with complete policies and guidelines. In her case, CPR would have caused not only increased pain, but other complications as well. Although she may have suffered from some initial pain, she was relieved from intricate attempts at revival. Instead, she was allowed to die peacefully.

History of the Essay

Lori Parsons' paper began as she visited her grandfather in the hospital and expanded from that very personal point to firsthand and library research. She talked to nurses in the hospital, telephoned authorities, interviewed faculty members, and read articles and books on the subject.

She had difficulty getting information, and what information she did obtain was often contradictory. She circled the subject, and then on deadline produced a draft for class consideration. Her commentary describes her dilemma:

> I had some difficulty in writing this first argument paper. I started out with mumbled thoughts, paragraphs on separate index cards. They did help a bit in organizing something. Once I did get started, I wasn't sure if I was sticking to one thing or if I got off on tangents. I still don't know how it is. The biggest problem was the ending. I have always followed the good ol' "say what you're gonna say, say it, then say what you've said." I did finally come up with an end which was not a conclusion, but it took some time. Something tells me I have quite a bit of revising to do, and something else tells me that that will be just as hard as the first-draft writing!

The student responses were supportive and helpful. They were also consistent. Most would agree with this one: "Excellent lead! I could tell your point of view without your actually coming out and saying it. Ending—a little unclear." Most readers wanted more development and clarity in the middle of the paper.

In the next draft she responded to the criticisms of the previous draft, and the students responded well to it. "Great paper. Like the way Marion was used throughout the paper, made it more personable. I like this ending better than the first one. It is clearer and more effective."

Still there were questions. "Very clear and organized. The case study was used well. How do you feel about DNR? Your point is made—I think. That DNR is good for some people—but who? How sick should a person be to have a DNR code? The paper is informative about DNR, but has little opinion."

Final Commentary

> To reach my final topic, I trudged through many other subjects, beginning with the broad and multi-sided topic of life-sustaining machinery. I had considered the life-prolonging kidney dialysis machines, which my grandfather uses, to ventilators. Unable to narrow my subject, or get information to lead me in one direction, frustration set in. However, when I spoke with Marc Hiller, Associate Professor of Health Administration and Planning, he stressed the importance of narrowing my subject. With his help, I finally decided to focus on the order not to resuscitate, otherwise known as DNR.
>
> During this time, my ideas for writing the paper went through several changes, often following tangents. One such tangent included living wills and guardians in dealing with comatose or incompetent patients.
>
> As for the surprises, religious views never entered my final paper. I had primarily considered religion to play a major part in my paper, especially when it came to the decision-making process. Also, beginning with life-sustaining machinery, my position leaned towards doing all possible to keep the person alive. Surprisingly

enough, my final opinion consisted of the importance of allowing an ill, elderly patient to die a "death with dignity."

Once I found my topic and a position, although not so clearly defined at the time, I began to run into some difficulty researching it. Many of the books which I found dealt primarily with the aspect of death itself. The only concrete information came from several magazine articles written on the subject of DNR. Also, the long-awaited articles from the Wentworth Hospital in Dover never arrived. Luckily the information I did find provided me with enough to write an argument supporting my opinion.

Argument itself was also something I had to focus. Just as my pre-conceived notion of a formal paper followed the "Say what you're gonna say, say it, then say what you've said" rule, my idea of an argument consisted of fighting with my mother, or something you may possibly do with your boyfriend. And, any such argument as written was found in the editorial pages, not as an article in a magazine. Needless to say, this point of view quickly changed. I learned that argument is just a written form of opinon. With a topic that you feel strongly about, writing an argument isn't too difficult either.

I also got rid of my high school style of formal introduction to conclusion writing. That took some time to adjust to, especially when it came to writing the ending. Since I have been used to writing a conclusion, it was always the endings that needed the most work. However, this did improve by my final paper.

Through this course, I realized that one can write a lot in a short period of time, and what is written doesn't have to be in order. Each piece may be arranged and rotated until it fits into place. This proved to be especially true in my case. I used one of the pieces that I wrote for an ending as the lead. I believe by doing this, my lead works effectively in capturing the audience's attention and drawing them into place.

The idea of using a case example in my argument came after writing a short story on the subject. I made many adjustments between the first and second draft, drawing the lead throughout the paper. Although that revision did flow well, changes were still needed in the lead and in the ending.

5

A Draft Developed

Now the writer stands at the edge of the high diving platform—and steps back. No matter how experienced the writer, there is always the terror of the blank page, the first line from which there seems no recovery. Writing is fearful public commitment, a revelation to others—and, worse still, to ourselves—of all we know and all we are.

The writer has to remember all that went before, the experience of writing other successful drafts, the subject that has been identified and the information that has been collected about that subject, the focus that has been found, the order that has been designed. At least 60 percent of the work of writing is done and it is time to attempt a draft.

The writer also has to remember that a draft is just that, a draft. It is an experiment in meaning and form. In writing a first draft, the writer discovers what may be said and how it may be said. There will be time to read the draft and toss it away or call it a final draft, time to eliminate part of the text and to insert new text, time for more research or more drafts, time to rearrange the order and to replace one word with another, time for revision and time for editing.

Remembering all that, the writer steps to the edge of the platform again, carefully trying not to look down, takes a deep breath and takes off into the draft.

With experience, the writer learns a ritual that works to get a draft down, the critical stage of writing that turns possibility into reality. Writers write by hand or word processor, type or dictate, use yellow paper or green, write early in the morning or late at night, play the radio or work in silence. There are a thousand ways to write, and all of them are right if the writer has a first draft at the end.

296

There are some tricks of the trade that may help:

1. *Write Fast* is the advice followed by many writers to achieve a first draft. The very act of writing fast gives the writing energy, an energy that gains momentum as it goes along. This energy creates a vital flow that brings together many bits of information into meanings that surprise the writer and may surprise the reader.

Of course, fast is a relative term, and writers do write at different paces. But the majority of writers produce the first draft at their top speed. You may be one of the minority of writers who write slowly, correcting each sentence, paragraph, or page until it is right. And obviously that is the right way for you to write if you, your editor or teacher, your readers are satisfied with what you are producing. But you should play around with increasing the speed of your writing. Slow writing can clog the pipes and block them completely. There are times when I write slowly, but my best writing always seems to come at top speed, after there has been time for conscious and unconscious immersion in the material and rehearsal about how the material will be used. Try it yourself. Write so fast that it is uncomfortable. Choose the form of writing—typing, handwriting, dictating—that is easiest for you to perform and then charge through a draft. When you go back to this top speed draft you may be surprised at what you have accomplished, at the meanings the speed has produced, and at the twists and turns of language it has also produced.

2. *Write Without Notes* is almost always good advice. Plodding writing is often turned out by a writer who plods through the notes conscientiously moving from one card file to another. The text becomes clogged with indiscriminate facts and references.

You have been absorbed in the subject. It is time to put the notes away and write what you remember—what the process of writing makes you remember. What you forget is probably what should be forgotten, and what you remember is probably that which is significant. When you come to a quotation or a statistic, don't go back to your notes; put a marker in the text so you'll know to look it up later. At *Time* magazine we would use the letters TK, for *to come*. For example, we might write "President's qte. TK." Work out your own system. Sometimes I put such a note to myself in parentheses, or I leave a big space and put a key word in the middle to trigger my memory at revision time, or make a note in the margin. It doesn't matter what you do as long as you do not stop the essential flow of the draft.

But no matter, after the crucial first draft is done you will be able to return to your notes, check the quotation, make sure the reference is right, double-check the statistic. The job now is to get a draft done, to think through writing. The producing of a draft, after all, is not a matter of reporting thinking that has been done; but it is an act of thinking, an act of intellectual exploration and discovery.

3. *Suspend Critical Judgment* while writing the draft. There are times in producing every draft when my stomach cramps up or a pair of great tongs start crushing my skull. I lose faith in what I am writing, and I lose faith in myself as

a writer. I feel despair, hopelessness, failure. I know that I cannot write this piece; I know that the draft is a mistake, that it will not work, that I cannot write it, that I cannot write. And sometimes I'm right. But I cannot know whether I am right or wrong until the draft is completed, and so I must force myself to keep the draft going until the end at any cost. And I must admit nine times out of ten, perhaps 19 times out of 20 I have a first draft that works. Of course, it needs revision and editing, sometimes a little, sometimes a great deal; but it is a working first draft. I no longer have an unachievable dream of what I may write, I have a text.

4. *When Interrupted* stop in the middle of a sentence so that you will be able to write the rest of the sentence when you get back to the text. There is an enormous inertia to overcome each time we sit down to write. The trick of stopping in the middle of a sentence that we know how to finish vaults us right into the act of writing, and we do not have to overcome the inertia of starting another draft.

5. *Develop With Information,* not inflated language, words that float off over the treetops like untethered hot-air balloons. Even the reader of poetry wants information. Notice how Mekeel McBride and Sharon Olds write their poems with specific information, details, images, the down-to-earth and solid, practical materials of our world. Readers need a fullness and a completeness that comes from documentation, evidence, description, reference, quotation, statistics, revealing details—all the many forms by which we can take information from our brain and our world and place it within the brain of a reader.

6. *Write With Your Ear* is the most important advice of all. Writing that is broadly read has the illusion of speech. The reader hears an individual writer speaking to an individual reader. The reader hears a writer's voice.

Voice is the element that makes writing most effective. Voice is the way language sounds from the page. It carries meaning to the reader, but also it carries the context, the concern, the emotion, the power of the text. When we write we should hear the evolving text. Listen to how Didion and Orwell, White and Shepherd, McBride, Olds, Dillard, and Updike sound. Each voice is different, distinctive; each voice is appropriate and strong.

I have picked out the best writers in a strange city room by observing those whose lips move while they write. They are not all the good writers, for some good writers have learned to speak the text as they write it without moving their lips. But it is a signal that the writer is hearing what is being said as it is being said.

We all have much more experience speaking and listening than we have writing and reading. We draw on this experience to achieve emphasis and grace, flow and feeling, pace and rhythm as we produce a draft—and later as we revise and edit that draft.

We should not in this society be producing a text that cannot be read aloud, because our readers are hearing the text. If we write sentences that are so long we cannot breathe, or so pompous we cannot read them aloud without laughing at ourselves, then we must revise the text.

Voice, of course, is not a simple matter. We begin with our own natural voice. The way we speak depends, in part, on our psychology. The timid do not speak with confidence, and the confident with anxiety. The way we speak reflects the way we respond to the world. Voice is also a matter of ethics. We may be honest or dishonest in our speech, authoritarian or passive, aggressive or receptive.

We also speak the way we do because of the way we have learned language—at home, on the street, in school. Our speech will be influenced by the language we speak at home—English, Spanish, French-Canadian, Japanese. Whatever language we learned at birth may affect our writing. It may cause some errors, but it can also cause a particular flavor and a wonderful effectiveness in how we speak. We are also influenced by the dialect of our family and our neighborhoods. We have regional dialects and racial dialects that can also produce problems, at times, in formal speech, but can give our language a special energy, music, and force. Out of all that we are we evolve a personal voice that is ours as much as a thumbprint is ours. We can identify the speaker in the next room or out of doors even without understanding the words if that person is a family member or a close friend. Each of us has a way of speaking.

We also have the ability to adapt that voice to the situation. Children, for example, have to learn to speak softly in public places. We all learn to adapt our voice to the playground, to the church, to the conversation with the best friend, to the visit to grandmother. We speak one way in a street argument, another way at a funeral. As we learn to write we have to adapt our voice, being formal when it is appropriate to be formal, and informal when it is appropriate. We have to learn to speak strongly and softly, smoothly or with a blunt edge, being patient or impatient, humorous or serious, angry or soothing, adapting the whole range of human interaction into our text. We do not lose our individuality, but adapt it to the task at hand.

As we produce a text we use what we have learned from our reading, not copying directly the way other people write, but learning from the voices we hear and read the ways in which we may speak, adapting what others have done to our own voices, our own readers, our own purposes. As writers we should constantly read, listening carefully to hear how others develop their texts with information and communicate that information in a voice that is their own.

Case Study: A Poet Writes and Reads

Mekeel McBride

Every teacher has those moments in class when a question comes off the wall. One question that startled me was "Who would you like to be?" I heard myself answer, without hesitation, "Mekeel McBride" and I knew I had answered right.

Yes, I'd like to be my colleague Mekeel McBride for her talent, her craft, and, most of all, for her attitude. Too many of my writer friends, and myself, wallow in despair, rise for a few moments on wings of self-adulation, then fall to self-pity, taking everything, especially ourselves, very, very seriously.

Mekeel McBride is a serious poet who has been published in the most competitive journals; has produced three books; won a Radcliffe Institute Fellowship and received an NEH grant; has taught at Harvard, Wheaton, Princeton, and is on the faculty at the University of New Hampshire. Yet she always seems to keep her work in perspective.

"I know so many writers who think that life is tragic and that only tragic life can produce great art," she says. "I think that's bullshit. I think that some people use writing as an excuse to live painful, complicated lives. I'm happy when I'm writing. That's why I do it. Some people feel good *only* when they're writing. When they're not writing, their lives are misery. That's not true for me."

She writes in great bound ledgers that she carries with her and she makes writing a natural part of every day. "Writing a poem is a process of discovery," she says as she continues to make discoveries, "and you don't know what you're going to learn about yourself or what you're going to learn about the world until you're through with that poem." We are fortunate that she agreed to share some of her poems with us. Mekeel agreed to contribute before the poem "Red Letters" began, so we have her journal entries and the twelve drafts from which we've published the ones reproduced on the following pages. We are also fortunate to have her account of how she read and wrote to produce that poem.

Lackawanna cars swollen with helpful too wheat
& faulty thunder.   1/11/84

Feet are invisible anyway & the newspaper reporter's feet
are never in one place long enough. The tight rope walker & the
avalanche expert wear different shoes but still experience
a spiritual horror at the notion of duplication. Amputee,
cripple & computer expert really don't care. Oh, there's a lover
somewhere, bare footed & careless, romancing simple grass
with earth-stained toes. And that person knows, yes knows
when to leave well enough alone.

    I don't suppose, in this case, that there will be any
new ground to stand on. Only the courage to walk [away]
although the earth under one's feet is always the same.
HE FEELS RELIEF. And you've got a full into life and
you've got a sense that in zero degree weather (& that is
the weather) you can still romp in the snow -- not duty --
but choice and that this all mattered, helped put the
tiger together together.

        Train whistle. Believe I will always
remember Anton Joseph with the sound of a train
passing. And then, the train gone. How to live with
the silence. The huge beautiful shatter of immense
presence & passage & the absence of past or future —
just freight train after freight train spilling
across faulty but audible rails, sailing away full of
Idaho potatoes, coffins, licorice & helpful wheat, Chamois
shirts & swollen oranges — yes, let's repeat that — oranges
Each click & spin of the train almost off the rail
something like my heart trying to keep keep track of
what is passing, what I'm in the presence of —

I am witness to every possible imagined loss·· cargo
hot· spit· and· damn flashing past with ignominys
blessing. The bridge I stand on snakes, almost
shatters with the passing. Gone. And then its gone.
And I could mourn. And I could play statue. (the)
orphan of silence. orphan of the storm. But it was there! that train
Rumbling plumetting out of pure summer air. thrust in
its passage. Ominous & luminous. Shook my bones. Blamed
my hair (thin) — only for a moment··· into a place down
birds might bless & bombast with open song shook me, stood
me up held me hopeless in one long "whistle blast" gave
me ripe oranges— promised nothing was itself in every
failling, made its way, was gone. But it who met.
never faltered!

[adored the tame lawns
  shuttered houses, tainted dreams]
shamelessly trespassing through
the small dreams of the unhappily married

hidden suitcases full of gladiolas & apples
tape measures & mexican jumping beans
French porcelain [coffee from Peru

Enough

[The] Train

just   *hope*
(And then the huge beautiful shatter of immense presence
and passage. Absence of past or future. Just freight
(A) train after freight car, spilling across faulty,
but durable rails, sailing away/full

of coffins and potatoes, (licorace and camisoles),
Irish linens and tangerines. Lackawana cars
swollen with helpful wheat and favorite thunder. [Yes,
and coal that will never be diamonds. Let's repeat that).

[Never be diamonds.] Each click and spill/of the train/
almost off the rail, some immense tattered heart
that keeps beating long after the date of its predicted
death, my heart trying to keep track of what

(s passing, what) I'm (n the presence of) witness
to every possible loss -- cargo not-spit-and-damn *of unchartable*
flashing past with lightnings blessing. Bridge   *cars*
I stand on shakes almost shatters with the passing.

Gone and then, it's gone.[I could mourn, play statue,
orphan of silence, orphan of the storm. But
it was here.] Train, train, rumbling, plummeting
out of pure summer air. Honest in (its) passage,

luminous and ominous. Shook my bones. Bloomed
my hair -- only for a moment -- into a place
dawn birds might bless and bombast with open song,
Shook me, Stood me up, held me hopeless in one blast

me   *made*
of whistle, getting there and getting, getting.
Gave me ripe oranges, a lust for the long, worthless
wheat fields of America. Sealed baggage cars
singing out the contents of locked suitcases:

(gladiola,s, apples, tape measures, the atom bomb,
gladiola, apple, Aunt So-andSo's life insurance,
the last letter from death row, the whole
secret of winter sealed into the Idaho potatoe.
history   *under the calm skin of an Idaho p.*
Shamelessly trespassing through the xxxii sleep
dreams of the unhappily married, violating   their
small violent dreams of parole. Prudence
absent even in the in-need-of-paint blue caboose.
I afraid of almost everything, I live anyway
Getting and getting there, itself in every
failing,/taking nothing with it that it can't
discard, mad parent to every steadfast oak it passes
wont' come back and always there. Sheep dozing

in the tiny meaodow of each box car alongside the cars *containing*
(that carry) the red letters of separated lovers.   xxx
Keeps to some kind of schedule. Bridge sinks into silence,
tracks, an utterly still lesson in the failure
Static   */stiffens*

future love the
seperate or parallel

of trying to stay/parallel. Still you saw
how in perspective that train spit its way into
the ~~horizon~~, dragged tracks and distance, and ~~even in~~   *topography*
sunset into one small dot on your visable ~~map~~   *the*
it all
~~married~~ in blaze, disappeared entirely, except
it

? even perspective ⟨ but not without

a struggle, not without the ~~fact for~~
unexpected surprise

of letting you know

dragged .... into a marriage of black vanishing

made of it all the small black dot where
all things married in blaze, scarcely hampered
by the gentle indigo haze that may have
born future or ~~simple~~ dusk (a ~~million disappointment~~
ordinary

simple portent of the   or the old ember without
in admitting that it was enough .. Enough.

shapeless
simpler residue of memory

II

MM

Jan 29 . 84

Princeton

③

Train

~~I'm trying to keep track of what~~ I witness passing --
~~the~~ Hot-spit-and-damn of unchartable cargo flashing past
with lightning's blessing. Bridge I stand on shakes,

almost shatters with the passing. Gone, and then it's
gone. Train, train rumbling, plummeting out of pure summer air.
Honest in its passage, luminous and ominous.

Shook my bones, bloomed my hair -- only for a moment --
into a place dawn birds might bless and bombast with open
song. Shook me, stood me up, held me hopless in one long

whistle blast, getting me there and getting, getting.   *other orchids*
Lackawana cars swollen with helpful ~~wheat~~ and favorite
thunder, coffins and ~~potatoes~~, camisoles and tangerines.

Gave me ripe ~~oranges~~ *plums*, a lust for the long worthless
wheatfields of America. Made sealed baggage cars sing out
the contents ~~of locked suitcases:~~ gladiola, appale,
aunt so-and-so's ~~life insurance~~, last letters from death row,
the whole secret of snow sealed under ~~the~~ calm skins
of ~~an~~ Idaho potato. Shamelessly tresspassing through the sleep
of the unhappily married, ~~violating~~ their small violent dreams
of parole. Prudance absent even in the ~~in need of pain~~ once-was
blue caboose. Getting and getting there, itself in every
                 free   *cant*
failing, afraid of almost everything, going anyway, taking
nothing with it that it ~~couldn't~~ discard, mad parent
to each steadfast oak it passed. Won't come back and ~~always~~ *with its*
here. Sheep dozing ~~inxto~~ the tiny meadow of a box car next *always here*
~~to cars containing~~ the red letters of separated lovers. ~~Keeps~~
~~to~~ no schedule, keeps nothing and keeps going.

Now the bridge I stand on stiffens into silence; tracks,
an utterly static lesson in the failure of trying to love
the parallel. Still, I saw that train spits its way
                                         with it   a vantage point   *&*
into the future, dragging tracks ~~and distance~~, sunset, even
perspective , married them all in a blaze of horizon
scarely hampered by the indigo haze that may have been
      leaving only a thickening haze   *black.*
simple portent of the future, or ordinary dusk
or the odd embarrassment of having to admit   *it was enough.*
that having been there in the passing was enough. enough.

3 MM Princeton

That was no birth of storm, just ordinary

(4)

Red Letters   *Seduces & then stands you up*

Hot-spit-and-damn of uncharable cargo flashes past
~~with~~ lightning ~~to~~ blessing. Bridge (~~I stand on~~) shakes, almost
shatters with the passing. Gone, and then it's

gone. Train, (~~train~~) rumbling, plummeting out of pure summer *almost*
air. Honest in its passage, luminous, ~~and~~ ominous. Shookes
~~my~~ bones, bloomed ~~my~~ hair ~~into a place dawn birds might~~

bless ~~and bombast with open song~~. Shook me, ~~stood me up~~,
held ~~me~~ hopeless in one long whistle blast, getting ~~me~~ there
~~and~~ getting, getting. Lackawana cars swollen with helpful

wheat and favorite thunder, coffins, ~~and~~ tomatoes, camisoles
and tangerines. Gave me ripe plums, a lust for the long,
worthless farmlands of America. Made sealed baggage cars

sing out their locked contents: gladiola, apple, Aunt So-
and-So's black lace-up shoes, last letter from death row,
complete lack of ~~quite~~ packed under ~~calm~~ silkskins *the silk skins*
of Maine potatoes. Shamelessly tres~~s~~passing ~~through the~~ sleep *invading* *bedroom*
of the unhappily married, inventing their small, violent (*tropical?*)
dreams of parole, Prudence absent even in the once-was-blue

bcaboose. Getting and getting ~~there~~, itself in every
failing, afraid of almost everything, going awyway, taking
nothing that it can't discard; mad parent to each steadfast *tree*

tree/it passes. Wond't be back with its bereaved sheep *grazing*
~~grazing~~ in the tiny meadow of a box car next to *the red letters*
~~the red letters~~ of separated lovers. ~~Always here~~. Keeps *no schedule, keeps*

~~bo schedule~~, keeps nothing and keeps going. Spits its way *into the future*
~~into the future~~, dragging with it tracks and vantage point,
sunset and/perspective, marries them all in a black blze *of closed*
~~of~~ horizon, leaves only a gentle haze that is not birth   *slight sigh*
of storm, just ordinary dusk and the odd embarassement
of having to dmit ~~athat~~ to witness the passing was enough. (It was) enough.
                                  witnessing passage
4│MM Princeton
January 31, 1984

admitting that to witness
passage was enough. Enough.   *in the shaken trees, no*

★ *in* *of having to admit that being witness was enough.*

Mekeel McBride

6

Red Letters

Hot-spit-and-damn of unchartable cargo flashes past,
lightning blessed. Bridge shakes, almost
shatters with the passing. Gone, and then it's

you're telling too much

gone. Train, rumbling and plummeting out of pure summer
air. Honest in its passage, luminous and ominous, shakes
bones, blooms hair. Seduces and then stands you up,

Why honest? in this list it seems to raise more questions than it answers.

helpful & favorite thunder just seem cute to me. I like the juxtaposition of wheat & coffins better. They seem like true & more surprising opposites — Then I like the list

holds you hopeless in one long whistle blast, almost
gets you there, getting and getting. Lackawana cars
swollen with helpful wheat and favorite thunder;

coffins, tomatoes, camisoles and tangerines. Gives you
ripe plums, a lust for the long Gethie
farmlands of America. Makes sealed baggage cars sing out

Here this might go over because it is more surprising to change the thought with "lust" not just continue the list.

seems wrong—maybe a physical image

This list is great. The order seems right.

their locked contents: gladiola, apple, Aunt So-and-So's
black lace-up shoes, last letter from death row,
nothing but snow sealed under the silk skins,

seems strange in this particular list because its mostly food & death

of Maine potatoes. Shamelessly invading bedrooms
of the unhappily married, inventing their semi-tropical
dreams of parole. Prudence, absent even in the once-was-blue

beautiful

nice!

caboose. Getting and getting, itself in every failing,
afraid of almost everything, going anyway, taking only
what it can discard, mad sweetheart to each steadfast tree

The language here seems flat to me. Also the effort seems too dramatic here, too hyped

I'm not sure you need this.

I like the image of the steadfast trees, etc. Maybe This can be worked in

it passes, won't be back, with its bereaved sheep,
grazing in the tiny meadow of a box car next to the red
letters of separated lovers. Keeps no schedule, keeps

can you link up "prudence won't be back"

nothing and keeps going. Spits its way into the future,
dragging with it tracks and vantage point, sunset
and perspective, marries them all in a black daze of closed

nice

horizon, leaving only a slight sigh in the shaken trees;
no birth of storm, just ordinary dusk and the odd embarrassment
of having to admit that being witness was enough.

great

nice ending!!!

I'm not sure I like this — definitely take out the word "odd" — each noun here is modified by an adjective so I'd have a noun free by itself. Is embarrassment really the word you want... How about the idea of burden? or something more complex? In other words human in its pain — not just embarrassment

I love this!

I like the idea of beginning in the poems of imagining the contents of the closed cars... imagining what is inside that is somehow hidden, inaccessible, flashing past.

This poem could stand losing one stanza, since it's about speed... + things flashing past... I think the changes would speed it up + also that way you won't get stuck in your lists — or being overly explanatory with other short passages.

Red Letters

Hot-spit-and-damn of unchartable cargo flashes past
lightning blessed. Bridge shakes, almost shatters
with the passing. Gone, and then its gone. Train

rumbling and plummeting out of summer air. Honest
in its passage, shakes bones, blooms hair. Seduces
and then stands you up, hopeless, in one long whistle blast,

almost gets you there, getting and getting. Lackawana/cars
swollen with foreign thunder, tangerines xxxx
camisoles and coffins. Gives you soot-stained wind,

a lust for the worthless gold wheatfields of America.
Makes sealed baggage cars sing out their locked contents:
gladiola, apple, Aunt So-and-So's black lace up shoes,

a last letter from death row, nothing but snow
sealed under the silk skins of Maine potatoes. Shamelessly
invades the bedrooms of the unhappily married, inventing

their semi-tropical dreams of parole. Prudence, absent
even in the once-was-blue caboose. Won't be back
with its bereaved sheep grazing in the tiny meadow

of a box car next to the red letters of separated lovers.
Keeps no schedule, keeps nothing, and keeps going,
mad sweetheart to each steadfast tree it passes,

spits its way into the future, dragging with it
tracks and vantage point, sunset and perspective,
marries them all in a black daze of closed horison

leaving only a slight sigh in the shaken trees, no birth
of storm, just ordinary dusk and the old burden
of having to admit that being witness was enough.

Draft 10
MM/Prince
MAR 21, 1984

Red Letters

1   Hot-spit-and-damn of unchartable cargo flashes past
lightning blessed. Bridge shakes, almost shatters
with the passing. Gone, and then it's gone. Train

2   rumbling and plummeting out of summer air. Honest
in its passage, shakes bones, blooms hair. Seduces
and then stands you up, hopeless, in one long whistle blast,

3   almost gets you there, getting and getting. Lackawanna
cars swollen with omniscient thunder, coffins, cheap
wine from Hungary. Gives you soot-stained wind,

4   a lust for the long worthless wheatfields of America.
Makes sealed baggage cars sing out their locked contents;
gladiola, apple, Aunt So-and-So's black lace-up shoes,

5   a last letter from death row, nothing but snow
sealed under the silk skins of Maine potatoes. Shamelessly
invades the bedrooms of the unhappily married, inventing

6   their semi-tropical dreams of parole. Prudence, absent
even in the once-was-blue caboose. Won't be back
with its bereaved sheep grazing in the tiny meadow

7   of a boxcar next to the red letters of separated lovers.
Keeps no schedule, keeping nothing, and keeps going,
mad sweetheart to each steadfast tree it passes,

8   spits its way into the future, dragging with it
tracks and vantage point, sunset and perspective,
marries them all in a black daze of closed horizon

9   leaving only a slight sigh in the shaken trees, no birth
of storm, just ordinary dusk and the common burden
of having to admit that being witness was enough.

❡ The poet's account of the poem's making: ❧

1   The countess in Giraudoux's *The Madwoman of Chaillot* explains to a
potential suicide:

2   *To be alive is to be fortunate. . . . all you need to feel the call of life once more is
a letter in your mail giving you your schedule for the day—your mending, your
shopping, that letter to your grandmother that you never seem to get around to
. . . then you're armed, you're strong, you're ready, you can begin again . . .*

3   Her grandmother is long dead and she writes these letters containing
schedules to herself, mails them, reads them, recreates herself daily. Like the
Countess, whose rather eccentric life depends somewhat on her ability to read

her own writing, I keep a journal and read it regularly. There I find I have invented myself.

4   And there, too, I find my own Countess who leaves me all sorts of odd messages. This, for instance, from some rainy evening late in December: "If you dare to romance the moon, then you have insinuated in a practical sort of way that you will spend your fair share of time waltzing with the dust-lovely, frayed and lonely broom." Here is evidence that I am concerned with planetary matters as well as solid earth. Here is evidence I am concerned.

5   Reading teaches me the present tense of things.

6   Zero degrees, January, midnight. I sit up late at the kitchen table writing in the journal. In a few weeks I have to move from Dover, New Hampshire, to Princeton, New Jersey. No wonder I write about various kinds of feet: the feet of dancers, tigers, newspaper reporters, avalanche experts. Frightened with movement, I'd like to disguise the magnitude of that fear and so speculate on exotic creatures walking about in imagined places. But then I hear the whistle from some freight train in the distance. Clear, cold air carries the sound close. Immediately I'm transported back to summer, late ripe summer and a train that I came upon and watched with a great deal of wonder.

7   In the journal, I forget feet and lapse into train-reverie, trying in any way possible to capture the exact memory. There's no critical part of me reading over my shoulder, saying, "But you're writing in sentence fragments. You've used the word *orange* three times. You have neglected sensible transitions." My only concern is to be back in the experience, back in summer, watching the train. I have no notion that I've begun a poem.

8   My handwriting disintegrates visibly as I become absorbed in the happiness of recording images, keys, and clues to the experience. But bad handwriting is a certain sign that I'll go back and try to write a poem. I never recognize that until later.

9   In this rush to get things down, I find that words seem to group by themselves and cause me a great deal of delight. "Luminous and ominous," for instance, rattle about in my head—summoning up miles of tumbling, purposeful boxcars somehow as shy as elephants, that unwieldy, that unexpected. And as they passed me then, and pass me now (in imagination), splendid in their uncompromising speed, their secret contents are almost a kind of taunt. So it is satisfying to read that the dark Lackawanna cars contain "potatoes, coffins, licorice, wheat, and camisoles."

10   Perhaps the biggest surprise is that I have associated the train, its whistle, its vibrant passage, and the summer day itself with a person who is, now, just as absent as the train. William Dickey asks, "Is the point of being a poet to clean your plate, use up things, make every loss valuable?" Not always, but in this case, yes. This draft, as rough and clunky and fast as the train, celebrates more than the mechanics of passage. I write until I've caught the memory and then, comforted, go to bed. Subsequent journal entries include detailed reports of trainless dreams, mention of a haircut, lists of things to take to New Jersey. I do not even reread what I've written about the summer train.

11   Less than a month later I'm in New Jersey, feeling homesick and displaced, up late again, writing in my journal, when I hear a train whistle. The
sound of Dover, the sound from summer. It's a shock to me how easily, sometimes, the most disparate landscapes and weathers can unite. The simple sound
of a passing train in the distance places me at home in a suddenly mild climate
and makes me aware that since I wrote the initial journal entry, there has been
the gentlest tugging going on, a tugging that I've not been paying attention to.
Simple—go back and write the poem.

12   An aside. As a poor speller, I grew up with an enormous hatred of the
dictionary. How, after all, do you look up pterodactyl when you're convinced
it starts with a *t*? As a writer, I've come to see the dictionary as a book of miracles. There, a word's origins may be discovered and words, like people, have
histories and patterns of growth. Although a word's original meaning may not
be relevant in contemporary usage, still, that initial meaning breeds and dreams
in the word as surely as any vivid experience from childhood informs the adult.

13   Since I am concerned here with how I read an experience, and how, then,
I read various drafts of the poem that translates that experience into words, I
look up *read* in the *Oxford English Dictionary*. And I find that *read* originally
meant "to deliberate, to consider, to attend to."

14   Good news. A correspondence right away. I attended the passage of that
train with such concentration that if an eight-foot giant, covered in sequins, had
approached me with news that I'd just won the New Hampshire lottery, I would
not have noticed. Perhaps I exaggerate but as Gaston Bachelard says, "Exaggeration is the surest sign of wonder," and wonder is surely what I felt in watching the train and later, in writing about it.

15   It is, as I had guessed and hoped, that *to read* is a verb that pertains to
more than the act of a student scanning fifty pages on the mating habits of
woodchucks. Another original meaning for *read*: "to make out or discover the
significance of . . ." So I read the train by attending fully to my experience of it
and I make out, or discover the significance of it by writing a poem, reading
draft after draft, rewriting until the discovery is complete. The happiest coincidence of all (I prefer to call it correspondence): just as a train stitches together
and connects the most unlikely destinations, so the act of reading concerns and
connects physical experience, active memory, writing and revision, and the finished poem.

16   I pull out my journal, read the train entry and begin to work on the second
draft. I want the lines to be long in order to imitate the railroad tracks. I need
a fast, snappy rhythm to catch the train's movement. Once, standing on an
Amtrak platform in Princeton, I witnessed an Amtrak commuter train shoot
through so quickly that the wind from it blew off my hat and pushed me back
on the platform. I asked a conductor how fast the train was going. "You don't
want to know," he said. I asked again. "One hundred and twenty-five miles."
That's how fast I want this poem to be.

17   Since this train represents marriage to the present moment, whatever that
moment may be, everyone and everything has to be on it; lovers, criminals,

relatives, sheep, tangerines, even the atom bomb. Well, it is a second draft, after all. When I read this draft, it becomes clear to me that there's a fairly large "atom bomb" category, that is, images and emotions and words I've tossed in during the exuberant process of trying to *get it all down,* strange little trespassers who slipped in past my notice.

18   Reading reveals them to be duds, imposters, uninvited, out of place. Why after all, should this particular train carry "coal that will never be diamonds," "tape measures," or "the atom bomb"? No good reason. I toss them all out and also begin to remove my irrelevant personal asides—"I could mourn, play statue/orphan of silence, orphan of the storm." Sentimental and forced. True, I like the sound of "mourn" with "storm" but as for the melodrama involved, I'm perfectly comfortable leaving that to the heroines of silent movies.

19   This first typed draft is as it should be, large enough to allow me a lot of cutting room. I need to be able to see the exaggerated poem so that I can read and reread it, discover what's bad, what needs to be taken out. I scarcely ever begin with a skinny poem and then fatten it up.

20   Titles, right from the start, are a tricky, difficult business. Usually I make myself write a minimum of twenty, then cross them off, starting with the corniest, worst ones and whatever gets left becomes the title—a process that I imagine beauty pageant judges use. Out go Miss Nebraska, Miss Idaho, and Miss Alaska, Leaving Miss California as the winner. This poem's title changes little. There are three weak initial attempts, "Train," "The Train," and "Enough" before I discover "Red Letters." It places appropriate emphasis on the letters of the separated lovers and only vaguely suggests "red letter" day—the habit of marking church holidays on the calendar in red ink. The vision of the train *was* a kind of spiritual holiday occurring with determined speed right in the middle of a perfectly normal summer afternoon when everything else was far too hot to move at all. Of course I'm making this up. The title simply announced itself. I liked it and kept it.

21   In early drafts, and all too frequently in later ones as well, I have an unerring ability to fall in love with my worst lines. Now, for draft three, I retrieve the line "my heart trying to keep track of what/is passing" from the fourth stanza and make it the first line with only a vague attempt to remove it from the maudlin. It reads, in the revised version, "I'm trying to keep track of what I witness passing." I won't realize until later that I've told the reader what to think, rather than evoking for him the feeling of being a witness. No matter. This is an early draft. Priority now is to place images in the best possible order. I read draft two over and over to hear what sounds silly. Quite a bit. The "immense tattered heart" sounds like it crept right out of a bad science-fiction movie and it is discarded. I love bad science-fiction movies the way I love bad lines in my poems. They are low-budget bridges, but fairly reliable and the imagination uses them to move to higher regions.

22   In the meantime, I toss out the tattered heart, licorice, Irish linens, and change the aunt's life insurance to black, lace-up shoes. I want the lines to be

longer, the entire poem to happen more quickly, to have more whoosh, one-hundred-twenty-five miles worth of whoosh.

23   How do I read a draft of a poem? I type it up, then read it over lunch, during dinner, while I'm waiting for a bus. Working on this essay, I discover I've typed *bud* instead of bus. Typographical errors are usually quiet, accurate little messengers from the mysterious part of the brain that harbors insight and inspiration. Bus is okay but bud is wonderful. I keep reading the poem in order to find out *what will blossom*. That means a lot of waiting around and daydreaming.

24   I pencil in a word and remove the word three hours later. For instance, the word camisole (as part of the train's cargo) appears in the original draft and nine more times in subsequent drafts. It's removed three times and does not appear in the final version. Originally it was included because I liked the idea that a huge, loud train might carry, as cargo, women's fragile dressing gowns. Ultimately I omitted it because I lost interest in the contrast. No bud.

25   In draft three I decide that "Bloomed/my hair only for a moment—into a place dawn birds might bless and bombast with open/song" are some of the best lines I've ever written and congratulate myself on them at some length. In draft four I toss them out. Sentimental. Suggests that birds or at least their songs are all tangled up in my hair which is funny, very messy, and bad writing.

26   I read the draft before I have coffee in the morning. I cross out and add. I scarcely know what I'm doing. This whole process involves the wedding of whimsy and intuition. It's the same way I buy a dress. Whimsy, or what seems like whimsy, says—That blue one, there, that looks like silk. Intuition has already secretly confirmed that the dress will fit and that I own matching shoes. And so, in the poem, whimsy invents sheep grazing in a boxcar and intuition places them next to the car containing letters of separated lovers. It's right, although I'm not sure why. Later, when the poem's finished, I can tell you that the unfortunate sheep are on their way to be slaughtered. The lovers, too, are in trouble, forced to maintain their connection through easily lost, necessarily fragmented letters. Somehow, sheep and lovers modify each other correctly. But when I discover the sheep and lovers while writing about them I know only that they belong where they are. That's all.

27   Constant rereading of a draft allows me to see what the poem really wants to say and helps me to remove what I'm trying to force it to say. I have written that the train trespasses through the sleep of the unhappily married, *violating* their small, *violent* dreams of parole. Reading it for the 10th or 20th time I realize that train-sound invents, in the sleep of the unhappily married, dreams of parole. Now I can leave them alone for awhile and search out other areas that need to be clarified.

28   Does this train pass mile after mile of nothing but oak trees? Of course not. Initially I wanted the trees to be oaks because the oak is a symbol of wisdom. A sure sign of trouble—trying to use symbols. So the oaks vanish in favor of the generic word *tree*. Now more work needs to be done with those sheep.

They have been, up to this point, dozing, but doze is a lazy, rather gentle word. A so-what word. These sheep, stationed as they are, next to the cars containing the letters of separated lovers, are actively upset sheep. I add "bereaved" to modify them correctly. I make them graze.

29   And it's clear that if I want this poem to have more movement than it does, I had best drop the turgid first line and begin with "Hot-spit-and-damn of unchartable cargo flashes past." I may fall deeply in love with rotten lines but, just as quickly, fall out of love and file rejects in folders titled "Failed." That's where "I'm trying to keep track of what I witness passing" goes. Into the "Failed" folder. Sometimes when I'm stuck, unable to work on a particular poem, I'll browse through the failed folders and find phrases, words, even whole stanzas that I can recycle and use in the new poem. These files are much like the Salvation Army, filled, for the most part with gawdy junk, but housing a few genuine treasures.

30   By draft six I've gotten rid of most of the offensive and/or sentimental garbage. The poem has attractive three-line stanzas; line breaks seem about right; rhythm's quick, smooth, trainlike; images are sharp and effective. Or so I think. I've worked on this poem so hard that I've become trapped *in it*. It's like being an architect caught ladderless in the attic of a half-built building of her own design. She can't stand on the lawn where she'd have the proper perspective to see that the builders have forgotten the back porch, that the southern wall needs another window, etc. From the inside, everything looks fine.

31   Being trapped *in* the poem results from taking myself and the poem too seriously; from working hard without allowing proper intervals so that I can "forget" the poem in order to see it correctly. Finally, there's only so much that I can do alone. This poem (any poem) is written with an audience in mind and so at some point in the reading/revision process I have to work up the courage to show the poem to an unbiased, honest friend.

32   I usually send work to my poet friend, Jane Shore. I send this particular poem when I'm almost certain it's quite likely to receive only the highest praise. I say "almost certain" because there's some small part of me that knows how much I need Jane's intelligent objectivity, need her to stand on the lawn and say, "Oh come on. Take that heart-shaped swimming pool out of the baby's bedroom. Let's have a screened-in front porch facing the mountains. I love the skylights over the kitchen working area." Etc.

33   Jane's a healthy balance to my own internal critic who thinks the poem is perfect, awful, finished, unfinishable, so busy sending me contradictory messages that if I listened with any seriousness, I wouldn't write at all. Even writing this essay causes me a great deal of anxiety. My own voice seems squeaky and simple-minded. Here's part of a journal entry (July 15, 1984) that talks about it:

34   *Worked all day on the "Red Letters" essay. Finished at quarter to eight. But still am not finished. Yes, I tortured myself the whole way through with the usual stuff: This is stupid. No one would ever want to read it. Etc. Nevertheless, the prism in the window threw rainbows all over the pages and I loved being in the*

clean writing room. And no matter what the voice of insecurity might say, also feels good to dream and invent my way through a draft.

35   *Disquieting to work so closely with ''Red Letters'' (essay) but comforting, too, because the whole point seems to be that you love people, places, things, and then, when it's time, let go. The man on the burning roof drifts away on his ladder of smoke. The white-haired man, Mr. King of the Moon, continues his jangly dance long past the brief span of road my eyes cover and I'll never know where he goes. W. shows up every six months or so to tell me I'm ''heaven'' and then he, too, vanishes. Strange life. In the meantime I eat salad for dinner, quilt, write and wonder. Yes, wonder.*

36   Well, let the critical voice babble on. Finally what always pulls me through (no matter how small or insignificant it may seem) is the pleasure of dreaming and inventing my way through a draft, the wonder. From that, I garden (and I mean *garden,* the difficult work of watering and weeding and tending) the courage that allows me to show imperfect drafts of this essay to my editor, Don Murray, and poem-in-process to Jane Shore.

37   The internal critic isn't really interested in discovery or creation of any sort. She wants me to buy a bag of potato chips and eat them while watching reruns of ''I Dream of Jeannie'' on a twenty-inch color TV for the rest of my life. Jane Shore and Don Murray, as objective critics and good writers, offer me many valid suggestions that mean I have to change my prejudices and work hard in order for the writing to succeed. They also offer necessary support and encouragement.

38   To put it another way, Jane and Don are the tough but honest umpires in a baseball game that I win, no matter what, as long as I keep playing. My internal critic's the thunderstorm that tries to disrupt the entire event.

39   Finally, Giraudoux's Countess has some good advice on this matter: ''Everyone knows that little by little, as one wears pearls, they become real.'' It means, trust yourself. And trust the world.

40   Back to the train poem. Jane returns it with responses written in all the margins. She has, with faultless precision, crossed out most of what I like best. About ''Honest in its passage, luminous and ominous'' she says ''Why *honest?* in this list . . . it seems to raise more questions than it answers.'' Black lines through my favorite stanza: ''Getting and getting, itself in every failing,/afraid of almost everything, going anyway, taking only/what it can discard . . .'' Jane's comments here ''The language seems flat to me. Also . . . the effort seems too dramatic, too hyped. I'm not sure you need this.''

41   At this point I am only able to see what I might mistakenly call negative criticism. But there are many things in the poem that she likes and she says so. For instance, she writes ''beautiful'' next to ''nothing but snow sealed under the silk skins/ of Maine potatoes.'' She thinks the 5th stanza is ''great,'' writes and underlines ''nice ending'' and at the end, writes ''I love this.''

42   I'm confused. I decide the poem stinks and put it in a drawer. Most of this is sulking. I'm still trapped *in* the poem, only able to see it one way, *my* way. I leave the poem in a drawer (and any drawer will do, cosmetics drawer in the

bathroom, cutlery drawer in the kitchen, pet-food cabinet, etc.—just to get the poem out of my sight) until I've regained some sense of perspective and play-fulness about the entire revision process. That means being able to re-see the poem as a movable, changeable thing: a river, rather than a stone.

43   Of "helpful wheat and favorite thunder" Jane says, "just seems too cute to me." Helpful wheat and favorite thunder sustained me through all of the beginning drafts but the more I think about it, I realize that, literally speaking, I'm suggesting that a stalk of wheat is capable of helping me into a chair and that I might, on some stormy evening wander out into a field and exclaim "Oh, why there's my favorite thunder!" Jane's right. Too cute. Something Shirley Temple might have dreamed up when she was six. I save thunder, make it "omniscient" and wheat works its way into an ordinary field.

44   Jane helps me the most with the last stanza. I had written "the odd embar-rassment/of having to admit that being witness was enough." She writes:

45   *I'm not sure I like this. Definitely take out the word odd. Each noun here is modified by an adjective. So I'd have a noun free by itself. Is embarrassment the word you really want . . . how about the idea of burden? or something more complex?*

46   Suddenly I'm embarrassed by the word embarrassment. Burden's what I want but it must be modified, because alone, it's too somber, too full of sym-pathy for its solitary unmodified self. Finally I discover "common burden" and that's it. Not just one light bulb switches on, but the entire chandelier.

47   In typing final versions there's a sense I'm moving almost effortlessly to some imaginary but real finish line. I've got the euphoria a runner feels in the last surge past ache, past doubt, past lack of breath. I've found what I need: this train's simply the metaphor for anything beautiful and transitory—love affair, movie with Fred Astaire, a sunset, a life, the process of writing a poem; there-fore, witnessing it, loving it and letting it pass is both shared gift and common burden. Roethke says it better:

48   *I cherish what I have*
        Had of the temporal:
        I am no longer young
        But the winds and waters are;
        What falls away will fall.
        All things bring me to love.

Five Other Poems by Mekeel McBride:

Black Boy's Death by Drowning
Walter Bridges
1958–1972

1

I wonder why I always do things wrong.
Davis and Earl kept on top
of the lake like rubber ducks.
I dived, watched them disappear.
They survived. Their legs
dangled from a bright sky
like bicycle handle bars far away.

2

I reached for air, caught only a rough rope
of water. Sky came back black as my hand
and a minute later I knew
something on the bottom wanted me.
Not the way rats used to hiss, nibbling
my sleep like I was their
gingerbread boy, brown enough and sweet.

3

I thought again of Earl, our
jelly sandwiches wax-paper wrapped,
my tennis shoes hidden on shore.
I tried to shout. My lungs filled
with water as easily as if it were air.
Afterwards I drifted to these weeds.
They wrapped me mummy-tight, murmuring apologies.

4

I never had a mother.
The weight of her presses me
as flat as freshly ironed sheets.
Dusky streets chalked for hop-scotch
tighten at my neck. I'm made of lead,
late for school, can't run.

5

There's something scared inside
wants out, can't shout anymore.
I am the one who got away
thin as the reeds that surround me.
Whoever I was, Walter Bridges,
now rises empty and aching
in the swollen sun.

The Need to Talk

1
The poem you asked me to write
places me at this plain table,
at a time when my neighbors lie blessed in pairs;
the evidence, Biblical,
their ark, sleep which eludes me.

2
Hardest to bear is the light from my lamp, late now,
in December. I live
alone, would like to believe
this light is more than the loosely woven cloth
of insomnia;

3
would like to believe my life
is more than
what surrounds me. My shoes
surround me, paired up like couples
at a private funeral
each with their own reasons for walking away.

4
For a moment I hold
my ground, gaze at the box of paper before me
as blank as calendar pages for next year.
Here, the funeral goes unattended;
love's body lies cold,
embossed by the kiss of a literary rose.

5
Nothing has died that I cannot do without
but even as I write this, I set my head
down on the table,
for a moment, for a moment only,
and wish there were
someone here to talk to.

The Knife-Thrower's Wife

1
The knife-thrower's wife stands
stranded in danger's glittery geography.
A paper heart is pinned in sequin
to her breast. She would be afraid
if she could see her husband caress
each knife, mouth her name before aiming.

2

But the spot-light sews her eyes shut.
"Slut," he says to himself, "you whore."
Now she hears them coming, a sound
like bees, a sound of bullets. She
wonders if there is a war somewhere.
Applause. A held-breath pause.

3

He places his blindfold carefully. He aims
as close to her heart as he can. And then
it is over. She steps forward, sees
her silhouette set out by ice-pick,
sword, all manner of sharp things. She
joins hands with her husband. They bow.

4

She sees he loves his knives more than
he loves life: his, hers, it doesn't matter.
This is what makes her take her place
again and again, glad for the knives
that need her, that wait to surround her
like a crowd of adoring suitors.

How Spring Appears This Time of Year in New England

1

In walks this lady, seventy five, maybe
eighty, wants the new look, something feisty.
Okay, so I roll her thin hair
then settle her under the dryer, old queen bee,
right out of a Saturday morning
monster movie.

2

She's a regular percussion section
rattling through movie magazines
like she's expecting some Latin type
named Rudolpho or Raoul to step out
of an illustration, sweep her off to a savannah,
scorch her with a lion-wild kiss.

3

I wasn't as careful as I should have been.
Her hair makes like lightning
in thin blue zig-zags, a real robot *do*.
She's got this smile would teach
a tornado patience. I try to give her
the messed up works for free but she pays

4   in full, washed cash, and you can see her
       doing it. She'd soap each bill, pin
       them all to a doll's laundry line, chirping
       away the whole time—crazy old parakeet
       so caught up in percolating her own song
       seems to have forgot she's caught in the cage

5   for keeps. She counts out every coin to the last
       shining dime, says, "Only three years old,
       I'd steal blueberries, stuff myself fat
       as a summer tick, just trying to turn some part
       of myself blue. Now you've done it. And you
       give it to me for a good price, too."

If I'd Been Born in Tennessee

1   I'd have long ago married somebody
       named Sweet Pea Russell. Sour mash, shoot,
       I guess. And my name'd be Rita Louise.
       I'd find me a Chinaberry to sit up in
       with old blind Henry's monkey and maybe
       I'd play the banjo and maybe I'd just talk
       monkey talk and wait for Sweet Pea to come looking.

2   There'd be no trouble telling how God's
       got hold of the mockingbird's throat
       making it tell its kinda repeat truth
       just in a way you can't quite get hold of.
       Or how the Lord's slinked his way
       up the spine of the sunflower that leans over
       eavesdropping on everything.

3   Reading aloud would be easier, too; vowels,
       those old wheels going no place special
       spinning their worn-outness on the red cart
       those idiot twins drive around in,
       their over-alls so dusty you ain't never
       gonna tell what color they was to begin with.
       There's rules. There's always rules.

4   But then there's what's got to be done.
       And if I went out into the honeysuckle-
       soaked night with someone I ain't naming.
       And if we laid down on Double Wedding Ring
       quilts and never slept the whole time and
       never made much mind of if we got caught.

Well, I guess that's my own business.
I could give up

5 reading altogether and look for Jesus
in the garden with his gold scissors
cutting June-bugs and poke brush, black
snakes outta my way. I could say
God damn, just like that and be old,
the oldest woman ever was, without getting tired
of discoursing with whatever passes by—

6 three legged mongrel, hunter's moon,
or the reverend who wears the eye patch,
although the Lord ain't taken no sight
out of that eye. Holy past all telling, he talks
with no patience for the primrose path
which I do believe I have walked
all my life. Sour mash, shoot, I guess.

Discussion

- Discuss how poetry compresses and distills experience. Consider how McBride's subjects would be expressed in an essay or in a short story. What would be lost by its expansion?
- Discuss the relationship between the sentence in prose and the line in poetry. How are they different? What do they each do well?
- Discuss how the poet uses specifics, a basic building block of much of the prose in this text. Is there a close relationship between the poet and the prose writer's use of specifics? What is it?
- What can the nonfiction writer learn from the poet?
- Have someone read the poems aloud and then discuss their music. Have several people read the poems aloud and discuss how the responses vary to each reading.
- Compare McBride to other writers in the book, such as Olds, McDermott, Morrison, Gibson, Baldwin, Baraka. Discuss how their voices and their visions of the world are similar and different.

Activities

- Write a poem of your own. Especially write a poem of your own if you have never written a poem. Do not worry about rhyme or meter. Create a list poem from specifics, or write with the line. Simply try to distill experience and write according to the music the poem provides for your dance.

- Play with McBride's poems. See how they would work if the line breaks came in different places, if the lines were shorter and the stanzas longer. Rearrange them to see how they were constructed.
- Rewrite the poems as prose. Then take a paragraph of writing from someone else in the book or from one of your own drafts and rewrite it as a poem.
- Read some other contemporary poets and write a page, telling yourself—and other prose writers—specific things they can learn to do because of what McBride and other poets show them.
- Write a page about an important experience in your life, then turn it into a poem by making it more concrete and more specific. (Nonpoets write poems with adjectives and adverbs, with flatulent language; most contemporary poets write with precise images.)

To Collaborate

- Write a poem by writing alternate lines to see how the text directs the writer, limiting choice and pointing toward alternatives.
- Write a poem as a dialogue, with alternative short stanzas responding to the preceding one.

Sharon Olds

One of the delights of a lifetime of reading is that I keep discovering new authors. Some of them, like Sharon Olds, I should have known earlier, but I no longer feel guilty. They seem to come to me when I need them.

My need may simply be for reading or for escape into another life and another world, for information or for instruction. When I discovered Sharon Olds I read her first for delight. She took me into her world and made me see and feel in a way that I had not before. Given the difficult and painful nature of many of her poems, *delight* may seem an inappropriate word, but it is not. We gain in appreciation of our life as others allow us into their lives.

Olds' poetry also instructs me as a poet. I was writing personal poetry and she supported me in that act of exposure and showed me how to to be tough and disciplined at our craft.

Sharon Olds has been a Lamont Poet of the American Academy of American Poets and she has won the National Book Critics award. She has received grants from the National Endowment of the Arts, a Guggenheim Fellowship, and the Pennsylvannia Council on the Arts and the San Francisco Poetry Center Award. In addition to her three books, her poems have been published in many major journals, including *The New Yorker, Poetry, The Atlantic Monthly,* and *The Paris Review.* She teaches poetry workshops at New York University, Columbia University, and Goldwater Hospital on Roosevelt Island in New York.

A Writer's Notes for a First Reading

Your reading of these poems will be your own, depending on your own personal history, your sex, age, relationship with your parents, your friends, whether you are married or have been or not, all the complex histories we bring to each moment in our lives.

You may not want to cloud your vision by reading my notes first. Good. Do not read them. But if you are curious about my own reading or inexperienced with poetry and want to know what I see in them, then read my notes first. In either case, read them quickly and loosely at first to let the poem act upon you. Read aloud to hear the music that carries the meaning. Then, read them carefully to see what you can learn from the poem as a human being and as a writer. And if your mind wanders during a reading, follow your mind. Works of art should stimulate us to recollect our lives. Perhaps you will even begin to write your own poem.

Feared Drowned—Another common experience, made uncommon by her discipline and craft. We are forced to go back in our own lives, to re-experience, and, because of what Sharon Olds has written, to re-understand.

The Blue Dress—It is a story that unfolds as the dress unfolds when it is taken from the box. I like the specificity of the world created in the poem and the ambivalence she captures in her feeling about her father.

My Father Snoring—My father snored, great, terrifying rumblings, and my daughters told me I snored, that my rumblings were a part of their childhood so I come to the poem with curiosity. Again I am struck by the skill with which she uses specifics and terror she manages to imply in the commonplace.

The Forms—This poem speaks to me because it expresses some powerful feelings about my own mother that I have never been able to put into words. The artist does that: expresses what we feel but have not expressed and through the artist's articulation we are somehow helped.

Bread—A celebration. And that is enough for me. A wonderful, lively, concrete recreation of an ordinary event that becomes extraordinary through its recreation. It reminds me to observe the ordinary in my life, discover its significance and celebrate it.

Sex Without Love—A central question asked and answered in a detached, clinical tone that is especially powerful for me—a tone that gives me the room to make my own moral judgments after I have experienced the poem. She doesn't preach but causes me to think.

Feared Drowned

1   Suddenly nobody knows where you are,
your suit black as seaweed, your bearded
head slick as a seal's.

2   Somebody watches the kids. I walk down the
edge of the water, clutching the towel
like a widow's shawl around me.

3   None of the swimmers is just right.
     Too short, too heavy, clean-shaven,
     they rise out of the surf, the water
     rushing down their shoulders.

4   Rocks stick out near shore like heads.
     Kelp snakes in like a shed black suit
     and I cannot find you.

5   My stomach begins to contract as if to
     vomit salt water.

6   when up the sand toward me comes
     a man who looks very much like you,
     his beard matted like beach grass, his suit
     dark as a wet shell against his body.

7   Coming closer, he turns out
     to be you—or nearly.
     Once you lose someone it is never exactly
     the same person who comes back.

The Blue Dress

1   The first November after the divorce
     there was a box from my father on my birthday—no card, but a
     big box from Hink's, the dark
     department store with a balcony and
     mahogany rail around the balcony, you could
2   stand and press your forehead against it
     until you could almost feel the dense
     grain of the wood, and stare down
     into the rows and rows of camisoles,
     petticoats, bras, as if looking down
3   into the lives of women. The box
     was from there, he had braved that place for me
     the way he had entered my mother once
     to get me out. I opened the box—I had
     never had a present from him—
4   and there was a blue shirtwaist dress
     blue as the side of a blue teal
     disguised to go in safety on the steel-blue water.
     I put it on, a perfect fit,
     I liked that it was not too sexy, just a
5   blue dress for a 14-year-old daughter the way

Clark Kent's suit was just a plain suit for a reporter, but I
felt the weave of that mercerized Indian Head cotton
against the skin of my upper arms and my
wide thin back and especially the skin of my
6   ribs under those new breasts I had
raised in the night like earthworks in commemoration of his name.
A year later, during a fight about
just how awful my father had been,
my mother said he had not picked out the dress,
7   just told her to get something not too expensive, and then
had not even sent a check for it,
that's the kind of man he was. So I
never wore it again in her sight
but when I went away to boarding school I
8   wore it all the time there,
loving the feel of it, just
casually mentioning sometimes it was a gift from my father,
wanting in those days to appear to have something
whether it was true or a lie, I didn't care, just to
9   have something.

My Father Snoring

1   Deep in the night, I would hear it through the wall—
my father snoring, the great, dark
clotted mucus rising in his nose and
falling, like coils of seaweed a wave
brings in and takes back. The clogged roar
2   filled the house. Even down in the kitchen,
in the drawers, the knives and forks hummed with that
distant throbbing. But in my room
next to theirs, it was so loud
I could feel myself inside his body.
3   lifted on the knotted rope of his life
and lowered again, into the narrow
dark well, its amber walls
slick around my torso, the smell of bourbon
rich as sputum. He lay like a felled
4   beast all night and sounded his thick
buried stoppered call, like a cry for
help. And no one ever came:
there were none of his kind around there anywhere.

The Forms

1
I always had the feeling my mother would
die for us, jump into a fire
to pull us out, her hair burning like
a halo, jump into water, her white
body going down and turning slowly,

2
the astronaut whose hose is cut
falling
         into
             blackness. She would have
covered us with her body, thrust her

3
breasts between our chests and the knife,
slipped us into her coat pocket
outside the showers. In disaster, an animal
mother, she would have died for us,

4
but in life as it was
she had to put herself
first.
She had to do whatever he
told her to do to the children, she had to

5
protect herself. In war, she would have
died for us, I tell you she would,
and I know: I am a student of war,
of gas ovens, smothering, knives,
drowning, burning, all the forms

6
in which I have experienced her love.

Bread

1
When my daughter makes bread, a cloud of flour
hangs in the air like pollen. She sifts and
sifts again, the salt and sugar
close as the grain of her skin. She heats the
water to body temperature

2
with the sausage lard, fragrant as her scalp
the day before hair-wash, and works them together on a
floured board. Her broad palms
bend the paste toward her and the heel of her hand
presses it away, until the dough

3
begins to snap, glossy and elastic as the
torso bending over it,
this ten-year-old girl, random specks of
yeast in her flesh beginning to heat,
her volume doubling every month now, but still

4   raw and hard. She slaps the dough and it
crackles under her palm, sleek and
ferocious and still leashed, like her body, no
breasts rising like bubbles of air toward the
surface of the loaf. She greases the pan, she is
5   shaped, glazed, and at any moment goes
into the oven, to turn to that porous
warm substance, and then under the
knife to be sliced for the having, the tasting, and the
giving of life.

Sex Without Love

1   How do they do it, the ones who make love
without love? Beautiful as dancers,
gliding over each other like ice-skaters
over the ice, fingers hooked
inside each other's bodies, faces
2   red as steak, wine, wet as the
children at birth whose mothers are going to
give them away. How do they come to the
come to the   come to the   God   come to the
still waters, and not love
3   the one who came there with them, light
rising slowly as steam off their joined
skin? These are the true religious,
the purists, the pros, the ones who will not
accept a false Messiah, love the
4   priest instead of the God. They do not
mistake the lover for their own pleasure,
they are like great runners: they know they are alone
with the road surface, the cold, the wind,
the fit of their shoes, their over-all cardio-
5   vascular health—just factors, like the partner
in the bed, and not the truth, which is the
single body alone in the universe
against its own best time.

Discussion

- Has your concept of what poetry is been changed by reading Sharon Olds? And Mekeel McBride? How has it changed?

- How does reading aloud help you experience and understand the poem? What is the role of music or voice in all forms of writing?
- How does Sharon Olds write about personal matters yet maintain a distance that allows you to react to the experience?
- What did Olds make you think about when you were reading her poems? How was your reaction different from that to Murray's? Was your reaction important to you, as Murray implies?
- What does Sharon Olds have to teach us about finding subjects to explore through writing in our ordinary worlds that aren't so ordinary after all?

Activities

- Put down specific details about an "ordinary" event in your life, then arrange them into a poem, leaving some out and adding new ones that come during the writing.
- Take one of her poems and turn it into prose, then decide what are the strengths and weaknesses of each form.
- Take a prose paragraph of your own and turn it into a poem.
- Compare a poem by McBride and Olds, perhaps McBride's "Black Boy's Death by Drowning" and Olds' "Feared Drowned," to see how they each develop the poem or to describe the differences between their voices.
- Play with one of Olds' poems, change the length of the lines, the form of the poem to see how it might have been written.

To Collaborate

- Work together on a statement arguing for inclusion of poetry in a public school curriculum.
- Share the task of taking a short poem and agreeing on a written analysis that states how each line moves the poem forward, how the line develops the meaning of the poem.

Annie Dillard

Annie Dillard, in all of her writing, combines a poetic and mystical understanding of the world with a down-to-earth practicality. And she goes about her writing in the same way: "I work mornings only. I go out to lunch. Afternoons I play with the baby, walk with my husband, or shovel mail."

Many times when I have despaired on a writing project I have turned to Annie Dillard's counsel: "Every single work: There's just some prohibitive and fatal flaw in the structure. And that's where most people quit. You just have to hang on, through that time, with faith. It happens every time—I think to everybody.

Maybe a quarter of the way through, the thing just dissolves in your hands. You have to be able to analyze out that problem and look at it bare—and roll up your sleeves and solve it intellectually. And you have to be able to separate yourself from your feeling of utter disaster when it happens."

She also reminds me about the priorities a writer must establish and hold to as the world's trivialities intrude: "I don't do housework. Life is too short and I'm too much of a Puritan. . . . *Let* the grass die. I let almost all of my indoor plants die from neglect while I was writing the book. There are all kinds of ways to live. You can take your choice. You can keep a tidy house, and when St. Peter asks you what you did with your life, you can say, I kept a tidy house, I made my own cheese balls.

Annie Dillard has obviously not concentrated on cheese balls. She won the Pulitzer Prize for her *Pilgrim at Tinker Creek;* the following excerpt is from her seventh book, *An American Childhood.*

An American Childhood

1   Throughout the long, deadly school afternoons, we junior and senior girls took our places in study hall. We sat at desks in a roomful of desks, whether or not we had something to do, until four o'clock.

> ❡ Note how Dillard sets the scene in a short paragraph, telling the reader here's the situation, remember what it was like? Then she expands on the theme—the world outside the classroom, the other girls. Then, in the third paragraph, she turns inward. The fourth paragraph echoes back to the shortbread but advances the text. And so the text moves forward, each paragraph expanding on what has gone before and moving into new territory. ❡

2   Now this May afternoon a teacher propped open the study hall's back door. The door gave onto our hockey field and, behind it, Pittsburgh's Nabisco plant, whence, O Lordy, issued the smell of shortbread today; they were baking Lorna Doones. Around me sat forty or fifty girls in green cotton jumpers and spring-uniform white bucks. They rested their chins on the heels of both hands and leaned their cheeks on curled fingers; their propped heads faced the opened pages of *L'Étranger, Hamlet, Vanity Fair.* Some girls leaned back and filed their nails. Some twisted stiff pieces of their hair, to stay not so much awake as alive. Sometimes in health class, when we were younger, we had all been so bored we hooked our armpits over our chairs' backs so we cut off all circulation to one arm, in an effort to kill that arm for something to do, or cause a heart attack, whichever came first. We were, in fact, getting a dandy education. But sometimes we were restless. Weren't there some wars being fought somewhere that I, for one, could join?

3   I wrote a name on a notebook. I looked at the study-hall ceiling and tried to see that boy's familiar face—light and dark, bold-eyed, full of feeling—on

the inside of my eyelids. Failing that, I searched for his image down the long speckled tunnel or corridor I saw with my eyes closed. As if visual memory were a Marx brothers comedy, I glimpsed swift fragments—a wry corner of his lip, a pointy knuckle, a cupped temple—which crossed the corridor so fast I recognized them only as soon as they vanished. I opened my eyes and wrote his name. His depth and complexity were apparently infinite. From the tip of his lively line of patter to the bottom of his heartbroken, hopeful soul was the longest route I knew, and the best.

4   The heavy, edible scent of shortbread maddened me in my seat, made me so helpless with longing my wrists gave out; I couldn't hold a pen. I looked around constantly to catch someone's eye, anyone's eye.

5   It was a provocative fact, which I seemed to have discovered, that we students outnumbered our teachers. Must we then huddle here like sheep? By what right, exactly, did these few women keep us sitting here in this clean, bare room to no purpose? Lately I had been trying to enflame my friends with the implications of our greater numbers. We could pull off a riot. We could bang on the desks and shout till they let us out. Then we could go home and wait for dinner. Or we could bear our teachers off on our shoulders, and—what? Throw them into the Lorna Doone batter? I got no takers.

6   I had finished my work long ago. "Works only on what interests her," the accusation ran—as if, I reflected, obedience outranked passion, as if sensible people didn't care what they stuck in their minds. Today as usual no one around me was ready for action. I took a fresh sheet of paper and copied on it random lines in French:

> Ô saisons, ô châteaux!
> *Is it through these endless nights that you*
> *sleep in exile*
> *Ô million golden birds, ô future vigor?*
> *Oh, that my keel would split! Oh, that I would*
> *go down in the sea!*

7   I had struck upon the French Symbolists, like a canyon of sharp crystals underground, like a long and winding corridor lined with treasure. These poets popped into my ken in an odd way: I found them in a book I had rented from a drugstore. Carnegie and school libraries filled me in. I read Enid Starkie's Rimbaud biography. I saved my allowance for months and bought two paper-bound poetry books, the Penguin *Rimbaud,* and a Symbolist anthology in which Paul Valéry declaimed, *"Azure! c'est moi . . ."* I admired Gérard de Nerval. This mad writer kept a lobster as a pet. He walked it on a leash along the sidewalks of Paris, saying, "It doesn't bark, and knows the secrets of the deep."

8   I loved Rimbaud, who ran away, loved his skinny, furious face with the wild hair and snaky, unseeing eyes pointing in two directions, and his poems' confusion and vagueness, their overwritten longing, their hatred, their sky-shot lyricism, and their oracular fragmentation, which I enhanced for myself by reading and retaining his stuff in crazed bits, mostly from *Le Bateau Ivre,* The

Drunken Boat. (The drunken boat tells its own story, a downhill, downstream epic unusually full of words.)

9   Now in study hall I saw that I had drawn all over this page; I got out another piece of paper. Rimbaud was damned. He said so himself. Where could I meet someone like that? I wrote down another part:

> There is a cathedral that goes down and a lake
>   that goes up.
> There is a troupe of strolling players in costume,
>   glimpsed on the road through the edge of
>   the trees.

10   I looked up from the new page I had already started to draw all over. Except for my boyfriend, the boys I knew best were out of town. They were older, prep-school and college boys whose boldness, wit, breadth of knowledge, and absence of scruples fascinated me. They cruised the deb party circuit all over Pennsylvania, holding ever-younger girls up to the light like chocolates, to determine how rich their centers might be. I smiled to recall one of these boys: he was so accustomed to the glitter of society, and so sardonic and graceful, that he carried with him at all times, in his jacket pocket, a canister of dance wax. Ordinary boys carried pocket knives for those occasions which occur unexpectedly, and this big, dark-haired boy carried dance wax for the same reason. When the impulse rose, he could simply sprinkle dance wax on any hall or dining-room floor, take a girl in his arms, and whirl her away. I had known these witty, handsome boys for years, and only recently understood that when they were alone, they read books. In public, they were lounge lizards; they drank; they played word games, filling in the blanks desultorily; they cracked wise. These boys would be back in town soon, and my boyfriend and I would join them.

11   Whose eye could I catch? Everyone in the room was bent over her desk. Ellin Hahn was usually ready to laugh, but now she was working on something. She would call me as soon as we got home. Every day on the phone, I unwittingly asked Ellin some blunt question about the social world around us, and at every question she sighed and said to me, "You still don't get it"—or often, as if addressing a jury of our incredulous peers, "She still doesn't get it!"

12   Looking at the study-hall ceiling, I dosed myself almost fatally with the oxygen-eating lines of Verlaine's "The long sobs / of the violins / of autumn / wound my heart / with a languor / monotone."

13   This unsatisfying bit of verse I repeated to myself for ten or fifteen minutes, by the big clock, over and over, clobbering myself with it, the way Molly, when she had been a baby, banged the top of her head on the crib.

> Ô world, ô college, ô dinner . . .
> Ô unthinkable task . . .

❡ To read this piece I have to put myself in a jazz mood. We have a common theme here, study hall, and Dillard plays variation after variation on this theme, following one thought of a daydream, coming back to another, all played in a before college mood. Beginning with this sentence, Dillard's variations turn inward, self-evaluative, the way a jazz soloist will draw away from the audience, following his music in a wonderful kind of loneliness he allows us to share.❡

14   Funny how badly I'd turned out. Now I was always in trouble. It felt as if I was doing just as I'd always done—I explored the neighborhood, turning over rocks. The latest rocks were difficult. I'd been in a drag race, of all things, the previous September, and in the subsequent collision, and in the hospital; my parents saw my name in the newspapers, and their own names in the newspapers. Some boys I barely knew had cruised by that hot night and said to a clump of us girls on the sidewalk, "Anybody want to come along for a drag race?" I did, absolutely. I loved fast driving.

15   It was then, in the days after the drag race, that I noticed the ground spinning beneath me, all bearings lost, and recognized as well that I had been loose like this—detached from all I saw and knowing nothing else—for months, maybe years. I whirled through the air like a bull-roarer spun by a lunatic who'd found his rhythm. The pressure almost split my skin. What else can you risk with all your might but your life? Only a moment ago I was climbing my swing set, holding one cold metal leg between my two legs tight, and feeling a piercing oddness run the length of my gut—the same sensation that plucked me when my tongue touched tarnish on a silver spoon. Only a moment ago I was gluing squares of paper to rocks; I leaned over the bedroom desk. I was drawing my baseball mitt in the attic, under the plaster-stain ship; a pencil study took all Saturday morning. I was capturing the flag, turning the double play, chasing butterflies by the country-club pool. Throughout these many years of childhood, a transparent sphere of timelessness contained all my running and spinning as a glass paperweight holds flying snow. The sphere of this idyll broke; time unrolled before me in a line. I woke up and found myself in juvenile court. I was hanging from crutches; for a few weeks after the drag race, neither knee worked. (No one else got hurt.) In juvenile court, a policeman wet all ten of my fingertips on an ink pad and pressed them, one by one, using his own fingertips, on a form for the files.

16   Turning to the French is a form of suicide for the American who loves literature—or, as the joke might go, it is at least a cry for help. Now, when I was sixteen, I had turned to the French. I flung myself into poetry as into Niagara Falls. Beauty took away my breath. I twined away; I flew off with my eyes rolled up; I dove down and succumbed. I bought myself a plot in Valéry's marine cemetery, and moved in: cool dirt on my eyes, my brain smooth as a cannonball. It grieves me to report that I tried to see myself as a sobbing fountain, apparently serene, tall and thin among the chill marble monuments of the

dead. Rimbaud wrote a lyric that gently described a man sleeping out in the grass; the sleeper made a peaceful picture, until, in the poem's last line, we discover in his right side two red holes. This, and many another literary false note, appealed to me.

17   I'd been suspended from school for smoking cigarettes. That was a month earlier, in early spring. Both my parents wept. Amy saw them weeping; horrified, she began to cry herself. Molly cried. She was six, missing her front teeth. Like Mother and me, she had pale skin that turned turgid and red when she cried; she looked as if she were dying of wounds. I didn't cry, because, actually, I was an intercontinental ballistic missile, with an atomic warhead; they don't cry.

18   Why didn't I settle down, straighten out, shape up? I wondered, too. I thought that joy was a childish condition that had forever departed; I had no glimpse then of its return the minute I got to college. I couldn't foresee the pleasure—or the possibility—of shedding sophistication, walking away from rage, and renouncing French poets.

19   While I was suspended from school, my parents grounded me. During that time, Amy began to visit me in my room.

20   When she was thirteen, Amy's beauty had grown inconspicuous; she seemed merely pleasant-looking and tidy. Her green uniform jumper fit her neatly; her thick hair was smoothly turned under; her white McMullen collars looked sweet. She had a good eye for the right things; people respected her for it. I think that only we at home knew how spirited she could get. "Oh, no!" she cried when she laughed hard. "Oh, no!" Amy adored our father, rather as we all did, from afar. She liked boys whose eyebrows met over their noses. She liked boys, emphatically; she followed boys with her big eyes, awed.

21   In my room, Amy listened to me rant; she reported her grade's daily gossip, laughed at my jokes, cried, "Oh, no!" and told me about the book she was reading, Wilkie Collins, *The Woman in White*. I liked people to tell me about the books they were reading. Next year, Amy was going to boarding school in Philadelphia; Mother had no intention of subjecting the family to two adolescent maelstroms whirling at once in the same house.

❦ A neat transition. We go outside the study hall. ❧

22   Late one night, my parents and I sat at the kitchen table; there was a truce. We were all helpless, and tired of fighting. Amy and Molly were asleep.

23   "What are we going to do with you?"

24   Mother raised the question. Her voice trembled and rose with emotion. She couldn't sit still; she kept getting up and roaming around the kitchen. Father stuck out his chin and rubbed it with his big hands. I covered my eyes. Mother squeezed white lotion into her hands, over and over. We all smoked; the ashtray was full. Mother walked over to the sink, poured herself some ginger ale, ran both hands through her short blond hair to keep it back, and shook her head.

25   She sighed and said again, looking up and out of the night-black window, "Dear God, what are we going to do with you?" My heart went out to them. We all seemed to have exhausted our options. They asked me for fresh ideas, but I had none. I racked my brain, but couldn't come up with anything. The U.S. Marines didn't take sixteen-year-old girls.

❦ And we are brought back to the study. As she plays we keep getting reminders of the tune but are shown it in different forms with different meanings.❧

26   Outside the study hall that May, a cardinal sang his round-noted song, and a robin sang his burbling song, and I slumped at my desk with my heart pounding, too harried by restlessness to breathe. I collected poems and learned them. I found the British war poets—World War I: Rupert Brooke, Edmund Blunden, Siegfried Sassoon, and especially Wilfred Owen, who wrote bitterly without descending to sarcasm. I found Asian and Middle Eastern poetry in translation—whole heaps of lyrics fierce or limp—which I ripped to fragments for my collection. I wanted beauty bare of import; I liked language in strips like pennants.

27   Under the spell of Rimbaud I wrote a poem that began with a line from *Une Saison en Enfer,* "Once, if I remember well," and continued, "My flesh did lie confined in hell." It ended, slantingly, to my own admiration, "And in my filth did I lie still." I wrote other poems, luscious ones, in the manner of the Song of Songs. One teacher, Miss Hickman, gave her lunch hour to meet with us about our poems.

28   It galled me that adults, as a class, approved the writing and memorization of poetry. Wasn't poetry secret and subversive? One sort of poetry was full of beauty and longing; it exhaled, enervated and helpless, like Li Po. Other poems were threats and vows. They inhaled; they poured into me a power I could not spend. The best of these, a mounted Arabic battle cry, I recited to myself by the hour, hoping to trammel the teachers' drone with hoofbeats.

29   I dosed myself with pure lyricism; I lived drugged on sensation, as I had lived alert on sensation as a little child. I wanted to raise armies, make love to armies, conquer armies. I wanted to swim in the stream of beautiful syllables until I tired. I wanted to bust up the Ellis School with my fists.

30   One afternoon at Judy Schoyer's house, I saw a white paperback book on a living-room chair: Lucretius, *On the Nature of Things.* Lucretius, said the book's back cover, had flourished in the first century B.C. This book was a prose translation of a long poem in Latin hexameters, the content of which was ancient physics mixed with philosophy. Why was this book in print? Why would anyone read wrong science, the babblings of a poet in a toga—why but from disinterested intellectual curiosity? I regarded the white paperback book as if it had been a meteorite smoldering on the chair's silk upholstery.

31   It was Judy's father's book. Mr. Schoyer loaned me the book when he was finished with it, and I read it; it was deadly dull. Nevertheless, I admired Judy's

lawyer father boundlessly. I could believe in him for months at a time. His recreation proceeded from book to book, and had done so all his life. He had, I
recalled, majored in classical history and literature. He wanted to learn the
nature of things. He read and memorized poetry. He quizzed us about current
events—what is your opinion of our new Supreme Court justice? On the other
hand, his mother's family were Holyokes, and he hadn't raised a hand to rescue
Judy from having to come out in Salem, Massachusetts. She had already done
so, and would not talk about it.

32   Judy was tall now, high-waisted, graceful, messy still; she smiled forgiv-
ingly, smiled ironically, behind her thick glasses. Her limbs were thin as stalks,
and her head was round. She spoke softly. She laughed at anything chaotic. Her
family took me to the ballet, to the Pittsburgh Symphony, to the Three Rivers
Arts Festival; they took me ice skating on a frozen lake in Highland Park, and
swimming in Ohiopyle, south of town where the Youghiogheny River widens
over flat rock outcrops.

33   After school, we piled in Judy's jeep. Out of the jeep's open back I liked
to poke the long barrel of a popgun, slowly, and aim it at the drivers of the cars
behind us, and shoot the cork, which then swung from its string. The drivers
put up their hands in mock alarm, or slumped obligingly over their wheels.
Pittsburghers were wonderful sports.

34   All spring long I crawled on my pin. I was reading *General Semantics*—
Alfred Korzybski's early stab at linguistics; I'd hit on it by accident, in books
with the word "language" in their titles. I read Freud's standard works, which
interested me at first, but they denied reason. Denying reason had gotten Rimbaud nowhere. I read without snobbery, excited and alone, wholly free in the
indifference of society. I read with the pure, exhilarating greed of readers sixteen, seventeen years old; I felt I was exhuming lost continents and plundering
their stores. I knocked open everything in sight—Henry Miller, Helen Keller,
Hardy, Updike, and the French. The war novels kept coming out, and so did
John O'Hara's. I read popular social criticism with Judy and Ellin—*The Ugly
American, The Hidden Persuaders, The Status Seekers*. I thought social and political
criticism were interesting, but not nearly so interesting as almost everything
else.

35   Ralph Waldo Emerson, for example, excited me enormously. Emerson
was my first crack at Platonism, Platonism as it had come bumping and skidding
down the centuries and across the ocean to Concord, Massachusetts. Emerson
was a thinker, full time, as Pasteur and Salk were full-time biologists. I wrote a
paper on Emerson's notion of the soul—the oversoul, which, if I could banish
from my mind the thought of galoshes (one big galosh, in which we have our
being), was grand stuff. It was metaphysics at last, poetry with import, philosophy minus the Bible. And Emerson incited to riot, flouting every authority, and
requiring each native to cobble up an original relation with the universe. Since
rioting seemed to be my specialty, if only by default, Emerson gave me heart.

36   Enervated, fanatic, filled long past bursting with oxygen I couldn't use, I hunched skinny in the school's green uniform, etiolated, broken, bellicose, starved, over the back-breaking desk. I sighed and sighed but never emptied my lungs. I said to myself, "O breeze of spring, since I dare not know you, / Why part the silk curtains by my bed?" I stuffed my skull with poems' invisible syllables. If unauthorized persons looked at me, I hoped they'd see blank eyes.

37   On one of these May mornings, the school's headmistress called me in and read aloud my teachers' confidential appraisals. Madame Owens wrote an odd thing. Madame Owens was a sturdy, affectionate, and humorous woman who had lived through two world wars in Paris by eating rats. She had curly black hair, rouged cheeks, and long, sharp teeth. She swathed her enormous body in thin black fabrics; she sat at her desk with her tiny ankles crossed. She chatted with us; she reminisced.

38   Madame Owens's kind word on my behalf made no sense. The headmistress read it to me in her office. The statement began, unforgettably, "Here, alas, is a child of the twentieth century." The headmistress, Marion Hamilton, was a brilliant and strong woman whom I liked and respected; the school's small-minded trustees would soon run her out of town on a rail. Her black hair flared from her high forehead. She looked up at me significantly, raising an eyebrow, and repeated it: "Here, alas, is a child of the twentieth century."

39   I didn't know what to make of it. I didn't know what to do about it. You got a lot of individual attention at a private school.

40   My idea was to stay barely alive, pumping blood and exchanging gases just enough to sustain life—but certainly not enough so that anyone suspected me of sentience, certainly not enough so that I woke up and remembered anything—until the time came when I could go.

> C'est elle, la petite morte, derrière les ro-
>   siers . . .
> *It is she, the little dead girl, behind the rose*
>   *bushes . . .*
> *the child left on the jetty washed out to sea,*
>   *the little farm child following the lane*
>   *whose forehead touches the sky.*

❧ This is a new chapter in her book. It grows directly out of the study hall in the last chapter. You can learn a great deal about writing—I have in rereading this—by studying the many ways Dillard weaves her spell on us, drawing on what has gone before to move and interest through what is now being discovered on the page. ❧

41   During classes all morning, I drew. Drawing deliberately, as I had learned to do, yielded complex, fresh drawings: the inevitable backs of my friends'

heads; their ankles limp at rest over their winter brown oxfords; the way their white shirts' shoulders emerged from their uniform jumpers. I roused myself to these efforts only once or twice a day. I drew Man Walking, too. During the other six or seven hours, when I wasn't fiddling with poetry, I drew at random.

42   Drawing at random, paying no attention, infuriated me, yet I never stopped. For years as a child I drew faces on the back of my left hand, on the tops of my knees, in my green assignment book, my blue canvas three-ring binder. Later I drew rigid faces on the Latin textbook's mazy printed page, down and across the spaces between lines and words. I drew stretchable cartoons on the wiggly and problematic plane of a book's page edges. Those page edges—pressed slats and slits—could catch and hold your pen the way streetcar tracks caught and held your bike's wheel; they threw you off your curve. But if you overcame this hazard, you could play at stretching and squeezing the Hogarthy face. I drew inside a textbook's illustrations, usually on the bare sky or on the side of a building or cheek. When I was very young, I sometimes drew on my fingernails, and hated myself for it.

43   I drew at home, too. My lines were hesitant. "You make everything out of hair," Amy complained. It was always faces I drew, faces and bodies, men and women, old and young, mostly women, and many babies. The babies grew as my sister Molly did; they learned to walk.

44   At Ellis, Molly was in the second grade. The little kids didn't wear uniforms; she wore pretty dresses. I was a forward on the basketball team. Standing around in front of the school, I used to dribble Molly. She bounced hopping under my hand; we both thought it was mighty funny. During class, I drew her hopping in a smocked dress.

45   If I didn't draw I couldn't bear to listen in class; drawing siphoned off some restlessness. One English teacher, Miss McBride, let me sit in the back of the classroom and paint.

46   I paid no attention to the drawings. They were manneristic, obsessive, careless grotesques my hand gibbered out like drool. When I did notice them, they repelled me. Mostly these people were monstrous, elongated or compressed. Some were cross-hatched to invisibility, cross-hatched till the paper dissolved into wet lint on the desk. They were swollen of eyelid or lip, megalocephalic, haughty, moribund, manic, and mostly contemplative—lips shut, full-lidded eyes downcast, as serene as I was excited. They wore their ballpoint-pen hair every which way; they wore ill-fitting hats or melting eyeglasses. They wore diapers and ruffled pants, striped ties, brassieres, eye patches, pearls. Some were equipped with hands on which they rested their weary heads or which they waved, shockingly, up at me.

47   Very often I connected these unwittingly formed people by a pen line leading from the contour of a neck or foot to a drawing of the pen that drew the line and thence to my carefully drawn right hand holding the pen, and my arm and sleeve. I loved bending my thoughts down that pen line and up, that

weird trail connecting and separating the conscious and unconscious: the wiggly face half-fashioned, and the sly, full-fashioned, and fashioning hand.

48   More than once, on family visits far away, or on the streets where I walked to school, or at Forbes Field, I saw a stranger whom I recognized. How well I knew that face, its bee-stung lips, its compressed forehead, its clumsy jaw! And I realized then, with a draining jolt of superstitious dread, that I was seeing in the flesh someone I had once drawn. Someone I had once drawn with a ball-point pen inside a matchbook, or on an overcrowded page, a scribbled face inside the lines of a photographed woman's skirt. Now here was that face perfectly molded and fleshed in, as private as the drawing and as sad, walking around on a competent body, apparently experienced here, and at home.

❦ Take note of how she uses the same words, the same notes, to restate her theme and move it forward toward the conclusion. This is a many-layered text but it always moves forward. ❧

49   Outside the study hall the next fall, the fall of our senior year, the Nabisco plant baked sweet white bread twice a week. If I sharpened a pencil at the back of the room I could smell the baking bread and the cedar shavings from the pencil. I could see the oaks turning brown on the edge of the hockey field, and see the scoured silver sky above shining a secret, true light into everything, into the black cars and red brick apartment buildings of Shadyside glimpsed beyond the trees. Pretty soon all twenty of us—our class—would be leaving. A core of my classmates had been together since kindergarten. I'd been there eight years. We twenty knew by bored heart the very weave of each other's socks. I thought, unfairly, of the Polyphemus moth crawling down the school's driveway. Now we'd go, too.

50   Back in my seat, I repeated the poem that began, "We grow to the sound of the wind playing his flutes in our hair." The poems I loved were in French, or translated from the Chinese, Portuguese, Arabic, Sanskrit, Greek. I murmured their heartbreaking syllables. I knew almost nothing of the diverse and energetic city I lived in. The poems whispered in my ear the password phrase, and I memorized it behind enemy lines: There is a world. There is another world.

51   I knew already that I would go to Hollins College in Virginia; our head-mistress sent all her problems there, to her alma mater. "For the English department," she told me. William Golding was then writer in residence; before him was Enid Starkie, who wrote the biography of Rimbaud. But, "To smooth off her rough edges," she had told my parents. They repeated the phrase to me, vividly.

52   I had hopes for my rough edges. I wanted to use them as a can opener, to cut myself a hole in the world's surface, and exit through it. Would I be ground, instead, to a nub? Would they send me home, an ornament to my breed, in a jewelry bag?

53   I was in no position to comment. We had visited the school; it was beautiful. It was at the foot of Virginia's Great Valley, where the Scotch-Irish had settled in the eighteenth century, following the Alleghenies south.

Discussion

- What words, lines, and techniques does Dillard use to establish her authority with the reader and connect with their study hall experiences?
- What are all the ways she develops her theme?
- What different kinds of specifics does she use? What are some of the specific details that are most effective?
- Discuss how Dillard makes this first-person piece of writing more than self-indulgent, how she establishes the universal in her private ruminations.
- Where do you see evidence of Dillard the naturalist, the close observer of the natural world, and where do you see evidence of Dillard the philosopher, the seeker of meaning in her world?

Activities

- Make a checklist of the different ways Dillard weaves her themes through the piece so that you can turn to this when doing a piece of your own writing when that would help.
- Diagram the piece to show the main theme and the variations, to reveal the way the piece is organized to produce a single master effect.
- Dillard is master of the quick scene (with the family) or the quick observation (her sister). Take a scene or person from your own life and try her technique—the quick, incisive, revealing stroke.
- Compare Dillard with another writer in the book, Baldwin perhaps, or Updike, any writer in the book, and note the ways in which the writers are similar—and different.
- Write your own study hall ruminations from your own senior year. Note how you are like and unlike Dillard in how you write. Remember there is no one way to write, only alternate ways that may be equally effective.

To Collaborate

- Draft together a news story that could be published in both black and white newspapers.
- Draft a policy statement for next year's graduation that would give guidelines for a new administrator.

———————————— ✒ ————————————

John Updike

John Updike is one the master stylists and most productive writers of our time. Year in and year out he produces novels, short stories, book reviews, critical articles, and poetry. "Creativity is merely a plus name for regular activity," Updike has said. "The ditchdigger, dentist, and artist go about their tasks in much the same way, and any activity becomes creative when the doer cares about doing it right, or better. Out of my own slim experience, I would venture the opinion that the artistic impulse is a mix, in varying proportions, of childhood habits of fantasizing brought on by not necessarily unhappy periods of solitude; a certain hard wish to perpetuate and propagate the self; a craftsmanly affection for the materials and process; a perhaps superstitious receptivity to moods of wonder; and a not-often-enough mentioned ability, within the microcosm of the art, to organize, predict, and persevere."

The following excerpt from "The Dogwood Tree" deals with some of the same experiences of childhood that other writers in this text have written about. I have included a number of such excerpts, because they demonstrate that the raw material of fine writing exists in the lives you have lived and are living, in the experiences, thoughts, feelings, facts of your own existence. We all have our own individual histories, and it should interest you to see the different ways such writers as Baraka, Baldwin, Gibson, and Updike—with others to come later in the book—see the common events and anxieties of childhood through their own eyes and how they report it with their own language.

Schools

1   The elementary school was a big brick cube set in a square of black surfacing chalked and painted with the diagrams and runes of children's games. Wire fences guarded the neighboring homes from the playground. Whoever, at soccer, kicked the ball over the fence into Snitzy's yard had to bring it back. It was very terrible to have to go into Snitzy's yard, but there was only one ball for each grade. Snitzy was a large dark old German who might give you the ball or lock you up in his garage, depending upon his mood. He did not move like other men; suddenly the air near your head condensed, and his heavy hands were on you.

2   On the way to school, walking down Lancaster Avenue, we passed Henry's, a variety store where we bought punch-out licorice belts and tablets with Edward G. Robinson and Hedy Lamarr smiling on the cover. In October, Halloween masks appeared, hung on wire clotheslines. Hanging limp, these faces of Chinamen and pirates and witches were distorted, and, thickly clustered and rustling against each other, they seemed more frightening masking empty air than they did mounted on the heads of my friends—which was frightening

enough. It is strange how fear resists the attacks of reason, how you can know with absolute certainty that it is only Mark Wenrich or Jimmy Trexler whose eyes are moving so weirdly in those almond-shaped holes, and yet still be frightened. I abhorred that effect of double eyes a mask gives; it was as bad as seeing a person's mouth move upside down.

3   I was a Crow. That is my chief memory of what went on inside the elementary school. In music class the singers were divided into three groups. Nightingales, Robins, and Crows. From year to year the names changed. Sometimes the Crows were Parrots. When visitors from the high school, or elsewhere "outside," came to hear us sing, the Crows were taken out of the room and sent upstairs to watch with the fifth grade an educational film about salmon fishing in the Columbia River. Usually there were only two of us, me and a girl from Philadelphia Avenue whose voice was in truth very husky. I never understood why I was a Crow, though it gave me a certain derisive distinction. As I heard it, I sang rather well.

4   The other Crow was the first girl I kissed. I just did it, one day, walking back from school along the gutter where the water from the ice plant ran down, because somebody dared me to. And I continued to do it every day, when we reached that spot on the pavement, until a neighbor told my mother, and she, with a solemn weight that seemed unrelated to the airy act, forbade it.

5   I walked to school mostly with girls. It happened that the mothers of Philadelphia Avenue and, a block up, of Second Street had borne female babies in 1932. These babies now teased me, the lone boy in their pack, by singing the new song, "Oh, Johnny, oh, Johnny, how you can love!" and stealing my precious rubber-lined bookbag. The queen of these girls later became the May Queen of our senior class. She had freckles and thick pigtails and green eyes and her mother made her wear high-top shoes long after the rest of us had switched to low ones. She had so much vitality that on the way back from school her nose would start bleeding for no reason. We would be walking along over the wings of the maple seeds and suddenly she would tip her head back and rest it on a wall while someone ran and soaked a handkerchief in the ice-plant water and applied it to her streaming, narrow, crimson-shining nostrils. She was a Nightingale. I loved her deeply, and ineffectually.

6   My love for that girl carries through all those elementary-school cloak-rooms; they always smelled of wet raincoats and rubbers. That tangy, thinly resonant, lonely smell: can love have a better envelope? Everything I did in grammar school was meant to catch her attention. I had a daydream wherein the stars of the music class were asked to pick partners and she, a Nightingale, picked me, a Crow. The teacher was shocked; the class buzzed. To their amazement I sang superbly; my voice, thought to be so ugly, in duet with hers was beautiful. Still singing, we led some sort of parade.

7   In the world of reality, my triumph was getting her to slap me once, in the third grade. She was always slapping boys in those years; I could not quite figure out what they did. Pull her pigtails, untie her shoes, snatch at her dress, tease

her (they called her "Pug")—this much I could see. But somehow there seemed to be under these offensive acts a current running the opposite way; for it was precisely the boys who behaved worst to her that she talked to solemnly at recess, and walked with after school, and whose names she wrote on the sides of her books. Without seeing this current, but deducing its presence, I tried to jump in; I entered a tussle she was having with a boy in homeroom before the bell. I pulled the bow at the back of her dress, and was slapped so hard that children at the other end of the hall heard the crack. I was overjoyed; the stain and pain on my face seemed a badge of initiation. But it was not. The distance between us remained as it was. I did not really want to tease her, I wanted to rescue her, and to be rescued by her. I lacked—and perhaps here the only child suffers a certain deprivation—that kink in the instincts on which childish court-ship turns. He lacks a certain easy roughness with other children.

8   All the years I was at the elementary school the high school loomed large in my mind. Its students—tall, hairy, smoke-breathing—paced the streets seemingly equal with adults. I could see part of its immensity from our rear windows. It was there that my father performed his mysteries every day, striding off from breakfast, down through the grape arbor, his coat pocket bristling with defective pens. He now and then took me over there; the incorruptible smell of varnish and red sweeping wax, the size of the desks, the height of the drink-ing fountains, the fantastic dimensions of the combination gymnasium-audito-rium made me feel that these were halls in which a race of giants had ages ago labored through lives of colossal bliss. At the end of each summer, usually on Labor Day Monday, he and I went into his classroom, Room 201, and unpacked the books and arranged the tablets and the pencils on the desks of his home-room pupils. Sharpening forty pencils was a chore, sharing it with him a solemn pleasure. To this day I look up at my father through the cedar smell of pencil shavings. To see his key open the front portals of oak, to share alone with him for an hour the pirate hoard of uncracked books and golden pencils, to switch off the lights and leave the room and walk down the darkly lustrous perspective of the forbidden. The very silence of the pavilion, after the daylong click of checkers and *pokabok* of ping-pong, was like a love-choked hush.

9   Reality seemed more intense at the playground. There was a dust, a daring. It was a children's world; nowhere else did we gather in such numbers with so few adults over us. The playground occupied a platform of earth; we were exposed, it seems now, to the sun and sky. Looking up, one might see a buzzard or witness a portent.

Three Boys

1   A, B, and C, I'll say, in case they care. A lived next door; he *loomed* next door, rather. He seemed immense—a great wallowing fatso stuffed with pos-sessions; he was the son of a full-fashioned knitter. He seemed to have a beer-belly; after several generations beer-bellies may become congenital. Also his

face had no features. It was just a blank ball on his shoulders. He used to call me "Ostrich," after Disney's Ollie Ostrich. My neck was not very long; the name seemed horribly unfair; it was its injustice that made me cry. But nothing I could say, or scream, would make him stop, and I still, now and then—in reading, say, a book review by one of the apple-cheeked savants of the quarterlies or one of the pious gremlins who manufactured puns for *Time*—get the old sensations: my ears close up, my eyes go warm, my chest feels thin as an eggshell, my voice churns silently in my stomach. From A I received my first impression of the smug, chinkless, irresistible *power* of stupidity; it is the most powerful force on earth. It says "Ostrich" often enough, and the universe crumbles.

2   A was more than a boy, he was a force-field that could manifest itself in many forms, that could take the wiry, disconsolate shape of wide-mouthed, tiny-eared boys who would now and then beat me up on the way back from school. I did not greatly mind being beaten up, though I resisted it. For one thing, it firmly involved me, at least during the beating, with the circumambient humanity that so often seemed evasive. Also, the boys who applied the beating were misfits, periodic flunkers, who wore corduroy knickers with threadbare knees and men's shirts with the top button buttoned—this last an infallible sign of deep poverty. So that I felt there was some justice, some condonable revenge, being applied with their fists to this little teacher's son. And then there was the delicious alarm of my mother and grandmother when I returned home bloody, bruised, and torn. My father took the attitude that it was making a boy of me, an attitude I dimly shared. He and I both were afraid of me becoming a sissy— he perhaps more afraid than I.

3   When I was eleven or so I met B. It was summer and I was down at the playground. He was pushing a little tank with moving rubber treads up and down the hills in the sandbox. It was a fine little toy, mottled with camouflage green; patriotic manufacturers produced throughout the war millions of such authentic miniatures which we maneuvered with authentic, if miniature, militance. Attracted by the toy, I spoke to him; though taller and a little older than I, he had my dull straight brown hair and a look of being also alone. We became fast friends. He lived just up the street—toward the poorhouse, the east part of the street, from which the little winds of tragedy blew. He had just moved from the Midwest, and his mother was a widow. Beside wage war, we did many things together. We played marbles for days at a time, until one of us had won the other's entire coffee-canful. With jigsaws we cut out of plywood animals copied from comic books. We made movies by tearing the pages from Big Little Books and coloring the drawings and pasting them in a strip, and winding them on toilet-paper spools, and making a cardboard carton a theatre. We rigged up telephones, and racing wagons, and cities of the future, using orange crates and cigar boxes and peanut-butter jars and such potent debris. We loved Smokey Stover and were always saying "Foo." We had an intense spell of Monopoly. He called me "Uppy"—the only person who ever did. I remember once, knowing he was coming down that afternoon to my house to play Monopoly, in order

to show my joy I set up the board elaborately, with the Chance and Community Chest cards fanned painstakingly, like spiral staircases. He came into the room, groaned, "Uppy, what are you doing?" and impatiently scrabbled the cards together in a sensible pile. The older we got, the more the year between us told, and the more my friendship embarrassed him. We fought. Once, to my horror, I heard myself taunting him with the fact that he had no father. The unmentionable, the unforgivable. I suppose we patched things up, children do, but the fabric had been torn. He had a long, pale, serious face, with buckteeth, and is probably an electronics engineer somewhere now, doing secret government work.

4   So through B I first experienced the pattern of friendship. There are three stages. First, acquaintance: we are new to each other, make each other laugh in surprise, and demand nothing beyond politeness. The death of the one would startle the other, no more. It is a pleasant stage, a stable stage; on austere rations of exposure it can live a lifetime, and the two parties to it always feel a slight gratification upon meeting, will feel vaguely confirmed in their human state. Then comes intimacy: now we laugh before two words of the joke are out of the other's mouth, because we know what he will say. Our two beings seem marvelously joined, from our toes to our heads, along tingling points of agreement; everything we venture is right, everything we put forth lodges in a corresponding socket in the frame of the other. The death of one would grieve the other. To be together is to enjoy a mounting excitement, a constant echo and amplification. It is an ecstatic and unstable stage, bound of its own agitation to tip into the third: revulsion. One or the other makes a misjudgment; presumes; puts forth that which does not meet agreement. Sometimes there is an explosion; more often the moment is swallowed in silence, and months pass before its nature dawns. Instead of dissolving, it grows. The mind, the throat, are clogged; forgiveness, forgetfulness, that have arrived so often, fail. Now everything jars and is distasteful. The betrayal, perhaps a tiny fraction in itself, has inverted the tingling column of agreement, made all pluses minuses. Everything about the other is hateful, despicable; yet he cannot be dismissed. We have confided in him too many minutes, too many words; he has those minutes and words as hostages, and his confidences are embedded in us where they cannot be scraped away, and even rivers of time cannot erode them completely, for there are indelible stains. Now—though the friends may continue to meet, and smile, as if they had never trespassed beyond acquaintance—the death of the one would please the other.

5   An unhappy pattern to which C is an exception. He was my friend before kindergarten, he is my friend still. I go to his home now, and he and his wife serve me and my wife with alcoholic drinks and slices of excellent cheese on crisp crackers, just as twenty years ago he served me with treats from his mother's refrigerator. He was a born host, and I a born guest. Also he was intelligent. If my childhood's brain, when I look back at it, seems a primitive mammal, a lemur or shrew, his brain was an angel whose visitation was widely hailed as wonderful. When in school he stood to recite, his cool rectangular forehead

glowed. He tucked his right hand into his left armpit and with his left hand mechanically tapped a pencil against his thigh. His answers were always correct. He beat me at spelling bees and, in another sort of competition, when we both collected Big Little Books, he outbid me for my supreme find (in the attic of a third boy), the first Mickey Mouse. I can still see that book, I wanted it so badly, its paper tan with age and its drawings done in Disney's primitive style, when Mickey's black chest is naked like a child's and his eyes are two nicked oblongs. Losing it was perhaps a lucky blow; it helped wean me away from hope of ever having possessions.

6   C was fearless. He deliberately set fields on fire. He engaged in rock-throwing duels with tough boys. One afternoon he persisted in playing quoits with me although—as the hospital discovered that night—his appendix was nearly bursting. He was enterprising. He peddled magazine subscriptions door-to-door; he mowed neighbors' lawns; he struck financial bargains with his father. He collected stamps so well his collection blossomed into a stamp company that filled his room with steel cabinets and mimeograph machinery. He collected money—every time I went over to his house he would get out a little tin box and count the money in it for me: $27.50 one week, $29.95 the next, $30.90 the next—all changed into new bills nicely folded together. It was a strange ritual, whose meaning for me was: since he was doing it, I didn't have to. His money made me richer. We read Ellery Queen and played chess and invented board games and discussed infinity together. In later adolescence, he collected records. He liked the Goodman quintets but loved Fats Waller. Sitting there in that room so familiar to me, where the machinery of the Shilco Stamp Company still crowded the walls and for that matter the tin box of money might still be stashed, while my thin friend grunted softly along with that dead dark angel on "You're Not the Only Oyster in the Stew," I felt, in the best sense, patronized: the perfect guest of the perfect host. What made it perfect was that we had both spent our entire lives in Shillington.

A Writer's Notes for a Second Reading

Updike is the master of the revealing detail. This paragraph teaches me every time I read it because I watch Updike manipulating detail to recreate a world.

All the years I was at the elementary school the high school loomed large in my mind. Its students—tall, hairy, smoke-breathing—paced the streets seemingly equal with adults. I could see part of its immensity from our rear windows. It was there that my father performed his mysteries every day, striding off from breakfast, down through the grape arbor, his coat pocket bristling with defective pens. He now and then took me over there; the incorruptible smell of varnish and red sweeping wax, the size of the desks, the height of the drinking fountains, the fantastic dimensions of the combination gymnasium-auditorium made me feel that these were halls in which a race of giants had ages ago labored through lives of colossal bliss. At the end of each summer, usually on Labor Day Monday, he and I went into his classroom, Room 201, and unpacked the books and arranged the tablets and the pencils on the desks of his homeroom pupils. Sharpening forty pencils was a chore, sharing it with him a solemn pleasure. To this day I look up at my father through the cedar smell of pencil shavings. To see his key open the front portals of oak, to share along with him for an hour the pirate hoard of uncracked books and golden pencils, to switch off the lights and leave the room and walk down the darkly lustrous perspective of the forbidden. The very silence of the pavilion, after the daylong click of checkers and pokabok *of ping-pong, was like a love-choked hush.*

Go back and read this paragraph. Note how the high school "loomed large in my mind," how the students were "tall, hairy, smoke-breathing," that his father "performed his mysteries" every day, "his pocket bristling with defective pens," how he still sees his father "through the cedar smell of pencil shavings." A writer delights in this skill the way a professional baseball player admires the ease with which an all-star scoops an impossible grounder and with practiced ease flips it to second to start the double play. I could study that paragraph again and again—and I have, learning each time.

Discussion

- Compare how Dillard and Updike deal with similar content.
- Choose a paragraph from Updike and a similar paragraph from other autobiographical writers in this book and discuss how these paragraphs were made, what they intended to say, and how they said it.
- Describe Updike's voice and discuss how much his white, middle-class, Pennsylvania background influenced his voice, as the racial, economic, and regional backgrounds of other writers have influenced their voices.
- Discuss the phrase, those groups of words that are less than a sentence that rub together and give off a particularly appropriate meaning. What are some of the ways to make a phrase work, weight playing against airy, hairy bumping against smoke-breathing, bristling fighting with defective, the smell of cedar and the sight of shavings. Select phrases from other writers in the book and see how they make a few words do more than those words alone could ever do.
- Discuss how Updike connects with his readers, involving their experiences in his text.
- Discuss how the autobiographical writers, such as Updike, use point of view to control the abundance of material their memories hold about their childhood.

Activities

- List as many specifics as you can about a schoolyard, a school, a classmate, a classroom, a teacher, and then write about that subject using some of the specifics and using some of the new ones that occur to you during the writing.

- Write an account of part of your schooldays, not imitating Updike or the other writers in the book, but being stimulated by their vision.
- Rearrange the phrases in an Updike paragraph—or a paragraph from another author—to see if you can carve a poem out of the prose.
- Make an outline of one of Updike's paragraphs to see how it is constructed. That could be very helpful, but don't think that that's the way he wrote it. The process of writing is much less rigid and more exciting than that. "Writing and rewriting are a constant search for what one is saying," Updike has said. At another time he said, "I don't make an outline or anything. I figure that I can hold the events in my head and then hope that things will happen which will surprise me, that the characters will take on life and talk." So go ahead and outline to see what he has constructed. That will teach you something about how effective writing works. Your own writing, however, will teach you how it is made.
- If you find outlining one of Updike's paragraphs helpful, try the same thing on paragraphs of other writers in the book that you have liked.
- Rewrite a paragraph of Updike as it might have been written by Baraka, McMillan, Baldwin, Gibson, or Dillard. And then be Updike and rewrite one of their paragraphs.

To Collaborate

- Each member of the team should brainstorm a list of revealing details they remember from school, then combine the best into the creation of an imaginary school that will make each reader see a real one when reading it.
- Work together to write guidelines for corporate writers, using a paragraph from Updike to show them how to use revealing details in such documents as annual reports and business letters.

E. B. White

E. B. White was once chosen as the writer most likely to survive from our century. No one should take bets on that, but the fact remains that E. B. White has influenced the way we use language. All nonfiction writers in our time have been students of his, whether they know it or not. His style, his tone, his ability to speak of heavy matters with a light touch has taught us all.

After he became a well-known writer he published *The Elements of Style,* a book that repeated the edicts of his writing teacher, William Strunk, Jr. For years I had a paragraph from Strunk, by way of White, over my desk.

Vigorous writing is concise. A sentence should contain no unnecessary words, a paragraph no unnecessary sentences, for the same reason that a drawing should have no unnecessary lines and a machine no unnecessary parts. This requires not that the writer make all his sentences short, or that he avoid all detail and treat his subjects only in outline, but that every word tell.

There is a whole semester of a writing course in that one paragraph.

In his own additions to that book White expanded from rules to philosophy. He wrote, "Style takes its final shape more from attitudes of mind than from principles of composition, for as an elderly practitioner once remarked, 'Writing is an act of faith, not a trick of grammar.' This moral observation would have no place in a rule book were it not that style *is* the writer, and therefore what a man is, rather than what he knows, will at last determine his style."

Once More to the Lake

1   One summer, along about 1904, my father rented a camp on a lake in Maine and took us all there for the month of August. We all got ringworm from some kittens and had to rub Pond's Extract on our arms and legs night and morning, and my father rolled over in a canoe with all his clothes on; but outside of that the vacation was a success and from then on none of us ever thought there was any place in the world like that lake in Maine. We returned summer after summer—always on August 1st for one month. I have since become a salt-water man, but sometimes in summer there are days when the restlessness of the tides and the fearful cold of the sea water and the incessant wind which blows across the afternoon and into the evening make me wish for the placidity of a lake in the woods. A few weeks ago this feeling got so strong I bought myself a couple of bass hooks and a spinner and returned to the lake where we used to go, for a week's fishing and to revisit old haunts.

2   I took along my son, who had never had any fresh water up his nose and who had seen lily pads only from train windows. On the journey over to the lake I began to wonder what it would be like. I wondered how time would have marred this unique, this holy spot—the coves and streams, the hills that the sun set behind, the camps and the paths behind the camps. I was sure that the tarred road would have found it out and I wondered in what other ways it would be desolated. It is strange how much you can remember about places like that once you allow your mind to return into the grooves which lead back. You remember one thing, and that suddenly reminds you of another thing. I guess I remembered clearest of all the early mornings, when the lake was cool and motionless, remembered how the bedroom smelled of the lumber it was made

of and of the wet woods whose scent entered through the screen. The partitions in the camp were thin and did not extend clear to the top of the rooms, and as I was always the first up I would dress softly so as not to wake the others, and sneak out into the sweet outdoors and start out in the canoe, keeping close along the shore in the long shadows of the pines. I remembered being very careful never to rub my paddle against the gunwale for fear of disturbing the stillness of the cathedral.

3   The lake had never been what you would call a wild lake. There were cottages sprinkled around the shores, and it was in farming country although the shores of the lake were quite heavily wooded. Some of the cottages were owned by nearby farmers, and you would live at the shore and eat your meals at the farmhouse. That's what our family did. But although it wasn't wild, it was a fairly large and undisturbed lake and there were places in it which, to a child at least, seemed infinitely remote and primeval.

4   I was right about the tar: it led to within half a mile of the shore. But when I got back there, with my boy, and we settled into a camp near a farmhouse and into the kind of summertime I had known, I could tell that it was going to be pretty much the same as it had been before—I knew it, lying in bed the first morning, smelling the bedroom, and hearing the boy sneak quietly out and go off along the shore in a boat. I began to sustain the illusion that he was I, and therefore, by simple transposition, that I was my father. This sensation persisted, kept cropping up all the time we were there. It was not an entirely new feeling, but in this setting it grew much stronger. I seemed to be living a dual existence. I would be in the middle of some simple act, I would be picking up a bait box or laying down a table fork, or I would be saying something, and suddenly it would be not I but my father who was saying the words or making the gesture. It gave me a creepy sensation.

5   We went fishing the first morning. I felt the same damp moss covering the worms in the bait can, and saw the dragonfly alight on the tip of my rod as it hovered a few inches from the surface of the water. It was the arrival of this fly that convinced me beyond any doubt that everything was as it always had been, that the years were a mirage and there had been no years. The small waves were the same, chucking the rowboat under the chin as we fished at anchor, and the boat was the same boat, the same color green and the ribs broken in the same places, and under the floor-boards the same fresh-water leavings and debris—the dead helgramite, the wisps of moss, the rusty discarded fish-hook, the dried blood from yesterday's catch. We stare silently at the tips of our rods, at the dragon flies that came and went. I lowered the tip of mine into the water, tentatively, pensively dislodging the fly, which darted two feet away, poised, darted two feet back, and came to rest again a little farther up the rod. There had been no years between the ducking of this dragonfly and the other one— the one that was part of memory. I looked at the boy, who was silently watching his fly, and it was my hands that held his rod, my eyes watching. I felt dizzy and didn't know which rod I was at the end of.

6   We caught two bass, hauling them in briskly as though they were mackerel, pulling them over the side of the boat in a businesslike manner without any landing net, and stunning them with a blow on the back of the head. When we got back for a swim before lunch, the lake was exactly where we had left it, the same number of inches from the dock, and there was only the merest suggestion of a breeze. This seemed an utterly enchanted sea, this lake you could leave to its own devices for a few hours and come back to, and find that it had not stirred, this constant and trustworthy body of water. In the shallows, the dark, watersoaked sticks and twigs, smooth and old, were undulating in clusters on the bottom against the clean ribbed sand, and the track of the mussel was plain. A school of minnows swam by, each minnow with its small individual shadow, doubling the attendance, so clear and sharp in the sunlight. Some of the other campers were in swimming, along the shore, one of them with a cake of soap, and the water felt thin and clear and unsubstantial. Over the years there had been this person with the cake of soap, this cultist, and here he was. There had been no years.

7   Up to the farmhouse to dinner through the teeming, dusty field, the road under our sneakers was only a two-track road. The middle track was missing, the one with the marks of the hooves and the splotches of dried, flaky manure. There had always been three tracks to choose from in choosing which track to walk in; now the choice was narrowed down to two. For a moment I missed terribly the middle alternative. But the way led past the tennis court, and something about the way it lay there in the sun reassured me; the tape had loosened along the backline, the alleys were green with plantains and other weeds, and the net (installed in June and removed in September) sagged in the dry noon, and the whole place steamed with midday heat and hunger and emptiness. There was a choice of pie for dessert, and one was blueberry and one was apple, and the waitresses were the same country girls, there having been no passage of time, only the illusion of it as in a dropped curtain—the waitresses were still fifteen; their hair had been washed, that was the only difference—they had been to the movies and seen the pretty girls with the clean hair.

8   Summertime, oh summertime, pattern of life indelible, the fade-proof lake, the woods unshatterable, the pasture with the sweetfern and the juniper forever and ever, summer without end; this was the background, and the life along the shore was the design, the cottagers with their innocent and tranquil design, their tiny docks with the flagpole and the American flag floating against the white clouds in the blue sky, the little paths over the roots of the trees leading from camp to camp and the paths leading back to the outhouses and the can of lime for sprinkling, and at the souvenir counters at the store the miniature birch-bark canoes and the postcards that showed things looking a little better than they looked. This was the American family at play, escaping the city heat, wondering whether the newcomers in the camp at the head of the cove were "common" or "nice," wondering whether it was true that the people who drove up for Sunday dinner at the farmhouse were turned away because there wasn't enough chicken.

9   It seemed to me, as I kept remembering all this, that those times and those summers had been infinitely precious and worth saving. There had been jollity and peace and goodness. The arriving (at the beginning of August) had been so big a business in itself, at the railway station the farm wagon drawn up, the first smell of the pine-laden air, the first glimpse of the smiling farmer, and the great importance of the trunks and your father's enormous authority in such matters, and the feel of the wagon under you for the long ten-mile haul, and at the top of the last long hill catching the first view of the lake after eleven months of not seeing this cherished body of water. The shouts and cries of the other campers when they saw you, and the trunks to be unpacked, to give up their rich burden. (Arriving was less exciting nowadays, when you sneaked up in your car and parked it under a tree near the camp and took out the bags and in five minutes it was all over, no fuss, no loud wonderful fuss about trunks.)

10   Peace and goodness and jollity. The only thing that was wrong now, really, was the sound of the place, an unfamiliar nervous sound of the outboard motors. This was the note that jarred, the one thing that would sometimes break the illusion and set the years moving. In those other summertimes all motors were inboard; and when they were at a little distance, the noise they made was a sedative, an ingredient of summer sleep. They were one-cylinder and two-cylinder engines, and some were make-and-break and some were jump-spark, but they all made a sleepy sound across the lake. The one-lungers throbbed and fluttered, and the twin-cylinder ones purred and purred, and that was a quiet sound too. But now the campers all had outboards. In the daytime, in the hot mornings, these motors made a petulant, irritable sound; at night, in the still evening when the afterglow lit the water, they whined about one's ears like mosquitoes. My boy loved our rented outboard, and his great desire was to achieve singlehanded mastery over it, and authority, and he soon learned the trick of choking it a little (but not too much), and the adjustment of the needle valve. Watching him I would remember the things you could do with the old one-cylinder engine with the heavy flywheel, how you could have it eating out of your hand if you got really close to it spiritually. Motor boats in those days didn't have clutches, and you would make a landing by shutting off the motor at the proper time and coasting in with a dead rudder. But there was a way of reversing them, if you learned the trick, by cutting the switch and putting it on again exactly on the final dying revolution of the flywheel, so that it would kick back against compression and begin reversing. Approaching a dock in a strong following breeze, it was difficult to slow up sufficiently by the ordinary coasting method, and if a boy felt he had complete mastery over his motor, he was tempted to keep it running beyond its time and then reverse it a few feet from the dock. It took a cool nerve, because if you threw the switch a twentieth of a second too soon you would catch the flywheel when it still had speed enough to go up past center, and the boat would leap ahead, charging bull-fashion at the dock.

11   We had a good week at the camp. The bass were biting well and the sun shone endlessly, day after day. We would be tired at night and lie down in the

accumulated heat of the little bedrooms after the long hot day and the breeze would stir almost imperceptibly outside and the smell of the swamp drift in through the rusty screens. Sleep would come easily and in the morning the red squirrel would be on the roof, tapping out his gay routine. I kept remembering everything, lying in bed in the mornings—the small steamboat that had a long rounded stern like the lip of a Ubangi, and how quietly she ran on the moonlight sails, when the older boys played their mandolins and the girls sang and we ate doughnuts dipped in sugar, and how sweet the music was on the water in the shining night, and what it had felt like to think about girls then. After breakfast we would go up to the store and the things were in the same place—the minnows in a bottle, the plugs and spinners disarranged and pawed over by the youngsters from the boys' camp, the fig newtons and the Beeman's gum. Outside, the road was tarred and cars stood in front of the store. Inside, all was just as it had always been, except there was more Coca Cola and not so much Moxie and root beer and birch beer and sarsaparilla. We would walk out with a bottle of pop apiece and sometimes the pop would backfire up our noses and hurt. We explored the streams, quietly, where the turtles slid off the sunny logs and dug their way into the soft bottom; and we lay on the town wharf and fed worms to the tame bass. Everywhere we went I had trouble making out which was I, the one walking at my side, the one walking in my pants.

12   One afternoon while we were there at that lake a thunderstorm came up. It was like the revival of an old melodrama that I had seen long ago with childish awe. The second-act climax of the drama of the electrical disturbance over a lake in America had not changed in any important respect. This was the big scene, still the big scene. The whole thing was so familiar, the first feeling of oppression and heat and a general air around camp of not wanting to go very far away. In midafternoon (it was all the same) a curious darkening of the sky, and a lull in everything that had made life tick; and then the way the boats suddenly swung the other way at their moorings with the coming of a breeze out of the new quarter, and the premonitory rumble. Then the kettle drum, then the snare, then the bass drum and cymbals, then crackling light against the dark, and the gods grinning and licking their chops in the hills. Afterward the calm, the rain steadily rustling in the calm lake, the return of light and hope and spirits, and the campers running out in joy and relief to go swimming in the rain, their bright cries perpetuating the deathless joke about how they were getting simply drenched, and the children screaming with delight at the new sensation of bathing in the rain, and the joke about getting drenched linking the generations in a strong indestructible chain. And the comedian who waded in carrying an umbrella.

13   When the others went swimming my son said he was going in too. He pulled his dripping trunks from the line where they had hung all through the shower, and wrung them out. Languidly, and with no thought of going in, I watched him, his hard little body, skinny and bare, saw him wince slightly as

he pulled up around his vitals the small, soggy, icy garment. As he buckled the swollen belt suddenly my groin felt the chill of death.

A Writer's Notes for a Second Reading

I am struck, on rereading E. B. White, by the quietness of his tone. There is humor—notice the third, fourth, and fifth lines of the piece—but it is quiet humor. He is reflective, nostalgic, sad in a quiet way. The text is subdued.

When I first taught E. B. White one student violently complained. He was too New Yorkish, too WASPish, too Eastern. I was defensive then and didn't understand what my student was trying to teach me. I do now.

Perhaps we should read White as an ethnic writer and appreciate the qualities of his upper-middle-class, suburban-New York, East-Coast, white, Protestant background. They should not be seen, as they were for too long, as the model for us all, but as an interesting—and often imprisoning—way of life.

White has style (I think I would always have been a bit uncomfortable in his presence, not knowing quite where to put my hands) and he is restrained, but his essay delights me for its celebration of a crucial moment in the life of a young person.

Discussion

- Discuss the idea that style is the person. Consider what White is and who others in this book are.
- Discuss how Strunk's edict for vigorous writing can be true of writers who communicate with a rich abundance of language. Do they make every word tell?
- Discuss how White's counsel about writing relates to Didion's and Orwell's.
- Consider whether White followed Strunk's advice.
- White has said, "When a mosquito bites me—I scratch. When I write something, I guess I'm trying to get rid of the itchiness inside me." What was itching White? How would writing stop the itching?
- Compare White's autobiographical piece about childhood to some of the other autobiographical pieces in the book.
- Consider White's point of view. What are its advantages and disadvantages?

Activities

- Rewrite a page of White from the son's point of view.
- Write a piece about an event that marked your moving into adulthood.
- Go through a paragraph of White and decide what every word tells. Do the same thing to a paragraph by another writer and to a paragraph of your own.

- Go through the White essay and make a note in the margin by every paragraph, telling how each paragraph prepares the reader for the last sentence of the essay.
- Rewrite the first paragraph using an entirely different environment, one that you know. Once more to the vacant lot, the ball field, the barroom, the abandoned farm, the amusement park, the alley.

To Collaborate

- Work as a team to write an anthropological report on what White's essay reveals of the way the boy is being brought up.
- Discuss the elements that would have to be changed to develop the essay into a short story or television play. Make plans to do so.

Jean Shepherd

Jean Shepherd is a member of the second oldest profession: storyteller. We depended on storytellers before we knew that a cave was a good place to stay out of the rain. They explained what we had done and what it meant. They chronicled our adventures, and each had an individual way of seeing the world. Shepherd sees the world with humor. He is a talker who is always creating and recreating the myths of his life, and therefore showing us the humor and the meaning in our own lives. Years ago he was on radio station WOR in New York, and I used to go to sleep listening to him talk, talk, talk, telling the same stories over and over again. I would go to sleep smiling. I remember first hearing the story that I later read and that is reprinted below. It has, in print, the same wonderful flavor of speech, of a story being told to a bunch of guys hanging out at the gas station. Shepherd has told his stories live to audiences, large and small. He has told them on radio and television, on tape and on record, and he has told them in print. Listen as he tells the story to you.

Hairy Gertz and the Forty-Seven Crappies

1   Life, when you're a Male kid, is what the Grownups are doing. The Adult world seems to be some kind of secret society that has its own passwords, handclasps, and countersigns. The thing is to get in. But there's this invisible, impenetrable wall between you and all the great, unimaginably swinging things that they seem to be involved in. Occasionally mutterings of exotic secrets and incredible pleasures filter through. And so you bang against it, throw rocks at it, try to climb over it, burrow under it; but there it is. Impenetrable. Enigmatic.

2   Girls somehow seem to be already involved, as though from birth they've got the Word. Lolita has no Male counterpart. It does no good to protest and pretend otherwise. The fact is inescapable. A male kid is really a *kid*. A female kid is a *girl*. Some guys give up early in life, surrender completely before the impassable transparent wall, and remain little kids forever. They are called "Fags," or "Homosexuals," if you are in polite society.

3   The rest of us have to claw our way into Life as best we can, never knowing when we'll be Admitted. It happens to each of us in different ways—and once it does, there's no turning back.

4   It happened to me at the age of twelve in Northern Indiana—a remarkably barren terrain resembling in some ways the surface of the moon, encrusted with steel mills, oil refineries, and honky-tonk bars. There was plenty of natural motivation for Total Escape. Some kids got hung up on kite flying, others on pool playing. *I* became the greatest vicarious angler in the history of the Western world.

5   I say vicarious because there just wasn't any actual fishing to be done around where I lived. So I would stand for hours in front of the goldfish tank at Woolworth's, landing fantails in my mind, after incredible struggles. I read *Field & Stream, Outdoor Life,* and *Sports Afield* the way other kids read *G-8 And His Battle Aces*. I would break out in a cold sweat reading about these guys portaging to Alaska and landing rare salmon; and about guys climbing the High Sierras to do battle with the wily golden trout; and mortal combat with the steelheads. I'd read about craggy, sinewy sportsmen who discover untouched bass lakes where they have to beat off the pickerel with an oar, and the saber-toothed, raging smallmouths chase them ashore and right up into the woods.

6   After reading one of these fantasies I would walk around in a daze for hours, feeling the cork pistol grip of my imaginary trusty six-foot, split-bamboo bait-casting rod in my right hand and hearing the high-pitched scream of my Pflueger Supreme reel straining to hold a seventeen-pound Great Northern in check.

7   I became known around town as "the-kid-who-is-the-nut-on-fishing," even went to the extent of learning how to tie flies, although I'd never been fly casting in my life. I read books on the subject. And in my bedroom while the other kids are making balsa models of Curtiss Robins, I am busy tying Silver Doctors, Royal Coachmen, and Black Gnats. They were terrible. I would try out one in the bathtub to see whether it made a ripple that might frighten off the wily rainbow.

8   "Glonk!"

9   Down to the bottom like a rock, my floating dry fly would go. Fishing was part of the mysterious and unattainable Adult world. I wanted In.

10   My Old Man was In, though he was what you might call a once-in-a-while-fisherman-and-beer-party-goer; they are the same thing in the shadow of the blast furnaces. (I knew even then that there are people who Fish and there are people who Go Fishing; they're two entirely different creatures.) My Old Man

did not drive 1500 miles to the Atlantic shore with 3000 pounds of Abercrombie & Fitch fishing tackle to angle for stripers. He was the kind who would Go Fishing maybe once a month during the summer when it was too hot to Go Bowling and all of the guys down at the office would get The Itch. To them, fishing was a way of drinking a lot of beer and yelling. And getting away from the women. To me, it was a sacred thing. To *fish*.

11   He and these guys from the office would get together and go down to one of the lakes a few miles from where we lived—but never to Lake Michigan, which wasn't far away. I don't know why; I guess it was too big and awesome. In any case, nobody ever really thought of fishing in it. At least nobody in my father's mob. They went mostly to a mudhole known as Cedar Lake.

12   I will have to describe to you what a lake in the summer in Northern Indiana is like. To begin with, heat, in Indiana, is something else again. It descends like a 300-pound fat lady onto a picnic bench in the middle of July. It can literally be sliced into chunks and stored away in the basement to use in winter; on cold days you just bring it out and turn it on. Indiana heat is not a meteorological phenomenon—it is a solid element, something you can grab by the handles. Almost every day in the summer the whole town is just shimmering in front of you. You'd look across the street and skinny people would be all fat and wiggly like in the fun-house mirrors at Coney Island. The asphalt in the streets would bubble and hiss like a pot of steaming Ralston.

13   That kind of heat and sun produces mirages. All it takes is good flat country, a nutty sun, and insane heat and, by George, you're looking at Cleveland 200 miles away. I remember many times standing out in center field on an incinerating day in mid-August, the prairie stretching out endlessly in all directions, and way out past the swamp would be this kind of tenuous, shadowy, cloud-like thing shimmering just above the horizon. It would be the Chicago skyline, upside down, just hanging there in the sky. And after a while it would gradually disappear.

14   So, naturally, fishing is different in Indiana. The muddy lakes, about May, when the sun starts beating down on them, would begin to simmer and bubble quietly around the edges. These lakes are not fed by springs or streams. I don't know what feeds them. Maybe seepage. Nothing but weeds and truck axles on the bottom; flat, low, muddy banks, surrounded by cottonwood trees, cattails, smelly marshes, and old dumps. Archetypal dumps. Dumps gravitate to Indiana lakes like flies to a hog killing. Way down at the end where the water is shallow and soupy are the old cars and the ashes, busted refrigerators, oil drums, old corsets, and God knows what else.

15   At the other end of the lake is the Roller Rink. There's *always* a Roller Rink. You can hear that old electric organ going, playing "Heartaches," and you can hear the sound of the roller skates.

16   "Shhhhhh . . . sssshhhhhhhh . . . sssssshhhhhhhhhhhhhhhh . . ."

17   And the fistfights breaking out. The Roller Rink Nut in heat. The Roller Rink Nut was an earlier incarnation of the Drive-In Movie Nut. He was the kind who was very big with stainless steel diners, motels, horror movies, and frozen

egg rolls. A close cousin to the Motorcycle Clod, he went ape for chicks with purple eyelids. You know the crowd. Crewcuts, low foreheads, rumbles, hollering, belching, drinking beer, roller skating on one foot, wearing black satin jackets with SOUTH SIDE A. C. lettered in white on the back around a white-winged roller-skated foot. The kind that hangs the stuff in the back windows of their '53 Mercuries; a huge pair of foam-rubber dice, a skull and crossbones, hula-hula dolls, and football players—Pro, of course, with heads that bob up and down. The guys with ball fringe around the windows of their cars, with phony Venetian blinds in the back, and big white rubber mudguards hanging down, with red reflectors. Or they'll take some old heap and line it with plastic imitation mink fur, pad the steering wheel with leopard skin and ostrich feathers until it weighs seventeen pounds and is as fat as a salami. A TV set, a bar, and a folding Castro bed are in the trunk, automatically operated and all lined with tasteful Sears Roebuck ermine. You know the crew—a true American product. We turn them out like Campbell's Pork & Beans.

18   This is the system of aesthetics that brought the Roller Rink to Cedar Lake, Indiana, when I was a kid.

19   About 150 yards from the Roller Rink was the Cedar Lake Evening In Paris Dance Hall. Festering and steamy and thronged with yeasty refugees from the Roller Rink. These are the guys who can't skate. But they can do other things. They're down there jostling back and forth in 400-per-cent humidity to the incomparable sounds of an Indiana dancehall band. Twelve non-Union cretinous musicians—Mickey Iseley's Montgomery Ward altos. The lighting is a tasteful combination of naked light bulbs, red and blue crepe paper, and orange cellophane gels.

20   In between the Roller Rink and the Dance Hall are seventeen small shacks known as Beer Halls. And surrounding this tiny oasis of civilization, this bastion of bonhomie, is a gigantic sea of total darkness, absolute pitch-black Stygian darkness, around this tiny island of totally decadent, bucolic American merriment. The roller skates are hissing, the beer bottles are crashing, the chicks are squealing, Mickey's reed men are quavering, and Life is full.

21   And in the middle of the lake, several yards away, are over 17,000 fisherman, in wooden rowboats rented at a buck and a half an hour. It is 2 A.M. The temperature is 175, with humidity to match. And the smell of decayed toads, the dumps at the far end of the lake, and an occasional *soupçon* of Standard Oil, whose refinery is a couple of miles away, is enough to put hair on the back of a mud turtle. Seventeen thousand guys clumped together in the middle fishing for the known sixty-four crappies in that lake.

22   Crappies are a special breed of Midwestern fish, created by God for the express purpose of surviving in waters that would kill a bubonic-plague bacillus. They have never been known to fight, or even faintly struggle. I guess when you're a crappie, you figure it's no use anyway. One thing is as bad as another. They're just down there in the soup. No one quite knows what they eat, if anything, but everybody's fishing for them. At two o'clock in the morning.

23   Each boat contains a minimum of nine guys and fourteen cases of beer. And once in a while, in the darkness, is heard the sound of a guy falling over backward into the slime:

24   SSSSGLUNK!

25   "Oh! Ah! Help, help!" A piteous cry in the darkness. Another voice:

26   "Hey, for God's sake, Charlie's fallen in again! Grab the oar!"

27   And then it slowly dies down. Charlie is hauled out of the goo and is lying on the bottom of the boat, urping up dead lizards and Atlas Prager. Peace reigns again.

28   The water in these lakes is not the water you know about. It is composed of roughly ten per cent waste glop spewed out by Shell, Sinclair, Phillips, and the Grasselli Chemical Corporation; twelve per cent used detergent; thirty-five per cent thick gruel composed of decayed garter snakes, deceased toads, fermenting crappies, and a strange, unidentifiable liquid that holds it all together. No one is quite sure *what* that is, because everybody is afraid to admit what it really is. They don't want to look at it too closely.

29   So this melange lays there under the sun, and about August it is slowly simmering like a rich mulligatawny stew. At two in the morning you can hear the water next to the boat in the darkness:

30   "Gluuummp . . . Bluuuummmp."

31   Big bubbles of some unclassified gas come up from the bottom and burst. The natives, in their superstitious way, believe that it is highly inflammable. They take no chances.

32   The saddest thing of all is that on these lakes there are usually about nineteen summer cottages to the square foot, each equipped with a large motorboat. The sound of a 40-horsepower Chris-Craft going through a sea of number-ten oil has to be heard to be believed.

33   RRRRRRRAAAAAAAAHHHHHHHHHWWWWWWWWWWRRRRRRRRR!

34   The prow is sort of parting the stuff, slowly stirring it into a sluggish, viscous wake.

35   Natives actually *swim* in this water. Of course, it is impossible to swim near the shore, because the shore is one great big sea of mud that goes all the way down to the core of the earth. There are stories of whole towns being swallowed up and stored in the middle of the earth. So the native rows out to the middle of the lake and hurls himself off the back seat of his rowboat.

36   "GLURP!"

37   It is impossible to sink in this water. The specific gravity and surface tension make the Great Salt Lake seem dangerous for swimming. You don't sink. You just bounce a little and float there. You literally have to hit your head on the surface of these lakes to get under a few inches. Once you do, you come up streaming mosquito eggs and dead toads—an Indiana specialty—and all sorts of fantastic things which are the offshoot of various exotic merriments which occur outside the Roller Rink.

38   The bottom of the lake is composed of a thick incrustation of old beer cans. The beer cans are at least a thousand feet thick in certain places.

39   And so 17,000 fishermen gather in one knot, because it is rumored that here is where The Deep Hole is. All Indiana lakes have a Deep Hole, into which, as the myth goes, the fish retire to sulk in the hot weather. Which is always.

40   Every month or so an announcement would be made by my Old Man, usually on a Friday night, after work.

41   "I'm getting up early tomorrow morning. I'm going fishing."

42   Getting up early and going fishing with Hairy Gertz and the crowd meant getting out of the house about three o'clock in the afternoon, roughly. Gertz was a key member of the party. He owned the Coleman lamp. It was part of the folklore that if you had a bright lantern in your boat the fish could not resist it. The idea was to hold the lantern out over the water and the fish would have to come over to see what was going on. Of course, when the fish arrived, there would be your irresistible worm, and that would be it.

43   Well, these Coleman lamps may not have drawn fish, but they worked great on mosquitoes. One of the more yeasty experiences in Life is to occupy a tiny rented rowboat with eight other guys, knee-deep in beer cans, with a blinding Coleman lamp hanging out of the boat, at 2 A.M., with the lamp hissing like Fu Manchu about to strike and every mosquito in the Western Hemisphere descending on you in the middle of Cedar Lake.

44   ZZZZZZZZZZZZZZZZZZZZZTTTTTTTTTTT

45   They *love* Coleman lamps. In the light they shed the mosquitoes swarm like rain. And in the darkness all around there'd be other lights in other boats, and once in a while a face would float above one. Everyone is coated with an inch and a half of something called citronella, reputedly a mosquito repellent but actually a sort of mosquito salad dressing.

46   The water is absolutely flat. There has not been a breath of air since April. It is now August. The surface is one flat sheet of old used oil laying in the darkness, with the sounds of the Roller Rink floating out over it, mingling with the angry drone of the mosquitoes and muffled swearing from the other boats. A fistfight breaks out at the Evening In Paris. The sound of sirens can be heard faintly in the Indiana blackness. It gets louder and then fades away. Tiny orange lights bob over the dance floor.

47   "Raaahhhhhd sails in the sawwwwnnnnsehhhht . . ."

48   It's the drummer who sings. He figures some day Ted Weems will be driving by, and hear him, and. . . .

49   ". . . haaaahhhhwwww brightlyyyy they shinneee . . ."

50   There is nothing like a band vocalist in a rotten, struggling Mickey band. When you've heard him over 2000 yards of soupy, oily water, filtered through fourteen billion feeding mosquitoes in the August heat, he is particularly juicy and ripe. He is overloading the ten-watt Allied Radio Knight amplifier by at least 400 per cent, the gain turned all the way up, his chrome-plated bullet-shaped crystal mike on the edge of feedback.

51   "Raaahhhhhd sails in the sawwwwnnnnsehhht . . ."

52   It is the sound of the American night. And to a twelve-year-old kid it is exciting beyond belief.

53   Then my Old Man, out of the blue, says to me:

54   "You know, if you're gonna come along, you got to clean the fish."

55   Gonna come along! My God! I wanted to go fishing more than anything else in the world, and my Old Man wanted to drink beer more than anything else in the world, and do did Gertz and the gang, and more than even *that,* they wanted to get away from all the women. They wanted to get out on the lake and tell dirty stories and drink beer and get eaten by mosquitoes; just sit out there and sweat and be Men. They wanted to get away from work, the car payments, the lawn, the mill, and everything else.

56   And so here I am, in the dark, in a rowboat with The Men. I am half-blind with sleepiness. I am used to going to bed at nine-thirty or ten o'clock, and here it is two, three o'clock in the morning. I'm squatting in the back end of the boat, with 87,000,000 mosquitoes swarming over me, but I am *fishing!* I am out of my skull with fantastic excitement, hanging onto my pole.

57   In those days, in Indiana, they fished with gigantic cane poles. They knew not from Spinning. A cane pole is a long bamboo pole that's maybe twelve or fifteen feet in length; it weights a ton, and tied to the end of it is about thirty feet of thick green line, roughly half the weight of the average clothesline, three big lead sinkers, a couple of crappie hooks, and a bobber.

58   One of Sport's most exciting moments is when 7 Indiana fishermen in the same boat simultaneously and without consulting one another decide to pull their lines out of the water and recast. In total darkness. First the pole, rising like a huge whip:

59   "Whooooooooooooop!"

60   Then the lines, whirling overhead:

61   "Wheeeeeeeeooooooooooooo!"

62   And then:

63   "OH! FOR CHRISSAKE! WHAT THE HELL?"

64   Clunk! CLONK!

65   Sound of cane poles banging together, and lead weights landing in the boat. And such brilliant swearing as you have never heard. Yelling, hollering, with somebody always getting a hook stuck in the back of his ear. And, of course, all in complete darkness, the Coleman lamp at the other end of the rowboat barely penetrating the darkness in a circle of three or four feet.

66   "Hey, for God's sake, Gertz, will ya tell me when you're gonna pull your pole up!? Oh, Jesus Christ, look at this mess!"

67   There is nothing worse than trying to untangle seven cane poles, 200 feet of soggy green line, just as they are starting to hit in the other boats. Sound carries over water:

68   "Shhhhh! I got a bite!"

69   The fishermen with the tangled lines become frenzied. Fingernails are

torn, hooks dig deeper into thumbs, and kids huddle terrified out of range in the darkness.

70   You have been sitting for twenty hours, and nothing. A bobber just barely visible in the dark water is one of the most beautiful sights known to man. It's not doing anything, but there's always the feeling that at any instant it might. It just lays out there in the darkness. A luminous bobber, a beautiful thing, with a long, thin quill and a tiny red-and-white float, with just the suggestion of a line reaching into the black water. These are special bobbers for *very* tiny fish.

71   I have been watching my bobber so hard and so long in the darkness that I am almost hypnotized. I have not had a bite—ever—but the excitement of being there is enough for me, a kind of delirious joy that has nothing to do with sex or any of the more obvious pleasures. To this day, when I hear some guy singing in that special drummer's voice, it comes over me. It's two o'clock in the morning again. I'm a kid. I'm tired. I'm excited. I'm having the time of my life.

72   And at the other end of the lake:

73   "Raaahhhhhd sails in the sawwwwnnnnsehhht . . ."

74   The Roller Rink drones on, and the mosquitoes are humming. The Coleman lamp sputters, and we're all sitting together in our little boat.

75   Not really together, since I am a kid, and they are Men, but at least I'm there. Gertz is stewed to the ears. He is down at the other end. He has this fantastic collection of rotten stories, and early in the evening my Old Man keeps saying:

76   "There's a kid with us, you know."

77   But by two in the morning all of them have had enough so that it doesn't matter. They're telling stories, and I don't care. I'm just sitting there, clinging to my cane pole when, by God, I get a nibble!

78   I don't believe it. The bobber straightens up, jiggles, dips, and comes to rest in the gloom. I whisper:

79   "I got a bite!"

80   The storytellers look from their beer cans in the darkness.

81   "What. . . ? Hey, whazzat?"

82   "Shhhh! Be quiet!"

83   We sit in silence, everybody watching his bobber through the haze of insects. The drummer is singing in the distance. We hang suspended for long minutes. Then suddenly all the bobbers dipped and went under. The crappies are biting!

84   You never saw anything like it! We are pulling up fish as fast as we can get them off the hooks. Crappies are flying into the boat, one after the other, and hopping around on the bottom in the darkness, amid the empty beer cans. Within twenty minutes we have landed forty-seven fish. We are knee-deep in crappies. The jackpot!

85   Well, the Old Man just goes wild. They are all yelling and screaming and pulling the fish in—while the other boats around us are being skunked. The fish

have come out of their hole or whatever it is that they are in at the bottom of the lake, the beer cans and the old tires, and have decided to eat.

86   You can hear the rest of the boats pulling up anchors and rowing over, frantically. They are thumping against us. There's a big, solid phalanx of wooden boats around us. You could walk from one boat to the other for miles around. And still they are skunked. *We* are catching the fish!

87   By 3 A.M. they've finally stopped biting, and an hour later we are back on land. I'm falling asleep in the rear seat between Gertz and Zudock. We're driving home in the dawn, and the men are hollering, drinking, throwing beer cans out on the road, and having a great time.

88   We are back at the house, and my father says to me as we are coming out of the garage with Gertz and the rest of them.

89   "And now Ralph's gonna clean the fish. Let's go in the house and have something to eat. Clean 'em on the back porch, will ya, kid?"

90   In the house they go. The lights go on in the kitchen; they sit down and start eating sandwiches and making coffee. And I am out on the back porch with forty-seven live-flopping crappies.

91   They are well named. Fish that are taken out of muddy, rotten, lousy, stinking lakes are muddy, rotten, lousy, stinking fish. It is as simple as that. And they are made out of some kind of hard rubber.

92   I get my Scout knife and go to work. Fifteen minutes and twenty-one crappies later I am sick over the side of the porch. But I do not stop. It is part of Fishing.

93   By now, nine neighborhood cats and a raccoon have joined me on the porch, and we are all working together. The August heat, now that we are away from the lake, is even hotter. The uproar in the kitchen is getting louder and louder. There is nothing like a motley collection of Indiana office workers who have just successfully defeated Nature and have brought home the kill. Like cave men of old, they celebrate around the campfire with song and drink. And belching.

94   I have now finished the last crappie and am wrapping the clean fish in the editorial page of the *Chicago Tribune*. It has a very tough paper that doesn't leak. Especially the editorial page.

95   The Old Man hollers out:

96   "How you doing? Come in and have a Nehi."

97   I enter the kitchen, blinded by that big yellow light bulb, weighted down with a load of five-and-a-half-inch crappies, covered with fish scales and blood, and smelling like the far end of Cedar Lake. There are worms under my fingernails from baiting hooks all night, and I am feeling at least nine feet tall. I spread the fish out on the sink—and old Hairy Gertz says:

98   "My God! Look at those *speckled beauties!*" An expression he had picked up from *Outdoor Life*.

99   The Old Man hands me a two-pound liverwurst sandwich and a bottle of Nehi orange. Gertz is now rolling strongly, as are the other eight file clerks, all

smelly, and mosquito-bitten, eyes red-rimmed from the Coleman lamp, covered with worms and with the drippings of at least fifteen beers apiece. Gertz hollers:

100 "Ya know, lookin' at them fish reminds me of a story." He is about to uncork his cruddiest joke of the night. They all lean forward over the white enamel kitchen table with the chipped edges, over the salami and the beer bottles, the rye bread and the mustard. Gertz digs deep into his vast file of obscenity.

101 "One time there was this Hungarian bartender, and ya know he had a cross-eyed daughter and a bowlegged dachshund. And this . . ."

102 At first I am holding back, since I am a kid. The Old Man says:

103 "Hold it down, Gertz. You'll wake up the wife and she'll raise hell."

104 He is referring to My Mother.

105 Gertz lowers his voice and they all scrunch their chairs forward amid a great cloud of cigar smoke. There is only one thing to do. I scrunch forward, too, and stick my head into the huddle, right next to the Old Man, into the circle of leering, snickering, fish-smelling faces. Of course, I do not even remotely comprehend the gist of the story. But I know that it is rotten to the core.

106 Gertz belts out the punch line; the crowd bellows and beats on the table. They begin uncapping more Blatz.

107 Secretly, suddenly, and for the first time, I realize that I am In. The Eskimo pies and Nehi oranges are all behind me, and a whole new world is stretching out endlessly and wildly in all directions before me. I have gotten The Signal!

108 Suddenly my mother is in the doorway in her Chinese-red chenille bathrobe. Ten minutes later I am in the sack, and out in the kitchen Gertz is telling another one. The bottles are rattling, and the file clerks are hunched around the fire celebrating their primal victory over The Elements.

109 Somewhere off in the dark the Monon Louisville Limited wails as it snakes through the Gibson Hump on its way to the outside world. The giant Indiana moths, at least five pounds apiece, are banging against the window screens next to my bed. The cats are fighting in the backyard over crappie heads, and fish scales are itching in my hair as I joyfully, ecstatically slide off into the great world beyond.

A Writer's Notes for a Second Reading

I revel in this piece and its difference from White's essay. There is nothing quiet about Shepherd's humor or style. This piece is Midwestern, middle-class [heading toward lower-], loud, boisterous, exaggerated. It is not better or worse than White, but different. And, as a writer, I delight in the difference.

It would be hilarious to sit on a dock while White sipped a glass of white wine and Shepherd guzzled a beer and listen to the music of their conversation.

White teaches me craft, taking care, shaping, polishing, choosing the right word, turning a phrase; and Shepherd loosens me up, returns me to the world of fun, where a mistake is not a crime but something that deserves a laugh.

I need both teachers in my workroom.

Discussion

- Discuss how Jean Shepherd fulfills Strunk's injunction.
- What are some of the distinctive elements of storytelling as demonstrated by Jean Shepherd? How is his work marked by the fact that he has spoken his stories so many times before writing them?
- In what significant ways do White's and Shepherd's essays differ? In what ways are they similar?
- How does Shepherd's essay compare to other autobiographical essays in the book?
- How is the Shepherd piece paced and organized?
- Is the importance of the last pages foreshadowed early in the piece? Where and how?
- What does voice do for Shepherd, White, and others in the book?

Activities

- Tape-record the best storyteller you know and study the tape to see what it may teach you about writing.
- Tape-record yourself telling a story to some friends. Examine the tape to see how the telling is different from your writing.
- Take a subject you've written a draft on and without referring to the text tape-record your telling of it. Compare the tape and the text to see what you can learn from the telling to improve the written text.
- Take a draft you have written and read it into a tape recorder, adding anything that comes to mind or dropping anything out. In other words, work over the text orally to see how speaking can change and improve the text.
- Listen to someone else telling a story and write it down later to see if you can capture the story and the way it was told.
- Write an account of an event that signaled your acceptance into adulthood.

To Collaborate

- Work with a partner and turn out a page or two of White and Shepherd, only use quotes to turn the pages into a dialogue between two fishermen.
- Write a brief collaborative sociological report predicting what the boys in the two essays learned from their trips to the lake and how it will influence their lives as adults.

Traci Tucker
STUDENT ESSAY

Someone Stop the Flow

1   Robert Anastas is the founder of Students Against Driving Drunk. He once said (this is directed towards parents), "believe in them as they believe in you." Most children do have a great belief in their parents. They do need to believe in their children just as their children believe in them.

2   The family is the basic unit in today's society. Preventing drinking begins at home. Parents have to take charge of their children's education from day one. Not only do they need a formal education but they also need to learn about the undesirables in the world we live in.

3   When children reach adolescence drinking should be high on the list of undesirables. Parents need to realize that if they give a fair lesson about drinking, providing their children with all the information possible, then they will be able to make some sort of decision about what is right for themselves.

4   Lessons can be given at home, but who can teach them outside the home? Teachers can try—but many times teens don't trust them. Friends can try— but they don't always give the whole story. Society can try—but there are pressures that often do more harm than good.

5   I was talking to a friend of mine the other day. He was a high school math teacher for many years. I asked him to speak at a function that I was organizing. He said that he couldn't speak in front of people. I reminded him that he used to be a teacher and he said, "Teaching isn't like talking to people." I couldn't believe he said that. Teenagers are people. They need to be treated with as much respect as any adult. They need guidance to be able to choose what is right for themselves.

6   Let's look at two situations involving drinking by teenagers. Try to think how you would handle the same situations.

7   1. Jeff was eighteen years old and felt that his mother was useless. She left him alone quite often with the refrigerator full of beer. She never noticed if one, two, or even all of them were missing. When he found out that she was going away for the weekend he was psyched. He could have all of his friends over and have a party the whole weekend. Just before his mom left she said, "No parties and no drinking." Jeff laughed in her face. Of course he had a party and of course he drank. At the end of the weekend he and four of his friends were passed out on the living-room floor. His last thoughts were if his mom didn't care why should he?

8   2. Joy was eighteen years old and had a great relationship with her parents. They were always honest with her and were always there when she needed

to talk. They didn't tell her she couldn't drink but they didn't tell her she could. They felt that they had given her a broad enough outlook on drinking to make a mature decision that would be right for her. She tried drinking not once but a few times. She knew deep down inside that it was not right for her. She chose not to drink. It felt good to be able to make an important decision on her own.

9   In both of these cases it is the parents who are the major factors, not the children. In the first case Jeff's mom took the subject of drinking lightly and so did he. In the second case Joy's parents treated her as an adult and she behaved like one.

10   It isn't always like this in many homes. Many times the Joys become drinkers and the Jeffs don't. This does not mean that parents should feel they can't help. They can. If they remain behind their children there isn't much they can't do or overcome.

11   If you are a parent or plan to be one would you behave like the first case or the second one? It is something to think about. We may think that as parents we will know what is best for our children but we also have to remember that they have a mind of their own. I would like to make sure that I teach my children to make their own decisions about drinking. Here are a few ways to assure yourself that you do all you can to influence their decisions.

12   Provide a positive role model for your children. Don't act as if drinking is important to living a normal life. If you act as if drinking is something that you do responsibly then they will feel the same, or at least it will give them something to think about.

13   See if they are receiving any alcohol-related education at school. If they aren't maybe you could suggest that they begin one. If you need help deciding what kind of program, could look into a Students Against Driving Drunk organization. This program involves both children and parents. It would be a way to show your child that you care enough to be involved.

14   Discuss the subject of drinking with them openly. Make sure that communication lines are always open. If your children know that you are available they might feel better about coming and talking with you.

15   Establish a parent support group in your town. It might be helpful to talk about your fears to people who are in the same position that you are. They also may have some ideas that would be helpful to your own situation.

16   These are just a few ways that you could help both yourself and other parents deal with the subject of teenage drinking.

17   One quote I found in a pamphlet entitled "Let's Talk About Drinking" said this: "The right to drink is also the right not to drink." This says a lot to me. It says that everyone has the right to think and choose for themselves.

18   Children need to be given the right to make their own decisions. If choices were made for you, how could you feel good about yourself. You wouldn't be an individual, you would be a puppet. It is important for you to teach your children before you preach to them. Then they will have the knowledge to ignore the preaching and make their own rational decisions.

19   Individuals are unique because they can think for themselves. Parents

need to provide guidance and if they have done this to the best of their ability the individual will prepare a mature and rational decision.

20   I feel that I need to share this one experience with you to show you the point of my whole paper. My parents are close to my brother and me. They have always had a very open relationship with us. They never really talked a lot about drinking, but we knew that they would always stand behind us in whatever we chose to do.

21   My brother was twelve years old when this particular incident occurred. We went to my boyfriend's house and he was having a huge party. I knew that my boyfriend drank but I loved him just the same. That night he told his friends to get my brother a beer. I started to get angry and he picked me up and carried me to the bathroom. Then he locked me in. I thought that they were doing terrible things to my brother and I started to shake. Finally I heard my brother say "I don't want a drink. Traci and I have to leave, NOW." I had started to cry. When we finally got outside I squeezed him so tightly that I felt he would burst. That night I realized that my parents had done a good job in bringing us up. I never thought that Robby was his own person until that evening.

22   That is the point I'm trying to get across. You can only do so much for your children, and then you just have to pray that they think enough of themselves to do what is best for them.

23   There is a fine line between right and wrong when you talk about drinking. Should teens be allowed to drink? Should drinking be outlawed to people under twenty-one? Can there be exceptions to the rules? So many questions and no real answers.

History of the Essay

Traci Tucker chose a topic she felt strongly about. She realized it was an emotional subject for her but wrote:

> I read a lot this week about teenage drinking and the statistics scared me. We have to find some way to stop this or at least control our youth. I realize now that I really need to take a different approach to this paper. I still don't condone teenage drinking but I know that I have to back my views with facts. I also have to propose some sort of alternative or solution before people will read my paper and think. That is my main goal. To make people sit and think when they are through reading.

As she went on she sounded like a writer veering between confidence and despair. Her commentary for her first full draft for class publication shows the writer at work:

> I sat down to write today having no idea where I was heading. I took Mr. Murray's advice and cut my paper up separating the paragraphs. It made my paper look a little better than it did in the old order. I sat down at the typewriter

feeling that I should rewrite my rough draft before typing but I just had no energy.

It started to flow. My story just started to form and take shape. There were many things that I left out though and that bothers me. I had piled up quite a few statistics and I wanted to use them but when it came time they just didn't look good on paper. I don't know if maybe some of them could be used. You might have some ideas.

The length bothers me. I don't know if it's long enough. You said that when it's done it's done and I'm glad this is only the first draft. I'll need some advice. Keep this, ditch this, and rewrite this. I hope it's not as bad as I think it is. Actually it turned out better than I thought it would.

At the start of last week I thought it would be great if I started to work on my rough draft early. As I went along it started to look terrible. I ended up leaving it until today and it took shape much better. I should probably always wait to the last minute and then I'll know that it has to be done.

I'm very glad that the first part of my final paper is finished. Now I have something to build on. I'm sure that the final draft won't look at all like this one—after all what are first drafts for?

Her readers were supportive but had good criticisms. She wrote in the commentary for her next draft that "with the help of the comments the class gives about this draft my final copy will flow easily."

Final Commentary

My paper has come a long way. It started out as a revolt against people around me drinking. I hate it. My problem was how to express that without seeming like a hypocrite. As I continued to research I decided to write about my own experience with drinking. That bombed also. It brought back too many bad memories and I was back to anger.

Finally it hit me. Your parents are so great. Why not write about how important parents are to the subject of drinking. Awesome. The problem now was information. I couldn't find much to correspond to this subject so I began to grasp for straws. Then just as I was to write my second draft what do I receive in the mail? Yes, I got more information. I was happy, to say the least.

I have now finished my final draft and I feel a sense of relief. It was fun to experiment with many different angles and drafts of this paper. I like the finished product.

What have I learned? Not to use the word very. *I wanted to write it ten times in my paper but refused. I have also come to a conclusion:* argument *is hard to spell. I have had to look it up every time I want to write it. On a serious note,* argument *is how you feel about a subject. You don't have to be angry, you just need to have an opinion. An opinion that you feel strongly about. It is easy to do if you don't think about it.*

Richard Dahl, Jr.
STUDENT ESSAY

Tough Isn't Enough

1   I drink. I admit it. Once in a while, I may drink more than a little. But I'm not stupid.

2   That's what I call drunk driving. Stupid. Senseless. 25,000 dead each year. 700,000 more injured or maimed each year. Why? From a disease for which we have no cure? No. But because people drink, and then aren't responsible enough not to drive. There's a simple enough cure if we choose to call it a disease: if someone's been drinking, they shouldn't drive; and if they're driving, they shouldn't drink. Yet people continue to mix the two, and so continue to kill innocent people. In two years, drunken drivers kill as many Americans as were killed in the entire Vietnam War, and some thought they died without reason.

3   Teenagers alone present a large problem. One out of four of the 70 percent that drink alcoholic beverages admits that he drives while intoxicated. 4,000 go on to die as a direct result of this decision to drive drunk, making it the leading cause of death among youths between fifteen and twenty-four, and accounting for nearly twice as many teenage deaths as any other cause. Yet it's not an uncontrollable plague that causes these deaths; it's something they choose to bring upon themselves.

4   Until fairly recently, no one really seemed to care about the havoc people were bringing to themselves as well as countless innocents, except for those directly affected. Back in 1978, two young students at a school in New York were killed by a reckless driver who was found after the crash to have a blood alcohol content twice that of the legal limit. No criminal charges were filed against that driver. In 1981, Idaho authorities arrested 1,800 people for drunk driving, convicted one-third of them, and jailed just two. One district attorney observed that killing ducks out of season could be seen by courts as more serious than killing people with a vehicle.

5   A lot has changed since then. Community outrage over statistics like these has prompted more prosecutors and judges to regard drunken driving accidents as violent crimes. It has brought the emergence of powerful and active groups such as MADD (Mothers Against Drunk Driving) and SADD (Students Against Driving Drunk). It has given birth to educational programs on drunk driving, and tougher laws to punish it. Thanks to this outrage, the problem has begun to be confronted, and statistics have begun to improve.

6   Some parts of the country, however, still balk at any attempt to deny what they see as the inalienable right to drive with a beer in one hand and a steering

wheel in the other. For example, only twenty-three states have open-container restrictions on the books. As a result, in states like North Carolina and Tennessee, gas stations sell iced-down beer from tubs right at the pumps. "You don't even have to open your door," Charles Hurley of the National Safety Council says, "just reach out and grab one." Thirty-some states have yet to legislate statutes that would force bars and tavern owners to ensure that their customers don't leave their barstools too intoxicated to drive. And in other states, the laws are full of loopholes, so that convicted drunk drivers can literally get away with murder and never spend a night in jail.

7   Nationally, the confidence of the drunk driver remains almost unshaken. Amazingly, four out of every ten drivers admit to driving while under the influence of alcohol, while 10 percent of all drivers on weekend nights can be legally defined as intoxicated. There are good reasons for this, one of which is brought out by a recent report from the National Transportation Safety Board. It found that only one in 2,000 who drive while intoxicated will be pulled over. And even with the most thorough police control and rigorous administration, it doesn't rise to more than one in 200. Yet, all too often, those who do escape arrest do not live to get home. Every year, about 25,000 do not, including 4,000 teens.

8   What more can we possibly do to stop drunk driving and its horrible consequences? Well, we could give up drinking and return to prohibition. Or we could stop driving, turn our cars over to the junkyard, and solve the oil shortage at the same time. I'm afraid I couldn't support either of these enthusiastically, though.

9   What we do need instead is a deep concern by all, and a strong commitment to do something, with which we can attack drunk driving from all sides. We must realize that drunk driving is everyone's problem, and it affects all Americans, whether they drink or not. So to protect not only other innocent people, but to protect ourselves also, we must work to make it tougher to drink and drive.

10   We can start by supporting efforts to check offenders on our roads, such as an increase of roadblocks, especially from 8 P.M. to 4 A.M., and on access roads to popular drinking places and to other states where the drinking age is lower.

11   We can help more directly, however, by working for new laws which make it tougher on drunk drivers and support efforts to enforce them. Probably the best way to do this is to join groups, such as MADD, which put pressure on legislators. Even on our own, though, we can apply pressure by writing our senators and representatives. They take such concern and interest quite seriously, especially if it is an opinion voiced by a thousand of us. Keeping their jobs is as important to them as it is to us, maybe more so.

12   More importantly, we need to put pressure on judges to enforce the laws once they are passed. Laws in many states now mandate jail terms for a convicted drunk driver. Nevertheless, a study by the National Institute of Justice shows that many judges and prosecutors ignore those provisions, even for

repeat offenders. We must make it known that we won't stand for this any longer. Edward O'Farrell, a municipal judge in New Philadelphia, Ohio, says "Most judges would get tougher on drunk drivers if people in their communities let them know that they are unhappy about leniency." He suggests that citizens ask local news media to publicize the sentencing records of judges. Then, if lenient judges don't get tough on drunk drivers, campaign against them.

13   But we need the laws first. An example of ones we need to work for is that which outlaws two-for-one specials at bars. New Jersey and Ohio have already passed such a law. Little laws like this have a large impact when put together. But we need to work for more significant laws even more.

14   To help counter teenage drinking and driving, for example, many states have raised their drinking age to 21. But many have not. The House and Senate have passed bills forcing all states to raise their legal drinking age to 21 by threatening to take away highway funds. A law is still far from passed, though, and some states, the liquor lobby, and campus organizations continue to fight its passage; so pressure is still needed. That pressure is equally important, for New Jersey reported that the number of drunk drivers eighteen to twenty-one years old involved in fatal accidents declined 39 percent in the first year. Candy Lightner, the founder of MADD, believes a national drinking age of 21 would save an estimated 1,250 lives in a year.

15   "21," as it's called, would also destroy blood borders (borders between states with different drinking ages). Every year thousands of teens die on their way back home after crossing the state border to go to bars where they can get served. In Kenosha County, Wisconsin, one of the primary liquor getaways for Illinois, 469 motorists were arrested for drunk driving in 1982, 119 of them were from Illinois. Many of them wouldn't have made it home if they hadn't been pulled over.

16   We should also work for new, tougher laws against those who are caught driving while intoxicated. Instead of making it possible for people to drink and drive the night after a conviction, we need to take them off the road. We also need to make them think twice about driving any time they've had more than a couple. To deal with these problems, the Senate proposal on the drinking age also rewards states with more highway funds if they enact mandatory penalties for drunken drivers: First offenders would spend two days in jail and lose their license for 90 days; a second conviction would lead to 90 days in jail and a license suspension of one year; and a third conviction would mean the loss of one's license for three years and four months in jail. To me, it seems as though it would be just as effective to reduce the jail sentence to one day for the first offense and to 30 days for the second, while also requiring mandatory attendance to a state program for alcoholic drivers and some community work. This seems especially suitable for youngsters. Something similar to this, however, is necessary to keep murderers off our roads and away from loved ones.

17   We can, and should, take an even more active role in accomplishing this task. We can notify police of any suspicious behavior on the part of other drivers. MADD publishes a card with tips for recognizing drunk driving. Oregon has

a toll-free hotline people can call to report drunk drivers. During 1982 and 1983, the first two years of the program, traffic fatalities were the lowest in twenty years. In Nebraska, fatalities dropped 26 percent in the first year of its drunk driver reporting program. So it works, but you don't need a program to get involved in making it tougher to drink and drive, just a concern for the welfare of yourself and thousands of other innocent people.

18   As we make it tougher to drink and drive, people will begin to take the crime more seriously, and realize it's not worth the risk or effort. People will begin to look down on those who combine alcohol and gasoline as the jerks and heartless criminals they really are. Through such social pressure, we can make it even tougher on drunk drivers. But these are all just wishes in the air if people aren't concerned enough about saving lives, possibly their own, to do something. 25,000 dead, another million injured or maimed—this must stop!

History of the Draft and Final Commentary

Well, I finally made it. Tomorrow I hand in the final draft of my argument paper, a paper we've spent most of the semester laboring on in one way or another. Sometimes I seriously wondered whether I'd be able to come up with anything that even slightly resembled what the professor fantasized about receiving at that last class. Now that it's finished, though, and our last class is tomorrow, I feel more a sense of accomplishment than anything else.

It all started just a few weeks into the semester, when our mission—an accurate word for it, I think—was first explained to us. It would be completed in five steps. The first of these was the collection of information, which lasted three weeks. First, we had to choose a topic: something that was important to us, something which affected us, and something we wanted to spend the semester on. I chose drinking, simply because it goes on all around me. I then spent the three weeks doing my research on it, collecting facts on anything about drinking, but especially alcoholism and drinking habits.

After the research, and not before, we were supposed to choose a position from which to argue, and then spend two weeks developing it. This was the second stage. When I looked over my information, though, I had trouble finding anything to argue about. The facts I had found on alcoholism and drinking habits were interesting, but I couldn't find a strong opinion within them which could be argued. And because I drink myself, I could not comfortably argue against the evils of alcohol use in general. So I came up with a position that the 21-year minimum drinking age was ineffective because 18–21-year-olds could get their hands on alcohol any time they wanted it. In the back of my mind, though, I knew it was a weak argument, and never once did I feel strongly about it, thinking that the law kept those under 18 from drinking and so was at least in part effective.

Nevertheless, I stuck with it, and tried to develop it somewhat, even though we were now into the third stage, where we were to develop our strategy of argument for two weeks. I continued to play around with and research my position. Unfortunately, I was finding more facts in favor of the 21-year drinking age than against it. This, and the fact that the fourth stage and development of all we had into a first draft was only one week away, brought me to change my position one more time.

Now, I would argue that we needed to make it tougher to drink and drive. Not only was it a strong argument, but one I felt strongly about too. I spent the next week doing my research over again, and this time I found more than enough. The last couple of days before the paper was due, I spent my time sorting out my information and then piecing it together until it was written and handed in on Thursday, November 13.

We finally entered the fifth and final stage on this day: clarifying the paper and making its argument as effective as possible for a second draft, and then a final draft due about four weeks later. On this day and the day the second draft was due, class served as a workshop in which students made comments on what worked, what didn't work, and what needed work and how for other students' papers. Both times, we also met with the professor in conference for more ideas on how to improve the paper. As suggested, I concentrated on adding more specifics and examples to my facts, and putting more of myself into the paper. With this, I finally handed in the final draft on December 11.

For three months I worked on this paper, and in that time, I learned a great deal about writing argument. In my opinion, the most important thing to be remembered about writing an effective argument paper is that it needs a good balance between powerful facts and information on the one hand and a strong voice that forces its way through on the other.

A lot of time needs to be spent on research. The writer has to get everything he possibly can on the topic and not worry about what will be or won't be effective in the paper. Later, this information can be sorted out, but he can't be caught with too little an amount of facts. Then by using outlines, the facts can be put in some sort of order, from which they can be tied together with the writer's own feelings and personal experience with the subject. These opinions provide the medium through which the writer can put himself into the paper and make it his own until his personality comes shining through.

Not all I have learned is about writing argument, though, but writing in general also. Here, I think the most important thing is to have room to experiment with one's writing. This allows for the person to break out of their shell, inside of which all writing is not their own, but something devoid of personality, created to please the teacher only. Writing should be done first and foremost for the writer, so that it pleases him. Keeping this in mind will not only create a stronger piece of writing, but make writing in general a much easier and more enjoyable process.

6

A Meaning Made Clear

The most satisfying part of the writing process comes when there is a draft that can be shaped into meaning by the writer's hand. After all the planning, the collecting, the focusing, the ordering, and the drafting, there is at last a text. The writer is no longer dealing with intangibles, but with the reality of language.

The first thing the writer has to do is to stand back and read the entire text at a distance, sometimes even role-playing a particular reader to discover what has been said, which is never quite the same as what the writer intended to say. The reading writer is usually disappointed, for the text rarely matches the dream that was in the writer's mind, but the writer is often intrigued by the unexpected that appears on the page. The text is not the dream, it is something both less and more than the dream.

It is helpful if the writer can avoid asking if the text is right or wrong, good or bad. More helpful questions are "What works?" and "What needs work?" The writer has, first of all, to recognize those elements in the text, such as subject, or organization, or voice, that are strong or potentially strong in the draft. Once the writer has discovered the strength of the text the writer can go on to discover its weaknesses. Drafts are not so much corrected against some absolute scale as they are improved on their own terms, worked over until the strengths are made stronger and the weaknesses made strong. School too often gives the young writer an idea that a text can be corrected as if there were an absolute right or wrong. But what works and doesn't work in writing is a complicated matter of context. What works changes according to the writer's purpose, the needs of the reader, the demands of the subject matter itself, the traditions of the form, and the interaction of all the elements in the writing—fact against fact, large structure against small structure, line against sentence, word against phrase. A piece of writing is a living organism, growing to fulfill its own needs.

The writer has to see the entire text. Usually it is helpful for me to sit back in a comfortable chair, to read it as fast as a reader will read it, not putting pen to paper, but swooping over the landscape of the text, seeing the bigger accomplishments and larger failures. The writer, of course, is asking at this stage, "Do I have anything to say? Do I have the information with which to say it? Can it be said?"

The Craft of Revision

If the answer is no, then the writer has to revise, and revise means going back through the planning process, making sure that there is a subject, that there is an adequate inventory of information about the subject, that the piece of writing has a focus and a structure that supports that focus. Too often revision is thought of as a separate writing act that occurs after a draft. It does occur at that time, but it is a reseeing and a rewriting that means, for the writer, replanning.

Rewriting is too often seen as punishment. It is not. It is opportunity, a chance to make meaning clear. As Neil Simon says, "Rewriting is when playwriting really gets to be fun. In baseball you only get three swings and you're out. In rewriting, you get almost as many swings as you want and you know, sooner or later, you'll hit the ball." When rewriting, the writer has the chance to use all the elements of craft, and watching that craft at work is like seeing a photograph coming clear in a tray of chemicals.

Many people make the mistake of plunging immediately into editing. If there is no subject, no information, no structure, then it is impossible to do effective line-by-line editing. The writer saves time by scanning the piece first and answering the larger questions of content and form before attempting to clarify the meaning line by line.

The Craft of Editing

When the larger questions are answered, the writer can go to work, reading the piece carefully paragraph by paragraph, sentence by sentence, phrase by phrase, word by word. Now the writer has the delight of doing the fine work, the cutting and adding and reordering which, when the writing is successful, makes the meaning come clear with an invisible skill. The writer, as editor, is continuously trying to remove the writer from the text, finding a way to make the text immediate to the writer. The writer usually does not want to be standing between the subject and the reader pointing out what is important, but revealing the importance to the reader so the reader discovers the significance directly.

All the selections in this chapter are designed to show how meaning can be made clear. A science writer and a scientist write each in their own way on the same subject. Two journalists report on the bombing of Japan. Members of two ethnic communities reveal their Americas. All of these matters are complicated and could be written in a complicated way. But these writers have found how to make the complex clear.

Denise Grady has revealed some of her craft to us, but behind all of these pieces, all of the other pieces in this book, and all of the effective writing you read there are many acts of craft that have been performed and then made invisible. The work has been done and the craftsperson has cleared up afterward, so that what remains appears natural—the shelf looks as if it had always clung to that wall.

Many writers do not know what they do; they just do it, the way a basketball player doesn't think "I have to shift the ball to my left hand and get my body between the ball and the guard." The guard moves and the experienced player reacts. Here are some pieces of advice and some tricks of the trade that may be helpful as you edit your own text, reacting to your draft in such a way that your meaning is made to come clear:

- *If It Can Be Cut, Cut It.* Everything in a piece of writing should advance the meaning. That does not mean that you should write in a staccato style likeamachinegun, but that everything in the text must contribute to the clarification of meaning. There may be a time to slow the text down, to repeat, to turn a fine phrase, but whatever is done must make the meaning clear.
- *Define* those words, ideas, or pieces of information that are essential to the reader's understanding of the text. But try, whenever possible, to work the definition right into the sentence at the time the reader needs to know it, sometimes using clauses. A definition should rarely be a big chunk of material dumped on the reader before the reader needs to know it, or when it is too late to assist the reader in understanding the text.
- *Be Specific.* The reader needs accurate, concrete information. The reader wants the authority of such specific details, and the reader needs information on which to base the reader's own conclusions. Specific information gives a piece of writing vigor and liveliness. Although it is logical to write in generalities and abstractions when appealing to a large audience, every writer has learned that the larger the audience the more important it is to reveal the subject in specific terms.
- *Document* each point with evidence that will convince the reader of the authority of the text. Readers cannot be expected to take a piece of writing on faith. They need facts, statistics, quotations, description, anecdotes, all sorts of documentation.
- *Write Short* for emphasis. Brevity gives vigor and clarity. The more complicated the subject, the harder to understand, the more important it is to use the shortest words, the shortest sentences, the shortest paragraphs that communicate the meaning without oversimplifying and distorting it.

- *Achieve Brevity by Selection*. Inexperienced writers try to compress everything into tiny pellets of text. Experienced writers achieve brevity by selecting those pieces of evidence, for example, that are necessary to the reader, and then develop them fully.
- *Edit with Your Ear*, reading and rereading aloud so that the final text has the flow and ease of natural speech. The reader should have the illusion of hearing the text, the illusion of an individual writer speaking directly to an individual reader.
- *Write with Verbs and Nouns*, active verbs and proper nouns whenever possible. Lean on verbs and nouns and avoid adverbs and adjectives, especially at important points in the text. Do not try to put words on the page that may surround a meaning, but try to find those words that precisely express meaning.
- *Respect the Subject-Verb-Object Sentence*. Turn to it when meaning becomes unclear or where an important point has to be made. Beware of sentences that are unnecessarily complex and go in circles of clauses, like a puppy chasing its own tail.
- *Aim for Simplicity*. You want to make the writing look easy. Of course you don't want it so easy that it does not tell the truth of your subject, but you should not write to complicate or to impress; you should write to communicate.
- *Say One Thing* and say it well. There should be a dominant meaning in your piece. Your sentences should carry one bit of information to your reader. Your paragraphs should develop one idea. Of course there are exceptions. There must be variety in writing, but the focus of the writing should be in the development of single pieces of information that add up to one overall meaning.
- *Clarify* what you have to say and you will find that you are following the traditions of language most of the time. When the writing doesn't come clear look to what you have to say and make sure that you know what you want to say. If it still isn't clear, look to the traditions of language to see what principles and rules may help you clarify the text. But, as George Orwell reminded us, never follow a rule that does not help make meaning clear.
- *Write the Truth*. People sometimes feel that writing is a dishonest trade. Certainly there are politicians, public relations spokesmen, and advertising writers who try to use language in a dishonest way. And sometimes they succeed. But the fact that some drivers drive to endanger does not mean we should imitate them. The most effective writing is honest, and the reader recognizes that honesty.

The lessons of a lifetime spent in the pursuit of craft, a lifetime of trying to write with increasing clarity, vigor, accuracy, and grace cannot be summed up in a few pages, but the counsel of experienced writers expressed in the list above and practiced in the texts that follow express attitudes as well as skills. The purpose of writing is to learn and to share that learning. The purpose of revising and editing is to make meaning come clear, first to the writer, then to the reader.

Case Study: A Science Writer Writes and Reads

Denise Grady

Many of our best writers were not English majors. (The reverse is also true: many of our worst student writers are English majors.) Denise Grady majored in biology at the State University of New York at Stony Brook and worked as an editor at *Physics Today* before going to the University of New Hampshire, where she received a master's degree in writing and also taught writing. Grady was an assistant editor at the *New England Journal of Medicine,* a senior editor of *Medical Month,* and a staff writer for three years at *Discover,* a science magazine published by Time Inc. and is now on the staff of *Time.* She is the author of more than 50 magazine articles, most of them dealing with science and medicine. The article published here is a health column written for *Newsday.*

Grady does a lot of writing in her head, which is a fine place to work, but she has given us some interesting examples of false starts with her marginal comments saying why she found them false.

FALSE STARTS

wrong focus. — not a piece about infertility

Today, more and more couples are finding out that they cannot have children.   According to WHOEVER TK, some TK% of American couples are infertile, a TK% increase over the YEAR TK figure.   The rise has two probable causes: an increase in the rates of sexually transmitted diseases, which can damage the female reproductive systems, and

wrong focus, too slow — not about multiple births

An Australian woman who thought she would never be able to have children gave birth to ~~spiriotipul~~ quadruplets last winter, four little boys who were conceived outside her body when doctors mixed her eggs and her husband's sperm in laboratory dishes.

Just too flat.

And it's a lazy + a cop-out to start with a question.

Has medical technology solved the problem of infertility? Clinics specializing in in vitro fertilization--"test-tube babies"--are springing up across the United States, offering hope to the NUMBER TK Americans couples who cannot have children on their own.   According to the American Fertility Society, there are now NUMBER TK hospital based in vitro programs in TK states.   And private clinics are also getting into the business.

❦ Grady has also provided some early drafts of the paragraphs she reworked the most, with marginal comments showing the problems she experienced. ❧

Early

Draft of paragraph 3, 4

I thought of leaving this paragraphs the last but decided that's a tired device

She was, the doctors said, an ideal candidate for in vitro fertili~ation. All that kept her from getting pregnant were blockages in the Fallopian tubes, the ~~passages~~ ~~an egg would normally travel through in order to get from~~ ~~the ovary to the uterus~~

the passages where an egg is normally fertilized, *on its way from* ~~and through~~ ~~which it must pass to get from~~ the ovary to the uterus ~~.~~ ~~the passages leading from ovary at to uterus~~

The in vitro procedure would, ~~in essence~~ bypass the blocked tubes: eggs would be surgically removed from her ovaries, *fertilized with what?* → fertilized in a dish outside her body, and, if fertilization occurred, transferred back into her uterus. With luck, one would implant itself there and grow into a ~~normal,~~ *redundant* healthy baby.

→ She and her husband decided to try it. (They had been trying to conceive for several years; surgery could not open her tubes,) surgery had not helped, she was in her mid-thirties, and time was running out. The couple traveled from New York to the Yale University *Just seems to read better* Medical Center, in New Haven. The procedure seemed to go well: hormone treatments before surgery made ~~the ovaries~~ *makes* ~~release~~ four eggs, ~~simultaneously, instead of the usual~~ *is this?* *makes them mature; they don't want them released.* (one a month, and all four fertilized and were placed into her uterus.

Early draft of paragraph 8 (p. 4 of final version)

Like Linda and Bill, some NUMBER OR % TK American couples are infertile. Their numbers are growing, probably because of the increase in sexually transmitted infections that damage the female ~~rpaax~~ reproductive organs, and because more women are ~~trying to start their families later in life~~, ~~start families in~~ their thirties, *postpone preceding until* when fertility may begin to decline. Many of these couples look to in vitro fertilization clinics for a solution. For some, the procedure works. But most wind up like Linda and Bill.

(tighten)

But I haven't said how these 2 wound up yet.

❦ What follows are several pages from Grady's last draft before the final version, with the changes she edited into the text and her comments about why she made those *changes.* ❧

They may well be the happiest parents in the world--

the couples who, once told they would never have

children, have now become families with the aid of

the ~~pree~~ medical technology known as in vitro

fertilization. ~~Their appearances~~ on television~~,~~   pictures of them and their babies

more definite this way, with "the"--and there are thousands

and in newspapers and magazines have undoubtedly

→ *the thousands*

~~spurred~~ inspired ~~hundreds~~ of other childless couples *who have put*

their names on waiting lists

~~to check in~~ at ~~the~~ in vitro clinics that are

America ⊙

opening all across ~~the country.~~

a new piece of information

But how many of these couples ~~really~~ understand

what they're getting into--the physical and emotional

will have to

stress, and the expense they incur for what amounts

For

to a small chance of getting pregnant? ~~Xixiaxx~~ One

∧

New Yorker, ~~xxx has described~~ in vitro fertilization *turned out to be*

~~as~~ "one of the most emotionally disturbing things

my husband and I have ever been through."

Doctors ^had told ~~Linda~~ ^Linda she was an ideal candidate for
~~in vitro fertilization~~. *the procedure.* All that kept her from having

a baby were ~~blockages in her~~ *blocked* Fallopian tubes, the two

passages where eggs are normally fertilized on their

way from the ovaries to the uterus. The in vitro ~~procedure~~

would ~~essentially~~ bypass the ~~blocked tubes~~ eggs would

be surgically removed from ~~Linda's~~ *Linda's* ovaries, mixed with

her husband's sperm in a laboratory dish, and, if

fertilization occurred, transferred back into her

uterus. With luck, one would implant itself ~~itself~~

there and grow into a ~~normal~~ healthy baby.

She and her husband Bill decided to ~~try~~ it, ~~She~~

was in her mid-thirties, and time was running out.

~~They couple traveled from Manhattan to~~ *at* the Yale Univer-

sity Medical Center, in New Haven. There, the pro-

cedure seemed to go well. Hormone treatments before

[handwritten margin note, left:] I'm trying quickly to define & explain procedure.

[handwritten margin note, right:] A little more dramatic this way, somehow?

surgery made ~~his brain ovaries release four eggs, instead~~ four of Linda's eggs mature simultaneously (one a month is usual)

~~of the usual one at a time,~~ and all four were fertilized

and placed into her uterus.

Then she and Bill waited. Two weeks later, the dream

was over. She was not pregnant. But she thought, she had consoled herself with the fact

come close enough to make it worth another try.

"This time," she says, "We decided to ~~go to~~ try the very

best experts in the country, to the oldest and most suc- Late last year, she and Bill went to

cessful in vitro fertilization clinic in the U.S., established

in 1980 at the Eastern Virginia Medical School. Again, in Norfolk.

the prospects looked good. Doctors said ~~she had plenty~~

~~of healthy-looking ovarian follicles~~ seemed to have

plenty of eggs that could be ~~matured~~ ripened with hormone shots.

But they operated too late. The eggs, already

matured and released from the ovaries, were lost. ~~Jeannie~~ Linda

and Bill were devastated. "The doctors said, 'Please She recalls,

come back and let us try again. You're such a good

candidate.' They said they were learning that they

[handwritten margin note: Why introduced "follicles," which would simply need defining?]

There is no professional body that enforces

practice standards at these clinics or keeps track

of how well they are doing, so patients have no *sure*

checking out clinics other than calling to ask

~~way of telling whether or not they are in exper-~~

~~ienced hands.~~ *Their success rates. Calls to the*

three clinics that opened in the New York area in

early 1983 yielded the following information.

Unfortunately, the only way to get good at in vitro is to practice on patients.

most of which opened in 1983, have been going through

similar periods of trial and error. When ~~they~~ novices do

achieve a ~~fixsi~~ first pregnancy, they may not be sure

what ~~they-fin~~ they've finally done right.

insert

~~Sucess rates vary.~~ In the New York area,

three hospitals opened in vitro clinics ~~in~~ early in

1983. At North Shore University Hospital, in Manhasset,

TK patients have tried the treatment; TK got pregnant, TK

miscarried, and TK have given birth. At Manhattan⅛s
already

Columbia Presbyterian ᴹedical Center, - ----

Statistics to come

Finally, at the Mount Sinai Medical Center, also in

Manhattan, -----

but they are difficult to compare, because they depend

to some degree on the cause of the infertility. Women
and the patient's age.

under 40 with blocked tubes have the best chance.o⨍x

❧ Here is Grady's final draft of the column. ❧

In Vitro Fertilization: It Doesn't Always Work

1   They may well be the happiest parents in the world—the couples who, once told they would never have children, have now become families with the aid of the medical technology known as in vitro fertilization. Pictures of them on television and in the newspapers, cuddling their babies, have undoubtedly inspired the thousands of other couples who have put their names on waiting lists at in vitro clinics that are opening all across America.

2   But how many of these couples understand what they're getting into—the physical and emotional stress, and the expense they will have to incur for what amounts to a small chance of getting pregnant? For one New Yorker, in vitro fertilization turned out to be "one of the most emotionally disturbing things my husband and I have ever been through."

3   Linda's doctors had told her she was an ideal candidate for the procedure. All that kept her from having a baby were blocked Fallopian tubes—the two passages where eggs are normally fertilized on their way from the ovaries to the uterus. Surgery had failed to open the tubes. But the in vitro technique would bypass them: eggs would be surgically removed from Linda's ovaries, mixed with her husband's sperm in a laboratory dish, and, if fertilization occurred, transferred back into her uterus. With luck, one would implant itself there and grow into a healthy baby.

❧ Note how neatly Grady works in the scientific exposition, relating the explanation to a single human being. Grady provides definitions at the point the reader needs them and they are woven right into the text. ❧

4   Linda was in her mid-thirties, and time was running out. She and her husband Bill decided to go for it, at the Yale University Medical Center, in New Haven, which opened its in vitro clinic in the spring of 1982. There, the procedure seemed to go well. Hormone treatments before surgery made four of Linda's eggs mature (one a month is usual), and all four were fertilized and placed into her uterus.

5   Then she and Bill waited. Two weeks later, the dream was over. She was not pregnant. But she consoled herself with the thought that she had come close enough to make it worth another try.

6   "This time," she says, "we decided to try the very best experts in the country." Late last year, she and Bill went to the oldest and most successful in vitro fertilization clinic in the United States, established in 1980 at the Eastern Virginia Medical School, in Norfolk. Again, the prospects looked good. Doctors said she seemed to have plenty of eggs that could be ripened with hormone shots.

7   But they operated too late. The eggs, already matured and released from the ovaries, were lost. Linda and Bill were devastated. She recalls, "The doctors said, 'Please come back and let us try again. You're such a good candidate.' They said they were learning that they couldn't assume all their patients ran on the same timetable, and next time around they'd operate on me sooner." Linda and Bill made an appointment to return to Eastern Virginia a few months later. But she wasn't looking forward to a third round of hormone treatments, general anesthesia, and surgery, and she and Bill weren't sure they could face another disappointment.

8   Like them, some 15 percent of married couples in America are infertile. Their numbers are growing, probably because of the increase of sexually transmitted infections that damage the female reproductive system, and because more women are postponing pregnancy until their thirties, when fertility may begin to decline. Many of these couples are heartbroken, and willing to put up with any hardship for even the smallest chance of having a baby. They see in vitro fertilization as their only hope.

❧ Grady gives us the background to understand the subject in context. ❧

9   How realistic is this hope? For some, the procedure does work: more than 100 in vitro babies have been born in the United States. But most couples are not so lucky. Indeed, the standing joke among gynecologists is that more women get pregnant on the waiting lists than in the clinics. Actually, pregnancy rates range from zero to 20 percent at in vitro clinics, according to a survey of 37 hospital-based clinics published last spring in *Medical Month* magazine. Eastern Virginia is the exception, reporting an overall pregnancy rate of 30 percent, and a rate of 38 percent during the past six months, among women who had three embryos transferred to the uterus. This appears to be even better than nature, which gives a couple trying to conceive the usual way about a 20 percent chance of success each month.

10   But these clinic rates are inflated, because they don't include all patients. Rather, the figures are based only on the number of women able to have fertilized eggs transferred into the uterus. Patients at Eastern Virginia are not even counted if, as happened on Linda's second try, eggs cannot be recovered, or if they are recovered but fail to fertilize. Moreover, not every pregnancy survives: miscarriage rates can run as high as 30 percent to 50 percent, two to three times the rate in naturally occurring pregnancies. Many women who have had children by in vitro fertilization have undergone the procedure—including surgery and general anesthesia repeatedly, some as many as seven times. And they are charged about $5,000 for each attempt; insurance coverage varies.

11   The disappointing statistics reflect the difficulty of the procedure. It may sound like a straightforward matter to take an egg from a woman, fertilize it, and put it back. But it's not that simple. While the patient is taking hormones, she has to have daily blood tests and ultrasound exams to monitor the ripening

of the eggs, which must be removed during the short period when they're mature but not yet released from the ovaries. Then the eggs are incubated in a nutrient solution for a few hours before being mixed with a measured amount of specially treated sperm from the patient's husband. Forty hours later, if fertilization has occurred and the embryos have begun dividing normally, they're transferred into the woman's uterus.

12   Things can go wrong at any point—with the hormonal stimulation, egg retrieval, fertilization, or implantation. Even if they all go well, the woman can still miscarry. Failures are rarely explainable. Was it timing, temperature, nutrients, or handling? A defective egg or sperm? Or something in the woman's physiology?

❦ With the subjects Grady writes about, she must document what she has to say. Note how skillfully—and gracefully—she does that. ❧

13   Each new in vitro clinic has to work the bugs out of its techniques. Even Eastern Virginia had its growing pains—namely, a year and a half during which none of its patients got pregnant. The other 35 clinics polled by *Medical Month* magazine, most of which opened in 1983, have been going through similar periods of trial and error. Unfortunately, the only way to get good at in vitro is to practice it—on patients. When novices do achieve a pregnancy, they may not be sure what they've finally done right. There is no professional body that enforces practice standards at in vitro clinics or keeps track of how well they are doing, so patients have no easy means of checking up on the clinics.

14   In the New York area, four hospitals have in vitro programs: North Shore University Hospital, in Manhasset; Glen Cove Community Hospital; and the Mount Sinai and Columbia Presbyterian medical centers, both in Manhattan. At North Shore, 35 patients have been treated, but the hospital will not reveal how they've fared, because they're already under stress, according to a spokesman, and "we don't want to put them under a microscope." At Glen Cove, about a dozen patients have been treated, and the team is hoping that a recent, promising one will be the first to get pregnant. The Mount Sinai program has treated 42 couples and produced one pregnancy; because of this low success rate, the program stopped temporarily to analyze its problems, and is about to reopen, with an emphasis on new methods of hormone therapy and selection of younger patients. At Columbia, 15 patients had undergone embryo transfer as of last January, and three were pregnant. Many others had begun the program but never made it to the transfer stage, a spokesman says. New figures are not available because of the current hospital strike.

❦ Grady has to know her audience and answer its questions. *Newsday* is published on Long Island, near New York City. The reader asks, "Where can I get help or information near here? How are our local centers doing?" Grady hears her readers' questions and answers them. ❧

15   The one encouraging note is that success rates are climbing, gradually, at most clinics, as medical teams learn more about handling human eggs and sperm and using hormones to prime the body for pregnancy. In fact, Dr. Victor Reyniak, head of the team at Mount Sinai, says it is reasonable for women under the age of 36 to postpone in vitro for a year or two, to take advantage of the better odds that the future will bring.

❧Grady ends on a note of hope, and ties this technical subject back to an individual couple so that the medical facts are related to a person. She also shows, rather than tells, about one alternative: adoption.❧

16   For those who can't seem to beat the odds, there may be other solutions. Linda and Bill, for instance, were packing for a return trip to Eastern Virginia when a phone call from their lawyer changed their plans. They emptied the suitcases, cancelled the appointment in Norfolk, and went out to buy clothes for the newborn baby who was waiting for them to adopt him.

How the Column Was Written

1   Whenever I sit down to write an article or an essay, I force myself to write a sentence or two summarizing what I'm trying to say. If I can't do it, or if I have to keep rethinking my purpose as I write, I know I'm in trouble; I've got some long nights and a lot of false starts ahead of me. When I'm really struggling I feel like the college student who, going over a paper with a writing-teacher friend of mine, blurted, "Why does everything have to have a goddamn *point?*" and burst into tears.

2   The piece included here is a health column I wrote on assignment for the Long Island, New York, newspaper *Newsday*. The choice of subject was mine, and I started out with a pretty clear idea of what was on my mind: "In vitro fertilization requires a lot of time and money, and involves risk and pain, all for a very small chance of success. Some hospitals are a lot better at it than others."

3   I wanted to write the column because research I'd done previously on the topic for a medical magazine convinced me that all the media hype about test tube babies is obscuring the truth about this procedure. I hoped especially to make readers aware of the extent to which in vitro teams are using patients for on-the-job training. This is apparently the only way they can learn the techniques, and I'm not condemning that. What does disturb me is the impression I've gotten, that these patients—who are so desperate for babies that they'll try anything—think the in vitro doctors know exactly what they're doing. I know what it is to want children, and I'm not trying to destroy the hopes of childless couples. But I am trying to destroy false hopes.

4   One issue I often grapple with in reporting on medicine is what to say about medical practices that look bad to me. In researching this subject, for instance, I saw a surgical resident teaching a medical student how to work a trochar—a metal tube with a point attached to one end, which is used by in vitro surgeons to punch through a woman's navel and introduce other instruments into the abdomen. The unconscious patient they were practicing on was a woman about my age. I had talked to her before the operation; she was trusting and optimistic and very eager to have a baby. They poked that thing around inside her like a pair of plumbers. Later, the photographer I was working with described their technique to another surgeon, who said, "Well, you can do it that way nine times out of ten. But the tenth time you might puncture the patient's gut." Which might kill her, or at least make her very sick.

5   Is it fair to report this? Only if you're sure it's bad practice. To find out, you've got to watch more operations, talk to more surgeons, give the plumbers a chance to defend themselves. What's the right way to handle a trochar? Have there been mishaps? Do most hospitals let students practice on unconscious patients? Had the patient given permission?

6   Some people would say it's unfair *not* to report this, because the public has a right to know what goes on in hospitals. But people also have a right not to be scared unnecessarily by sensationalistic reporting. The fact is, most surgery looks shocking. The first time I saw an operation, I was stunned by how crude and violent it seemed, how roughly the body was handled. Anybody who watches surgery—and I mean first-rate surgery—could describe it honestly in terms that would make an audience swear off doctors and hospitals for life. So I would have to do a lot of research to feel confident enough to write a story portraying a particular surgeon as a clod. It's just not enough to know in my gut that he is a clod.

7   But I can't turn every assignment into an exposé. Investigative reporting takes time, patient editors, lots of room for the story, and lots of money—either the publication's, or mine if I'm working free-lance and the fee is the same regardless of how much time I spend reporting.

8   So sometimes I wind up compromising. I stick to what I *can* say, ever mindful of what I *want* to say, the gut feeling that would influence my choices if I were the patient or if I were speaking privately to a friend. Within my own arbitrary bounds of fairness I let what I want to say help shape the piece—the tone, the selection of material, the topic sentences that set the course for each paragraph. In this case, the job was not difficult, because the failure rates at the clinics tell their own story.

9   As I reread my drafts, I'm constantly checking to make sure I can back up what I've said, and have been faithful to what I perceive as the spirit of the piece.

10   So much for the moral tribulations of a medical reporter. I fret just as much over technical matters of writing. Like most writers, I can't really get anywhere until I've come up with a decent lead. I want those first few paragraphs to be

interesting, and also to reveal where the piece is going. I've come to despise myself for resorting to the hack medical writer's anecdotal lead of the "Mary woke up one morning with a pain in her toe" variety. I almost gave up and used one for this in vitro piece. Paragraph three was nearly the lead, but it made me cring every time I reread it. And it took too long to get to the point. So I wrote two opening paragraphs and stuck them in front of the sad story of Linda, and found myself in business.

11   Once I'm satisfied that the lead has put an article on course, the most important things I look for are organization and something that writing text-books call "coherence." I don't think I got control of these until I began writing articles regularly and seeing editors turn them inside out regularly. Wounded pride and frustration made me determined to put my pieces together so tightly and logically that they would need no rearranging, and editors would find them hard to cut. I accomplished one of these goals: I learned how to organize an article and construct paragraphs well enough so that editors would leave the structure alone. But editors always want to cut, and as my sense of structure became stronger and stronger, I found that the cutting was more and more often left to me. Which is both a reward and a punishment.

12   I find that to organize an article I need a thorough understanding of my material and what I'm trying to do with it. Then I've got to figure out what my main ideas are, how they're related to one another, and the most logical way to order them. I usually do this by drawing up lists or even writing a series of rough topic sentences to be fleshed out into paragraphs. I rarely follow these to the letter; sometimes the ideas change in the writing.

13   Coherence pertains more to the paragraphs themselves. I use the term to mean a smooth, logical flow of ideas that lets the audience read without having to double back, skip ahead, or stop to wonder if the piece is going anywhere. Every sentence has a reason for being where it is, a link to the one before and one after. The transitions from one paragraph to another are strong—and by strong I don't mean heavy-handed, just clearly reasoned.

14   Once I've got a piece put together to my satisfaction, I look at stylistic details like punctuation, word choice, and conciseness, and I labor over spon-taneous touches of grace and wit, which I think I manage to achieve about once every three articles. I can't explain every change; some just feel right, and I trust my instincts. I look for places to plug in leftover facts, and I check to see if my explanations and definitions—especially of scientific concepts—make sense. But I have to confess that I've never disciplined myself to ignore these things while writing, and I do slow myself down by diddling with words and semicolons and phrases all along the way. This is a particularly stupid waste of time, because it hurts much more later to drop a paragraph I've labored over than one I've whipped out.

15   By the time I'm through with all this reading and rereading, I've practically memorized my article. The drafts are usually black with cross-outs, because I'm so humiliated by my mistakes that I have to obliterate them. Once an article is

published, I usually try to avoid reading it again, because I know I'll find things I should have said better.

Discussion

- Discuss the problems of the science writer whose job is to communicate complex information that is important to the reader.
- Discuss the ways in which the reader can be given definitions when needed.
- Discuss how Grady paces the piece, getting the reader interested in the human problem with a large proportion of information about the effect on people, and then switches gears to deliver a large proportion of exposition. Consider how this can be applied to other forms of writing.
- Compare Grady's problems and techniques to Freda's, Selzer's, and those of other writers in the text.
- This column was written for a newspaper, as was Scanlan's. Are there any generalizations you can make from these two pieces about newswriting as compared to other forms of nonfiction writing?
- How might this piece be written differently if Grady had done it for a science magazine? For a book on in vitro fertilization?

Activities

- Write a newspaper column on a subject of importance to readers on which you are an authority or can become an authority. Submit it to a campus or local newspaper.
- Choose a complicated subject you know or care about and use Grady's techniques to write about it.
- Choose a subject you and your readers need to know about and list the places where you can get information on it.
- Go through one of your drafts and see if there are places where the reader needs a definition woven into the text.
- Go through a draft of your own and list the questions the readers will ask in the margin. Answer them.

To Collaborate

- Split the job up and each research both sides of a controversial issue, then draft a text combining both points of view.
- Work together to write a position paper opposing what Grady said.

Lewis Thomas

Dr. Lewis Thomas, President of the Memorial Sloan-Kettering Cancer Center in New York City, is a distinguished scientist whose collections of essays have won national awards and made him a best-seller. In this short essay he writes in the same territory as Grady from his own perspective.

On Embryology

1   A short while ago, in mid-1978, the newest astonishment in medicine, covering all the front pages, was the birth of an English baby nine months after conception in a dish. The older surprise, which should still be fazing us all, is that a solitary sperm and a single egg can fuse and become a human being under any circumstance, and that, however implanted, a mere cluster of the progeny of this fused cell affixed to the uterine wall will grow and differentiate into eight pounds of baby; this has been going on under our eyes for so long a time that we've gotten used to it; hence the outcries of amazement at this really minor technical modification of the general procedure—nothing much, really, beyond relocating the beginning of the process from the fallopian tube to a plastic container and, perhaps worth mentioning, the exclusion of the father from any role likely to add, with any justification, to his vanity.

2   There is, of course, talk now about extending the technology beyond the act of conception itself, and predictions are being made that the whole process of embryonic development, all nine months of it, will ultimately be conducted in elaborate plastic flasks. When this happens, as perhaps it will someday, it will be another surprise, with more headlines. Everyone will say how marvelously terrifying is the new power of science, and arguments over whether science should be stopped in its tracks will preoccupy senatorial subcommittees, with more headlines. Meanwhile, the sheer incredibility of the process itself, whether it occurs in the uterus or *in* some sort of vitro, will probably be overlooked as much as it is today.

❨ It is instructive to follow how Thomas develops his idea and the way he uses specific images to allow us to see the wonders to which he is calling our attention. ❩

3   For the real amazement, if you want to be amazed, is the process. You start out as a single cell derived from the coupling of a sperm and an egg, this divides into two, then four, then eight, and so on, and at a certain stage there emerges a single cell which will have as all its progeny the human brain. The mere existence of that cell should be one of the great astonishments of the earth. People ought to be walking around all day, all through their waking hours,

calling to each other in endless wonderment, talking of nothing except that cell. It is an unbelievable thing, and yet there it is, popping neatly into its place amid the jumbled cells of every one of the several billion human embryos around the planet, just as if it were the easiest thing in the world to do.

4   If you like being surprised, there's the source. One cell is switched on to become the whole trillion-cell, massive apparatus for thinking and imagining and, for that matter, being surprised. All the information needed for learning to read and write, playing the piano, arguing before senatorial subcommittees, walking across a street through traffic, or the marvelous human act of putting out one hand and leaning against a tree, is contained in that first cell. All of grammar, all syntax, all arithmetic, all music.

5   It is not known how the switching on occurs. At the very beginning of an embryo, when it is still nothing more than a cluster of cells, all of this information and much more is latent inside every cell in the cluster. When the stem cell for the brain emerges, it could be that the special quality of brainness is simply switched on. But it could as well be that everything else, every other potential property, is switched off, so that this most specialized of all cells no longer has its precursors' option of being a thyroid or a liver or whatever, only a brain.

6   No one has the ghost of an idea how this works, and nothing else in life can ever be so puzzling. If anyone does succeed in explaining it, within my lifetime, I will charter a skywriting airplane, maybe a whole fleet of them, and send them aloft to write one great exclamation point after another, around the whole sky, until all my money runs out.

Discussion

- To me, this piece of writing defines the essay, a form of writing in which the writer thinks about a subject and invites the reader to think as well. Discuss the qualities of an essay and consider how an argument, for example, differs from an essay. Discuss what other pieces in the book might be called essays, and why.
- Compare how the Thomas essay differs from Selzer's, from Grady's, from Freda's.
- Consider how the Thomas piece is similar to Trillin and White.
- Discuss how Thomas makes complicated matters clear.
- Discuss how important Thomas' voice is in the piece. Identify examples of that voice. Imagine how the piece might have been written by Jean Shepherd.

Activities

- Write a short essay making readers aware of the wonderment of something in their life, being as specific as Thomas.

- Look at one of your drafts and imagine what Thomas might say about it. See if what he says makes sense and improves the draft.
- In a piece of writing explain why you feel strongly about something in such a way that the reader will feel strongly too.
- Redraft Thomas' piece as the introduction to a proposal for research funding in embryology.
- Use Thomas' words to make a short poem from his piece.

To Collaborate

- Write a memo as publishing company editors, specifically suggesting how Thomas' piece could be developed into a book.
- Write a memo for technical writers explaining what the Thomas piece has to teach them.

William L. Laurence

I remember how excited I was when I met William L. Laurence of *The New York Times*. I was a young editorial writer, writing pieces on science and the military, and here was the dean of science writers, the journalist who had been chosen to be allowed behind the scenes of the creation of atomic power and its terrible weapons. What do I remember of the meeting? Not much. He seemed a shy man who was obviously a good observer and a good listener, the sort of ordinary man with whom you'd like to talk, a person who would nod and grunt in delight at your explanations. He was like other journalists I know who are reprinted in this book—Scanlan, Quindlen, Clark, and Grady—the kind of person who would sit beside you on a long plane flight, and after you got off the plane, you realized how much you talked and how much your companion seemed to enjoy your talking. As you read the article below, note how much Laurence has observed and how well he must have listened to deliver the information he had to report to the world.

Atomic Bombing of Nagasaki Told by Flight Member

1   With the Atomic Bomb Mission to Japan, Aug. 9 [1945] (Delayed)—We are on our way to bomb the mainland of Japan. Our flying contingent consists of three specially designed B-29 "Superforts," and two of these carry no bombs. But our lead plane is on its way with another atomic bomb, the second in three days, concentrating in its active substance an explosive energy equivalent to 10,000 and, under favorable conditions, 40,000 tons of TNT.

❧ This is simply not a great example of a news lead. It backs into the story and is rather clumsy, but remember that the dropping of the bomb has been announced. This is the story of the flight to drop the bomb. Laurence was not expected to be a great prose stylist. He was expected to report complex stories with clarity and accuracy. ☙

2   We have several chosen targets. One of these is the great industrial and shipping center of Nagasaki on the western shore of Kyushu, one of the main islands of the Japanese homeland.

3   I watched the assembly of this man-made meteor during the past two days, and was among the small group of scientists and Army and Navy representatives privileged to be present at the ritual of its loading in the "Superfort" last night, against a background of threatening black skies torn open at intervals by great lightning flashes.

4   It is a thing of beauty to behold, this "gadget." In its design went millions of man-hours of what is without doubt the most concentrated intellectual effort in history. Never before had so much brainpower been focused on a single problem.

❧ Note the tone of voice, which may be offensive now but may have been appropriate in wartime. At one moment he is objective and then he uses words such as *beauty*. Note the description of the natural thunderstorm. Be aware of the context in which this story was written; a war was being fought in which Americans were being killed. Now we can question the dropping of the bomb in the context of history, a perspective we did not have in 1945. ☙

5   This atomic bomb is different from the bomb used three days ago with such devastating results on Hiroshima.

6   I saw the atomic substance before it was placed inside the bomb. By itself it is not at all dangerous to handle. It is only under certain conditions, produced in the bomb assembly, that it can be made to yield up its energy, and even then it gives only a small fraction of its total contents—a fraction, however, large enough to produce the greatest explosion on earth.

7   The briefing at midnight revealed the extreme care and the tremendous amount of preparation that had been made to take care of every detail of the mission, to make certain that the atomic bomb fully served the purpose for which it was intended. Each target in turn was shown in detailed maps and in aerial photographs. Every detail of the course was rehearsed—navigation, altitude, weather, where to land in emergencies. It came out that the Navy had submarines and rescue craft, known as Dumbos and Superdumbos, stationed at various strategic points in the vicinity of the targets, ready to rescue the fliers in case they were forced to bail out.

8   The briefing period ended with a moving prayer by the chaplain. We then proceeded to the mess hall for the traditional early morning breakfast before departure on a bombing mission. . . .

In Storm Soon After Take-off

9   We took off at 3:50 this morning and headed northwest on a straight line for the Empire. The night was cloudy and threatening, with only a few stars here and there breaking through the overcast. The weather report had predicted storms ahead part of the way but clear sailing for the final and climactic stages of our odyssey.

10   We were about an hour away from our base when the storm broke. Our great ship took some heavy dips through the abysmal darkness around us but it took these dips much more gracefully than a large commerical airliner, producing a sensation more in the nature of a glide than a "bump," like a great ocean liner riding the waves, except that in this case the air waves were much higher and the rhythmic tempo of the glide much faster.

11   I noticed a strange eerie light coming through the window high above the navigator's cabin and as I peered through the dark all around us I saw a startling phenomenon. The whirling giant propellers had somehow become great luminous disks of blue flame. The same luminous blue flame appeared on the plexiglass windows in the nose of the ship, and on the tips of the giant wings it looked as though we were riding the whirlwind through space on a chariot of blue fire.

12   It was, I surmised, a surcharge of static electricity that had accumulated on the tips of the propellers and on the di-electric material in the plastic windows. One's thoughts dwelt anxiously on the precious cargo in the invisible ship ahead of us. Was there any likelihood of danger that this heavy electric tension in the atmosphere all about us might set it off?

13   I expressed my fears to Captain Bock, who seems nonchalant and imperturbed at the controls. He quickly reassures me.

14   "It is a familiar phenomenon seen often on ships. I have seen it many times on bombing missions. It is known as St. Elmo's Fire."

15   On we went through the night. We soon rode out the storm and our ship was once again sailing on a smooth course straight ahead, on a direct line to the Empire.

16   Our altimeter showed that we were traveling through space at a height of 17,000 feet. The thermometer registered an outside temperature of 33 degrees below zero centigrade; about 30 below Fahrenheit. Inside our pressurized cabin the temperature was that of a comfortable air-conditioned room, and a pressure corresponding to an altitude of 8,000 feet. Captain Bock cautioned me, however, to keep my oxygen mask handy in case of emergency. This, he explained, might mean either something going wrong with the pressure equipment inside the ship or a hole through the cabin by flak.

17   The first signs of dawn came shortly after 5 o'clock. Sergeant Curry, who had been listening steadily on his earphones for radio reports, while maintaining a strict radio silence himself, greeted it by rising to his feet and gazing out the window.

18   "It's good to see the day," he told me. "I get the feeling of claustrophobia hemmed in in this cabin at night."

19   He is a typical American youth, looking even younger than his 20 years. It takes no mind-reader to read his thoughts.

20   "It's a long way from Hooperston, Ill.," I find myself remarking.

21   "Yep," he replies, as he busies himself decoding a message from outer space.

22   "Think this atomic bomb will end the war?" he asks hopefully.

23   "There is a very good chance that this one may do the trick," I assure him, "but if not, then the next one or two surely will. Its power is such that no nation can stand up against it very long."

24   This was not my own view. I had heard it expressed all around a few hours earlier, before we took off. To anyone who had seen this man-made fireball in action, as I had less than a month ago in the desert of New Mexico, this view did not sound overoptimistic.

25   By 5:50 it was real light outside. We had lost our lead ship, but Lieutenant Godfrey, our navigator, informs me that we had arranged for that contingency. We have an assembly point in the sky above the little island of Hakoshima, southeast of Kyushu, at 9:10. We are to circle there and wait for the rest of our formation.

26   Our genial bombardier, Lieutenant Levy, comes over to invite me to take his front-row seat in the transparent nose of the ship and I accept eagerly. From that vantage point in space, 17,000 feet above the Pacific, one gets a view of hundreds of miles on all sides, horizontally and vertically. At that height the vast ocean below and the sky above seem to merge into one great sphere.

❧ Do you thing *genial* is used ironically? I think not, but I may be wrong. I don't think it was read ironically then, but it would be today. ❧

27   I was on the inside of that firmament, riding above the giant mountains of white cumulus clouds, letting myself be suspended in infinite space. One hears the whirl of the motors behind one, but it soon becomes insignificant against the immensity all around and is before long swallowed by it. There comes a point where space also swallows time and one lives through eternal moments filled with an oppressive loneliness, as though all life had suddenly vanished from the earth and you are the only one left, a lone survivor traveling endlessly through interplanetary space.

28   My mind soon returns to the mission I am on. Somewhere beyond these vast mountains of white clouds ahead of me there lies Japan, the land of our enemy. In about four hours from now one of its cities, making weapons of war for use against us, will be wiped off the map by the greatest weapon ever made by man. In one-tenth of a millionth of a second, a fraction of time immeasurable by any clock, a whirlwind from the skies will pulverize thousands of its buildings and tens of thousands of its inhabitants.

29   Our weather planes ahead of us are on their way to find out where the wind blows. Half an hour before target time we will know what the winds have decided.

30   Does one feel any pity or compassion for the poor devils about to die? Not when one thinks of Pearl Harbor and the Death March on Bataan.

> ❡ Here Laurence anticipates a reader's question and answers it in a wartime context. ❡

31   Captain Bock informs me that we are about to start our climb to bombing altitude.

32   He manipulates a few knobs on his control panel to the right of him and I alternately watch the white clouds and ocean below me and the altimeter on the bombardier's panel. We reached our altitude at 9 o'clock. We were then over Japanese waters, close to their mainland. Lieutenant Godfrey motioned to me to look through his radar scope. Before me was the outline of our assembly point. We shall soon meet our lead ship and proceed to the final stage of our journey.

33   We reached Hakoshima at 9:12 and there, about 4,000 feet ahead of us, was The Great Artiste with its precious load. I saw Lieutenant Godfrey and Sergeant Curry strap on their parachutes and I decided to do likewise.

34   We started circling. We saw little towns on the coastline, heedless of our presence. We kept on circling, waiting for the third ship in our formation.

35   It was 9:56 when we began heading for the coastline. Our weather scouts had sent us code messages, deciphered by Sergeant Curry, informing us that both the primary target as well as the secondary were clearly visible.

36   The winds of destiny seemed to favor certain Japanese cities that must remain nameless. We circled about them again and again and found no opening in the thick umbrella of clouds that covered them. Destiny chose Nagasaki as the ultimate target.

37   We had been circling for some time when we noticed black puffs of smoke coming through the white clouds directly ahead of us. There were fifteen bursts of flak in rapid succession, all too low. Captain Bock changed his course. There soon followed eight more bursts of flak, right up to our altitude, but by this time were too far to the left.

38   We flew southward down the channel and at 11:33 crossed the coastline and headed straight for Nagasaki about 100 miles to the west. Here again we circled until we found an opening in the clouds. It was 12:01 and the goal of our mission had arrived.

39   We heard the prearranged signal on our radio, put on our arc-welder's glasses and watched tensely the maneuverings of the strike ship about half a mile in front of us.

40   "There she goes!" someone said.

41   Out of the belly of The Great Artiste what looked like a black object went downward.

42   Captain Bock swung around to get out of range; but even though we were turning away in the opposite direction, and despite the fact that it was broad daylight in our cabin, all of us became aware of a giant flash that broke through the dark barrier of our arc-welder's lenses and flooded our cabin with intense light.

43   We removed our glasses after the first flash, but the light still lingered on, a bluish-green light that illuminated the entire sky all around. A tremendous blast wave struck our ship and made it tremble from nose to tail. This was followed by four more blasts in rapid succession, each resounding like the boom of cannon fire hitting our plane from all directions.

 ❦ It is Laurence's job to report on what was going on in the plane: Someone else's job to report what was happening on the ground. Do you agree? ❧

44   Observers in the tail of our ship saw a giant ball of fire rise as though from the bowels of the earth, belching forth enormous white smoke rings. Next they saw a giant pillar of purple fire, 10,000 feet high, shooting skyward with enormous speed.

45   By the time our ship had made another turn in the direction of the atomic explosion the pillar of purple fire had reached the level of our altitude. Only about forty-five seconds had passed. Awestruck, we watched it shoot upward like a meteor coming from the earth instead of from outer space, becoming ever more alive as it climbed skyward through the white clouds. It was no longer smoke, or dust, or even a cloud of fire. It was a living thing, a new species of being, born right before our incredulous eyes.

46   At one stage of its evolution, covering millions of years in terms of seconds, the entity assumed the form of a giant square totem pole, with its base about three miles long, tapering off to about a mile at the top. Its bottom was brown, its center was amber, its top white. But it was a living totem pole, carved with many grotesque masks grimacing at the earth.

47   Then, just when it appeared as though the thing had settled down into a state of permanence, there came shooting out of the top a giant mushroom that increased the height of the pillar to a total of 45,000 feet. The mushroom top was even more alive than the pillar, seething and boiling in a white fury of creamy foam, sizzling upward and then descending earthward, a thousand Old Faithful geysers rolled into one.

48   It kept struggling in an elemental fury, like a creature in the act of breaking the bonds that held it down. In a few seconds it had freed itself from its gigantic stem and floated upward with tremendous speed, its momentum carrying into the stratosphere to a height of about 60,000 feet.

49   But no sooner did this happen when another mushroom, smaller in size than the first one, began emerging out of the pillar. It was as though the decapitated monster was growing a new head.

50   As the first mushroom floated off into the blue it changed its shape into a flowerlike form, its giant petal curving downward, creamy white outside, rose-

colored inside. It still retained that shape when we last gazed at it from a distance of about 200 miles.

Discussion

- What other evidence is there of the wartime context in which this piece was written and read?
- Take a piece from the morning newspaper and show how it reveals its context. Discuss how it might appear 40 or 50 years later.
- Take an article written in class that is not a news story. Discuss how it reveals context.
- What obligations does the writer have to be aware of context?
- Discuss how the reader's context changes the way the same piece of writing may be read. How is this story read by a pacifist and a soldier, a Japanese and an American, an anti-Bomb demonstrator and a pro-Bomb activist, a veteran and a civilian, a German or a Russian or a citizen of the Third World, someone 65 years old and someone 19 years old?
- Discuss how Laurence makes complicated information clear.
- Consider how narrative is used in this story. What does it do for the writer and the reader? What are its dangers?

Activities

- Do a similiar story by riding an ambulance, a police car, a tugboat, a train, a ferry, reporting on what happened in narrative form. Write it in another form.
- Take a story of your own or of a classmate and mark the spots where the context of the story is revealed.
- Write an explanation of a complicated technical subject for a nontechnical reader.
- Take a news story or one of your own pieces of writing and write it in a different context: from the point of view of a different person, a different place, a different time.

To Collaborate

- Each take one side of the issue of whether we should or should not have dropped the Bomb and use material from this article to document each case.
- Write a position paper showing the strengths and weaknesses of a news story written about a major event in history.

John Hersey

When I heard an atomic bomb had been dropped on Japan, I was delighted. Of course I didn't know what it was—just another big bomb—but I was in the paratroops in combat in Europe where 90 percent of our division had been killed or wounded. We had seen so much of bullets and bombs and rockets and grenades and shells and flamethrowers we could not be shocked by any other way man could dream up to kill each other. And we were scheduled to go to the Pacific and jump into Tokyo.

Even after we marched in the Victory Parade in New York and were discharged, and read stories such as the one by William Laurence published on page 396, few veterans had any idea that there was anything special about the atomic bomb. I went back to college and one night a group of us met for a regular meeting of a literary club at the home of Professor Carroll Towle, and without much introduction he started reading the entire issue of *The New Yorker* to us. I was appalled at that idea, but within paragraphs, I was caught up in the text of John Hersey's *Hiroshima,* which was later published as a book. Hersey is a major journalist and novelist, but I can't imagine anything he could write that would be more important than this article. The editor of *The New Yorker* felt that it was important enough to toss everything else out and devote an entire issue to it. The text proves writers *can* make a difference, and Hersey's report was really the beginning of our education to the meaning of the atomic age, an education that is still going on today. We have reprinted the first part of the book, which catches that second when our world was forever changed.

A Noiseless Flash

1   At exactly fifteen minutes past eight in the morning, on August 6, 1945, Japanese time, at the moment when the atomic bomb flashed above Hiroshima, Miss Toshiko Sasaki, a clerk in the personnel department of the East Asia Tin Works, had just sat down at her place in the plant office and was turning her head to speak to the girl at the next desk. At that same moment, Dr. Masakazu Fujii was settling down crosslegged to read the Osaka *Asahi* on the porch of his private hospital, overhanging one of the seven deltaic rivers which divide Hiroshima; Mrs. Hatsuyo Nakamura, a tailor's widow, stood by the window of her kitchen, watching a neighbor tearing down his house because it lay in the path of an air-raid-defense fire lane; Father Wilhelm Kleinsorge, a German priest of the Society of Jesus, reclined in his underwear on a cot on the top floor of his order's three-story mission house, reading a Jesuit magazine, *Stimmen der Zeit;* Dr. Terufumi Sasaki, a young member of the surgical staff of the city's large,

modern Red Cross Hospital, walked along one of the hospital corridors with a blood specimen for a Wassermann test in his hand; and the Reverend Mr. Kiyoshi Tanimoto, pastor of the Hiroshima Methodist Church, paused at the door of a rich man's house in Koi, the city's western suburb, and prepared to unload a handcart full of things he had evacuated from town in fear of the massive B-29 raid which everyone expected Hiroshima to suffer. A hundred thousand people were killed by the atomic bomb, and these six were among the survivors. They still wonder why they lived when so many others died. Each of them counts many small items of chance or volition—a step taken in time, a decision to go indoors, catching one streetcar instead of the next—that spared him. And now each knows that in the act of survival he lived a dozen lives and saw more death than he ever thought he would see. At the time, none of them knew anything.

2   The Reverend Mr. Tanimoto got up at five o'clock that morning. He was alone in the parsonage, because for some time his wife had been commuting with their year-old baby to spend nights with a friend in Ushida, a suburb to the north. Of all the important cities of Japan, only two, Kyoto and Hiroshima, had not been visited in strength by *B-san,* or Mr. B, as the Japanese, with a mixture of respect and unhappy familiarity, called the B-29; and Mr. Tanimoto, like all his neighbors and friends, was almost sick with anxiety. He had heard uncomfortably detailed accounts of mass raids on Kure, Iwakuni, Tokuyama, and other nearby towns; he was sure Hiroshima's turn would come soon. He had slept badly the night before, because there had been several air-raid warnings. Hiroshima had been getting such warnings almost every night for weeks, for at that time the B-29s were using Lake Biwa, northeast of Hiroshima, as a rendezvous point, and no matter what city the Americans planned to hit, the Superfortresses streamed in over the coast near Hiroshima. The frequency of the warnings and the continued abstinence of Mr. B. with respect to Hiroshima had made its citizens jittery; a rumor was going around that the Americans were saving something special for the city.

3   Mr. Tanimoto is a small man, quick to talk, laugh, and cry. He wears his black hair parted in the middle and rather long; the prominence of the frontal bones just above his eyebrows and the smallness of his mustache, mouth, and chin give him a strange, old-young look, boyish and yet wise, weak and yet fiery. He moves nervously and fast, but with a restraint which suggests that he is a cautious, thoughtful man. He showed, indeed, just those qualities in the uneasy days before the bomb fell. Besides having his wife spend the nights in Ushida, Mr. Tanimoto had been carrying all the portable things from his church, in the close-packed residential district called Nagaragawa, to a house that belonged to a rayon manufacturer in Koi, two miles from the center of town. The rayon man, a Mr. Matsui, had opened his then unoccupied estate to a large number of his friends and acquaintances, so that they might evacuate whatever they wished to a safe distance from the probable target area. Mr. Tanimoto had had no difficulty in moving chairs, hymnals, bibles, altar gear, and church records by pushcart himself, but the organ console and an upright piano required some

aid. A friend of his named Matsuo had, the day before, helped him get the piano out to Koi; in return, he had promised this day to assist Mr. Matsuo in hauling out a daughter's belongings. That is why he had risen so early.

4   Mr. Tanimoto cooked his own breakfast. He felt awfully tired. The effort of moving the piano the day before, a sleepless night, weeks of worry and unbalanced diet, the cares of his parish—all combined to make him feel hardly adequate to the new day's work. There was another thing, too; Mr. Tanimoto had studied theology at Emory College, in Atlanta, Georgia; he had graduated in 1940; he spoke excellent English; he dressed in American clothes; he had corresponded with many American friends right up to the time the war began; and among a people obsessed with a fear of being spied upon—perhaps almost obsessed himself—he found himself growing increasingly uneasy. The police had questioned him several times, and just a few days before, he had heard that an influential acquaintance, a Mr. Tanaka, a retired officer of the Toyo Kisen Kaisha steamship line, an anti-Christian, a man famous in Hiroshima for his showy philanthropies and notorious for his personal tryannies, had been telling people that Tanimoto should not be trusted. In compensation, to show himself publicly a good Japanese, Mr. Tanimoto had taken on the chairmanship of his local *tonarigumi,* or Neighborhood Association, and to his other duties and concerns this position had added the business of organizing air-raid defense for about twenty families.

5   Before six o'clock that morning, Mr. Tanimoto started for Mr. Matsuo's house. There he found that their burden was to be a *tansu,* a large Japanese cabinet, full of clothing and household goods. The two men set out. The morning was perfectly clear and so warm that the day promised to be uncomfortable. A few minutes after they started, the air-raid siren went off—a minute-long blast that warned of approaching planes but indicated to the people of Hiroshima only a slight degree of danger, since it sounded every morning at this time, when an American weather plane came over. The two men pulled and pushed the handcart through the city streets. Hiroshima was a fan-shaped city, lying mostly on the six islands formed by the seven estuarial rivers that branch out from the Ota River; its main commercial and residential districts, covering about four square miles in the center of the city, contained three-quarters of its population, which had been reduced by several evacuation programs from a wartime peak of 380,000 to about 245,000. Factories and other residential districts, or suburbs, lay compactly around the edges of the city. To the south were the docks, an airport, and the island-studded Inland Sea. A rim of mountains runs around the other three sides of the delta. Mr. Tanimoto and Mr. Matsuo took their way through the shopping center, already full of people, and across two of the rivers to the sloping streets of Koi, and up them to the outskirts and foothills. As they started up a valley away from the tight-ranked houses, the all-clear sounded. (The Japanese radar operators, detecting only three planes, supposed that they comprised a reconnaissance.) Pushing the handcart up to the rayon man's house was tiring, and the men, after they had maneuvered their load into the driveway and to the front steps, paused to rest awhile. They stood

with a wing of the house between them and the city. Like most homes in this part of Japan, the house consisted of a wooden frame and wooden walls supporting a heavy tile roof. Its front hall, packed with rolls of bedding and clothing, looked like a cool cave full of fat cushions. Opposite the house, to the right of the front door, there was a large, finicky rock garden. There was no sound of planes. The morning was still; the place was cool and pleasant.

6   Then a tremendous flash of light cut across the sky. Mr. Tanimoto has a distinct recollection that it travelled from east to west, from the city toward the hills. It seemed a sheet of sun. Both he and Mr. Matsuo reacted in terror—and both had time to react (for they were 3,500 yards, or two miles, from the center of the explosion). Mr. Matsuo dashed up the front steps into the house and dived among the bedrolls and buried himself there. Mr. Tanimoto took four or five steps and threw himself between two big rocks in the garden. He bellied up very hard against one of them. As his face was against the stone, he did not see what happened. He felt a sudden pressure, and then splinters and pieces of board and fragments of tile fell on him. He heard no roar. (Almost no one in Hiroshima recalls hearing any noise of the bomb. But a fisherman in his sampan on the Inland Sea near Tsuzu, the man with whom Mr. Tanimoto's mother-in-law and sister-in-law were living, saw the flash and heard a tremendous explosion; he was nearly twenty miles from Hiroshima, but the thunder was greater than when the B-29s hit Iwakuni, only five miles away.

7   When he dared, Mr. Tanimoto raised his head and saw that the rayon man's house had collapsed. He thought a bomb had fallen directly on it. Such clouds of dust had risen that there was a sort of twilight around. In panic, not thinking for the moment of Mr. Matsuo under the ruins, he dashed out into the street. He noticed as he ran that the concrete wall of the estate had fallen over—toward the house rather than away from it. In the street, the first thing he saw was a squad of soldiers who had been burrowing into the hillside opposite, making one of the thousands of dugouts in which the Japanese apparently intended to resist invasion, hill by hill, life for life; the soldiers were coming out of the hole, where they should have been safe, and blood was running from their heads, chests, and backs. They were silent and dazed.

8   Under what seemed to be a local dust cloud, the day grew darker and darker.

9   At nearly midnight, the night before the bomb was dropped, an announcer on the city's radio station said that about two hundred B-29s were approaching southern Honshu and advised the population of Hiroshima to evacuate to their designated "safe areas." Mrs. Hatsuyo Nakamura, the tailor's widow, who lived in the section called Nobori-cho and who had long had a habit of doing as she was told, got her three children—a ten-year-old boy, Toshio, an eight-year-old girl, Yaeko, and a five-year-old girl, Myeko—out of bed and dressed them and walked with them to the military area known as the East Parade Ground, on the northeast edge of the city. There she unrolled some mats and the children

lay down on them. They slept until about two, when they were awakened by the roar of the planes going over Hiroshima.

10   As soon as the planes had passed, Mrs. Nakamura started back with her children. They reached home a little after two-thirty and she immediately turned on the radio, which to her distress, was just then broadcasting a fresh warning. When she looked at the children and saw how tired they were, and when she thought of the number of trips they had made in past weeks, all to no purpose, to the East Parade Ground, she decided that in spite of the instructions on the radio, she simply could not face starting out all over again. She put the children in their bedrolls on the floor, lay down herself at three o'clock and fell asleep at once, so soundly that when planes passed over later, she did not waken to their sound.

11   The siren jarred her awake at about seven. She arose, dressed quickly, and hurried to the house of Mr. Nakamoto, the head of her Neighborhood Association, and asked him what she should do. He said that she should remain at home unless an urgent warning—a series of intermittent blasts of the siren—was sounded. She returned home, lit the stove in the kitchen, set some rice to cook, and sat down to read that morning's Hiroshima *Chugoku*. To her relief, the all-clear sounded at eight o'clock. She heard the children stirring, so she went and gave each of them a handful of peanuts and told them to stay on their bedrolls, because they were tired from the night's walk. She had hoped that they would go back to sleep, but the man in the house directly to the south began to make a terrible hullabaloo of hammering, wedging, ripping, and splitting. The prefectural government, convinced, as everyone in Hiroshima was, that the city would be attacked soon, had begun to press with threats and warnings for the completion of wide fire lanes, which, it was hoped, might act in conjunction with the rivers to localize any fires started by an incendiary raid; and the neighbor was reluctantly sacrificing his home to the city's safety. Just the day before, the prefecture had ordered all able-bodied girls from the secondary schools to spend a few days helping to clear these lanes, and they started work soon after the all-clear sounded.

12   Mrs. Nakamura went back to the kitchen, looked at the rice, and began watching the man next door. At first, she was annoyed with him for making so much noise, but then she was moved almost to tears by pity. Her emotion was specifically directed toward her neighbor, tearing down his home, board by board, at a time when there was so much unavoidable destruction, but undoubtedly she also felt a generalized, community pity, to say nothing of self-pity. She had not had an easy time. Her husband, Isawa, had gone into the Army just after Myeko was born, and she had heard nothing from or of him for a long time, until, on March 5, 1942, she received a seven-word telegram: "Isawa died an honorable death at Singapore." She learned later that he had died on February 15th, the day Singapore fell, and that he had been a corporal. Isawa had been a not particularly prosperous tailor, and his only capital was a Sankoku sewing machine. After his death, when his allotments stopped coming, Mrs.

Nakamura got out the machine and began to take in piecework herself, and since then had supported the children, but poorly, by sewing.

13   As Mrs. Nakamura stood watching her neighbor, everything flashed whiter than any white she had ever seen. She did not notice what happened to the man next door; the reflex of a mother set her in motion toward her children. She had taken a single step (the house was 1,350 yards, or three-quarters of a mile, from the center of the explosion) when something picked her up and she seemed to fly into the next room over the raised sleeping platform, pursued by parts of her house.

14   Timbers fell around her as she landed, and a shower of tiles pommelled her; everything became dark, for she was buried. The debris did not cover her deeply. She rose up and freed herself. She heard a child cry, "Mother, help me!" and saw her youngest—Myeko, the five-year-old—buried up to her breast and unable to move. As Mrs. Nakamura started frantically to claw her way toward the baby, she could see or hear nothing of her other children.

15   In the days right before the bombing, Dr. Masakazu Fujii, being prosperous, hedonistic, and at the time not too busy, had been allowing himself the luxury of sleeping until nine or nine-thirty, but fortunately he had to get up early the morning the bomb was dropped to see a house guest off on a train. He rose at six, and half an hour later walked with his friend to the station, not far away, across two of the rivers. He was back home by seven, just as the siren sounded its sustained warning. He ate breakfast and then, because the morning was already hot, undressed down to his underwear and went out on the porch to read the paper. This porch—in fact, the whole building—was curiously constructed. Dr. Fujii was the proprietor of a peculiarly Japanese institution: a private, single-doctor hospital. This building, perched beside and over the water of the Kyo River, and next to the bridge of the same name, contained thirty rooms for thirty patients and their kinfolk—for, according to Japanese custom, when a person falls sick and goes to a hospital, one or more members of his family go and live there with him, to cook for him, bathe, massage, and read to him, and to offer incessant familial sympathy, without which a Japanese patient would be miserable indeed. Dr. Fujii had no beds—only straw mats—for his patients. He did, however, have all sorts of modern equipment: an X-ray machine, diathermy apparatus, and a fine tiled laboratory. The structure rested two-thirds on the land, one-third on piles over the tidal waters of the Kyo. This overhang, the part of the building where Dr. Fujii lived, was queer-looking, but it was cool in summer and from the porch, which faced away from the center of the city, the prospect of the river, with pleasure boats drifting up and down it, was always refreshing. Dr. Fujii had occasionally had anxious moments when the Ota and its mouth branches rose to flood, but the piling was apparently firm enough and the house had always held.

16   Dr. Fujii had been relatively idle for about a month because in July, as the number of untouched cities in Japan dwindled and as Hiroshima seemed more

and more inevitably a target, he began turning patients away, on the ground that in case of a fire raid he would not be able to evacuate them. Now he had only two patients left—a woman from Yano, injured in the shoulder, and a young man of twenty-five recovering from burns he had suffered when the steel factory near Hiroshima in which he worked had been hit. Dr. Fujii had six nurses to tend his patients. His wife and children were safe; his wife and one son were living outside Osaka, and another son and two daughters were in the country on Kyushu. A niece was living with him, and a maid and a manservant. He had little to do and did not mind, for he had saved some money. At fifty, he was healthy, convivial, and calm, and he was pleased to pass the evenings drinking whiskey with friends, always sensibly and for the sake of conversation. Before the war, he had affected brands imported from Scotland and America; now he was perfectly satisfied with the best Japanese brand, Suntory.

17   Dr. Fujii sat down cross-legged in his underwear on the spotless matting of the porch, put on his glasses, and started reading the Osaka *Asahi*. He liked to read the Osaka news because his wife was there. He saw the flash. To him— faced away from the center and looking at his paper—it seemed a brilliant yellow. Startled, he began to rise to his feet. In that moment (he was 1,550 yards from the center), the hospital leaned behind his rising and, with a terrible ripping noise, toppled into the river. The Doctor, still in the act of getting to his feet, was thrown forward and around and over; he was buffeted and gripped; he lost track of everything, because things were so speeded up; he felt the water.

18   Dr. Fujii hardly had time to think that he was dying before he realized that he was alive, squeezed tightly by two long timbers in a V across his chest, like a morsel suspended between two huge chopsticks—held upright, so that he could not move, with his head miraculously above water and his torso and legs in it. The remains of his hospital were all around him in a mad assortment of splintered lumber and materials for the relief of pain. His left shoulder hurt terribly. His glasses were gone. . . .

A Writer's Notes for a Second Reading

Laurence's piece may or may not be objective in your opinion, but Hersey makes no such attempt. Yet his clear argument against atomic war is not made through rhetoric but by simple storytelling, which is simple to read but not so simple to write.

I am struck again by the power of narrative. We learn how people survived and through those almost dispassionate stories feel the horror of the Bomb.

Hersey doesn't tell us how to think or feel or what to think or feel. He gives us an experience that will cause us to think and feel. We might not listen to a sermon against war, but we aren't likely to put down the story of those who survived the worst weapon in the history of man.

He gives us room to react and allows us unspoken trust to react in the way he expects. The more I write, the more I think it important to give the reader room and trust the reader to respond in an appropriate manner.

Discussion

- Compare the Laurence piece written from the bomber with the Hersey piece that reconstructs the scene on the ground. Compare the piece written *during* the war with the one written after the war.
- It often helps to know something of the time in which a piece is written. This piece is very much a 1946 piece of writing, although it hits the reader with great impact today. What were some of the problems Hersey faced in writing *Hiroshima* when he did?
- This is an example of journalism—history written in a hurry. What are some other examples of journalism in the book? What are the advantages and limitations of journalism?
- What are the advantages and disadvantages of the method of focusing on a few individuals that Hersey has chosen?
- What other ways could Hersey have written his article?
- What techniques has Hersey used to make the people sympathetic?
- Is narrative the best way to tell the story? What other choices did Hersey have?
- How is the exposition—the background material you need to know—woven into the article?

Activities

- Write about an individual, catching that person at an important moment.
- Write a page about the Hiroshima bombing without using Hersey's method: a page from a play, a history book, a news story, an editorial, a sermon, a poem, a short story, a government report (from the Japanese government and the U.S. government).
- Rewrite a page from Hersey as it might be written by someone else in the book.
- Interview the survivors of a fire or the victims of a crime to report on the effect of a story reported in the paper.
- Go to the library to see how the Hiroshima bombing was reported in local newspapers. Compare that coverage to Hersey.

To Collaborate

- Write a one-page statement on atomic war using material from Hersey.
- Brainstorm alternate ways that Hersey might have used to tell the story of Hiroshima; decide which ways are best and explain why.

Enrique Hank Lopez

We often make the mistake of taking seriously only those writers who make publishing a career, but each year there are hundreds of writers who publish only a piece or two of writing—an article, a poem, a short story, perhaps a book—then go on to other things. The pieces they publish usually have special authority: they demand to be written. The writers have obvious talent but they do not choose to continue to publish. Such a person was the late Enrique Hank Lopez, a lawyer whose account of his return to Bachimba continues to be reprinted and reread. You should all take comfort in the fact that you do not have to be a writer to write—and to write with such skill that the reader is forced to think and to care.

Back to Bachimba

1   I am a *pocho* from Bachimba, a rather small Mexican village in the state of Chihuahua, where my father fought with the army of Pancho Villa. He was, in fact, the only private in Villa's army.

2   *Pocho* is ordinarily a derogatory term in Mexico (to define it succinctly, a *pocho* is a Mexican slob who has pretensions of being a gringo sonofabitch), but I use it in a very special sense. To me that word has come to mean "uprooted Mexican," and that's what I have been all my life. Though my entire upbringing and education took place in the United States, I have never felt completely American; and when I am in Mexico, I sometimes feel like a displaced gringo with a curiously Mexican name—Enrique Preciliano Lopez y Martinez de Sepulveda de Sapien (—de Quien-sabe-quien). One might conclude that I'm either a schizo-cultural Mexican or a cultured schizoid American.

3   In any event, the schizo-ing began a long time ago, when my father and many of Pancho Villa's troops fled across the border to escape the oncoming *federales* who eventually defeated Villa. My mother and I, traveling across the hot desert plains in a buckboard wagon, joined my father in El Paso, Texas, a few days after his hurried departure. With more and more Villistas swarming into El Paso every day, it was quickly apparent that jobs would be exceedingly scarce and insecure; so my parents packed our few belongings and we took the first available bus to Denver. My father had hoped to move to Chicago because the name sounded so Mexican, but my mother's meager savings were hardly enough to buy tickets for Colorado.

4   There we moved into a ghetto of Spanish-speaking residents who chose to call themselves Spanish-Americans and resented the sudden migration of their brethren from Mexico, whom they sneeringly called *surumatos* (slang for "southerners"). These so-called Spanish-Americans claimed direct descent from the original conquistadores of Spain. They also insisted that they had *never*

been Mexicans, since their region of New Spain (later annexed to the United States) was never a part of Mexico. But what they claimed most vociferously—and erroneously—was an absence of Indian ancestry. It made no difference that any objective observer could see by merely looking at them the results of considerable fraternization between the conquering Spaniards and the Comanche and Navaho women who crossed their paths. Still, these *manitos,* as they were snidely labeled by the *surumatos,* stubbornly refused to be identified with Mexico, and would actually fight anyone who called them Mexican. So intense was this intergroup rivalry that the bitterest "race riots" I have ever witnessed—and engaged in—were between the look-alike, talk-alike *surumatos* and *manitos* who lived near Denver's Curtis Park. In retrospect the harsh conflicts between us were all the more silly and self-defeating when one recalls that we were all lumped together as "spiks" and "greasers" by the Anglo-Saxon community.

5   Predictably enough, we *surumatos* began huddling together in a subneighborhood within the larger ghetto, and it was there that I became painfully aware that my father had been the only private in Pancho Villa's army. Most of my friends were the sons of captains, colonels, majors, and even generals, though a few fathers were admittedly mere sergeants and corporals. My father alone had been a lowly private in that famous Division del Norte. Naturally I developed a most painful complex, which led me to all sorts of compensatory fibs. During one brief spell I fancied my father as a member of the dread *los dorados,* the "golden ones," who were Villa's favorite henchmen. (Later I was to learn that my father's cousin, Martin Lopez, was a genuine and quite notorious *dorado.*) But all my inventions were quickly uninvented by my very own father, who seemed to take a perverse delight in being Pancho's only private.

6   No doubt my chagrin was accentuated by the fact that Pancho Villa's exploits were a constant topic of conversation in our household. My entire childhood seems to be shadowed by his presence. At our dinner table, almost every night, we would listen to endlessly repeated accounts of this battle, that stratagem, or some great act of Robin Hood kindness by *el centauro del norte.* I remember how angry my parents were when they saw Wallace Beery in *Viva Villa!* "Garbage by stupid gringos" they called it. They were particularly offended by the sweaty, unshaven sloppiness of Beery's portrayal. "Pancho Villa was clean and orderly, no matter how much he chased after women. This man's a dirty swine."

7   As if to deepen our sense of *Villismo,* my parents also taught us "Adelita" and *"Se Ilevaron el canon para Bachimba"* ("They took the cannons to Bachimba"), the two most famous songs of the Mexican revolution. Some twenty years later (during my stint at Harvard Law School), while strolling along the Charles River, I would find myself softly singing *"Se Ilevaron el canon para Bachimba, para Bachimba, para Bachimba"* over and over again. That's all I could remember of that poignant rebel song. Though I had been born there, I had always regarded "Bachimba" as a fictitious, made-up, Lewis Carroll kind of word. So that eight years ago, when I first returned to Mexico, I was literally stunned when I came to a crossroad south of Chihuahua and saw an old road

marker: "Bachimba 18 km." Then it really exists—I shouted inwardly—Bachimba is a real town! Swinging onto the narrow, poorly paved road, I gunned the motor and sped toward the town I'd been singing about since infancy. It turned out to be a quiet, dusty village with a bleak worn-down plaza that was surrounded by nondescript buildings of uncertain vintage.

8   Aside from the songs about Bachimba and Adelita and all the folk tales about Villa's guerrilla fighters, my early years were strongly influenced by our neighborhood celebrations of Mexico's two most important patriotic events: Mexican Independence Day on September 16, and the anniversary of the battle of Puebla on May 5. On those two dates Mexicans all over the world are likely to become extremely chauvinistic. In Denver we would stage annual parades that included three or four floats skimpily decorated with crepe-paper streamers, a small band, several adults in thread-bare battle dress, and hundreds of kids marching in wild disorder. It was during one of these parades—I was ten years old then—that I was seized with acute appendicitis and had to be rushed to a hospital. The doctor subsequently told my mother that I had made a long impassioned speech about the early revolutionist Miguel Hidalgo while the anesthetic was taking hold, and she explained with pardonable pride that it was the speech I was to make at Turner Hall that evening. Mine was one of the twenty-three *discursos* scheduled on the postparade program, a copy of which my mother still retains. My only regret was missing the annual *discurso* of Don Miguel Gomez, my godfather, a deep-throated orator who would always climax his speech by falling to his knees and dramatically kissing the floor, almost weeping as he loudly proclaimed: *"Ay, Mexico! Beso tu tierra, tu mero corazon"* ("Ah, Mexico! I kiss your sacred soil, the very heart of you"). He gave the same oration for seventeen years, word for word and gesture for gesture, and it never failed to bring tears to his eyes. But not once did he return to Chihuahua, even for a brief visit.

9   My personal Mexican-ness eventually produced serious problems for me. Upon entering grade school I learned English rapidly and rather well, always ranking either first or second in my class; yet the hard core of me remained stubbornly Mexican. This chauvinism may have been a reaction to the constant racial prejudice we encountered on all sides. The neighborhood cops were always running us off the streets and calling us "dirty greasers," and most of our teachers frankly regarded us as totally inferior. I still remember the galling disdain of my sixth-grade teacher, whose constant mimicking of our heavily accented speech drove me to a desperate study of *Webster's Dictionary* in the hope of acquiring a vocabulary larger than hers. Sadly enough, I succeeded only too well, and for the next few years I spoke the most ridiculous high-flown rhetoric in the Denver public schools. One of my favorite words was "indubitably," and it must have driven everyone mad. I finally got rid of my accent by constantly reciting "Peter Piper picked a peck of pickled peppers" with little round pebbles in my mouth. Somewhere I had read about Demosthenes.

10   During this phase of my childhood the cultural tug of war known as "Americanization" almost pulled me apart. There were moments when I would

identify completely with the gringo world (what could have been more American than my earnest high-voiced portrayal of George Washington, however ridiculous the cotton wig my mother had fashioned for me?); then quite suddenly I would feel so acutely Mexican that I would stammer over the simplest English phrase. I was so ready to take offense at the slightest slur against Mexicans that I would imagine prejudice where none existed. But on other occasions, in full confidence of my belonging, I would venture forth into social areas that I should have realized were clearly forbidden to little *chicanos* from Curtis Park. The inevitable rebuffs would leave me floundering in self-pity; it was small comfort to know that other minority groups suffered even worse rebuffs than we did.

11   The only non-Mexican boy on our street was a negro named Leroy Logan, who was probably my closest childhood friend. Leroy was the best athlete, the best whistler, the best liar, the best horseshoe player, the best marble shooter, the best mumblety-pegger, and the best shoplifter in our neighborhood. He was also my "partner," and I thus entitled myself to a fifty-fifty share of all his large triumphs and petty thefts. Because he considered "Mexican" a derogatory word bordering on obscenity, Leroy would pronounce it "Me sican" so as to soften its harshness. But once in a while, when he'd get angry with me, he would call me a "lousy Me sican greasy spik" with the most extraordinarily effective hissing one can imagine. And I'm embarrassed to admit that I would retaliate by calling him "alligator bait." As a matter of fact, just after I had returned from the hospital, he came to visit me, and I thoughtlessly greeted him with a flippant "Hi, alligator ba—" I never finished the phrase because Leroy whacked me on the stomach with a Ping-Pong paddle and rushed out of my house with great, sobbing anger.

12   Weeks later, when we had re-established a rather cool rapport, I tried to make up for my stupid insult by helping him steal cabbages from the vegetable trucks that rumbled through our neighborhood on their way to the produce markets. They would come down Larimer Street in the early dawn, and Leroy and I would sneak up behind them at the 27th Street stop sign, where they were forced to pause for cross traffic. I would be waiting below to catch them with an open gunny sack. Our system was fabulously successful for a while, and we found a ready market for the stolen goods; but one morning, as I started to unfurl my sack, a fairly large cabbage conked me on the head. Screaming with pain, I lunged at Leroy and tried to bite him. He, laughing all the while—it was obviously a funny scene—glided out of my reach, and finally ran into a nearby alley. We never engaged in commercial affairs thereafter.

13   Still and all, I remember him with great affection and a touch of sadness. I say sadness because eventually Leroy was to suffer the misery of being an outsider in an already outside ghetto. As he grew older, it was apparent that he longed to be a Mexican, that he felt terribly dark and alone. "Sometimes," he would tell me, "I feel like my damn skin's too tight, like I'm gonna bust out of it." One cold February night I found him in the coal shed behind Pacheco's store, desperately scraping his forearm with sandpaper, the hurt tears streaming

down his face. "I got to get this off, man. I can't stand all this blackness." We stood there quietly staring at the floor for a long, anguished moment, both of us miserable beyond word or gesture. Finally he drew a deep breath, blew his nose loudly, and mumbled half audibly, "Man, you sure lucky to be a Me sican."

14   Not long after this incident Leroy moved out of Denver to live with relatives in Georgia. When I saw him off at the bus station, he grabbed my shoulder and whispered huskily, "You gonna miss me, man. You watch what I tellya." "Indubitably," I said. "Aw, man, cut that stuff. You the most fancy-pants Me sican I know." Those were his last words to me, and they caused a considerable dent in my ego. Not enough, however, to diminish my penchant for fancy language. The dictionary continued to be my comic book well into high school.

15   Speaking of language, I am reminded of a most peculiar circumstance: almost every Mexican-American lawyer that I've ever met speaks English with a noticeable Spanish accent, this despite the fact that they have all been born, reared, and educated exclusively in America. Of the forty-eight lawyers I have in mind, only three of us are free of any accent. Needless to say our "cultural drag" has been weighty and persistent. And one must presume that our ethnic hyphens shall be with us for many years to come.

16   My own Mexican-ness, after years of decline at Harvard University, suddenly burst forth again when I returned to Chihuahua and stumbled on the town of Bachimba. I had long conversations with an uncle I'd never met before, my father's younger brother, Ramon. It was Tio Ramon who chilled my spine with eyewitness stories about Pancho Villa's legendary *dorados,* one of whom was Martin Lopez. "He was your second cousin. The bravest young buck in Villa's army. And he became a *dorado* when he was scarcely seventeen years old because he dared to defy Pancho Villa himself. As your papa may have told you, Villa had a bad habit of burying treasure up in the mountains and also burying the man he took with him to dig the hole for it. Well, one day he chose Martin Lopez to go with him. Deep in the mountains they went, near Parral. And when they got to a suitably lonely place, Pancho Villa told him to dig a hole with pick and shovel. Then, when Martin had dug down to his waist, Villa leveled a gun at the boy. "Say your prayers, *muchacho.* You shall stay here with the gold— forever. But Martin had come prepared. In his large right boot he had a gun, and when he rose from his bent position, he was pointing that gun at Villa. They stood there, both ready to fire, for several seconds, and finally Don Pancho started to laugh in that wonderful way of his. "Bravo, bravo, muchacho! You've got more guts than a man. Get out of that hole, boy. I need you for my *dorados.*"

17   Tio Ramon's eyes were wet with pride. "But what is more important, he died with great valor. Two years later, after he had terrorized the *federales* and Pershing's gringo soldiers, he was finally wounded and captured here in Bachimba. It was a bad wound in his leg, finally turning to gangrene. Then one Sunday morning they hauled Martin Lopez and three other prisoners to the plaza. One by one they executed the three lesser prisoners against that wall. I was up on the church tower watching it all. Finally it was your uncle's turn. They dragged him off the buckboard wagon and handed him his crutches.

Slowly, painfully, he hobbled to the wall and stood there. Very straight he stood. 'Do you have any last words?' said the captain of the firing squad. With great pride Martin tossed his crutches aside and stood very tall on his one good leg. 'Give me, you yellow bastards, give me a gun—and I'll show you who is the man among . . .' Eight bullets crashed into his chest and face, and I never heard that final word. That was your second cousin. You would have been proud to know him.''

18   As I listened to Tio Ramon's soft nostalgic voice that evening, there in the sputtering light of the kerosene lamp on his back patio, I felt as intensely Mexican as I shall ever feel.

19   But not for long. Within six weeks I was destined to feel *less* Mexican than I had ever felt. The scene of my trauma was the Centro Mexicano de Escritores, where the finest young writers of Mexico met regularly to discuss works in progress and to engage in erudite literary and philosophical discussions. Week after week I sat among them, dumbstruck by my inadequacy in Spanish and my total ignorance of their whole frame of reference. How could I have possibly imagined that I was Mexican? Those conversations were a dense tangle of local and private allusions, and the few threads I could grasp only magnified my ignorance. The novelist Juan Rulfo was then reading the initial drafts of his *Pedro Paramo,* later to be acclaimed the best avant-garde fiction in Mexican literature. Now that I have soaked myself in the *ambiance* of Mexico, Rulfo's novel intrigues me beyond measure; but when he first read it at the Centro, he might just as well have been reading ''Jabberwocky'' in Swahili for all I understood of it. And because all of the other Mexican writers knew and greatly appreciated *Paramo,* I could only assume that I was really ''too gringo'' to comprehend it. For this reason, I, a person with no great talent for reticence, never opened my mouth at the Centro. In fact, I was so shell-shocked by those sessions that I even found it difficult to converse with my housekeeper about such simple matters as dirty laundry or the loose doorknob in the bathroom.

20   Can any of us really go home again? I, for one, am convinced that I have no true home, that I must reconcile myself to a schizo-cultural limbo, with a mere hyphen to provide some slight cohesion between my split selves. This inevitable splitting is a plague and a pleasure. Some mornings as I glide down the Paseo de la Reforma, perhaps the most beautiful boulevard in the world, I am suddenly angered by the *machismo,* or aggressive maleness, of Mexican drivers who crowd and bully their screeching machines through dense traffic. What terrible insecurity, what awful dread of emasculation, produces such assertive bully-boy conduct behind a steering wheel? Whatever the reasons, there is a part of me that can never accept this much celebrated *machismo.* Nor can I accept the exaggerated nationalism one so frequently encounters in the press, on movie screens, over the radio, in daily conversations—that shrill barrage of slogans proclaiming that ''there is only one Mexico.''

21   Recently, when I expressed these views to an old friend, he smiled knowingly: ''Let's face it, Hank, you're not really a Mexican—despite that long, comical name of yours. You're an American through and through.'' But that, of

course, is a minority view and almost totally devoid of realism. One could just as well say that Martin Luther King is not a Negro, that he's merely an American. But the plain truth is that neither I nor Martin Luther King can escape the fact that we are a Mexican and a Negro whose roots are so deeply planted in the United States that we have grown those strong little hyphens that make us Mexican-American and Negro-American. This assertion may not please some idealists who would prefer to blind themselves to our obvious ethnic and racial differences, who are unwittingly patronizing when they insist that we are all alike and indistinguishable. But the politicians, undoubtedly the most pragmatic creatures in America, are completely aware that ethnic groups *do* exist and that they seem to huddle together, and sometimes vote together.

22 When all is said and done, we hyphenated Americans are here to stay, bubbling happily or unhappily in the great nonmelting pot. Much has been gained and will be gained from the multiethnic aspects of the United States, and there is no useful purpose in attempting to wish it away or to homogenize it out of existence. In spite of the race riots in Watts and ethnic unrest elsewhere, there would appear to be a kind of modus vivendi developing on almost every level of American life.

23 And if there are those of us who may never feel completely at home, we can always make that brief visit to Bachimba.

A Writer's Notes for a Second Reading

Often a piece of writing will make my mind wander and I hear my elementary school teachers trying to get me to concentrate on the teacher's subject. I always feel guilty when my eye wanders, and yet that is the writer's way of life. Writers deal with what is caught out of the corner of the eye, half overheard from the next restaurant booth, what is partially remembered.

Ours is the wandering mind, and so when I read this piece my mind wanders. I think of my own ethnic background, my own family history, my own private alienation within the many worlds in which I have lived.

And of course, the author should be pleased. He has made me think—and perhaps write. That's a greater compliment than if I merely studied his text, always staying on his page.

Discussion

• What problems of clarity face Lopez that are different from ones that faced the writers of the other autobiographical pieces in the book? How does he solve them?

• What is the meaning of this article? What do you think Lopez wanted to say? Do you think he has said it?

• What other ways could Lopez have organized his article to make his meaning clearer?

• What questions did you want Lopez to answer in the piece? Did he answer them? If not, how could he have answered them?

• Are there places where your attention wandered? If so, what could Lopez have done to hold it?

Activities

• Write an article that explores your ethnic background and what it has meant to you.

• Outline the article as Lopez has written it. See how many outlines you can make to organize the article.

• Edit a page of Lopez to improve the text if you can.

• Edit a page of Lopez as it might have been written by the author of another autobiographical piece in the book.

• Write a piece about going back to a place where you used to live.

To Collaborate

• Interview people from other countries to see if their feelings are similar to those of Lopez. Write a collaborative report on your most significant findings.

• Work with a partner to co-edit the piece. Cut, reorder, or indicate what needs to be developed to make the piece clear.

Maxine Hong Kingston

Maxine Hong Kingston's first book, *The Woman Warrior,* became an instant classic when it was published, winning the National Book Critics Award for "the best book of nonfiction published in 1976." Its subtitle was *Memoirs of a Girlhood Among Ghosts* and it was a book that combined the experience of being a Chinese-American with the experience of being a woman, and its prose was woven with a wonderful combination of myth and reality. I can remember reading it sitting in a car, parked on a city street waiting for a member of my family; I can see the brick walls, the crowds on the sidewalk, hear the traffic. Somehow, when the writing or reading goes well it stimulates all my senses and I not only remember what I wrote or read but where and how I felt. *The Woman Warrior* was that kind of a book.

From *The Woman Warrior*

1   We were working at the laundry when a delivery boy came from the Rexall drugstore around the corner. He had a pale blue box of pills, but nobody was sick. Reading the label we saw that it belonged to another Chinese family, Crazy

Mary's family. "Not ours," said my father. He pointed out the name to the Delivery Ghost, who took the pills back. My mother muttered for an hour, and then her anger boiled over. "That ghost! That dead ghost! How dare he come to the wrong house?" She could not concentrate on her marking and pressing. "A mistake! Huh!" I was getting angry myself. She fumed. She made her press crash and hiss. "Revenge. We've got to avenge this wrong on our future, on our health, and on our lives. Nobody's going to sicken my children and get away with it." We brothers and sisters did not look at one another. She would do something awful, something embarrassing. She'd already been hinting that during the next eclipse we slam pot lids together to scare the frog from swallowing the moon. (The word for "eclipse" is *frog-swallowing-the-moon*.) When we had not banged lids at the last eclipse and the shadow kept receding anyway, she'd said, "The villagers must be banging and clanging very loudly back home in China."

2   ("On the other side of the world, they aren't having an eclipse, Mama. That's just a shadow the earth makes when it comes between the moon and the sun."

3   "You're always believing what those Ghost Teachers tell you. Look at the size of the jaws!")

4   "Aha!" she yelled. "You! The biggest." She was pointing at me. "You go to the drugstore."

5   "What do you want me to buy, Mother?" I said.

6   "Buy nothing. Don't bring one cent. Go and make them stop the curse."

7   "I don't want to go. I don't know how to do that. There are no such things as curses. They'll think I'm crazy."

8   "If you don't go, I'm holding you responsible for bringing a plague on this family."

9   "What am I supposed to do when I get there?" I said, sullen, trapped. "Do I say, 'Your delivery boy made a wrong delivery'?"

10   "They know he made a wrong delivery. I want you to make them rectify their crime."

11   I felt sick already. She'd make me swing stinky censers around the counter, at the druggist, at the customers. Throw dog blood on the druggist. I couldn't stand her plans.

12   "You get reparation candy," she said. "You say, 'You have tainted my house with sick medicine and must remove the curse with sweetness.' He'll understand."

13   "He didn't do it on purpose. And no, he won't, Mother. They don't understand stuff like that. I won't be able to say it right. He'll call us beggars."

14   "You just translate." She searched me to make sure I wasn't hiding any money. I was sneaky and bad enough to buy the candy and come back pretending it was a free gift.

15   "Mymotherseztagimmesomecandy," I said to the druggist. Be cute and small. No one hurts the cute and small.

16   "What? Speak up. Speak English," he said, big in his white druggist coat.

17   "Tatatagimme somecandy."

18   The druggist leaned way over the counter and frowned. "Some free candy," I said. "Sample candy."

19   "We don't give sample candy, young lady," he said.

20   "My mother said you have to give us candy. She said that is the way the Chinese do it.

21   "What?"

22   "That is the way the Chinese do it."

23   "Do what?"

24   "Do things." I felt the weight and immensity of things impossible to explain to the druggist.

25   "Can I give you some money?" he asked.

26   "No, we want candy."

27   He reached into a jar and gave me a handful of lollipops. He gave us candy all year round, year after year, every time we went into the drugstore. When different druggists or clerks waited on us, they also gave us candy. They had talked us over. They gave us Halloween candy in December, Christmas candy around Valentine's day, candy hearts at Easter, and Easter eggs at Halloween. "See?" said our mother. "They understand. You kids just aren't very brave." But I knew they did not understand. They thought we were beggars without a home who lived in back of the laundry. They felt sorry for us. I did not eat their candy. I did not go inside the drugstore or walk past it unless my parents forced me to. Whenever we had a prescription filled, the druggist put candy in the medicine bag. This is what Chinese druggists normally do, except they give raisins. My mother thought she taught the Druggist Ghosts a lesson in good manners (which is the same word as "traditions").

28   My mouth went permanently crooked with effort, turned down on the left side and straight on the right. How strange that the emigrant villagers are shouters, hollering face to face. My father asks, "Why is it I can hear Chinese from blocks away? Is it that I understand the language? Or is it they talk loud?" They turn the radio up full blast to hear the operas, which do not seem to hurt their ears. And they yell over the singers that wail over the drums, everybody talking at once, big arm gestures, spit flying. You can see the disgust on American faces looking at women like that. It isn't just the loudness. It is the way Chinese sounds, chingchong ugly, to American ears, not beautiful like Japanese sayonara words with the consonants and vowels as regular as Italian. We make guttural peasant noise and have Ton Duc Thang names you can't remember. And the Chinese can't hear Americans at all; the language is too soft and western music unhearable. I've watched a Chinese audience laugh, visit, talk-story, and holler during a piano recital, as if the musician could not hear them. A Chinese-American, somebody's son, was playing Chopin, which has no punctuation, no cymbals, no gongs. Chinese piano music is five black keys. Normal Chinese women's voices are strong and bossy. We American-Chinese girls had to whisper to make ourselves American-feminine. Apparently we whispered even more softly than the Americans. Once a year the teachers referred my

sister and me to speech therapy, but our voices would straighten out, unpredictably normal, for the therapists. Some of us gave up, shook our heads, and said nothing, not one word. Some of us could not even shake our heads. At times shaking my head no is more self-assertion than I can manage. Most of us eventually found some voice, however faltering. . . .

29   We have so many secrets to hold in. Our sixth-grade teacher, who liked to explain things to children, let us read our files. My record shows that I flunked kindergarten and in first grade had no IQ—a zero IQ. I did remember the first-grade teacher calling out during a test, while students marked X's on a girl or a boy or a dog, which I covered with black. First grade was when I discovered eye control; with my seeing I could shrink the teacher down to a height of one inch, gesticulating and mouthing on the horizon. I lost this power in sixth grade for lack of practice, the teacher a generous man. "Look at your family's old addresses and think about how you've moved," he said. I looked at my parents' aliases and their birthdays, which variants I knew. But when I saw Father's occupations I exclaimed, "Hey, he wasn't a farmer, he was a . . ." He had been a gambler. My throat cut off the word—silence in front of the most understanding teacher. There were secrets never to be said in front of the ghosts, immigration secrets whose telling could get us sent back to China.

30   Sometimes I hated the ghosts for not letting us talk; sometimes I hated the secrecy of the Chinese. "Don't tell," said my parents, though we couldn't tell if we wanted to because we didn't know. Are there really secret trials with our own judges and penalties? Are there really flags in Chinatown signaling what stowaways have arrived in San Francisco Bay, their names, and which ships they came on? "Mother, I heard some kids say there are flags like that. Are there? What colors are they? Which buildings do they fly from?"

31   "No. No, there aren't any flags like that. They're just talking-story. You're always believing talk-story."

32   "I won't tell anybody, Mother, I promise. Which building are the flags on? Who flies them? The benevolent associations?"

33   "I don't know. Maybe the San Francisco villagers do that; our villagers don't do that."

34   "What do our villagers do?"

35   They would not tell us children because we have been born among ghosts, were taught by ghosts, and were ourselves ghostlike. They called us a kind of ghost. Ghosts are noisy and full of air; they talk during meals. They talk about anything.

36   "Do we send up signal kites? That would be a good idea, huh? We could fly them from the school balcony." Instead of cheaply stringing dragonflies by the tail, we could fly expensive kites, the sky splendid in Chinese colors, distracting ghost eyes while the new people sneak in. Don't tell. "Never tell."

37   Occasionally the rumor went about that the United States immigration authorities had set up headquarters in the San Francisco or Sacramento Chinatown to urge wetbacks and stowaways, anybody here on fake papers, to come to the city and get their files straightened out. The immigrants discussed

whether or not to turn themselves in. "We might as well," somebody would say. "Then we'd have our citizenship for real."

38   "Don't be a fool," somebody else would say. "It's a trap. You go in there saying you want to straighten out your papers, they'll deport you."

39   "No, they won't. They're promising that nobody is going to go to jail or get deported. They'll give you citizenship as a reward for turning yourself in, for your honesty."

40   "Don't you believe it. So-and-so trusted them, and he was deported. They deported his children too."

41   "Where can they send us now? Hong Kong? Taiwan? I've never been to Hong Kong or Taiwan. The Big Six? Where?" We don't belong anywhere since the Revolution. The old China has disappeared while we've been away.

42   "Don't tell," advised my parents. "Don't go to San Francisco until they leave."

43   Lie to Americans. Tell them you were born during the San Francisco earthquake. Tell them your birth certificate and your parents were burned up in the fire. Don't report crimes; tell them we have no crimes and no poverty. Give a new name every time you get arrested; the ghosts won't recognize you. Pay the new immigrants twenty-five cents an hour and say we have no unemployment. And, of course, tell them we're against Communism. Ghosts have no memory anyway and poor eyesight. And the Han people won't be pinned down.

44   Even the good things are unspeakable, so how could I ask about deformities? From the configurations of food my mother set out, we kids had to infer the holidays. She did not whip us up with holiday anticipation or explain. You only remembered that perhaps a year ago you had eaten monk's food, or that there was meat, and it was a meat holiday; or you had eaten moon cakes or long noodles for long life (which is a pun). In front of the whole chicken with its slit throat toward the ceiling, she'd lay out just so many pairs of chopsticks alternating with wine cups, which were not for us because they were a different number from the number in our family, and they were set too close together for us to sit at. To sit at one of those place settings a being would have to be about two inches wide, a tall wisp of an invisibility. Mother would pour Seagram's 7 into the cups and after a while, pour it back into the bottle. Never explaining. How can Chinese keep any traditions at all? They don't even make you pay attention, slipping in a ceremony and clearing the table before the children notice specialness. The adults get mad, evasive, and shut you up if you ask. You get no warning that you shouldn't wear a white ribbon in your hair until they hit you and give you the sideways glare for the rest of the day. They hit you if you wave brooms around or drop chopsticks or drum them. They hit you if you wash your hair on certain days, or tap somebody with a ruler, or step over a brother whether it's during your menses or not. You figure out what you got hit for and don't do it again if you figured correctly. But I think that if you don't figure it out, it's all right. Then you can grow up bothered by "neither ghosts nor deities." "Gods you avoid won't hurt you." I don't see how they kept up a continuous culture for five thousand years. Maybe they didn't; maybe

everyone makes it up as they go along. If we had to depend on being told, we'd have no religion, no babies, no menstruation (sex, of course, unspeakable), no death.

A Writer's Notes for a Second Reading

When the book from which this excerpt is taken was first published every writer I know who read it was astonished at the wonderful way the author played her two cultures against each other. It seemed to me that she did just what writers want to do but rarely accomplish. She found a way to combine form and meaning. Her "ghost" stories were just right. She wasn't telling us about one culture or the other, she had found a way to see the cultures in action.

Maxine Hong Kingston lets us share her private explorations with her. It is a magic thing when the writer allows you into the process of making meaning that takes place in every text. Most writers make the reader stay outside the text. They present the text to the reader. This author opens the door and invites us in.

It is texts such as hers that I go to for inspiration. It's not that I copy another writer—I *never* do that intentionally—but other writers make me see the possibilities in my material, give me the courage to face my own material in my own way. The artistic courage of Maxine Hong Kingston inspires other writers, not to be her but to be like her in having the courage she had to be herself.

Discussion

- Compare the Lopez piece with Kingston's. What works in each piece? What needs work? Which probes deeper? How?
- How do Lopez and Kingston reveal a culture that is alien to most readers? What other techniques could be used to do this?
- This is the last autobiographical piece in the book. How does Kingston compare with the other writers? What could they—and you—learn from her? What could she—and you—learn from them?
- List the principal problems of writing autobiography. List a number of ways each problem can be solved.
- Discuss the ways Kingston makes complicated material clear.

Activities

- Write an incident from your childhood that reveals how your family's ideas or standards were different from the neighbors'.
- Interview a foreign student in your school or someone who comes from a culture different from yours. Write a story that reveals that difference.
- Take a draft you have written and write it as it might be written by someone with a different cultural background.

- Rewrite a fragment of the scene in the basement from the other girl's point of view.
- Interview someone in your family or someone else who came to this country from another culture to discover a problem they had adjusting. Write about that problem.

To Collaborate

- Interview foreign students on your campus to discover what they find difficult to understand about our culture. Write guidelines for understanding American culture.
- Have one person on the team from another cultural background or play the role of someone from another culture. Prepare guidelines for an American going to that other real or imaginary culture.

Mark Davidson
STUDENT ESSAY

A Change Is Needed

1   Leeches and parasites, that's all they are. In today's society, a great deal of importance is placed upon a person's ability to support oneself and be self-sufficient. The jobless are seen as spongers who would rather suck money out of the system than earn it themselves. The vision of an unemployed person, reclined in an easy chair, leisurely watching an afternoon soap, is easy for a laborer to imagine.

2   Though it holds true for some, the majority of unemployed people do not fit this description. There is a different side to unemployment that is often over-looked by proud, employed Americans. The recessions of 1980 and 1981–1982 are part of the harsh reality of unemployment. Jobs that once provided millions of people with work that paid middle-class wages have disappeared from the market.

3   Twenty years ago, manufacturing jobs employed one third of the work-force in the United States. Today, only one fifth of employed Americans make their living in the factories and on the assembly lines. In the past ten years, more than two million jobs have been lost in manufacturing throughout the United States. Products once made with pride by human hands are now system-atically assembled by machines. The result: many skilled men and women have no place to apply their craft or earn money.

4   But isn't the unemployment percentage following a downward trend? The unemployment rate which was over 10 percent five years ago now holds firm at 6.4 percent. As much as one would hope to trust in its validity, this statistic is deceptive. It does not paint an accurate picture of the present employment situation.

5   To be considered employed, one must work only one hour per week. Many frustrated blue-collar workers have tried to re-enter the workforce on a part-time level. Though now counted among the employed, these people have little hope of ever receiving the salaries they once made. They are accepting service, maintenance, and fast food job opportunities that pay only minimum wage. Flipping burgers, sweeping floors, and other part-time jobs do not provide enough money to support an individual, let alone a family. In many cases, a person would be better off financially on welfare than being employed part-time.

6   Welfare was originally designed to help those who needed financial assistance when they were unable to work, or temporarily out of a job. It has evolved into the sole means of support for countless thousands of American families. These people who collect welfare are willing to work, but in many cases are not able. Former Green Bay Packer star Travis Williams has turned to the Department of Welfare to help him support his family. Each day he actively pursues any job opportunity that will allow him to provide for his nine children.

7   Others are equally deserving, but oftentimes this sort of financial assistance is hard to come by. In twenty-six states, a family with two unemployed parents and two children would not qualify for welfare. Those who do qualify can only expect an allowance significantly below the poverty level. Richard Gorin, an associate professor in the Social Service Department at the University of New Hampshire, observes, "Nobody out there is getting rich off of welfare." Barring the cheaters of course, Mr. Gorin.

8   Those who still believe that the unemployed are home, sitting in armchairs, living a carefree life are invited to read *Mental Illness and the Economy* by Harvey Brenner. Mr. Brenner found, in a study that covered a period of 13 decades, that mental hospital admissions are highly inversely correlated with the index of employment. In everyday terms, this means that when the number of unemployed people rises, so too do the admissions to mental institutions. This is hardly characteristic of a class of people that is comfortable with their situation.

9   More people than ever before have exposed themselves to higher education as a help in finding jobs. Though this method has been of some help, it is not reasonable to assume that these opportunities apply to everyone. Many people are beyond the traditional educating age and are responsible for supporting entire families. They are too late. They must neglect the future and live each day as it comes.

10   Job opportunities in technological fields are expanding at a high rate. Michael Papia of the Hewlett Packard Corporation says that the only openings

in his company are in the engineering departments. "MBAs won't get you very far these days. We're laying off everywhere except engineering." As the high-tech jobs expand, more jobs are taken from manufacturing and the basic indus-tries. Meanwhile, the technical jobs are being filled and must brace for the inev-itable glut of qualified applicants. Eventually, engineering will have to face layoffs too.

11   Capitalism is a competitive form of society. It adheres to the rules of sur-vival of the fittest, the best person winning, and forcing the competition to fold. When there are thriving companies in a growing economy, others must falter. And with corporative hardship, observes Gorin, there is job loss. "The economy cannot provide sufficient jobs for the people in this country."

12   A *U.S. News & World Report*/CNN News poll has found that 77 percent of the people in our nation believe that unemployment is among the most serious problems our country faces. Unfortunately, many people see it only as a plague to society and not as people struggling to stand on their own financially. The only effects they comprehend are the ones that appear in the headlines and in their pocketbooks. The employed people need to see the reality of the issue and change their attitudes toward unemployment and the people it affects.

History of the Draft and Final Commentary

The idea for the paper before you now was originated one Sunday night in September on the third floor of the Dimond Library. I was sitting with two friends who were hard at work on their own English assignments. I had planned to work on English too, and use my time at the library wisely by doing research on my topic. Unfortunately, the topic had yet to be determined. I resorted to brainstorming and soliciting ideas from friends. I wanted to make sure that my topic was different, original, and interesting (at least to me). The effort got me nowhere; two hours and nothing. As we left the building it hit me. Unemployment. But why? I couldn't answer the question then, but somehow I knew it would be what I would write my paper on.

When I told people I was writing about unemployment, I began to hear things that concerned me. "What unemployment?," "Why don't they just get jobs?," and "Maybe the unemployed just don't want to work" were common responses. I was intrigued. I questioned my own beliefs concerning the issue. I wanted to see if these people were right. It gave me a way to approach my research.

Current information would be very important for my argument, so I began my research with periodicals. I conducted a fairly brief but interesting interview with associate professor Steve Gorin of the Social Service Department here at UNH. He was very informative and interested in the way I was thinking of approaching my assignment. Unemployment was a great concern of his and he talked empathetically about the people and their problems. He also led me to a book by

Harvey Brenner called Mental Illness and the Economy. *His comments and suggestions proved to be of great value.*

During the research phase, I found some facts that can only be described as shocking. It was becoming clear to me that the assumptions I heard from friends and classmates were more than a little off base. They needed to be convinced that an unemployed life was not an easy one to lead. It was not a choice, it is more like a sentence. I had my information; I could make my stand.

The strategy I chose for writing the paper was simple. I would begin with the opposing view. I thought that this would best serve my interests by giving the reader a documentation of their own assumptions, allowing them to readily compare them with my argument. From there I would relate my information in what I hoped to be an effective manner. My conclusion would be a statement that encompassed all of the material presented. Hopefully, it would be the strongest element and leave the reader with no doubts about what he had read.

The first draft, as Murray promised, did not take long to write. I based my first two paragraphs on the game of "Scruples." It didn't work as well as I hoped. It filled the entire page with the second person. Aside from that, the paper was decent for a first draft. Granted it was wordy and awkward at points, but there was some good writing and solid information.

The second draft scrapped the scruples idea in favor of a more appropriate, yet equally weak beginning. I managed to catch most of my wordiness and awkward phrases as I rewrote the paper. I utilized the example in "One Writer's Notes" by making crossouts and additions quite freely. I finished it feeling extremely pleased with myself. This feeling lasted only until workshop, where I was hit with many criticisms. I swallowed my pride and faced their validity. On to the third draft.

The beginning and ending are much different. The first paragraph is more biting and more direct. The last is not as wishy-washy; it has more substance. Again I went through the paper looking for useless sentences, wordiness, and awkward phrases. I found nearly as many as before. I think my point is easier to see now and without most of the garbage, the paper is stronger. Certainly having three chances to write it has increased its quality considerably. I'm proud of it. I've deposited a great deal of time into its writing and I think that shows. I must also add that I'm glad it is done.

The most important thing I've learned about argument is that clarity is key. This has been most evident in my work recently. People have been a bit confused when reading my drafts as to what I was trying to say. You can't convince anyone by confusing them. A clear ordered piece is certainly best.

Empathy is another important feature of argument. People can be more persuasive if they care about what they are saying. By identification with people or a problem, the writer can incorporate a voice that will better influence a reader. If the reader feels the same empathy after reading a piece, odds are the argument was a success.

Sure I've learned a lot in this class. I've learned argument, I've improved my focusing abilities, I've learned to edit, and I've learned about unemployment. I think the most important thing I've learned, though, is the desire to write. Every time I witness or am involved in something interesting, I think of what a good paper it would make. The ideas begin to pop into a semblance of order before they hit the page. It has made me a more analytical person; I look for some meaning that I can relate to others. I value this, and I think it will last a great many years.

Stacy Kendall
STUDENT ESSAY

Corruption in the Market: Inside Trading

1   1986 has been a year of mergers, takeovers, and heavy trading in the stock market. It has also been a year during which inside trading has increasingly been in the public eye.

2   It is illegal for persons learning of big corporate developments such as takeovers, in the course of business or from tips, to trade securities on that news before it has been made public. This action is known as inside trading.

3   Inside trading is a very hazy area. Many times it is hard to draw the line between what is right and what isn't. It may be one thing when you overhear a conversation about what stocks are good to invest in on the train to work, but it is different when you purposely tell a friend to invest in a prospective takeover stock before it has been publicly announced. Unfortunately, there are many in the business world who do not view it in that way, and unless they have a change of morals they will continue with their acts.

4   However, it must be noted that not all speculation is bad. For speculation is what makes the market work. There is a definite difference between when a person who is knowledgeable in the stock market takes a risk with his money because he thinks a possible buyout may be underway and when a person who sits on the board of a takeover company invests in the market before the information is public, because he knows it is a sure thing. It is the latter of the above we must stop.

5   In the past several months many lawyers, newspaper journalists, arbitrageurs, and especially investment bankers have been caught for inside trading, but many more have gone unnoticed. The traders have not been old institutions on Wall Street but rather young, aggressive executives eager to make a quick fortune (often in addition to the ones they already have). Most of the offenders have been under age forty and fit into the "yuppie" class.

6   Dennis Levine, 33, was an investment banker for Drexel Burnham until he was caught on inside trading deals in early June of 1986. The Securities and Exchange Commission (SEC) charged that he had made $12.6 million in the last five years by buying stocks of takeover targets before the bids were announced.

7   Earlier that spring the eighth largest investment bank, First Boston, was charged with inside trading. The SEC claims that Cigna, a client, told the bank of an impending $1.2 billion writeoff. Prior to the news going public, First Boston traded Cigna stocks for a $132,138 profit.

8   R. Foster Winans, a former *Wall Street Journal* reporter, was convicted last year of a fraud and conspiracy for leaking the contents of his articles before publication to two New York stockbrokers, who traded on the information and made nearly $700,000 in illegal profits. Winans received $30,000 of that money.

9   Also in June of 1986, four men, all under the age of 27, were charged with inside trading. The "Yuppie Scam," as it is called, involved the passing along of pending mergers through different firms.

10   Those on Wall Street aren't the only ones passing along inside information. The Commerce Department is firing three employees for allegedly using confidential economic statistics to profit in the bond market.

11   In November of 1986 the biggest insider trading case ever was uncovered. Ivan Boesky, a prominent Wall Street businessman, was charged for inside trading activities. He apparently paid Dennis Levine and others for information on pending mergers. Boesky was charged an unprecedented $100 million, $50 million in illegal profits and an equal amount in civil indemnities. He is also barred from trading stock in the U.S. for the rest of his life.

12   Although many people have been caught in the past year for inside trading, many have not. One Manhattan banker said in reference to the Boesky case: "There'll be people named from almost every firm on Wall Street before this is over—including mine." Inside trading may be more widespread than we believe, and there is substantial information to prove it is going on.

13   With the increase of mergers and takeovers in the past year we can see by looking at the volumes and prices of certain stocks that someone knew that something was soon to take place.

14   One month before Capital Cities announced a takeover of ABC the stock of ABC was priced at $66, one week before $70.72, two days before $73.72, and on the day of the announcement the price of the stock had reached $107. One month before Philip Morris announced a takeover of General Foods the General Foods stock was priced at $77.12, one week before it was valued at $88.72, two days before it was at $84.72, but on the day of the announcement the price of the stock was $106.72.

15   A third example is seen in the days prior to the General Electric bid to take over RCA. In the following graphs we see the price and volumes of the RCA stock prior to the bid.

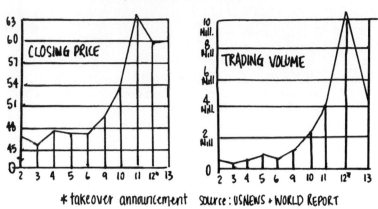

RCA STOCK, DEC. 1985

* takeover announcement   source: USNEWS + WORLD REPORT

16   From these graphs we can see that someone knew of information about the pending merger and used this information to buy the RCA stock, driving it up to a higher price so as to profit from the expected takeover by General Electric. While both RCA and GE say that the leaks have not come from their merger teams or employees the SEC is still conducting further investigations.

17   The probe has at least had some lasting effects. Surveys have shown a definite slowdown in the trading of stock of major corporation takeovers immediately before the announcement of merger bids.

18   At any rate the public is becoming worried, and they should. A *Business Week*/Harris poll asked the public if they felt they stood a fair chance on Wall Street and over half felt they did not. Inside trading creates a climate of distrust in which investors are reluctant to buy or sell on the basis of analyses of a company's outlook for profits. Inside trading also deprives those who sell stock to the insiders their potential profit. Inside trading is a serious problem and actions must be taken to stop it from occurring.

19   At present the New York Stock Exchange (NYSE) monitors every trade and tracks abnormal volume and price movements. The NYSE may ask for brokers' records, but they have no legal power. If they suspect any inside trading they are to report it to the SEC.

20   Investment banking firms have also increased security in order to save their reputations. Reviewing current employees, enacting new tougher guidelines for new employees, conducting internal investigations, and hiring internal auditors have been among the measures taken.

21   Other than the above measures, the Securities and Exchange Commission is responsible for the cracking-down on inside trading. The SEC depends highly on the information that they receive from those already convicted for inside trading. A perfect example of this is the Dennis Levine case, which has led to the recent Boesky case. Since his conviction earlier this year he has been supplying the SEC with much information on other insiders. His testimony has led

directly to the snaring of Boesky, and others such as Ira Sokolow with Shearson Lehman Bros. and Robert Wilkis, formerly with E. F. Hutton.

22   In turn the Boesky case has had similar developments. The Wall Street office of Drexel Burnham Lambert has had several of its top executives served with subpoenas from both the SEC and the U.S. Attorney's office. The Los Angeles-based brokerage house Jefferies & Company is also under investigation, as it has reportedly played a role in a number of corporate takeovers. Jefferies & Company is what is known as a "third market." This means that because it is not a member of the NYSE it is able to make trades on the exchange before it officially opens for the day and after it has closed. Exchange members are forbidden to make such transactions outside the official hours. The fact that Boesky may have used the firm is under probe.

23   Although the SEC has cracked down on insider trading in the past few years, it cannot rely totally on those who have been caught for all the information.

24   At present the SEC is severely short-staffed. Richard Phillips, a former SEC official, says "From 1975 to 1985 securities trading has increased by 700 percent and the number of investment companies by 600 percent; there is only one statistic that has receded, and that is the size of the SEC." The SEC does not have the manpower to conduct deep investigations so they will have to depend on other methods to combat inside trading.

25   The Securities and Exchange Commission needs to make their laws much clearer and stronger if they plan to stop insiders from trading on inside information. And it seems as if they are headed in the right direction, as we can see in the Boesky case. A fine of $100 million and being barred from the stock market for life was enough to make Boesky talk, and hopefully it will stop others from acting. For the insiders may not see the line between what is right and wrong, but steep fines and punishments may make them become more ethically conscious.

26   It is possible for an insider to make a fortune from just a few deals, and if the SEC plans to stop them they are going to have to do a lot more than just slap wrists. Insiders will have to be hit where it hurts them the most—in the wallet.

History of the Draft and Final Commentary

During the past three months I have learned much about the craft of writing argument. From the researching and writing of my "Argument Paper" I have learned that argument doesn't have to be a hostile debate. In my case, it is the presentation of facts and ideas in attempt to persuade the reader to agree with you, to see your point of view.

I have learned from my paper and from reading others that argument comes in many ways. It can be so subtle that you are barely aware of it until the end, it can be in the form of a story, it can be through facts, or it can be through opinion statements.

I enjoyed writing this paper very much. It was hard but rewarding. The hardest parts were finding a topic and deciding how to argue it. After I found a position I gathered as much information as possible. For me reading the daily newspaper and current magazines was most helpful. Although I questioned three people they seemed indifferent to the matter.

After putting the piece together the most helpful thing was having my classmates read and comment on my paper. Not only did they make suggestions for my piece, but it enabled me to see what other people did and how they did it.

Writing these commentaries has also been a great help. They allow me to take a step back and look at my paper from a different perspective. In them I find my weaknesses as well as my strengths. They help me to evaluate what I have done and to see what still needs to be done.

Most of all I have become much more confident about my writing. I realized I am not the only one lacking self-assurance. I don't mind other people reading my writing as much as I used to and I don't feel so hesitant to turn it in. My writing is a reflection of myself, and with it I have become more comfortable.

7

Watch Out: After School May Come Reading and Writing

For some of you, especially some of you who do not think it possible, coming to the end of this book will mean the beginning of a lifetime of writing and reading. You will be lucky if that is the case, for in writing you will hear your own voice and you will be able to make your voice heard. You will be able to join and influence communities of engineers, poetry lovers, businessmen, voters, football fans, educators, soldiers, environmentalists, speaking of your concerns to those who can affect the world in which you are interested.

As writers, you will learn by writing, finding out what you know when it appears on your page, reading, rewriting, and rereading as your meanings come clear. You will think by writing and therefore change and grow in your understanding and appreciation of your world. Writing increases awareness and the more you write, the more you see and feel. At times this is painful and you may wish for a numbing oblivion, but in the long run you will see those about you paralyzed by boredom and you will be grateful that you will never be bored, that there are always people to watch, questions to ask, places to observe, processes to follow, all sorts of material for the writing you have yet to do.

As a reading writer, you will learn from others, living their lives, hearing their counsel, enjoying their individual and diverse voices. In addition, you will be able to go behind the scenes, reading with a special understanding of the problems faced and solved by the writer. You will have a particular appreciation of the text that flows toward meaning with a simple, unaffected, and appropriate grace, for you will know something of the invisible craft that made that text come clear. You will become a member of the community of writers, living and dead, in your language and others, who have labored at your craft.

If you wish to know more about what writers say about their own books, their reading of other books, and the process with which they write, there is an abundance of material available. Interviews with writers have become an entire genre of its own. Each month, it seems, new collections of interviews with writers are published. The basic collection is the series of eight *Paris Review* interviews published by Viking Penguin. Everyone seriously interested in writing should have those books on the shelf. There are many collections of articles by writers. One of the best is *The Writer on Her Work,* edited by Janet Sternberg and published by Norton in 1980. There are also collections of interviews by individual writers.

In addition to interviews, there are the published journals of writers, their letters, the prefaces and commentary they have written on their own work and on the work of others, their autobiographies and biographies, the reproductions of their own manuscripts with the crossings out and insertions that reveal the creative process in action.

The writers' own works, of course, are most important, but the evidence of why and how they wrote puts the writing itself in context. Even more is your own writing. And from this interaction of reading and writing you will stay alive intellectually and artistically, enjoying the perpetual youth of the artist who always discovers the world anew.

Others of you will not write but only read. I hope that this text has helped you see something of what goes into the creation of an effective text, that you will read with increased skill and enjoyment because of what you have seen, while reading this book, happen on your page and on the pages of other writers in your class and in this text.

Reading is a way of escaping lifetime imprisonment in your present world. By reading, you can live other lives, see with other eyes, visit other places, consider new and old information, new and old ideas. Reading is a private activity that allows us to change and grow in our own way, escaping the loneliness of our lives, reaching out to other people across the barriers of time or place.

Be comforted in the fact that you will never be able to read all the books you should read. Read for fun and escape, read for stimulation and comfort, read for information, read for belief and disbelief, for confirmation and for challenge, read for all the hundreds of reasons you will need to read in school and beyond.

When you discover an author who speaks to you, see what else that person has written and read those books. When you discover a genre you enjoy—science fiction or history, poetry or books on how to succeed in business, autobiography, or novels—see what else has been written in that form and read some of it. When you find a subject that interests you—big business or little business, psychology or theology, sports or science—read other works on the same subject. Follow your own interests and then, through reading, reach out, exploring the subjects that interest you.

It's all there in paperback or hardcover, bookstore or library, in magazine or newspaper, waiting to catch your eye—and your mind.

And watch out. As you live and as you read there will probably come a time—especially if you don't believe such a time could come for you—when you will be invited to write or commanded to write or when you will simply have the itch to write. Then write. When you are in terminal middle age or beyond you may not be able to dance as you once intended to dance or twist and turn toward the goal line as you once believed you could, but it is never too late to write—and all that reading you have done is stored away, waiting to be called upon as your words move across your page.

436

Terry McMillan, "What Is Perfect Anyway? Simply Being Beautiful?" *Hers* column essay, *The New York Times,* November 5, 1987. Reprinted by permission of the author.

Toni Morrison, from *The Bluest Eye* by Toni Morrison. Copyright © 1970 by Toni Morrison. Reprinted by permission of Henry Holt and Company, Inc.

Donald Murray, "Victims of the Age of Prosperity," *The Boston Globe,* September 15, 1987. Reprinted by permission of the author.

Sharon Olds, "Feared Drowned," reprinted from *Satan Says* by Sharon Olds, by permission of the University of Pittsburgh Press. Copyright © 1980 by Sharon Olds. "The Blue Dress" reprinted from *The Gold Cell* by Sharon Olds. Copyright © 1987 by Sharon Olds. Reprinted by permission of Alfred A. Knopf, Inc. "My Father Snoring," "The Forms," "Bread," and "Sex Without Love" reprinted from *The Dead and the Living* by Sharon Olds. Copyright © 1983 by Sharon Olds. Reprinted by permission of Alfred A. Knopf, Inc.

George Orwell, "A Hanging" and "Why I Write," from *Shooting an Elephant and Other Essays* by George Orwell, copyright 1950 by Sonia Brownell Orwell, renewed 1978 by Sonia Pitt-Rivers, reprinted by permission of Harcourt Brace Jovanovich, Inc. and the estate of the late Sonia Brownell Orwell and Martin Secker & Warburg.

Anna Quindlen, "This Child I Carry, Like My Other Two, Is Wanted. Healthy or Not," by Anna Quindlen, *The New York Times,* May 12, 1988. Copyright © 1988 by The New York Times Company. Reprinted by permission.

Christopher Scanlan, "The Young Who Died Delivered Us," reprinted by permission of the author.

Richard Selzer, "Letters to a Young Surgeon III," from *Letters to a Young Doctor.* Copyright © 1982 by David Goldman and Janet Selzer, Trustees. Reprinted by permission of Simon & Schuster, Inc.

Jean Shepherd, "Hairy Gertz and the Forty-Seven Crappies" by Jean Shepherd. Originally appeared in *Playboy* magazine. Copyright © 1964, 1965, 1966 by HMH Publishing Company, Inc. From *In God We Trust—All Others Pay Cash* by Jean Shepherd. Reprinted by permission of Doubleday, a division of Bantam, Doubleday, Dell Publishing Group, Inc.

Charles Simic, "In the Beginning . . . ," first published in *Antaeus* #58, Spring, 1987. Copyright © 1987 by Charles Simic. Reprinted by permission of the author.

Lewis Thomas, "On Embryology" from *The Medusa and the Snail.* Copyright © 1978 by Lewis Thomas. All rights reserved. Reprinted by permission of Viking Penguin Inc.

Alice Trillin, "Of Dragon and Peas" in the *New England Journal of Medicine.* Vol. 304; pp. 699–701; 1981. Copyright 1984 Massachusetts Medical Society. Reprinted by permission of the *New England Journal of Medicine.*

Barbara W. Tuchman, from *A Distant Mirror: The Calamitous 14th Century.* Copyright © 1978 by Barbara W. Tuchman. Reprinted by permission of Alfred A. Knopf, Inc.

John Updike, from *Five Boyhoods* (Doubleday) edited by Martin Levin. Copyright © 1962 by Martin Levin. Reprinted by permission of Martin Levin.

E. B. White, "Once More to the Lake," from *Essays of E. B. White.* Copyright © 1941 by E. B. White. Reprinted by permission of Harper & Row, Publishers, Inc.

Writing Problems Solved

There are twelve writing problems most beginning writers seem to have difficulty defining and solving. Writers are so close to their material they may sense something is wrong but read what they hope is on the page, not what actually appears in print. In this index we will describe each of these key problems so that students may recognize them in the papers of their classmates as well as their own. We also suggest a few practical solutions to each problem and identify selections in the reader that demonstrate the problem solved. Students should be reminded, however, that they have to solve the problem in their own way, learning from the model but not copying it.

The problems are organized in a process sequence, working from subject through final copy, but we should remind ourselves that the students problems will not necessarily follow such an order. This is a convenient way to recover the information. Each student will have an individual process that depends on the students cognitive style. And that process will change with the writing task and the writer's experience in responding to it.

This index is built on the assumption of revision. We write, we read, we rewrite. This is the way we learn and what we learn carries over to other texts we draft. Some of us do more rewriting than others. There is no virtue in many revisions or evil in none. Each draft has its own demands. Some writers, experienced with a particular writing task, can prerewrite—anticipating and solving problems in advance of encountering them or revising as they go, maintaining a split vision involved and detached at the same time. But even such writers will produce texts that may require many rereadings and rewritings after they appear finished.

One of the most difficult problems for beginning—and many experienced writers—is to stand back from a draft and see it as a reader. I need good editors and test-readers who can see what I have written as a reader will see it. To achieve that essential detachment I also role play a specific reader and read my draft through those critical eyes. After writing, scan your draft to see if your reaction fits any of these categories, then try one of the solutions and read a selection to see how another writer has solved your problem.

Almost every selection in this reader can demonstrate all of the key writing problems solved, but the selections I have identified make that solution clear.

1. No Subject

Description

The draft establishes no territory, there are no horizons. It seems to be about one subject, then another, then still another. The writer seems to have no confidence in saying something worth reading. There is no context for the piece of writing—it appears to have no significance. The reader feels lost; the writer does not seem to have command of what is being said.

Solutions

- State the territory of your writing in one sentence.
- Define your territory by default: list what you are not going to be concerned with in rewriting the draft.
- State why you are an authority on this subject. Describe how you can revise the piece to take advantage of what you know.
- State why the subject is important. What is its context?

Demonstrations of an Effective Subject

- "Salvador" (Joan Didion),   76–83
- "Of Dragons and Garden Peas" (Alice Stewart Trillin),   219–225
- "An American Childhood" (Annie Dillard),   329–339

2. No Surprise

Description

There is no edge, no tension, no news, no surprise that demands the reader's attention. The text may be correctly written but it is bland, boring. A reader will know what the writer will say before it is said.

Solutions

- What surprised you in writing the text? Build on that surprise in the revision.
- Describe the tension central in the topic. Make it central in your draft.
- Decide on something that can make your draft different from other pieces written on the same subject.
- What would like more of in the draft? Deliver it to the reader.

Demonstrations of Appropriate Surprise

- "A Hanging" (George Orwell),   66–69
- "In the Beginning . . ." (Charles Simic),   179–187
- "Feared Drowned," "The Blue Dress," "My Father Snoring," "The Forms," "Bread," and "Sex Without Love" (Sharon Olds),   323–327

3. No Awareness of Reader

Description

The writing is private. The author talks to the author, unaware of what the reader may know or need to know. The writer has not entered into a dialogue with the reader.

Solutions

- Anticipate the questions the reader will ask. Answer them.
- Climb into the head of a reader and read the draft from that perspective.
- Write in the margin by each paragraph what a reader needs to know to understand your point.
- Read fast as a reader will, marking where a reader might stop, get mad, become puzzled, yawn, want more information. Revise to satisfy the reader.

Demonstrations of Reader Awareness

- "The Child I Carry, Like My Other Two, Is Wanted, Healthy or Not" (Anna Quindlen), 101–103
- "In Vitro Fertilization: It Doesn't Always Work" (Denise Grady), 387–390
- "Photo Decisions Are Careful, Deliberate" (Daryl Frazell), 146–149

4. No Form

Description

The reader doesn't know what the text is supposed to be. Each genre—story, poem, essay, report, argument—tells the reader how to read the draft. Experimental or artful writing may work against these expectations, but they are there in the writer's and reader's mind. The prose poem, the story that rejects chronological narrative, the essay that appears as story are all using form. The reader needs a feeling of form, a sense of familiarity that is comfortable or allows purposeful discomfort.

Solutions

- Reconsider your genre. If you have the choice, should the essay become a story, the poem an essay, the letter a report?
- List your expectations when you read something in the genre in which you are writing. Check to see if you have fulfilled them or dealt with them.
- Imagine the most important element in the genre when it deals with your subject. It might be chronology in a narrative, exposition in an essay, logic in an argument. Strengthen that element in your draft.
- Read the suggested pieces and list their basic elements. See if following them would help your piece.

Demonstrations of Effective Form

- "That Night" (Alice McDermott), 266–270
- "Red Letters" (Mekeel McBride), 309
- "Black Boy's Death by Drowning, Walter Bridges, 1958–1972," "The Need to Talk," "The Knife-Thrower's Wife," "How Spring Appears This Time of Year in New England," and "If I'd Been Born in Tennessee" (Mekeel McBride), 317–321

5. No Beginning

Description

The first lines hold no promise for the reader. The reader has no incentive to read on. The first lines of a piece of writing entrap the reader—or allow the reader to escape. In those

first lines, the voice, the topic, the dimensions, the form, the direction are established—
or the reader stops reading.

Solutions
- Draft fifteen first sentences as fast as you can, a minute, two minutes, three each. Discover the possibilities, then follow one.
- Draft titles to discover the essential tension within the draft.
- Tell what you have written to a friend. Notice how you begin to capture the friend's attention.
- Go through the reader and list what writers do in their first lines. Try some of their techniques.

Demonstrations of Skillful Beginnings
- "Letter to a Young Surgeon III" (Richard Selzer),   254–256
- "That Lean and Hungry Look" (Suzanne Britt Jordan),   258–260
- "Schools" and "Three Boys" (John Updike),   340–345

6. No Sequence

Description
There is no trail through the text, it meanders without charm or purpose. The reader has
no sense that one thing leads to another, that a meaning is being built by the writer. The
draft is a jumble without structure.

Solutions
- Try an outline of the main points in the text, then jiggle them around so they lead the reader in a natural order.
- Decide on the ending, then list the landmarks that will lead the reader to that end. See if your draft has them. If it doesn't, make sure it does.
- In a complicated piece it may be helpful to use headings or other typographical or rhetorical signals in the text to make sure the reader sees and follows your structure.
- Develop and clarify those transition paragraphs that summarize what has been said and point the reader towards a new point.

Demonstrations of a Clear Sequence
- "The Young Who Died Delivered Us" (Christopher Scanlan),   39–44
- "A Noiseless Flash" (John Hersey),   403–409
- "Back to Bachimba" (Enrique Hank Lopez),   411–417

7. No Information

Description
The text is general and vague. There are no revealing details, no interesting and significant
specifics, no concrete information that teaches the reader the subject. The reader's hunger
for information is not satisfied.

Solutions
- Brainstorm a list of twenty-five, fifty, one hundred revealing details you can use to rebuild the piece.
- Read through the draft slowly, making every generalization as specific as possible.
- Insert facts of details where they will support, qualify or illustrate a point.
- Use quotations, descriptions, anecdotes, and similar devices to make the text come alive with information.

Demonstrations of Delivering Specific Information
- "The Sad Irons" (Robert A. Caro),   52–59
- "'This Is The End of the World': The Black Death" (Barbara W. Tuchman),   211–218
- "The Bluest Eye" (Toni Morrison),   272–285

8. No Point of View

Description

The reader has no sense of where the writer stands in relation to the subject. The writer may be objective and detached but the reader needs to know this. The problem text does not reveal from a consistent, interesting, or informative point of view; the reader has no idea of the writer's authority, thoughts, or feelings toward the subject. The writer is not involved and the reader, therefore, is not either.

Solutions
- Make your opinion of what you are writing clear to the reader.
- Be sure the reader knows where you stand and where you expect the reader to stand as you view the subject together.
- What is your reaction to the draft? What does it make you feel? Think? Tell the reader that or imply it.
- Insert material that implies or states your authority to write this text. Does the reader know that you experienced it first hand, researched it, discovered it by imagination?

Demonstrations of Using Point of View
- "School" (Amiri Baraka),   84–91
- "Long Live High School Rebels" (Thomas French),   92–95
- "Atomic Bombing of Nagasaki Told by Flight Member" (William L. Laurence),   396–402

9. No Development

Description

The points made are not documented but are simply statements that float on the page. There is no evidence provided for the reader's examination. The draft is without pace and proportion. Some elements are read too fast, others lingered over too long; some points need to be more carefully led up to, others need to be shown or explained at greater length.

Solutions
- Select the main points and make sure you develop them in greater detail so the reader has the material and the time to understand what you have said.

- Pace the piece so the information doesn't just rush by like a blur of traffic on a super-highway but moves quickly when the reader's attention might wander, slows down when the reader needs more information and time to reflect on it.
- Try different forms of documentation, ones that are appropriate to the point you are making. Consider, for example, anecdotes or small narratives, quotations or scholarly citations, statistics, lists of causes or implications, the whole range of documentation.
- In the margin, note the kind of evidence that would make you believe each key point. Provide it for the reader.

Demonstrations of Well-Developed Writing
- "The Underside of Journalism" (Roy Peter Clark),   137–140
- "My Mother, in Memory" (Richard Ford),   189–208
- "Once More to the Lake" (E. B. White),   348–353

10. No Voice

Description
The draft has been written by machine, it has no more individuality than another Big Mac®. The text is not heard. We do not hear the voice of the text, the music that communicates and supports meaning. There is no sense of individual writer speaking to individual reader.

Solutions
- Read the text aloud and put in the music that supports and communicates your meaning.
- Tell all or part of your story to a tape recorder, play it back and compare it with your written draft. See if there is anything in the oral text that will improve the written one.
- Have someone read your text to you. Listen to hear what needs to be changed to give the text an appropriate, consistent human voice.
- Read authors' works who have strong voices aloud, or use the ones below. Listen as a writer to hear the music of their draft and decide what techniques they use that might work in your text.

Demonstrations of Writing in an Individual Voice
- "Notes of Native Son" (James Baldwin),   150–166
- "What is Perfect Anyway? Simply Being Beautiful?" (Terry McMillan),   261–263
- "Hairy Gertz and the Forty-Seven Crappies" (Jean Shephard),   354–363

11. No Clarity

Description
We simply do not understand what is being said. We do not recognize the work or understand it in context. The phrase does not qualify or develop. The sentence takes us away from the text, the paragraph brings us no delivery of information, thinking, or feeling. Our language, in the text, becomes foreign.

Solutions
- Read the text fast to see what is left out, what might be cut, what needs to be in a different place.

- Read the text to see what needs checking, what needs to be put in context so that it is clear.
- Read the text slowly, to make sure that each paragraph, sentence, word, every break in the text, every mark of punctuation, the spelling of every word, the preparation of the manuscript clarifies and advances the meaning.
- Read aloud so that your ear will help you catch what is awkward, clumsy, confused and read aloud as you edit to make sure your changes bring clarity and grace to your page.

Demonstrations of Clear Writing
- "The Colorization of Films Insults Artist and Society" (Woody Allen), 97–99
- "What is DECpage?" (Joseph Freda), 244–249
- "On Embryology" (Lewis Thomas), 394–395

12. No Ending

Description
The reader enjoys no sense of completion and, at the same time, no launching into contemplation, imagination, exploration, further reading, thinking, or feeling. We are neither stimulated or satisfied; there is no conclusion to the experience of reading the draft.

Solutions
- Close with a specific—a fact, a quotation, a scene, an anecdote, a description—that doesn't tell the reader what to think or feel but makes the reader think and feel.
- Think back to the leads from which you chose your beginning to see if one of them would make an effective ending.
- Look for something in the text that contains the meaning of the draft and that will make the reader think. Move it to the end.
- Cover the last paragraph with a piece of blank paper. See if the draft ends before the last paragraph. Move it up and do it again until you come to the paragraph that must be the end.

Demonstrations of Skillful Endings
- "Why I Write" (Joan Didion), 71–77
- "Victims of the Age of Prosperity" (Donald M. Murray), 109–110
- "Sunset I Saw By" (William Gibson), 168–177

Index

445

Instructor's Manual

READ TO WRITE

A Writing Process Reader

SECOND EDITION

DONALD M. MURRAY

Holt, Rinehart and Winston, Inc.
Fort Worth   Chicago   San Francisco   Philadelphia
Montreal   Toronto   London   Sydney   Tokyo

CONTENTS

Chapter 6   A MEANING MADE CLEAR   42

Chapter 7   WATCH OUT: AFTER SCHOOL MAY COME READING AND WRITING   50

USING THIS BOOK

Read to Write is designed to support composition instructors who teach in many different ways. I have always believed in diversity while teaching students and supervising staffs of composition teachers. There is no one way to teach, and I hope this book will help both teachers and students as they find their own ways to learn and instruct.

Each selection is followed by questions for discussion, writing activities, and suggestions for collaborative writing that are designed to be used by students on their own and to help the teacher with topics for classroom consideration. All the activities are designed to make connections between reading and writing. The questions and the activities will also help the instructor make connections between the selections in the text and will also help instructor and student examine published writing from a writer's point of view.

"What should I do next?" was my desperate question when I began as a freshman English instructor. I kept asking my colleagues what they did, but in those days it was the policy of the department not to discuss such matters. Academic Freedom was cited by the Head (Yes, no chairperson in those days: Head). He also felt any discussion of methods was undignified for an English professor. Such matters, he felt, belonged in the Department of Education.

Today we discuss methods and learn from each other, and this practical orientation has influenced each page in this instructor's manual. Teaching, like writing, may become an art but first it is a craft. The material at the end of each selection is designed to help the instructor learn the craft of teaching. It is designed to be practical and to help the teacher answer that recurring question: "What should I do next?"

Using *Read to Write* with *Write to Learn*

This reader will supplement and extend my text *Write to Learn*. It is organized on the same process model, with examples of writing that demonstrate effective solutions to the problems writers encounter as they work through the writing process.

vi

In *Write to Learn* I have used examples of my own writing to demonstrate each strategy and skill introduced in the book. There are also case histories of students' writing. The introductions to each stage of the writing process in this reader reinforce what has been said in *Write to Learn.*

Most important, each section in this reader is headed by a case history that reveals how five very different published writers write. Each section closes with two student case histories, ten in all, that demonstrate how students write effectively under conditions comparable to students using this text. All these case histories reinforce and contradict each other in a stimulating and instructive manner. It will also help the students see how they may adapt the writing process to their own writing tasks.

The anthology also extends *Write to Learn,* because it deals with the reading skills that are essential to effective writing. These skills are introduced in *Write to Learn,* but developed and demonstrated in *Read to Write.*

The special index "Writing Problems Solved" in the reader reinforces and support the indexes "Help for Your Writing Problems" and "Writing Techniques" in *Write to Learn.*

Specific suggestions for using this reader with *Write to Learn* are included after discussion of the introduction and before discussion of the individual selections in this manual. These suggestions will help the instructor integrate these texts so they reinforce and enrich each other.

Using *Read to Write* with Other Writing Texts

Read to Write will supplement other writing texts, rhetorics, and handbooks. The introductions to the sections will allow the instructor to support or introduce the process approach to writing. If the instructor, however, is not interested in that approach to the teaching of composition, the material in those introductions responds to common writing problems; for example, all writers must learn to structure and order their material. The introduction to Chapter 4 deals with the problems of bringing order to a draft.

The case histories of published writers also relate to the writing tasks of students who are writing in many disciplines across the curriculum. Students will be able to see writers at work and compare what they do and what they say they do with their own drafts and the instructions in their own texts.

Every writer must be a reader of other writers and of the evolving page. This text discusses both kinds of reading, suggests how it may be done effectively, and demonstrates one writer's response to the text—as a writer. This anthology is designed to help the student develop the parallel but different skills a writer uses to learn from the texts of others, and to learn from the writer's own evolving drafts.

The selections are designed to reach a broad range of students, students from different backgrounds, students studying different disciplines. The readings show successful student and professional writers solving the most common writing problems that face all writers, student and master, unpublished and published.

Using *Read to Write* as a Composition Text

Read to Write may be used as a writing text. The student may follow the writing process, using the introductions to Chapters 2-6 as the principal writing text. The teacher may follow the process approach as described in this text or ignore it and use the counsel in those introductions to fit the instructor's own approach to teaching composition.

There is a great deal of material in the book about writing in addition to the chapter introductions. Each of the case histories—student and professional—not only demonstrates writers at work but also includes an essay by each contributor discussing the writing. There are introductions to narrative and argumentative writing, as well as essays on writing such as "Why I Write" by George Orwell and "Why I Write" by Joan Didion and autobiographical pieces by George Orwell, Amiri Baraka, James Baldwin, William Gibson, Charles Simic, Richard Ford, Terry McMillan, Annie Dillard, John Updike, Enrique Hank Lopez and Maxine Hong Kingston that reflect on how writers develop.

Many of the introductions to writers in the book include counsel on writing, including James Baldwin, Barbara Tuchman, Richard Selzer, Toni Morrison, John Updike, George Orwell, Joan Didion, and E. B. White.

All of the discussion questions, activities, and collaborative suggestions are designed to support and stimulate the student's own writing. The writing problem index will not only help students respond to their own writing problems, but also will allow the instructor to introduce and demonstrate writing skills to the class or to individual students.

Aids to Help All Instructors

Instruction in Reading

Although composition is usually required of most freshmen, instruction in reading is not. Yet we know that students often have as much difficulty in reading as they do in writing. And we also know that an effective writer must be an effective reader of the writer's own evolving prose.

The first chapter of the book is designed to help the student learn to read, so that the student can appreciate writing models, comprehend the texts that the student must read to gain an education, and to read the student's own drafts in process so they can be improved.

The instruction in reading continues through the book. The authors who provide their case histories discuss and demonstrate their own readings of their evolving text. I have analyzed several pieces of writing in detail and have written "Notes for a Second Reading" on the other selections to show how one writer may read other writers.

Case Histories of Published Writers

The case histories of the published writers will be a valuable resource during the entire writing course. All of the instructors are extremely successful in their own fields of writing. They demonstrate some of the different problems of writing journalism, nonfiction essays, computer software manuals, poetry, and science writing. They also demonstrate the common discipline shared by writers in all forms of writing.

They reveal their work before it is finished, showing the student that it is not only permissible but usually necessary to write badly to write well. Their commentary is candid and individual, and it is enriched by the fact that they are not only writers but also teachers. They know where they are, and they know where students will be.

McBride is a college professor and one of the best teachers I have ever known. Clark was a college professor who has become an authority on writing and heads a program that teaches professional writers to write better. He also inaugurated a summer program for public school students and their teachers. Freda and Grady were outstanding graduate teaching assistants who were later hired as instructors of composition. Although they have left teaching for full editorial careers, their experience as teachers is revealed by the way in which they talk to students in their commentaries. Scanlan has not taught in school, but he has served as an instructor of writing within the city room and spoken in that role to many journalism groups.

One of the most effective teaching techniques is for the instructor to supplement the writing text with his or her own case history of a piece of writing, allowing the students to see the abundance of notes and drafts that are usually necessary to produce a piece of writing.

The instructor should also consider inviting people from the faculty and from the community—journalists, children's book writers, business writers, poets, technical writers, historians, scientists, novelists, environmentalists, judges—to share their own case histories of writing with the class. If they contradict what is said in this text or others, in your class or mine, so much the better. We then have another topic for discussion—and further evidence there is no one way to write well. Composition pedagogy and theory are, after all, not a matter of theology, there is no absolute right and wrong—and students need to know that. They should steal from us all, but write in the way that allows them to produce effective writing.

One of the most helpful exercises is to have students compile case histories. This can be done in two ways. One is to invite a student who has written a successful piece to share the case history of that successful draft in conference. This is especially valuable when the class has been impressed with the piece of writing in workshop. Often I am asked, "I don't know how to write, and I've been hired to teach composition; how do I start?" I suggest that the beginning instructor ask the students who have written the best pieces of writing—not perfect pieces of writing, simply those which are the best each week—to tell the instructor how they were written.

The second way is to have the student present this testimony to the class. Writing is not an unintellectual act. Students can tell what they have done to identify and solve their writing problems. The act of reconsidering what they have often done unconsciously and articulating it reinforces their skills and introduces those skills to the instructor and the other members of the class.

Why the Selections Are Paired

Each of the selections in the book is matched against another selection. It is my belief that there is no one way to write, but several ways. This pairing allows the student to see two writers at work, and it will stimulate productive discussion when the two pieces are assigned together.

The instructor may wish to work through the book sequentially, but no matter how sturdy the syllabus and how determinedly it is followed, the instructor should take advantage of situations within the class to assign readings individually, in small groups, or to the class as a whole.

These assignments can be made in response to a number of situations. For example, if a student is writing about the death of a parent it may be helpful to drop the regular reading assignment for that student and to assign James Baldwin and William Gibson, who are both writing about the death of a father. If there are several students dealing with such a topic, then they may be assigned to read Baldwin and Gibson and discuss those texts in a small group, talking about how those experienced writers have solved the problems they faced. In my experience, if a quarter to a third of the class is interested in a subject or faces a writing problem, then it is worthwhile to have the whole class deal with that topic or problem.

A number of students, for example, may be interested in the question of distance; how do you get close to a subject or how do you step back from it? Suggest the class read Barbara Tuchman and Alice Trillin to see how Tuchman deals with death in a historical manner and how Trillin deals with a life-threatening disease in a personal way. The question of voice may be introduced or responded to by reading E. B. White and Jean Shepherd. Both have strong, individual voices. A student interested in narrative may be encouraged to read Alice McDermott in combination with Toni Morrison. Students interested in poetry should read Sharon Olds and Mekeel McBride. Those interested in science should read Denise Grady and Thomas French. Throughout the book, I will point out other uses of these pairings.

Thematic Table of Contents

The thematic table of contents will make it possible for those instructors who take such an approach to the teaching of composition to use this text. It will also make the book more useful to all instructors and students because they will be able to see how writers of different backgrounds and voices explore common themes.

The thematic approach can be introduced deductively with the teacher, for example, assigning a paper on alienation. That assignment can be supplemented by the readings listed under alienation. The thematic approach can also be used inductively when some students, given the opportunity to write without assignment, write, for example, about alienation. The teacher can take advantage of this spontaneous interest and support it with the readings listed under that topic.

Students should also be encouraged to roam through the book on their own, using the thematic table of contents to explore and extend threads from their own lives.

Writing Problems Index

It is difficult for students to understand many of the rhetorical models given in traditional textbooks, because they have no context. In this reader we have tried, through the "Writing Problems Solved" index, to show writing at work, to reveal how writers use rhetorical devices and other skills of the writer's craft to discover meaning and make it clear.

This index is designed to supplement the special indexes—"Help for Your Writing Problems" and "Writing Techniques"—in *Write to Learn*. Students who have used that text have found it helpful to be able to refer to these reference lists when they encounter a problem in their own writing. This index in *Read To Write* is designed to serve the same purpose.

Students and teachers should supplement the index, making other references to the solutions of writing problems they face and references to rhetorical devices that are demonstrated in the reader. This text should be a working reference book for the student writer's desk.

If the reader is also used as a composition text, the"Writing Problems Solved" index is of special value in introducing students to the techniques of effective writers.

Making the Book Your Own

Most teachers will want to use this reader for the first time as it is organized, beginning with the first chapter on reading techniques and then moving from collecting information through focusing, ordering, developing, and clarifying that information. This organization presents the writing process in a logical sequence that students can understand. It also corresponds to the natural order of the students' learning in a writing course. At first the students need to find a subject (focusing and collecting), then they need to structure and draft what they have to say (ordering and developing). And finally they need to make their meaning clear (clarifying).

As you teach the book you'll find what works for you and your students. You may want to get students to read a number of autobiographical pieces first, perhaps showing how different writers—Baraka, French, Dillard, and Updike—respond to school, a subject common to all students.

It might be helpful to have the students individually read a selection that interests them. Students interested in political science or the problems of nuclear energy might read Laurence or Hersey. A computer science major might read Freda. Then the class could discuss the common elements of good writing in a variety of forms and topics.

The course might begin with the students writing on the first day without instruction. Ideally the instructor would write with the students, and they would share what they had written. I think this is the ideal way to begin any class in writing and an excellent way to begin a class in reading. People who are in the act of making meaning with language will understand composition instruction and also appreciate effective writing. Once the class has written and heard each other's writing the instructor, or the instructor and the class, can discuss what they need to study, and the reader can be used as a resource.

If the class reveals a lack of interest in writing, it may be helpful to read Orwell's and Didion's "Why I Write." A class that is having difficulty in finding a subject might benefit from reading Jordan and McMillan or Allen and Quindlen. If a number of students are using narrative as a simple account without revealing meaning, it might be helpful to read "A Note on Narrative" and the White and Shepherd selections, which find meaning in similar experiences.

Some instructors will find it helpful to work through the five case studies first, assigning one for each class meeting and discussing what these writers have done. If the class is using *Write to Learn*, it may be interesting for students to compare the processes of other writers to my own. Students should also read the introductions to the chapters, which precede the case histories. These introductions will put the case histories in context and will allow the students to discuss writing methods in the light of their own background and experience. The instructor, of course, can introduce other writing techniques that are helpful but have not been included in this book.

Students should be invited to bring in other pieces of writing to share with the class and to compare to pieces of writing in the book. An example from a software manual might be compared to the Freda selection. A story on a local racial incident might be read together with the Hersey and Laurence selections to see how the incident might be dealt with by a detached reporter or from the point of view of a victim. That newspaper report on a racial incident could also be studied in the context of Baraka, McMillan, and Baldwin.

The students should be reminded, again and again, that the primary text in the composition course is their own writing. They should read each selection, and all the instructions in this book and any other text, in the light of their own experience as writers. They should see published writers, not as magicians, but as masters of the craft, individuals who have faced and solved, each in their own way, the writing problems that face the student.

Chapter 1

READING AS
A WRITER

Most students have learned that the text has a single, secret truth and their job is to discover it. The teacher knows the secret and the students must find it — or guess until they get it right.

That may not be what their teachers have thought they were teaching, but that unfortunately is what students too often learn.

If students are to share our delight in reading and to find reading personally significant for them, they must first of all be brought to realize that just as writers bring all of their experience, all of their intelligence, feelings, and living to the text, so should the student.

Each student, in a sense, creates a different text as the life of the student interacts with the life of the author as represented by the text. Teachers should encourage the students to read the text, first of all, in their own individual way.

The teacher should invite the class to read the same text—a good choice would be Baraka or French or both from Chapter 2—and make notes of their emotional, experiential, and intellectual reactions as they read. Then they should write one paragraph giving their strongest reaction documented by something in the text that sparked the reaction.

Then each member of the class should read their paragraphs and the instructor should lead the way in delighting in different responses. At the end the instructor should share his or her personal response, not as the right response but one of many correct responses.

The student as reader and writer should begin with an individual response to the world, later learning how to distance that response in tune with the purpose of the writing and the needs of the reader.

The Writer's Promise

Once students have discovered their own individual responses to the text, they can begin to investigate the writer's individual reasons for writing the text. Effective writers discipline their reasons into a promise made to the reader.

Students should examine texts, perhaps the same texts to which they have just responded, to see what writers promise readers and how they express that promise and deliver on it.

They should put the promise into written language, using quotations from the text or their own paraphrase. Then they should mark the text or create a diagram to show how that promise is delivered, laying free the skeleton on which the text has grown.

Two-Step Evaluation

It is worth pointing out here, by demonstration if possible, that all of us as writers appreciate the reader/editor/teacher/colleague who can understand what we are trying to do in text and how we are trying to do it, *then* help us see where we have succeeded and failed *in our own terms*.

Too often the reader approaches the text with a preconceived expectation of what the writer wants to say and how the writer should say it. Each text should be evaluated in terms of its own purpose, its own promise.

To help fellow writers we should first read as the writer, then read critically as a reader. Too often we leap to the second level of evaluation and ignore the first. That is not fair to the published writer and not helpful to the writer in process.

The Voice of the Text

To help readers and writers, we should deal directly with the issue of voice, a term most writers use instead of style. Style seems something that you can buy off the rack, while voice is more individual and personal.

The individuality and personal nature of voice is important but it can lead to an excessive emphasis on personal voice, avoiding the fact that we all have many personal voices. What we should work at is tuning our personal voice in a written text to our purpose and our reader.

To teach voice, students (first of all) have to hear their own voice, the voices of others around them, and eventually the voices of the texts they read.

Here is a way to introduce voice:

- Say nothing about voice, but have each student write about an experience, an event, a place, a person that had a powerful effect on his or her life. Pass out three-by-five cards and have the students write quickly. Five minutes should be enough. You write, too.

• Have the students read their paragraphs without comment or programmed reaction. Read your own. I have often worried that nothing will happen. I may go two-thirds of the way around the class before anything happens, but then a student reads something that makes everyone laugh, or grow quiet, or respond, and then another, then perhaps another.

• Discuss the common elements in those paragraphs and the class will discover a special individual blending of content and language, an especially effective voice. Discuss the importance of a personal voice in writing.

• For another class, have the students choose a reader or publication for their paragraphs. Tell them to revise or completely rewrite the paragraph for the reader or publication.

• Have each student announce the reader or publication, then read the new paragraph. Again, the class will respond to those that are most effective.

• Now, building on the most effective paragraphs measured by class response during the reading, you will be able to explore the concept of the voice of the text.

During the entire term or semester it will be important to read at least some parts of most texts aloud, to urge your students to read aloud, to listen to the music that not only supports the meaning, like background music in a movie, but actually communicates the meaning of the text to the reader.

The Other Elements of the Promise

It may be possible to introduce all the other elements of the promise in terms of the two or three paragraphs to which the class responded most strongly. You may be able, after the class has read the chapter, to discuss how the paragraphs demonstrate

Authority

Tension

Significance

Technique

Surprise

Not each text will display all of these elements—and that should be made clear. They don't have to. They are elements that often occur in different degrees.

The Promise Fulfilled

It may be helpful to have the two or three paragraphs that demonstrate promise distributed to the class and then discuss the way the promise might be fulfilled with them. That discussion will be more productive if the class is prepared. They may, individually or in small groups, decide on specific ways the promise may be developed, referring to the chapter's explanation of

Texture

Development

Structure

Context

Solutions

Closure

The time spent introducing this new concept of reading will be worthwhile. And it will be especially valuable if the students begin with their own writing.

If they do this they will see the relationship between reading and writing. They will become reading writers, able to perceive the author's intent and techniques. And they will be able to work back and forth between their writing and their reading so that each activity will illuminate the other.

Chapter 2

INFORMATION
COLLECTED

This chapter and the four following each introduce a stage in the writing process, but whether or not you are using the process approach to teach writing it is important to help the students to find the information from which they may construct effective writing.

Finding a subject and then finding the information with which to write about that subject is a common problem for all writers. This chapter deals with those problems in a manner that should appear logical to the student. The subject is found through a process of searching, and then the information is collected through a process of exploration.

This chapter introduction can be assigned by itself in advance of a class discussion or student activity in finding a subject to write about. If it is assigned it may be helpful to assign it with a selection or selections from the chapter, so that the student can consider how the writer found the subject and found the information from which to build a good piece of prose. All of the pieces in this section are worth looking at from the point of view of exploration. Scanlan is particularly helpful, because he reveals so much of the search for information. Baraka and French are motivating because they show how a subject familiar to each student can turn into a piece of significant writing.

The chapter may also be used inductively. After students have attempted to find and explore their own subjects they may better appreciate the counsel given in the chapter introduction.

Each selection is followed by some suggested activities and discussion points, but there are some overall things that can be done. Students may, for example, be encouraged to attempt an outward search, and it may be helpful for them to use the questions to see what subjects they might develop.

Sometimes the academy values one form of searching over another. The important thing for students to realize is that there are different ways of getting information, and both the inward and the outward search should be considered on any topic.

If the reader is being used as a composition text, students will need to be introduced to additional collecting skills. These may be introduced by class presentation, handouts, assignments, class exercises, or a combination of all of these. It is usually profitable to draw out of the class the kind of activities they will need to perform, and have them suggest the way to learn those skills. You may say, for example, go to the library and do the library exercises. But it may be more motivating if the students realize they need to get information from written sources and if they have heard of a library exercise that shows students what is in the library and how it can be found.

Some additional skills that students may need to know:

The Outward Search

Awareness

Students need to collect information by becoming consciously aware of the world around them. The best way to do this is for them to sit in a familiar place for a limited amount of time—an hour, or a half hour—and write down as many concrete details as they can. The class may all go to the same place—the student union or the quadrangle, or a campus hangout—or they may go to separate places—a supermarket, night court, an accident ward, a basketball game, a pizza parlor.

Students should come to realize the brain stores many more specifics than anyone can write down, and that they will be able to draw on those specifics when they write. At first, most students will only use the sense of sight, but they should be encouraged to listen, to smell, to touch, to taste.

They should also note down what isn't happening, what is missing as well as what exists. And they should pay close attention to that which surprises them, is unexpected, is in conflict with other specifics. They should pay attention to what groups together and what separates, for as the specifics order themselves they may reveal a topic for writing.

The Interview

Students should be aware of live sources, and they should be encouraged to overcome their natural shyness by having it pointed out that it is flattering to interview someone, because you are saying that person is an authority, and you want to learn from the authority.

It is often a good idea to have students interview each other. Sometimes I begin a class this way, having each student interview another student, and then introduce that student to the class, through either a written or oral report. At other times I have the students interview me, as a sort of press conference, to get to know me, or I role-play a well-known person, and they can see how questions can reveal information.

They should discover how to ask questions that cannot be answered with a yes or no. Not "Did you accept the job as basketball coach?" but "Why did you accept the job as basketball coach?" It may be helpful for them to prepare for the interview by planning the five questions (or four, or six) that the reader must have answered.

Library Research

Unfortunately, most students do not spend Saturday night at the library. They need to be encouraged to use the library to discover what is there and, even more important, to discover how to find out what is there. Most libraries have exercises or brochures that can help the student learn how to use this central intellectual resource. If this doesn't exist at your institution then it's worth spending a little time on the obvious—the card catalogue, the reference library, *The Reader's Guide to Periodical Literature*.

It may be helpful to have the students research their name or a topic of interest to them, so that they can discover library sources that have particular meaning to them.

Connecting *Read To Write* with *Write To Learn*

Chapter 2 of *Read to Write*, entitled "Information Collected," develops and documents Chapter 2 of *Write to Learn*, entitled "Collect." The introduction to Chapter 2 in the reader, "Information Collected," attempts to cover in abbreviated form the topic covered in Chapter 2, "Collect," of *Write to Learn*. Students using both books should read this introduction in the reader to see if there is new material, to see if there is clarification, and to discover contradictions which may provoke good class discussion. Students may be interested in knowing that I purposely wrote these introductions without referring to *Write to Learn* so that I might achieve freshness in dealing with a topic that is familiar to me.

The process of recollecting described in *Write to Learn* is documented by all the pieces listed under autobiography in the Thematic Table of Contents of the reader.

Christopher Scanlan's journalistic case study shows the newspaper reporter searching for new information, using some of the techniques discussed in *Write to Learn*.

All of the selections, of course, are built from specific, accurate information that has been collected by the writer. You may wish to suggest the students look at some essays or paragraphs in areas that interest the student to see the importance of information and how it is used to create an authoritative, interesting piece of writing. The instructor or the students may wish to use the Thematic Table of Contents in the reader to choose the selections.

All the case studies show the writer collecting and using information. The Tuchman selection shows a historian at work. The Thomas selection reveals the thinking of a scientist. McBride's and Olds' poems show how poets use the specific information they have collected.

Discussion Questions and Activities

At the end of each selection there are a number of discussion questions and suggested activities. These are designed to help you make use of the essays in your class meetings and to connect the student writers in your class with the published writers in the book. I hope you will find the suggestions both practical and stimulating. They were written with realistic teaching conditions in mind. They should, when they work best, spark your own discussion points and writing activities.

A Note on Collaborative Writing

If you want to introduce collaborative writing, it will be useful for the class to discuss some of the places where it may be appropriate:

- A team of detectives writing a report on a murder.

- A consulting group that has observed a supermarket in operation.

- A legislative committee, perhaps in the student senate, that is writing a proposed law.

- An engineering group writing a report on a text.

- A group of students petitioning for a university requirement to be set aside.

Then the class should break up into groups, pick a collaborative assignment, and write out rules and procedures for their collaboration. Each group should present their rules and procedures to the class for discussion, realizing that there is no one right way but a number of effective possibilities.

The discussion should illuminate the basic issues underlying effective collaborative writing.

A Note on Writing Argument

In my experience, students do not understand the concept of academic argument. It may be instructive to the class and to you to take time to draw from the students their ideas about argument. You may discover that they feel argument is impolite, not good form, something to be avoided.

One issue that has come up in my own teaching is that a large proportion of female college freshmen, many who may be the brightest and most outspoken students in the class, will resist writing argument.

We must remember that our students, male and female, who resist the writing of argument have good reasons, reasons that grow out of their background and the way society has formed them. We must listen and respond to their beliefs and feelings with courtesy and respect if we are to persuade them to attempt to learn the skills of written argument and to understand its importance in the academy.

Sometimes it is useful to have the class plan an argument, both pro and con, on a current, local controversy, with you recording on two greenboards the points to be made on each side. Then you can show how the opposition's points may be anticipated and answered and how the order of the points is vital to the effectiveness of argument.

You also may find it helpful to jump ahead and look at my *Notes on a Course in Argument* that comes later in this chapter.

Case Study: A Journalist Writes and Reads

CHRISTOPHER SCANLAN

In using this first case history students should be assigned the complete selection: the pages of notes and drafts, the article itself, and the author's commentary. They will get more from this, however, if they are encouraged to reread it in the light of discussion questions at the end, or to perform an activity suggested at the end.

The essay written by the writer comes at the end after the notes and the drafts. Your students may find it more valuable to read Scanlan's own account of the writing of the article, and then go back and read the early drafts and the article itself.

Another way to have the students look at the article is to concentrate on the collecting process and identify the ways in which Scanlan has collected material and used the material he has collected. Students might suggest other sources he could have used.

Students can take a particular part of the draft, the first three paragraphs, for example, or the last four paragraphs, and see what evidence appears in the notes or the drafts that leads to their use in the article. Students should also look in the author's commentary to see what he has to say about writing the beginning or the end.

It may be valuable for students to discuss Scanlan's traveler's log and to compile their own notes of a trip on or off campus. Then they can see what kind of material is valuable for a writer.

Although this article is placed at the beginning of the chapter on collecting, it ranges through the whole writing process, and can be an introduction to that process.

Students may be invited to write down the process they go through when they write, and then describe Scanlan's process on this assignment, comparing their problems and solutions, their method of discovering meaning and making it clear, with Scanlan's.

Students should have an opportunity to discuss what surprised them in the way that Scanlan works or in what he says about how he worked on this particular piece. They should also be invited to revise or edit his piece. Throughout this book students should be encouraged to break through the printed page, to enter into the writing of the writers in this book.

It is important to help the students make connections with the writers they are studying. Whenever possible the teacher, classmates, or the students themselves should compare their writing to the writing in the book. The best way to do this is to define the problem the writer is solving, then to consider alternative ways of solving that problem. The class—and individual students—will find they have the ability to define and solve writing problems. Many of the solutions—for example, using shorter words and shorter sentences when a subject is complicated, adding more concrete specifics when the writing is dull, adding documentation when the piece is hard to believe—is nothing more than a matter of common sense.

ROBERT A. CARO

Students may need to have this selection put in context. The selection is from the first volume of a biography of Lyndon Johnson, who rose from Congressman from Texas to President of the United States. This particular section describes the conditions suffered by farm wives in the hill country of Texas before electricity. We forget how recently rural electricity was made available. I studied by oil lamp during the summers in rural New Hampshire after World War II. It is hard for women nowadays to remember the conditions under which women labored only a few decades ago.

In assigning this piece students may be invited to compare it to Scanlan. The relationship of journalism to the writing of history is close. It may be useful to discuss the difference between journalism and history, and the ways in which writers in both fields get their information.

In looking at this piece, try to figure out where the writer got the information. It can be helpful to take just one or two paragraphs and discuss how the information was collected.

Paragraph length may be worth discussion here. Caro is writing a book, and he can have long, fully developed paragraphs. Scanlan's piece was published in a newspaper magazine with narrow columns. The paragraphs had to be small. Students may want to consider the advantages and disadvantages of short and long paragraphs. Many times, of course, we vary paragraph length, using shorter paragraphs for emphasis, and Caro does this dramatically.

This is a well-developed piece of writing, and it may be interesting to chart or outline the structure Caro uses to develop his point. It is also useful to be aware of the forms of development, or documentation, Caro uses, such as statistics, quotation, pure description, anecdotes (little stories), and so on.

The class may perform a variation of the last activity following the Caro selection. Also, the class may write a 500-word, extremely detailed description of an activity common to our times, for example, shopping in the supermarket, or hanging out at a fast food restaurant. The class should use a variety of documentation and compare their version with Caro's. They will need to look for the accuracy and impact of specific details, and then consider how those specifics work to reveal a truthful context. In other words, the class needs to learn how to use specifics to create or document an accurate picture of our times.

Students may begin to see that there is not one truth, but many truths. One student can document that the supermarket demonstrates that the United States is blessed with a healthy food distribution system, and another can use similar and sometimes the same facts to reveal that the United States has an exploitive, artificially treated and irresponsible, materialistic food distribution system. Students should realize the power of the specific and the importance of using specifics in a fair and accurate context.

Students may, if they get interested in this topic, spend one assignment analyzing news magazine, newspaper, or television journalism to show how specifics are used to create a variety of truths.

GEORGE ORWELL

There are a number of different ways to assign the Orwell and Didion essays. Some of them are:

• Read Orwell's "Why I Write," then "A Hanging" to see, among other things, if and how it fits his reasons for writing. Discuss the relationship between these essays. Read Didion's "Why I Write" and then "Salvador" to see if and how it fits her reasons for writing. Discuss the connections between the two essays.

• Read all four essays and compare them.

• Assign yourself and your students to write a one-page statement of why you write, and then have the students read the "Why I Write" essays by Orwell and Didion. Have them discuss their reasons in comparison with Orwell and Didion. Don't worry if you get essays that give such reasons as "to pass this course," or "to get through school." Those may be the real reasons students write, and you can deal with those questions in comparison to the questions of others, such as Orwell and Didion. Then have your students write a page demonstrating the reason they write, and then read "A Hanging" and "Salvador," and discuss the relationship between the reasons for writing and the practice of writing.

• Have the students read "A Hanging" and "Salvador," and discuss why Orwell and Didion write as they do. Then have them read the authors' essays on why they write.

Orwell plays an interesting role in the essay "A Hanging," for he writes as both an observer and a participant. I don't believe this is an autobiographical incident but an account of what others did. By taking the point of view of an observer/participant, Orwell gains a special authority and involves the reader in a special way. Students should consider those advantages. Students should also understand the special difficulties of this role. They should see that they are often in this role themselves when they are hanging out with their peers and observing the scene at the same time. Young people are especially caught in this participant/observer role. They are studying themselves to see how they fit in and studying others at the same time to see what fitting in means—a situation that is close to Orwell's essay.

Orwell never lets himself off the hook as a human being, and students should realize the authority that comes from this. He is not giving a sermon, pointing out the evils of other people; he is exposing the evils and insensitivities that are within all of us.

JOAN DIDION

Students should realize that both Orwell and Didion are novelists as well as nonfiction writers. This may be a good time to reconsider the techniques of fiction that work in nonfiction and the techniques of nonfiction that work in fiction.

Didion, unlike Orwell, was not a participant. She is a reporter who spent only a few weeks in El Salvador. She does not presume to be an expert, merely a reporter recording what she saw in precise detail. Both the Orwell and Didion pieces give students another opportunity to appreciate the power of the specific detail to stimulate and inform. This may also be a good place to consider how the detail may have an illusion of authority and may convince and misinform. Are Orwell and Didion writing objective accounts; are they writing propaganda; are they telling the truth or their truths?

AMIRI BARAKA

In considering this piece of writing it may be helpful for the students to see where they discover in the text that the author is black and where they also discover his feeling about being black in a white society. Both Baraka and French, who is white, are critical of present society, but their concerns are far different.

This text has a number of pieces that deal with the issue of alienation. These pieces are listed in the thematic index, as are the pieces on childhood and school. The alienation of segments of our society is one of the central concerns of our time, and students should find that writing and reading are ways of learning about alienation and exploring their own experiences and feelings about alienation. The same thing is true of education. Our students have been "schooled" for many years, and that is a topic on which they are all authorities. These selections throughout the book attempt to make contact with all students, not just those who fit into our society and into our schools, but those who, like myself, a high-school flunkout, did not.

Central to writing well and to writing so that readers are attracted and held to our text is the issue of voice. We have seen a number of different voices in the selections in the book so far, but in these paired selections the differences become most marked.

THOMAS FRENCH

Often we appreciate the craft of a piece of writing better if we have written on the same subject ourselves. The class may benefit from writing, in class, a specific memory of high school. You should emphasize the specific—an event, a class, a teacher, a fellow student—and go to the center of the incident—the crucial moment of confrontation between student and teacher or student and student, the three minutes in class when something was learned or a teacher self-destructed, the seconds when the game was won or lost, the moment of the automobile accident.

The class can share and discuss these pieces, discussing how significance—documented, convincing generalizations—might grow out of their writing.

This "writing" may be done orally as you and the class share their high school experiences.

And, of course, such discussion can take place after the pieces have been written. A valid response to French or Baraka might be a brief paper of an experience the student remembers after reading the text.

WOODY ALLEN

It is worth discussing the strategy Allen employs in disarming the reader who says his issue—the colorization of films—is not significant.

Allen's argument is brief—approximately 1,000 words—because it was written for a newspaper. It is, however, effectively developed and documented.

The design of the argument is so clear, in fact, it can easily be charted in the margin of the article. It may be helpful to have each student make their own chart, noting paragraph by paragraph what Allen was doing to move his argument forward, then compare what they have decided.

It is vital for reader and writer to see the skeleton that lies beneath each effective piece of writing. Sometimes it is arrived at instinctively by the writer, other times it is calculated in advance, often it is a combination instinct and calculation; but argument or essay, poem or news story, science report or short story, autobiography or company report, it is there.

ANNA QUINDLEN

Students should see how a professional makes a personal paper available to the reader. Some questions to help the student see this might be:

- How does Quindlen establish the context for her personal experience so that the reader understands the issues are larger than one person?

- How does she use her voice to establish a distance that is far enough removed that we do not feel uncomfortable about invading her privacy yet close enough to make us concerned as we identify with her?

- How does her organization draw us into the piece?

- How does her pace help us to understand each point before moving on to the next one?

- How does she allow the reader to have his or her opinions that may be contradictory to Quindlen's?

These are a few of the questions that might be asked and answered with specific documentation from the text.

The letters allow students to realize the possibility of writing letters to a newspaper or magazine and getting their own opinions in print. They may use these letters and letters from local papers to see what kind of writing is most effective in this genre. It might be helpful to invite the editor of a campus or local newspaper to discuss how letters are chosen for publication, what he or she looks for in letters to the editor, what effect they have on editorial policy.

Notes on a Course in Argument

Students should realize that these notes provide a context for all the student papers in the book. They—and you—should understand that I am not advocating this as the one way to teach the writing of argument. There are many effective ways to teach writing. They may be interested in knowing that I had a visitor who came to that class and kept asking me how this or that had worked in the past and was shocked when I often answered, "I don't know, I haven't tried it before." I always felt that teaching—and writing—were experimental activities. And I taught myself as much as or more than I taught my students.

DONALD M. MURRAY

I have come to realize that the line that starts me going usually has a built-in tension. In this case, the tension is between the idea of victim and prosperity.

Once I had the idea that these students, who appeared prosperous—not all were by a long shot—who were in a good university, who were headed for the upper middle class, who lived a wealthy, powerful nation in which they had many more opportunities than most of their parents, were victims, I had something to explore—to think through—by writing.

That is where I start writing: with a problem, a question, an idea, a situation that I need to consider. As I got to know my students better and better I was struck by the differences between their world and mine at their age. I had my own family struggles, grew up in the Depression, would soon be headed to combat, but I was struck by their own struggles in a period of peace and comfortableness and was impressed by their courage and resiliency.

It may be interesting to invite students to try my way of writing a column. Have them think overnight about something that interests them, something that bugs them, that they keep thinking about, something they find funny or irritating or worrisome or wrong, something that is changing, something they want to think about, to understand better, to share.

When I have an area in mind I make notes, reading the fragments I have written in my Daybook to see "lines," small units of language that contain tension within them: "victims of prosperity."

Then I write fast, as fast as possible, not worrying about grammar, spelling, mechanics, typing, not worrying about being silly or making sense, just encouraging language to lead me toward meaning. I am happiest when I am surprised by what is appearing on the page: it is evidence of thought. I am making a meaning I have never made before.

Then I read what I have read to see if I have made sense or how it can be made to have sense. I focus on the one, most important thing I have said, organizing it, developing it, and making it clear and attractive to my readers. And I worry about spelling, grammar, mechanics, typing when I have a message that deserves to be made clear.

STUDENT ESSAY: MAUREEN HURLEY

Some teachers may want to have their students read the material that follows the essay first. I have chosen to place it first in each case so that students can read the essay quickly, read the material on the essay, then return to a careful reading of the essay.

Each of the student arguments are paired, as are all the selections in the book, to demonstrate how writers dealing with similar subjects or facing similar writing tasks can write effectively in different ways that are both interesting and worthy of study. You may want to have your students read both Hurley and Keiski, then discuss them together.

Some may be concerned that the topics the students chose are grim or depressing. These are the issues that they wanted to explore and in my class that is where we start. I did find that other students in the class were interested in such papers and identified with the writers' need to explore such depressing topics as suicide in writing.

You may want to point out that Hurley went beyond self-exploration and included material that is of service to the reader. We need, whenever possible, not only to explore problems but to also point the reader toward possible solutions.

STUDENT ESSAY: LISA KEISKI

In both student essays, the reader can see the writer exploring something of personal importance in a way that allows the reader to enter into the thinking that is within the text.

It is natural for the class to leave the text and focus on the issue within the text, discussing it in terms of their own personal experiences. I used to worry that we were just throwing the bull and not being rigorously academic. I have come to realize that such talk is a necessary part of writing and that the students, in their oral stories, are drafting their own essays.

We need to point that out to students. Most writing is a product of our talking to ourselves. When we are able to sit down and write something quickly, it is usually a subject that we have "written" in our minds and our conversations many times. These oral drafts are an integral part of the writing process.

Students should examine Keiski's text to see how she is able to give enough distance to her private concerns that the reader is able to learn from the text.

Chapter 3

A FOCUS
FOUND

Writers and editors often declare that an effective piece of writing should say just one thing. That is not true, of course, because an effective piece of writing says many things to many different readers. It is true, however, that a piece of writing should have a single, dominant meaning. John Steinbeck used to capture the meaning of a book in one sentence, on a single three-by-five card, he was going to write. He'd change that sentence as he wrote the book and discovered its meaning, but it did provide him with a North Star to guide his writing. It helps me to do the same thing. I need a sense of destination as I plan to write, as I write, as I rewrite, as I edit.

Students often begin to understand the need for this one overall meaning when they read models such as those included in this book and compare them to their classmates' early drafts which ride off in all directions.

One question that students should ask in conference or workshop is: Why should I read this? Whatever the reason—this is information you need to know, this is an experience you need to share, this is an argument you need to hear—it may provide the focus for a draft.

It is possible to force focus in a late revision, but it is much more efficient to decide on the focus early in the writing process. Sometimes the assignment gives the focus, and so the student will get the focus and then collect the information to fulfill it. Most assignments, however, have to be narrowed and limited, and the decision on how to do that best comes in response to the information the writer is finding.

Students who are using this text as a writing text as well as a reader, and those who are using it in combination with another text, will both find it helpful to go through the questions in the self-interview at the beginning of this chapter as well as the ways of finding a focus that follow.

The student may simply take the subject that he or she has discovered and work through these questions and activities. It is also helpful for students in peer conferences and workshops to see what other ways the piece of writing could be focused. It can be useful to have the class choose a subject common to them all— a specific problem faced during the first year of college—and go through the questions and the activities on the board, so that the students can see that material may be focused in many different ways.

Students should understand that focusing activities are central to critical thinking. The student, while writing, is not reporting what has been previously thought so much as thinking. The skill of focusing is to catch an idea on the fly so it can be developed and tested in drafts which stand up to the author's—and, later, the reader's—critical eye.

Students from the class may be able to contribute valuable insights to the focusing process. Photographers and artists may be able to show the class how a photograph or a painting improves when the artist focuses on a particular point and allows everything else to lead to that point. (Leonardo da Vinci's painting, *The Last Supper*, is a good example of focus, for everything in the painting leads to the head of Christ.) Engineering students may be able to show how engineers focus on a problem; premedical students may be able to show how doctors diagnose a disease. Each experiment in science, each football game planned, each marketing plan, each military campaign has to have its own focus.

Students should realize that a focus is not a final conclusion; it is a direction, a hypothesis which may be struck down, reinforced, or qualified during the writing process. And it is important that students realize that the focus may be found or will be refined and redirected during the process of writing and reading, because reading and writing are thinking activities.

Connecting *Read to Write* with *Write to Learn*

Chapter 3 of *Read to Write*, entitled "A Focus Found," is designed to develop and document Chapter 3 of *Write to Learn*, entitled "Focus."

The introduction to Chapter 3 in *Read to Write* is designed to cover the same material that is covered in *Write to Learn*. It will be helpful for the students to use this brief introduction in the reader as a review of what has been introduced in *Write to Learn*. Students should also see that I have not condensed what is in *Write to Learn*, but have written new material on the same subject. They should be interested in seeing where I have clarified—or confused—a point, where I have developed what I have to say, and where I have contradicted what I have to say, what I have added and what I have left out. Each of those points could spark an interesting discussion.

Students should discuss which of the suggestions about finding your own subject relate to the essays the students have read in the reader. The student essays and the one by Tom French may be especially helpful to the beginning student who has trouble finding a focus.

In Scanlan's essay he talks about making use of the problem of finding the grave in helping him organize the piece. Baraka and French both look backward. Each of the essays has connections with some of the techniques we have introduced as subject finders.

The suggestion of using a reader in *Write to Learn* is discussed in both Scanlan's and McBride's accounts of how they write. The instructor should help the student see that published writers and student writers face the same problems and use similar techniques to solve them.

Students should be encouraged to work alone, in small groups, and as a class to make their own list of essays in the book and from the class which demonstrate different ways of finding a focus. It is hard for many students to see the importance of having a focus, and then it is difficult for them to execute that need. The reader illustrates these points.

Students should not, however, just look for essays or selections which demonstrate the ways of finding focus in *Write to Learn*. They should look at the essays they are reading to discover the focus, and then to look back at how that focus helps the writer make choices as the material is ordered, developed, and clarified. Each of the selections in this chapter has a clear focus, and that focus helps the writer and the reader. Much of the discussion of the selections in this chapter should deal with the question of focus.

Students should also see other ways that the writer could have focused the subject, and how it would have changed Baldwin's essay, for example, to focus on the race riots rather than using the death of his father as a focal point.

At the end of each selection there are a number of discussion questions and suggested activities. These are designed to help you make use of the essays in your class meetings and to connect the student writers in your class with the published writers in the book. I hope you will find the suggestions both practical and stimulating. They were written with realistic teaching conditions in mind. They should, when they work best, spark your own discussion points and writing activities.

CASE STUDY: ROY PETER CLARK

When Roy Peter Clark first began to consider this subject seriously, I asked him to keep his notes and track his explorations as he used this topic as the subject of oral and written argument. I thought the documentation of how one scholar and professional writer works on an argument would be a valuable contribution to our literature, and I think it is.

The case history worked out better than I could have hoped as Clark's notes, texts, and his own account show a writer thinking. We do not just record thought as many students believe; we use writing as the most disciplined and effective way of thinking.

It is worth taking plenty of time to study this detailed case history of an evolving opinion on a subject that is significant, of personal and public concern. Here we can see a writer using the personal experience—the point at which most beginning writers start—and distancing himself from that experience as he writes a piece of more than personal confession or concern.

The students, through this case history and the others in the text, can be taken backstage and shown writers at work. They should, however, be constantly reminded that they do not have to work as Clark does. Each of us has our own process patterns and they change with personality, experience with a writing task and the nature of that writing task. The point is to be aware that there is a process, a way of making writing.

Students should be encouraged to share their writing habits and procedures. In studying this case history they will see that they face the same problems as a professional and that they may solve them in the same way - and they may not. In some wonderful way the knowledge of one writer's eccentricities allows the rest of us to develop and make use of our own writing quirks and methods.

In this text I hope we strip much of the mystery from writing. It is a craft that can be learned. Mystery may, in rare cases, rise out of the craft but as writers we must concentrate on the craft and accept the gift of mystery on those rare occasions when it occurs.

It will be helpful to your students if you are willing to share your own notes, false starts, abandoned drafts, extensive revisions with your students. They should not see you so much as one who knows how to write—I've published for more than 50 years and I'm still learning—but as a fellow writer, an experienced learner who is still studying the writing craft.

DARYL FRAZELL

Now we have a chance to observe an editor answer Clark with an argument of his own. It is always helpful to have students read different writers on the same subject so that we see how each of them uses the material in their own way. Students may not have been taught that the text is sacred but that is what they have often learned before they come to us. They are obsessed with rightness; they believe the printed word is final, finished, elevated above criticism.

In seeing different writers on the same subject, as we do in the student case histories in this chapter as well as in the professional case history, we see that writing is a matter of alternatives.

Students should also see that Frazell is a defense attorney, a common role in argument in which someone defends against an argument. His strategies are effective, I think, but open the door to discussion of other tactics he might have employed to make his point.

JAMES BALDWIN

I had wanted to include this essay in its entirety in the first edition, but the fee the author's lawyer asked was far beyond our budget. I cut the piece so we could include part of it—for a smaller fee—but James Baldwin didn't want his piece cut, and he negotiated a compromise fee. I'm glad, because it is a classic American essay, a well-formed piece of writing that deserves to be published without cutting.

This piece of writing should spark pieces of student autobiography. Of course, they will not be able to write at this length or with this skill, but they can take incidents from their lives that they remember while reading this essay, and develop a scene as Baldwin has developed his scenes.

A title can be a valuable focusing device, although I discuss titles under the next stage in the writing process. The line between using a title to order the piece and using a title to find the focus is blurred indeed. Baldwin has an ideal title here. The term "Notes" allows him to present the information to us in the tone of a message sent back from the front. Here are the notes of a participant, the description and documentation of a life. It has an authority to it. You can hear the writer saying, "Here it is. Here is my truth." And the phrase "a Native Son" has irony and anger in it. Here is an alien native—note the tension between those two words. This is the story of an insider who is an outsider. James Baldwin is a native American, an American citizen born in this country, and listen to what he has to tell you. I don't know whether he wrote that title before or after he wrote the essay; I do know that it could have given him the focus before or during the writing.

Students may want to list 10 or 20 or 50 titles—sometimes I do 150—that might appear on a piece they're intending to write. They may see how each title makes a change in the direction and the voice and the content of a piece of writing. For example, I might list these titles for this book:

Reading for Writing	A Writer's Reader
A Guide for Reading Writing	How Some Writers Wrote
Read to Learn	Reading While Writing
Read to Write	Read, Then Write

Students should see how much a title can help. I never require titles, but I do have my students write titles so they can see the value of brainstorming different titles in short periods of time. Often I make a game of it. Students might, for example, suggest titles for a common subject, and I would record them on the board:

Attending a Community College	A Freshman with White Hair
Getting a Third Chance	Housework and Homework
I Married My Roommate	The Job of Learning

Another focusing device is the lead, the first sentence or paragraph of a piece of writing that leads the reader right into the writing. Baldwin's lead is a classic one. Again students may be invited to write a lead for a story on their life. I ask my students to write 10, 15, or 25 leads, keeping them short, having fun (silly is okay), seeing how each lead predicts a different piece of writing.

Almost any paragraph in this piece can be analyzed profitably. Each of the paragraphs has a clear purpose, and it delivers a satisfying amount of information to the reader. Students may want to list what each sentence, even what each clause, and in some cases each word adds to the meaning of the paragraph. Students, by analyzing the paragraphs of master writers and their own paragraphs can see how an effective paragraph has a sense of destiny or destination, or how it moves the reader with information placed in context toward a meaning.

WILLIAM GIBSON

William Gibson's piece makes a fascinating match to Baldwin's. Both of them are dealing with the death of a parent in the same city in the same generation. Students should consider which elements are common in these experiences, which elements come from a different context—white and black, Catholic and Protestant—and which elements come simply from the fact that the writers are different human beings.

Both essays demonstrate how a powerful focus—the dying of a parent —can keep the reader moving forward toward the inevitable. That narrative drive allows the writer to bring in a richness of material that makes the experience special, and allows the reader to have the experience of the author.

Both of these essays demonstrate an interesting contradiction that students need to learn. If you want to write for a general audience you should be specific. Many students understandably believe that if you want to write for a large audience you should write in general terms. That's logical, but the opposite is true. Both Baldwin and Gibson write of their own private experiences, but the specifics will cause us not only to respond to their experiences, but will ignite memories of our own experiences. These pieces of writing make us relive our lives.

Another element in focus is distance. The camera has to be far enough away from the subject so we can see it in context. We have to understand the meaning. Yet the camera has to move in close enough so that we are given the details of the experience, so that we feel. If the camera is too close everything will be blurred, or we will be too involved and embarrassed. Our feelings will be emphasized at the expense of our intellect. If we are too far away we will not really see the experience, and we will not care about it. We'll be detached in the way that William Laurence is detached observing the dropping of an atomic bomb in his report in the last chapter. Students are sophisticated TV and movie viewers. It can be useful for them to consider where the camera is placed in these essays, how it moves in close, and how it comes back. I often find it helps my writing to consider where the camera is as I am "photographing" a scene or an opinion.

Both of these powerful pieces of writing should be read with a delight in the writer's craft. Students should be invited to choose a sentence that surprises them, a sentence that catches a meaning that you wouldn't think a writer could catch. The essays are filled with such fine sentences, and the class should share their favorites, saying why they thought they were particularly effective.

CHARLES SIMIC

Charles Simic is a world-famous poet in the English language although he came to this country as an immigrant when he was a boy. His poetry is usually brief, imagistic, surreal. His eye and his tongue catch quick, significant visions of our world and preserve them for our study.

Students should read his piece to see how, in prose, he captures glimpses from his experience with poetic economy and power.

Many people think poetry is all bonbons and flowers, an excess of feeling and language. Contemporary poetry often understands, it pares life down, distills it, until a few words, a line, an image, stands for a whole world.

Students might appreciate Simic better and improve their writing if they took a few paragraphs as he does to document an event of importance in their own childhood. They do not have to have survived a great war to have something to write about. Most of us are survivors of wars in our neighborhood, in our family, within ourselves.

RICHARD FORD

Richard Ford looks back on his youth as Simic does but he is a storyteller, one of our best novelists and short story writers whose style is always appropriate to his subject. In each of his books you know it is Ford writing, but they are significantly different in voice.

He, like Simic, and most effective writers, is a master of the revealing detail and the student might well be assigned to identify and mark such revealing specifics, but he is a master of narrative. He tells a story. Simic's writing is episodic, Ford weaves a tale. Both are effective ways; both methods work.

Students should see how Ford develops his narrative, especially using scenes to document and move his story forward. It will be helpful for students who know the literature of drama from film and TV, although they may not know it, to take a scene and analyze how Ford constructed it so the reader could observe what was happening and understand its significance.

BARBARA W. TUCHMAN

Tuchman and the next selection by Trillin work against each other in an interesting way. Tuchman writes of disease from a historian's point of view, documenting The Black Death, which swept Europe centuries ago. Trillin speaks, from personal experience, of cancer, one of the great fears of our time. Students should think of that camera again, moving in close in Trillin's case, standing back in Tuchman's. But in both cases the camera moves to reveal close-up details and to put those details into context.

Students should be invited to list the different forms of documentation Tuchman uses to make her case. They should see that they have a variety of documentary tools at hand when they write. The reader should also be aware of how some of the sources of the information are woven gracefully into the text. A good example is in paragraph 23.

Students should also discuss how Tuchman uses specific details to let us see and understand the disease. They should also see how details are used to document the spread of the disease.

History majors in the class may be invited to lead a discussion of how historians collect and present information, using this text and possibly bringing in others. It may be interesting to apply her statements about the writing of history in the biographical introduction to her text and others.

ALICE STEWART TRILLIN

This is a masterly example of that Freshman English form so many critics of current teaching fear: a personal narrative. It is, however, a personal narrative that has meaning; in fact, it has several meanings. It may be helpful for the reader to list the different meanings it has, and then to attempt to understand which one is dominant, and how each is woven together so that the entire piece has a depth and density appropriate to the subject.

Some teachers will say they are uncomfortable using this piece. It comes too close to a fear of the teacher, to an experience of the teacher, to a problem in the life of a student. Then don't use it. This is powerful writing and it may well be too powerful for a particular teacher, class, or time. No guilt is required. If you are uncomfortable, pass over it.

Others, however, will find this essay constructive and helpful to students who are writing about problems in their own lives. I suspect that the writing of the piece was good therapy for the author, and students might be invited to discuss why that might be so. On one level they can see in the piece the author thinking the narrative is the story of her own understanding. The class should also discover understandings through their own writing, and should appreciate how the act of writing may help one deal with painful realities. Writing can be therapy for both the writer and the reader. Each time I read this essay it helps me put the pressures of my daily life into a productive context.

Students should also consider how her original audience of doctors affected the writing of the piece.

Another significant consideration is the way in which she uses personal experience to document her case, yet uses this personal material in such a way that the reader is not embarrassed. She is able, for example, to deal with the question of alienation without rage or anger, but with understanding.

As professional writers and readers, teachers, critics and editors, we analyze writers but we should never feel that analysis is always necessary. I have simply read this essay to a class, not to analyze it or teach it, simply to share it, to respect it, to learn from it, to hear a powerful individual voice speaking of issues vital to us all.

STUDENT ESSAY: ANONYMOUS

Writing, real writing, is important. It deals with subjects that are close to the bone, matters of life and death, survival and loss, commitment and rejection.

These student essays show writers dealing with subjects that are of importance to them in the hope that the writing will, first of all, help them understand and, then, help the reader understand.

Students should be allowed to respond autobiographically if they want to, at first, then to become aware, through your comments and perhaps your own narrative, that they are responding in a genre: narrative.

They should understand the power of story and begin to see that is a form that passes through all other genre: fiction, poetry, drama, nonfiction. It can stand whole, as in a novel, or it can be a form of documentation as an anecdote serves the reader of a magazine article.

Students should build on their own experience and its telling to learn from this argument, discovering for themselves and in the class what works, in their opinion, and what needs work.

STUDENT ESSAY: PAMELA DEKONING

It may be helpful to compare this essay to Keiski's with the attention on the person near the victim or to compare these essays with the two in the previous chapter as they show how personal experience can be made to serve the reader.

All these essays can be seen in the light of Clark's case history, where he moved even further from the personal but maintaining its energy and concern.

All effective writing is ultimately personal. The tone should be appropriate to the subject and audience and that may make it detached but beneath that is always the involved writer.

Chapter 4

AN ORDER
DESIGNED

Most students write too early, and it isn't their fault. We require it. We demand premature first-draft writing, and then we are unhappy when we receive premature, first-draft writing. The writer needs time:

- to find a subject on which the author is an authority or can become an authority.

- to gather an abundance of information from which the writer may choose the information with which to build the piece of writing.

- to discover the focus or meaning in the information.

- to design an order that will develop and deliver the information to the reader.

When the writer has completed those tasks the writer is ready to begin a draft that will develop and test the planning that has preceded the draft.

The students learn the skills of planning best if they understand the need for planning. That need would seem obvious, but it isn't. Students have been urged or required to write without planning, and they need to see that planning is as important as rehearsal is to a play or practice to a football team.

Planning activities are best presented as a sort of classroom game, in which the students can participate with the teacher in whole-class activities, and with each other in small-group activities. Such work may be checked, but it shouldn't be graded. It's merely an introduction to techniques that will help the students. Sometimes I require these activities; for example, a dozen leads to be passed in with a draft. But most of the time I introduce these skills in activities, and do not require them. They will help the student, and students will discover that as they try to organize a piece of writing.

I've mentioned in the last chapter ways to play with titles and leads. The same thing can be done with endings, outlines, reader's questions, and genre. The students should discuss what happens, for example, when you use the form of an argument, a lyric poem, a familiar essay, a news story, a research paper, a narrative—fictional or nonfictional—a critical essay to organize a subject. Students should realize that there is not an aristocracy of forms. The right form is the one that clarifies the meaning for the writer and the reader.

It can be helpful to outline a selection from the book to see, for example, how Selzer, Jordan, or McMillan have developed their subjects. The students can also outline a piece they have already written to see how it was made, or, by creating two outlines, to see how it could have been made. Another way to do this is to have the student mark down in the margin of a piece in the book and/or a piece of their own how each paragraph has advanced the meaning. Students should see, at least once in the writing/reading course, how a piece of effective writing is constructed.

Connecting *Read to Write* with *Write to Learn*

Chapter 4 of *Read to Write,* entitled "An Order Designed," develops and documents Chapter 4 of *Write to Learn*, entitled "Order."

The introduction speaks in a different way of what is covered in *Write to Learn*. Students may be interested in comparing these two texts.

Students may want to look at the titles in the selections in the reader to see how the title helps the writer as well as the reader. One of the weakest points of the reader, I think, is the quality of the titles. Many of them, such as "On Embryology" and "School," are simply labels. It will be helpful for students to decide which titles might have helped the writer and which title will cause the reader to pick up the piece. Students should, of course, be invited to come up with better titles.

The selections in the book do include excellent leads, and the students should look backward and forward, picking leads which helped the writer and leads which attract the reader. They may, of course, be the same lead. Students should be invited to get into the game and write a number of leads of their own for selections in the book.

It may be helpful for students to consider the categories of leads in *Write to Learn* and give a name to the leads they see in the reader. They may also want to discuss the leads in terms of the lead writer's checklist in *Write to Learn*.

It may be helpful for them to look at the endings of some of the selections in this chapter to see how they might have given the writer a sense of destination, and how they give the reader a sense of satisfaction or closure.

Students should pick a selection in the chapter and then outline it, perhaps even using several forms of outlines, as described in *Write to Learn*. Outlining a published piece is a helpful way to discover the skeleton that is hidden within an effective piece of writing.

Students should also discuss how what they have learned about one writing task may help them on another.

At the end of each selection there are a number of discussion questions and suggested activities. These are designed to help you make use of the essays in your class meetings and to connect the student writers in your class with the published writers in the book. I hope you will find the suggestions both practical and stimulating. They were written with realistic teaching conditions in mind. They should, when they work best, spark your own discussion points and writing activities.

Case Study: A Technical Writer Writes and Reads

JOSEPH FREDA

Writing is writing is writing, and students should realize that once they have discovered their way to write effectively they can apply it to a great variety of writing tasks. They should realize from the introduction that Freda was trained as a fiction writer, and that he continues to write novels as he has become an award-winning technical writer and editor. Different forms of writing have their own emphases, but fundamentally they are the same.

I have had a class list their own writing processes on the boards around the classroom. We studied the different descriptions and became fascinated with many of the similarities. Engineering students started by visualizing, and poetry students started with images. As we discussed these differences we were struck by the similarities. The poets and the engineers, who dressed differently and talked differently, thought in the same way.

In the other case histories you have the alternative of assigning the author's commentary first instead of leaving it to last, as we have. This is not a choice in the case of Freda. His commentary and demonstration are integrated, and should be read from beginning to end.

This may be a good time in the course to discuss the effect of the computer or word processor on composition. The best way to begin such a discussion is to have those students who use word processors to testify about their advantages and disadvantages, describing the effect of this writing tool on their work. Most of us who use word processors have discovered that they increase productivity, because it is easier to write, and because we can get copy down on the page—or the tube—quickly. It is forgiving. We can write stuff we think is bad, and then revise it easily. Quite often I discover that what I thought was bad when I wrote it isn't that bad after all. It makes it possible for us to forgive ourselves and to get on with the task of producing a draft. In all, it simply makes writing and rewriting easier, and therefore allows us to spend more effort on that critical writing task of thinking.

After students have read Freda they may want to interview writers in many different fields, or to bring in examples of writing from fields that interest them, so the class can discuss the particular demands of different writing tasks.

Students may be encouraged to pick a form of writing that interests them, or that is required in a course or major, and then discuss how very specific selections can be adapted to their own writing. What are, for example, the tools available for the writer of the critical essay, the police report, the business letter, the historical research paper, the laboratory report?

RICHARD SELZER

This essay gives the student another chance to consider the advantages of writing in the first person. It is also an opportunity to discuss the structure or order of the information, and to consider how specific details are put into context so that the reader will understand their meaning.

Students may profitably consider the use of language in this essay, which is both technical and poetic. Students should consider what devices the writer uses to make a highly specialized task available to the general reader, and what devices he uses to deal with those mysterious and vague philosophical implications that cannot be talked about in precise terms.

It is interesting to compare this piece with Freda's, because both of them are writing about technical subjects, but their purpose and audience are different, and that makes the writing different. Students may want to compare the Selzer piece with the selection by Lewis Thomas. He is another doctor who is a master essayist, yet in tone and approach they are very different writers.

It might be interesting in class to consider how the piece would be written from the point of view of the young surgeon, a nurse observing the operation, or the patient. Each subject can be approached from many different points of view, and in planning the writer should move around like a cameraman, seeing how the scene looks from different angles.

SUZANNE BRITT JORDAN

This humorous essay provides a wonderful opportunity to consider the role of point of view or angle of vision, the place where the writer stands to view the subject. Students know a great deal about angle of vision from watching film but they don't know they know it. You have the chance to show them how smart they are.

It also shows the reader how a good piece can result from moving away from the expected angle of vision. They can imagine college as observed by a janitor, their home as seen by a social worker, themselves from the point of view of a great-grandparent.

Angle of vision is a great organizing device. Once you have a particular vantage point there is a lot that cannot be seen from there and other things that are seen with great clarity from another perspective.

TERRY MCMILLAN

McMillan is a fine fiction writer who, incidently, was trained in filmmaking. Students should see how she uses narrative to organize the piece and uses it as a documenting form within the essay.

Students should attempt to define her tone and to discuss alternative tones she might legitimately used to write this piece. What are the advantages and disadvantages of each?

It's worth considering how she uses herself in the piece. What are the possibilities and dangers in this for the writer and the reader?

Notice how many levels she uses to reach different readers. She writes of the experience of being black, of being young, of being a woman, of being a mother. How does she weave all this together into such an effective piece of writing?

A Note on Narrative

Narrative belongs in the composition course because it is the primary writing form, although much of the prose that students will write is not obviously narrative. Almost all effective writing, even the science report, the critical essay, the bluebook examination, the business letter, the software manual, has an invented narrative thread that draws the reader through the piece of writing. We learn to write primarily from our fiction writers and our poets, and then apply the lessons we learn from them to the less sophisticated forms of writing we use in our academic or professional lives.

A good way to make students aware of the power of narrative is to tell an anecdote or experience that you had in high school and then go around the class, having others tell their stories. They will be able, afterwards, to understand that they are storytellers and story receivers, that this is the way they record their life and culture, and pass it on to others. The history of our lives is a long living narrative told in brief narratives, a quilt of story sewn by language.

ALICE MCDERMOTT

It may be worthwhile to read this selection aloud so that the class can follow in their text but hear the music of the story and understand the role of voice, that the written story is still told by the writer and then heard by the reader.

It may be helpful to read a paragraph at a time if the class has read "That Night" through and comment on the paragraph, inviting discussion.

After reading the first paragraph you might say, "Notice how McDermott sneaks you right into the story. You are in the head— and the voice of a girl [and that's hard]—hearing her thoughts. She's not telling you *about* the story, she's revealing it to you. And then notice the specifics, the way she lets them build up and then makes their significance clear—but remains in the mind of the narrator. What surprises you about this paragraph as you hear me read it?"

"What are you discovering about the story—or the writing of the story?"

"What works best in that paragraph? Why?"

TONI MORRISON

Some pieces of writing deserve more than one reading. Students should realize this and not think of it as punishment or that they have failed in the first reading. McDermott's style is deceptively simple, Morrison's deceptively complex. Toni Morrison's voice is so strong and so different, and the world which she is revealing is superficially so alien from the world of many students, that this selection may need to be read at least twice, each time with delight, but with a different delight.

My students are surprised when I tell them I often read poetry or fiction, not understanding it the first time, but enjoying it just the same. I compare it to seeing a different movie, one that is unfamiliar, disturbing, confusing, and yet worth seeing. I don't try to understand it, I simply experience it. Students do the same thing when they hear a popular song for the first time. Often the lyrics are confusing and unclear the first time you hear them—or even the tenth—but gradually they come clear, and the listener appreciates more and more clearly the meaning of the song.

The selection from *The Bluest Eye* is probably best read fast just to hear its music. The first sentence, for example, stunned me when I read it. I'm not sure even today if I "understand" it, but the images are so powerful they have become part of my experience, and each time I read that sentence it has an impact on me.

Should the student learn from this that it's okay to write sentences that don't mean anything? Of course not. This sentence has a meaning; it sets a scene on the street where the selection is starting. That first paragraph is finished, and you are inside childhood [as you are in McDermott's narrative], inside a particularly frightening and fascinating world, inside a conflict that is black and white and universal at the same time. The sentence does its job, and does it brilliantly. It doesn't have an intellectual meaning; it has an imagistic meaning, and the more you read that sentence and see it the more impressive it becomes. It would take me paragraphs to describe all that comes to my mind as I read and reread the 21 words in that sentence. I see the street, the neighborhood, the people passing by, the rundown hotel, the abandoned men sitting in the lobby waiting, waiting, waiting.

As students read fiction and poetry they may be tempted to try their hands at these forms of writing, because they are— and have been for centuries—extremely contagious. Governments, religious institutions, and most schools have tried to keep people from writing fiction and poetry, but they haven't succeeded, not yet, and they won't succeed. People need to tell stories and write songs.

Most of us belong to an academic organization which outlaws the writing of fiction and poetry in the courses in composition we teach. We are not allowed, in my university, to teach fiction or poetry in Freshman English or in our advanced composition classes. Although I am a novelist, and I do publish poetry, I am not supposed to teach these in my courses, and I do not. The issue is so powerful a theological issue that I haven't been able to fight it, or even discuss it with those who feel most strongly about it.

It is hard for me to discuss it, because those people who feel most strongly are teachers of literature and poetry, and generally teach very little nonfiction in their literature classes. In fact, as a nonfiction teacher I'm often amazed at their ignorance of the literature of nonfiction. They seem to scorn the genre, yet they think that this is the form of writing that students must practice exclusively.

Since I do not understand this difference I would allow in my ideal class the student to write in that form which seems appropriate to the subject and the audience, or in that form which seems to allow the greatest possibility of discovery by the writer. I do not find that students who write poetry or fiction well cannot write nonfiction. The very opposite is true. Joseph Freda, whose technical writing case history is included in this book, studied fiction writing at the university, and was hired by Digital as a technical writer because of it. Denise Grady studied nonfiction writing at the university, and did an excellent job in a fiction workshop. Mekeel McBride, in her essay, obviously demonstrates her ability to write prose as well as poetry. Joseph Freda is a fiction writer who works as a technical writer.

We should in the basic writing courses simply work with our students on writing. If we are restricted to nonfiction writing, then we should enforce that restriction. There is plenty of room for good writing. And if our students choose, during the course or after the course, to write poetry or fiction, that work will benefit from what they are learning in their writing courses.

STUDENT ESSAYS: VALERIE GILLAM AND LORI PARSONS

Both these student essays deal with the issue of euthanasia, this one with an infant, the next with an elderly lady. Both combine case histories with a great deal of background information, presented in a clear and disciplined prose in an almost detached tone that allows the reader to consider the issues with sensationalism or a play to emotion.

Students may want to discuss other ways these arguments might be made, not saying these papers are wrong but to see the range of choices available to the writers.

This may be a good chance to discuss audience. What tone and approach is most effective for an audience? How might the piece change if written for a nursing magazine, a religious publication, a law journal, a parent publication, a magazine for the elderly? How would it change as a government report, a speech by a politician proposing a change in the law, a lawyer appealing to a jury in case of euthanasia?

Chapter 5

A DRAFT
DEVELOPED

There is a contradiction at this stage of the writing process. The first 60% of the process—obviously that can vary from 30% to 90% depending on the writer and the task—is spent planning, and now we say, "Let 'er rip."

Exactly. Now the planning will pay off. All the preparation should be internalized and will influence the writing in a natural way. Practice is over and the halfback and the violinist play "instinctively." Planning and rehearsal are over and it is time to produce a complete draft.

The wise writer hesitates. Fear is normal from the high diving board and before the first draft. At this moment everything that is planned will be tested; everything the writer knows and does not know will be revealed. And yet the writer has to write; the writer has to find out what the test of the planning shows, what the text reveals.

Writers' block is an understandable condition, but it must be overcome by habit and discipline. Habit and discipline must be combined with a change in attitude. Students feel that the first draft is the final draft, because they have usually been graded on the first draft. I like the term discovery draft to describe the process of exploration for meaning that goes on in the first draft, and students have to realize that the drafts can rarely be perfect.

The biggest problem I have with writers' block comes when I am trying to write to impress. If I want to show someone how well I can write, and I am aware of that during the writing, the writing stops. I can also turn off the writing by establishing ridiculously high standards. I had trouble getting started on this manual because I wanted to write a poem of a manual, an opera of a manual, a manual like no one had ever written, a manual that would make instructors all over the country cheer out loud — "M_U_R_R_A_Y, Murray, Murray" — when they read it. Finally I came

down to earth and just tried to write a good manual. I needed to have a standard—
"good"—but that standard had to be achievable, not impossible. I carry with me at
all times William Stafford's counsel:

> ...one should lower his standards until there is no felt threshold
> to go over in writing. It's *easy* to write. You just shouldn't have
> standards that inhibit you from writing.

The feelings we have about writing have to be dealt with as much as our skills.
It is important to get your students talking about how they feel about writing and how
they deal with those feelings, or might be able to deal with them, as well as to talk
about the procedures they use for writing, the tricks of the trade that they can share
with the class. We learn to write from each other, from the ways in which others
solve the problems we face. We take their methods and solutions to our common
writing problems and adapt them to our personalities and our tasks. The sharing of
feelings and techniques is best initiated by sharing ourselves, by our being honest
as teachers about how we feel and work as writers.

You may want to refer at this time to paragraphs 33-39 in Mekeel McBride's
essay. It is perfectly all right to admit our own feelings of inadequacy and to admit
that we write differently than the books say. Students should be aware that each of
the case histories were written by friends of mine, people whom I have chosen for
the book, yet there are contradictions in what they say and what I say in *Write to
Learn*. And that's exactly why they are in this book. I have written a text in which
I describe in detail ways in which I write, and I propose a process of writing in that
book and this one, but the process must be adapted and contradicted by the writer's
experience. This doesn't destroy my ideas; it makes use of them, even the
contradictions are playing against my ideas and teaching me.

I think it is valuable to look at writing as a process, and I think this is one of the
most effective ways to study writing. I never thought, however, it was the only way,
and my own views of how people write have not only changed from my continuing
observations, but from the challenges that colleagues and students have given me.

The tenor of the writing course should be write in your own way and see if it
works. If it works, fine. Share how you did it with us so we can see if it will work
for us. If it doesn't work, fine. Share with us why you think it doesn't work and how
you might make it work, and we will share with you our suggestions as we learn from
each other.

Never let the students forget that writing is a constant search for meaning. You
see this search in action in Mekeel McBride's poem and you heard it discussed
earlier in Joan Didion's "Why I Write."

Connecting *Read to Write* with *Write to Learn*

Chapter 5 of *Read to Write*, entitled "A Draft Developed," develops and
documents Chapter 5 of "Write to Learn," entitled "Draft."

Students should be invited to critique the introduction to Chapter 6 of *Read to*

Write in the light of what they read in *Write to Learn*. They should always be encouraged to report their own writing experiences and to see what in any text fits or does not fit their own experiences.

Students should take at least one selection and go through "A Checklist for Writing Readiness," to consider how the writer might have satisfied the points on that checklist. All of the selections in this chapter quite easily can be matched to the items on the checklist.

The "Writing the Draft" in *Write to Learn* should be discussed in terms of the writers' and students' case histories in this book. Many of the case histories discuss the issues raised in this section. Scanlan and McBride, for example, both write accounts which relate to lowering your standards.

All of the selections in the reader demonstrate a writer's voice, but some of the selections are particularly valuable in discussing voice. I particularly enjoy hearing E. B. White and Jean Shepherd deal with the same male rite of passage story in very different, yet equally strong, voices. Most of the paired selections offer an interesting contrast in the voices of individual writers facing similar writing tasks or subjects.

Students may be interested in considering my voice in both texts. I've received many letters from students that indicate that they find my voice different from the voices in many texts. It may be interesting for them to describe my voice, and to discuss some of its advantages and disadvantages. Students should see that there are many examples of writing around them. Writing is not just that which is done by master writers who are anthologized, but that which exists in radio commentaries, in the lines spoken on television or in the movies, in magazines and newspapers, in car repair manuals, and company brochures, even in textbooks.

At the end of each selection there are a number of discussion questions and suggested activities. These are designed to help you make use of the essays in your class meetings and to connect the student writers in your class with the published writers in the book. I hope you will find the suggestions both practical and stimulating. They were written with realistic teaching conditions in mind. They should, when they work best, spark your own discussion points and writing activities.

Case Study: A Poet Writes and Reads

MEKEEL MCBRIDE

One of the great advantages of poetry to a teacher is that it is short. An entire text can be studied in a class period. We have the same advantage in the book. Unlike the other case histories, this one can demonstrate the writer's search for meaning and document it with a series of complete drafts. Here we have the most complete case history in this text, and one that is worthy of extensive study.

Mekeel McBride's account of how she wrote this poem is, in itself, an extraordinary essay. And it may be helpful for most students to read this in advance of reading the drafts of the poems. Seeing the poet at work may make poetry more accessible to students unfamiliar with this form or uncomfortable with it.

It is important that students hear poetry read aloud. Most students do not know how to listen to a poem on the page, because they have only read prose, or the worst kind of rhymed verse. They do not know how to hear contemporary poetry. You might begin this chapter by reading the poem "Red Letters" or one of the other McBride poems if you find that one more accessible. I would ask the students just to hear the poem first, not to look at the text, but to shut their eyes and just listen to it. I'd also tell them to try not to "understand" the poem at first, but simply to experience it. A poem is experience; a poem is music.

Next I'd have the students look at the text while you read it aloud, twice. At this point you may want to get students to say what it means to them. The best way to do this in a class unfamiliar with poetry, or frightened by it, is to have everyone write down what it means in one sentence. Tell them the sentences are anonymous. Then collect the sentences and share them with the class. I would not at this time react to the meaning, but simply read the poem again after the class has heard the various meanings. There's nothing wrong with you putting your sentence into the pot. Then the students should be assigned to study the author's commentary, the drafts of the poem, and the poem itself to prepare themselves to discuss what they have learned from the case history of the writing and from the poem itself.

One of the reasons that many people in our society, and even in our English departments, are frightened of poems is that they are contagious. Students may want to try their own poems; the instructor may even want to write a poem. Perhaps the writing of a poem cannot count in the course you are teaching. It's probably better if it doesn't demand a grade, but the experience of writing a poem is valuable for the student, no matter what writing they intend to do in college and afterward.

When I work as a writing coach for newspapers people always ask if it is all right to show me poems and short stories. Every management I work with thinks that's just fine. They know that work on poetry and fiction will make their employees better writers of nonfiction.

Poetry requires the most disciplined kind of thinking. It is language honed to reveal significant meaning. Poetry is the distillation of meaning. It is a high form of thinking and a high form of art. Above all, it is fun.

If students want to try poetry, you may want to suggest it as a way of practicing distillation and discipline. A good way to get into poetry is simply to start playing with lists. You can demonstrate this yourself on the board, listing specific details and images in a random way, and then reordering them, adding and cutting, until you achieve something that resembles a poem. You can do this as a demonstration on your own, or invite suggestions from the class.

Poetry is, above all, a sublime form of play. It allows us to play with our world, the images of our world, and to play with our language, so that meaning may be discovered. Song reveals meaning, and meaning refines song. Whatever you do with poetry, remember that it is far too serious a matter to be dealt with seriously. It must be fun for instructor and student alike.

If you do work on poetry you should keep reminding your students of the connections poetry makes with nonfiction. Poetry forces the writer to get to the meaning immediately, to reveal it without an excess word, to have everything advance the meaning to achieve a coherence and clarity and sense of completeness at the end.

You may be interested in my personal reactions to McBride's poems:

Black Boy's Death by Drowning

I admire the courage of the writer as well as her skill. She immediately places the reader inside the head of a boy who is drowning. This is a remarkably effective example of a writer making use of an unusual angle of vision. And the poem is believable because of the rightness of the authoritative details.

The Need to Talk

Here is an exploration and celebration of loneliness in which the writer escapes the trap of self-pity because of the way is which she uses language. The poem is carried forward by action as much as recollection. We see the poet at the table, see her head resting, for a moment, on the table.

The Knife-Thrower's Wife

This poem haunts me and each time I read it I see it differently. We should remember that a poem is not a regulation or a sermon that is supposed to be understood in one way, but a moment snatched out of time, to which we bring our ever-changing personal history and read it for what we need at that moment.

How Spring Appears This Time of Year in New England

Now we are within the head of a hairdresser. Note how quickly the reader is placed there. Mekeel is having fun but it is fun with insight and compassion.

If I'd Been Born in Tennessee

Voice. You want a poem about voice, here it is.

Students should be invited to try their own poems, humorous, sad, whatever they need to write. Rhyme is not necessary, neither is meter, but poetry is music and the line its measure.

Let them sing, dance the words on the page but not to tell us how to feel, but to capture a fragment of life and place it on the table so that we will feel.

SHARON OLDS

Students should not feel they have to come to poetry because it is poetry, but because it is the most disciplined form of writing. In poetry, the writer does the most with the least and by attempting poetry and reading poetry we do not only have the experience of the poem, we see writing at its best and can learn from it.

Poets get right to it. They have to. No time in a poem for fooling around. At the poetic moment the writer has to place the writer in the poem and each word, each space between each word, each line has to carry its burden of meaning.

It is also vital that students read poetry aloud to hear the poem's music and, perhaps, to realize that all effective writing, poetry or prose, has its own music. That music, however, is not a frill. It is essential, for the music carries meaning to the reader.

Olds' poetry is a lesson in how powerful feelings can be captured and communicated. She does it with her disciplined vision and her disciplined language; she sees and captures her vision with accurate, concrete pieces of information. The reader is allowed, invited, to live the poet's experience and then to make us his or her own opinion of what has been experienced.

Some people may be offended by Sharon Olds' content or her feelings. Good. Poetry is tough; language is important. Some of her poems are terrifying, the more so when they come close to the hidden feelings we have about parents or sex.

ANNIE DILLARD

Students understand a sport, a concert, a skill if they have participated themselves. Every student can write with Annie Dillard. That doesn't mean they can write as well as Dillard, it does mean they can take a paragraph such as #10 and write their own version from their own experience.

This will give them an insight into the text and allow them to build a bridge between reading and writing. To be responsible to our students we must keep passing back and forth over that bridge so that our students, by reading, will improve their writing and, by writing, improve their reading.

This may be a good point in the term to have class discussion of how students are seeing reading, writing, and their relationship differently than they did at the beginning of the term.

It is often at this time in the year that I pass out three-by-five cards and ask students to write down questions they have about subject matter of the course. Then I go through the cards and answer them spontaneously. It tells me where the class is and gives me a chance to answer important questions that never would be asked orally.

JOHN UPDIKE

This piece, compared with Dillard and other selections such as Baraka and French in the book, should show students how writers can, in recounting a common school experience, find meaning in it. Students may need to be reminded that the same thing happens in writing that is neither personal nor autobiographical.

The scientist, writing up an account of an experiment, understands the experiment better than he did when performing it. Often, the scientist is given a significant insight during the recording or reporting process. The same thing is true for the business executive writing a marketing strategy, a diplomat predicting the implications in a change in Kremlin leadership, a scholar examining the work of Emily Dickinson.

Dillard and Updike are not merely describing. They are thinking about childhood experiences through writing. They are capturing what happened so it can be held still and studied.

E. B. WHITE

Talking about humor can be a very humorless business indeed, but the students in reading this piece and the one that follows should realize that they are reading articles by humorists. The meaning of both essays is profound, but the manner is light.

Students should see the clue in the E. B. White article in the second sentence, which contains surprise coming after the first sentence. He uses unpleasant experiences to come to a conclusion that is the opposite of what the reader might expect.

Since E. B. White's humor is subtle, quiet, and sophisticated, students may understand this better if they first read Jean Shepherd, which is built on wild and unsubtle exaggeration.

It's great fun and freeing for the writer to read paragraphs from both essays aloud; for example, paragraph 3 of White and paragraph 13 of Shepherd, paragraph 11 in White and paragraphs 15-17 of Shepherd. It's best for the students to pick their own paragraphs, and to read them aloud. A sort of competition can take place with one student finding the paragraph from one author and other students competing to find a matching paragraph in the other.

Students may be invited to write their own description of a place in the style of White, in the style of Shepherd, in the style of the teacher, and in the style of the student himself or herself. Small groups could pick the best of these and share them with the class. The teacher should share his or her paper with a paragraph in the style of one of the student writers in the class.

These selections probably should be assigned together, because they show the same subject—a boy being taken through a rite of passage into manhood by his father. The students should see how this same story is told in two such different ways, each appropriate with the experience, the background, and the voice of the author.

This is a good chance for students to write an account of a rite of passage. The obvious should be pointed out, that these two essays reflect a male experience, and it's worth taking some time to discuss similar experiences that mark the development of girl to woman. You may want to discuss this in terms of the selection from *The Bluest Eye* by Toni Morrison.

JEAN SHEPHERD

Some of Jean Shepherd's monologues have been recorded, and it may be fun to play one or two for the class so they can hear the relationship between his spoken and written voice.

Students should discuss the advantages and disadvantages of using humor to comment on life. Students may want to bring in examples of their favorite humorists and to discuss the difficulties of writing humor. They also may want to discuss the role of humor in sermons, political speeches, TV commercials, and perhaps in life itself.

It is important, however, for students to realize that most humor, and certainly the examples here, are rooted in real experience. These experiences between father and son are distant in tone, but not in importance, from the pieces by Baldwin and Gibson. These humorists are talking about significant human relationships between parent and adolescent, and what they say is serious.

As we approach the end of this chapter it's important to reinforce not only the role of voice, but also to emphasize the development of writing. Both White and Shepherd give the reader a fullness of information, so that they are able to experience the text. The experience may be largely intellectual or it may be autobiographical as in these essays, but in any case the reader is given a satisfying amount of information.

It is not just a matter of length; White accomplishes as much as Shepherd in a shorter essay. He writes as a Yankee intellectual in a spare and somewhat removed style. Shepherd writes with hyperbole, a glorious overabundance of information, a hilarious exaggeration. When you sit down with White you have a gourmet dinner, a filet of fish, a neat salad, a few small potatoes sprinkled with parsley, some sauteed sugar-snap peas. There's plenty of white space on the plate between the food. On Shepherd's place are fried pork chops, mashed potatoes, gravy, beans, and a thick slab of homemade bread. There's a heaping cucumber salad on the side, and the plate is crowded, everything running into everything else. Instead of wine there is beer, a pitcher of beer.

A subtheme, of course, should be the importance of diversity. There is no one voice, no superior subject, no inferior form. There is not right or wrong, but choices that are judged by what works to fulfill the writer's purpose and the reader's needs.

STUDENT ESSAY: TRACI TUCKER

Tucker uses an interesting and obvious technique to draw readers in by inviting them to consider alternative case histories. This is an opportunity to reconsider other essays and how the writer involves the reader.

We have often said that the purpose of much writing is not to tell the reader how to think but to extend the process of exploration or thinking the writer went through in writing the piece: to make the reader think.

I feel I should bring the reader into the text, to stimulate the writer to use the text as a springboard for the reader's own thinking. There are many ways to do this and it may be profitable to have the students identify many of the ways it can be done that are demonstrated in the pieces they have read and discussed.

STUDENT ESSAY: RICHARD DAHL, JR.

Dahl has brought the reader into the text through the first-person lead that should make the reader identify with the writer. In the piece the writer speaks directly to the reader. This gives the class a chance to consider the effectiveness of a range of options, from revealing a situation and allowing the reader to make up his or her own mind to the opinion piece in which the writer shares an opinion and urges the reader to agree.

Again, there is no one way to write. In another case, Dahl might use Tucker's strategy and she might use his.

Chapter 6

A MEANING
MADE CLEAR

It is important that students realize the difference between revision and editing. Many people who are inexperienced with writing confuse these two activities.

Revision involves the consideration of the larger questions of the text, and it looks at the text entire. Revision is that which has to be done to produce a draft worthy of editing. The writer is still engaged in thinking about the subject. Revision involves a great deal of significant discovery of meaning.

Editing is what the writer does to a draft which is ready for publication but needs that final polish, line by line, to make the meaning clear. The writer is concerned with the smaller questions of clarity that will interfere with the reader's understanding. At this point the writer may make discoveries, but they are usually questions of definition and refinement that are answered. The delights of editing are small but satisfying, because they allow the first reader, the writer, to see the meaning made clear and to feel the satisfaction of a job well done.

The Craft of Revision

In revision the writer re-sees the entire text according to a specific sequence.

- First, the writer reads the text to see if there is a subject and to see if there is enough information to develop that subject. If the writer cannot gather enough information to satisfy a reader, then the writer has to go back and do more research, literally re-searching for an adequate inventory of information from which to build the article. There is no point in going on until there is enough information on hand.

• Next the writer has to re-read the draft to see if it has a meaning or focus. If there is no significance in the piece of writing, no point of view from which the material can be viewed by the writer and the reader, then the writer has to go back and search for a focus or meaning in the material. It is a waste of time to go on, because all of the decisions in the writing which will follow are made to develop and clarify the meaning. If the meaning is not known there is no way for the writer to make the editorial decisions that are required at the end of the writing process.

• Finally, the writer has to go through the article to see if the genre, form, and structure allow the writer to develop the meaning and reveal it to the reader. The structure is built so that the writer can make the reader think and feel by recreating an ordered experience, with each point being developed in a convincing manner. (If there is no focus there is no way a writer can construct an effective piece of writing.) If the structure does not bring order to chaos and allow the writer to develop the meaning in such a way that the reader can enjoy it, then the writer must go back and reconstruct the piece of writing.

Revision must not be seen as a punishment. The grading system should neither reward nor penalize the student who revises. Revision is what writers have to do. Some pieces do not have to be revised, and I worry about a course that seems to indicate that revision is virtuous and must always be attempted. It is true, on the other hand, that most writers, especially inexperienced writers, have to revise again and again to discover what they have to say and how they may be able to say it.

Revision requires a constructive reading. The students should see what works first. Revision is not so much a matter of correcting error or removing failure as it is a matter of seeing what is effective in a piece of writing, and then building on that.

The student and the student's readers—the instructor and the classmates—should help the writer see the most effective element in the draft. It may be the amount of authoritative material, or the focus of the piece of writing, or its ordering, or its voice, or the way it involves the reader, or any number of other elements. Then the writer can work to bring up the other elements in the piece to the standards of the most effective element. Revision is not punishment but opportunity.

Revision may mean extensive cutting or reordering; it may mean lengthy inserts or a recasting of the entire voice; it may mean, for example, changing from first person to third or back. Sometimes the genre has to be changed. A personal narrative may work better as an argument, or vice versa. In some cases a revision will mean an hour's work; in other cases it may mean an entire new piece, with little remaining of the original draft. Students should remember that those discarded drafts were essential parts of the process of seeking and discovering meaning.

A course should allow for revision. I think it's best if a revision counts as a new paper. If revision is required of all students it becomes an academic exercise, with a certain number of revisions demanded regardless of the need of the text. If revisions, on the other hand, are simply demanded or allowed on certain papers by individual students, then those students end up having to produce new drafts and revisions, and revisions of previous pieces, doubling, tripling the work and making revision punishment.

Revision will be the most valuable skill many students will learn, and it should count as much as a new draft. You and the students should remember that revision is not editing, but a re-seeing and recasting of the entire text.

The Craft of Editing

Many students have difficulty understanding the skills and satisfactions of editing, because they think that they are merely following arbitrary rules which they do not understand and which are not worth understanding. They should realize that the purpose of editing is to make meaning clear. That is the challenge of the writer, to make the writer's own language reveal the writer's own meaning. That is not trivial or arbitrary work, but a significant, exciting, and satisfying part of the process.

Before working on editing students may look ahead to the editing Denise Grady does and read what she has to say on it. It is a good time to review all of the case histories, paying attention to the reproductions of the writers' drafts, where students can see experienced writers cutting, adding, and reordering—the three basic techniques of the editor. Students may also be referred to Orwell's counsel in the biographical introduction and to the E. B. White counsel on conciseness in the biographical introduction.

This may be a good time to revise some sample paragraphs from the text, from your own writing, or from your students', using an overhead projector so that students can not only observe but also participate in the exercise, suggesting changes that should be made. I find it helpful to edit the same paragraph a number of different ways, showing what happens when you make sentences shorter, for example, and then longer, revealing the effect of increasingly active verbs, then decreasingly active verbs. They should see a paragraph that speeds up, and then what happens when it slows down. Specifics should be piled in until there are too many specifics, and then taken out until there are too few. The voice should be polished until it is too consistent, too bland to be read, and then hyped up until it is too distinctive, too inconsistent to be worth reading.

The one goal of all editing is to make the writer's meaning clear. This is the one rule of all editing exercises, and students should be allowed to play with editing.

Students should discover the play that is important to revision and editing. They should not worship text, but get in there and mess around with it. They should revise pieces in the book, writing them in a radically different way. And they should edit pieces in the books, or at least parts of selections, making significant line-by-line changes.

These activities should extend to the students editing drafts written by the instructor, or by their classmates. They may find that they learn a great deal from the activity of editing copy written by someone else. It is almost always easier to operate on someone else's prose than on one's own. And so students can learn the game of editing on other texts, and then apply it to their own writing.

Connecting *Read to Write* with *Write to Learn*

Chapter 6 of *Read to Write*, entitled "A Meaning Made Clear," develops and documents Chapter 6 of *Write to Learn*, entitled "Clarify."

Students should read the introduction to Chapter 7 in *Read to Write* in the light of what has been discussed and demonstrated in *Write to Learn*. Contradictions or discrepancies may be helpful points for discussion, with each student adapting the counsel on revision or editing to the student's own writing tasks.

The three readings of my piece on my grandmother demonstrated in *Write to Learn* should be compared to the edited pages in the case histories: Scanlan, Clark, Freda, McBride, and Grady. Students should scan all of the commentaries in the five case histories to see what the writers say about revising and editing.

All the selections that are published are merely the version the writer could deliver on deadline. They can all be revised and edited. Students should pick a selection which they particularly like, take out a pen and, in the text or on a photo copy, work over their favorite piece of writing, putting in and taking out, reordering and reshaping, so that they begin to understand how a well-made piece of writing is put together. Students should learn that they don't have to worship the printed page, that they can and should second—and third and fourth—guess the published writer.

At this stage in the course the students should have quite a bit of experience in writing. It may be good to invite them to revise or edit some of my own text, so that they think it would be more effective in helping their classmates. Invite them to do this. I will be revising the text, why shouldn't they? Each of us should make our textbooks our own. The reader, not the writer, owns the text.

The section on test readers in *Write to Learn* should be reinforced by the comments of Scanlan and McBride.

Read to Write can be helpful in reviewing the whole writing process from the point of view of the last chapter, Chapter 7, in *Write to Learn*. The students can now make even more connections between what *Write to Learn* says and what *Read to Write* demonstrates.

At the end of each selection there are a number of discussion questions and suggested activities. These are designed to help you make use of the essays in your class meetings and to connect the student writers in your class with the published writers in the book. I hope you will find the suggestions both practical and stimulating. They were written with realistic teaching conditions in mind. They should, when they work best, spark your own discussion points and writing activities.

Case Study: A Science Writer Writes and Reads

DENISE GRADY

Since the pieces are short, it may be a good idea to assign the Grady and the Thomas selections simultaneously. Students should be able to identify the reasons for the differences between the two pieces.

Grady's purpose is to inform the public in a practical way. Readers can make use of the article to solve problems in their personal lives. Thomas' purpose is to inform in a less practical way. He wants the reader to understand, to appreciate, to think. There is no immediate practical action which can be taken as a result of reading the article.

Grady's article is to be published in a newspaper, Thomas' in a magazine. Grady's article is the result of specific research and interviewing; Thomas' article is the result of reflection. Grady works within the newswriting tradition; Thomas within the literary tradition of the personal essay. Grady's voice is direct, professional, informative; Thomas' voice is ruminating, speculative, discursive.

Both pieces of writing are good jobs of work in which the writer fulfills the purpose he or she has established and reaches the reader to whom the piece is directed.

Students should decide if they agree with Grady's own criticisms of her leads, and they should do the same second-guessing on the other drafts we've reproduced as they look at what she has done and what she says in the margin that she is doing.

Students have to develop this ability to stand back from the job, to become the reader of what has been written. This critical reader can't be too critical (I usually feel that everything is hopeless and horrible, and sometimes it is) or too confident (sometimes I think everything is just fine, and it is). But most of the time the writer has to identify what works and what needs work.

If I have difficulty with this essential detachment I role-play a specific reader, making myself into someone whom I know and respect who is intelligent, but not informed about my subject. I do not make this an abstract reader, but a specific person with a name, a person who is a good reader of mine. Sometimes I try to talk like that person, sit, or walk around the desk like that person, so that I can read my text and not see what I hope is there, or fear isn't there, but what is there.

This is a good time to review the case histories that have headed up each of the stages in the writing process. Students should identify what has surprised them in these case histories and what has helped them. They should mark up specific pieces of advice that they have followed. The class should then discuss what is learned from these glimpses backstage into the writer's workshop.

LEWIS THOMAS

This six-paragraph essay is worthy of careful analysis. Students should be able to see, paragraph by paragraph, how he establishes his voice, how he makes complex matters clear, how he speculates on the meaning of what he has described, how he invites the reader into the thinking process.

Students can be invited to write their own six-paragraph (five-paragraph, seven-paragraph) essay on the implications of something with which they are familiar. They can be invited to imitate Thomas' speculative, full-of-wonder tone and attitude, or to write from their own turn of mind with their own voices.

WILLIAM L. LAURENCE

Students must be prepared to read this piece and the one that follows. I am constantly amazed by our students' failure to have a historical context for their world. Some do not know who the President is, but they really get into trouble when they try to remember who the President was. Carter and John Adams and Lincoln and Johnson and Jefferson and Franklin Delano Roosevelt all become contemporaries. Viet Nam, Bull Run, Korea, and World War I are all part of World War II. Many students do not seem to know that there was a world without TV, paved roads, McDonald's, and the six-pack. To students who have no yesterday the next two pieces may be confusing, and so it may be necessary to have a brief history lesson. It's hard to do this without being sarcastic or patronizing, but you should certainly try. The need for the information is there. I had a freshman report me to the dean because he discovered I had fought on the side of Russia. He had a military father and was convinced I was a traitor. Although he thought of himself as a student of military affairs, he didn't realize that Russia was on our side in World War II. In a nation that drives Volkswagens and Toyotas, students may not remember that the German and the Japanese nations were our enemies.

The decision to drop the atomic bomb was made while the war was still going on, and Laurence's story puts us within that period. He wrote the official account of the development and utilization of atomic weapons. Students should realize that his story was written from the point of view of an American correspondent observing the dropping of a bomb against an enemy that was killing our troops, and he observed this from a plane where he could not see the effect of the bomb.

The John Hersey piece which follows was a reconstruction, written from the victims' point of view, revealing what had happened on the ground. It was written when the war was over.

Laurence's article is a good example of newspaper journalism, and may be compared in style to the articles by Scanlan and Grady. Scanlan's piece, although it is a Sunday magazine article that has been reprinted in magazines, is an example of news style at its best.

Students should consider the advantages and disadvantages of news style.

Students may also consider the role of the press as an observer and a chronicler, seeing where Laurence is detached and objective and where he crosses the line and becomes involved and allows his opinions to intrude. The story was written at a time when journalism was trying to maintain high standards of objectivity, and to keep opinion, the personal experience of the writer, and analysis by the writer, out of the news column.

JOHN HERSEY

John Hersey's piece is part history, part journalism. It may be compared in style to such biographers and historians as Caro and Tuchman. As a journalist he writes in the same tradition as Orwell and Didion. Students may want to discuss the elements in a writing tradition. What kind of standards are imposed by tradition? What elements—for example voice, distance of writer from the subject, length, involvement by the reader—are affected by a tradition? Students may profit from seeing how those traditions limit, but help, the writer.

Students may be interested in discussing Hersey's style. It seems to me that his writing is effective in this selection because of its flat, almost unemotional manner. The facts are so overwhelming that the writer has to deal with them in such a way that the reader gets the information directly. This brings up an interesting problem in writing. The inexperienced writer wants to put a lot of emotion and opinion into the writing, but the most effective writing often occurs when the reader presents information that will cause the emotional or the intellectual reaction of the reader to occur within the reader. This is the way most effective writers want to work. They do not want to do the feeling or the thinking for the reader as much as stimulate the reader to think or feel.

Students may want to think back through the book to discuss those writers who have had the greatest impact on them, and to see how they have made this impact on the students.

ENRIQUE HANK LOPEZ

Both this piece and the one that follows are trying to make clear to the reader what it is like to be part of a specific alien culture. Students should consider how Lopez, for example, uses Spanish words to document the difference between that world and the English-speaking one in which he also lived. It's also interesting to see how he defines or explains these Spanish expressions.

Students should realize that Lopez, writing in the first person, is writing *about* his subject. He is looking back at it from his present perspective. During the whole piece he stands between us and his subject, pointing out elements from his life and telling us what they mean. Although his piece is personal, he makes us think more than feel; for me, I guess it is about 60% of think and 40% of feel.

MAXINE HONG KINGSTON

Although this selection is autobiographical non-fiction, it borrows more from the novel than Lopez does. Kingston puts us immediately in the world. She tells us, but not as much as she shows us. She reveals, and this piece reverses the emphasis of the last one. In reading this piece I feel at least 60% and think about 40%.

Given the purpose of the piece, to record and reveal an alien nation within our own, Kingston has the greater impact on me. In the Lopez piece he stands between me and the subject; in the Kingston piece I feel it directly, and that causes me to think.

Students should see those elements that we usually think are fictional used in nonfiction writing—and used very effectively. The line between truth and nontruth, fiction and nonfiction, should not be crossed, but the stylistic lines between the two forms are often crossed. Students should identify the fictional techniques used in these pieces of writing.

STUDENT ESSAY: MARK DAVIDSON

Here is another strategy in argument. By now the students have had experience with many forms of argument and should be in a good position to second Davidson, identifying the strengths and weaknesses of his approach and describing the many alternatives before him.

It may be a good time to discuss, again, the influence of audience on argument and all writing. The writer should be able to identify with the audience for whom the piece is intended and select strategies appropriate for that audience.

STUDENT ESSAY: STACY KENDALL

In teaching writing I believe we should move from the autobiographical to the more impersonal forms of writing. Students learn best when they write from authority and during their education they should be able to extend their area of authority from the purely personal to the academic or professional.

This piece is an excellent one on an important issue. Kendall makes the complex remarkably clear. She is not in the piece, but of course she is. It is a subject that fascinates her. It was self-assignment and she brings to it her own motivation, her own intelligence, and her own concerns and sense of values. This combing of the personal and impersonal is exactly what we want to achieve in a writing course.

Chapter 7

WATCH OUT:
AFTER SCHOOL MAY
COME READING
AND WRITING

I always have a great deal of difficulty ending a course, and I haven't been able to get much help from my colleagues. I did spook one colleague by asking him what he did when his students applauded at the end of a course. Of course, my students do not applaud, but there are some techniques that may work.

Sometimes I ask for questions. It may take a bit of waiting, but they come. Other times I have the students write out questions, or bring written questions with them, to stimulate this concluding dialogue.

It's best if the course ends with the students doing most of the talking. I try to get them to tell me what they've learned about writing, what they need to remember, what they still need to learn. I invite them to evaluate the readings, talking about the pieces they remember and why they remember them. And I get in written and oral form suggestions about how to run the course in the future. Some of those suggestions are unrealistic, but many are helpful. Certainly my students have taught me how to teach.

Another way to end a course on reading and writing is to read a piece of writing, or pieces of writing, that is particularly exciting to you. Your excitement can be contagious, and the enthusiasm you have for reading and writing can leave a mark on your students. Not much comment is needed, not analysis, not interpretation, but a simple sharing, allowing your students to hear good pieces of writing. By doing this you compliment them, implying they are now writers and will appreciate a piece of well-made writing. The best text, of course, is those pieces which have come from the class itself, the pieces the class has heard in process, now in final form.

For Further Preparation

After I wrote *Write to Learn* I wrote the second edition of *A Writer Teaches Writing* [1985]. This is an entirely different book from my first edition, and it was greatly influenced by the writing of *Write to Learn*. It is, in a sense, an extended teacher's manual for *Read to Write* as well as *Write to Learn*. It provides a great deal of practical information on how to apply the process approach to writing and reading to the classroom situation.

Two collections of articles I have written on writing and teaching, *Learning by Teaching* [1982] and *Expecting the Unexpected* [1989] have been published. Many of the ideas in these essays relate to *Read to Write* and to what I have said in this instructor's manual.

I urge everyone who is teaching composition to participate in the profession of composition teachers. I didn't know there was such a profession when I was assigned to the teaching of composition as a chore which was not supposed to take time away from my major assignment. I found almost by accident that I had colleagues across the country and throughout Canada who were dedicated to the teaching of composition and to the intellectual investigation of how effective written composition is created.

I urge you to join the National Council of Teachers of English (1111 Kenyon Road, Urbana, Ill. 61801). College teachers should also join the Conference on College Composition and Communication, a group within NCTE. Attend local, regional, and national meetings whenever possible. Membership includes a subscription to an appropriate journal, such as *College Composition and Communication* for college instructors and the *English Journal* for secondary teachers. NCTE publishes other significant journals, including *College English, Language Arts, English Education,* and *Research in the Teaching of English.*

I find the profession of composition teaching stimulating and supportive. I learn from my colleagues and I am inspired by my colleagues. All composition instructors should participate in the profession by presenting papers and publishing articles so that we can all learn from each other and share with each other what we learn from our students.